In the Shadow of the Gods

In the Shadow of the Gods

The Emperor in World History

DOMINIC LIEVEN

VIKING

VIKING
An imprint of Penguin Random House LLC
penguinrandomhouse.com

First published in hardcover in Great Britain by Allen Lane,
an imprint of Penguin Random House Ltd., London, in 2022

First North American edition published by Viking, 2022

Illustration credits can be found on pp. xi–xiii

ISBN 9780735222199 (hardcover)
ISBN 9780735222212 (ebook)

Printed in the United States of America
1st Printing

Set in Sabon LT Std

This book is dedicated to Trinity College, Cambridge – to its Masters and Fellows, to its students, and to the college staff who did so much to make my time at Trinity so pleasant and productive.

Contents

List of Illustrations

1. The Assyrian king Ashurbanipal (r. 668–631 BCE) is shown killing a lion in a wall relief from his palace at Nineveh, c. 654–635 BCE. (*Copyright © Trustees of the British Museum*)
2. The earliest known pillar erected by Ashoka (r. c. 268–232 BCE) at Vaishali, India. (*Amaan Imam / Wikimedia Commons CC BY-SA 4.0*)
3. Roman Emperor Marcus Aurelius (r. 161–80 CE) shows his clemency towards the vanquished after his success against Germanic tribes. Bas-relief, c. 176–80 CE, from the Arch of Marcus Aurelius, Rome. Musei Capitolini, Rome. (*Luisa Ricciarini / Bridgeman Images*)
4. Emperor Taizong of China (r. 626–49 CE) receiving the ambassador of Tibet, in a contemporary scroll of the Tang era. (*Bridgeman Images*)
5. The Caliph Mu'āwiya I ibn Abī Sufyān (r. 661–80 CE) meeting his councillors, illustrated in a fifteenth-century manuscript from Herat, Afghanistan. (*Yale University Art Gallery, Gift of Mary Burns Foss (1983.94.4)*)
6. A portrait of Otto, Holy Roman Emperor (r. 996–1002) from his contemporary Gospel Book, depicts him between military men on one side and two clergy on the other. On the facing leaf, four figures resembling the Magi approach him, symbolizing the four provinces of his empire (Germany, France, northern Italy, and the Slavic east). (*Bayerische Staatsbibliothek, Munich (Clm 4453)*)
7. Entrants undertake Imperial Chinese civil-service exams, in a seventeenth-century copy of a painting dating from the period of the Song Emperor, Zhenzong (r. 997–1022). Bibliothèque Nationale, Paris. (*Bridgeman Images*)
8. Founding emperors of the Qin and Han dynasties, portrayed in an early fourteenth-century history book owned by the son of Timur, Shahrukh (r. 1405–47). Shahrukh's seal appears on the folio alongside a sketch of a face. (*The Khalili Collections (MSS 727 fol. 11a)*)

9. The Mughal Emperor Babur (r. 1525–30), celebrates the birth of his son and successor, Humayun (r. 1530–40 and 1555–6) in the royal gardens at Kabul. Miniature, c. 1590. The British Library, London (Or. 3714 Vol.2 f.295). (*Copyright © British Library Board. All Rights Reserved / Bridgeman Images*)

10. The Emperor Maximilian I (r. 1459–1519) with his wife Mary of Burgundy and their family, c. 1515–20. Below them are Philip's sons, the future emperors Charles V (r. 1519–56) and Ferdinand I (r. 1556–64). Kunsthistorisches Museum, Vienna. (*Bridgeman Images*)

11. Suleyman the Magnificent (r. 1520–66) with his faithful Janissaries during the Conquest of Belgrade, 1521. Topkapi Palace Museum, Istanbul. (*Bridgeman Images*)

12. In El Greco's painting *The Adoration of the Holy Name of Jesus*, 1577–9, Philip II of Spain (r. 1556–98) is shown kneeling at bottom centre. Monasterio del Escorial, Madrid. (*Bridgeman Images*)

13. Prince Khurram (later Emperor Shah Jahan, r. 1628–58) weighed in gold and silver (a Hindu royal ritual) before Jahangir (r. 1605–27), in a painting of c. 1615. The British Museum, London (1948,1009,0.69). (*Bridgeman Images*)

14. Louis XIV (r. 1643–1715) portrayed in triumph as the Roman god Apollo, 1664. Châteaux de Versailles et de Trianon, Versailles. (*Copyright © 2021 RMN-Grand Palais /Dist. Photo SCALA, Florence /Phot. Franck Raux*)

15. An eighteenth-century portrait of the Qing dynasty's Kangxi Emperor (r. 1661–1722). (*Pictures from History / Bridgeman Images*)

16. Kangxi's son, the Yongzheng Emperor (reigned 1722–35), from *An Album of the Yongzheng Emperor in Costumes*, by anonymous court artists, c. 1725. The Palace Museum, Beijing. (*Bridgeman Images*)

17. Peter the Great (r. 1682–1725). Portrait attributed to Jean-Marc Nattier, 1717. Hermitage Museum, St Petersburg. (*Ian Dagnall / Alamy*)

18. Maria Theresa, Archduchess of Austria, Queen of Hungary and Bohemia, and Roman-German Empress (r. 1740–80). Portrait by Jean-Étienne Liotard, 1747. (*Rijksmuseum, Amsterdam*)

19. Standing before the tomb of Peter the Great, Catherine (r. 1762–96) gestures towards the banners and other trophies of Russian victory over the Ottoman fleet in 1770. Painting by Andreas Huhne, 1791. Tsarskoye Selo, Pushkin. (*Photo Josse / Bridgeman Images*)

Preface and Acknowledgements

This book is about emperors. Probably most readers will come to the book believing that they know what an emperor is. No illusion could be more fatal. Emperors come in many different shapes and sizes. Empire is one of the most contested words in history and politics. In chapter 1 I will delve deeper into these questions. For the moment I will confine myself to saying that my book studies the hereditary holders of supreme authority in many of the most powerful and significant polities in history. In principle this is a global history of emperors. In practice I limit myself before the sixteenth century CE to Eurasia and north Africa. The surviving sources do not allow a historian to know much about the personalities of emperors in the Americas and sub-Saharan Africa before that time. Sheer despair at the already enormous scale of my project was an extra deterrent to extending its limits even further from my comfort zone.

The most obvious point about a topic of this scale is that much more needs to be left out than can be included. Some important empires even in Eurasia get barely a mention in this book. The Byzantine, Carolingian, Sasanian, Seljuk and south-east Asian empires head the list. Even among the empires I do study, I am forced to concentrate on specific periods and reigns. It is sometimes hard to avoid looking most intently at empires in their prime. Almost every sentence in this book deserves a paragraph. Nearly every statement ought to come with a string of qualifications, exceptions and nuances attached. The role of emperors in the history of the world is so vast and fascinating a topic that one is almost bound to feel a sense of failure when concluding a book on this subject. If most readers conclude that this book is a heroic, thought-provoking and sometimes amusing failure I will be more than content.

Inevitably, how I approached this topic and the themes I chose to emphasize to some extent reflect my own academic and personal background and experience. In academic terms I am above all a historian of imperial Russia and an international historian. Geopolitics, diplomacy and war loom large in this book, in my view correctly so, given their importance to the rulers of empires. In personal terms I come from a mixed background but one in which empire was an all-pervading theme. Ireland, British India, imperial Russia and the Baltic German community all lurked in my childhood and adolescence. In those years the dominant identities were British-imperial and Catholic, both of which to a great extent imploded in the late 1960s and early 1970s. Into the hole they left moved imperial Russia, the world of my father's family, to whose study I have devoted most of the past fifty years of my life. Nevertheless, tsarist Russia never occupied the whole space. In 1991 the Latvian government generously restored to me the citizenship which my father had possessed until his homeland was annexed by Stalin in 1940. The collapse of the Berlin Wall and the re-emergence of central Europe got me so excited that I christened my son Maximilian Leopold in honour of my Austrian godfather and the Habsburgs, the supreme embodiments of central Europe's history.

The memory of empire in our family was by no means simply triumphalist. Thanks to his wonderfully intelligent and humane education at an excellent French state lycée my father's mindset was that of a left-leaning Parisian intellectual, with little nostalgia for any old regime. The empires my family served had all collapsed, amidst considerable chaos and tragedy. Moreover, my father's family had never been unequivocally Russian in the modern meaning of the word and none of our ancestors were ever English. As children, we spent weeks of every summer at the house of Hubert Butler near Kilkenny. Hubert was a Protestant gentleman from a minor branch of a family whose heads had been the dukes of Ormonde. He was nevertheless a famous Gaelic scholar and a strong if idiosyncratic Irish patriot. Adolescent memories of Ireland were of large houses which were damp and cold for reasons of both tradition and penury. The strangest was 'Clonalis' in Roscommon, home of O'Conor Don, descendant of the High Kings of Ireland who reigned in the eleventh century before the English came. If you overslept in one of the four-poster beds at 'Clonalis' you were liable to be woken by guided tours of Irish-American tourists in search of their roots. On the other hand, if you ventured on to the top floor on a rainy day – Roscommon is about the rainiest county in Ireland – it was wise to take an umbrella.

My only middle-class great-grandfather, Pringle Kennedy, was the most interesting of the four. Born in India, he barely escaped death in the 1857 rebellion. A successful barrister but also a fine amateur scholar, after the death of my great-grandmother he had the considerable courage for a man of his class and era to marry an Indian woman. Both she and my grandmother's sister were assassinated in 1908 by an Indian nationalist who mistook their carriage for that of an unpopular British official. Both British and Indian accounts of the assassination – a *cause célèbre* at the time – had their reasons for not mentioning that one of the two victims was an Indian woman.

For more than half of my life I have been married to a Japanese woman and have spent at least one-third of every year in Japan. This has been an education. The past, present and future look different when viewed from Tokyo. More recently, a partly Jewish son-in-law and a mostly Filipina daughter-in-law have added happily to the mix. This book was largely written in our country home on what one might describe as a high hill or small mountain, depending on whether or not one is in a Romantic mood. As I look out through the windows of my study, Mount Fuji dominates the view in all its majesty and beauty. On a clear day one can see a hundred miles or more, out to the Pacific Ocean and beyond. During a pandemic this was a scholar's paradise. The awfulness of the pandemic of course interrupted life in this paradise. This is a good moment to pay tribute to two of my dearest friends, professors Hari Vasudevan and David Washbrook, both of whom died at this time. Donald Trump's rantings were an even greater source of long-term anxiety than the pandemic itself. I was sustained by my daily *Financial Times* and by a plentiful store of Marmite, surest of all English identity-markers.

Amidst this riot of conflicting identities and loyalties, on one point I have always been clear. I am a British and specifically Cambridge historian. Much of what has been most valuable in my life is owed to the education I received in the Cambridge history faculty. My deep thanks go to my former teachers (many of them now dead): Derek Beales, Neil McKendrick, Henry Pelling, Simon Schama, Jonathan Steinberg and Norman Stone. To these names must be added that of Christopher Bayly, one of the finest and most generous historians I have ever known. Also remembered with deep respect and gratitude are the supervisor of my PhD, Hugh Seton-Watson; my academic godfather at the London School of Economics, Leonard Schapiro; and my history teacher at Downside, Desmond Gregory.

A number of friends and colleagues read my manuscript. The book's emphases and errors are mine, but without those readers it would have been much worse. The list includes Peter Fibinger Bang, Jeroen Duindam, Alan Forrest, Garth Fowden, Janet Hartley, Glen Rangwala and Peter Sarris. Cumhur Bekar was an extremely efficient research assistant and guided me on a wonderful expedition around Istanbul, helped by my former PhD student Serkan Kececi. Nivedita Chakrabarti was hugely helpful during my struggles with the technology of the Anti-Christ (IT) in the latter stages of writing this book. Among others who helped me in writing the book, the names of Christopher Clark, Jonathan Daly, Oliver Haardt, John Hall and Nicholas Postgate stand out. My friends Kyoji Komachi and Iehiro Tokugawa gave me valuable and deeply appreciated help in Japan. Vincent Haegele, Curator of the Versailles City Library, and Gérard Robaut took me on a truly memorable private tour of the backstairs at the palace of Versailles, including the royal library, Louis XVI's workshop, and the apartments of mesdames de Pompadour and du Barry. A number of members of staff at the *Financial Times* helped me to make comparisons between my topic and contemporary problems of leadership and geopolitics. Rather than mentioning individuals, perhaps a word of thanks to their employer is in order. A daily newspaper which can often keep me reading and thinking for ninety minutes is a wonder in today's world.

Very great thanks are also due to my agent, Natasha Fairweather, and to my publishers, Wendy Wolf and Simon Winder. In particular, Simon's advice on the manuscript went far beyond a publisher's call of duty and has made this book much better than it would otherwise have been. Very great thanks are also due to the labours of my eagle-eyed copy-editor Richard Mason, and to Eva Hodgkin and Cecilia Mackay. My family has put up with my obsession with emperors for many years with good humour. My wife has reconciled herself to living in homes whose walls are covered by portraits of Romanov and Qing monarchs and whose living rooms are occupied by vast-scale matryoshka dolls, beautifully painted in Moscow, which celebrate inter alia the Habsburgs, Ottomans, Mughals and Qing. Only a polite request that a third wave of Russian and Austro-Hungarian pre-Dreadnought battleships (wonderfully re-created in wood by Vietnamese boat-builders) be allowed to live in our bedroom caused a squeak of disquiet.

The greatest of all my debts as regards writing this book comes last. It is to Trinity College, Cambridge. For eight years I was a Senior

Research Fellow at Trinity – in other words a de facto research professor at Cambridge University with no administrative or teaching responsibilities. In all circumstances this is a position of privilege almost unequalled among Humanities professors in British academia. Given the state of my eyes, there is no chance that this book would have been written had I carried a normal load of administration and teaching. So, in the most literal sense, this book is owed to Trinity. In a broader sense, my eight years at Trinity were enormously fruitful and pleasant, thanks to my colleagues and Fellows, to the Masters (Lord Martin Rees and Sir Gregory Winter), to the history students, and to the wonderful college staff who did so much to help me at every turn. To all of them, and above all to Trinity itself, this book is dedicated.

Along with thanks there must also be apologies. Even when I began my last book, *Towards the Flame: Empire, War and the End of Tsarist Russia*, I was having increasing eye and deep ear/balance problems. These were greatly exacerbated by high-intensive work in the Russian archives on old manuscripts and microfilm. When I returned from the archives I was unable to read at all for a month. Subsequently things improved and during most of my research for this book I was able to read for six hours a day so long as I was careful. For a book of these dimensions that barely sufficed. Just as I was beginning work on this book Frederik Paulsen gave me an immensely generous donation to set up a foundation to help Russian (especially young) historians. Running this foundation out of my old university home – the London School of Economics – was a great honour and added purpose and value to my life. Inevitably, however, it also added to the pressure on my eyes and my time. Senior academics are drowned in appeals to read manuscripts, write references, examine theses, act on appointment committees and in general respond to a wide range of requests for advice and assistance. It quickly became clear to me that if I continued to yield to these appeals in previous fashion then I had no conceivable chance of writing this book. In the past six years I have continued to assist former students and close colleagues and have always tried to be helpful in cases where my knowledge was genuinely essential, but I have had to say no to far more requests than I would have wanted.

A parallel apology is due to the many scholars whose work has been of value to me but who are not mentioned in the endnotes. This book is the product of six years' labour but in many ways it sums up almost everything I have studied, taught and written about in a career of nearly fifty years. If I had listed all the works on which I have drawn, any ensuing bibliography would have been many times longer than the book itself. So I have been forced to confine myself to referencing all direct quotations and works that I would otherwise have been plagiarizing to a scandalous degree. I have largely limited my very brief suggestions on further reading to works in English, and I have spelled the names of people and places in the manner that is most familiar and accessible to an English-speaking readership.

Given the enormous complexity of this topic, I have also opted for the simplest possible structure for the book – a chronological narrative – to the extent possible. Some exceptions to this rule are inevitable. Chapter 1 is an introduction to the themes that run throughout the book. It explains what the job of being an emperor entailed, as well as what factors and qualities contributed to the success or failure of the enterprise. The rest of the book tackles the same issues on a case-by-case basis, which requires an understanding not just of individual personalities and dynastic traditions, but also of the challenges, resources and opportunities faced by specific emperors.

Chapters 2, 3, 4, 5 and 6 cover the millennia from the first empires down to the collapse of the (Western) Roman Empire and the Han Empire in China between the third and fifth centuries CE. Chapters 2, 3 and 4 look at the imperial monarchies of the Near East and Mediterranean from earliest times down to Rome. Chapter 5 covers the Mauryan dynasty of ancient India and chapter 6 investigates the origins and establishment of empire in ancient China. Traditionally, this whole period was usually described in the West as antiquity or the ancient world. The idea of a sharp break between this era and the following age made some sense from a Western perspective. After the fall of Rome, Europe was almost without empires for a millennium, thereby establishing a deep-rooted non-imperial tradition at the extreme western end of Eurasia. The emergence of Islam also marked a vital and dramatic break with antiquity. It is much harder to see so sharp a break between Han-dynasty and Tang-dynasty China. The book's structure and periodization in most cases are a matter of convenience, rather than an effort to impose a plan of history.

Nomadic empires, the subject of chapter 7, burst through the book's chronological structure. This chapter covers the whole period from the beginning of the first millennium BCE to the fifteenth century CE. During those 2,500 years nomadic military power was a crucial element in the history and geopolitics (by which term I mean the impact of geography on politics and policy) of Eurasia and northern Africa. One of the last nomadic empires – that of the Mongols – was also the largest empire thus far in history, subsequently being surpassed only by the British Empire.

Chapters 8 and 9 look at the two greatest non-steppe imperial monarchies of the millennium between the demise of the ancient world and what historians often call the early modern era, and they date from the sixteenth century CE. These two empires were Tang- and Song-dynasty China and the Islamic caliphate. Chapters 10, 11, 12, 13 and 14 cover the five greatest imperial monarchies of the so-called early modern era – namely the Habsburgs, Ottomans, Mughals, Qing and Romanovs. To some extent it is fair to identify a major break between this era and the previous period. With the Spanish conquest of the Americas in the sixteenth century begins what one might describe as global history. From this period also there commences the sharp decline of nomadic military power, which in time transformed Eurasian geopolitics. By the second half of the eighteenth century, European power was casting its shadow across ever more of the globe. Nevertheless, for most of the period covered by these five chapters the history of the great Eurasian empires of the Mughals and Qing was driven by local factors, not by European influence or power. For obvious geographical and geopolitical reasons this was less true of the Ottomans and Romanovs. The manner in which they responded to European challenges is an important element – though far from the only one – in my chapters on these two great imperial monarchies.

Once one reaches chapters 15 and 16 periodization becomes more clear-cut. Chapter 15 looks at the last two generations of the Habsburg dynasty before the French Revolution and concludes by discussing the Revolution itself and Napoleon. The ideology of the French Revolution is often seen as one of the two key ingredients of modernity. The other, even more fundamental, is the Industrial Revolution. Chapter 16 looks at imperial monarchy between 1815 and 1945 in the era when Europe ruled the globe and when society, culture and politics were transformed by the impact of the two great modern revolutions. There is a fundamental difference between the agrarian and pastoral societies and economies which sustained all pre-nineteenth-century empires and the world created by the Industrial Revolution. One key theme running through chapter 16 is that, in this radically new era, hereditary, sacred imperial monarchy was no longer viable. Another theme is that the strategies and decisions adopted by imperial monarchies to survive this era's challenges were enormously important at the time and have left many a mark on our contemporary world.

In the Shadow of the Gods

I

Being an Emperor

This book is a collective biography of emperors and an anatomy of hereditary imperial monarchy as a type of polity. Empires and imperial monarchies had existed since ancient times, but the last true empires disappeared in the twentieth century. In this book I cover the history of empire across the millennia and throughout most of the world. At the book's heart lies a key tension. To make any sense of so vast a topic requires concepts, comparisons and generalizations. But this book is less about empires than about the people who ruled them. It is to some extent possible to generalize about emperors and divide them into distinct groups and categories. Individual dynasties, for example, had specific traditions. But in the end monarchs were human beings and their individual personalities were crucial. One way of approaching this book is to see it as a contribution to the old debate about the roles of impersonal forces and human agency in history.[1]

Sometimes when dining at Trinity College, Cambridge, I was asked about my research by other Fellows who were natural scientists. I tried to argue that their research and mine were similar. Often they were experimenting with how materials behaved at extreme temperatures and I was doing the same to human beings. Being an emperor often strained an individual beyond what the human frame was designed to tolerate. The results could be spectacular. One happy example must suffice. Writing this book in isolation in my house on a Japanese mountain during the pandemic I often had recourse to the BBC's international news. For many months before news bulletins there frequently appeared a clip from the admirable Prime Minister of New Zealand, Jacinda Ardern, in which she said that she was only the second national leader in history to bear a child when in office. Her intention – to act as a role model for young women – was splendid, but I felt it a shame to ignore the story of Empress Maria Theresa of Austria (r. 1740–80). When she inherited the throne aged twenty-three she had no experience or training in government. Her father, the Holy Roman Emperor Charles VI, considered this inappropriate for a female. So he had appointed her husband, Prince Francis Stephen of Lorraine, to the key imperial council rather than her. Maria Theresa loved Francis Stephen deeply but after her father's death in 1740 she quickly made it clear that she was the boss. Four enemy armies – Prussian, French, Bavarian and Saxon – invaded her empire, since a woman's claim to inherit a crown was easily disputed. Courage and strong leadership qualities rescued Maria Theresa and her empire from near catastrophe. She ruled for forty years, playing the leading role in government and administration, and leaving behind an empire which was not just much more powerful and prosperous than before but also more humane. During these years she gave birth to sixteen children. What can it have been like, to live such a life and work in such an extraordinary role? What qualities did it take to perform this role successfully? These are key themes of this book.

Most of what we know about emperors relates to how they did their jobs. Even today, the personalities of top leaders often disappear behind the office they hold and the behaviour it imposes on them. An emperor's personality was even more likely to be subsumed in the majesty of his office, for which he had usually been prepared since childhood and which he held until he died. Even in modern times a monarchy's aura and legitimacy require an element of mystery. In the past that was even more the case, since the monarch was in general both a semi-sacred figure and the supreme political leader. No monarch could safely reveal his innermost thoughts to his subjects. Although there are a few exceptions, in general the further back one goes in history the scantier becomes the evidence about the inner man behind the royal mask. Nevertheless, enough evidence does exist to enable me to present a rounded and plausible picture of some emperors. As always with human beings, their personalities were formed by a combination of inherited genes, upbringing and the cultural norms of their families, societies and eras. My task is to place these personalities within the context of the specific challenges, constraints and opportunities they faced.[2]

I have been studying aspects of imperial monarchy for much of my academic life. Even so, the sheer scale and complexity of this book makes writing it a challenge. My first chapter is an attempt to guide the reader across a vast and complicated terrain. Fortunately this terrain does have many common features. Emperors often faced similar challenges. They often used comparable means and tactics to achieve their goals. All of them operated within powerful and sometimes typical constraints. The most obvious of these constraints were external: they included pre-modern communications and the power of foreign states and domestic vested interests. Constraints were also internal, meaning an emperor's own values and intellectual horizons. In this chapter I introduce some of the key themes that run through my book: these include the human life cycle, the dynamics of family politics, the role of women, the politics of succession and the training of heirs. Leadership is also a key uniting theme in this book. For emperors, leadership usually came in many guises. To varying degrees and in different combinations emperors could be sacred symbols, warrior kings, political leaders, chief executive officers of the government machine, heads of a family, impresarios directing the many elements of 'soft power' essential to any regime's survival. Tracing the different and shifting balance between these elements of an emperor's role, across individual monarchs, dynastic traditions and eras, is one of the main tasks of the book.

Four key elements went into the make-up of an emperor. First, he was a human being, and in the great majority of cases a male. Second, he was a leader. Third, he was a hereditary monarch. Fourth, he ruled over an empire. In this book, and especially when constructing bio-graphical sketches of emperors, all four elements in his make-up merge. For now, however, addressing them separately helps us to understand who emperors were and what their role entailed.

The most important similarity between emperors was also the most banal. The emperor was a human being. He therefore had the basic human need for food, drink, sleep and sex. Humans are social animals and most emperors needed company and even friendship. They were also usually capable of appreciating beauty and feeling love. Each stage of human life has its specific features. The child is vulnerable, the young man seeks to assert himself, the older one can gain a measure of wisdom from his experience, old people lose physical and mental endurance. Being humans, emperors did not live long and had to face the prospect of death, but they also contemplated the mystery of birth and fertility among humans, animals and plants. From earliest times emperors like other human beings looked at the stars and wondered about the meaning of life and earth's relationship to the heavens.

Of course, human nature and, above all, the human mind did not remain static over the millennia covered by this book. Most monarchs in prehistory were semi-sacred figures who mediated between living humans and the spirits permeating the world of nature, the realm inhabited by dead ancestors and the forces in the heavens that directed affairs on earth. These monarchs provided a link to mysterious powers such as the sun, fire and fertility. In modern parlance they were shamans. The only emperor still reigning on earth is the Japanese monarch, Naruhito. In terms of status and antiquity his closest contemporary rivals are Britain's Queen Elizabeth II and King Philip VI of Spain. As is the case with all the older European dynasties, the British and Spanish monarchs are the descendants of leaders of war-bands who were semi-domesticated by one of the great salvation religions, Christianity. Emperor Naruhito's lineage dates to a more ancient and animist world of sacred monarchy.[3]

In the centuries between roughly 500 BCE and 700 CE there emerged the great religions and ethical systems that to a significant degree still define the world's major cultural zones: Buddhism, Hinduism, Confucianism, Christianity and Islam. All the great empires in time adopted one or other of these religions. In the Chinese case a synthesis between Confucianism and Buddhism evolved over time. These religions offered rulers explanations of life's meaning, a degree of inner calm and purpose, a system of ethics and a cosmology. But these religions were forced to cohabit with an older world of magic and astrology. Until the sixteenth century even Christian and Islamic theologians admitted that the stars might be a part of the divine message and plan. The Scientific Revolution and the Enlightenment undermined this belief and created a fundamental shift in thinking. As regards both personality and policy there are some similarities between the Roman emperor Julian I ('the Apostate': r. 361–3 CE) and Joseph II of Austria (r. 1765–90 CE). Both were intelligent and thoughtful men, but their impatience and excitability could at times verge on hysteria. Unlike most hereditary emperors, they both came to the throne with radical plans for domestic reform. Julian sought to restore paganism, Joseph to implement fundamental reforms based on Enlightenment principles of utility, uniformity and progress. In both cases the emperors' domestic programmes were wrecked by their adventurous foreign policies and the wars these caused. In one sense, therefore,

Julian and Joseph are good subjects for comparison. But a chasm divided the world of classical pagan gods and neo-Platonic metaphysics inhabited by Julian from the secular, utilitarian and rational world view which Joseph imbibed from the Enlightenment.[4]

Normal human attributes could have dramatic consequences when the human was an emperor. For a man who was lord of all he surveyed on earth, death could be even more intolerable than for ordinary mortals. Some monarchs killed themselves swallowing elixirs in order to gain eternal life. The great religions – Buddhism, Hinduism, Christianity, Zoroastrianism and Islam – provided answers to questions of death and immortality. Even so, one reason why emperors built palaces, mausolea and monuments of vast scale was their desire to leave their imprint for eternity. Usually educated by the leading cultural figures of their era and possessing vast means, emperors often patronized the finest artists and musicians of their day.

For a monarch, being a patron was much easier than being a friend. Friendship usually entails some degree of equality, along with a measure of banter, repartee and criticism. An insecure or jealous ruler might be especially prone both to yearning for friendship and resenting anyone whose behaviour suggested a degree of intimacy, let alone equality. Some tutors of princes warned them that, once they ascended the throne, they could never have true friends. On the other hand, second-century (CE) Roman thinkers claimed that the four great emperors of Rome's classical era (Trajan, Hadrian, Antoninus Pius and Marcus Aurelius) were immune to flattery because they opened themselves up to true friendship. Roman aristocratic culture liked to think of the emperor as merely *primus inter pares*. Most imperial traditions were less 'egalitarian'. A monarch's search for friends might well prove frustrating and fruitless. Given the potential power and patronage of the monarch's 'friends', the search could also have great political consequences. Even more dangerous might be a monarch's quest for sex and love. Louis XIV (r. 1643–1715) warned his heir that he must never allow any friend to become a 'favourite' and control the channels of information and patronage on which royal power rested. Still more fatal was a mistress who occupied this position, given that the charms natural to the female sex gave her a uniquely strong hold over a monarch.[5]

This is a reminder that the emperor was not just a normal man but a leader. Much of what is taught about leadership in business schools or written in the memoirs and biographies of present-day presidents and CEOs is relevant to emperors. Manfred Kets de Vries is a professor at INSEAD, one of the world's leading business schools, but also a practising clinical psychoanalyst with a PhD in psychology. His main focus as both professor and psychiatrist is leadership. In his most recent book, *The CEO Whisperer*, he compares his role in advising and analysing CEOs to that of the fool in a Renaissance monarch's court: he has a licence to speak truth to power. Power is the essence of leadership. The corruptions and temptations of power are one of the oldest tropes in political thinking. Reflecting on his reading about the Nazi leaders but also his lifetime spent in analysing and advising CEOs, Kets de Vries writes that 'it is a sad truth that our inner wolf doesn't need much encouragement to be set free and start devouring everybody who stands in its way'. The education of an emperor was designed in part to control the wolf and even turn him into a sheepdog.[6]

Some of the CEOs whom Kets de Vries describes and analyses had personalities similar to a number of well-known monarchs. Louis XIII of France (r. 1610–43) reigned at a vital time for France and Europe. During his reign the French monarchy regained its power, laid many of the foundations of the modern French state, and successfully led European resistance to possible Habsburg hegemony in Europe. The decisive victory at Rocroi just five days after Louis XIII's death and his son's ascent to the throne was by no means the end of the process by which France replaced the Habsburgs as Europe's leading power, but it marked, in Winston Churchill's words about the victory at El Alamein in November 1942, 'the end of the beginning'. The mastermind of Louis's successes both at home and abroad was his chief minister, Cardinal Richelieu. The first half of France's struggle with the Habsburgs put enormous strains on French society and aroused great opposition. Success often hung by a thread and would not have occurred without Richelieu. His hold on power depended on the king's support alone. It was rooted in the shared commitment of monarch and minister to royal power and France's glory. But it also required the minister's expert handling of his king's fragile and unpredictable character.[7]

Louis XIII found living difficult and ruling an excruciating challenge. Physical defects did not help: the king's tongue dangled and he was inclined to slobber. His painful stammer was an everyday reminder of his inner nervousness and lack of confidence. He worshipped his father,

Henry IV, and no doubt suffered greatly from his assassination in 1610, as a result of which the already troubled nine-year-old heir suddenly found himself king of France. His mother, Catherine de' Medici, made no secret of her preference for Louis's younger brother, Gaston of Orléans, and became the leader of elite opposition to Louis's policies. Louis was bisexual. His life was punctuated by intense emotional relationships with male and female courtiers, all of which ended badly. The king desperately needed emotional support, resented this need, and had a high sense of his status as monarch.

Implacable determination to achieve his goals for France and defend monarchical power against all challenges were the main features of Louis XIII's reign. Kets de Vries describes a similar personality mix of inner fragility, near-obsession at defending their power and deep-rooted stubbornness among some CEOs. Given 'these stubborn people's vulnerable mental equilibrium, you have to be extremely careful not only about what you say but also when to say it. And when the time is right to present a different opinion, it should be done very respectfully.' Kets de Vries calls advising such leaders an 'exercise in emotional judo'. In time, Richelieu became his king's mentor and father figure, in the process exploiting his position as a cardinal and the king's need for spiritual guidance and comfort. He studied Louis's character with great psychological insight, came to know his every mood, and 'took extreme care to avoid giving any impression that he was trespassing on the king's authority'. Richelieu played the role not just of Louis's minister but also his equivalent of a Kets de Vries. In his case, however, the stakes were far higher – not just the fate of a company but the future of the French state and the European balance of power.[8]

Among the many pearls of wisdom in his book is Kets de Vries's warning that in almost any hierarchical organization the leaders' 'subordinates are likely to tell them what they want to hear'. Successful leaders must therefore operate and create a culture which checks this weakness. All competent emperors would have agreed with this. So does Barack Obama in his memoirs. Most emperors would also have nodded at the comments in Obama's memoirs about the fickleness of political friendships, the role of luck and chance in politics, the loneliness of supreme power, and the need to preserve both inner and outer calm in the face of adversity and the need to make difficult decisions. Some emperors trod the same path as Tony Blair as they tired of the pettiness and the frustrations of domestic government and concentrated their attention on the grander and more satisfying arena of international relations. Armies and diplomats then as now usually operated under a leader's direct control and obeyed his orders, unlike the vested interests confronted in domestic policy. It is true that a monarch, let alone an emperor, almost always enjoyed a status and aura far superior to a contemporary British or American politician or CEO. This guaranteed that he would very seldom be openly contradicted by his subordinates, but it increased the chances that they would not tell him unpalatable truths. Publicly prostrating oneself before the monarch and then in private sabotaging his wishes in order to serve the interests of oneself and one's clients was the oldest trick in the politics of imperial elites and courts.[9]

To rule effectively, the emperor required many of the contemporary attributes of a successful leader. Politics and government are a gruelling business: a ruler needed stamina, mental and physical toughness, and self-confidence. He needed to have a sound judgement of problems and people, which is partly innate but also the product of education and experience. A good brain was essential for setting priorities, weighing conflicting advice and matching ends to needs. Resolution was needed to implement policies in the face of inertia and opposition. As important was the emotional intelligence to choose and manage wise and loyal advisers and lieutenants. In any government, let alone any far-flung empire, no leader could rule effectively without such followers. Appointing subordinates whom one knows to be abler than oneself requires not just self-confidence but also humility. Unlike a contemporary political or business leader, the emperor's status meant that at least he did not need to see such men as potential rivals or successors. One impressive work on leadership stresses the need but also the difficulty for a CEO to achieve an 'appropriate balance between warmth and distance'. This was even harder for emperors, who were simultaneously sacred figures and deeply embroiled in government and politics. Nevertheless, the most successful emperors knew how to inspire and manage human beings, and to retain their loyalty. In his study of recent British and American prime ministers and presidents, David Runciman writes that 'self-knowledge may be the most valuable political commodity of all'. Kets de Vries agrees, quoting Confucius in support: 'He who conquers himself will be the mightiest warrior.' This too was true of emperors. After many years in power some contemporary leaders and CEOs lose their sense of reality and fall victim to arrogance and megalomania: 'their grandiose sense of self-importance and their feelings of entitlement are ultimately self-damaging'. Emperors had far more reason to succumb to these temptations. But the surest path to disaster for an emperor was to believe the official ideology that proclaimed him to be virtuous, all-powerful, all-seeing and almost divine.[10]

Just as contemporary business school studies of leadership have much to say about how to be a successful emperor, so too Louis XIV's memoirs have good advice for anyone attempting to be a leader. They are a goldmine for those interested in an intelligent insider's view of how best to be a great monarch. These memoirs were never intended for publication. They were written as a guide to rulership for Louis's heir. The king wrote that the monarch of a great state needed to set himself high and ambitious goals and then focus his attention and resources on achieving them. The state's interests must always take precedence over the king's pleasures or inclinations. Statesmanship required fixed resolution about goals but flexibility as regards tactics. Circumstances changed constantly in politics and the ruler must adapt to them. In matters of foreign policy and war – which Louis saw as the core of a great monarch's activity – reason and caution must prevail as regards tactics, though the status and glory of France and its kings were vital strategic goals. Decisions must be taken after weighing all the available evidence. Choosing able ministers was 'the principal function of a monarch'. He must encourage his advisers to give him honest advice, rewarding and promoting men who disagreed with him and told him things he did not want to hear. The monarch must not hesitate to appoint strong, ambitious and intelligent ministers. His status and his hold on the levers of patronage and reward gave him the means to control them. But to do this effectively he must be knowledgeable and well-informed. This demanded both hard work and keeping many channels of information open. Most important, monarchs must know themselves and 'learn to examine ourselves very strictly'. Louis's role was on the one hand exalted, on the other deeply mired in the realities of human nature and politics. He warned his heir that a monarch was besieged by applicants for patronage. It was always easiest to say yes, thereby gaining a comfortable life and a reputation for generosity, but no state's coffers were sufficient to satisfy most of those in search of favour. One of a monarch's hardest tasks was to defend the treasury but to do so in a graceful manner that did not offend the proud aristocrats who were always first in the queue of applicants.[11]

Of course, Louis XIV was not just a politician or chief executive. He combined in his person the modern roles of sovereign, head of state and head of government. He ruled with an assurance born of the fact that he was God's anointed and that his family had reigned over France for more than seven hundred years. Not all monarchs were as secure. The most famous book on royal leadership ever written is probably Niccolò Machiavelli's *The Prince*. This work has some value for any leader. Jeffrey Skilling, formerly the CEO of Enron and now serving a long gaol sentence, in his heyday was 'sometimes also known as "The Prince" after Machiavelli's famous study. In fact, new recruits were encouraged to read *The Prince* from beginning to end as part of an indoctrination method.' In some respects the dog-eat-dog world in which Enron thrived was similar to the world of Italian sixteenth-century newly minted city-state despots and dynasties in which Machiavelli lived. There were similarities also to the world of the Roman emperors from which Machiavelli drew many examples in his book. As Machiavelli himself recognized, there were major differences between the politics of an Italian despotism and the Roman Empire on the one hand, and the politics of a long-established and legitimate dynasty on the other. For example, Machiavelli warned a prince never to appoint a prime minister to run his government or a general to command his army for fear of having his throne usurped. If their empire and dynasty were to survive, emperors often had to do both these things. Most of the dynasties and emperors studied in this book had a legitimacy strong enough to make this possible. We have seen in the case of Louis XIII and Richelieu how important this could be. Just as France's rise to first position in Europe depended on their relationship, the same was true in the Prussian case as regards Otto von Bismarck's relationship with the king and subsequently emperor William I.[12]

The emperors who came closest to Machiavelli's model were the founders of dynasties. Unlike the great majority of the emperors whom I write about, they inherited neither office nor legitimacy and their rule did not rest on inertia or habit. By definition, they struggled in the snake pit of politics rather than standing above it, as a legitimate emperor from an old dynasty could partly do. Dynastic founders needed all of Machiavelli's dark arts. They also usually needed some degree of charisma. The idea of charisma was introduced into political debate by Max

Weber, the most famous sociologist of the early twentieth century. Weber's own definition of charisma was not entirely clear and subsequent use of the concept has further extended its meaning. In its origin the word and idea of charisma dates back to ancient Greece. It denoted a person of such superhuman qualities and deeds that he must have been touched by the gods. Charisma was closely linked to heroism on the battlefield. It was largely confined to males. Weber himself drew on the Old Testament prophets as early examples of charisma. A leader's charisma drew supporters to him, especially in times of turmoil when established authority, laws and norms had broken down.[13]

Weber made a sharp distinction between authority which was based on personal charisma and authority rooted in ancient traditions, institutions and hierarchies. Of course, he knew that occasional hereditary monarchs also possessed and exploited a strong degree of personal charisma, Alexander the Great being the most famous example. The distinction made by Weber between the two types of authority is nevertheless real and important. Charismatic authority was personal, fleeting and very often both the result and the cause of disruption. A hereditary dynast must on the contrary subordinate his personality to the interests of collectives – meaning the family to which he belonged and the realm which he had inherited from his ancestors and for whose fate he was responsible. Hereditary monarchy usually rested on order, stability and custom. The classical Greek hero stood above all rules and norms. He was the prototype of nineteenth-century Europe's Romantic genius. One author refers to 'the madness and excess of charisma'. Such a man might use his charisma to inspire widespread disobedience or even revolt against established dynastic authority. Still more frightening for a ruler was the link made by Weber between charisma and prophecy. Mass millenarian revolts sparked by charismatic prophets were the nightmare of emperors. These occurred periodically, for example in China. The last such revolt, the so-called Taiping, occurred between 1845 and 1864 and has been described as the largest uprising in human history, reputed to have killed more people than died during the First World War. Islamic empires were especially vulnerable to the threat of charismatic prophets. One of them, the Safavid leader Ismail, transformed Middle Eastern politics in the early sixteenth century and turned Iran into the homeland of the Shiite faith.[14]

In this book I pay relatively little attention to the founders of dynasties. By definition, these men were untypical of the great majority of history's emperors. They were different in upbringing, mindset and talents to the hereditary monarchs who are the subjects of this work. Their position as hereditary monarchs is the third of the four key elements in the make-up of the emperors whom I study. The politics specific to hereditary monarchy are one of the core themes of this book. Hereditary monarchy means families holding power over the generations, in other words dynastic politics. Families in power share some of the dynamics of families in general and in their case these dynamics can have major political consequences. Brothers can be either close friends or rivals. Which tendency prevailed among royal brothers had dramatic consequences for the stability and even survival of dynasties. In monarchies whose system of succession required an emperor's sons to fight for the throne, bitter enmity was inevitable since those who failed the competition died. The Mughal and Ottoman dynasties followed this tradition. Both ordinary and royal mothers-in-law and daughters-in-law can compete to influence their son and husband. Even in the first years of the twentieth century the rivalry between the wife and mother of the last Russian emperor, Nicholas II (r. 1894–1917), mattered, above all because the two women came to espouse diametrically opposite political strategies and therefore supported different candidates for high office. For the first ten years of his reign Nicholas was more influenced by his mother. For the remainder he listened more to his wife.[15]

In imperial monarchies, as in all pre-modern polities, women were usually subordinated to men. Female rulers were rare. Unlike in some smaller African countries, succession was never by preference in the matrilineal line. Nevertheless, the core realities of hereditary monarchy gave great power to women. Very few official posts were open to females, but in most dynastic states politics was at least as much concerned with patronage as with policy. Women at court were often formidable patrons who stood at the centre of the royal and elite family networks that formed the core of the political system. The monarch was the supreme source of patronage and policy. Access to him was the greatest of prizes. Having the monarch on one's own for hours on end was a courtier's dream. In the nature of things, the ruler's sexual partners were best placed to live this dream. Succession is always at the core of politics. Today's democratic politicians obsess about opinion polls and elections. In hereditary monarchies succession was determined by biology. The basic point is simple. Historically it was never difficult to exclude women from armies, bureaucracies and law courts, but no one has ever devised a way to remove them from the business of family and reproduction.[16]

For enemies of hereditary monarchy, female power was all the more insidious for being partly informal and hidden from view in the monarch's private apartments. Like British puritans in the seventeenth century, French Jacobins associated monarchy with female intrigue and the corruption, vice and luxury of the court. They contrasted this world to their wholly masculine ideal of the sincere and dutiful, republican citizen-in-arms. Many ministers in hereditary monarchies shared the Jacobins' distrust of women. Confucian official ideology was no less puritan and misogynist than Jacobinism. For Confucian officials, an emperor who spent time dallying with his concubines, let alone listening to their advice on policy and appointments, was betraying the right order of the universe. In the Chinese case, female influence was especially detested because it operated behind the walls of the harem, from which all men except the emperor and eunuchs were banned. Nevertheless, though ministers might resent female influence, they knew that they had little alternative but to cultivate good relations with the females who had the emperor's ear.[17]

Assessing female influence quickly confronts the tension at the heart of this book between structure and biography. In most empires the emperor's mother outranked his wife. This was always the case in the Chinese and Ottoman harems. The position of a European queen-consort was in principle stronger than that not just of Ottoman, Mughal or Chinese concubines but even of Chinese empresses in most dynasties. In Christian monarchies the ruler could have only one wife, divorce was extremely difficult, and only legitimate children could inherit the throne. In China the empress-consort's status was lower than that of her mother-in-law, wives could be dismissed, and in some dynasties their sons did not even have precedence over the sons of concubines as regards inheriting the crown, though in other cases empresses were allowed to 'adopt' – in other words partly expropriate – the sons of concubines. Nevertheless, such generalizations are at most only part of the story. A woman's influence depended above all on her personal relationship with the man who had supreme power. Of all aspects of life, none is less susceptible to generalization than the relationship between a man and a woman. The status and position of Louis XV's queen, Marie Leszynska, was in one sense untouchable: she was queen for life and the mother of the heir. But no one doubted that she had far less influence on patronage and policy than the king's favourite mistress, Madame de Pompadour.[18]

In principle the most powerful women of all were Christian consorts whom their husbands loved and to whom they were faithful. Adding the institutional status of a Christian queen to monopoly of the monarch's sexual and even emotional life was a powerful combination. Resentment at these women's influence on patronage and policy was inevitable. Immediately the names spring to mind of Henrietta Maria, wife of England's Charles I (r. 1625–49); Marie-Antoinette, wife of Louis XVI of France (r. 1774–92); and Alexandra, wife of Tsar Nicholas II (r. 1894–1917). All three women were notorious in their time and their unpopularity played an important part in their husbands' downfall.[19]

Of course, the British, French and Russian monarchies did not collapse just because monarchs were overly influenced by their wives, but there was nevertheless some connection. To run his government successfully a monarch needed many of the qualities of a lion-tamer. He had to be able to dominate the tough, determined and sometimes ruthless men who often reach the top of political systems. In deeply misogynist cultures the perception that Charles, Louis and Nicholas could not even tame their wives was a blow to their authority. It also mattered greatly that Henrietta Maria, Marie-Antoinette and Alexandra were foreign princesses who nevertheless operated at the centre of the political system and played a crucial role in the upbringing of their son, the future monarch. As political tensions rose these women could be pilloried as agents of an enemy power. Xenophobia combined with misogyny. The accusation had some grain of truth in the case of Marie-Antoinette, very little as regards Henrietta Maria, and none whatsoever where Empress Alexandra was concerned. Even less just were the accusations made against them of sexual depravity. In the last years of the Romanov dynasty Empress Alexandra, Queen Victoria's prudish granddaughter, was even widely credited with being the mistress of Rasputin. Such accusations had an old lineage. Right back in the thirteenth century, at the very origins of what one might call Parisian public opinion, Queen Blanche of Castile, the relentlessly pious mother of Saint Louis (Louis IX, r. 1226–70), was accused both of debauchery and treason. Her main lover, so it was claimed, was the Papal Legate – a perfect target for xenophobia and prurience.[20]

The politics of hereditary monarchies was greatly influenced by the marriage strategies of dynasties. Some dynasties married members of the aristocracy. This boosted the power and arrogance of aristocratic magnates and their followers. It caused intense jealousy within the aristocratic elite. It even on occasion led to the throne being usurped by royal in-laws. To avoid these dangers some dynasties 'married down'. Before the time of Peter I 'the Great' (r. 1682–1725) Russian tsars usually married girls from respectable families of the middle gentry. This avoided stirring up aristocratic rivalry and jealousy. His modest in-laws were no threat to the tsar but could on the contrary become useful and dependable allies. The most extreme version of 'marrying down' was provided by the Ottomans, who avoided marriage and instead produced heirs from slave concubines. In the era of greatest Ottoman power each concubine was only allowed one son and the man who won the competition to succeed his father killed all his half-brothers. Inevitably, Ottoman court politics became a particularly vicious zero-sum game. At the opposite end of the spectrum was the European tradition of royalty only marrying their peers. This was only possible in a multi-polar international system in which rival monarchs nevertheless respected each other (and no one else) as equals. By marrying only royalty Europe's dynasties emphasized their superior status to even the grandest aristocrats. But royal intermarriage had its dangers, of which accusations of treason against foreign consorts was only one. Repeated intermarriage between dynasties could mean inbreeding and loss of fertility. Combined with Christian monogamy this could lead to dynasties dying out in the male line. The nearest relatives in the female line were then by definition foreign princes. The result was often wars of succession that by the eighteenth century spread their devastation across much of the globe.[21]

In the great majority of imperial dynasties succession descended from father to son. This gave immense political importance to the father–son relationship. The heir was his father's pride and joy, the future of his dynasty and part of the monarch's own place in eternity. But he could also be a major threat. As the monarch aged and his grip on affairs weakened, his courtiers' attention could easily turn towards the young prince who represented the future. The prince himself might feel increasing impatience with his father's rule. The accession of a new monarch had the advantage that it could bring new ideas, new energy and new groups into a dynasty's government and patronage system. It could also promote into top office a young man generally seen as a pale imitation of his father. As in all political systems, succession was the cause of much instability and intrigue. How much instability depended greatly on a dynasty's laws and conventions as regards succession.

At one extreme was the prevailing European system of male primogeniture. This maximized stability but ensured that the throne would sometimes be occupied by children or incompetents. At the other extreme was the Ottoman and Mughal practice of forcing the rulers' sons to fight for the throne. This ensured that succession would go to men who were competent generals and political leaders but at the price of periodic civil wars. From the ruler's perspective the European system, deeply rooted in law and tradition by the seventeenth century, reduced his hold over his heir but made it less likely that he himself would be deposed as his sons competed to succeed him. This sometimes happened to Ottoman and Mughal emperors. Even if they avoided this danger, the latter part of their reigns became increasingly agonizing as the struggle to succeed them undermined political stability and loyalties. Some dynasties attempted a compromise solution to the dilemmas of succession, allowing the emperor to choose his heir. In principle this introduced an element of merit into inheriting the throne while reducing the risks of conflict. To achieve this result an emperor needed to choose his ablest son rather than the one he himself, his favourite concubine or key court factions liked best. This was far from certain. Nor could any system guarantee that a monarch's choice would prevail after his demise, especially if the designated heir was still a child. In all hereditary monarchies stability was threatened if a monarch lived into his dotage or died so young that his heir was still a child. For all their misogyny, most political cultures recognized that a mother was her child-son's legitimate guardian and placed regency in her hands. Pragmatic considerations reinforced cultural norms. Mothers were far less likely to usurp the child's throne than uncles. But regencies were usually a time of weakness for hereditary monarchies. For newer and less legitimate dynasties they might prove fatal.[22]

However it selected the heir to the throne, a political system was likely to put great effort into preparing him for his future role. On the frail shoulders of this child, once he came to the throne, would rest the fate of his dynasty and empire. Once he was emperor no human being would have the right to criticize or control him. He would have access to every luxury, vice and temptation that the world could offer. Especially in dynasties where succession was fixed, the heir would know from his earliest years that he was a very special person. In time he would come to realize that most people he encountered hoped to use him for their personal goals and ambitions. The discipline, balance and sense of responsibility essential for his future calling would have to come from within. These qualities needed to be instilled in the child and adolescent by adults for whom he felt trust and affection. Winning the child's trust in the early, innocent years was the foundation for many brilliant careers. Some tutors later became chief ministers. The best job at court for a woman was to be governess of the royal children. In Europe this post was always held by aristocrats. Many governesses filled a deep emotional void in the prince's life and they and their kin often benefited from this greatly. Governesses and tutors needed to instil into the child a deeply felt sense of religious and dynastic obligation if the royal ego was not subsequently to run amok. On the other hand, creating a dutiful, pious and obedient young man was insufficient and even dangerous. A future ruler needed a strong will, self-confidence and resolution. Educating a future autocrat is a formidable challenge. Some dynasties trained their heirs much better than others. Studying princes' education provides unique insights into the values, culture and self-belief of the elite world in which their dynasty and polity were rooted. In today's business schools the question of whether leadership can be taught or is a quality inherent in the genes is much debated. Studying the education of heirs to imperial thrones approaches this question from an unusual angle.[23]

Perhaps the most important question about hereditary monarchy is why such a self-evidently flawed system of government should nevertheless have been by far the most prevalent type of polity in history. After all, if the aim of politics was to give power to the virtuous and the competent, no rational person could believe that this was best achieved through the principle of hereditary succession. Self-evident to modern minds, this truth was equally evident not just to the ancient Greeks but also to many ancient Chinese and Indian thinkers. Nevertheless, in almost all ancient civilizations sacred and hereditary monarchy dominated political thinking. In most parts of the world its basic principles went almost unchallenged until the second half of the eighteenth century. Not until the twentieth century, however, did sacred, hereditary monarchy cease to be the predominant form of polity on earth.[24]

One key reason why hereditary, sacred monarchy prevailed was that in the majority of pre-modern societies political thinking was practically a sub-branch of theology. In most cultures explanations and justifications for events and institutions on earth were generally found in some version of Heaven. Things happened because the gods willed or at least allowed them to do so. The Christian anointed monarch, the Buddhist wheel-turning king, the Muslim Caliph and the Chinese son of Heaven linked humans to Heaven. Monarchs were seen as agents of divine and human order and essential for their preservation. If the gods had created humans then divine and natural law must at least overlap. Human society could not survive without a just but, where necessary, stern hereditary ruler, wrote Louis XIV. The king was no doubt sincere in writing that by preserving and defending the social order the Christian monarch was allowing true religion and morals to flourish and thereby serving God. In addition, nothing seemed so natural as that son should succeed father. This was after all the near-universal rule of everyday life in most societies ruled by emperors. Aristotle wrote that any king would wish his son to succeed him. From very ancient times heredity, in the form of lineage, played a big role in the organization of society and the legitimation of authority. The earliest origins of monarchy were often related to claims to belong to a tribe's senior lineage, the one most directly related to some mythical and usually semi-divine founder.[25]

Natural law and divine blessing overlapped and merged with pragmatic and prudential reasons for supporting hereditary monarchy. The alternative was generally seen to be chaos. Few political thinkers had any faith in the people's rationality, self-discipline or capacity for self-government. Elected monarchy was seen as an invitation to civil war within the elite and the weakening of royal power. Monarchy emerged in response to the needs of increasingly large and complex societies for a supreme adjudicator of disputes, guardian of order and defender against external threats. Countless historical examples existed of the chaos that happened when monarchies fell. Not just thinkers drawn from the elite but popular wisdom and legend also often sustained monarchy. Ancient dynasties became entwined in the legends and the identities of the communities they ruled. Local elites were usually much greater exploiters than a distant monarch. Only a powerful hereditary monarch might be able to constrain their exactions and their conflicts with each other. The greatest victims of anarchy and invasion were in general the masses. Confucian political thinking and ancient Chinese legend emphasized the need for wise and virtuous rulers. This need had to be balanced against the requirements of filial piety and hereditary right. Chinese 'abdication legends' told of mythical ancient kings who handed power not to their son but to their wisest minister. In the late fourth century BCE the ruler of the state of Yin followed this path. Unsurprisingly, his son objected and the result was civil war. The lesson seemed clear: hereditary right could not safely be challenged.[26]

The Greeks were unique among political thinkers of the ancient world in often defending democracy. Aristotle believed in the self-governing, participatory Greek city state and saw the Greeks as 'the best-governed of any nation'. He added that 'the best political community is formed by citizens of the middle class' and that when a city had a large number of middle-class males the move towards democracy was almost inevitable. This is the 'Washington Consensus' in ancient form. On the other hand, Aristotle believed that democracy was only viable in medium-sized city states, which could 'be taken in at a single view'. Even large city states were almost impossible to govern well. Plato had less sympathy for middle-class democracy than Aristotle. He wrote that there would never be good government 'unless either philosophers become kings in our cities, or the people who are now called kings and rulers become real, true philosophers'. His philosopher-rulers would require a long and austere education to achieve the true wisdom and understanding needed to govern. By far the most important and successful philosopher-guardians in history were the Confucian elite of scholar-officials. They too had a long and austere education in what we now call 'the Humanities'. These men ruled China for two millennia in alliance with emperors who claimed to be guided by Confucian philosophy. If Confucian elites – sometimes grudgingly – supported the principle of hereditary emperorship this was partly because it seemed the only way to achieve one of their most treasured goals, the unity of the entire, vast Chinese cultural space in a single polity.[27]

European elites were brought up on the lessons of classical history. That history showed that city states could not defend themselves for long against external enemies. Nor were the fractious Greek city-state democracies capable in the long run of sustaining lasting alliances to defend their security. European history as viewed from the eighteenth century seemed to confirm the Greek lesson that city states were not viable and that the future lay with monarchy. By then the British monarchy had even perfected what had long seemed to be one of the few power-political advantages of the city state, namely its ability to oversee and sustain an effective system of public debt. As befitted the age of the Enlightenment, the guardian of the Habsburg heir and future emperor Joseph II cited rational and historical justifications for hereditary monarchy, simply noting that on balance it had proved more successful than any other type of polity. If Joseph required any convincing he needed only to reflect on the weakness of the Holy Roman Empire and Poland, homes of Europe's last two elected secular monarchs. Given the enormous difficulties of governing far-flung empires, a powerful, hereditary autocrat seemed even more essential to their survival than was the case with smaller polities. Montesquieu made this point explicitly, but his argument would have been taken as self-evident by most emperors in history.[28]

This brings me to the fourth key element in the make-up of the human beings who are the subject of this study. They were humans, leaders and hereditary monarchs but in addition they were emperors. Defining what an emperor is and, above all, what distinguishes him from a mere king is no easy matter. In most respects the emperor was a king writ large. He usually ruled over more lands and peoples. Because he commanded greater resources he could field larger armies and build greater palaces. But in most ways his job was similar to that of a king. Much of his attention was devoted to preserving his dynasty and maintaining its status. Kings and emperors performed many similar rituals and acted as the source of legitimacy and the embodiment of sovereignty in their domains. As political leaders they needed to choose, manage and direct their ministers skilfully if they were to achieve their goals. War and diplomacy in general stood high on their list of priorities and were areas in which they were likely to leave the strongest personal imprint.

The difference between an emperor and a king was in principle one of hierarchy and status. The word 'emperor' derives from the Latin 'imperator' who in Roman eyes towered above all other rulers on earth and had many kings who served as his clients and lieutenants on the periphery of his empire. The Holy Roman Empire, initially created by

Charlemagne, was in part an attempt to revive the Roman heritage. It was also linked to Charlemagne's claim to be the secular leader of the Christian world community, though in the Latin Christian case overall leadership was shared with the pope. The Iranian monarchical and imperial tradition is one of the most long-lasting and important in history. Its monarch from Achaemenid times was described as *Shahanshah*, in other words, King of Kings. He was the equal of the Roman emperor in power and status.

The greatest of all imperial traditions, that of China, provides a still better guide to what differentiated an emperor from a king. When he united all China in 221 BCE the ruler of the Qin monarchy, King Zheng, took on the title of *Huangdi*, often translated as 'August Thearch'. Not just his new title but the king's entire propaganda machine and many aspects of his policy were designed to emphasize that his empire and reign marked a new era in history and were a sharp break with all that had gone before. In this case the First Emperor's claim was correct. The new empire was far more powerful than any of the kingdoms into which China had been divided for centuries. In creating the foundations of lasting empire in China the First Emperor's role in world history was of enormous significance. Like the Christian Roman emperor, the Chinese emperor knew that there were other rulers on earth who were not directly under his control. Also like his Roman counterpart, the Chinese emperor believed that the civilization he headed was the only true civilization on earth, uniquely blessed by Heaven. All humans who sought to be civilized and live according to correct principles owed him respect and should follow his guidance. This represents what historians call universal empire in its purest form.[29]

Before adopting a claim to universal empire as the mark of any true emperor we must, however, turn from the world of ideas to that of material realities. Many rulers and dynasties made claims to universal dominion and the superior status it entailed. They included, for example, a raft of petty kings on the island of Bali who are the subject of a famous and influential study by the anthropologist Clifford Geertz. These kings competed through the staging of spectacular ceremonies and rituals to place themselves at the centre of the imaginative universe and cosmic consciousness of Bali's Hindu population. Among what Geertz calls 'these localized, fragile, loosely interrelated petty principalities' ceremonial competition was the stuff of politics. In his famous phrase, 'power served pomp, not pomp power'. To put his words in contemporary jargon, this was universal empire in a parallel, virtual reality. Anthropology has much to contribute to the study of monarchy and empire. Ceremonial grandeur was not just part of imperial soft power but also central to the mindset of many emperors. Nevertheless, the rulers discussed in my book were in most ways very different to Geertz's princelings. There are many other examples closer to home of the mismatch between an emperor's claim to pre-eminent status and his actual power. Mere kings could sometimes be much more powerful than rulers who held the title of emperor. In the last five hundred years of the Holy Roman Empire, for example, the emperor was usually weaker than his arch-rival, the king of France.[30]

When Queen Victoria came to the throne in 1837 she reigned directly or indirectly over an empire which was already more extensive than any other in history. Victoria believed unequivocally in the superiority of European, and within it specifically British, civilization. At the core of this civilization stood Protestant Christianity and private property, together with liberal political, economic and cultural principles – of course, in the nineteenth-century definition of 'liberal'. These principles in time came to conquer far more of the globe than had the values and beliefs propagated by any previous empire. This included areas never subject to British rule. In the nineteenth century their spread was sustained by the immensely powerful British navy, by the financial strength and networks of the City of London, and by Britain's position as the first industrial power. In the terms in which I define emperorship, Queen Victoria was an empress decades before she acquired the title of Empress of India in May 1876. The British monarchy was changed in important ways by becoming the centrepiece of one of the greatest empires in history. Even so, its fundamental role remained the same, and so, for the most part, did the daily work and lives of British monarchs. Princes went on grand imperial tours, but only one emperor ever visited India. Victoria cared greatly about the empire, but she spent most of her time worrying about her dynasty, working alongside her British ministers especially where foreign policy was concerned and, after her retreat into solitary widowhood ended, performing a ritual and ceremonial role in London. Yet, even at its most extravagantly imperial and neo-feudal apogee, royal ceremony never envisaged the monarch swaying down the streets of London mounted on an elephant.

Empire is a difficult and slippery concept to define. Empires have existed since ancient times and have taken many forms. Individual empires were by definition diverse and their various territories were often governed in different ways. Great empires survived for centuries, often changing fundamentally in the process. Trying to find a few words which will accurately define the essential features of this multi-faceted kaleidoscope is near-impossible. Almost any definition, unless it is so general as to be almost useless, is likely to fit some empires and some features of empire better than others. This is true even when one remains within the constraints of structure and analysis. Roaming the minds of monarchs and the world of the imagination further complicates matters. Although I must be among the least post-modern of historians, there are moments when I believe that empire needs not only to be defined in words but also seen, felt and imagined. For me, the essence of empire is best encountered when sitting overlooking the Golden Horn at Istanbul or standing on the steps of the Temple of Heaven in Beijing where the Chinese emperors made their great annual sacrifices. In those surroundings it is hard not to sense the power, magnificence, confidence and beauty of imperial monarchy, together with the sense of history and destiny that fuelled great empires. In more prosaic terms, one reason why biography plays a big role in this book is that it brings into play empathy, imagination and the senses in a way that analysing political structures never can.

Nevertheless, it is essential that readers of this book should be clear at least about what I do and do not mean by empire. Tracing the key similarities and differences between the empires discussed is a good way to start this quest. It also allows useful insights into the context in which the individual emperors operated. In most of the contemporary world the word 'empire' is linked above all to the history of the European trans-oceanic empires that began their conquest of the rest of the globe at the end of the fifteenth century. The conquest of the Americas by Europeans and the expropriation and development of a whole hemisphere to serve European power and prosperity in time transformed global geopolitics. In 1500 Europe came a distant third on the ladder of world civilizations. China and the Islamic world competed for the top spot. Latin Europe was hemmed in by the steppe nomads to the east and Islamic empires to the south. In the late fifteenth century maritime technology opened up the oceans to west Europeans. These oceans were a broader and more frictionless highway even than the steppe. They allowed Europeans to descend on the far less powerful and unprepared peoples of the Americas and expropriate the resources of two vast continents at what was, in terms of most imperial conquests, minimal cost. For the first time American silver provided Europeans with something that the Chinese and Indians wanted badly. The unprecedented movement across the Atlantic Ocean of labour (very often African slaves) in one direction and plantation produce in the other began the process that turned the Atlantic world into the centre of an increasingly integrated global economy.

In this book we first encounter the European trans-oceanic empires in the person of their first emperor, Charles V of the House of Austria (Habsburg). For Charles and his son King Philip II of Spain the empire in the New World was above all a milch-cow from which they could draw resources for their attempt to assert the hegemony in Europe of their dynasty and Counter-Reformation Catholicism. Fear of the Habsburgs' power was a big incentive for the dynasty's rivals to create trans-oceanic empires of their own. Until the end of the seventeenth century the greatest Eurasian empires held their own against the Europeans. In 1700 the Ottoman Empire was still almost a match for the Austrian Habsburgs and remained more formidable than the Russians. All Europeans behaved humbly when faced by the majesty and power of the Mughal and Qing emperors. In the eighteenth century the balance of power tilted strongly in Europe's favour. By 1800 the British were taking over most of the former Mughal Empire while Ottoman relative power was in steep decline. Britain's defeat of Napoleon depended greatly on its ability to draw huge wealth from its trans-oceanic trade and empire. This story is told at the end of chapter 15. Most of the nineteenth-century world was increasingly dominated by European empires, of which the British, Russian and German were the most powerful. They are the subject of the book's last and longest chapter.

In the European trans-oceanic empires the distinction between metropolis and colonial periphery was stark. It was marked by geography, race and increasingly enormous differences in wealth. By 1900 there was also a clear distinction between the peoples of the metropolitan state, who were often citizens, and non-White colonial subjects. The White settler colonies represented by far the greatest example in history of the ethnic cleansing, expropriation and sometimes annihilation of indigenous peoples by conquerors. These empires fit snugly the definition of empire as the political conquest, economic exploitation and cultural domination of peripheral peoples by a metropolitan state and nation. This definition fits the other empires encompassed in this book to varying degrees.[31]

For roughly two millennia before 1500 CE the most basic fact about Eurasian geopolitics was the superior military power of warrior nomads over sedentary societies. The vast steppe lands that stretch across northern Eurasia from Hungary to Manchuria were the greatest home on earth for nomads. The semi-deserts of Arabia and north Africa were a smaller but still substantial base for nomadic military power. Much of Eurasian history revolved around whether a sedentary society was within easy range of nomads. Most of Eurasia was. Western Europe, South-East Asia and Japan were not. Nomad empires and dynasties are the subject of chapter 7. The Ottomans (chapter 11), Mughals (chapter 12) and Manchus (Qing; chapter 13) were dynasties whose origins lay on or near the steppe. Their empires had much in common with European trans-oceanic empire. They were created by conquest and driven by the rulers' desire to exploit the conquered peoples and their lands. But in key respects they diverged radically from European overseas empire. The conquerors sometimes even saw themselves as inferior in cultural terms to the great sedentary civilizations that they ruled. At its most extreme, this type of empire witnessed the assimilation and ultimate disappearance of the conquering people.[32]

The word 'empire' is derived from the Latin 'imperium'. Rome stood out in the European imagination as the model empire and the one which early modern Europeans sought to emulate. In key respects the early Roman Empire was similar to the later European empires. The Romans were a clearly defined nation which conquered a swathe of other peoples. Roman elites derived immense wealth from these conquests. Even ordinary Romans received generous food subsidies from the exploitation of conquered territories. The Romans could be exceptionally ruthless, in some cases resorting to near-genocidal policies to conquer and suppress their enemies. A sharp divide existed between the privileges of Roman citizens and non-Roman subject peoples. However, over the centuries the Roman Empire changed radically. Above all, the Romans showed a rare willingness not just to grant citizenship to conquered peoples but also to allow native elites admission to the empire's metropolitan aristocracy. In 212 CE nearly all non-slaves were granted

Roman citizenship. By the third century most senators and even emperors were no longer Italian, let alone Roman. At least as regards the elites, a consolidated imperial nation emerged, increasingly known as 'Romania' from the mid-fourth century. Had the Roman Empire survived, one might perhaps imagine an evolution similar to that of China, whose elites in time inculcated a sense of ethno-national identity into the Han Chinese masses. In fact, the Roman Empire began to contract under the impact of external invaders. It lost its western provinces in the fifth century and its more important provinces in Africa and the Levant in the seventh. Nevertheless, the later Roman (usually described as Byzantine) Empire survived for further centuries. It called itself an empire and proudly identified with the Roman imperial heritage. But one of Byzantium's leading contemporary historians sees it not as a multi-ethnic empire on the early Roman or later European model, but rather as a large but mostly homogeneous political community which is called an empire simply because its ruler styled himself 'emperor'.[33]

Only China has three chapters in this book (6, 8 and 13). That is a measure of the unique longevity, nature and importance of the Chinese tradition of empire. Two thousand years ago the Roman and Han empires controlled the eastern and western quarters of Eurasia. It is of vast contemporary importance that whereas the Roman Empire disintegrated into a long-lasting multi-polar international order, the Chinese tradition of empire survived. The debate over why the European and Chinese paths diverged is relevant to this book. One key point is that whereas in Europe spiritual and secular power were divided between pope and monarch, in China they were united in the person of the emperor. If I hesitate to call the Chinese emperor a priest-king that is because the word 'priest' is closely linked to the Judaeo-Christian monotheist tradition. The emperor conducted rituals which included Confucian, Daoist, Buddhist and (if his dynasty came from beyond the Great Wall) shamanic elements. That in turn raises the thought-provoking but unanswerable question whether polytheism in its Chinese variant was inherently better suited than monotheism to the governance and survival of empire.

Beyond any doubt there was a Chinese imperial tradition. It was rooted in ancient Confucian and legalist thought and in the evolving institutions and practices of successive dynasties. Even a cursory knowledge of Chinese history, however, shows that a clear divide existed between Han Chinese dynasties (above all, the Song and the Ming) and dynasties (Mongol, Qing, Tang) whose roots lay wholly or in part in the nomadic warrior world of the Eurasian steppe. These latter dynasties ruled empires that were far bigger and more multi-ethnic than the realms of the Song or the Ming. The Ming Empire at its apogee covered 3.1 million square kilometres. Its successor, the Qing (Manchu), covered 14.7 million by 1790. The native Chinese dynasties ruled over what was at least in embryo a vast but relatively homogeneous Chinese ethno-national community with a few non-Han territories attached. One recent work studies the emergence of a specifically ethno-national Chinese identity under the Song in the tenth and eleventh centuries. It argues that the Song regime's obsessive desire to regain the sixteen north-eastern prefectures lost to the Kitan confederation was rooted in the fact that (unlike most former Tang possessions) these were seen as ethnic Chinese lands. Conceivably, parallels exist as regards contemporary China's fixation on Taiwan (a de facto independent state since 1948) and its seeming acceptance of the loss of the Mongolian, Amur and other northern regions previously ruled by the Qing. China provides its own twist to the complex relationship between empire and nation. Part of my academic life has been devoted to studying why the core peoples of former empires welcome some aspects of imperial history into their national pantheon and exclude others, but defining what empire and nation mean is not just a game for professors. These definitions can have crucial political consequences. Taiwan's status is the likeliest cause of what would be the ultimate catastrophe, namely war between the USA and China.[34]

My own understanding of empire should by now be apparent. It is tied to clarifying the challenges and temptations that emperors faced. Vast territory was a key mark of empire. It implied great resources and power. Given pre-modern communications, empire's immense size was also a big challenge to its rulers. Traditionally imperial rule was of necessity 'light-touch'. It left most aspects of government to local elites and communities, concentrating instead on squeezing enough tax from the population to sustain the emperor's armies and palaces. Ever since the ancient Greeks, Europeans have tended to see despotism as the necessary corollary of empire's scale. Montesquieu agreed but, unlike the Greeks, he saw city states as unable to defend themselves and believed that a medium-sized polity such as France was best able to balance the needs of internal liberty and external power and security. In the century following Montesquieu's death it seemed clear that medium-sized European states could be far more intensively governed and developed than vast, sprawling and under-governed empires. The European nation state ruled supreme. In the second half of the nineteenth century the pendulum of power swung back towards large, continental-scale polities. The many reasons for this will be discussed in the book's last chapter. A crucial one was that modern technology, meaning above all the railway and the telegraph, made it possible to colonize, exploit and develop continental heartlands. The geopolitical realities that underpinned the so-called era of High Imperialism (c. 1870–1918) still govern today's world. As the co-editor of the outstanding new *Oxford History of World Empire* puts it, a 'pre-condition for projecting power in the current international order is, increasingly, sheer mass. The great and coming powers of the moment are all such empire nations – the United States, Russia, China, India.'[35]

A second mark of empire was rule over many and diverse peoples. Caution is required in weighing the significance of this fact. In pre-modern polities elites were usually much more politically significant than the mass of the population. Emperors spent considerable time winning the support of these elites by carrot-and-stick policies, as well as by promoting all-imperial ideologies and identities. The ethno-linguistic criteria that define most modern nations seldom meant much to either elites or masses in the pre-modern world. An occasional mass rebellion, like the Jewish revolt of the first century CE, might have proto-nationalist aspects, but emperors usually had far more to fear from mass uprisings driven by economic pressures or millenarian religious excitement. Emperors acquired pride and status from proclaiming themselves to be the lords of many lands and peoples. This situation was transformed in the nineteenth century. Increasingly the nation – defined by ethno-linguistic criteria, citizenship and history – was seen as the only fully legitimate polity. This was a huge and ultimately fatal challenge to both empire and anything but a largely symbolic monarchy that identified itself with the nation. Nationalism acquired the strength of a religion, giving meaning and purpose to many people's lives. Its push to break up existing multi-national empires collided with the geopolitical forces that pointed towards continental scale as the only way to be a modern great power, with all that meant in terms of status, security and prosperity.

This collision underlay much of the conflict and instability that culminated in the First World War. It continues to play a key role in destabilizing contemporary politics.

Above all, in my opinion, empire means power. Unless for a significant part of its life a state played a major role in the history of a sizeable slice of the globe it does not deserve the name of empire. Almost all empires were created by conquest and none of them survived without formidable armies. The glory that empire offered to rulers and the security it brought for their subjects were key elements in empire's legitimacy and *raison d'être*. But military power was never sufficient even to create an empire, let alone to sustain it over the generations. Not just political and economic but also cultural and ideological power were also crucial. The most important empires were linked to some great universal religion or splendid civilization. In that case an empire's rule determined not just who ruled the world but what beliefs, values and culture dominated. The Mongols ruled the largest empire in history until it was surpassed by the British in the nineteenth century. Some traces of the Mongol Empire still influence the present-day world. In the long run, however, it pales into insignificance beside the Arab caliphate. Although militarily much less formidable than the Mongols, by allying themselves with Islam the Arab nomads fundamentally transformed global geopolitics and culture in ways that remain crucial in the contemporary world. In this book I devote some attention to the Mongol emperors but much more to the caliphs. That is partly because it is easier to gain a sense of the personalities of some caliphs. But it is also because I have tried to focus my attention on the empires and emperors that mattered most.

Defining empire clarifies the roles that emperors played. The emperor was a dynast, the head of a family. Managing the succession, controlling his close relations, and training his heir were among his most vital tasks. To what extent he subsumed his own ego in service to the dynasty differed from emperor to emperor and from dynasty to dynasty. The descendants of Timur (Tamberlane) were notorious both for their pride in their dynasty and for their unwillingness to sacrifice personal ambition and ego to preserve its heritage. In 1808 the childless Ottoman sultan Mustapha IV ordered the murder of the two other remaining Ottoman princes, placing his own survival above that of a dynasty which had ruled for over five hundred years. By contrast, the Habsburgs generally showed great dynastic loyalty and solidarity. Of course, it helped that no Habsburg emperor or prince risked having his throat slit by his relations.

Emperors were in one sense or other sacred beings, blessed by one version or another of Heaven. Even Napoleon, heir to a revolution that had been at war with the Catholic Church, insisted on the pope officiating at his coronation. A dynasty with no sacred aura and legitimacy was unlikely to last long. In the first centuries of the common era German kings were essentially elected military leaders whose legitimacy rested on success in war. War is a risky and uncertain business and the kings' tenure in office was about as assured as that of contemporary English Premier League football managers. Emperors carefully cultivated their legitimacy as sacred rulers and needed the support of religion, but they were sometimes at odds with the various 'priesthoods' as to whose authority was supreme across a range of issues. Conflicts over the enormous wealth often held by official priesthoods were also frequent.

Most emperors were the chief political officers of their realms, though the Japanese emperors and the late-Abbasid caliphs lost almost all their political power and for centuries acted as sacred symbols whose role was to legitimize the rule of those who wielded real political power. In the nineteenth century the British and Dutch imperial monarchies evolved into playing a similar role. At a minimum a royal chief political officer usually reserved to himself the final word on foreign and military policy, top appointments and matters concerning members of his dynasty. Monarchs in well-established dynasties could safely devolve most of the business of government on a chief minister, though they often faced (usually whispered) criticism for not doing their royal duty if they behaved in this way. Whether a monarch chose to employ a chief minister or to play the role of autocrat himself depended on personalities, dynastic traditions, and whether he could find a deputy whom he trusted to do the job well. There was something to be said for both options. The greatest danger came when the monarch felt that it was his duty to act as autocrat but lacked the ability to do so. No emperor was a CEO in the full modern sense. Whether his role can be compared in some respects to that of a CEO depends on whether he headed a large and complex government machine. Chinese emperors led the way here. No European leader since the fall of the Roman Empire deserved this title until at least the growth of the Spanish administration in the sixteenth century. Nor did the caliphs and the early Ottomans and Mughals.

Most empires and imperial monarchies were founded by military leaders. This was true of even the indigenous Chinese Han, Song and Ming dynasties. In the longer run religious and cultural norms usually prevailed. The Confucian and Buddhist monarch was a sage and a moral exemplar, not a soldier, though some Chinese monarchs from wholly native dynasties yearned for military glory and most retained the final say on questions of grand strategy and top military appointments. European feudal monarchs and the descendants of nomad-warriors on the contrary treasured their military traditions and needed to sustain them if they were to retain the respect of aristocratic elites. Yearning for military glory could lead monarchs to disaster. On the other hand, victory on the battlefield in almost all empires brought the greatest glory and legitimacy. In a military camp an emperor might find the camaraderie and freedom that was so difficult to experience in his palace and court. Moreover, a ruler with military experience might be better equipped by training and temperament when it came to crisis management and the need to make decisions rapidly in the face of great danger and uncertainty.

To an even greater degree than in most states, an empire needed powerful but loyal armies which would defeat foreign enemies but pose no threat to their own governments. The Roman imperial monarchy was least successful in combining military power and loyalty. Repeated military coups and civil wars among generals aspiring to the throne did huge damage. A major cause was the weakness of the dynastic principle in Rome. Among all the empires studied in this book, dynasty was strongest in 'feudal' and early modern Europe. That goes far to explain why European armies in the early modern era could be simultaneously both formidable and loyal. Monarchs and noble officers shared the same 'feudal' warrior origins, values and pride. They were bound together by shared experience, rituals, stories of courage, traditions and the sense of being merely the latest actors in a long-running, epic, family drama. Both in reality and symbolically these armies represented the tight alliance between the monarchy and the noble-landowning class that was the foundation of most early modern European states. The officer's uniform bound him to his monarch and had great symbolic meaning. The uniform contained many semi-hidden codes: if the royal cipher and crown were the most obvious, the gorget that hung around the officer's throat, for example, was the last relic of the feudal knight's armour. Prussian, Russian and Austrian monarchs from the mid-eighteenth century onwards were increasingly seldom seen in public except in military uniform. Nor should one forget the banal but powerful sex appeal of military uniforms. In the nineteenth century, as formal menswear became ever drabber and more 'uniform', military costume took off in the opposite Romantic and exotic direction. Semi-colonial Highland kilts and Cossack cloaks added an extra touch of glamour to the outfits of British and Russian monarchs in the era of High Imperialism.[36]

Successful empires rested on a close and stable alliance between the monarchy and landowning elites. In the long term it was impossible in pre-modern times to sustain an empire-wide bureaucratic machine sufficiently large and efficient to ignore these elites and deal directly with the peasants. The alliance between monarchy and local elites required a stable agreement on sharing the surplus extracted from the farming community. This was difficult to achieve. The peasants should not be so exploited that they were ruined or forced into revolt or flight. Pre-modern monarchies were always hierarchical, exploitative and dominated by self-serving elites. But they also usually rested on a claim to justice which resonated among the mass of the population. The myth of the just and benevolent emperor was almost always central to the way imperial regimes represented themselves to their subjects in word, ritual and image. If practice too flagrantly contradicted this myth then danger loomed. This was especially the case if long-established norms of exploitation suddenly increased. Even leaving aside the greed and fecklessness of monarchs and aristocrats, the problem was that poor harvests, the weather or any number of other natural disasters could easily undermine the always fragile customary modus vivendi between emperor, elites and peasants. So too could growing external threats that forced the monarchy to increase its demands for soldiers and taxes.[37]

Elites were naturally disinclined to hand over part of their surplus to a monarch, especially if he was seen as a foreigner and lived far away. They had to be persuaded to do so. Some coercion was usually needed, especially in a dynasty's early decades. In the longer run elites had to be bound to the monarchy by a sense both of self-interest and of cultural, religious and ideological solidarity. Royal courts often played a central role in cementing the alliance between monarchs and the upper echelon of the elite. The court was the centre for distributing the patronage that underpinned the politics of imperial monarchy. It could be a splendid marriage market for aristocratic families. The court brought monarch and aristocrat into personal and even sometimes informal contact. It was often a venue for every kind of amusement: music, theatre and conversation. The monarch could act as generous host. The royal hunt, almost universal in Eurasian monarchy, was a semi-substitute for the battlefield, as an outlet for male camaraderie and displays of courage and horsemanship.[38]

Courtiers were both spectators and participants in a splendid and carefully choreographed ballet at whose centre was the monarch. On formal occasions his every step and gesture was designed to radiate majesty, awe and benevolence. Raised on a throne, he was surrounded by gorgeously uniformed guardsmen and by courtiers ranked in precise order of precedence. This reflected the key principle of hierarchy defined by closeness to the monarch. To some extent the same principles ruled courts from the Achaemenid emperors in the fifth century BCE down to Louis XIV and beyond. When we look today at some massive painting of a court event thronged with aristocrats in elaborate wigs and immense skirts, it looks ridiculous to us because the codes that lie at the heart of the event have ceased to have any relevance or plausibility. But at the time those featured in the picture would have 'read' it in minute detail, with the positioning, clothing and chivalric orders of each figure speaking volumes about their rank and significance at that moment.

Nevertheless, there are dangers of being too beguiled by the example of Louis XIV and taking the idea of the royal impresario too far. Even by European standards the French king was uniquely on display. The Chinese or Ottoman emperor, to take but two examples, was much less visible. Outside Europe a monarch might disappear for weeks behind the walls of his harem. Even when seen in public, he might be as immobile as a statue. Louis XIV's ambassadors to the Thai king in the 1680s 'were entering into another world of sacred kingship altogether. Here they encountered kings who sat on their thrones like gods.' The Thai king's ambassadors to Versailles in turn were astonished by the informality of a court where the monarch could be waylaid by jostling courtiers seeking patronage as he walked the corridors of his palace chatting to his intimates. Comparisons between the main palaces of the contemporary British and Japanese monarchs are to the point. Buckingham Palace and its approaches are built for public ceremony and display. The Japanese emperor lives in a modest group of smallish, contemporary buildings hidden from view behind the trees of the imperial garden. Elizabeth II's coronation, in line with European tradition, was a vast-scale pageant on the streets of London. The most important and sacred elements in the Japanese emperor's accession rituals are performed in semi- or sometimes complete privacy. They are not performed for an audience and they cannot be described as theatre. Heaven rather than courtiers, let alone the public, was the intended onlooker.[39]

A banal but crucial point is that whereas some elements of the monarch's ceremonial role could be performed by anyone not actually physically or mentally defective (including a child), other aspects of the job of royal impresario required great skill. A good posture and a strong sense of duty sufficed to prepare a ruler for many elements in his ceremonial role. A prince's education usually emphasized both. Great efforts often went into teaching the young prince and princess to stand, move, gesture and smile in a graceful and appropriate fashion. How to wear clothes and robes to best effect was another lesson taught in childhood and adolescence. The best parallel in the contemporary world is a would-be beauty queen or young model's training in how to discipline and display her body to maximum effect. Especially for naturally shy and clumsy royal children, this training in royal theatre could be a great strain. Nevertheless, whereas an average person could perform the monarch's ceremonial functions successfully, management of the courtiers and the patronage system was one of the ruler's most important and delicate tasks. This book is in one sense a collective biography of emperors. It certainly does not ignore their ceremonial roles but it places greater emphasis on those aspects of their job where personality and talent mattered most.[40]

Being a successful emperor meant doing a difficult job well. Louis XIV enjoyed being a monarch and was good at his job. This was far from always the case with emperors. As this chapter illustrates, they were expected to shine in a variety of roles, some of which required different, even contradictory attributes. Simultaneously to be a hard-working head of government, almost iconic symbol of sacredness, a paragon of piety and morality, supreme military commander and the centre of patronage and sociability was a tall order. Something had to give. There was also often a huge gap between the monarchy's claims to semi-divine power and its ability to enforce and implement its wishes and policies. 'All political lives end in failure' is a watchword to which many of the more intelligent and introspective monarchs would have subscribed. The problems of governing empires were immense. A young monarch might well seek refuge in debauchery. As the years passed, a sense of fatigue, frustration and failure could easily take hold of an ageing monarch. 'Burnout' is a term often now used for hard-driving CEOs. But, unlike a contemporary CEO, a monarch was usually unable to retire even if he so wished. Political weakness and even collapse in the last years of a long reign is a recurring theme in imperial history.

Nevertheless, failure and powerlessness were by no means the full picture. The emperor's power could be formidable and effective. Unsurprisingly, it is most often visible as regards military affairs and foreign policy. At moments of crisis too, when decisive action by the supreme power-holder was essential, the emperor's competence or otherwise could decide a dynasty's fate. Leadership could also matter hugely to the longer-term rise and decline of empires. Some decisions made by monarchs hundreds or even more than two thousand years ago still leave a big mark on today's world. Sam Finer, former Regius Professor of Politics at Oxford University, called the founding emperor of the Qin dynasty (r. 221–206/7 BCE) the most important political leader in history because he created the model of imperial statehood that ultimately preserved China as a united country and thereby had a decisive impact on global geopolitics. The religions chosen by monarchs for themselves and their empires sometimes still define the borders of the world's cultural regions. The conversion to Christianity of Emperor Constantine is a case in point. Without Emperor Ashoka, Buddhism would probably have remained one of many sects confined to one region of India and would probably in time have disappeared. Instead it spread across most of South-East and East Asia, with enormous consequences for the culture and belief-systems of this vast region. More recent examples can be drawn from sixteenth- and seventeenth-century Europe. The adoption of the Shi'i faith for themselves and Iran by the Safavid shahs in the sixteenth century probably remains the single most important factor in the geopolitics of today's Middle East. Emperors mattered.[41]

2

Cradle of Empire: The Ancient Near East and the World's First Emperors

Agriculture, towns, writing systems and most other elements of what we call civilization first emerged in the Near East. The earliest core of this region was Mesopotamia, literally the land between the rivers Tigris and Euphrates. Without the rivers neither agriculture nor towns would have been sustainable in this semi-arid area. In time the term 'Near East' came to include present-day Iraq, Syria, parts of Anatolia and Elam (southwestern Iran). Although many peoples and languages existed across this region it was united by close trade links, periodic unification under one or other empire, and by use of the same cuneiform writing system, a clumsy mixture of short wedge-topped lines combined into symbols.

The basic political unit in this region was the city state, each with its own city god. Even by the beginning of the third millennium BCE monarchy was the universal system of rule. The heavens and earth were seen as parallel realms, with the king as the intermediary between the two. The rituals and sacrifices he performed placated the gods and secured the well-being of his subjects. As deputy and steward of the city god, the king provided order, justice and security. Kingship everywhere had both religious and secular attributes. In a manner to be repeated in only slightly different terms across most of the world in the following millennia an Assyrian proverb stated that 'a people without a king is like a flock without a shepherd, a crowd without a supervisor, water without a pipe . . . a house without a master, a wife without a husband.' A contemporary historian comments that 'kingship seemed so obvious and right to the Mesopotamians that they believed it had been invented by the gods, that it had come "down from heaven".' In the ancient Near East as in most other pre-modern societies we can only guess the extent to which royal and elite ideology was internalized and accepted by the mass of the population, but no record survives of opposition or altern-atives to this ideology.[1]

Although the idea of sacred monarchy dominated the city-state world and was in practice often hereditary, the belief that some version of divine right inhered in a specific family or lineage seems to have come from the tribal and semi-nomadic peoples who periodically conquered and ruled the urban communities. A historian of ancient Babylonia, in many respects the heartland of Near Eastern culture, comments that, in the third millennium BCE, although 'it was a matter of human nature that fathers often wished their sons to succeed them and groomed them to that end', never before the Amorite conquest (early second millen-nium BCE) did there exist 'any hint that a certain family line was divinely endowed with a right to kingship'. He adds that this idea of a sacred lin-eage was common to many of the region's semitic and pastoral peoples, was associated with ancestor cults, and spread to the city-state peoples, including the Assyrians.[2]

Some city states expanded by taking over their neighbours. A very few were so successful at this game that they created the world's first empires. The history of empire is usually reckoned to begin with Sargon of Akkad (r. 2334–2279 BCE). Whereas previous kings had at most ruled a handful of city states, Sargon's empire included all of today's Iraq and Syria. For Sargon empire paid handsomely: he amassed a rich hoard of booty and tribute. He sought to portray himself as unlike any previous ruler and used religion to underpin his legitimacy, installing a daughter as high priestess of the moon god in the temple-city of Ur. Sargon's dynasty and empire lasted for over a hundred years. We do not know the specific reasons for its fall but they will certainly have included deep resentment in the city states he conquered, both at the brutality of his rule and the heavy tribute he imposed. Nevertheless, in time Sargon became a hero, at least in elite eyes. 'His was a life to idolize and, for kings, to emulate. More than 1,500 years after his death, the stories of Sargon's deeds continued to be told.' We cannot know how the mass of the population viewed Sargon either in his lifetime or in retrospect. Quite possibly with loathing, indifference or even incredulity: here, as in most of history, our sources are almost by definition written by elites close to the rulers. This is a deformation with which we historians simply have to live.[3]

Over the next 1,500 years kingdoms, dynasties and empires came

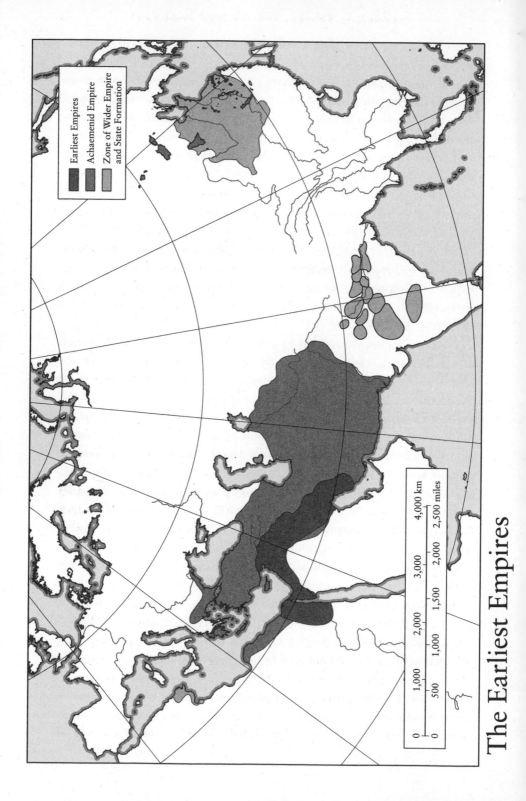

The Earliest Empires

and went in the Near East. Probably the most famous Near Eastern emperor in the eyes of distant posterity was the Amorite King of Babylonia, Hammurabi (r. c. 1792–1750 BCE). His fame rests less on the fact that he ruled over most of Iraq and much of Syria than on the code of laws which he wrote down and which has survived, having been rediscovered by archaeologists in 1901. Hammurabi was very concerned for his reputation among not just his contemporaries but also following generations. He portrayed himself less as a conqueror than as a ruler who provided his subjects with public works (water supplies and canals), protected the weak and, above all, served the royal and sacred ideal of justice.

The biggest of the Near Eastern empires was the so-called Neo-Assyrian, which existed from 972 until 612 BCE. It was four times larger than any previous Near Eastern empire, covering the whole region from the Mediterranean to the Gulf but also ruling territories beyond the borders of the historic Near East. For many centuries Assyria was a city state of medium power, situated not far from the modern city of Mosul in northern Iraq. Early Assyria's main claim to fame was the extensive commercial networks established by its merchants in both Anatolia and southern Iraq. By the thirteenth century BCE Assyria had become a large and formidable kingdom, one of a handful of such kingdoms which dominated the region at that time. After 1200 BCE a general crisis seems to have afflicted the Near East, for reasons which remain unclear, though serious drought in Iraq and attacks by Mediterranean sea-raiders played a part. The Hittite Empire and the Egyptian kingdom disintegrated, Babylonia was conquered by Elamites from south-western Iran, and Assyria shrank back towards its original city-state limits. Recovery began in the early tenth century and the empire reached its fullest extent in the seventh. It collapsed suddenly at the end of the seventh century for reasons that remain disputed.

The Neo-Assyrians seem to have pursued an exceptionally ruthless system of exploiting conquered territories. Official ideology stressed allegiance to the Assyrian god Assur, in whose service conquest and plunder were virtues. The Assyrian language was unique to them and was a dialect of Akkadian. The original Assyrian city state had no natural defences and had on occasion been conquered by outsiders. 'A dark blend of religious and militaristic ideology placed the king in the centre of the universe and presented Assyria as a land enclosed by a ring of evil.' Assyrian propaganda revelled in tales of the savage torture and execution of anyone who opposed its rule. Mass deportations of conquered peoples were also frequent. Among these peoples were the Jews: given the Bible's impact on the Christian world (to which most historians and archaeologists studying the ancient Near East belonged), it is hardly surprising that the Assyrians have gone down in history as especially vicious imperialists – as exemplified in Byron's line, 'The Assyrian came down like a wolf on the fold'. Terror and cruelty were to varying degrees policies pursued by all empires. Nevertheless, as one historian comments, no previous dynasty in the Near East had boasted about inflicting such terrible sufferings on its enemies, nor did any Assyrian propaganda ever echo King Hammurabi of Babylon's stance as defender of widows, orphans and the weak. Unmitigated terror, exploitation and expansion is usually fatal for any empire in the long run.[4]

The sources available usually make it far easier for a historian to gain a sense of what ancient monarchs did and how they presented themselves to the world than of the inner man. This is certainly true of the Assyrian emperors. Many of these men were clearly fine generals as well as skilful and ruthless political leaders. In certain cases we can identify them as the authors of specific political programmes. King Tigrath-Pileser III (r. 745–727 BCE), for example, was a formidable leader who extended the empire's borders and tightened control over peripheral territories. He also reduced the power of the Assyrian aristocracy by concentrating top office and the rewards it provided in the hands of royal officials of varied origin, many of whom were eunuchs and thus believed to be totally loyal and dependent on the monarch. This policy increased royal power in the short run but by weakening the dynasty's support within the social elite it 'led to a situation in which the collapse of the court equalled the collapse of the empire'.[5]

The only Assyrian monarch whose personality does to some extent reveal itself is Ashurbanipal (r. 669–631? BCE). Ashurbanipal was a very unusual Assyrian monarch in that he prided himself far less on his military prowess (he may never have commanded armies on campaign) than on his skill as a scholar: 'in the traditional scenes portraying the king as warrior and protector of his people, Ashurbanipal uniquely chose to have himself depicted with a stylus tucked into his belt'. The monarch boasted in public of his qualifications as astrologer, diviner, mathematician and literary expert. Some of these skills were closely related to policy-making. All governments make calculations and predictions about the future when adopting policies. For Assyrians the key was to understand the gods' intentions through examining the stars and studying the entrails of sheep. A ruler who grasped the principles of astrology and divination was better placed to judge between the advice he received from rival experts and the factions that might be standing behind them.[6]

To the modern eye this might seem a strange and primitive example of a ruler's unavoidable dilemma as to how best to weigh expert advice from his officials. Other dilemmas facing Ashurbanipal are more familiar. As the supreme source of power, status and wealth a monarch was always a target for flattery, intrigue and slander. In royal courts disputes over policy and position might often be resolved by whispers in the monarch's ear. The ruler needed to keep at least one ear open but to filter out mere jealousy and slander. Ashurbanipal had come out on top in a vicious struggle to succeed his father on the throne. He knew that the losers in that struggle had not all been destroyed and that some of his royal ancestors had fallen victim to court conspiracies. Insight into other humans' hearts and minds was the key not just to success but often to survival as a ruler. Confronted with the fears of one old and trusted official about a rival's slanders, Ashurbanipal sought to reassure him: 'Don't be afraid! What can this villain say against you? Don't I know that you . . . stayed awake, kept my watch, and (have) been driven and hard pressed, through no fault of your own, on behalf of the house of your lord? What could he say against you? Why would I listen? . . . Do not fear his return; your life is with me.'[7]

The Assyrians were the first Near Eastern empire to conquer Egypt, though their hold was brief and insecure. Egyptian civilization was distinct and ancient. It had its own gods, its own cultural and political traditions, and its own completely different writing system. Although trade between Egypt and Mesopotamia had existed for millennia, what brought Egypt out of its geopolitical isolation was the invasion and conquest of Lower Egypt by the so-called Hyksos – Mediterranean seafaring peoples mostly based in the Levant – in the seventeenth century BCE. The Hyksos brought with them technologies – in military terms above all the chariot and the composite bow – which a native dynasty based in Thebes in Upper Egypt subsequently used to expel these foreigners in the sixteenth century BCE. This ushered in the so-called New Kingdom era of

Egyptian history (1550–1069 BCE), probably the most glorious and certainly the most studied era in the history of ancient Egypt.

For most of this era Egypt was the richest and potentially the most powerful state in the eastern Mediterranean and Near East. Stung by memory of Hyksos rule the early New Kingdom pharaohs prioritized military power and portrayed themselves primarily as warrior-kings. Egypt dominated the region we now call Israel, Palestine and Lebanon. Its armies on occasion campaigned as far away as the Euphrates. However, Egypt was never more than *primus inter pares*. A balance of power existed between a number of powerful realms, including the Mittani and Hittite kingdoms, Babylonia and Assyria. Conventions emerged to underpin relations between the monarchs of these 'great powers'. Kings addressed each other as brother and exchanged gifts and ambassadors. Dynasties sometimes intermarried. Alliances and non-aggression pacts for generations allowed states to pursue their divergent interests within a relatively stable international system. Like most such balance-of-power systems in international relations, the Near Eastern system in time collapsed. The Mittani kingdom was gobbled up by the Hittites. Then ecological and economic crisis undermined all the larger states in the region. Finally, a renewed Assyrian Empire (972–612 BCE) overran the entire region, Egypt included.

It is a moot point whether ancient Egypt can ever truly be called an empire. Certainly, it was in key respects a different kind of empire to that of Sargon or the Assyrians. In the Near East city states founded empires, but Egypt was already a large territorial kingdom at the beginning of the third millennium BCE. At that time Upper and Lower Egypt had just been unified politically but even before that time they already formed a single cultural unit. The Nile and the extremely productive agriculture it sustained along its banks created Egypt and underpinned its unity in political, economic and cultural terms. The river was navigable in both directions for 800 kilometres. The Egyptian monarch was portrayed as a divine figure who had the power to control the Nile's annual flooding, on which the Egyptian people's well-being depended. From early days the Egyptian kings conquered and ruled Nubia, above all because they coveted its gold and other minerals. In the New Kingdom era they ruled indirectly over wide territories in Asia. But by the standards of Near Eastern and many subsequent empires their core 'national' territory was very large and their empire rather small.[8]

A historian of ancient political thought calls Egyptian political thinking the most extreme theory of absolute monarchy anywhere in the
ancient world. Even in the sacred monarchies of the Near East, the
monarch was very seldom regarded or worshipped as a god. But 'in
Egypt the king was more closely identified with the gods than in any
other culture. He was the incarnation of Horus and Osiris, the son of
the supreme god', Amun-Ra, and he would return to his father in the
heavens after his brief stay on earth. Historians have traditionally been
inclined to stress the cosmic role of the pharaoh and to compare it to the
more mundane Near Eastern tradition in which kings above all were
military and political leaders. This contrast should not be pushed too
far. Most ancient Near Eastern kings – and especially the rulers of
empires – were anything but mere mortals in royal propaganda and in
the eyes of their subjects. Meanwhile the pharaoh in principle also performed the key tasks of an earthly ruler: he was the final decision-maker
as regards policy and the distributer-in-chief of the state's patronage.
The ancient Egyptian sources (almost all archaeological) that remain to
us portray the pharaoh much more in his sacred and cosmic role than
as the central figure in the dangerous world of court politics, but occasional hints of the latter intrude. The Egyptian monarch, like his peers
across the millennia, had to manage the ambitions of members of his
own dynasty, as well as the military and priestly elites on whom his
throne depended. In the Egyptian case, at least under the New Kingdom, it seems to have been the priestly elites and their vastly rich and
powerful temples which were the biggest threat. Indeed, by the end of
the era their power eclipsed that of the pharaoh.[9]

Just occasionally, fragments of a pharaoh's personality reveal themselves. As a young man King Thutmose IV (r. c. 1400–c. 1391 BCE) was
a passionate chariot-racer. His son, Amenhotep III, ascended the throne
aged twenty and ruled for the next thirty-eight years. Amenhotep's
biographer writes that surviving sources allow us to know more about
him than most contemporary humans know about their great-
grandfathers, which is encouraging until one remembers that most
people in today's First World have at best a very sketchy outline of their
great-grandfathers' lives and very little understanding of the inner men.
But aspects of Amenhotep's personality do emerge plausibly from the
biography. Like many members of his (so-called eighteenth) dynasty,
Amenhotep III was club-footed. His son and successor, Amenhotep IV

(Akhenaten), had (among other medical problems) a cleft palate. His grandson, Tutankhamen, was 'a frail boy with a left clubfoot and painful Kohler's disease in his right foot'. With Tutankhamen the eighteenth dynasty died out, which is unsurprising since the pharaohs practised intermarriage on a scale unimaginable even to the Habsburgs. Some monarchs married their sisters or even their daughters. Tutankhamen was probably the product of three generations of intermarriage between first cousins.[10]

Despite this inbreeding, Amenhotep III was an able ruler and an inspired patron of the arts, with a fine eye for beauty, proportion and craftsmanship. Perhaps it helped that for the first twelve years of his life he was one prince among others and not the heir apparent. His early education was rather democratic by the standards of most princes we will encounter. Princes and young aristocrats were taught alongside the sons of royal officials and household staff. Possibly this helped Amenhotep in later life to judge people and to choose able lieutenants, some of them from non-elite backgrounds. The boys received a good grounding in arithmetic, music and drawing. Above all they were educated in the classic texts of ancient Egypt, each of which had morals and instructions to be learned by the children. From his elementary 'nursery', Amenhotep graduated first to the palace school at Memphis and finally to his father's old alma mater and tutors at the Mut temple school in Thebes. Apart from his academic education, the young prince was taught the etiquette of the royal court and aristocratic sports such as archery and charioteering. In Thebes and Memphis Amenhotep lived amidst many of the greatest splendours of ancient Egyptian culture. His chief tutor, Hekareshu, was famous for his deep respect for the earliest history and traditions of the Egyptian monarchy and seems to have passed this respect for antiquity on to Amenhotep. In a manner typical of hereditary monarchs, some of Amenhotep's mentors in his youth held high office in his reign and enjoyed his special trust.

As heir, Amenhotep may have served briefly as viceroy of Nubia. Early in his own reign he campaigned against Nubian rebels. But Amenhotep III had no wish to extend Egyptian territory or to play the role of warrior-king. Instead he devoted his energies to architecture, sculpture and the decorative arts, leaving to posterity a vast cultural heritage that combined ancient Egyptian traditions with Nubian and Near Eastern borrowings. Amenhotep's artistic inclinations, his lack of interest in playing the part of warrior-king, and the role played by the dynasty's women in his reign led some old-school British Egyptologists to dismiss him as effete and effeminate. In reality, royal women were a powerful presence throughout Egyptian dynastic history and never more so than in the New Kingdom. Amenhotep's senior wife, Queen Tiy, seems to have had a close personal relationship with her husband, bore him many children, and was the first Egyptian queen to be deified in her lifetime. Her own family, military aristocrats, played key roles in Amenhotep's army and administration. Possibly this alliance with military aristocrats was seen by Amenhotep as a means to balance the powerful priestly elite.[11]

Hostility to senior clergy and their vast wealth was a major theme in the reign of Amenhotep's son and successor, Amenhotep IV (Akhenaten). Amenhotep IV changed his name to Akhenaten (chief-priest of the Aten) to signify his abandonment of Egypt's old senior god, Amun, and his allegiance to the worship of the sun-god Aten. Out with Amun went all the mythologies and the human-like qualities of the old world of Egyptian gods and cosmology. The pharaoh elevated the god Aten to supreme, quasi-monotheistic status. He abandoned the old capital, Thebes, and the vast religious establishment there dedicated to Amun. Instead he built a new capital at present-day Amarna, devoted to Aten. This represented a huge blow to the status and wealth of the old priestly elite. It was also a shocking blow to Egyptian religious sensibility since the new supreme god and creator was a purely abstract concept, represented by the sun-disk, who was never depicted in human or animal form and never spoke. Akhenaten's attempt to transform Egypt's religion had many parallels in the later history of emperors. In his case it is impossible to say to what extent personal and spiritual motives played a role in his policy. One obvious lesson of his reign – repeated in many other political systems – is that emperors with grandiose conceptions of their majesty who attempt head-on assaults on core elites and deeply rooted public beliefs are unlikely to succeed. Akhenaten's attempted revolution failed completely. After his death the old religious beliefs and elites reasserted themselves. Akhenaten himself became one of the great hate-figures in Egyptian history.[12]

Archaeology has revealed much about the monuments, rituals and ceremonies of ancient Egyptian monarchy. The scale and symmetry of the pyramids still inspire awe. New Kingdom remains at Luxor and Karnak, together with surviving reliefs and inscriptions, convey a good sense of how rituals were performed and the messages they were designed to convey. Order, hierarchy, splendour and majesty were common motifs, all of them centred around the pharaoh's person. Monuments, buildings and public spaces conveyed this message permanently in stone but they also provided the setting in which ceremonies could be performed and messages thereby reasserted among both participants and onlookers. Key festivals were linked to cosmic and natural forces: for example, the end of the Nile's flood season when the river receded and planting began. Ceremonies linked the pharaoh to the gods, the cosmos and his ancestors: the pharaoh himself took part every day in the rituals to feed and sustain his divine father.[13]

Most of these motifs recur over and over again in imperial monarchies during the subsequent millennia, of course in specific religious and cultural idioms. Nicholas II of Russia was one of the world's last emperors. In the early twentieth century he participated in many ceremonies and rituals designed to convey messages similar to those proclaimed and acted out by the pharaohs. For example, every January at the Feast of the Epiphany he performed the central role in the so-called Blessing of the Waters on the River Neva, which ran beside the Winter Palace in St Petersburg. The waters of the Neva symbolized those of the Jordan where Christ was baptized. Orthodox religious ritual and robes merged with court ceremonial. Next to the Orthodox clergy, court officials were ranked around the emperor and dressed in their most splendid uniforms. Earthly and heavenly hierarchy and truth was confirmed. The immense squares and palaces of St Petersburg provided an awe-inspiring setting. Like most imperial capitals its buildings conveyed both general messages about the dynasty's antiquity, majesty and sacredness and a specific content. In the Russian case, St Petersburg's wholly European aspect was designed to show that Russia was a European Great Power. The obelisks that dotted the city's landscape were a physical reminder of the long history of imperial monarchy. Originating in ancient Egypt, some of the pharaohs' greatest obelisks had been carried off to Rome and Constantinople as trophies. The obelisk became a feature of imperial architecture and monument-building. The Romanovs constructed obelisks to assert their claim to be a great empire and, specifically, an empire whose lineage stretched back to Rome and Byzantium.[14]

3

The Persian Emperors and Alexander of Macedon

Between 550 and 530 BCE the entire Near East was conquered by the Persian Achaemenid dynasty. Egypt's conquest followed shortly after. The Persian Empire was by far the largest yet seen in history. It stretched in the east across all of present-day Iran and into Afghanistan and Central Asia. Only the caliphate was to equal the Achaemenids in combining in one empire the two great regional power centres of the Iranian plateau and the Mediterranean. Not even the Romans managed this, the Arcacid and Sasanian empires in Iran proving to be their most formidable and longest-lasting enemies.

The western half of the Achaemenid Empire was a world of city states but in the east there were few towns and many peasants and aristocratic estates. The Persians originated in the Caucasus region and Anatolia. They were from the Aryan branch of the Indo-European language group. The nomadic Scythians were cousins. The Persians themselves were probably nomads in origin but by 550 BCE they had lived in south-west Iran for centuries and had absorbed many influences – both political and cultural – from the settled peoples of the region, and above all the Elamites. The Persian model of a conquering people on the edge of a sedentary civilization who combined their ancestors' warrior skills with political institutions, technologies and concepts drawn from the settled world was to be repeated many times in Eurasian history.

At the beginning of the sixth century BCE south-western Iran was dominated by neighbouring kingdoms of the Persians and the Medes. The Achaemenid Empire's founder, Cyrus II 'the Great' (r. c. 560–530 BCE), was the heir to both these kingdoms, since his mother was the only child of the Medean king. Cyrus was a bold and inspirational leader, an excellent military strategist and tactician, and a shrewd politician. This much it is possible to intuit from the record of his life and campaigns. More than this it is impossible to say, though the king was the subject of what is sometimes called the first biography, the famous work of the Greek author Xenophon. Xenophon's book is also sometimes described as a primer on leadership. The problem is that although some of the historical background is accurate, the character of Cyrus as depicted by Xenophon is better described as historical romance than biography. Moreover, it is a historical romance set within the classical Greek norms of heroic leadership. After Cyrus's death a combination of imperial overstretch, succession struggles, and the sudden death in 522 BCE of his successor, Cambyses, without obvious heirs, almost led to the early collapse of the Achaemenid Empire. Instead it was reconquered and then refounded on a more lasting basis by Cyrus's distant Achaemenid kinsman Darius I. Darius proved an outstanding political and military leader, as well as an excellent administrator. He created the political, ideological, military and administrative framework which sustained the empire for the rest of its existence. Luck was on his and the Achaemenids' side, in that, after grabbing power in 522 and defeating many rivals and rebels in civil war, he then lived and ruled until 486 BCE. In the pre-modern world, the fate of all hereditary monarchies depended greatly on medical chance.[1]

As with the Egyptians and Assyrians, the Achaemenid regime was a sacred monarchy.[2] Although the dynasty claimed neither to be divine nor even descended from the gods, it based its legitimacy in part on the blessing of the supreme god of the Zoroastrian religion, Ahura Mazda. Raised far above ordinary men, the emperor had a charisma – summed up by the word *Farr* – that came straight from God and was often symbolized by the sun-disk. Zoroastrianism was in key respects still in the process of formation in Achaemenid times and its sacred texts, the Avesta, were not to be written down for another millennium, so it is difficult to be precise as regards many aspects of the religion in this era. Zoroastrianism addressed the same key questions as Buddhism, Christianity and Islam. It provided a cosmology and explained the beginning and the end of the world. It told a dramatic tale of the struggle between good and evil on earth, and of the fates of good and wicked people after death. The king's roles included that of high priest and mediator between Ahura Mazda and His people. But Zoroastrianism, at least in Achaemenid times, was a tolerant religion and accepted other lesser gods even among the Persians. Achaemenid ideology and practice, for example, gave honoured space to the mostly Medean god Mithras. The Persian kings also made a point of not just tolerating the gods of the peoples they conquered but also of worshipping them when their imperial tours took them to the gods' home cities.[3]

This was the ideological element in what was a relatively tolerant and benevolent version of empire. The dynasty and the Persian elite had conquered an empire in order to win for themselves wealth and status. Conquered peoples who rebelled or refused to present their tribute and military recruits were repressed. But Darius I set tribute payments at a relatively modest level and Achaemenid propaganda (unlike Assyrian) stressed not ruthless repression but rather the peace and harmony provided by empire. The Achaemenids conciliated local elites and ruled through them. Given the scale of the empire and the size of the Persian elite this was realistic, but it meant that the rulers must never press too hard. So long as they restrained their demands and retained the aura of power their subjects were unlikely to rebel. On the other hand, if antagonized, non-Persian regional elites could mobilize great resources behind a rebellion. Moreover, the dynasty, the Persian elites and an imperial ideology could not penetrate deeply into non-Persian society. The rulers could not expect deeply committed loyalty from the conquered peoples.

This was a dynastic and Persian Empire. Its basis – like those of most of the empires we will study – remained always the alliance between the royal dynasty and the aristocratic service and landholding elite. The Achaemenids and the Persian aristocracy needed each other. The vast spoils of empire were shared out largely within this narrow group and were the political foundation of the imperial system. Almost all top officers at court and in the central army and administration were Persians and the great majority of them were aristocrats. So too were almost all the provincial governors (satraps). The core Persian elite was still semi-tribal and largely hereditary. Meritorious service and the king's favour brought some 'new men' into the elite. An aristocratic family and its wealth always remained vulnerable to royal caprice and unchecked power. But no Achaemenid king either wished or would have dared to challenge the aristocracy as a group. The Persian elite never questioned the Achaemenid dynasty's right to rule but the position of individual kings was far less secure. Few monarchs died in their beds and most fell victim to court conspiracies. Persian aristocrats served the

Achaemenids because service had much to offer but their ultimate loyalty was to their own aristocratic family and clan.[4]

The Achaemenid court possessed most of the features and functions of imperial courts throughout history. The court brought together the monarch, his family, his ministers and the social elite. It was at one and the same time a family's residence, a centre of government, the fountain of patronage, and a theatre of propaganda and spectacle. Gorgeously dressed and in full majesty, the king sat on a throne which was itself raised above his courtiers on a dais. He walked on carpets that were reserved for him alone. He was surrounded by superbly uniformed guards and courtiers. Everyone's place and movement were strictly choreographed. Status was defined by where a courtier stood in relation to the king, what type and colour of costume he wore, and whether he bore emblems and titles (such as Friend of the King) which signified special intimacy and favour. At banquets, too, strict precedence prevailed but after dinner a small group of roughly twelve senior courtiers could be chosen by the king to join him in a private drinking session. Honour and influence, politics and sociability were combined, as was usually the way at royal courts: during these private parties (symposia) important questions of patronage and policy were discussed. Queens and princesses participated in life at court. Only the royal concubines were half-confined to a form of harem. Rivalries and hatreds between siblings, royal mothers and in-laws could turn deadly, especially when succession to the throne was at stake. It was at this point that an ageing or newly enthroned king was most at risk. The absence of a fixed law of succession inevitably contributed to instability: even nomination as heir in his father's lifetime did not guarantee a smooth transition. Still less did primogeniture. Although the sons of wives took precedence over those of concubines, on occasion the latter inherited the throne.[5]

No surviving evidence allows us a reliable view of an Achaemenid monarch's personality or innermost thoughts. The inscriptions on the tomb of Darius I do allow an insight into how the greatest of the dynasty's monarchs perceived the nature of kingship and the qualities needed to fulfil the king's role successfully. Darius defined himself first by his ancestry as an Achaemenid, member of an ancient dynasty with many royal forebears. Next came the fact that he was a Persian and then – a bow perhaps primarily to the Medes – that he was an Aryan. Here as elsewhere, Darius added that he ruled over wide territories and many peoples, thereby deserving the title of 'King of Kings' and near-universal ruler. He derived his power from the appointment of Ahura Mazda, who had bestowed upon the king 'wisdom and energy'. Darius was a friend of 'the right' and the enemy of 'the lie', punishing the wrongdoer and rewarding the virtuous. Physically strong, a good horseman, archer and spearman, he was also a good commander. In war he was intelligent, full of commanding authority, and not inclined to panic when faced by the enemy. He had a ruler's necessary ability to restrain his anger, avoid hot temper and punish and reward in measured fashion. In addition, Darius never believed accusations or slander until he had heard both sides of the story.[6]

The tale that was traditionally told about the Achaemenids read like that of a Chinese dynasty's winning and then losing the mandate of Heaven, or indeed the rise and fall of a great modern family firm. A bold and innovative founder (Cyrus II) was succeeded by a formidable administrator and consolidator of the family's business (Darius I), but after this decay set in. The problem is that the traditional story was overwhelmingly dependent on Greek sources and these were in general heavily biased. In the first place they concentrated almost exclusively on Persian policy in the west, and especially towards the Greeks. They tell us next to nothing about the empire's huge eastern wing. Secondly, the tale they told was infused with the Greek belief that, whereas they themselves were manly, freedom-loving, disciplined and austere, the Persians were the precise opposite – given over to luxury, opulence, cowardice and softness. This was both the cause and effect of living in an absolute monarchy in a court plagued by women, eunuchs, servility and intrigue. The juxtaposition of Persian vices against Greek virtues was a wonderful rhetorical device whereby the Greeks could praise themselves and what they claimed as their core characteristics. The extraordinary cultural impact of these descriptions continued for more than two millennia to assign specific vices to 'the East' and its rulers even when Europe's own kings and elites often themselves behaved in similar fashion.

Darius I's successor, Xerxes I, whose invasion of Greece was defeated in 480 BCE, was derided by Plato as ruined by 'a womanish education', and his reign was described as the beginning of a sharp decline in Achaemenid power and leadership which culminated in the dynasty's destruction by Alexander of Macedon (r. 336–323 BCE) in the 330s. In a manner familiar to historians of the Ottoman Empire, Western bias telescopes a long period in the history of an 'eastern' dynasty into a single narrative of decline in a way that is both untrue and unhistorical. The story of decline included murderous rivalries between royal women, the intrigues of eunuchs and waning royal control over courtiers and satraps. Alexander's destruction of the Persian Empire was partly ascribed to the cowardice and poor reputation of the last Achaemenid king, Darius III, many of whose Persian lieutenants were said to have deserted him because they saw his rule as illegitimate. Much of this story is clearly wrong. The Persian Empire remained immensely strong after the relatively minor setback against the Greeks in 480. In the first half of the fourth century the Persians exercised great indirect power over the Greek mainland and regained control of Egypt, which had been lost for decades as a result of a weakening of central power during a war of succession within the Achaemenid dynasty. As for Darius III, he is now usually portrayed as a legitimate and competent leader, who had the misfortune to face the formidable Macedonian military machine, built up and trained to perfection by King Philip II and then led during the campaigns of the late 330s by his son, Alexander, one of history's greatest generals.[7]

Alexander's Argead dynasty had ruled Macedonia for well over two hundred years. The monarchy had touches of sacredness: 'religion and rituals that the kings uniquely performed, sacrifices and celebrations, were vital' elements in the role and the legitimacy of the Argeads. On the other hand, rules of succession were unclear: the ruler's sons often competed to succeed him. Even once established on the throne, the king's 'government was personal, his authority as absolute as he could make it'. Success was vital to consolidate a king's power and this meant, above all, success in war. First and foremost, the Macedonian monarchy inherited by Alexander was a variant of warrior-kingship. The Macedonian royal war-band, expanded and perfected by Philip II, looked to its king to provide successful leadership in battle. Philip also fed its expectation that a king would lead from the front, himself losing an eye and suffering other wounds on the battlefield. Philip sought legitimacy beyond Macedon in the broader Greek world: for example, he competed successfully in the Olympic games and thereby established himself as a hero-athlete. Well before Philip's reign the Argead kings had for a long time patronized and hosted Greece's leading artists.[8]

The Argead court and elite in Philip's day combined Macedonian martial toughness and Greek high culture. Alexander embodied both. Aristotle was his tutor. Throughout his life Alexander loved Greek poetry, music and literature. 'Alexander could quote Euripides's plays by heart and would send for his plays, together with those of Sophocles and his greater predecessor Aeschylus, as his leisure reading' when on campaign in the furthest eastern reaches of Iran. As a prince, Alexander was brought up among Macedonian aristocratic boys: training in war, shared bravery at the hunt, and Greek literary and artistic culture dominated his youth. He became one of the greatest generals in history, famous for his boldness, his strategic insight and the speed of his armies on campaign, but also for his tactical flair on the battlefield. He was also famous for his courage. Leading from the front and sharing his soldiers' dangers and burdens, he was adored, trusted and followed by his men. Even his vices – including mammoth drinking bouts – were on a more than human scale. Alexander was the charismatic Greek hero in its most perfect embodiment. Like the best Romantic heroes, he conquered the world and died young, aged thirty-two.[9]

Alexander's greatest long-term contribution to history was the spread of Greek culture across much of Asia. Above all this meant the territories of the Achaemenid Empire: the king established Greek colonies across these lands and the dynasties of his generals Seleucus and Ptolemy ruled them for generations after his death. But traces of Alexander's legacy lived on in regions his armies never reached, even in China: 'there is clear evidence now that some more complicated western art practices – hollow-cast moulding etc. – were learned by China from the west, from sources that owed their establishment and continued industry in Central Asia to Alexander's conquest'. As usual with conquering empires, the spread of cultural influences in all directions has to be balanced against the devastation wrought by the conquerors. In Alexander's case this included the destruction of the fabulous palace complex at Persepolis. His efforts to spread Greek culture had great long-term effects that he could never have envisaged. Perhaps the most important is that without the Greek lingua franca that Alexander established across much of the Near and Middle East, 'Christianity could never have spread beyond Judaea.'[10]

The family of Alexander's mother, Olympias, claimed Achilles as an ancestor. The Macedonian dynasty of his father claimed descent from Heracles, a son of Zeus. Performing deeds of heroism on the battlefield and wearing spectacular armour was in part royal theatre designed to impress not just his Macedonian soldiers but also a Greek world steeped in Homeric legends. Alexander himself internalized these legends and was driven above all by thirst for a personal glory which would outdo even that of his heroic ancestors and Greek legend, not to mention his father, Philip. A recent historian of Alexander and the 'Great Man' in classical Greece writes that 'Alexander seems to have wanted to be considered a god in his own right, probably while he was still alive. The imitation and surpassing of Achilles, Heracles, and Dionysus strongly implied it and the claims of direct descent from the divine pressed his case.' His obsessive and megalomaniac drive for personal glory grew with time and success. His campaigns in India were more bloody and less linked to achievable objectives than his earlier conquest of the Persian Empire. At this point even Alexander's devoted soldiers had had enough and demanded to turn back, many of them calling for a return to Macedonia. Nevertheless, even this did not stop Alexander's lust for glory. He died in the midst of planning the conquest of Arabia.[11]

Beyond question Alexander was a genius who made a great impact on history. Whether he was a good hereditary monarch or empire-builder is another matter. No doubt most founders of empires or contemporary corporations have a touch of megalomania. This needs to be shed if the empire or company is to survive. Alexander left behind on his death few institutions and two infant sons to sustain the empire he had conquered. The inevitable result was civil war and disintegration. His sons, together with his halfwit brother and sister, were all in time murdered, so his dynasty lost even their ancestral throne in Macedonia. Macedon itself was very soon less powerful after his demise than it had been when he ascended its throne.

To what extent Alexander can be blamed for this is debatable. He understood and sought intelligently to surmount the challenge of evolving from being a mere Macedonian 'national' king to becoming the emperor of the vast and multi-ethnic Achaemenid realms. As was often the case, a newly created empire disintegrated because of a succession crisis – in this case Alexander's lack of an adult male heir. In one sense Alexander can hardly be blamed for dying young. On the other hand, the recklessly heroic style in which he commanded his armies on the battlefield made a premature death likely.

As with most great historical figures, Alexander has his admirers and his critics among historians. For my purposes, the key point is to explore the way in which his life and reign illuminate key themes of this book. Alexander was both a hereditary monarch and a charismatic leader. He showed just how formidable this combination could be. His death at an early age and the resulting lack of adult heirs is a reminder of the inherent fragility of hereditary monarchy, unless it was buttressed by powerful institutions and well-established rules of succession. Alexander's life also illustrates the tensions between hereditary monarchy and charisma as sources of authority and principles of leadership. The hereditary monarch must owe allegiance to something greater than himself, which usually means to his dynasty and community. The survival of the state is essential to the community's well-being and cannot be risked like a private company, let alone in a leader's pursuit of heroic personal status. The Greek tradition of hero-worship was 'the cult of the individual, and the hero is always imagined standing alone'. Aristotle called Achilles, the alleged ancestor and role model of Alexander, 'a non-cooperator like an isolated piece in a game of draughts'. As an expert on Greek heroes notes, 'the responsibilities of government do not combine well with the individualism expected of the hero'. Among later rulers in the Roman, Christian and Muslim worlds no ancient emperor would enjoy more fame and allure than Alexander, but his influence was often nefarious. In conceptual terms, charisma and hereditary monarchy are inherently in conflict. On a more down-to-earth level, a man brought up on the steps of a throne already risked megalomania and needed no encouragement from misleading Homeric role models. Moreover, unlike Alexander, he was most unlikely to be a military genius and to inherit the best army in his region of the world.[12]

4

The Roman Imperial Monarchy

In this book I concentrate on the history of the Roman Empire from the last decades of the first century BCE until the 630s CE, in other words from Augustus's creation of a monarchy until the eruption of Islam across the Near East. Whereas starting with the first emperor is an obvious choice given the subject of this book, opting for the 630s might be challenged. The western Roman Empire after all fell in 476 CE. I follow here in the footsteps of the great Belgian historian Henri Pirenne, who long ago argued that the arrival of Islam in the seventh century meant the real end of the ancient world.[1] From it came in time the division of the previously united Mediterranean world into a Christian northern and Muslim southern shore. Although this division – both ideological and geopolitical – was never total, it has remained a key divide in global history to this day. In comparison, 476 CE was of minor importance. By that time the geopolitical and economic core of the Roman Empire was no longer Italy but rather Constantinople, the eastern provinces and north Africa. These remained part of the (eastern) Roman Empire until the rise of Islam. In the period between 476 and the 630s it was easy to believe that one day the core provinces of the old empire would reconquer its western territories, as Justinian I partly did in the mid-sixth century.

Like many empires in the ancient Near East, the Roman Empire was created and initially ruled by a city state largely for the benefit of that city state's elites. By the time of Augustus it had evolved into a vast empire, 1.35 million square miles in area, stretching from Britain to the Red Sea and from Portugal to Armenia. This territory needed to be governed to a degree sufficient to yield the taxes and recruits required for its defence. The Roman Empire rested on an iron-age, agrarian economy. Its economic base was not necessarily superior to that of its potential enemies, nor in this era did economic superiority always translate into military might. In Augustus's reign roughly half the state budget went on the armed forces, sustaining 300,000 troops. These were now long-service professional soldiers, more competent but also much more expensive than the armies of the former republic. A republican-style army made up of Italian citizen-soldiers could never be expected to patrol the far-flung borders of empire. Some 300,000 soldiers, however professional, were barely sufficient to defend 17,000 miles of borders. In Augustus's era external threats were limited. When under later emperors they grew, so too did the tax burden.

Britain was a nuisance because difficulties of rapid reinforcement meant that it needed a far bigger permanent Roman garrison than its size or strategic value warranted, but the two key military theatres were the Rhine and upper Danube in Europe and the Persian front in Asia. The main headquarters for the two fronts were Cologne and Antioch respectively. It was impossible for reinforcements to move between the two in the course of a single campaigning season. Nor could reserve forces reach either front from the empire's capital and core region in central Italy if faced by a sudden attack: Cologne was 67 days' march from Rome and Antioch 124 days. The passage across the Mediterranean was shorter but too dangerous to be used for half of the year given the ships of that era. Strategic crisis for the Roman Empire above all meant simultaneous threats on the Persian and European fronts. At such times two big and independent armies had to be positioned in the Persian and European theatres. A divide always existed in the Roman Empire between the Greek-speaking east and the Latin-speaking west, though this was attenuated by the co-option of eastern elites into the imperial senatorial class and by the fact that the old Roman aristocracy was itself deeply influenced by Greek high culture, which it often acknowledged to be superior to its own. After Emperor Constantine's acceptance of Christianity in 313 with the Edict of Milan the whole empire evolved over the course of the fourth century into a polity united by allegiance to a religion of salvation that originated in the east. Perhaps in the long run ethno-cultural differences might have sundered the Roman Empire, but the initial split between the eastern and western empires was owed to geopolitical rather than ethno-cultural or religious factors.[2]

The Roman imperial monarchy was military through and through.

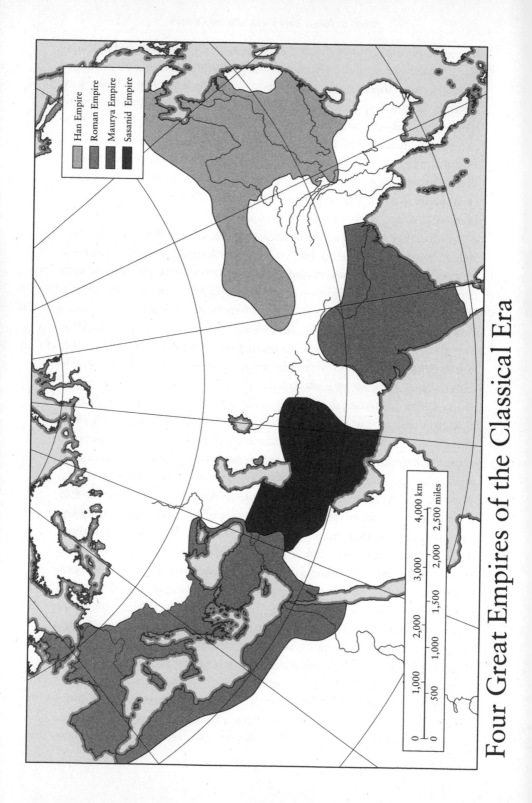

Four Great Empires of the Classical Era

0   1,000   2,000   3,000   4,000 km
0   500 1,000 1,500 2,000 2,500 miles

Not all the most famous and successful emperors were successful generals but most were. Nothing gained more legitimacy for an emperor than victory in war and this was especially true at times of crisis. Trajan and Hadrian in the first half of the second century CE were the first emperors from outside Italy and both were famous generals. It was their crushing victories over Rome's enemies that gave Diocletian and his network of generals from Illyria the legitimacy which enabled them to save the empire and reform the system of government in the face of the existential crisis of the late third century. For roughly a century after Diocletian's accession in 284 CE the empire was ruled by warrior-emperors. After 395 CE, however, monarchs mostly gave up commanding armies in the field. One historian of the late Roman Empire comments that as 'emperors ceased to take part in campaigns themselves and became palace-based, the empire's ability to defend the northern frontier and retain the western provinces was critically reduced'.[3]

This points to a key dilemma of empires in general and to the Roman Empire's fate in particular. The history of empire is one long illustration of the dangers of emperors commanding in the field. The chances for stability and long-term survival of empires were greatly increased if they evolved institutions and conventions that made this unnecessary. Rome failed in this respect and this was probably its greatest weakness. The Latin word for 'emperor' (*imperator*) was the same as the word used for 'victorious general' in the republican era. Most emperors and dynasties established themselves on the throne by civil wars and military coups. The Imperial Guard, the so-called 'Praetorians', were so adept at this game that 'Praetorian' has become a synonym for 'putschist' in the English language. Both Roman history and the Roman monarchy's weak dynastic legitimacy meant that any successful general might dream of becoming an emperor and was likely to be suspected of such ambitions even when he did not have them. On many occasions this resulted in political instability, poor strategy and the huge waste of resources caused by civil war. Compared to other great empires the average length of Roman emperors' reigns was short. In its first 311 years, the era of the so-called Principate – dating from the reign of Augustus in 27 BCE to the end of the Imperial Crisis in 284 CE – Rome had fifty-three emperors. In roughly the same length of time (1710–2021) the United Kingdom had just twelve monarchs. Perhaps a fairer comparison is with Rome's greatest enemy, the Sasanian dynasty in Iran. If one excludes the chaotic last decade of the Sasanians, then thirty monarchs ruled in just over four hundred years between 224 and 628 CE. The Roman imperial monarchy survived for almost five hundred years even in the West, so it would be absurd to call it fragile. The strength of the elites' commitment to the empire added to the exceptional quality of many of the empire's monarchs for a long time more than offset the vulnerability caused by the weakness of the dynastic principle.

Historians have long since divided the Roman monarchical regime's history into two eras, those of the so-called 'Principate' and 'Dominate'. The former was the system of rule created by Augustus four years after he emerged victorious in 31 BCE from the civil wars that followed the assassination of his uncle and adopted father, Julius Caesar, in 44 BCE. Augustus was a ruthless and skilful politician whose power rested ultimately on victory in the civil war and continuing control of the Roman army. Once his enemies were defeated in the field he turned to legitimizing and consolidating his regime. He understood that Roman traditions and the elite's values would made a naked military dictatorship or absolute monarchy unpopular and vulnerable. While retaining the core elements of power for himself, he therefore conceded to the senatorial aristocracy a small share of that power and a much greater helping of top jobs and patronage. He was also careful not to wound their aristocratic pride or self-respect and behaved in his relations with the senatorial aristocracy as if he were merely the empire's friendly first citizen rather than its monarch. Learning from Julius Caesar's mistakes, he resolutely refused to allow himself to be officially proclaimed a living god or to assume the manners or trappings of royalty in the city of Rome, though he happily accepted the divine status officially proclaimed by local elites in the eastern half of the empire and the private cults that worshipped him as a deity even in Rome and across the empire's western half.

Augustus was a subtle and effective politician but he did not need to be a true chief administrator. The central administration was tiny, rudimentary and personal: at its core were Augustus's own household freedmen and slaves. The empire was governed on a highly decentralized basis. Cities ran their own affairs, appealing to the emperor where disputes either within the community or with other cities required an arbiter. Augustus was commander-in-chief, patron-in-chief, chief priest and director of the empire's foreign policy, but in internal affairs he was closer to supreme judge than chief administrator. In this the Principate was not an exception among imperial monarchies even at their apogee but rather an empire towards the more decentralized end of the spectrum. The luck and physical toughness that allowed Augustus to live to the extraordinary (for Roman times) age of seventy-seven enabled the Principate to put down deep roots.[4]

The regime created by Augustus mostly survived until the last quarter of the third century when it was replaced by the so-called 'Dominate', whose founder was Diocletian (r. 284–305 CE). The most important reason for the shift was the growing external threat to the empire. In deeply impressive fashion, Roman elites adapted to this new challenge just as Augustus and his allies had adapted to the new challenges thrown up against the republican regime in the first century BCE. After the replacement of the Arsacid (Parthian) dynasty by the much more formidable Sasanians in 224 CE, the Persian threat grew significantly. In 260, for example, the Sasanian king, Shapur I, sacked Antioch, Rome's greatest city in the east and the base for all military operations in the region. He defeated and captured Emperor Valerian. Simultaneously the European theatre became more dangerous as Germanic tribes formed into larger units, partly in response to the challenge but also the example presented by the Romans themselves. Increased external challenges put pressure on the Roman regime to generate more taxes and soldiers. Combined with succession struggles and military revolts the result was great internal instability and conflict. Between Caracalla's assassination by a disaffected soldier in 217 and Diocletian's accession in 284, emperors succeeded each other with dizzying speed. On many occasions rival generals ruled parts of the empire and fought each other. In Diocletian the Roman elite once again found a ruler who could save the empire and refashion it to meet new challenges.

The system of rule that was consolidated under Diocletian was different in its public face and administrative methods to the regime created by Augustus. By the third century the army was no longer commanded by aristocratic senators from Rome. The generals were now hard-bitten professional soldiers of provincial origin. These men often lacked the cultural sophistication of the old senatorial elite but they were fully devoted to the Roman imperial idea. The officer corps saved the Roman Empire in the third century and Diocletian was its very competent leader and representative. Such men had no sense of the Augustan fiction that the monarch was merely the first aristocrat of his empire and they felt a great need for rituals and ideologies that would raise them high above their subjects. Imperial portraits now showed rulers 'in a rigid, frontal stance, towering over all others'. Diocletian was addressed as 'master and god'. Whereas Augustus (and the more sensible of his successors under the Principate) at receptions allowed himself to be addressed by 'the traditional greeting of patrons by their favoured friends and clients', even members of the elite prostrated themselves before Diocletian and kissed the hem of the emperor's robe at court ceremonies. 'The wearing or display of purple became an imperial monopoly.' The emperor's image was no longer that of a benevolent first citizen described in traditional Roman terms as just, generous, virtuous and wise, though with the addition of the monarchical quality of mercy. Under Diocletian and his successors the monarch was depicted as 'a distant, god-like, aggressively militaristic, and mostly terrifying autocrat'. Living up to this image put an extra strain on an emperor.[5]

From Diocletian's reign onwards the emperor moved towards becoming a chief administrator, while retaining his other roles. Although the imperial administration had grown in size and complexity under the Principate, its numbers and activity now increased significantly. Even in the late second century there had been only a few hundred salaried imperial officials, with a much larger number of slaves and seconded soldiers acting as messengers, clerks and porters. By the end of the fourth century the number of salaried imperial officials was 30,000–35,000. Through this apparatus the emperor was able to collect most of the extra revenue he now needed to recruit and supply his soldiers, and to maintain a degree of control and order across his territories. It remains in dispute among historians whether the cumbersome new administrative arrangements actually accomplished anything but a short-term increase in the emperor's disposable income. What seems beyond question is that the weight of this administrative machine bore down not just on his subjects but also on the monarch himself. In one historian's words, 'the paper trail surged'. Elite bureaucrats in the imperial capital were generally competent but they were also highly political and self-interested. Divided formally by department and specialization, they also created powerful patron–client networks in pursuit of promotion, pay and perks. Expanding a department's remit meant to increase its officials' income from the areas of economy and society they oversaw. Vicious turf-wars were the result.[6]

A leading contemporary expert on the late imperial government describes graphically the late-Roman variant on a theme which recurs throughout this book: an emperor, in theory all-powerful and sur- rounded by sacred ceremonial, was often the captive of his officials: 'Bureaucracy, with its predictable rules and established norms, had little room for the caprice of autocracy. Emperors risked being pavilioned in splendour within an inaccessible court; trapped unwillingly in a shim- mering web of ritual, their capacity, their inclination, and simply their time for intervention subordinated to an endless round of pomp and circumstance.' Most emperors felt and resented this gilded cage. Many of them intervened arbitrarily and frequently in order to show their subordinates who was boss. Intervention could have other causes. Some problems and most emergencies could not be solved by applying bureau- cratic rules and norms. Arbitrary use of the emperor's power might be essential for the speedy and coordinated response to crises that threat- ened the state's survival. Above all, the ruling bureaucracy was a political as well as an administrative body. For an emperor, getting policy right often mattered but patronage always did. Politics and patronage had their own 'logic' which for an emperor would usually override bureau- cratic rules.[7]

Of course, caprice and cruelty might be just the mere whims of a monarch unconstrained by any laws and drunk on power. They could also be a response to fear of the conspiracies and hidden dangers that often lurked behind his courtiers' deference, or simply a means to impose the monarch's will on his bureaucrats. Ammianus Marcellinus, a shrewd and well-informed observer of the fourth-century imperial court, recalled that Constantius II was in many ways a moderate man and ruler, until he smelled the slightest whiff of conspiracy, at which point he turned savage. Even in normal times the emperor and his spies constantly sniffed, listened and investigated in search of conspiracy. Val- entinian I was infamous for his rages: minor mistakes might be punished by hideous tortures and executions. The emperor kept 'Goldflake' and 'Innocence', two savage and underfed man-eating bears, outside his bedroom as a warning to his entourage.[8]

Inevitably, the eras of both the Principate and the Dominate had their good and bad emperors. Nevertheless, the principle of monarchy quickly gained near-universal recognition. When Nero's suicide extinguished Augustus's 'Julio-Claudian' dynasty in 68 CE and led to civil war, no significant voices called for a return to the republic. By now monarchy was accepted as necessary to restrain the conflicts within the elite that had nearly destroyed Rome in the last generations of the republic. The history of the republic's death agonies had become a political and moral tale universally known both to emperors and the Roman elites. It was now widely recognized that the institutions of the old Roman city state could not govern a vast empire. From the provincial perspective the monarchy offered more efficient government and placed constraints on the unlimited rapaciousness of the senators sent out from Rome as provincial governors. The cry that went up in 68–9 CE was not for a republic but for the 'good old days' of Augustus.

Although monarchy – in the discretely camouflaged form created by Augustus – now had great legitimacy, individual monarchs and dynasties did not. Rome was 'the least ideological monarchy of the ancient world', sustained above all by the consensus within the elite that in practice monarchy was merely the least bad option available. The Roman state since time immemorial had its city gods and possessed a sacred aura. When imperial monarchy was established the emperors personified the state and shared its aura. First Augustus and subsequently all emperors who died on the throne were deified posthumously. They thereby became part of the imperial cult, whose temples and rituals spread across the empire. But 'worship' and 'divinity' in the eyes of Romans did not have the connotations they possess in the great monotheistic religions. For the Romans no vast chasm divided the worlds of gods and men. Divine status was conferred on outstanding humans once they were dead: they were supermen rather than gods in the Christian sense. No Roman believed that an emperor, living or dead, was the creator and ruler of the universe. Members of the Roman elite were realistic and politically shrewd. Once mediocre and even disastrous emperors were deified posthumously the honour lost all meaning. No member of this elite – including even the priests who officiated at sacrifices in its name – was much impressed or much inhibited by a monarch's supposedly semi-sacred status when the moment came to plunge a dagger in his back.[9]

If religion provided a Roman emperor with limited support, dynastic legitimacy was even weaker. The Roman state and empire had existed long before Augustus created the monarchy. They far overshadowed any dynasty. The Roman elite identified totally with state and empire. It came to accept monarchy as essential to the state and empire's preservation.

Only the maddest and most autocratic emperor could think of the Roman state and empire as his family's creation or possession in later European feudal style. Rulers with such pretensions generally came to a sticky end. Occasionally an emperor might attempt to divide rulership between two of his sons but this strategy never prevailed.

By imperial standards the lifespan of Roman dynasties was very brief. Augustus's dynasty, the Julio-Claudians, reigned for ninety-five years and lasted longer on the throne than any dynasty that succeeded them. Since a dynasty's antiquity was almost everywhere a vital factor in its legitimacy this helps to explain why Roman dynasties had little hold on the public imagination or loyalty. Even in the case of the Julio-Claudians, since Augustus had no sons the line of succession was anything but clear-cut. Driven by feuds, adoptions, assassinations and unexpected deaths the succession passed to and fro within his and his wife Livia's descendants for four generations before ending with Nero. This too was typical of later dynasties. Astonishingly, in our entire period the imperial throne never passed from father to son for even three generations.[10]

The failure of imperial dynasties to reproduce themselves was true of the Roman elite as a whole. Men married late and died early. The city of Rome was especially unhealthy in this regard. In the first century CE only one Roman in ten was born in the lifetime of a paternal grandfather. Roughly three-quarters of consular families disappeared in the male line in each generation. Given low life expectancy, women needed to have five to six children to sustain the population level. The norm among aristocratic females was three or fewer. Roman women were far from equal to men but they had much greater power than in many ancient societies. For example, they could and often did divorce their husbands at will, retaining their property after doing so. Conservative male critics complained that elite women preferred a life of ease and luxury to child-bearing. Augustus twice issued laws requiring married couples to have at least three children and imposing fines and other penalties if they failed to do so, but his efforts had little long-term effect. No ruler of any other empire whom I have encountered needed to issue such orders to elite families. If the Roman elite's attitude to reproduction was unique, that was probably partly owed to Rome's equally unique law of adoption. 'There was no distinction drawn between sons by birth and sons by adoption in Roman law or in public perception.'[11]

The law on adoption had great advantages for an imperial dynasty.

If the imperial couple were childless or their sons died, it was possible to adopt suitable candidates for the throne. Usually though not always these candidates were kinsmen. Some of the most famous and successful emperors in Roman history were adopted by their predecessor on the throne: this was true, for example, of the four great monarchs of the second century CE – Trajan, Hadrian, Antoninus Pius and Marcus Aurelius. The one chink in the otherwise splendid principle of adoption was that this was only resorted to if a man had no natural and legitimate sons to inherit his property and status. Displacing a natural son by an adopted one was generally seen as impious.

As a result, when natural heirs did exist they almost always succeeded their fathers on the throne. Given average life expectancy, most natural heirs succeeded when still very young men or, more often, adolescents. Inevitably they lacked the knowledge, maturity or confidence to live up to their role. The temptations lying in wait for a young emperor were immense. Self-discipline and self-knowledge were vital for a monarch: neither comes easily in adolescence. Supreme products of the Roman *jeunesse dorée*, Caligula, Nero and Commodus neither wanted nor were temperamentally suited to buckling down to the hard grind of rulership. Unlike their peers in other imperial systems their position was not buttressed by traditions, institutions and ideologies. As already noted, dynastic and religious legitimacy were weak. In addition, since Augustus's monarchy rested on the fiction that it was the republic restored, it could not claim a law of succession to the throne, leaving the young monarch even further exposed.

The Roman emperor's role was extremely demanding. He was expected to reign, rule and lead in both the political and military fields. A crucial element in his job was the management of proud and experienced senators and generals. The Roman elite still retained many attitudes inherited from the republican aristocracy. An insecure or arrogant young emperor who put on airs or struck out against potential conspirators raised many hackles. To a great degree an emperor's legitimacy depended on his performance. Murder was the only way to remove an incompetent or oppressive monarch and Roman political culture was bloody. The three first dynasties of the Principate – the Julio-Claudians, Flavians and Antonines – all ended in the violent deaths of young emperors (Nero, Domitian and Commodus) who had antagonized key individuals and interests within the elite.

The father of Commodus was Marcus Aurelius, who was born in 121 CE, ascended the throne in 161 and died in 180. Of all Rome's emperors he has the highest reputation. This is owed partly to his achievements, partly to the admiration expressed for him in surviving contemporary sources, but also because his *Meditations* offer a unique glimpse into the mind and soul of a ruler. This document is a personal confession, never edited or intended for publication. To put things in Catholic terms, to read the *Meditations* is almost to be a priest hearing the emperor's confession.

Written towards the end of Marcus Aurelius's life, these are the words of a tired and ageing man, often in pain and contemplating death. Pessimism comes naturally to many men in this condition. But the emperor's words also reflect all the frustrations of a life spent in politics. 'A king's lot,' he reflected, was 'to do good and be damned.' An unphilosophical but emotionally satisfying reason for not fearing death, he added, was that it would be a relief from a life lived amidst politics, surrounded not by men of the mind like himself but by people obsessed by wealth, status, fame and power. Even some of his advisers and ministers, men on whom he had spent so much 'effort, prayer and thought', would be glad to see him gone. He imagined their inner thoughts: 'we can breathe again now, rid of this schoolmaster . . . I could feel his silent criticism of us all.' Marcus Aurelius had always been a conservative, proud of Rome's laws and traditions. At the peak of Roman power and confidence, this was the near-universal stance of Roman aristocrats. The exceptions were reactionaries who yearned for an imagined earlier golden age in culture and politics. No emperor would have survived had he challenged the principles or institutions underpinning a grossly unequal society which rested partly on slavery, but probably such an idea never entered Marcus Aurelius's mind. An enormously conscientious and fair supreme judge, he was deeply committed to the idea of justice as this was understood in his time, society and class. In his *Meditations* he expressed the near-impotence of the supposedly all-powerful monarch: 'Don't hope for Plato's Utopian republic, but be content with the smallest step forward, and regard even that result as no mean achievement.'[12]

The future emperor had been a serious, hard-working and disciplined boy. He chose to sleep on a camp bed, covered only by a cloak. In this he stood out among the aristocratic youth of his day. The Roman aristocracy had become hugely wealthy in the first century CE, far wealthier than either its contemporary peers in the Chinese imperial elite or the sixteenth-century European aristocracy. Marcus Aurelius was a throwback to the austere discipline of the republican elite amidst a *jeunesse dorée* grown accustomed to luxury and pleasure. Together with his obvious intelligence, this was no doubt why the childless emperor Hadrian singled him out as a future monarch when Marcus was still an adolescent.[13]

Since Marcus was still too young to rule, Hadrian chose a worthy but elderly aristocrat, Antoninus Pius, to act as stop-gap emperor after his death (which came in 138 CE). Antoninus was Marcus's uncle by marriage but now adopted him as his son and married him to his daughter. Antoninus was fifty-one at the time and by Roman standards approaching old age, so no one expected him to live for another twenty-three years. Most heirs would have chafed at this drawn-out wait for the throne, some would have conspired to remove an adopted father. Marcus on the contrary was totally loyal to a man whom he regarded with deep affection as father, mentor and model ruler. His comments about Antoninus in the *Meditations* describe not just the man but also Marcus's own perception of the qualities required in a ruler. 'A man of mellow wisdom and mature experience', Antoninus was kind, patient, and 'an accurate judge of men's character and actions'. He ignored gossip, accepted criticism even when it was unfair, and stood far above jealousy, pettiness or anger. Tireless, thrifty and deeply responsible, he studied issues in great detail but was quick to grasp their essential principles. In council he encouraged debate but showed 'an immovable adherence to decisions made after full consideration'. Disliking pomp and circumstance, Antoninus behaved like the president of an aristocratic republic rather than an absolute monarch. This example Marcus took to heart, writing that he himself stood for 'a monarchy which valued above all the liberty of the subject'.[14]

For all Marcus's praise of his adopted father, in some important respects Antoninus had neglected to prepare his heir for his future role. Marcus had never travelled outside Rome before his accession to the throne in 161 and had been given no military experience or training. The three previous decades had been entirely peaceful but the new emperor was immediately faced by major invasions on both the Danube and Persian fronts. The Persians and the Germanic tribes were each driven into aggression by internal factors but they may also have sensed that Rome's army had gone a little flabby after decades of peace and decided to test the empire's power. Soon afterwards, a plague epidemic devastated the empire. Rome was faced with its most dangerous security threat thus far in the second century though one which did not yet have the deep-rooted structural elements that lay behind the long crisis of the third century. Marcus disliked military life but his sense of duty drove him to take command on the European front. He spent much of his reign commanding armies, in time proving himself to be a competent and successful general who won the loyalty and respect of his soldiers.

Since he could not command simultaneously in Europe and Asia, the emperor appointed an experienced and skilful general, Avidius Cassius, to face the Persians. Avidius was not just a Roman aristocrat but also a descendant of the Greek Seleucid dynasty that had ruled Persia for generations after Alexander's death. He succeeded brilliantly and was richly rewarded and praised, remaining in the east as supreme commander after the Persians were defeated. In 175, with Marcus ageing and the issue of succession coming on to the agenda, Avidius rebelled and proclaimed himself emperor. Many of the key eastern generals and governors supported the rebellion, though in some cases this was due to rumours that the emperor had died. Marcus Aurelius was as legitimate and benevolent a ruler as any Roman emperor could ever be, so Avidius's rebellion is a stark illustration of the monarchy's inability to control or trust its generals. Avidius failed and the rebels were treated leniently but Marcus moved immediately to secure the succession of Commodus, his only surviving son out of the fifteen children born to him and Empress Faustina. Aged only fifteen, Commodus was appointed co-emperor in 177. Three years later he ascended the throne on his father's death. Subsequently it was sometimes argued that Marcus Aurelius's only major blemish was to appoint so unsuitable an heir, but in fact he had little choice. Roman custom insisted that son should follow father. Moreover, to set Commodus aside was also probably to sign his death warrant since his survival would be a huge threat to any other man who succeeded Marcus on the throne.

Marcus Aurelius saw philosophy as a far higher calling than rulership: 'Alexander, Julius Caesar, Pompey,' he wrote, 'what are they to Diogenes, Heraclitus, Socrates? These men saw into reality, its causes and its material, and their directing minds were their own masters. As for the former, they were slaves to all their ambitions.' The emperor regretted that his station in life did not allow him to retreat in solitude to 'the country, by the sea, in the hills' and have time to think and read. He loathed rulers' pursuit of fame and glory, mocking men who sought immortality through the eyes of posterity. All fame was shallow and fleeting in his view. True fulfilment lay within a man and in his mind. The emperor is usually categorized as a Stoic, a philosophical school that was Greek in origin but made a great impact on Roman elites. Its basic tenet was that humans were rational and social beings. Their nature required them to value reason above everything and to act with benevolence towards their fellow men. The Roman Stoics were mostly interested in Stoicism as an ethical system and a code of public service. In principle the Stoics believed in the universal community of mankind, though, unlike the later Christian Roman emperors and churchmen, they did not see their empire as the political face of the universal human community.[15]

There was something of a chasm between Roman Stoics' belief in a theoretical universal human community and their absolute assumption that Roman male aristocratic culture represented the pinnacle of human civilization. They saw reason and self-discipline as the unique attributes of the male Roman cultural and social elite. On the contrary, barbarians, the Roman plebs and women were the slaves of their passions. This was to be a very familiar and widespread conceit in the history of empire. No emperor ever existed whose power did not rest on an ideology based on hierarchy, and with an entirely man-made yet deeply felt set of assumptions – about sex and class – that made the hierarchy 'natural'. Even Empress Maria Theresa in eighteenth-century Austria subscribed to this idea, though her behaviour contradicted it. Probably Empress Wu Zetian in seventh-century Tang-dynasty China believed instinctively that females were fully as competent to rule as males. Perhaps Catherine II of Russia was the first empress both to believe this and to be able to articulate ideas to sustain this belief. In a misogynist world she was far too intelligent and cautious to make such claims in public.

Marcus described the four greatest virtues as 'justice, truth, self-control, courage'. His philosophy left no place for the senses or the emotions. In Book One of his *Meditations,* where he writes at length about the people who most influenced his life, the only females to get a mention are his mother and his wife, and even they get far less mention than a bevy of male former tutors, mentors and role models. At the same time Marcus despised homosexuals. Probably for that reason his old mentor Hadrian, the most famous homosexual emperor in history, gets no recognition in the *Meditations*. Marcus Aurelius's philosophy offered little comfort or consolation and no warmth amidst life's troubles or in the face of death. Looking back on his life from the perspective of old age, he wrote, 'my soul ... will you ever taste the disposition to love and affection?' His was very much the code of a male ruling class, with many similarities to both Confucianism and to the values inculcated into a later imperial elite by the English public school. Not surprisingly, Matthew Arnold, the Victorian educational evangelist, saw Marcus Aurelius as 'perhaps the most beautiful figure in history'.[16]

In the second half of the period covered in this section – in other words the 'Dominate' and the early Byzantine centuries – the Roman Empire was ruled by a number of formidable monarchs. Diocletian, Constantine, Theodosius I and Justinian I immediately spring to mind. We cannot know any of these men, however, as well as we know Marcus Aurelius. In this book's context the most interesting aspect of Diocletian's reign was his attempt to solve two great problems that threatened the empire's survival, namely succession and the need to have a competent emperor-leader on the spot both in the east and the west. The system of rule he devised to answer this challenge was the so-called 'Tetrarchy', roughly translated as the Rule of Four.

Seizing the throne in 284, Diocletian concentrated on restoring Rome's position in the east and immediately established Maximian, his close friend and fellow Illyrian general, as junior emperor in the west. In 293 he and Maximian were recognized as co-emperors and each had a deputy emperor with the title of Caesar to aid them in their task and succeed them when they died. In 305, uniquely for a Roman emperor, the ill and aged Diocletian decided to abdicate and twisted Maximian's arm to do the same. Immediately conflict broke out over the succession. Rivalries to dominate the college of four flared and sons insisted on their right to replace deceased fathers. The Tetrarchy was too novel and artificial an institution to constrain ambitious generals and deep-rooted beliefs in a son's rights. Its existence depended on Diocletian's personal authority as undisputed senior monarch. Probably, had he possessed a natural son of his own he would not have established the Tetrarchy in the first place.

The wars of succession were won by Constantine I, who finally established his power over the whole empire in 323–4. His dynasty ruled until the death of his nephew Julian in 363. The history of this dynasty is dominated by Constantine's conversion to Christianity and Julian's attempt to overturn his uncle's legacy and steer the empire back to the old Roman religion. Constantine's life and reign are deeply hidden beneath Christian hagiography and legend. We cannot hope to know the man or be sure as to his motives. His mother is usually claimed to have been a strong Christian: if so, he had been familiar with the religion since childhood. On the other hand, from the mid-third century emperors had been attempting to strengthen their positions by associating themselves with some variant of a supreme god and claiming to be his deputy. Diocletian chose Jupiter. Constantine's father, who had served as deputy emperor (Caesar) to Maximian, was a devotee of 'Sol Invictus' (the Unconquered Sun). Constantine himself identified with this deity even to some extent after his conversion to Christianity. But in the last years of his life and reign he became an ever-more unequivocal Christian. Of course, like every emperor in history, he found that political necessity often overrode strict adherence to religious doctrine. Constantine's Christian faith did not, for example, stop him from executing his oldest son.

For the Christians the emperor's conversion and support was an immense benefit. Nevertheless, the creation of a Christian monarchy confronted both the emperor and the Christian bishops with questions that were difficult and novel. Maybe Constantine himself at first only dimly understood the unique character of Christian belief, let alone the implications of establishing Christianity as his empire's privileged religion. Christian monotheism was unlike any previous religion with which a Roman emperor had identified. It could not live alongside other religions harmoniously on earth or in its version of Heaven. Even more dangerous were believers who subscribed to incorrect doctrines. Failure to worship the true God in the right way made eternal damnation certain. Conceptions of 'orthodoxy' and 'heresy' were fundamental to Christianity but wholly alien to traditional Roman religion.

The emperor soon became involved in the struggle to create institutions and define true doctrine in order to unite and direct the Christian community. This was a much needed but difficult task since the widely dispersed Christian groups combined an intense aspiration to unity with 'wild disparities' of actual opinion and belief. At the request of the bishops Constantine called and presided over the crucial first universal church council at Nicaea in 325. The bishops welcomed the emperor's support but they also feared that he might usurp their authority over the Christian community and its doctrines. Questions emerged which would continue throughout the history of Christian and, in somewhat different form, Islamic monarchy. Given that both monarch and bishops were chosen and blessed by God, what were their proper relationship and roles? Was the monarch a priest and, if so, was he a high priest with responsibility to define Christian doctrine? Should he appoint bishops or, on the contrary, was it the bishops' blessing at some version of coronation which conferred legitimacy on the monarch? These and related questions will recur many times in this book. They were inherent in the fact that both rulers and priests drew their authority directly from the same god. Often they were the most important and contested political but also religious issues of their day.[17]

We often gain more insight into Emperor Julian from his own writings than from the evaluations of contemporaries or even later historians. The man who attempted to dethrone Christianity and restore the pagan gods is one of the most contentious figures in antiquity. The polemics that surround him go as far as radically different descriptions of his appearance and mannerisms, not to mention his psyche. Julian was six years old when his uncle the Emperor Constantine died in 337. The late emperors' three sons presided over the immediate massacre of Julian's father, uncle and cousins. Only he and his elder brother Gallus survived, since they were children. We can only guess as to the impact of these deaths on Julian's personality but he is often described as highly strung, excitable and sensitive. Few have denied his intelligence. Although brought up as a Christian and confined to a country villa for years in semi-isolation, he was given a good education in the Greek and Roman classics. His enthusiasm for the old Graeco-Roman civilization led in time to commitment to restoring its pagan gods.

Constantine's son Constantius II came out on top in the struggle with his brothers and by 350 ruled over the whole empire. Childless and forced to turn most of his attention to the affairs of the eastern empire, he took the risk of appointing Julian (his last male kinsman) to be his deputy in Gaul, where Roman authority was threatened by both

Germanic tribal invasions and ineffective administration. Despite having no military or administrative training or experience, Julian seems to have performed well, though just how well is hotly disputed between his admirers and enemies. The crucial moment came early in 360 when Constantius ordered Julian to send much of his army to the east to help defeat a Persian invasion. Whether Julian was already contemplating rebellion we cannot know. He had some reason to fear for his fate if deprived of his troops. But it may well be that his decision to rebel was partly driven by his soldiers' great reluctance to be deployed away from their garrisons and families to a far-distant theatre. Fortune favoured Julian when Constantius II died suddenly and the crown fell into his hands.

Once installed in Constantinople as emperor in 361, Julian revealed his religious sympathies and policy. Since he ruled for only twenty months this policy had no time to be fully developed. Later Christian depictions of brutal persecution are untrue. But Julian did encourage conflicts between Christian sects and he re-established and subsidized pagan temples. His aim was to marginalize Christianity and to restore the old Graeco-Roman gods to primacy within the state. Noting the prestige that Christianity had acquired through the piety of its priests and the distribution of charity, he urged similar action by the pagan temples he subsidized. Given his deep interest in philosophy and Graeco-Roman culture, it is not surprising that Julian saw Marcus Aurelius as the greatest of Rome's emperors. Marcus himself had viewed Christianity as a crudely theatrical religion without philosophical substance. He would certainly have seconded Julian's opinion that it was 'the creed of the countryfolk' and that 'he whom one holds to be a god can by no means be inserted into a woman's womb'.[18]

Historians debate what chance Julian's counter-revolution had of success. By now Christianity had existed for 350 years, despite periods of vicious persecution. For the last forty years it had enjoyed powerful backing from the state. Moreover, for all the changes Julian intended in the activities and organization of the pagan priesthood, his belief system was still essentially that of Marcus Aurelius. A religious counter-revolution on this basis would be hard pressed to compete with the power of the Christian message or its appeal far beyond the world of the male social elite. On the other hand, one should not underestimate the impact of imperial patronage and subsidy, if pursued over the course of a long reign. Since his reign was so short we cannot know for certain whether Julian's counter-revolution could have prevailed. Julian was killed in a skirmish near present-day Baghdad in 363. His decision to mount a full-scale invasion of the Persian Empire was not dictated by strategic necessity. It seems in part to have been driven by a quest for increased legitimacy and prestige at home. Certainly, the emperor had no reason to risk his life in the front lines of a minor skirmish. But along with Marcus Aurelius, Julian's other emperor-hero was that fatal role model Alexander of Macedon. Attempting to inspire his troops and emulate Homeric heroes by his courage, Julian was killed by a spear thrust into his liver. With him died any hopes for a pagan counter-revolution.

5

Ashoka, India and the Origins of Buddhism

The rich soil of the north Indian plain has always been a centre of world civilization. By the middle of the third millennium BCE the so-called Harappan culture centred on the River Indus had reached similar levels of urbanization and sophistication to Sargon's Akkad, the world's first empire. After ecological crisis destroyed Harappan society the centre of north Indian civilization moved to the basin of the River Ganges. By 1000 BCE the initially nomadic peoples who inhabited this region had created a rich agrarian society, the beginnings of urban settlement, and a unique religious culture which is often called 'Vedic' after the songs of praise and sacrifice (*vedas*) that shaped its core beliefs and traditions. Among the latter was the division of society into four castes (*varnas*), of which the two senior were the priests (*Brahmins*) and warriors (*Kshastriyas*). These hereditary castes were believed to have existed since creation and to be divinely sanctioned. Antony Black, in his comparative history of ancient political thought, calls the Vedic tradition 'the strongest manifestation in any recorded ideology of status and hierarchy'.[1]

During the first millennium BCE similar developments occurred in a number of regions of the world, which led some historians to call this era the 'Axial Age'. North India, Greece and northern China were among the leaders in this process. The Achaemenid Empire provided a link between the cultures of Greece, India and the Middle East. Cultural developments went alongside the increasing use of iron tools. Growing prosperity and urbanization created clusters of what we might call intellectuals who discussed and refined fundamental conceptions about religion, ethics and politics. Ideas and beliefs that had previously been enshrined in oral myths and songs were written down and became more focused, abstract and sophisticated. In India as elsewhere kingdoms and even empires sometimes replaced a world of city states. The most significant Indian polity in this era was the Mauryan Empire, which existed from 321 to 187 BCE. The first three Mauryan emperors were Chandragupta (r. 321–297 BCE), his son Bindusara (r. 297–273 BCE) and his grandson Ashoka, who was consecrated as emperor in 269 or 268 BCE and reigned for almost four decades.

Ancient India produced one of the most remarkable works of 'political science' in the ancient world, the *Arthashastra*. The author's name has come down to us as Kautilya, which in the past was often seen as a version of the name of Emperor Chandragupta's chief minister, Chanakya. In fact the *Arthashastra* in the form in which we know it was probably written in the second or third centuries CE. The book's history is contested, but our version is probably the final reworking of a text which dated back many centuries. The Mauryan Empire had only a limited impact on subsequent Indian history. Unlike King Ying Zheng of the Qin dynasty, who united China in 221 BCE and laid the foundations for later empires, the Mauryans did not create a lasting tradition of empire in the Indian subcontinent. On the other hand, the key role played by Ashoka in Buddhism's emergence as one of the world's great religions makes him one of the most important emperors in history.[2]

The *Arthashastra* is mostly 'a meticulous, methodical, rigorous and logical' study of statecraft and kingship. It is the Indian version of the famous ancient Chinese work on war by Sun Tzu but covers a much wider canvas. In European terms it combines Machiavelli's *The Prince* with eighteenth-century cameralist literature on how states could encourage economic development. About one-third of the *Arthashastra* is devoted to war and diplomacy, discussing everything from what we would call grand strategy down to planning campaigns and battlefield tactics. Kautilya also discusses at length the qualities necessary for a king and the ways to manage his family, government, court and officials. Developing the economy and tapping its resources to enhance the state's power is a core concern, but Kautilya also goes into detail on a frequent challenge of pre-modern government – how to reconcile sacred, state and customary law. Above all, the *Arthashastra* is about power and how a ruler can best retain, increase and use it. Apart from the extraordinary range and intelligence of the *Arthashastra*, its great value in the context of this book lies in the fact that, much more than either Machiavelli or Chinese political writings, its focus is on dynasty and

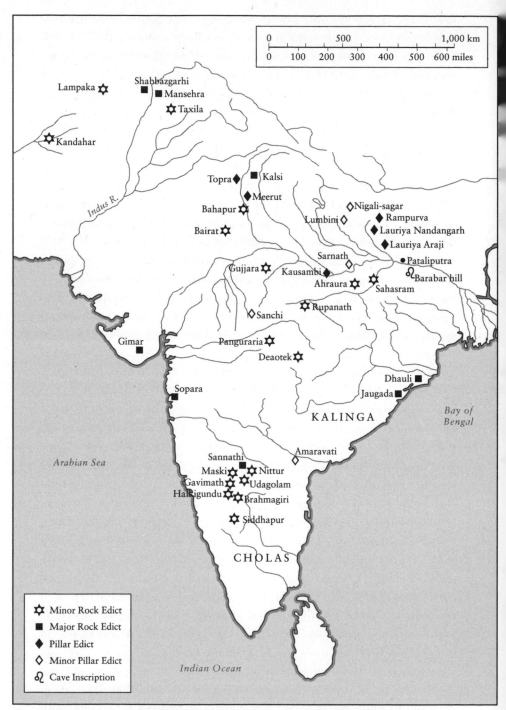

Ashoka and the Mauryan Empire

hereditary monarchy, just as its most important intended reader is a dynast who seeks to flourish in a harsh world of Realpolitik.[3]

At the core of the *Arthashastra* is the belief that without the king's coercive power anarchy would destroy society: 'people without a king devoured each other like fish'. International relations was the struggle for power and domination between states. Weak kingdoms were swallowed by strong ones. Territorial expansion brought wealth and power. Empire was the necessary and inevitable ambition of any powerful state. It required monarchs who were 'energetic', possessed 'a sharp intellect' and 'strong memory', and were 'free from passion, anger, greed, obstinacy, fickleness, haste and back-biting habits'. To succeed, they needed where necessary to be ruthless, crafty and two-faced. But the king was not a bandit-chief: 'In the happiness of his subjects lies his happiness.' The state's power rested on society's prosperity and neither was possible under the rule of a king who ignored justice and put his own pleasure above the community's interests. To be a conqueror and create an empire was the monarch's necessary and laudable ambition, but empires were not sustained by force alone. On the contrary, the emperor must provide justice, peace and security to his new subjects. Not only must he respect their religion and property, 'he should adopt the same mode of life, the same dress, language and customs as those of the people'.[4]

The king was the core of the polity and its success depended hugely on his abilities and his sense of duty. No institutions could sustain the polity against a wayward king. Although Kautilya believed that succession was best managed through male primogeniture, he also believed that it was fatal to allow an undisciplined or stupid prince to ascend the throne. In that case, the state 'perishes like a worm-eaten piece of wood'. If no alternative prince was available, a daughter's son could be chosen. In the last resort, if the king was sterile, it might be necessary to sneak a suitable man into the harem to impregnate one of his wives. Kautilya stressed the great temptations lying in wait for a monarch. The main ones were drink, gambling, women and hunting. The first step in a princely education was to inculcate a sense of self-discipline and duty. Monarchs who could not control their own emotions and senses had no chance of controlling their government and kingdom. A monarch's decisions must be measured and they must be based on cool calculation, never on anger, dislike or lust. He must take advice and weigh it carefully but he must also make decisions in good time and stick to them. In judging individuals he must neither arouse contempt by excessive mild-ness nor hatred by harshness or bias. He must be seen to be just. Although character training was essential, it was far from sufficient. The boy-prince must be taught martial arts but also writing and arithmetic. As he approached adolescence these basic subjects must be supplemented by the study of philosophy, economics and politics. Lessons in the last two fields should be taught not just as theory but also by experienced offi-cials. Ashoka's own education was thorough and successful: 'his inscriptions reveal a deep interest and understanding of statecraft, phil-osophy, and ethics.'[5]

The *Arthashashtra* warned the king that he faced many dangers, the worst of which came from within the inner circle of his dynasty and regime. He must remember that he was often most vulnerable when resting or enjoying himself in his palace. A close watch must be kept especially on all comings and goings in his harem. Members of the royal household, especially disloyal queens and disaffected, rebellious princes, were an acute danger: 'Princes like crabs have a notorious tendency of eating up their begetters,' but a seemingly loving queen might be even more of a danger, especially when the issue of succession came on to the agenda. Ministers must be carefully selected, balanced against each other but never fully trusted. The *Arthashastra* is full of advice on how to set up and control a secret police to spy on the ruler's family, minis-ters and courtiers. The loyalty of the army and its commanders was also vital. If troops went unpaid they would revolt. Generals in particular must be very well paid to secure their faithfulness. Although dangers were greatest when within the monarch's palace and inner circle, in-justice and impoverishment would result in mass rebellion. His subjects' loyalty and quiescence depended above all on whether their stomachs were full.[6]

The little we know about Ashoka's life before the Kalingan war of 260 BCE chimes with the principles of Indian politics depicted in the *Arthashastra*. After a thorough education Ashoka was sent by his father to suppress a rebellion at Taxila in the Punjab, subsequently serving as a provincial governor. For most empires there were both risks and bene-fits in using royal princes in this way. A loyal prince could hold a key, outlying region for his dynasty while simultaneously training himself in the business of government. On the other hand, the political experience and the following he would build up in the process could be a threat to the monarch, especially when the question of succession came over the horizon. This happened in Ashoka's case. His father intended to follow the usual though not invariable custom of passing his crown to his eldest son, Prince Susima. As Emperor Bindusara aged, however, Ashoka returned to the capital and organized sufficient support to seize and hold the crown after his father died in 273 BCE. We cannot know how many of his brothers were killed in the struggle for succession but the conflict appears to have been bloody and protracted.[7]

The Kalingan war occurred nine years after Ashoka was consecrated as ruler and is the first event in his reign of which we have certain knowledge. The conquest of Kalinga, a large state in eastern and coastal India, brought big strategic and economic benefits to the Mauryan Empire and was a military triumph. Almost every other emperor we will encounter would have used so victorious a war to proclaim his glory as warrior and conqueror. Instead, in the first of his many inscriptions on rocks and pillars, Ashoka stated his grief and guilt at the bloodshed and misery he had caused: 'A hundred and fifty thousand people were deported, a hundred thousand were killed and many times that number perished ... On conquering Kalinga the Beloved of the Gods [i.e. Ashoka] felt remorse, for when an independent country is conquered the slaughter, death and deportation of the people is extremely grievous to the Beloved of the Gods and weighs heavily on his mind.' Still worse was the fact that most of the victims were innocent, law-abiding civilians who lived moral lives and behaved 'well and devotedly towards their friends, acquaintances, colleagues, relatives, slaves and servants – all suffer violence, murder, and separation from their loved ones'. He added that even if the death and misery had been one thousand times less than was actually the case, the victory would not have been worth the price. Although Ashoka was in his mid-forties during the Kalingan war and had seen much bloodshed in his life, the war's carnage caused or at least greatly deepened his conversion to Buddhism.[8]

When Ashoka ascended the throne Buddhism had already existed for over 200 years. Its spread had been steady but not dramatic and Buddhists were still just one of a number of sects outside the Indian religious ('Hindu') mainstream. Capturing the emperor for their faith was therefore an immense coup for the Buddhist community. In the Buddhist pantheon, Ashoka ranks second only to the Buddha himself. He looms even larger than Constantine in the story of his religion and is deeply buried in hagiography. Certainty about the reasons for his conversion is in any case impossible at a remove of more than two millennia. Still, it is improbable that any monarch converted to a religion without an eye to the political consequences.[9]

Like Christianity, Buddhism was a salvation religion open to all. At its core were answers to the deepest human concerns: the transience of life; suffering in this world; where we humans come from before birth and will go to after death; what is our place in the cosmos. These answers had a powerful philosophical and emotional foundation. The Buddhist belief in reincarnation differed radically from Christianity or Islam but, like them, it linked ethical behaviour in this world to reward in its version of life after death. As the representative of the Buddhist divinity on earth the monarch could claim a more powerful and more universal legitimacy than anything available to a mere tribal king. Buddhism suited the needs of a ruler like Ashoka who needed to consolidate and legitimize his rule over a newly established, diverse and far-flung empire. In 'Hindu' tradition the sacredness of the social (i.e. caste-based) order tended to overshadow the king's aura, so Ashoka might conceivably have seen Buddhism as improving the monarchy's status. It is also fair to point out that by the time of Ashoka's reign the Mauryan Empire was already huge and was approaching its natural limits: adopting Buddhism with its prohibition of aggressive war and internal feuding was therefore fitting.[10]

Nevertheless, most contemporary historians believe that Ashoka's personal faith in Buddhism was at the heart of his policies. He grew up in a world of intense religious debate and commitment. His grandfather had favoured Jainism and Ashoka himself had other options than Buddhism. For much of the rest of his long reign we can trace how his commitment to Buddhism deepened and influenced his policies through the many statements he had inscribed on rocks and pillars that have survived to this day. In his inscriptions he made clear that concern for salvation in the afterlife was partly responsible for his zeal. Almost all monarchs encountered in this book boasted about their dynasty and its lineage, but Ashoka makes no reference to either. He seems 'born-again', uninterested in the past and intent on his duty to spread the Buddhist religion of compassion and non-violence. A sense both of the man and his faith come down to us powerfully over the millennia through the inscriptions. 'The personality of ancient Indian kings is usually difficult to identify behind their carefully epigraphic masks. Ashoka is an exception. The frequent use of the first person and the strong personal tone in his ... inscriptions leave no doubt that they were not composed by an inspired ghost-writer but represent the emperor's ideas, desires and commands, tempered occasionally by ... candour and self-reflectiveness.'[11]

The key message in Ashoka's inscriptions was his dedication to spreading true Buddhist understanding (*Dhamma*) among his subjects. 'The Beloved of the Gods ... sets no great store by fame or glory, except in that he desires fame and glory both now and in the future in order that his people may obey *Dhamma* and follow the way of *Dhamma*.' Ashoka created a new branch of officialdom to carry this message across his empire and make sure it was heard and respected. His frequent tours around the empire were in part pilgrimages to Buddhist sites and in part designed to allow him to distribute charity and spread the Buddhist faith. The emperor had no doubt that his personal commitment to the true faith made it his duty to lead his subjects in the same direction. In time he exercised both disciplinary and doctrinal authority within the Buddhist community, using both to defend its unity against 'heresies'. 'Whoever creates a schism in the Order [i.e. among Buddhist monks], whether monk or nun, is to be dressed in white garments' and exiled from their communities, 'for it is my wish that the Order should remain united and endure for long'. Nevertheless, in comparison to many religious converts, let alone emperor-converts, Ashoka was tolerant of other faiths. This helped to establish a norm for later Buddhist missionaries. Buddhism's strategy was always to envelop and absorb other faiths rather than seeking to conquer them in the spirit of Judaic monotheism. Ashoka's decrees stressed the need for mutual respect between religions. He emphasized that other religions than Buddhism also sought spiritual understanding and lived moral lives. Aggressive missionaries who disparaged other faiths only did harm. 'The Beloved of the Gods ... honours all sects ... whosoever honours his own sect or disparages that of another man, wholly out of devotion to his own, with a view to showing it in favourable light, harms his own sect even more seriously. Therefore, concord is to be commanded, so that men can hear another's principles.'[12]

Compassion rather than a narrowly dogmatic Buddhism was Ashoka's core ideal and message. Ethical behaviour in everyday life, whose essential principle was not to harm other sentient beings, was the foundation on which any search for higher spiritual understanding had to rest. Buddhism was less sharply removed from the animist religious mindset than Judaism, Christianity and Islam. In the Buddhist view, rationality distinguished humans from animals or plants but all life was precious. Many of Ashoka's edicts contain prohibitions on killing animals or needlessly cutting down forests. This distinguishes Buddhism from the Christian message that God had placed the animal and natural world at human disposal. Ashoka's edicts chime with contemporary ecological sensitivities.

Christianity and Buddhism were, however, at one in preaching a degree of equality among humans that conflicted with the hierarchical order of their era. Ashoka did not openly denounce Brahmins any more than Christ attacked the Roman emperor or the Jewish social order. Even so, Ashoka's assertion that truth and salvation were equally available to human beings of all castes was subversive. In mainstream 'Hinduism' the four-caste social hierarchy was divinely created and each caste had its own canon of proper behaviour and belief. In his so-called Tenth Major Rock Edict, Ashoka wrote that achieving true understanding was hard for all men, 'whether humble or highly placed, without extreme effort and without renouncing everything else, and it is particularly difficult for the highly placed'. For later generations of Buddhists the memory of Ashoka was conveyed above all in a number of legendary tales, initially passed down orally but subsequently written down. Of these, none was more important than the *Asokavadana*, which was finally committed to writing in the second century CE but whose origins go back to the emperor's lifetime. In this tale Ashoka upbraids his chief minister in the following terms: 'You, sir, look at the caste and not at the inherent quality of the monks. Haughty, deluded and obsessed with caste, you harm yourself and others . . . For *Dhamma* is a question of qualities and qualities do not reflect caste.'[13]

In all sacred monarchies there was a big divide between the realities of political life and the high religious and ethical principles that the sacred monarch was supposed to embody and promote. The contrast between Ashoka's inscriptions and the *Arthashastra* represents this in the sharpest form. As in all the salvation religions, the highest ideal of Buddhism is to rise above and renounce the things of this world, but among these religions it is in principle the least political or worldly. Nevertheless, it is important that, unlike his grandfather, Ashoka did not abdicate and spend his last years seeking spiritual fulfilment. Chandragupta in his twilight years had lived the life of a Jain ascetic. Ashoka remained in this world and sought to promote the Buddhist message of compassion by personal example and the power inherent in his wealth and position.

Ashoka's inscriptions and policies recognized that a monarch must compromise to achieve his overall goals. Banning the killing of all animals was impossible. But he could try to protect some species and could himself set a good example by becoming a vegetarian. Capital punishment could not be abolished entirely but it could be better regulated and limited. No monarch could abolish his armies or entirely renounce war. But Ashoka denounced needless aggression, sought to limit the use of violence, and stressed that the most lasting conquests stemmed from the triumph of true religion. In Buddhist lore, Ashoka became the model emperor or 'wheel-turning king' (*chakravartin*). The wheel in this Buddhist conception is the great symbol of sovereignty and hangs over the emperor's palace at the imagined centre of the universe. In the Golden Age the *chakravartin* ruled over the whole earth through the strength of *Dhamma* alone and his wheel was sheathed in gold. Ashoka by contrast, though the greatest and most admirable of emperors, lived in less ideal times and had to use force on occasion to uphold the *Dhamma*. His wheel was sheathed in iron and he ruled only over one-quarter of the earth, namely the Indian subcontinent. This was a Buddhist variant on the theme of universal, imperial monarchy as both ideal and reality.[14]

The enormous contrast between Ashoka and Alexander in many ways defined the subsequent difference between 'western' and Buddhist monarchy, at least as ideals. On the one hand stood the warrior, on the other the spiritual guide and embodiment of compassion. The late King Bhumibol of Thailand (r. 1950–2016) in many ways spoke and acted in public in Ashoka's tradition. The Western tradition of military monarchy was in time influenced by Christian calls for humility and acceptance of the principle of 'just war'. Even so, Saint Louis (Louis IX: r. 1226–70), the paragon of Christian monarchs, achieved sanctification in good part because of his crusades against the infidel. Nor was the contrast between Alexander and Ashoka just that between a warrior and a man of peace. Alexander was a larger-than-life example of heroic individualism. He sought glory and fame in the eyes of contemporaries and history. Buddhism and its search for *Nirvana* is on the contrary driven by a desire to escape from subjection to the bustle and trivia of this world, including public glory and reputation. It looks instead to inner balance and calm as the basis for higher spiritual understanding. Ashoka would have shared Marcus Aurelius's disdain for Alexander. But Buddhism went deeper than Marcus's Stoicism and offered more comfort to a far wider range of human beings.

Ashoka's legacy was stronger outside India than within it. The Mauryan dynasty did not long outlive him. Not until the Mughals in the sixteenth century CE was an empire of comparable scale and power seen again in India. Buddhism continued to flourish for many centuries in the subcontinent. Even in the eleventh century the monastic complexes of Bengal and Bihar were still among the most powerful centres of Buddhism in the world. Subsequently, however, these centres were devastated by nomad invaders across the north-west frontier and Buddhism itself faded away in India. Centuries later, Jawaharlal Nehru proclaimed the Gandhian principle of non-violence and supra-ethnic spirituality to be part of an Indian tradition traceable back to Ashoka, and he incorporated Ashokan symbols into independent India's flag and official heraldry. In the era of Narendra Modi, Ashoka's creed of renunciation, religious tolerance and non-violence seems less relevant. More than two thousand years after Ashoka the caste system still has a big impact on Indian society. At a high level of generalization one might even compare Ashoka to the Egyptian pharaoh Akhenaten, whose attempt to impose monotheism in Egypt foundered against the opposition of priestly elites and deeply rooted popular beliefs and customs.[15]

That comparison of course makes no sense at all if one looks beyond India and sees the immense impact of Buddhism in East and South-East Asia. Ashoka put great stress on encouraging missionary efforts beyond his realm. In Buddhist legend, his sons are credited with leading missionary expeditions that converted Sri Lanka and Myanmar to Buddhism, but Ashoka's missions went far further afield too. Subsequently, one of the two main branches of Buddhism, the so-called *Mahayana* (Great Vehicle) school, built on Ashoka's commitment to remaining in the world and conducting missionary work. In time it spread Buddhism across Central Asia, China, Korea and Japan. By the twentieth century Buddhism was beginning also to make inroads in Europe and North America. Contemporary Western psychiatry and even neuroscience often has considerable respect for Buddhist techniques of meditation and the search for detachment and calm that lies beneath them. So-called Tantric Buddhism emerged in seventh-century India and subsequently spread to China and Japan, being called *Chou* in the former and *Zen* in the latter. The last truly great Chinese emperor, Yongzheng (r. 1723–35), drew much of his inner strength and calm from this strand of Buddhism.[16]

6

The Origins of Chinese Emperorship

In the English language the rulers of the Roman and Chinese empires are both called emperors. In their own Latin and Chinese languages the differing nature of rulership in the two traditions becomes much more clear. The Latin word 'imperator' originally meant 'victorious general'. The Chinese term 'huangdi' had a variety of sacred and cosmological associations, which was why King Zheng of the Qin kingdom chose this title after uniting the whole of China in 221 BCE. However, not all Roman emperors were generals. All of them had a role as priestly sacrificers to the imperial cult. Equally, some Chinese monarchs, and almost by definition the founders of dynasties, were military leaders. But most monarchs, not only of the Han dynasty, which ruled from 202 BCE to 220 CE, but also later Chinese emperors, were first and foremost sacred rulers. Their key role was to legitimize state authority by conducting the rituals and sacrifices that linked Heaven and Earth, as well as the present generation to its ancestors. A famous eleventh-century Confucian thinker stated: 'in the office of the Son of Heaven, nothing is more important than ritual.'[1]

The statement is true as a broad generalization but it has its dangers. Confucian thinkers and officials wanted emperors to concentrate on ritual and leave governing to themselves. Both the Roman and the Chinese emperor was in principle a political leader. All public authority was legitimized and executed in his name. But most emperors of the Han dynasty played a less active role in government and politics than was the case with Roman monarchs. To some extent this was the inevitable result of some Roman emperors being adopted as heirs by reigning monarchs precisely because of their political and military talents. Many others seized the throne through military rebellions or coups. The Chinese hereditary monarchy could not hope to produce a succession of rulers of equivalent energy and competence. The Confucian tradition of political thought was always suspicious of overly autocratic monarchs who failed to bend to the wise advice of ministers trained in the Confucian canon. The Daoist tradition regarded imperial activism with even greater suspicion. The Chinese emperor was much less visible and accessible than his Roman counterpart. He lived, for example, in a 'forbidden city', out of bounds to all but a chosen few. Many Han monarchs ascended the throne as children and often did not survive until adulthood. Some adult monarchs were happy to leave the coordination of government to chief ministers. Even conscientious, adult Han emperors usually acted as arbiters of disagreements among their advisers rather than as initiators of policy. On the other hand, the last decades of the Han dynasty showed that, in the absence of an adult emperor who either himself ruled or gave full support to a competent chief minister, effective government became increasingly impossible.[2]

To some extent it is possible to construct a genealogy of the empires studied in earlier chapters. The Persians were in a line that stretched back to Sargon of Akkad. Alexander of Macedon saw himself as taking over the Achaemenid heritage and his legacy had an impact both on the Mauryan Empire in India and on the Romans. The Chinese imperial tradition by contrast was self-contained. Not until Buddhism began to make a major impact on China in the period after the demise of the Han Empire were Chinese society and politics greatly affected by outside influences. In some respects the closest comparison to China was Old and Middle Kingdom Egypt, whose ancient and powerful political traditions were substantially self-contained. In Egypt as in China the ancient traditions of sacred native monarchy loomed very large in the minds of later rulers. But Egypt was a small and easily ruled country by Chinese standards. Almost all its inhabitants lived on a flat plain within thirty miles of the River Nile. Even Han-dynasty China was vastly bigger and was divided into diverse regions by mountains, rivers and forests. The Yellow River meant almost as much to ancient Chinese government and civilization as the Nile did to Egypt, but it was far more treacherous and difficult to manage. Holding together this vast country within a single state for most of the last two millennia was an extraordinary achievement. One present-day historian rightly calls it 'the political miracle of the Chinese empire'. Many of the key elements that underpinned that miracle already existed, at least in embryo,

The Han, Tang and Song Empires at their Wide

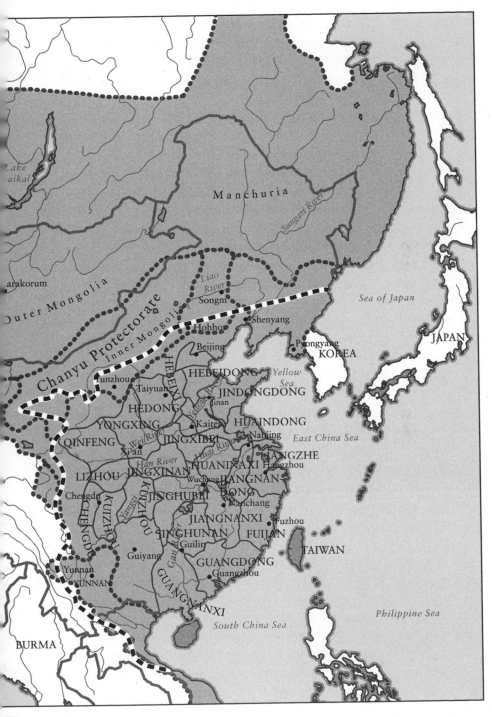

Extent

during the Han era. They included a sacred monarchy, a dominant ideology that saw empire ('all under Heaven') as the only legitimate polity, and officials increasingly imbued with that ideology and its commitment to imperial unity.[3]

For most Chinese thinkers in the centuries both before and after unification in 221 BCE there existed a golden age located in legend and ancient history. This age began with the rule of the mythical 'Yellow Emperor' and passed through other partly mythical dynastic eras until rule was transferred from the Shang to the Zhou dynasty in the eleventh century BCE. Many of the principles on which Chinese political thought was based right down to the twentieth century CE were derived from tales of this golden age. One such principle was the so-called Mandate of Heaven, which gave the emperor his mandate to rule. What Heaven gave, it could also take away should a monarch fail to live up to his responsibilities. Underlying this idea was the belief that Earth, humans and Heaven were part of a single universe whose elements must live in harmony with each other. An emperor's misbehaviour disturbed Heaven and resulted in natural disasters, strange apparitions in the skies and other warnings of trouble to come. The fall of the villainous last king of the Shang dynasty and his replacement by the virtuous first ruler of Zhou was the master-tale of the Mandate of Heaven. Not just in legend but also in reality it coincided with 'very rare astronomical phenomena'. In a very Chinese way the theory of Heaven's mandate combined cosmology, realism and political ideology. Chinese thinkers were all too aware of the fallibility and potential for tyranny of kings, but they were too terrified of the people's ignorance and potential for anarchy to support the right to rebellion even against tyrants. Arguing that nature and Heaven would in time bring down a tyrant was a convenient compromise.[4]

In the centuries between the break-up of the Zhou Empire in 771 BCE and reunification under the Qin in 221 BCE there were significant differences in popular culture and even in the written script between the various Chinese states. But the intellectual class that emerged in these centuries – the *shi*, who are sometimes called gentlemen-scholars or literati in English – mostly remained loyal to the idea of a single, united China. They looked to some version of wise imperial monarchy which would restore and sustain the unity of what they perceived as the single Chinese cultural space. This allegiance to a vision of unity was partly a reaction to the increasingly devastating wars between the rival Chinese great powers during the fourth and third centuries BCE.[5]

In the centuries preceding unification intellectual debate and diversity flourished. Many rival conceptions of the good life, the good society and the nature of rulership competed. Only after unification in the Han era were the various thinkers corralled retrospectively into rival 'schools' of thought. Even so, there was some reality to these attempts to divide thinkers into schools, as well as to the view that the three key schools that influenced Chinese history and philosophy in the long run were Daoism, Legalism and Confucianism. At the risk of a truly gross generalization, Daoism proclaimed a 'way' for humans in accord with the rhythms of nature and the cosmos. In political terms it condemned overactive and intrusive government. Legalism stressed human foolishness and investigated the best ways to manage bureaucracies and mobilize resources from the population to feed the state's war machine. Confucius lived from 551 to 479 BCE. It is important not to conflate his own opinions with the orthodox Confucian ideology adopted by the Han dynasty in the second century BCE, let alone with the 'neo-Confucian' ideas that became standard under the Song dynasty more than a millennium later. Nevertheless, some ideas were fundamental to the Confucian world view from Confucius's own times onwards.[6]

Confucius's views of the good society and legitimate political order were based on an idealized vision of ancient China as a world of families. Family life was hierarchical: emperor headed society, father led family and husband ruled over wife. Proper behaviour and ritual demanded and embodied respect for these hierarchies. They alone guaranteed social stability and economic prosperity. But hierarchy entailed obligations on both sides and was sustained by mutual affection. At its core Confucianism was an ethical system and one which gave a high status to public service. The gentlemen-scholars (literati) who were its paragons and teachers were urged to serve virtuous rulers in defence of the public welfare. Of the world's great 'religions' – including Buddhism, Christianity and Islam – it was the one most easily adaptable to the requirements of rulers and governments. It was in many ways close to Stoicism and not least in the rather weak comfort it provided for humans suffering torments in this life and fears about death. On the other hand, Confucianism was a less jealous 'religion' than Christian or Islamic monotheism. In time it absorbed some elements of Buddhism and Daoism. In China it came to a modus vivendi with both these religions in a manner unthinkable in monotheistic cultures.[7]

Unsurprisingly, it was Legalist thinkers and their disciples who found favour from the rulers of the rival states in the centuries before unification. When the old Zhou kingdom evaporated in the early decades of the eighth century BCE it was initially succeeded by some 150 city states. By the final brutal phase of inter-state conflict (the so-called Warring States era of 481–221 BCE) only twelve independent states existed, of which five could be seen as serious contenders for dominion over the whole region. The era of all-out conflict began with the disintegration of the Jin state into three separate countries in 453 BCE because of rivalries between three great aristocratic lineages. Deeply sensitive to the dangers of aristocracy, the rulers of the most powerful of the three successor states, the kingdom of Wei, created a bureaucratic regime designed to discipline society and mobilize all available resources for the country's military needs. The fact that Wei was situated at the centre of the Chinese states system and surrounded by potential enemies was an additional reason to pursue this policy. The Wei reforms and the political model they created proved extremely successful. For the next fifty years Wei was the most powerful and aggressive state in the region. Among the greatest victims of Wei aggression were their neighbours to the west, the Qin state and dynasty, which lost most of its borderlands to Wei in the late fifth and early fourth centuries BCE.

To survive, the rulers of the Qin decided they must import the Wei model of government. The process was begun by Duke Xian (r. 384–362 BCE), who had spent thirty years in exile at the Wei court before ascending the Qin throne. The decisive change came under his successor, Duke Xiao (r. 361–338 BCE), and was driven forward by his chief minister, Shang Yang. The latter became the model and hero for later Legalist thinkers and statesmen. His writings were collected into what became a handbook, or perhaps even a bible. Shang Yang himself was a gentleman-scholar from Wei whose family was a junior branch of the Wei royal dynasty. Like most gentlemen-scholars, his major allegiance was to the Chinese cultural region as a whole, not to his own kingdom. Directed by Shang Yang, the Qin bureaucracy penetrated deep into society, which it regulated minutely in order to maximize the state's military power. At the bottom of society peasants were organized into groups of families which bore collective responsibility for providing conscripts and taxes but were rewarded by land grants and public honours if they performed well in the army. Even members of the dynasty had to serve with merit in the army to retain their royal status.

The Qin's exceptionally radical reforms were vital to its triumph over its rivals but other advantages also counted. The Qin's core territory was fertile, ringed by mountains and easily defended. Above all the Qin had the advantages often possessed by countries on the periphery of a system of states. They could use the war machine honed by conflicts within the system to conquer usually weaker neighbours to their west and beyond the Chinese core area. In the Qin's case the weak neighbouring tribal 'kingdoms' ruled over a rich and strategically vital region that today is called Sichuan. Conquering Sichuan gave the Qin control not just of its fertile lands and rich deposits of salt and iron but also of the upper reaches of the River Yangzi. This opened an invasion route into the heart of the formidable Chu kingdom, which Qin generals exploited to good effect in a brilliantly planned and executed campaign in 278 BCE. In comparison to some of their rivals, geography favoured the Qin. By contrast, the powerful Zhao kingdom on the north-western periphery of the Chinese state system had as its neighbours the formidable nomad warriors of the Xiongnu confederation. Much of its army had to be deployed far away on its northern borders to keep the nomads at bay. In the decades that followed the Qin's conquest of Chu a combination of ruthlessness, military effectiveness and subtle diplomacy swallowed up the other great powers, which proved unable to match the Qin or to unite against them. King Zheng's final campaign of the 220s BCE, which created a united imperial state and made him the 'First Emperor', was almost a foregone conclusion.

The First Emperor, the former prince Ying Zheng, was born in 259 BCE and ascended the Qin throne thirteen years later after his father's death. His mother was notorious for her sexual adventures, including an affair with her husband's chief minister. One historian comments that 'due to the strange background of his childhood, Ying Zheng was naturally cruel, suspicious, lacking affection and willing to take risks'. One of his leading generals described the emperor as having 'the heart of a tiger or wolf'. Ruthlessness was combined with immense energy and single-minded purpose. In his eleven-year reign as emperor Ying Zheng went on six long tours of inspection across his vast dominions. He introduced new standardized administrative institutions and weights and measures for the whole empire. He also greatly extended its roads and frontier walls, and he launched grand-scale military offensives across his empire's northern and southern borders. Given that the Great Wall of China is generally assumed to have been a purely defensive rampart, it is worth noting that the First Emperor's massive extension of fortifications northwards was designed to protect vast grasslands that he had annexed from the Xiongnu nomads.[8]

For some historians the First Emperor's most decisive step was to reverse the trend towards regional literatures and regional diversity in the Chinese written script that had emerged in the Warring States era. Without his reimposition of a single standard script, 'it is conceivable that several regionally different orthographies might have come into permanent existence. And had this happened, it is inconceivable that China's political unity could long have survived.' Ying Zheng saw himself as a unique historical figure embodying the age-old Chinese yearning for a monarch of superhuman wisdom who would reunite the Chinese cultural world and thereby restore the ancient ideal of imperial peace and stability. He proclaimed this achievement on stone tablets planted on the highest mountain peaks of his empire. He embodied his vision of everlasting, all-encompassing and cosmic empire in the many vast palaces he built and above all in his mausoleum, which was probably the biggest burial complex of a single ruler ever to have been constructed anywhere in the world.[9]

Hubris was quickly followed by nemesis. The First Emperor had proclaimed that his dynasty would survive for generations beyond count. In fact it collapsed just two years after his death in 210 BCE. The reasons are not difficult to find. The non-Qin dynasties and elites had not merely lost their independence and status but were also deported in their thousands to the Qin heartland after 221 BCE. The claim of the ruthless and tyrannical First Emperor to be the manifestation of Chinese intellectuals' long-held yearning for a wise and virtuous unifier of the Chinese lands was scorned by most literati. His infamous 'burning of the books' campaign was aimed at confiscating private libraries, ending public debates about history and imposing a single, state-dominated set of ideological principles. This increased his unpopularity among the literati, especially of course among scholars (including those belonging to the Confucian tradition), whose beliefs he was seen to belittle. His wars and vast construction projects put immense pressure on the masses.

At one estimate 15 per cent of the entire population was conscripted by the Qin state after 221 BCE to build roads, fortifications and palaces. The emperor's mausoleum complex alone covered 25 square miles and required 700,000 labourers for its construction, many of them highly skilled.

One modern historian comments that 'no regime of such callousness could survive for long', but more was involved than mere cruelty and exploitation. To some extent the fate of the Qin has parallels with the collapse of the Neo-Assyrian dynasty and empire. Over-centralization and the concentration of power in the hands of an emperor and his court brought short-term gains in state power at the expense of long-term vulnerability. Attempting to micro-manage society meant that the bureaucracy's operating costs had been high even in the pre-unification Qin kingdom. Trying to extend this principle to a huge empire was a hopeless endeavour in the pre-modern world. To survive, the Qin dynasty needed to adapt rapidly to the realities of governing an empire. Above all, this meant creating a stable alliance between the monarchy and regional elites. Probably Qin traditions made rapid adaptation impossible but the dynasty destroyed any chance of survival by indulging in a vicious succession struggle after the First Emperor's death. With the regime at war with itself, the floodgates were opened and rebellion burst forth on all sides.[10]

Despite the rapid demise of his dynasty, the First Emperor was undoubtedly one of the most significant rulers in world history. Empire remained the predominant and only legitimate form of polity in China into modern times, with enormous consequences for the twenty-first-century world. Later emperors and dynasties were in key respects Ying Zheng's heirs and based their rule on precedents he established. But his reputation for tyranny was so black that his legacy could never be admitted. The legitimacy of the Han dynasty partly rested on loudly proclaimed rejection of Qin principles. The Confucian literati who came in time to dominate the Han ideological apparatus had every reason to blacken the First Emperor's memory. Since variants of Confucianism defined Chinese state ideology down to the twentieth century – and even to some extent to the present – the ironic result was that the world's greatest imperial tradition condemned the founding father of the Chinese Empire.

In the civil war that followed the First Emperor's death the final victor was Liu Pang, who founded the Han dynasty that was to rule China with just a sixteen-year intermission for the next four centuries. Liu Pang, who as emperor assumed the name Gaozu ('Founder'), was a man of peasant origin who had served the Qin as a minor official. Driven into rebellion by fear of execution for a minor infraction, he triumphed through a mixture of political skill, courage, intelligent leadership and luck. In the last years of the civil war Liu Pang's key rival was Xiang Yu, a man of much higher social standing who probably commanded more formidable armies and had earned a justified reputation as an outstanding general. Many years later, Liu Pang spoke to his intimate circle of advisers about the reasons he had defeated a rival who on paper had most of the advantages. The emperor accepted that Xiang Yu was in many respects more inspiring and outwardly impressive than himself as an individual leader but added that – unlike himself – Xiang had proved unable to create and direct a team of top-class military and bureaucratic lieutenants and advisers. That was partly because his rival's personality made it hard for him to give credit to his advisers and share with them the spoils of victory. Gaozu added that, by avoiding this weakness, he had been able to recruit and hold the loyalty of key lieutenants who were superior to him as diplomats, generals and administrators but who worked together effectively under his leadership. Many successful chief executives and rulers in history could justifiably have said the same. But perhaps a man who had risen by his own efforts was more likely than a prince brought up on the steps of the throne to possess the modesty and self-awareness to speak in this fashion. Such a man at least knew that he had to create a team. An unwary emperor might put too much faith in his right to command obedience.[11]

Liu Pang had to accommodate the widespread reaction against Qing centralization. Just as Augustus learned from Julius Caesar's mistakes and disguised his power behind a republican facade, so Liu Pang maintained some elements of the Qin system of government under camouflage and amidst loud denunciations of Qin tyranny. But the founder of the Han dynasty had to concede more real power than was the case with Augustus. Political realities and the strategy that brought Liu Pang victory in the civil war meant that he was forced to assign more than half his empire as autonomous fiefs to his main supporters. Perhaps his personal and un-autocratic style of management contributed to this too. His three successors made it their priority to reassert control over these fiefdoms, whose initially great autonomous power and resources were a major threat to the survival of the Han dynasty and empire. Urged on by their ministers, Gaozu's two sons and grandson had achieved this goal by the time the seventh Han monarch, Emperor Wu, ascended the throne in 141 BCE.[12]

The fifth Han monarch, Emperor Wen, ruled successfully from 180 to 157 BCE. A conversation is recorded that took place between him and his chancellor (i.e. chief minister), Chen Ping. The emperor asked the Chancellor what in his opinion was the true role of a monarch. In response Chen Ping stated that the emperor's key duty was to act as the chief ritualist and performer of sacrifices in the state's great ceremonies. As regards governance, the ruler's main responsibility was to appoint the chancellor, who would direct the government in accordance with cosmic and ethical principles of harmony, and who was responsible for ensuring that ministers worked together and that administration flowed smoothly and efficiently. This definition of the monarch's role was advanced by many Confucian (and other) famous literati in the Warring States era. It was the conception of emperorship cherished by Confucian ministers throughout the history of imperial China. An expert on imperial Chinese political institutions comments, 'when this political arrangement worked well, it looked very much like modern constitutional monarchy'.[13]

The problem was that, to 'work well', the system required a monarch sufficiently informed and intelligent to appoint an effective chancellor. Although Chen Peng remained tactfully silent on this point, it was presumably also the monarch's responsibility to decide when the time had come for his chancellor to retire. It was hard to see what other institution or individual in China could fulfil this role, one which demanded great political awareness and sensitivity. A ruler with sufficient insight to make these decisions was nevertheless expected to leave governing to the chancellor and confine himself to the performance of rituals and sacrifices. Presumably he must shut his ears to the torrent of criticism, jealousy and slander which a chancellor and his policies were bound to attract. On the other hand, at least one of the emperor's ears must be left half-open, otherwise a chancellor could serve into his dotage and lead empire and dynasty to disaster. Finding a ruler who was willing and able to follow these somewhat contradictory guidelines was not easy. Since the emperor was in principle an absolute monarch, unconstrained by legal restrictions and the source of all legitimate authority, it was in any case up to him to what extent he played a personal role in governing his empire. Contemporary Western readers may be inclined to assume that a bureaucracy and its ministers will govern more effectively than a hereditary autocrat. Much of Chinese (and other) history contradicts this assumption. Left to their own devices, bureaucratic factions could easily paralyze and corrupt government. Confucian officials and scholars shared some assumptions – including for example a commitment to very low taxes – which could wreck a government's effectiveness.[14]

Emperor Wen's grandson Wu ruled for fifty-four years and is usually depicted as the most active monarch of the Han dynasty. We have very little information about Wu's personality. By far the best source for the history of the Qin and early Han dynasties is Sima Qian's *Historical Records (Shiji)*, but the chapter on Wu's reign has disappeared. Perhaps this is not an accident. The great historian disapproved of Wu's despotic character and policies. When the general whom Sima Qian had recommended for high command against the nomads was defeated in battle, an angry Emperor Wu ordered his court historian's castration. Serving in Wu's vicinity was therefore nerve-racking. During the course of his reign the emperor executed six of his chancellors. In 113 BCE – to take one example – his unannounced personal tour of inspection in the provinces resulted in two governors and several lower officials either committing suicide or facing execution. In a manner typical of activist monarchs, Wu boosted the role of his private secretariat at the expense of his chancellor, ministers and government institutions. This was to place power within the so-called Inner Court, which was mostly staffed by eunuchs. In similar fashion the emperor appointed his in-laws to top positions, especially in the army. In-laws, like eunuchs, were seen (not always correctly) as operating outside bureaucratic networks and having a strong personal loyalty to the monarch.

It is possible to point to key policy shifts in Wu's reign and to assume that these could not have occurred without the emperor's strong support. By re-creating the iron and salt monopolies Wu's regime committed itself to a significantly more activist economic policy, for example. Relations with the Xiongnu nomads were the biggest foreign policy issue in Wu's reign. After Emperor Gaozu's defeat by the Xiongnu in 202 BCE, Han policy had been to appease and buy off the nomads. By the time of Wu's accession the benefits and costs of appeasement were increasingly debated within the government. The policy was expensive, humiliating, and even so did not stop almost constant minor raids by nomad bands, not to mention occasional larger invasions. With the treasury full and the problem of autonomous princely fiefdoms resolved, many officials argued for a more aggressive military stance, but the potential risks and costs of war against the Xiongnu were frightening. In imperial monarchies such crucial decisions for peace and war were the quintessential preserve of the monarch. One immediate result of the decision to switch to an aggressive, military strategy was a swingeing 1.2 per cent levy on all property to fund what were bound to be extremely expensive military offensives deep into Xiongnu territory.

These offensives nevertheless paid rich dividends and were often planned and executed with great skill. The decisive campaign of 119 BCE, for example, entailed pushing 250,000 men deep into Xiongnu territory, 870 miles from their starting point and across the Gobi desert. A combination of military skill, political subtlety and excellent logistical organization in time destroyed the Xiongnu Empire and brought stability to the northern frontier for decades. One result of this victory was the extension of Chinese territory far to the north-west, with Chinese influence spreading deep into Central Asia. This was a prerequisite for the opening up of the so-called Silk Route, which stretched all the way to Rome. But it was in the nature of Chinese and Eurasian geopolitics that triumphs over the nomads could only be temporary. In time new nomadic empires would form and the security threat to China's northern frontier would resume. From Emperor Gaozu's shocking defeat in 202 BCE down to the Qing dynasty's final destruction of nomadic power in the mid-eighteenth century CE, defence of the northern border against the nomads was by far the biggest geopolitical challenge faced by China's rulers.[15]

In the long run Emperor Wu's most vital input into government policy concerned ideology. It was in his reign that Confucianism became what one might call the state religion. Very important to this development was the fact that many of Wu's favourite childhood tutors were strong Confucians. Influencing the heir's education and capturing him for one's cause was always a crucial element in imperial politics. From early in his reign Wu showed a strong commitment to Confucianism, appointing well-known adherents to Confucian doctrines to key positions in government. In his reign the imperial university was established, designed to study and edit the Confucian classics and to teach Confucian wisdom to the thousands of candidates for official positions who entered the university every year. Posts in central government were increasingly confined to men with satisfactory knowledge of Confucian principles and sacred texts. The emperor played a major role in introducing and refining a number of key rituals and sacrifices which remained of vital significance down to the twentieth century CE. Perhaps most important, he was a generous patron of the scholars who developed and synthesized Confucian ideas during his reign. Of these scholars Dong Zhongshu was probably the most important. Emperor Wu sought his advice and supported his scholarship for decades. More than anyone else, Dong was responsible for fusing Confucian ethics, natural philosophy, political ideas, rituals and cosmology into a single coherent guide to belief and behaviour.[16]

There is here an obvious conundrum. Wu was the most autocratic of Han emperors. Confucianism on the contrary stressed the monarch's ritual role and pressed – at least implicitly and quietly – for governance to be left largely to officialdom. Common sense suggests that the Confucian scholars and officials surrounding Wu must have kept a sharp curb on their tongues and their innermost thoughts. The alliance between imperial monarchy and Confucian officialdom was the bedrock of the Chinese Empire. From the start it contained deep tensions. We simply lack the sources to understand in any detail how these tensions worked out in Wu's reign.

None of the women whom Emperor Wu had promoted to the status of empress gave birth to sons who survived. When Wu died in 87 BCE he was therefore succeeded by the child-son of a concubine. This was to be the norm during the remainder of the Han era. With concubines' sons succeeding to the throne, the competition within the harem to catch the emperor's eye became a vital aspect of political life. The occupation of the throne by children placed enormous power in the hands of their mothers (and sometimes grandmothers), since Chinese custom in practice gave them guardianship over their sons and grandsons so long as they remained children. Given the strength of kinship ties in China, these women inevitably relied heavily on their own male relations to govern the state. The power of imperial in-laws was a key theme of Chinese politics in both the Western Han era and again after a cadet branch of the imperial family was restored after a sixteen-year interlude between 9 and 25 CE during which one in-law, Wang Mang, seized the throne and attempted to establish his own dynasty.

The Wang family were middle-ranking gentry landowners and state officials. They rose to prominence after Wang Zhengjun entered the harem of the heir to the throne, Prince Yuan, who succeeded his father as emperor in 49 BCE. Zhengjun gave birth to the later Emperor Cheng in 51 BCE and was proclaimed empress three years later. When Emperor Yuan died in 33 BCE, Prince Cheng succeeded to the throne, aged almost eighteen. Real power rested with the Wang family: one uncle succeeded another as de facto regent until 8 BCE when the older Wang generation died out and power was transferred to the most able male in the younger generation, Wang Mang, who was Dowager Empress Zhengjun's nephew. The emperor himself was perfectly content with these arrangements: 'Cheng . . . proved himself to be a charming and pleasure-loving man, easily dominated by women. He had no stomach for government and was content to let his uncles rule for him.' The situation in which Han emperors reigned but the Wang family ruled looked set to continue indefinitely when Wang Mang married off his daughter to the boy-emperor Ping in 7 BCE. It was only Ping's death and the likelihood that the throne would now pass to a distant Han cousin that spurred Wang Mang into usurping the crown.[17]

Initially his move was widely accepted. Wang was a highly competent political leader and administrator. The Han dynasty had not produced an effective ruler for generations and this could be seen as evidence that the Mandate of Heaven was shifting. What destroyed Wang Mang was partly elite opposition to his attempted land reform but above all a vast natural disaster, when the Yellow River burst its banks and permanently shifted its course between 3 and 11 CE, killing or displacing millions of people. Not merely did this unleash anarchy and massive deprivation across several densely populated provinces, the disaster was also used effectively by Wang's enemies as a sign of Heaven's displeasure at his usurpation. Nevertheless, if a distant cadet branch of the Han dynasty was now restored to the throne, this had less to do with deep dynastic loyalism than the fact that restoration of the Han was the compromise solution least unacceptable to the many strands of opposition to Wang Mang.[18]

In the second half of the Han era (known as the Eastern Han period) many earlier elements of political tension in time re-emerged. Court politics often turned on struggles between families and factions linked to empresses and empress dowagers. Monarchs once they reached adulthood sometimes attempted to reassert their personal power by using Inner Court eunuchs in key positions of power. The prestige and legitimacy of the dynasty declined, not least among state officials with Confucian values. Deeper structural issues also served to undermine the regime. Before unification the Qin state had protected the peasantry from pressure by rural elites since it was the foundation of the state's army and tax system. With unification disappeared the need for large infantry armies made up of conscripted peasants. The key security issue now became the defence of the distant northern frontier against nomadic invasions and raids. As in the Roman case, Han-dynasty military power came to rest on tribal cavalry auxiliaries and hard-bitten veterans. These soldiers' loyalties were to their chiefs and their generals, not to a distant Han emperor, especially when that emperor could no longer always pay them on a regular basis. By the second century CE this was becoming the case as big landowners squeezed out much of the free peasant farming community in the Yellow River core of Han China. Wang Mang's efforts to reverse this trend failed and the restored Han regime had neither the means nor the will to oppose the growing power of landowning elites. Its inability to persuade or coerce this elite into paying sufficient taxes undermined the state's army and administration, thereby greatly con- tributing to the demise of the Han Empire.[19]

Although its last decades were melancholic, the Han dynasty never-theless made a big long-term contribution to the triumph of empire in East Asia. Before 221 BCE the literati had dreamed of a united China: four hundred years of Han rule had made that dream a reality and pro-vided a model to which all later Chinese rulers aspired. For most of four centuries the Han regime had brought the peace of empire to a world previously ravaged by constant devastating wars. Peace had allowed growing prosperity and the flowering of a magnificent high culture. China had expanded deep into Central Asia, in the process helping to link the two ends of Eurasia through the Silk Route and open itself to outside influences. The emergence of a coherent Confucian state ideol-ogy and of a bureaucracy increasingly loyal to its values were vital for the long-term viability of the Chinese imperial state and for its crucial alliance with China's social and intellectual elites. What one might call the Chinese imperial model had not fully developed by the time the Han dynasty collapsed in 220 CE. For this one needs to wait until the evolution of the civil-service examination system, the emergence of neo-Confucian thought, and economic and cultural development under the Song dynasty (tenth–thirteenth centuries). But the Han era proved to be a mighty step in that direction.

7

Nomads

From early in the first millennium BCE nomad warriors dominated the northern Eurasian grasslands. They continued to do so for another 2,500 years. These grasslands stretched in a wide corridor for over 3,000 miles from Hungary in the west to Mongolia in the east. Nomad power extended far beyond the borders of these grasslands. For this whole era a key question in Eurasian geopolitics was whether or not a sedentary society was within range of nomad warriors. Above all, this was a matter of distance but also of climate, topography and vegetation – nomads flourished in flat grasslands where they could feed their horses and deploy cavalry armies to best effect. In the previous chapters the nomads' impact on the ancient Near East and on the Roman and Han empires was noted. This theme looms larger still in much of the rest of this book. The Ottomans and Mughals were the descendants of Turkic nomad warriors from Inner Asia. The Qing (Manchu) came from the forests and grasslands of Manchuria. In later chapters we will look at how these dynasties sought to combine the equestrian-warrior values of their ancestors with the culture and political heritage of the sedentary peoples whom they ruled. In the present chapter, however, I concentrate on Inner Asia itself and on the empires that nomad warriors created in this region.

The greatest problem is evidence. Written sources are far fewer than for sedentary societies. In the overwhelming majority of cases they were written by outsiders to the steppe world. As a result, they were usually ill-informed and hostile. The Greco-Romans, Persians and Chinese saw themselves as civilized peoples faced by nomad barbarians. Their contempt for these barbarians was compounded by fear. In the Old Testament the Prophet Jeremiah wrote that 'at the sound of horsemen and archers every town takes to flight . . . Their quivers are like an open grave ... Look, an army is coming from the land of the north ... they are armed with bow and spear; they are cruel and show no mercy. They sound like the roaring sea as they ride on their horses.'[1] The sources we do possess allow us to understand much about the social structure and material culture of the steppe world. The impressive luxury items found by archaeologists in royal and aristocratic burial sites, for example, prove that hierarchy and inequality reigned on the steppe, as in sedentary societies. It is harder to get a sense of nomad values and impossible to gain any insight into the personalities and the inner worlds of the rulers of steppe empires. For this we will have to wait until a later era when sources on Ottoman, Moghul and Qing monarchs are far more abundant. I hope it is not mere prejudice that persuades me that these later dynasts, who embodied a complex mixture of steppe warrior and sedentary cultures, were more interesting human beings than their more simple and rugged warrior ancestors.

Keeping tabs on the tribes and peoples of Inner Asia is difficult. The steppe was a highway. Nomadic tribes could move vast distances along this highway at great speed. These tribes were in general ill-defined and unstable groupings, much inclined to split in bad times and incorporate outsiders in good ones. The larger tribes in particular were seldom mono-ethnic or monolingual. Pushed out of its existing pasturage by aggressive neighbours, a tribe (or parts of it) might ride thousands of miles to find a new home, in the process scattering other tribes that stood in its path and setting off a chain reaction of migrations that rippled across vast areas. To make matters even more complicated, a tribe might be identified by one name by its own members and by a variety of different names by its nomadic neighbours and the sedentary societies it encountered. To this day, arguments rage among historians, archaeologists and philologists as to what (if anything) was the relationship between the Xiongnu steppe empire that confronted imperial China from the third century BCE to the first century CE and the nomadic Huns who played a big role in destroying the western Roman Empire more than three hundred years later.[2]

The Tatars are merely one of many examples of just how confusing tribal names can be. Narrowly defined (which inter alia was the Mongols' usage) the term 'Tatar' meant a large tribe that lived just to the east of the Mongols in what is now the Mongolian heartland. Although in origin Mongolian speakers, Tatars are recorded in the eleventh century

CE as also speaking a Turkic dialect. The Mongols and their richer Tatar neighbours were bitter rivals. It was Tatars who treacherously poisoned the father of Chinggis (Genghis) Khan. The steppe was a world of the family vendetta: memories were long and revenge was sweet. When he crushed the Tatars on the road to building his empire Chinggis exterminated the tribal elite and distributed the rank and file among other tribes. That might lead us to expect that the term 'Tatar' would disappear from the history books but quite the opposite occurred. The Tatars' neighbours to the east, the Kitans, had always used the term 'Tatar' to describe a larger and more mixed group of Mongolian tribes. Meanwhile, in Chinese and Islamic sources the term Tatar 'served . . . as a convenient label for all the peoples of the eastern steppe, in particular those who were not Turkish'. The 'Mongol' armies that conquered 'Russia' in the 1230s and 1240s were largely made up of Turkic speakers. In time even the originally Mongol leaders of the so-called Golden Horde, which dominated the Russian lands for two hundred years, became Turkic in language and customs. In Russian memory this period is described as the Tatar Yoke and their Turko-Mongol rulers are called Tatars. Latin Europe adopted a roughly similar terminology, calling the entire Mongol Empire 'Tartary'. In today's world Tatars still exist, the two largest groupings being the Volga and Crimean Tatars. The innocent outsider, remembering the age-old links between Tatars and Mongols, will probably be surprised to discover that today's Tatars look much more like Italians than Chinese.[3]

Amidst the fog, some basic points stand out. Nomadic societies required wheeled transport to carry tents and other necessities of life. The immensely long steppe corridor sustained great numbers of cattle, sheep and horses. In Chinggis's lifetime probably half the world's horses lived on the Eurasian steppe. Steppe horses were extremely tough and had great stamina. They remained unstabled in the winter, using their unshod hooves to dig under the ice for grass and roots. Given the steppe's climate and vegetation, horses and cattle needed to shift from one area to another in order to survive. At a minimum, herds had summer and winter pasturages. Already by the end of the first millennium BCE, there were no unutilized and unclaimed pastures anywhere in Eurasia, so life on the steppe entailed a constant struggle to defend one's pasture lands from neighbouring nomadic tribes. Men on horseback could manage far larger herds than men on foot. Over many centuries,

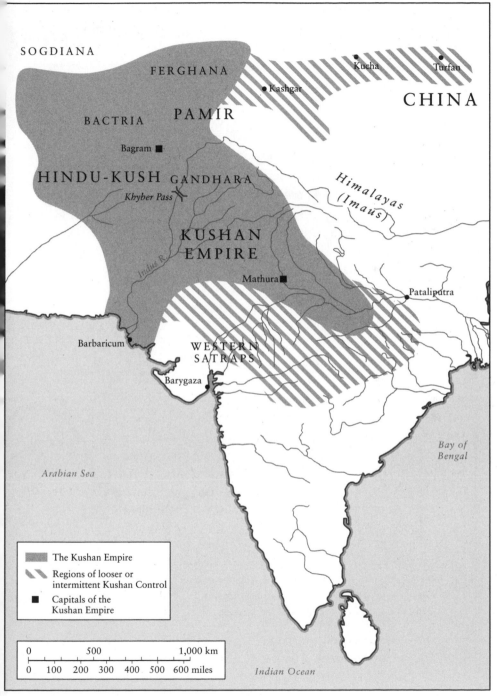

SOGDIANA

FERGHANA

BACTRIA

PAMIR

Kashgar

Kucha

Turfan

CHINA

Bagram ■

HINDU-KUSH GANDHARA

Khyber Pass

Indus R.

Himalayas
(Imaus)

KUSHAN
EMPIRE

Mathura ■

Pataliputra

Barbaricum

WESTERN
SATRAPS

Barygaza

Arabian Sea

Bay of
Bengal

The Kushan Empire

Regions of looser or
intermittent Kushan Control

Capitals of the
Kushan Empire

0   500   1,000 km

0   100   200   300   400   500   600 miles

Indian Ocean

The Kushan Empire

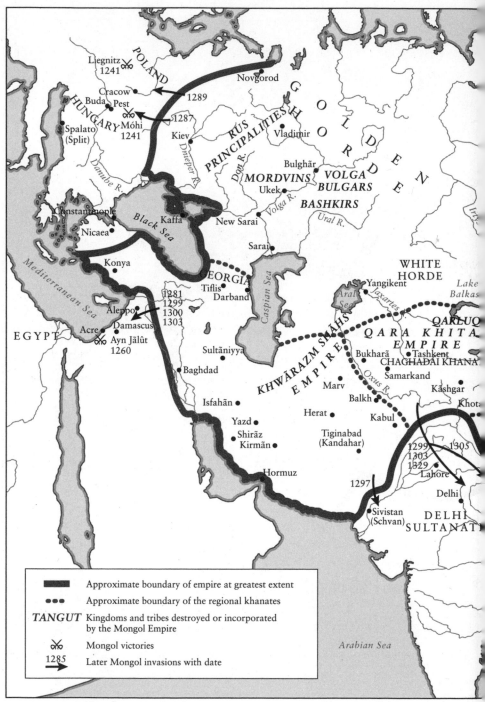

The Mongol Empire

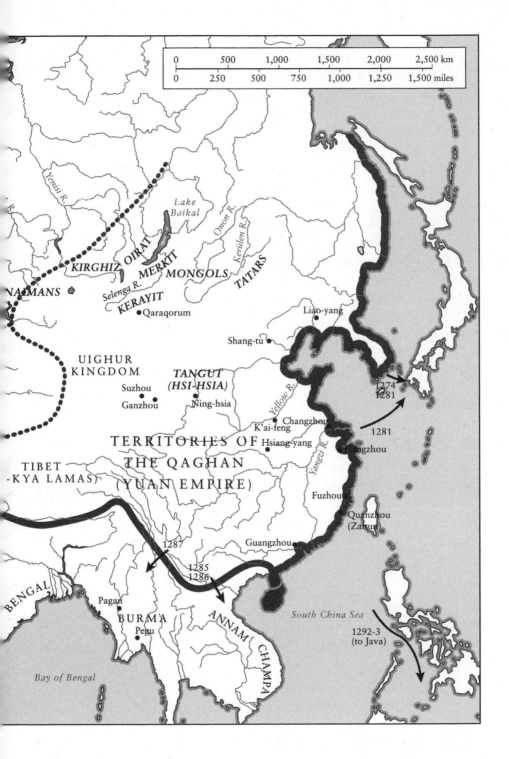

Yenisi R.

Lake
Baikal

Onon R.

Keriilen R.

KIRGHIZ   OIRAT

MERKIT

MONGOLS

Selenga R.

KERAYIT

TATARS

NAIMANS

Qaraqorum

Liao-yang

**UIGHUR
KINGDOM**

Shang-tu

1274
1281

Suzhou

**TANGUT
(HSI-HSIA)**

Yellow R.

Ganzhou

Ning-hsia

1281

K'ai-feng

Changzhou

Hangzhou

TERRITORIES OF

Hsiang-yang

Yangzi R.

**TIBET
-KYA LAMAS)**

THE QAGHAN

(YUAN EMPIRE)

Fuzhou

Quanzhou
(Zaitun)

1287

Guangzhou

1285
1286

BENGAL

Pagan

BURMA

Pegu

ANNAM

CHAMPA

South China Sea

1292-3
(to Java)

Bay of Bengal

bits, harnesses and stirrups evolved to ease the rider's task. Skilled riders and herdsmen had no difficulty morphing into formidable cavalry. Men used to fighting their nomad neighbours for pasturage turned easily into predators who raided towns and agricultural settlements, plundering and extorting protection money as they passed. Predatory warrior nomadism started at the eastern end of the steppe and the eastern region also gave birth to the greatest steppe empires – above all, the empires of the Xiongnu, the Turks and the Mongols. In the European and west Siberian steppe-lands, pastures were lusher and the climate milder and less capricious than in Mongolia. Ecological, political and military factors combined to ensure that the basic pattern of migration on the steppe was in a westward direction.[4]

Nomad society at the bottom was made up of individual tented households united in small groups at campsites in order to herd their cattle. Above this level formed clans, tribes and the multi-tribal confederations that were the penultimate stage before true statehood and empire. Although in mythology tribal solidarity was rooted in shared kinship, in reality it was usually only the tribe's elite which was united by a strong sense of family relationships and common ancestry. Much of the rank and file were taken over after successful wars and some might be slaves. Leadership in clans and tribes was hereditary and the same was even more true in nomadic empires. Only men from the core royal lineage had any right to rule. Nomadic elite society attached very great importance to sacrifices to ancestors, genealogy and bloodlines. The royal lineage was generally traced back at least partly to the spirit world and supernatural forces that intervened in human affairs. In this sense it is correct to describe nomadic society as dynastic and aristocratic, but use of the latter word has its dangers. To the modern ear, aristocracy implies rootedness and permanence whereas steppe society was above all fluid and mobile. Tribal elites might or might not survive when conquered and absorbed by hostile neighbours.[5]

There were also countervailing currents undermining aristocracy even within the tribal and imperial elites. A core institution of warrior nomadism was the war-band that surrounded the leader and pledged unconditional allegiance to him unto death. These war-bands were made up of warriors who joined voluntarily across tribal, linguistic and social barriers. They bore some similarities to the knights and retainers of a European feudal king's household, and even more to the slave-warriors who filled the ranks of many Islamic rulers' households. In steppe empires war-bands could grow to a great size, in the extreme case of Chinggis Khan numbering 10,000 men. From the ranks of his war-band came the emperor's bodyguard and the innermost core of his army but also many of the trusted lieutenants whom he used to govern his empire. To hold the loyalty of his war-band the leader needed to share their dangers in war-time and to distribute generously the booty that victory provided. Another way of putting this is to say that the leader of a war-band needed to display charisma, camaraderie and success. The legitimacy of hereditary monarchy and aristocracy is rooted in very different principles. Admittedly, if their leader triumphed and created an empire, key members of his war-band might found dynasties which became part of that empire's hereditary aristocracy. This was to be the fate of leading members of Chinggis Khan's war-band.[6]

Sedentary societies and their rulers above all feared nomad aggression and military power. The sources are therefore dominated by accounts of war. The relationship between nomadic and sedentary societies entailed much more than this and was by no means always hostile. In general, stable nomadic regimes protected and policed long-distance trade because they knew just how much they could benefit from taxing it. Often subsumed under the term 'Silk Route', the trade links between the Mediterranean, the Near East, and Inner, South and East Asia flourished by the end of the first millennium BCE. The most famous element in this long-distance trade was Chinese silk, for which the Roman elites had an insatiable appetite, but many other luxury items were involved. So too were slaves and horses, both of which had the huge advantage of not requiring transport. In this era as later, international trade flourished under the protection of nomad empires. At the time of the Romans and the Han, this meant above all the so-called Kushan Empire that, at its height, ruled over today's Pakistan, Afghanistan and much of northern India and Inner Asia. Nomads also traded directly with neighbouring sedentary societies, sometimes for basic necessities such as grain but more importantly for the luxury goods which a war-band leader needed to distribute among his retinue, thereby displaying the generous patronage on which his followers' loyalty and his own legitimacy depended.

Nevertheless, it would be naïve to downplay the role of warfare in the relationship between the nomadic and sedentary worlds. For the warrior-predators of the steppe sedentary societies offered juicy targets. If very wealthy and sophisticated China, positioned on the borders of the steppe, was usually the juiciest target of all, Iran and northern India came not far behind. Even nomads bent on trading with sedentary societies knew that a military threat could tilt the terms of trade sharply in their favour. Whether tribal chieftains or budding emperors, the rulers of nomadic polities were aware that their survival depended on tapping the wealth of neighbouring sedentary societies in order to secure the trophies and luxury goods demanded by their followers. Extortion and plunder were built into the political economy of the steppe world. The balance of power between sedentary and steppe empires fluctuated. In both cases there were powerful internal forces that dictated the emergence, waxing and waning of imperial power. Looking at the whole span of 2,500 years of nomad–sedentary relations it is nevertheless a fair generalization that, whereas nomad empires usually had the edge in terms of military power, in political terms the sedentary empires were mostly more resilient.

Nomadic military superiority persisted despite the fact that sedentary societies had far larger populations. Although the Xiongnu emperor (*chanyu*) ruled over 1 million people and the Han emperor over 54 million, for eighty years it was the Xiongnu who dictated terms to the Chinese. Every able-bodied adult male in the nomadic world was a cavalryman, trained from early childhood to ride a horse, use a bow, and participate in the hunting expeditions that were a good training for warfare. In the composite bow, nomad cavalry had the most formidable hand-held weapon created by humans before the invention of firearms. Nomad mounted archers were a terrifying enemy whose skilful coordination of horse and bow took years of training to perfect. If necessary, a nomad ruler could enrol one-quarter of his entire population in his army, leaving the women to mind the herds. A cavalry army operating with many remounts could manoeuvre with a speed, flexibility and endurance that the armies of sedentary societies found very hard to match.[7]

The peasants who made up the great majority of sedentary populations were less suited for warfare, nor could they easily abandon their farms for year-long campaigns. Unlike hunting and cattle-herding, farming taught few basic military skills. Even many years of training could not turn peasants into cavalry capable of matching nomad warriors. For a sedentary society the only answer to the nomad threat was to rely on a professional army, usually including large numbers of 'native' horsemen. Sustaining large professional armies was ruinously expensive. A sedentary society could seldom put more than 1 per cent of its population in the field, though much larger numbers might be mobilized in an emergency in a defensive role behind city walls. These armies were also difficult to control and a threat to their own rulers.

Even professional armies were generally at a disadvantage when faced by nomads. Large-scale invasions by nomad armies occurred intermittently in most eras. Sometimes a whole generation could pass with most of a sedentary empire's professional army sitting quietly in its barracks. Not only was this extremely expensive, it also created great difficulties as regards maintaining morale, discipline and military competence. Operating on the offensive and enjoying great mobility, a nomad ruler usually had a choice of targets against which he could concentrate his strike force. A sedentary society had fields and many towns which had to be defended. Over time nomads built up considerable knowledge about their sedentary neighbours. Merchants could easily double as spies, warning a nomad khan as to which city or region was most vulnerable to attack. Although initially baffled by siege warfare, nomad rulers soon found refugees and captives from the sedentary world to teach them its craft. By contrast, the frustrations faced by King Darius of Persia in the sixth century BCE as he pursued Scythian nomads deep into the steppe without being able to bring them to battle, as described by Herodotus, were an early example of how hard it was to defeat nomads. In any major advance across the steppe against the nomads logistics would matter even more than fighting skill. Nevertheless, one should not exaggerate: 'hard' did not mean impossible. In 121 and 119 BCE the well-trained Han army crossed the Gobi desert in brilliantly planned and executed operations. Penetrating deep into the Xiongnu heartland, it destroyed or captured millions of livestock and killed 100,000 nomad warriors. The Xiongnu never recovered from this massive blow to their wealth and their pool of military manpower.[8]

The simplest and most important reason for nomadic political weakness was succession crises. Some nomadic empires managed succession better than others. For eighty years in the second century BCE the Xiongnu passed power across the generations of the royal lineage without a political breakdown or civil war. In nomad terms this was a great and unusual achievement. The two brothers who founded the Turk Empire in the sixth century CE collaborated amicably and transferred power peacefully to the next generation. But in hereditary monarchies the usual rule was that although such informal arrangements could sometimes work between brothers, they almost always broke down in the next generation and resulted in wars of succession between cousins. This was always the case in the nomadic world. The basic problem was that nomads believed that sovereignty belonged to the ruling lineage as a whole. All princes in theory had a claim to rule. To challenge this principle was to confront fundamental nomad conceptions of justice and equity. In no major nomadic polity did an ordered and generally accepted system of succession emerge which would avoid civil war within the royal clan for many generations. This was the most frequent cause of the collapse of nomad polities, including nomad empires.

There were also other sources of political weakness. Nomad polities were most stable when engaging in successful raids and conquests. To a certain extent this reflects the truism that success unites any group and legitimizes its leaders' authority. In all pre-modern societies which believed that gods somewhere in the sky intervened in events on earth, success was seen as a sign of heaven's blessing. The Mongols' belief that their sky-god, Tengri, commanded them to rule the whole earth was far cruder than the Islamic call to jihad, but it had some of the same effects as regards providing supernatural backing for the very human urge to conquer and plunder.

When conquests stopped, rulers somehow had to devise a way to satisfy and control highly mobile nomadic warriors, armed to the teeth and scattered across an enormous area. Plunder was vital to raising the ordinary warrior nomad above a life of bare subsistence. Above all, rulers had to placate tribal elites and leaders who commanded their own small armies (including their own war-bands) and could easily rebel or transfer their allegiance to a neighbouring ruler. These local elites must now be paid off from taxes and tribute levied from conquered sedentary subjects. Creating effective fiscal and administrative institutions to achieve this could be difficult. If his regime was to last, the ruler must ensure the prosperity of his newly conquered sedentary subjects and legitimize his rule in their eyes. In his attempts to do this a monarch might easily alienate the nomad warriors on whom his power depended.

Even if he achieved a workable balance his problems might not be over. The fourteenth-century north African thinker Ibn Khaldun devoted part of his life to investigating the dynamics of nomadic politics. He believed that once they had conquered and begun to rule over sedentary societies, nomads lost their military qualities. Not only did they soften, they also lost the sense of elan and solidarity that had fuelled their military triumphs. Ibn Khaldun drew his examples from north Africa but the nomads of the Maghreb and the Sahara were close cousins of the nomads of the steppe. Nizam al-Mulk, the great Iranian vizier of the Seljuk Empire in eleventh-century Anatolia, urged the Seljuk sultan to encourage his nomad subjects to engage in constant warfare with the Byzantines in order to stop them going soft. This was sound advice but it could be dangerous. It was the inability or unwillingness of the Xiongnu emperor to stop his subjects from raiding the Han Empire that contributed to the devastating Chinese campaigns that destroyed Xiongnu power in 121 and 119 BCE. Moreover, however well a nomad ruler managed his own subjects, disruption could easily come from outside. Battles between other nomadic polities could unleash a chain of migration across the steppe. So could even minor shifts in the weather in Mongolia and the eastern steppe where pasturages were arid, the climate was extreme, and the nomads lived on a permanent ecological knife-edge.[9]

The three most important steppe empires were the Xiongnu, the Turk and the Mongol. The Xiongnu ruled Mongolia from 209 BCE until 91 CE and dominated the Tarim basin and parts of northern China for the first half of this period. They provided a model for future steppe empires. Their empire came into existence largely as a result of the nomads' need to defend themselves against attack by China's First Emperor (Qin Zheng/Shihuangdi) in the 210s BCE, and in particular his annexation of the nomads' richest pasture lands in the Ordos region just south of the Yellow River. The first true Xiongnu emperor (*chanyu*) was the bold and charismatic Modun, who seized power from his father in 209 BCE, exploited the civil war in China that erupted after the fall of the Qin and regained the Ordos region. His subsequent defeat of the Han armies led to a peace treaty heavily tilted in the Xiongnu's favour. The tribute payments it entailed were crucial to the *chanyu*'s ability to retain the loyalty of his large personal warrior retinue and the tribal elites. Although never as institutionalized as later Turko-Mongol empires, the Xiongnu polity was more than just a tribal confederation. The monarch did usually dominate military and diplomatic policy-making. Nor was he simply the leader of a war-band: he also carried out religious rituals and sacrifices. He structured his empire as if it was an army, creating a hierarchy of theoretically non-tribal decimal units all the way from squads of ten up to units of 20,000 households. These units were designed to fulfil both military and administrative functions. Nevertheless, given the scale of his dominions and the lack of any effective bureaucracy beyond the royal court, the emperor inevitably remained very dependent on local leaders. In practice these leaders remained hereditary chieftains. In the end the Xiongnu Empire disintegrated in the face of Chinese military power, succession struggles and the Han dynasty's success in buying the allegiance of significant sections of the Xiongnu elite.[10]

An early step in the Xiongnu's rise to empire was the crushing of their most significant nomadic rivals, the Yuezhi. Ejected from China's north-western borderlands by the Xiongnu, in time-honoured nomadic fashion the Yuezhi fled more than 750 miles westwards in search of alternative pastures. When their further westward expansion into Iran was blocked by the Parthian Empire, the Yuezhi turned south where opposition was less formidable. In time they formed a vast empire of their own which stretched all the way from Samarkand in Inner Asia to the eastern limit of the north Indian plain, including Ashoka's old capital city of Pataliputra (Patna). This empire has gone down in the history books as the empire of the Kushans. It lasted from roughly 80 BCE until well into the third century CE, when the Kushans fell victim to the aggression of the formidable Iranian Empire of the Sasanians. For well over two centuries the Kushan Empire played a vital role in opening up and protecting long-distance trade routes in Asia. Thanks to the Kushans, vast amounts of Chinese silk were transported across their empire to ports on the Indian Ocean, from where they were shipped to the Arabian Gulf, Egypt and the Mediterranean world. While preserving elements of their steppe cultural identity and remaining tolerant in religious matters, by the time their empire reached its apogee in the second century CE the Kushans had ceased to be nomads. They still offered strong protection to merchant communities across their empire. The patronage offered by the Kushans to Buddhist merchants and monks was vital in the religion's spread from India to China.[11]

After the fall of the Xiongnu, the Turks were the next tribe to establish an empire on the steppe. The first Turk Empire existed from 552 until 630 CE. Its eastern half, conquered by China's Tang dynasty, revolted in the late 670s and created a new (albeit smaller) empire that lasted until 745. Important in itself, the Turk Empire is significant also as the first certain sighting of Turkic-speaking peoples in Inner Asia. Originating in Mongolia, the Turks migrated westwards across most of northern Eurasia, in the process assimilating huge numbers of other nomadic peoples. Of the many nomadic tribes in northern Eurasia, only the Mongols and the Hungarians resisted Turkification and survived as major, separate peoples into the modern era. From their Inner Asian base, the Turks also migrated across much of sedentary Asia. Starting in the eleventh century, Turkic dynasties were to rule many of the lands between the Mediterranean and northern India for hundreds of years. The first Turkic inhabitants of the Near East were ninth-century slave soldiers in the military retinue of the Abbasid caliphs. Subsequently Turkic slave soldiers were to give a new and crucial twist to the steppe tradition of the war-band. From the tenth century Turks began to convert to Islam in large numbers. The alliance between Turkic military nomadism and the Islamic faith was to have an enormous impact on Eurasian history in the following centuries. The founder of the Seljuk dynasty was the leader of an insignificant war-band dwelling in today's Kazakhstan who converted to Islam in 985. His followers were 'universally described as a bedraggled, sorry lot, driven by desperation and impending starvation to conquest'. In time his descendants created a great empire in Iran and Anatolia. In their wake came the equally insignificant Ottoman war-band, which fled the Mongol advance across Inner Asia in the early thirteenth century and ended up founding the greatest and longest-lasting of all the Turko-Islamic empires on the shores of the Bosphorus.[12]

Inevitably, we know far more about the Seljuks, Ottomans and other later Turkic dynasties than we do about the first Turk empires on the steppe. The name 'Turk' initially only applied to the ruling Ashina clan but in time was ascribed to their diverse subjects too. The language they spoke is the ancestor of modern Turkish but many distinct Turkic dialects already existed on the steppe. The best-known myth of origin of the Ashina royal clan traced their ancestry back to the Xiongnu and attributed the family's survival to the miraculous intervention of a compassionate she-wolf, who saved the only survivor of a massacre carried out by a rival tribe and in time bore him ten sons, of whom the wisest and bravest – in other words Ashina – became the hereditary leader of the clan. With many variations, similar myths of origin, often involving wolves, existed among other steppe dynasties. They generally linked the dynasty's origins both to the animal world and to supernatural forces.

The religious beliefs and rituals of the Turks were complex. Ordinary Turks performed rites – for example, offerings to their ancestors – at home and without need for shamans. The latter were only called in during emergencies such as epidemics among people or animals, when their ability to address and placate the spirit world was needed. The Ashina rulers (the khagans) used shamans more, above all because they were believed to be able to predict the future and were therefore consulted on military and political questions. But the Ashina khagans and the shamans were also to some extent in competition as regards religious leadership. The khagans claimed to be the representatives on earth of the sky-god, Tengri, and of Umay, the goddess of fertility. When the ruler, as high priest of the imperial cult, made annual sacrifices to Tengri at the holy Otukan mountain in Mongolia, shamans (along with women and children) were excluded. Buddhism made many inroads among the Ashina's subjects but also aroused hostility within the Ashina elite because of its pacifist creed and support for monasticism. In the long run, Turkic nomadic warriors were always more likely to be attracted to Islam, with its call to Holy War and the respect it paid to the Islamic warriors (*ghazi*) who fulfilled their religious duty to spread the domain of the true faith across the globe.[13]

The political history of the Turk Empire followed patterns familiar in the steppe world. A vast empire was created at breakneck speed. For a brief period the Turks dominated all northern Eurasia from Crimea to Manchuria. Between 626 and 630, for example, their intervention in the Byzantine–Sasanian war was vital to the final victory of Emperor Heraclius. Like their predecessors, the Kushans, the Turks allied themselves to local (mostly Sogdian) merchant communities and did everything in their power to encourage long-distance trade. But the vast scale and sparse warrior population of this empire made it very hard to hold together. In the absence of any inherited all-imperial bureaucracy, princes of the Ashina clan acted as local viceroys. Inevitably this encouraged the development of autonomous hereditary fiefdoms. From its inception the empire was divided between two brothers (Bumin and

Ishtemi) into eastern and western khaganates. Although the eastern khagan was initially recognized as the senior emperor and head of the royal clan, this arrangement did not survive for more than two generations. As always, a key cause of instability was succession struggles in both the eastern and western khaganates. No rules for succession were created, above all because of the strong belief that the empire was the common patrimony of the royal clan. In this era and region, no one had a conception of the state, in other words a public authority and set of institutions perceived as separate from the reigning dynasty. When the dynasty imploded due to constant succession struggles, so too did the empire.

As usual, the rise and decline of steppe empires was closely related to the waxing and waning of Chinese power. When the Turk Empire emerged in the mid-sixth century China was divided. The Ashina khagans drew immense tribute payments from the feuding kingdoms of northern China. When China was reunited first by the Sui and then the Tang dynasties, Turk power declined. The eastern Turk Empire was destroyed in 629–30 by a combination of a well-planned invasion by Emperor Tang Taizong, unusually heavy snowfall which devastated the nomads' herds, and widespread anger among the nomad elites at the khagan's deference to the interests of his sedentary Sogdian subjects. From 630 until 679 the Turks were controlled indirectly by the Tang regime. The foundation of this control was military power but its effectiveness was enhanced by the attraction of part of the Turk elite to Chinese high culture and lifestyles. In the 670s, when the Tang were threatened from the west by the Tibetans, the Turks took the opportunity to regain their independence, which they preserved until 745. In this so-called Second Turk Empire there were frequent warnings from the khagans and their advisers against succumbing to the lures of Chinese sedentary culture. If they lost the mobility and the warrior qualities of their nomad ancestors, it was urged, the Turks could not hope to defend themselves against overwhelming Chinese numerical superiority. If they became fixed to towns and temples, the Turks would be defenceless against Chinese invaders. 'Besides, the teachings in the Buddhist and Daoist temples only make people gentle and submissive.'[14] Ibn Khaldun would have endorsed these warnings. But in the end the attractions of Chinese culture proved too strong. In addition, the Second Turk Empire soon became embroiled in succession struggles that wrecked its power and unity.

Among steppe nomads, the Mongols created the largest and most famous of all empires. The tribe of Chinggis Khan, the empire's founder, dwelled in north-eastern Mongolia at the extreme, harshest eastern corner of the Eurasian steppe. Chinggis was probably born in 1162 and died in 1227. Thanks above all to *The Secret History of The Mongols*, the first book written in Mongolian, we know more about him than about any previous steppe monarch. But although *The Secret History* was written shortly after his death and is sometimes surprisingly honest about darker aspects of his rise to power, we nevertheless know much less about him than is the case with many rulers of sedentary societies, let alone that small minority of monarchs whose own writings give us direct access to their inner thoughts.

From *The Secret History* (and a handful of other Mongol sources) we learn that 'his strengths are stamina, determination and shrewdness. He repeatedly demonstrates that he knows how to run, when to attack, when to make peace, and how to manipulate alliances to his own advantage.'[15] In steppe terms Chinggis was an aristocrat: he came from the core of the Mongol tribe's ruling Borjigid lineage. On the other hand, his success was due above all to his personal qualities and efforts. After the death of his father, when Chinggis was nine years old, he faced a harsh struggle to survive, let alone ultimately regain leadership over the Mongols. He was beyond question a charismatic figure, able to draw people to him and inspire their devotion and their confidence in his leadership. Of course, he could also be ruthless and treacherous in his pursuit of power. Like all steppe leaders he created a war-band of loyal followers drawn from every background. He shared these men's hardships in his rise to power, rewarded them generously and appointed them to the key positions in his government and army. He had the ability to spot good advisers and listen to their advice. This included advisers who could guide him as regards the unfamiliar challenges of waging war and governing in the sedentary world.

The Mongol military machine became the most formidable yet seen in history. It built upon the long-established strengths of nomadic armies: the number and resilience of steppe horses and the toughness and skill of nomad mounted archers. In the thousand years since the fall of the Xiongnu some aspects of nomad arms and equipment had improved substantially: this included iron stirrups, wooden saddles and ever more sophisticated composite bows made from wood, horn, sinew and glue which could regularly hit targets at a range of 325 metres. The vast number of horses available on the steppe allowed Chinggis's armies to set out on campaign with five horses for every man, and thereby to outmanoeuvre and exhaust enemy cavalry. Superior cavalry meant better intelligence about enemy deployments and denial to enemy generals of knowledge about the strength and movements of Mongol forces.

Under Chinggis's command Mongol armies acquired the additional skills and cadres necessary for warfare away from the steppe: above all that meant expertise at siege warfare. Even more important, he instilled tight discipline and coordination at tactical, operational and strategic levels. On the battlefield the so-called 'chisel formation', allowing ranks of mounted archers to fire their arrows, wheel to the rear and reload before returning to loose further volleys, required drill and training not seen in Europe until the seventeenth century. Victories inspired morale, rich plunder increased motivation, but discipline ensured that victorious soldiers did not stop to loot a defeated enemy's camp before total victory and rout had been achieved. The penalty for doing so was death. At a higher tactical level the feigned retreats that often lasted for many days and lured the exhausted pursuing armies to their doom required not just discipline but also impressive coordination of the movements of the Mongol army's units. Both on the battlefield and in the planning and execution of campaigns Mongol generalship was superior to that of all the enemies they encountered. Armies would move in widely dispersed divisions which would bewilder, outflank and surround the enemy but nevertheless converge on the battlefield. This was to anticipate Napoleon's rule of marching separately but fighting united. It was also to anticipate the principles of the *Blitzkrieg*, in which the speed, surprise and scale of operations paralyses enemy commanders. Also as in *Blitzkrieg*, terror was used systematically and on a grand scale in order to undermine future resistance. One historian comments that carnage on the scale sometimes employed by Chinggis's armies had not been seen since the days of the Neo-Assyrian Empire.[16]

The devastation and cruelty caused by Mongol invaders must not be ignored in modern historians' attempt to 'be fair' to the nomadic world, but it does not weaken Chinggis Khan's undoubted right to be considered one of the greatest warrior-emperors in history. Although he inherited the ingredients of military power, he fused them into one of the greatest armies in history. He led that war machine on campaign for decades.

After his death the army and the generals he had created conquered much of sedentary Eurasia in the following three generations. Chinggis's military innovations were accompanied by policies which moved the Mongol nomadic polity further towards becoming an imperial state than anything previously seen on the steppe. Sometimes Chinggis built on long-established methods but he took them further. This included the scale of his war-band (*keshik*) and the uses to which he put it. It also included the reorganization of his army into decimal, non-tribal units. The Xiongnu had done this a thousand years before, but Chinggis went a step further by applying de-tribalization even to units made up of his own Mongol tribesmen. He also, however, introduced a comprehensive imperial law code (the so-called Blue Book/*koke debter*) and what amounted to a manual of instructions for his successors as to how to govern his empire. As regards the ideological underpinnings of empire, the astonishing triumphs of Chinggis Khan convinced the Mongol elite that their great sky-god, Tengri, had given them the obligation to conquer the universe in his name.[17]

Civil institutions of government reached their highest point of development in the reign of Chinggis's grandson Mongke (r. 1251–9). Chinggis had divided his empire into appanages for his four sons (Jochi, Chaghatai, Ogodei, Tolui) but appointed Ogodei as his successor as Great Khan and overall ruler. The richest sedentary lands conquered by the Mongols (above all northern China and Iran) were not included in the appanages and remained mostly under central control. Ogodei built a capital in Karakorum and established permanent institutions of central government there. He also oversaw the perfection of an all-imperial postal system to facilitate rapid communication across the empire. Mongke carried the process further, establishing a regular administrative system to oversee the appanages, protect the sedentary population from plunder, and establish uniform and moderate taxes. One historian comments that, had Mongke's policies been continued, the Mongol Empire would have developed 'an extensive bureaucracy and centralisation of authority',[18] the path subsequently taken by the Ottoman and Moghul empires by the seventeenth century.

Given the unprecedented size of the Mongol Empire, one has to wonder whether any system of government possible in the pre-modern world could have held it together for long. But the absolute prerequisite for survival was to overcome the traditional inability of nomadic polities to create a stable system of succession. Chinggis Khan passed his undivided empire to Ogodei with the consent of his remaining sons but the empire's founder and world conqueror enjoyed an authority that none of his successors was likely to match. When Ogodei died, his wife Toregene became regent until a new great khan was recognized. This illustrates the prominent and public role the dynasty's women played in the Mongol Empire. Thanks partly to her efforts and partly to his own reputation, her son Guyuk succeeded to his father's throne, but when Guyuk died in 1248 after only two years in office the system of orderly succession collapsed.

In the end the throne went not to one of Guyuk's sons but instead to Mongke, the eldest son of Ogodei's brother Tolui. Mongke was victorious partly because of his undoubtedly superior qualities but above all because the 'Toluid camp' proved much abler at political manipulation than Ogodei's descendants and their supporters. The succession crisis was resolved without civil war but not without conspiracies, demotions and executions among members of the imperial family and their households. When Mongke himself died in 1259, four years of civil war followed between his brothers Khubilai and Arig-Boke. During this civil war the appanages ruled by the descendants of Jochi, Chaghatai and Ogodei threw off any allegiance to the Great Khan. Khubilai Khan, victorious in the civil war, concentrated on the conquest of China rather than on even attempting to reunite Chinggis's empire. Khubilai's brother Hulegu, who had conquered Iran, did recognize Khubilai's higher status as Great Khan but in practice the Chinese and Iranian branches of the Toluid line now acted as independent, albeit allied, states. In large part due to ferocious conflicts within the dynasty, the Iranian branch of the Chingissid dynasty died out in 1335. Khubilai's descendants were driven out of China in 1368 and replaced by a native Chinese dynasty, the Ming. In their case, however, the Black Death and other natural disasters beyond their control were more responsible for the end of Mongol rule than the dynasty's own failings.

The true heir of Chinggis Khan was Tamerlane (Timur the Lame), whom his biographer correctly describes as 'the last of the great nomad conquerors'. Tamerlane was born probably in 1336, in other words over a century after Chinggis's death. He was a member of a now Muslim but still nomadic clan of Mongol descent which dwelled in the region of Samarkand and had close ties to the largely Iranian sedentary population of the city and its neighbourhood. This was part of the former appanage of Chinggis's son Chaghatai, but by the time Tamerlane was born the Chaghatayids (i.e. Chaghatai's descendants) had lost most of their territories and all of their power. Nevertheless, the Chingissid name and bloodline still carried great prestige and the Great Khan's descendants were widely regarded as the only men with a legitimate right to rulership. Tamerlane conquered a vast swathe of Eurasia. He defeated Ottoman and Mamluk armies in Anatolia and the Levant, sacked Delhi and penetrated deep into European Russia to rout the army of the Golden Horde, which was the westernmost part of Chinggis's former empire and ruled by descendants of his eldest son, Jochi. Shortly before his death in 1405 Tamerlane was planning the conquest of China. Nevertheless, to acquire legitimacy he both married a Chingissid and until very late in his career claimed to be the mere chief servant of his sovereign, the Chaghatayid khan.[19]

Tamerlane's goals, methods and ideology were drawn from Chinggis's example and the Mongol heritage. Although illiterate, he had a highly intelligent and inquisitive mind, surrounded himself with scholars and was passionately interested in history. He also commissioned some of the finest examples of Islamic architecture. He combined 'a persona which deliberately echoed Genghis Khan with religious and cultural patronage based largely on Perso-Islamic norms'. Ibn Khaldun, who spent thirty-five days with him in 1400, recalled in his memoirs that 'Timur is one of the greatest and mightiest of kings ... he is highly intelligent and very perspicacious, addicted to debate and argumentation about what he knows and what he does not know.' Within a century of Tamerlane's death, his descendants had frittered away almost all his vast empire, not least through incessant succession struggles. On the other hand, they had overseen and encouraged the flowering of a superb literary and artistic culture, which combined Turkic, Persian and Islamic elements in a unique synthesis. Babur, the founder of India's Moghul dynasty, was the proud descendant of Tamerlane and Chinggis Khan and the product of this Turko-Persian-Islamic high culture.[20]

8

Imperial Civilization and Chinese Tradition: The Tang and Song Dynasties

From the abdication of the last Han emperor in 220 CE until the enthronement of the first Sui-dynasty emperor in 581 CE, China was divided into a number of dynastic states. The most fundamental split was between north and south. 'North' meant the grain-growing region around and north of the Yellow River. 'South' was defined as the rice-growing region around and south of the River Yangzi. During these three and a half centuries many peoples of Turkic and Mongolian nomadic origin settled in the northern region, and most of the dynasties that established states in the north were at least partly Turko-Mongolian in origin. They in general combined the aristocratic and military traditions of their ancestors with deep respect for Chinese high culture. In the eyes of southern elites these northern dynasties nevertheless remained semi-barbarian and southerners saw their region as the heartland of Chinese civilization and refinement.

Because the northern population was both bigger and more militarized the drive to reunify China was always likely to come from the north. Between 557 CE and 581 CE the so-called Northern Zhou dynasty went some way towards achieving this goal, only to be undermined by the untimely death of a competent young monarch whose heir was a child. In a pattern frequently repeated in the previous three centuries the 'prime minister', Yang Jian, usurped the throne and founded the Sui dynasty. Unlike long-established dynasties, a young hereditary monarchy was vulnerable to Machiavelli's warning that allowing the emergence of a prime minister was to invite him to seize the throne.[1]

Yang Jian's subsequent reunification of north and south was endangered by the catastrophic failure of attempts by his son, Yang Guang, to conquer Korea. There are parallels here with Napoleon's debacle in

Russia in 1812. Operating far beyond its core region and in unfamiliar terrain and climate, the Sui army was destroyed by an enemy who understood the theatre of operations and in its planning and operations exploited all its advantages. The enormous expense of these campaigns between 612 and 617 and the damage inflicted by defeat on Emperor Yang Guang's prestige undermined the Sui dynasty. Widespread revolts were followed by a civil war from which a senior official and general in the Sui regime, Li Yuan, emerged victorious. Li Yuan, known to posterity as Emperor Gaozu, established his Tang dynasty, which ruled China from 618 until 907 CE and is often seen as the greatest dynasty in China's imperial history. At its apogee in the mid-eighth century the Tang ruled a vast empire stretching far into Central Asia. Not for another thousand years when the Qing (Manchu) emperor Qianlong conquered the region now known as Xinjiang was a Chinese dynasty to match this feat, but the Tang era also witnessed great economic advances and a superb flowering of Chinese literary and artistic high culture.

The Tang dynasty – whose family name was Li – was of mixed Chinese and Turkic origin. It claimed descent from senior generals of the Han era and from the founder of Daoism, Laozi. The Li/Tang family was one of the leading aristocratic houses of north-western China in the sixth century CE, though not quite in the very top group. The first Tang empress came from the even more aristocratic Tou family, which had intermarried over the generations with many of the reigning dynasties of the northern region. The second Tang emperor, Taizong, was her son and embodied the mixed Chinese and Turkic traditions of the Li and Tou families.

An excellent calligrapher and poet, Taizong was also well educated in the Chinese classics and Chinese history. He was famous, too, for his skill at archery and horsemanship. Taizong consciously but also naturally embodied a range of identities. His poems – an important source of legitimacy among a Chinese elite which valued poetry above all other literary and artistic forms – combined the moral earnestness of northern Confucianism with southern poetic style and frequent allusions to southern scenery and nature. Taizong was bilingual in Chinese and Sarbi (a Mongolian dialect) and may well also have spoken Turkish. He exchanged refined poetic compositions with his Chinese advisers and swore oaths of blood-brotherhood with Turk warrior leaders. As the emperor of China from 626 CE, after defeating the Turk Empire he was proclaimed 'Heavenly Qaghan' of the steppe lands and peoples at a huge and carefully choreographed tribal assembly in 630. Chinese and Turko-Mongol conceptions of divinely appointed monarchy and universal empire had much in common, but Taizong also looked and played the part of an emperor whose power stretched across the known world. 'He had a truly imperial bearing and cut an intimidating and magnificent figure at court. Highly emotional and easily provoked, his face would turn purple with rage and strike fear into those around him. Much of his success in dealing with the Turks derived from his forceful personality and heroic presence.' In the world of the steppe nomads personal charisma and personal loyalties generally counted for more than allegiance to institutions or ideologies. Taizong matched both the image and the reality of a nomad warrior emperor.

In the years of civil war that preceded the final establishment of Tang rule Emperor Gaozu had recognized his eldest son by the empress as his heir. This was to follow Confucian norms about seniority and succession. Once the war was over Gaozu seems, however, to have reverted to the steppe and Turkic tradition of allowing his sons to compete for the throne. He did nothing to confirm his eldest son's claims. His main intervention was to make sure that the competition remained within the palace and the capital, refusing to allow any son to mobilize support across the empire. Since any competition that went beyond the palace's walls could easily have resulted in civil war and the collapse of the dynasty this was a wise precaution. Gaozu was already fifty-one when he rebelled against the Sui in 616 so the issue of succession could not be postponed. The new Tang dynasty had little legitimacy, which made a competent successor vital for its survival. In 626 the conflict was resolved: Prince Li Shimin, the future Emperor Taizong, ambushed and killed his two elder brothers at the gate of the palace. Maybe Gaozu believed Li Shimin's (possibly correct) claim that his brothers were plotting to poison him. In any case he accepted not just his sons' death but also his own subsequent replacement with seeming good grace. Already sixty-one, he may even have welcomed the comfortable and honourable retirement granted by Taizong. Certainly, he will have rejoiced that the dangerous question of succession had been resolved and that his dynasty's future rested in very competent hands.[2]

Taizong was beyond question one of history's greatest emperors. Formidable later Chinese monarchs such as Khubilai Khan of the Yuan (Mongol) dynasty, Qianlong of the Qing (Manchu) dynasty and Yongle of the Ming dynasty took him as their role model. A leading Western expert on Chinese military history calls him a 'genius' and 'one of the most celebrated military leaders in all of Chinese history', but he was also an extremely effective administrator and political leader. Taizong 'had an unquestioned flair for the dramatic, flamboyant gesture'. He was his regime's chief propagandist. In 628 many provinces were devastated by a plague of locusts. Bemoaning the miseries this plague was inflicting on his peasant subjects, the emperor very publicly devoured a meal of locusts: he proclaimed that 'the people regard grain as life itself, yet you devour it. Better that you devour my own lungs and bowels.' This and other stories about Taizong were widely publicized, sunk deep into popular legend and contributed to his fame and legitimacy.[3]

Taizong first established his name as an outstanding general during the civil war, during which his military genius played a decisive role in Tang victory. He commanded armies from the age of nineteen. The chaos caused by the civil war greatly weakened China and left it open to invasion by the Turks, whose armies came close to taking the capital, Changan, in 620 and 626. On the latter occasion the Turk Qaghan had to be bought off with a hefty ransom, which Taizong found deeply humiliating. Exploiting divisions within the Turk Empire over succession and the impact of drought on the nomads' horses, Taizong quickly turned the tables and within four years his counter-offensive brought down the Turk Empire and opened the way for Tang domination of the northern borderlands. Taizong's only failure as a general came in his first campaign in Korea in 645, when he was confounded by the same combination of distance, climate and logistics that had destroyed the last Sui emperor. When Taizong died in 648 he was preparing for a further massive offensive designed to bring Korea to its knees. Although there were strategic reasons for imposing Tang overlordship on Korea, considerations of personal prestige and dynastic legitimacy counted for more.

In comparison to the northern steppe frontier, Korea was of secondary importance and the massive invasions mounted by the Sui and the Tang were a misuse of resources. By contrast, Taizong's victories on the northern front opened the way to dramatic Chinese expansion far to the north-west. One outcome was the reopening of the Silk Route across Eurasia. The strategic consequences of Chinese expansion were more important even than the growth in external trade. Once established on the borders of Inner Asia the Chinese could gather intelligence about their nearer and further neighbours and pursue a shrewd but cheap divide-and-rule diplomacy designed to secure the empire's borders. Expansion brought Tang control over the mountain passes and fertile corridors that led from the steppe into China's heartland. Dominating these key strategic points both enhanced security and reduced its costs. Control over the vast grasslands north of the Yellow River allowed the Tang to create a network of 'ranches' where horses, camels and mules could be concentrated, bred and trained. In 725 CE these ranches are estimated to have contained 430,000 horses and 336,000 other animals. Since horses were the key to warfare on the northern steppe front, while camels and mules played a vital role in military transport, Tang control over these northern grasslands was of immense strategic importance.

In his campaigns Taizong tried to lure enemies to advance against him so that he could delay and wear down their armies by skilful use of fortifications and by sending light cavalry to raid their communications. Patience, caution and subtlety were combined with detailed planning of his army's operations, supplies and logistics. Among his greatest qualities were Taizong's ability as a grand strategist and planner of campaigns, together with his skill in choosing first-class generals as his lieutenants. Taizong had an acute sense of timing and psychology, and an instinctive feel for his enemy's vulnerabilities. Offensive and defensive tactics were equally legitimate in his eyes, and in most cases had to be combined if victory was to result. When the moment came to counter-attack, caution turned into fearsome and confident aggression. Taizong attacked ruthlessly, subsequently using his fast-moving cavalry to turn an enemy's defeat into rout. Taizong was a courageous soldier who knew how to lead by example on the battlefield but he was never reckless in the fashion of Alexander of Macedon. He was very much the product of a cool and realistic Chinese tradition of military thinking that stretched back to Sun Tzu and beyond. He understood that war was not a game of dice, still less a theatre for male egos. It must be analysed, calculated and planned. Above all, it must always serve realistic political goals. Unlike Alexander, Taizong had a strong sense of responsibility for the fate of his dynasty and the community over which he and they reigned.[4]

In the Tang era the great majority of civil officials were recruited on the basis of recommendations by ministers and provincial elites. An exam system also existed through which a small percentage of 'outsiders' could enter the civil service and rise to senior positions on merit. Taizong interviewed each candidate for the annual metropolitan examinations that formed the summit of this system. By so doing he came personally to know and subsequently employ some of his empire's brightest young officials. He also put much effort into personally reviewing the qualifications of candidates for provincial governorships and choosing between them himself. Above all, he showed excellent judgement in his choice of ministers, building a stable inner circle of trusted and wise advisers who served him loyally throughout his twenty-two-year reign. This group included men who had previously served his father and brothers, as well as his own long-term clients.

Taizong was devoted to his consort, the Wengde empress (born Zhangsun), who played no overt political role but who helped him to control his emotions. Her brother Zhangsun Wuzhi was the emperor's close and lifelong friend and probably his most influential adviser. Fang Xuanling, a highly intelligent and pragmatic veteran official who combined long experience in senior central and provincial posts with great skill as a drafter of official documents, remained at Taizong's side throughout his reign. Also crucial but from a very different background was General Li Zhi, a middle-ranking Sui official of humble origin who went over to the Tang during the civil war and proved himself not just an excellent general but also rock solid in his loyalty to Taizong and his dynasty. From 626 until 641 Li Zhi served as commander of the crucial Taiyuan region, which both protected the capital (i.e. Changan) from nomadic incursions from the north and controlled much the most formidable military forces in Changan's vicinity. Taizong once commented that Li Zhi was far more reliable than any Great Wall when it came to keeping the Turks at bay, but the control exercised over all military forces in and near the capital by this loyal general and his reliable network of lieutenants was also of vital importance at any moment of political tension or weakness. After fifteen years of service in Taiyuan, Li Zhi moved to Changan to serve as minister of war and the emperor's chief military adviser. In moments of rest the empire's two greatest soldiers enjoyed discussing past campaigns and the keys to success in warfare. As regards victory on the battlefield, they agreed that the crucial point was to constrain and trick your enemy into fighting at the time and on terrain that played to your strengths and his weaknesses.

A rather different group were the more orthodox Confucian scholar officials who staffed the upper ranks of the Censorate and the emperor's personal secretariat, the so-called College of Literary Studies. The Censorate was a branch of the Chinese government inherited from the Han dynasty which survived all subsequent dynastic changes until the end of Chinese imperial monarchy in 1911. In part it served as a procuracy, designed to ensure that not just officials but even the monarch adhered to Confucian ethical norms and the bureaucracy's rules and conventions. To an extent the censors' role vis-à-vis the emperor was that of a European court fool, licensed to tell truth to power, but Chinese censors' perception of their role was deeply serious, even puritanical. In a political order without public scrutiny or an autonomous legal system, the censors to some extent operated as representatives of Confucian elite opinion. Telling hard truths to an emperor could be dangerous but a monarch who turned a deaf ear or persecuted his censors lost legitimacy and encouraged rumours that his dynasty was losing the Mandate of Heaven.

The senior censor for most of Taizong's reign was Wei Zheng. In the first years of his reign Taizong was on his best behaviour and anxious to live down Confucian criticism that in killing his brothers and replacing his father he had acted in disgraceful fashion. The emperor lived frugally and often deferred to his ministers' advice. Inevitably, over the years Taizong grew fonder of luxuries and amusements, and more confident in his own opinions. He bore the criticisms of Wei Zheng and other censors about his growing arrogance and self-indulgence less willingly. The basic point is, however, that though he often ignored these criticisms, he never punished his censors for making them. In this he stands out from most imperial autocrats across the ages. Sometimes Taizong even corrected his behaviour – for example by not allowing his love of hunting to damage agriculture and farmers. Taizong was very concerned about his historical reputation and often pressed his official diarist, Zhu Suiliang, to change the Court Record (on which subsequent official dynastic histories were largely based) in order to enhance his future image. Zhu Suiliang was a gifted and famous scholar, calligrapher and historian. He did his best to limit such changes and persuade Taizong that the emperor's reputation would suffer if these attempts became public knowledge. The emperor did not always listen to this advice but he did not resent it. He trusted and admired Zhu Suiliang, who by the time of Taizong's death had become a very influential member of the emperor's inner group of advisers.[5]

Taizong is a rewarding monarch to study not just because of his importance and his fame. His voluminous writing allows some insight into his personality and a strong sense of how he understood the responsibilities, pitfalls and possibilities of the emperor's job. Even his poetry helps one to understand the emperor as well as the man. Many of his poems turn on the conflict between the luxuries and temptations that surround him and the demands on a Confucian monarch for duty, self-mastery and frugality. The appeal to all his senses of the harem, with its beautiful women, exotic perfumes, sensual dances and shimmering silks stands in contrast to the harsh discipline of military command on the steppe. In his poems as well as his prose writing he shows an acute awareness of the short lives of most Chinese dynasties and his strong ambition that the Tang should survive long enough to emulate the achievements of the Han. But some poems speak to the yearning of an ageing monarch for tranquillity and meaning amidst an exhausting work schedule: Taizong searches the stars and the moon at night, and writes that the peace which his empire has given to its subjects during his reign justifies the sacrifices that he has demanded both of them and himself.[6]

By far the most important of Taizong's writings for a historian of emperorship are the two long pieces he wrote shortly after coming to the throne in 626 and in the last months of his reign in either 647 or early 648. The title of the first document is usually translated into English as 'The Golden Mirror'. His second document, basically a last testament addressed to his heir and his ministers, is sometimes translated as 'Plan for an Emperor' (*Ti-Fan*). The ideas expressed in both these documents are repeated, and sometimes supplemented, by the collection gathered posthumously of Taizong's conversations with his key advisers.[7]

In 'The Golden Mirror' the newly enthroned young monarch strikes a Confucian tone. No doubt he was anxious to legitimize his rule in the eyes of his officials, though this does not mean that the ideals he expressed were necessarily insincere. The emperor, wrote Taizong, must cultivate virtue, wisdom and self-mastery. He must never sacrifice his people's well-being to his own desire for amusement, rest or luxury. Ordinary people were in dire need of mentors and teachers if they were to live orderly and virtuous lives. The emperor was the supreme teacher of his people. His greatest lesson was the model of wisdom, virtue and self-discipline his own behaviour provided. Among his greatest challenges was to find able and moral ministers: 'a wise monarch seeks out men of talent like drought-stricken sprouts longing for the rain'. He must not fear to appoint ministers who are cleverer than himself. Next came the imperative need to encourage honest advice and criticism: 'if he blocks the path for direct and straight speaking, those who act loyally towards him will be few, while if he opens the road for fawning flattery, those who will become obsequious and false will be many ... enlightened rulers ponder upon their own shortcomings, and improve their good qualities'. In line with Confucian tradition, Taizong wrote that if the emperor behaved badly – for instance disregarding or showing disrespect 'towards the deities and spirits, tempests and rains will occur in response to his violence'.[8]

Taizong was no innocent. By the time he ascended the throne aged twenty-six he already had seven years' experience of top military command, government and court politics. An emperor, he wrote, could not simply follow the moral code of a Confucian gentleman. Virtue alone would not guarantee the security of his empire's borders. The interests of the state and the community had to come first. Although moderation was vital, humanity had to be tempered by toughness and, where necessary, ferocity. 'If he restrains his emotions and acts generously and kindly, then the laws and regulations will not be put into effect.' Men in general and effective ministers in particular were not cast as black or white. One had to accept human frailties and choose the right man for the job. The emperor should not expect to be loved. Acting always in the public eye, he would inevitably be the butt of never-ending criticism. His successes would be ascribed to luck, his failures to stupidity or malice. Following the advice of one minister or group would invariably arouse the resentment and jealousy of others. If he was too easy-going with his officials, then his subjects would suffer. Listening to whispers from family and friends against his ministers was a recipe for injustice and inefficiency. But ministers could be treacherous and deceitful, so the emperor had to remain alert. In a very obvious allusion to recent events, Taizong noted that one bureaucratic vice that deserved severe punishment was ministers' opposition to the choice of an effective heir and their preference for a weakling whom they could control. Above all, the ruler must remember the fragility and uncertainty of human, and especially political, life: 'one who is flourishing at dawn may be filled with anxiety by evening'. He concluded this missive to his ministers with the words, 'we present this summary in rough outline just to set forth what preoccupies our heart' and represents 'our deepest concerns'.[9]

Between the time he wrote his first and second memorials Taizong gained twenty-one years of experience as a ruler. In the 640s he faced major setbacks. The failure of his invasion of Korea in 645 was his first significant defeat in war. Above all, the emperor faced that perennial nightmare of ageing monarchs, the question of the succession. Immediately after his accession, Taizong appointed his eldest son by his empress as his heir. This was a bow to Confucian principles and to Taizong's determination to present himself to the Chinese elite as a model monarch. By 640, however – at least if the official record is to be believed – the heir was showing strong signs of mental imbalance. Chinese courtiers were scandalized by his preference for all things Turkic, not to mention a homosexual affair in which he indulged. Facing his father's growing wrath, the crown prince bungled a rather pathetic plan to displace Taizong and was confined to gaol.

The emperor's attempts to find a mature and capable substitute heir among his older sons failed: at least in one case, a dangerous faction promptly formed around the prince whom Taizong was currently favouring. Finally, and with many misgivings, the emperor was prevailed upon by his most trusted advisers to appoint the fifteen-year-old Prince Li Chi as heir and to hand him over to trusted tutors so he could be prepared for his future role. With the empress dead, her brother Zhangsun Wuzhi was the man whose advice the emperor most trusted in this matter. Taizong himself played a significant role in Prince Li Chi's training: the heir was given rooms next to his father and attended councils and audiences by the emperor's side. Taizong tutored his son in the business of rulership in their private apartments but in public asked his opinions on the issues to be decided and praised his judgement. Nevertheless, right down to his death in 648 Taizong harboured deep fears as to whether his adolescent son had the personality, let alone maturity, to be an effective emperor and ensure the Tang dynasty's survival. This is the backdrop against which Taizong's second memorial, the 'Plan for an Emperor', has to be understood.

The 'Plan' was addressed by Taizong both to his son and to the heir's tutors and future ministers. The emperor wrote that 'when I was eighteen, I was still living among the people, and I knew everything true and false about their weariness and suffering. Yet when I came to occupy the

Great Position, and had to make decisions about the business of the world, I still made errors. How much more will be the case with the heir-apparent, who was born and has grown up in the depths of the palace. Since he has never experienced with his own eyes and ears the hardships of the common people, how can he be expected not to be arrogant and disposed to idleness. You will not fail to admonish him with the utmost strictness.' To his son, Taizong wrote that his youth and upbringing meant that he could not yet understand how to act as a ruler, manage his ministers, or grasp the realities of his subjects' everyday lives and needs. Above all, so much of a ruler's effectiveness depended on understanding human beings, but this was the hardest to acquire of all forms of knowledge and wisdom. 'This is something that really needs to be carefully considered.'[10]

Much of Taizong's 'Plan for an Emperor' repeated points he had made in his 'Golden Mirror' and in his conversations with his ministers. Above all, this meant the personal qualities and ideals essential to effective but moral rulership. But Taizong's testament was infused with a greater sense of urgency and pessimism as he recalled his own struggles and considered the enormous responsibilities that would soon confront his young heir. The emperor wrote that 'the empire is a sacred vessel' and the monarch was therefore responsible before Heaven for its survival. In one sense divine, the empire had also been created by the heroic efforts of monarchs stretching back to the legendary Yellow Emperor but including Li Chi's own father and grandfather. To them too the heir owed a deep sense of obligation. The imperial office must seem to his subjects to be like the great sacred mountain peaks, 'lofty and towering and unmoveable'. The monarch must exude a power so awesome that his commands would be heard and obeyed across a vast empire but he must also be benevolent and cherish his people. High ideals and great self-discipline must somehow be combined with realism and suppleness in his management of his ministers. We cannot know what impact these warnings and injunctions had on Taizong's still adolescent heir. It would be strange if he – and many other heirs to imperial thrones – was not at times overwhelmed by the immensity of his future responsibilities. Taizong was a devoted and highly conscientious mentor. Nevertheless, for his son a sense of inadequacy in the face of his future role must surely have been compounded by the fear that he could never live up to the awe-inspiring model of his father.

Alongside moral injunctions Taizong added down-to-earth practical advice born of long immersion in politics and administration. Even more dangerous than the flattery and ambitions of individuals was the power of factions. 'Forming cliques', warned Taizong, officials and courtiers 'support one another (in their evil ambitions), and there is no place so deep that they cannot penetrate it. Partisan and unable to grasp broader principles, they work with one another.' Taizong cited a saying of the ancients: 'it is not that knowing is difficult, only that putting it into practice is not easy'. Getting policies launched was far harder than devising them. Bringing them to a successful conclusion was hardest of all. But amidst all the endless frustrations of guiding men and institutions, the ruler must not waver, despair or take the easy and seductive path to self-indulgence, idleness or failure to do his duty. All human beings must follow the true Way if they were to lead a moral and worthwhile existence. The hardest Way of all was that of the emperor. Taizong took the responsibilities of emperorship no less seriously than did Marcus Aurelius. His values were no less hierarchical and, to use a modern term, elitist. On the whole both men fulfilled their duties as ruler superbly well. But Taizong's personality and ideals did not force him to repress or deny his emotions to anything like the same degree as was true of Marcus. He certainly enjoyed life more than did his Roman counterpart.[11]

When Taizong died in 649 he was succeeded without any opposition by the twenty-year-old Prince Li Chi, who adopted the regnal name of Emperor Gaozong. The new monarch had been well-trained for his job and was well-meaning, dutiful and by no means stupid. But he was far less forceful a personality than his father and he was physically frail. Understandably, in the first years of his reign the young emperor was overawed by Taizong's surviving group of veteran ministers, headed by Gaozong's maternal uncle Zhangsun Wuzhi. Subsequently he was dominated by his formidable consort, Wu Zetian. His infatuation with Wu had led Gaozong to push aside his empress, who though childless came from the very influential and aristocratic Wang family. This scandalized most of Gaozong's advisers, headed by his uncle. As a result, Zhangsun Wuzhi was forced into exile and then suicide in 654, and his sons were executed. These were to be the first of many deaths among those who opposed Wu's ambitions. So long as Gaozong lived, Wu's position depended on him. But the emperor's growing frailty after he suffered his first stroke in 660 increased his dependence on his wife. As Wu's power grew, so did the circle of ambitious and often very able courtiers and officials who joined her camp. After Gaozong's death in 683 she dominated Tang government and politics, at first from behind her son's throne but from 690 explicitly as sovereign empress and founder of a new reigning dynasty, the Zhou. For the next fifteen years she reigned as the only sovereign empress in Chinese history.

All the pre-modern dynasties and cultures that are described in this book were misogynist. They all gave men a higher status than women. Male rulers' sexual appetites were allowed almost free rein. Even in monogamous Christian dynasties a monarch's mistresses and illegitimate children were not just tolerated but publicly honoured. So long as a male ruler's sexual appetites did not result in gross mismanagement of policy and patronage they were accepted. The only truly mortal sin for a monarch was to allow his infatuation for a mistress to persuade him to alter the order of succession. Female sexual appetites by contrast were heavily constrained, denounced and feared. Except in very limited and specific circumstances (above all when a mother acted as regent for her child-son) any female wielding power was almost certain to be condemned. Almost always such denunciations included lurid and usually false accusations of sexual depravity. Chinese Confucian scholar-officials were an extreme example of misogyny. They wrote most of the history books. Inevitably, the picture they painted of Wu Zetian was entirely black and lurid. That has to be borne constantly in mind when investigating Wu's life and reign, and most of all where her sexuality is concerned.

Nevertheless, it would be a huge mistake to ignore this side of Wu's personality. To do so detracts from understanding a fascinating individual and distorts the truth as regards her rise to power. Even more important, it ignores a key element in the dynamics of imperial monarchy. The basic point is simple. Sexual allure seldom had any connection to the positions held by male monarchs and ministers or the power they exercised. This was true of some influential women too. Above all, this meant the monarch's sisters, daughters and, above all, his mother. A small minority of much-loved former governesses also became recipients of extraordinary favour and patronage. In the great majority of cases, however, it was precisely sexual allure that won women favour, patronage and power in imperial monarchies. The power even of a

Christian queen was greatly strengthened if she had a sexual and emotional hold on her husband. In a few cases concubines and mistresses were even able to persuade their royal lover to make their son his heir, thereby attaining the position of empress-mother, the highest status open to a woman in almost all dynastic courts. Wu Zetian was one of the most spectacular examples of this phenomenon.

Wu Zetian 'was exceptionally gifted, with a natural genius for politics and brilliantly adept at manipulating the power structure at court. Her phenomenal rise to power resulted from her sharp intelligence, determination and excellent judgement of men, combined with ruthlessness, unscrupulousness and political opportunism.' The empress was a totally extraordinary and exceptional individual but to understand her life one does also need to understand the culture of the Tang-era elite to which she belonged. The non-Chinese, initially nomadic element in that elite's make-up had a big influence on the freedoms and public role enjoyed by women, which stood in stark contrast to the Confucian ideal of subordinating females wholly to males and constricting them to the inner family world. Tang aristocratic women moved comfortably in mixed society and played an overt role in court politics. They even competed in polo matches and they enjoyed a significant degree of sexual freedom too, much to the chagrin of Confucian scholars.[12]

Wu was born in 624. Her father, Wu Shiyue, was a man of middling merchant origin who was a trusted client of the founder of the Tang dynasty, Gaozu, from the years when the future emperor was still serving the Sui. His lifelong, loyal and effective service to Gaozu brought him in time a post as a senior minister in the Tang government, wealth and a title, Duke of Ying. Wu Shiyue then married into the Yang family, a collateral branch of the former Sui reigning dynasty. Early Tang-era society was dominated by the old aristocratic families of northern China, but men who rose to the top of the Tang government and army merged into this elite, often through marriage. Inevitably the process was not without friction: Wu herself was initially looked down on by members of the great aristocratic families as a merchant's daughter. She did not forget these slights and subsequently made some of these aristocrats pay dearly for their snubs. Wu had no brothers, so her doting mother gave her daughters an excellent education in poetry, history and the Buddhist religion. Combined with great beauty and intelligence, these made her a very attractive young woman. For this reason she was taken into Emperor Taizong's household as a junior consort in 637, aged thirteen. Although she made no great impact on Taizong, who liked more demure women, her moment came when the fifteen-year-old Prince Li Chi took up quarters next to his father from 645 to train for his future role as monarch. Four years younger than Wu, Prince Li Chi fell for her totally and remained both emotionally and sexually dependent on her for the rest of his life. Their last child, the Taiping princess, was born in 664, when Wu was already forty years old. Although at times Gaozong (i.e. the former Prince Li Chi) bridled at his wife's cruel treatment of anyone who stood in her way, the emperor could never withstand his wife's powerful and magnetic personality, let alone contemplate the idea of living without her.

When Gaozong died in 683 Empress Wu was not yet all-powerful at court and in the upper reaches of government. Had her eldest son, the able and popular Crown Prince Li Hung, not died prematurely in 675 it is likely she would have had to yield her place to him. Her third son, Prince Li Xian, who adopted the regnal name of Emperor Zhongzong, was far less of an obstacle. There is in fact some dispute as to whether Zhongzong really was the son of Gaozong and Wu. During her pregnancies Gaozong took her elder sister, the so-called Lady of Han, as a secondary consort and Zhongzong may actually have been her son. Probably this mattered far less to Empress Wu than the fact that the new emperor was wholly in thrall to his wife, who came from the powerful Wei aristocratic house. Zhongzong's first act as emperor was to make his father-in-law prime minister and shower favours on his wife's relations. This infuriated not just Empress Wu but also other key ministers and she had no difficulty in putting together a coalition that forced Zhongzong off the throne after two months, replacing him with Wu's youngest son, Prince Li Dan, who took the regnal title of Ruizong.

Li Dan had no political experience or ambition, and was totally dependent on his mother, who had always regarded him as her favourite son. Initially the new emperor and his mother were on good terms but as opposition inevitably mounted to her increasingly evident ambition to take the throne, Wu's suspicion of Ruizong grew. Although he survived her reign under what amounted to dignified house arrest, his wife and his senior consort (the mother of the future Emperor Xuanzong) were both murdered on trumped-up charges. So were hundreds of members of the Tang dynasty from the family's collateral branches. It says something about the relative weakness of dynastic legitimacy in Chinese history that Wu's usurpation of the throne from her son and her founding of a new dynasty was accepted without greater opposition within the elite. No doubt the executions and torture directed against suspected enemies played a major role in this quiescence, but they were not its sole cause. As in Rome, albeit not to the same extent, dynasties were small against the backdrop of the imperial state, its myths and its traditions.

When Gaozong died in 683 Empress Wu was fifty-nine years old. Nevertheless, she took several lovers during her widowhood, at least one of whom she inherited from her husband's aunt. Later Confucian critics denounced all these lovers as young men who fed the empress's lusts and no doubt some were no more than sexual partners. But some of those described in these terms, especially the architect Xue Huaiyi, were clearly intelligent and amusing companions as well as lovers. No one need doubt Wu's strong sexual appetites or the power of her allure. She was famous for her skilful use of cosmetics and for long retaining her beauty. But Wu was always deeply interested and credulous about sorcery and the supernatural. Although initially she showed little favour to Daoism, which was closely linked by tradition to the Tang dynasty, as she aged and became more scared of impending death she grew ever more disposed to a religion which abounded in prophecies, mysticism, magic and recipes for immortality. One esoteric element in the Daoist religion of nature was the belief that ageing in females was kept in check by male sperm.

The sexual exploits of an imperial grandmother against a background of sorcery, torture and executions takes us deep into the world of *Game of Thrones*. This was undoubtedly part of the reality of Wu's court (and of many other imperial courts too). But it is important to remember that Wu's regime also patronized and appreciated the exquisite Chinese artistic and literary culture of the era. As important, though she destroyed many lives in her pursuit of power, the struggle and the victims all came from the small world of the court. Not only was the vast majority of the population untouched but so was the machinery of government and its ability to react effectively to crises. Her regime responded decisively and successfully to threats from Tibet in the west and the Khitan nomads in the north. Wu selected first-class generals to command her armies. Suspicious of the aristocratic clans that had dominated Tang government, she also extended the civil-exam system in order to draw on a wider pool of talent and one whose loyalty to her could be trusted. Holders of higher exam degrees made up 23 per cent of Taizong's senior ministers and 40 per cent of those who served Empress Wu. The able young officials she promoted played a big role in the long reign of her grandson Emperor Xuanzong. Among her chief ministers was Di Renjie, to whose fight against nepotism and corruption in government she gave full support, despite his loyalty to the Tang dynasty. Di Renjie has a special fame in the West as the hero of the detective stories of Robert van Gulik, the Sinologist who also served for many years as Dutch ambassador in Beijing. Van Gulik's depiction of 'Judge Dee' as a cultured, incorruptible and efficient public servant is of course fictional but it is nevertheless an accurate picture of much of the government elite moulded and promoted by Empress Wu.[13]

One very significant aspect of Wu's rule was the strong support she gave to Buddhism. By the 690s the Buddhist religion had been making ever greater inroads into Chinese society and culture for 500 years. Its powerful belief system, rituals and artistic culture satisfied emotional, spiritual and intellectual needs that Confucianism could never reach. Like early Christianity, it also attracted groups that the existing order and ideological regime subordinated, and especially women. Although Buddhism certainly did not preach equality of the sexes, it did offer women greater freedom and respect than Islam or Christianity, let alone Confucianism. Wu had been immersed in Buddhist religion and culture since childhood. By the time she set up her dynasty in 690, Buddhism had become an extremely powerful force in Chinese society with millions of disciples and great wealth. Wu befriended famous Buddhist monks, built scores of temples, statues and pagodas, and gave generous gifts to existing Buddhist institutions. Her propagandists linked Wu to Buddhist texts and 'saints', thereby enhancing her legitimacy. One such 'saint' was Emperor Ashoka: invoking his memory, Empress Wu gave great prominence in her official title to her role as a Buddhist universal monarch (*chakravartin*). But her propaganda machine also mined Daoist and Confucian traditions in order to glorify the empress and link her to many powerful elements in Chinese historical memory and the Chinese belief system.

For many years Empress Wu pondered how to establish her new 'Zhou' dynasty. The key problem was that this would entail disinheriting her sons in favour of her Wu nephews. Perhaps if one of her nephews had been a sufficiently strong and impressive personality then Wu Zetian would have appointed him her heir. But none of them were and their arrogance won them many enemies. Wu's reluctance to appoint them her heirs was probably also owed to deeper-rooted religious concerns. For all her Buddhist beliefs, Wu was a product too of the Confucian system of values and rituals. The ageing empress was deeply concerned with her place in the afterlife, which was tied closely to her position in her family's ancestral temple. Sacrificial offerings to ancestors could only be made by sons and grandsons. If a nephew inherited her throne, there would be no one to make sacrifices at her tomb or tend to her spirit in the afterlife. In 698 she accepted chief minister Di Renjie's proposal to recall her son, the former emperor Zhongzong, from fourteen years of exile and subsequently to reappoint him as her heir.[14]

By 1705 the eighty-year-old Wu was visibly losing her ability to run affairs. A coup in the name of the former emperor Zhongzong removed her from power. She was allowed to go into comfortable retirement and when she died ten months later her dying wish to be buried alongside her husband, Gaozong, was honoured. Even more remarkably, a reconciliation of sorts occurred between some of her Wu nephews and the Tang dynasty. The power behind Zhongzong's regime was not the lacklustre emperor but his wife, Empress Wei. She was apparently the mistress of Empress Wu's nephew Wu Sansi. Her only surviving child, the Anle princess, was married to Wu Sansi's son. Empress Wu's former female private secretary, Shangkuan Wanerh, became in theory a consort of Emperor Zhongzong but in practice she managed the examinations for elite civil-service candidates on Empress Wei's behalf. Nevertheless, although Emperor Zhongzong was a cipher, being able to capture him and use his name was vital for his wife, daughter and 'consort'. Serious consideration was given to appointing Princess Anle as her father's heir, but it was decided that this remained impossible given Chinese tradition and values. Instead, when Zhongzong died suddenly in 710 Empress Wei attempted to install his youngest son, still too young to rule, as his successor in order to preserve her power. Her plans were destroyed by a coup plotted by Empress Wu's daughter, the Taiping princess, which resulted in the murder of Empress Wei, the Anle princess and Shangkuan Wanerh, and the reinstatement of former emperor Ruizong, Wu's youngest son and the Taiping princess's brother.

Ruizong was as much of a cipher as his brother Zhongzong and longed to abdicate and retire to a peaceful life. Terrified by a comet which he interpreted as a warning from Heaven, he insisted on doing this in 711. He was succeeded by his third son, Prince Li Lungchi, the future Emperor Xuanzong, whose mother had been killed on Empress Wu's orders. Lungchi had played a vital, if subordinate, role in the coup that overthrew the Empress Wei because he had many friends and clients in the Guards units, whose role in palace coups was always vital. The Taiping princess realized that unless she could speedily remove the young and able Xuanzong her hold on power was doomed. She strove to turn the new emperor's half-brothers against him without success. In a rare but admirable show of solidarity, all his half-brothers united behind Xuanzong as the best candidate to defend their common cause, though Prince Li Chengchi actually had a better claim to the throne since he was Ruizong's son by his empress. Perhaps Prince Li Chengchi felt that a quiet life as a senior prince was a better option than ruling China. Surprisingly in the context of dynastic politics, since in the years to come Li Chengchi could very easily have been regarded as a threat by Xuanzong given his superior claims to the throne, the two half-brothers remained on the closest and most trusting terms for the rest of their lives.

With time running against her the Taiping princess attempted a preemptive coup in 713. She had inherited both her mother's intelligence and much of her network. Had she been a man the coup might well have succeeded. But even at the apogee of female power a princess could not mingle with the Guards units nor actually lead assassination squads. The Taiping princess had to delegate these roles and delegation increased the risks of betrayal. In the event her plot was betrayed and she was allowed to die by 'honourable' suicide. An extraordinary half-century of female dominance of Chinese government and politics thereby came to an end.

Emperor Xuanzong's reign lasted for forty-five years. In these decades the Tang empire reached its furthest extent. In terms both of raw power and the spell cast by Tang high culture these were the dynasty's years of greatest glory. Tang China became the creator and centre of an East Asian cultural zone, rooted in Confucian beliefs, the Chinese variant of Buddhism, the Chinese written script and the enormous prestige of Tang literary and artistic refinement. Xuanzong's court made an impact throughout the East Asian region just as Louis XIV's Versailles was later to do across Europe. Xuanzong himself was an impressive figure: he was a skilled musician, a poet, a calligrapher, and a patron of many outstanding artists and writers. He was also a successful political leader. The emperor chose competent and forceful ministers who, with his unwavering support, solved key challenges such as the reform of the crucial land-tax system and the threatened breakdown of the network for feeding and supplying the huge population of the empire's capital city, Changan. Xuanzong worked hard to manage his ministers and he did so patiently and on the whole humanely, without resorting to excessive violence: he adjudicated their conflicts, flattered their egos and balanced them off against each other, allowing none of them unchecked power and reserving for himself the overall direction of policy and top-level appointments.

If only Xuanzong had died in 740 he would have gone down in history as one of China's most admired emperors. Instead he lived for another sixteen years and the familiar story of a tired and ageing monarch played out. Managing competing ministers and complex administrative issues for thirty years had taken its toll. The emperor increasingly withdrew from politics and concentrated on his inner life and religious questions. In his late fifties he became infatuated by Yang Yuhuan, the beautiful wife of one of his sons, took her into his own harem and catered to her whims. The story of the ageing male who seeks the elixir of youth in the arms of a young woman and makes a fool of himself in the process is familiar. Men in powerful positions have historically used this power to satisfy their sexual and emotional urges. Emperor Xuanzong's behaviour followed a familiar human pattern but had huge consequences, contributing to the near destruction of one of history's greatest empires.

A minor whim of the emperor was having fresh lychees delivered to his beloved by special mounted couriers from the furthest south-eastern corner of the empire. More serious were her interventions in top-level patronage and appointments. The situation cried out for a trusted and experienced heir who would take over most of the burdens of government, but this seldom happened in China. The rules of succession were too uncertain, harem politics and rivalries intervened, and crown princes were very often not trusted by their fathers. Inevitably the emperor's 'friends' and clients did their utmost to make sure that he clung to the levers of power and patronage. Perhaps too, the Confucian stress on filial piety made it harder for a son to exercise effective power while his father reigned.

As a result of Xuanzong's withdrawal, factional politics escalated during the last years of his reign. Had this simply entailed a temporary loss of the government's focus and effectiveness matters would not have been too dire. Unfortunately, the battle between court factions compromised the monarchy's control over its military commanders, leading to the revolt of its most senior general, An Lushan, in 755. To any historian of empire the pattern taken by events is familiar. The military logic of protecting far-flung borders and deploying cavalry armies capable of operating deep into steppe territory necessitated the formation of a professional army with large contingents of non-Chinese mounted tribesmen in its ranks. Great autonomous power had to be granted to commanders operating so far from the capital. In the first half of the eighth century the Tang army evolved in this direction and in military terms proved formidably effective. The most senior and successful Tang general by mid-century was An Lushan, a man of partly Turkic-nomad and partly Sogdian origin.

An Lushan was allowed to extend his control to a dangerous degree over most of the empire's armies and horse ranches in the 740s and early 750s. With Xuanzong less involved in political management, power from 736 to 752 was exercised in an increasingly unchecked manner by Li Linfu, a competent administrator and a junior member of the Tang royal lineage. Inevitably, Li Linfu's rivals hated and envied the power and patronage possessed by him and his clients. Faced by many enemies, Li Linfu was happy to allow An Lushan to extend his control over the empire's armies: the general was Li Linfu's most trusted military client and was fully loyal to his patron. An Lushan did also have some sense of loyalty to Emperor Xuanzong. Unfortunately, as was the norm in steppe culture, An Lushan's allegiance was to individuals, not to dynasties, let alone to institutions such as the Tang state or empire. When Li Linfu died in 752, rival factions attacked his network of clients. The leader of this attack was the new chief minister, Yang Guozhong, the cousin of Xuanzong's beloved young consort. Since the aged emperor seemed unable to protect him and could not live much longer, An Lushan decided to strike first while his power base was still intact. Although in the end the Tang regime survived his rebellion, it never recovered anything approaching its previous power. In typical imperial fashion, as the centre weakened it lost control over many of its provinces, beginning with the periphery but spreading to core regions too. Local warlords and elites took over, often recognizing Tang sovereignty but hanging on to local revenues for themselves and denying the emperor any jurisdiction in their territories. One immediate result of greater weakness was Chinese withdrawal from Inner Asia and the north-western borderlands, which thereby became irrevocably part of the Islamic world.[15]

After generations of decline, the Tang dynasty finally fell in 907 CE. Not until 960 was part of the core of the Tang Empire reunited under the Song dynasty. The Tang and Song regimes are always seen as glorious episodes in the history of Chinese Empire. This interpretation is mostly justified. The two dynasties ruled over the same core region, which was inhabited by people we today call Chinese. Their courts sustained a common, superb Chinese high culture. Both dynasties saw themselves as heirs of an imperial tradition stretching back to the Yellow Emperor and legitimized by Confucian ideals. They also shared many institutions inherited from the Han era, of which the emperorship was the capstone. Nevertheless, in many respects the empires they ran were very different. Most obviously, the Song Empire was far smaller, having lost all its northern borderlands and their non-Chinese population. As always, China's scale confounds easy comparisons. The Song Empire may in territorial terms have been small by Tang standards but it contained one-third of the world's population.[16]

Nevertheless, though vast by European standards, the Song Empire was only one-quarter the size of today's People's Republic of China. If one applied the usual definition of empire supported by most contemporary Western historians, one might well conclude that the Song polity was not so much an empire as a Chinese proto-nation. In the Song era there were signs that an ethno-national Chinese identity was growing among the new upper class formed by the now much more extensive civil-service exam system and the streamlined, 'neo-Confucian' values on which it was based. One element in this national consciousness was the strong conviction that the sixteen ethnic Chinese prefectures in the north-east which the semi-nomadic Khitan Empire had annexed between 906 and 960 belonged 'naturally' to the Chinese state and community and must therefore be reconquered. This became a top priority – even sometimes an obsession – for Song monarchs and ministers.[17]

The Tang regime had been dominated at least in its first centuries by a hereditary aristocracy rooted in the northern and north-western regions and their great capital cities, Luoyang and Changan. Historically, the Tang were not even quite in the very top rank of this aristocratic elite, which may be an additional reason why their dynasty could be rather easily displaced by Empress Wu Zetian. The old aristocratic families were destroyed in the ninth century, however, amidst the anarchy unleashed by the decline and fall of the Tang and a new elite was formed in the Song era.[18]

This new 'bureaucratic' elite that emerged in the first 150 years of Song rule (the so-called Northern Song era) was drawn from across the empire and many of its members had started their careers by passing the highest levels of the civil-service examination system. By 1100 CE roughly 200,000 students were enrolled in schools whose curricula were designed to prepare young men for the triennial civil-service exams. Every three years some 80,000 candidates took these exams. In the Tang era, Buddhism and Daoism had challenged Confucianist doctrines as the core ideology and value system of the state and the elites. Under the Song, Confucian intellectuals fought back, refining their doctrines, absorbing some elements of the two rival religions but strongly reasserting Confucianism's central role as the source of the rational and ethical principles on which the community and the state rested. The neo-Confucian school's two founding fathers were Cheng Yi (1033–1107) and Zhu Xi (1130–1200). For that reason some historians call neo-Confucianism 'Cheng-Zhu learning'. Although this was becoming the unchallengeable ideological basis of the political and social order by the last century of Song rule, the process was only completed under the next native Chinese dynasty, the Ming, during the fifteenth century. Passing the exams became the greatest source of status and respect for members of the Chinese elite and their extended families. The exam system and the neo-Confucian ideology and high culture it promoted became a very powerful force for consolidating the Chinese elite and linking it to the imperial political order. A loose comparison might be made with the role of the public schools and Oxbridge in nineteenth- and twentieth-century Britain.[19]

For the Northern Song monarchs the emergence of this new order was a double-edged sword. On the one hand, the demise of the Tang-era aristocracy raised the dynasty far above all other groups in society. In principle all power derived from the monarch and was executed by civil servants whose careers he controlled. The bureaucracy enabled the emperor's writ to run across a large empire. Its institutions, ideology and prestige were of vital importance in holding his empire together. In a sense the emperor was not just the chief executive officer but also the high priest of a powerful corporation whose core belief was that a united imperial China was the only legitimate form of statehood and that the monarchy was its essential capstone. But although ideal in principle as a bastion of imperial union and monarchical rule, the bureaucratic machine was often in practice a nightmare for an emperor to manage.

The Song bureaucracy was more sophisticated than any other on earth at that time. Under the early Song there were perhaps 13,000 professional, civilian officials, roughly the same number as in the much larger Tang Empire at the height of its power. By 1112 there were 43,000 officials. The Song state was attempting to do things beyond the imagination, let alone the capacity, of any European government. A standing, professional army of one million men needed to be paid, supplied and equipped. Managing the empire's waterways created enormous organizational and technological challenges. When the Yellow River burst its banks in 1048 maybe 20 per cent of the population of the huge Hebei region died or were displaced and this was only one of many such disasters in the Song era. Planning and carrying out the engineering works required to cope with such challenges required great professional skill, organization and expertise. Under the Song the Chinese economy developed to a level seen nowhere else on earth until late eighteenth-century Britain. The Song state successfully created a sophisticated tax machine to tap this non-agricultural wealth. Coming to the study of Song China can be confusing. On the one hand one confronts a world which seems all the more distant for being from an alien culture as well as a past era. On the other hand, aspects of Song society, government and emperorship seem surprisingly modern.[20]

The job of being an emperor had changed in significant ways from the Tang era. In the Introduction to this book I explained the four identities of an emperor. He was a human being, a leader, a hereditary monarch and the ruler of an empire. With the Song, for the first time in this book we encounter leaders who can in some real sense be called chief executive officers – in other words the heads of large and complex bureaucratic organizations, staffed by professional officials chosen by examination and in principle promoted according to strict impersonal criteria. Of course, there were huge differences between a Song emperor and a modern president, let alone the head of a private corporation. Even comparisons with modern European emperors have their difficulties. Unlike the German and Austrian emperors in the late nineteenth century, the Song monarch was not constrained by constitutions or parliaments. Even so, to run large and complex bureaucracies of this sort means experiencing some specific challenges. As leader of the Song state the emperor faced difficulties which were not encountered by any European monarch until the eighteenth century – and even then seldom on a Chinese scale.

The story of how Northern Song emperors managed their government machine provides a foretaste of how European emperors reacted when faced with similar challenges in the nineteenth century. In both cases emperors found the bureaucratic apparatus extremely hard to direct, control and manage. This caused them great frustration and absorbed a good deal of their time and energy. Emperors usually entrusted coordination of government policy to a chief minister, reserving for themselves the final say as regards decisions they considered crucial. Above all, that meant foreign policy and questions of war and peace. Appointing and dismissing a prime minister and usually some other top ministers remained a royal prerogative and represented some degree of control over a government's overall policy line. Song emperors, like nineteenth-century European monarchs, continued to fulfil many ceremonial roles and legitimizing rituals. At moments of crisis they were forced to play a more prominent and active role than was otherwise the case, taking overall and final responsibility as supreme crisis managers. In 1940 this happened even to the well-established constitutional monarchs of Belgium and Norway, Leopold III and Haakon VII. As the Song dynasty entered the near terminal crisis of 1125–7 it happened to Emperor Huizong.

Inevitably, running the Song government had its own specific challenges. The bureaucracy drowned in paper and so did the emperor. This was partly because of the recent spread of printing but also because of the convoluted procedures of the official machine. Decision-making required multiple signatures, with documents shuffling to and fro between offices. Even middle-ranking bureaucrats could often bring matters to a halt if they refused to sign documents which, so they claimed, violated bureaucratic norms and principles. A bureaucratic machine set up with multiple checks and balances invited potential paralysis. Since, for all its high moral rhetoric, the bureaucracy was riven by patron–client networks, it was inevitable that their struggle for power and patronage included many opportunities for sabotage. Built into the system there was also the 'censorate', whose remonstrance officers existed to hold ministers and even the emperor to account before elite public opinion if they infringed Confucian ideals. Used as a weapon in factional struggles, the censorate had the potential to bring government to a halt. Among the world's bureaucracies, Confucian state officials had an exceptionally high sense of esprit de corps, mission and status. They were imbued with an almost religious ideology that gave officialdom the duty to make not just subjects but also emperors behave according to correct ethical principles. They believed that failure to do this would result in disharmony in the natural order of the cosmos and catastrophe on earth. Running a government machine that sees itself as a semi-priesthood has special frustrations. Differences in policy were soon transformed into mutual denunciations for unethical principles and incorrect thoughts, couched in high-flown and didactic Confucian rhetoric.

The emperor's life was made even harder by the deep ideological and policy rift within the bureaucracy caused by the introduction of the so-called 'New Policies' in 1069. This programme called for radical state intervention in the economy and society in order to foster economic growth, the people's welfare and the state's tax revenues. Opponents of the programme denounced it as not just unworkable and a source of corruption but also as a betrayal of Confucian principles and a reversion to the reviled Legalist policies of the Qin regime and the First Emperor. Political conflict revolving around the proper role of the state in the economy and society has very modern echoes. Powerful vested interests supported the idea of the minimalist state both then and now. The sixth emperor of the Song dynasty, Shenzong (r. 1067–85), backed the New Policies instituted in 1069 but wished to keep their opponents within his circle of advisers in order to gain an all-round perspective on policy, thereby improving the quality of decision-making. Bitter factional hatreds wrecked his efforts. To force the New Policies through the bureaucracy he had to set up what was in many ways a parallel, 'emergency' set of institutions headed by the so-called Finance Planning Commission. He was also forced to emasculate the censorate. Shenzong's two sons, Zhezong (r. 1085–1100) and Huizong (r. 1100–25/6), followed their father's policy partly out of filial piety but also as a means to increase revenue in order to sustain the state's military power and its ability some day to regain from the Khitans the lost sixteen prefectures in the north-east.[21] The emperors' support ensured that supporters of the New Policies remained in power, but the government machine in the end proved unable to deliver either the economic or the social welfare benefits the reformers had promised.

Emperor Huizong came to the throne unexpectedly in 1100 as a result of the sudden death without heirs of his half-brother, Zhezong, aged only twenty-three. We know rather more about him than about other Song emperors, but far less than is the case with some Roman emperors and all the emperors who reigned from the sixteenth century and are the focus of later chapters in this book. We even know significantly more about Tang Taizong. The Song dynasty barred all younger sons of emperors from involvement in politics, government or military affairs and encouraged them to become pillars of Chinese arts and high culture. Even heirs to the throne had no military training or experience. There is evidence that the seventeen-year-old Huizong was very unhappy at suddenly being dragged from the world of culture and placed on the throne. When Emperor Zhezong died, Huizong was in principle second in the line of succession but his elder half-brother had eye problems, potentially a major disadvantage for a man fated to head a bureaucratic apparatus so obsessed with written documents. The final decision between the two half-brothers was made by the dowager empress, the dynasty's senior matriarch. Even misogynist China recognized the rights of motherhood and seniority in such a matter. But she sat down with the senior ministers to discuss the strengths and weaknesses of the two candidates in sensible and down-to-earth fashion. In this case too, Song China seems a strange mixture of the modern and familiar in some respects – and deeply ancient and alien in others.

In Chinese elite circles calligraphy was regarded as an art form displaying an individual's learning and cultivation but also providing insights into his character and conduct, so many emperors were good amateur calligraphers. Huizong was the most elegant and famous imperial calligrapher of all, with a unique style of writing that is still widely admired today. Far less common was the emperor's skill as a painter. He is the only emperor to stand in the first rank of Chinese artists. Huizong was a generous and subtle patron of the arts, an avid collector of antiquities, and a passionate planner of buildings and gardens. The emperor was much attached to Daoism, with its belief in the links between Heaven, humans and the natural order: his garden-park was not just a hobby and a source of aesthetic pleasure but also reflected his religious beliefs and sensitivities. After the catastrophic defeat in the 1125–7 war against the Jurchens – a mostly pastoralist people who lived in Manchuria and were formidable cavalrymen – the emperor was blamed by Confucian scholars for neglecting state business in favour of his expensive and time-consuming aesthetic pursuits. This was mostly unfair. Huizong was by no means an earlier Chinese version of Ludwig II of Bavaria – Richard Wagner's patron and an avid builder of Romantic castles who was finally declared insane by his ministers. He performed both his ritual and governmental duties conscientiously. It is true that Huizong placed great faith in his chief minister, Cai Jing, and kept him in office for most of his reign, but there is no reason to believe that matters would have gone better if the emperor had attempted to play a more autocratic role.

The disaster that destroyed the Northern Song regime actually occurred because Huizong in 1121–5 overruled the more cautious older generation of advisers and supported the younger 'war party' in entering into an alliance with the Jurchens to destroy the Khitan Empire and fulfil the Chinese dream of recovering the sixteen lost prefectures. In almost any empire, such fundamental military and foreign policy decisions ultimately lay with the monarch. To some Song ministers the emergence of a powerful Jurchen potential ally at the back of China's Khitan rivals seemed providential. Huizong's policy was based on the old principle that the enemy of my enemy is my friend, but it miscued horribly. The Song army proved ineffective and when the Jurchen saw its weakness, after crushing the Khitans they invaded and conquered all Song territory north of the Yangzi. Huizong compounded his initial mistake of choosing an adventurous military policy by putting his faith in poor generals and failing to act decisively when defeat and crisis required a fundamental choice between last-ditch defence or peace at any price. The emperor had no military education or insight. Neither by temperament, training nor experience was he equipped to manage a crisis. Unnerved and exhausted by his failings and the disaster to which they had contributed, he was easily persuaded to abdicate in the midst of the crisis by advisers weary of his mistakes and in need of a scapegoat.[22]

One undoubted lesson of the debacle was that the Song got a poor return for the money they lavished on defence: in the early twelfth century they spent over four-fifths of what must surely have been the biggest budget of any government of that era on the army. To some extent the Song problem with their army was that of the Tang in reverse. Memories of An Lushan's rebellion had burned deep into Chinese consciousness. The Song dynasty had itself come to power through a military coup and its rulers were obsessed with the need to subject their army to civilian control. This they achieved but at great cost in military effectiveness. Placing civilian controllers at key places in the military hierarchy, rapidly rotating generals, and allowing no permanent military units above regimental level were no way to prepare for war. Regimes since time immemorial have faced the conundrum of needing armies for external defence while distrusting the loyalty of these armies and their generals. Empires faced this dilemma in acute form because by definition they employed large, regular armies on faraway borders where central government found it very hard to oversee them. Among the imperial monarchies studied in this book, Rome managed this problem worst and early modern Europe did best. China lay somewhere in the middle, oscillating between the models of military management offered by the Tang and the Song.

In partial excuse of the army's failures, the strategic dilemma facing the Song was exceptionally difficult. As always, defence of the northern borderland dividing China from the steppe was the overwhelming strategic priority. The Great Wall of China, the only human construction visible from space, is a monument to the fixation of all Chinese rulers on keeping the nomads at bay. Defensive strategies had inherent problems given the nomads' mobility and their ability to strike at whatever point they chose. But the Song dilemma was worse than that of most dynasties. Without the empire's northern borderlands the Song were deprived of the reserve of horses essential for warfare against nomads. Dealing with borders now far to the south of the steppe, Song diplomacy and intelligence inevitably lost the Tang regime's knowledge of steppe politics and its ability to play off enemies against each other. All the key passes and corridors which led from the steppe towards the North China plain were in enemy hands. In strategic terms the forced retreat to the line of the River Yangzi in 1125 after the crushing defeat by the Jurchens made defence far easier. The Song regime regrouped south of the Yangzi and survived for almost another 150 years. In the end the Southern Song succumbed to the Mongols, but so did every other polity that stood in the way of Chinggis Khan and his successors.

Ironically, though at enormous human cost, the Mongol conquest served the age-old dream of imperial unity. In the thousand years between the fall of the Han dynasty and the Mongol conquest, China at a generous estimate had been united for only 460 years. After the Mongol conquest the empire remained united until the end of the imperial age in 1911, admittedly under partly alien rule in the case of the Mongol and Manchu (Qing) dynasties. Like so many human beings, Huizong was crushed by long-term geopolitical trends which he could neither predict nor comprehend. After his capital fell to the Jurchens, the emperor spent the last eight years of his life in bleak and humiliating captivity far to the north in the Jurchen homeland.[23]

9

The Islamic Caliphate: The Ultimate Universal Empire

No empire in earlier history had spread so far or so fast as the Arab caliphate. Within three generations of Muhammad's death his heirs ruled over everything from Spain and north Africa in the west to the borders of India and China in East and South Asia. For two hundred years the whole of the former Achaemenid territory and the richest provinces of the late Roman Empire were combined under one ruler. Never again in history was any empire to equal the caliphate's achievement in being simultaneously the dominant power on the Iranian plateau and the southern shore of the Mediterranean. Nor was the caliphate's impact to be brief or confined mostly to geopolitics. On the contrary, it laid the foundations for the vast Islamic cultural and religious zone which remains of crucial significance in today's world.

It is true that Arab expansion benefited greatly from the exhaustion of the two empires that lay directly in its path – East Rome (Byzantium) and Sasanian Iran. Repeated epidemics of plague had devastated these empires in the sixth century and continued to do so in the first decades of the seventh. Even worse, the centuries-old rivalry between Rome and Iran came to a head in a destructive series of campaigns in the first three decades of the seventh century. By 619 CE the Sasanians had taken Syria, Egypt and Anatolia and stood at the gates of Constantinople. The Roman Empire appeared to be doomed. Emperor Heraclius restored the situation by a daring and brilliant invasion of Iran across its northern frontier in 624, combined with an alliance with the steppe empire of the Turks and exploitation of conflict between the Sasanian king and aristocracy. By 629 the Iranians had capitulated and Heraclius travelled to Jerusalem in triumph to restore the True Cross to its rightful resting place. Seldom has the fickleness of political fortune been so cruelly and rapidly displayed.

Suddenly an enormous, new and totally unpredictable threat in the form of Islam erupted out of Arabia, which had previously been a strategic and cultural backwater.[1]

Although Islam's eruption across Eurasia was helped by Byzantine and Sasanian exhaustion, its two key elements were the enormous impact of the new Islamic religion and the military strength of nomads. Of these two elements the religious factor was most important. This is obviously true as regards the long-term impact of the Arab Empire. Most nomadic conquerors in history were themselves to a great degree conquered in cultural and linguistic terms by the sedentary communities over which they ruled. On the contrary, despite overrunning the centres of ancient civilization, the Arabs preserved much of their culture and their language. Although previously of minimal cultural influence, Arabic came to dominate a vast region as the language of government and – above all – of Holy Scripture. The Arab nomads who conquered this empire had no previous history of statehood. Feuding between tribes was endemic. Islam and loyalty to the Muslim community (*Umma*) provided a focus for a supra-tribal unity that had never previously existed.

The tribesmen of the Arabian desert had the same toughness, mobility and warrior ethos as their nomadic cousins on the Eurasian steppe but in other respects were weaker in military terms. They were much less numerous and although they travelled to the battlefield by horse and camel, they usually fought on foot. Their victories cannot therefore be explained with reference to the composite bow, or the devastating proficiency at mounted archery and cavalry tactics which made the Eurasian steppe nomads so formidable. Whatever its causes, military victory and conquest on the scale achieved by the Arabs was bound to be seen as a mark of Heaven's favour and the caliphate's legitimacy. Although any people and religion would have believed this, Islamic doctrine was especially open to this view. Unlike Christianity, Zoroastrianism or Buddhism, the Islamic religion was involved in high politics and government from its earliest days. When Muhammad fled Mecca as a result of a breakdown in relations with the city's elites and took up residence in Medina in 622 CE, he very soon became the political, judicial and military leader of his new home city. War was a key responsibility of Muhammad, as of any other ruler. The duty to defend and extend Islam – *jihad* – figures prominently in the Qur'an. This contributed to the enormous sense of confidence and elan that drove forward the Islamic armies of conquest.[2]

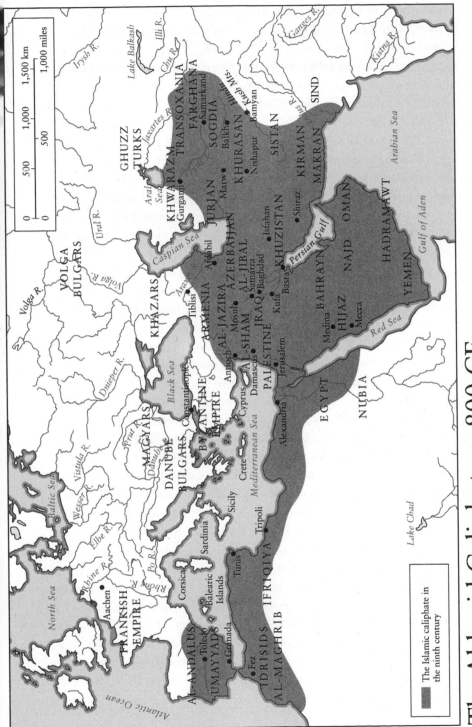

The Abbasid Caliphate c. 800 CE

The Islamic caliphate in the ninth century

Although Muhammad was a political leader, the Qur'an says little about government. Still less does it provide any guidelines for an emperor. It is a matter of deep disagreement between the majority (Sunni) and minority (Shi'i) traditions in Islam as to whether Muhammad nominated a successor. The Shi'i claim that the Prophet clearly indicated his desire to be succeeded by his son-in-law and cousin Ali, the husband of Fatima, Muhammad's only child who survived to adulthood. The Sunni deny this. The great internal conflicts that split early Christianity in ways that survive to this day usually concerned doctrine, and above all disagreements about the precise mixture of the divine and human in Jesus Christ. Islamic doctrine is clearer, sparser and more unequivocally monotheist. It contains no such tortured theological oddity as the Trinity. The great, early and permanent cleavage in Islam concerned succession. In many ways the Sunni-Shi'i split is the most important monarchical succession struggle in history.

As with all monarchical succession struggles, this one divided the Prophet's family. His favourite wife, Aisha, was on bad terms with his son-in-law, Ali. Muhammad's successor, the pious Caliph Abu Bakr, was chosen by an ad hoc meeting packed by his supporters. The new caliph was Aisha's father. The rivalries between members of the Prophet's family were partly linked to different factions and groups within the new Islamic elite. One element in the succession struggle was opposition among the broader Quarysh tribe to the idea of hereditary leadership of Islam being confined to one of its sub-groups, namely the Hashem clan to which both Muhammad and Ali belonged. The *Muhajirun* (Companions) who had accompanied Muhammad on his flight from Mecca to Medina commanded great prestige, but they were not united on the succession issue. All of the first four caliphs – Abu Bakr, Umar, Uthman and Ali – were Companions: three were murdered amidst feuding about power and the spoils of conquest in the new polity. Native Medinans who had given shelter to Muhammad could easily resent Meccan attempts to dominate the Islamic polity. Many of the Companions and the Medinans might to some extent unite in resenting the claims to leadership of the Meccan elite, most of whose members had been slow to accept Muhammad and Islam. On the other hand, in the traditional Arab tribal world aristocratic lineage counted for much.

To the divisions within the Arabian elite were soon added disagreements across their realms over the distribution of the enormous spoils

of conquest. The third caliph, Uthman, came from the traditional Meccan elite but was a Companion. One cause of his growing unpopularity
was his tendency to favour his own relations, but he was killed by rebels
from Egypt and Iraq (Kufa) who were angry at his intervention in local
disputes over power and booty. Uthman was succeeded as fourth caliph
by Ali, but this was never accepted by part of the Islamic elite, and civil
war soon erupted. The eventual victor of the civil war was Mu'āwiya,
Uthman's cousin and the governor of Syria. He created the Umayyad
hereditary monarchy which ruled the Islamic world until 750. One victim of the civil war was Ali. Subsequently his son, Huseyn, was also
killed. The story of their 'martyrdom' and the belief in the fundamental illegitimacy of all Islamic regimes which followed their deaths
formed the core element in the Shi'i communal identity and belief
system.[3]

In the decades following Muhammad's death there was a great
danger that the Islamic community and religion would disintegrate.
Personal, factional and tribal rivalries divided its Arab core. Not for at
least another century did the conquered, non-Arab peoples begin to
convert en masse to Islam. The Qur'an itself was completed twenty
years after the Prophet's death and was the first book written in Arabic.
Constructed in rhymed prose and full of allusions and symbolism it was
often hard to understand and open to many interpretations. Not for
another century would the authority of the Qur'an be supported by the
Hadith, considered to be authoritative compilations of the sayings and
decisions of the Prophet and his Companions. It would be even longer
before an official and generally accepted Islamic set of doctrines was
clearly established in written form by recognized 'schools' of religious
scholars (Ulama) who drew inspiration from the four eighth- and early
ninth-century 'founding fathers' of Qur'anic and Hadith study. In the
interim the institution of the caliphate was vital for Islam's survival. By
guaranteeing the unity and security of the Islamic community and supporting religious learning for over two hundred years, first the Umayyad
and then the Abbasid hereditary monarchy made possible the flourishing of an Islamic cultural and religious commonwealth long after their
dynasties and empire had passed away.[4]

Although the dynastic monarchy of the Umayyads and Abbasids was
vital for Islam's well-being in these early centuries, it inevitably distressed many true Muslims. Muhammad was one of the most important

leaders in history but he was in no sense a hereditary monarch, let alone a hereditary emperor. Max Weber singled out Old Testament prophets as the most striking examples of his concept of charismatic leadership. Like most charismatic leaders, they were a disruptive force in the Jewish society of their time. Muhammad was a prophet and disrupter on the grandest possible scale. Muslim theologians stressed the fact that, unlike Jesus Christ, Muhammad made no claims to divinity. But in the minds of most of the Islamic community his status was little short of that occupied by Jesus in the minds of Christians. No caliph could hope to equal Muhammad's charisma or authority. The first four caliphs drew their legitimacy from the fact that they were Muhammad's Companions and his closest lieutenants. Their personal piety and the support they possessed in the Islamic community were also key elements in their authority, though the conflicts surrounding the succession introduced questions of lineage and hereditary right into Islamic politics. With the Umayyads came the triumph of hereditary monarchy. The caliphs were not just hereditary emperors but also rulers of one of the greatest and most significant empires in history. Their empire was in territorial terms the largest yet seen. It was the launching pad for a far broader Islamic community which in time included much of Eurasia and Africa. Not until the British Empire and the liberal and capitalist civilization it helped to spread across the globe did any empire have a wider or deeper impact on humanity. In other words, the caliphs were model universal emperors.[5]

The caliphate always legitimized itself in strictly Islamic terms as the heir to Muhammad and as the guardian of the Muslim community. Nevertheless, as time passed, its rituals and values drew heavily from the tradition of Middle Eastern, and especially Persian, imperial monarchy. The ruling dynasty accumulated immense wealth and lived a life of luxury and refinement, especially after the Abbasids moved the empire's capital to Baghdad. The huge palaces they built were largely constructed of mud brick and have mostly crumbled away from sight. Unlike in the case of the Pyramids or even the stone ruins of the Roman Empire we cannot share the impact they made on the people of their era. This was all very far removed from the simple and comparatively egalitarian world of Muhammad and the Arab tradition. It was even further from the millenarian hopes and dreams of so many early adherents of this great – and in key respects egalitarian – religion of human salvation.

Many religious scholars and true believers kept their distance from the dynasty and its court, even if they often continued to see its existence as unavoidable and even necessary. A significant section of Muslim society called the Kharijites never accepted the legitimacy of hereditary monarchy, and for generations after the Prophet's death they carried out an underground war against the reigning dynasty and the social order it supported.[6]

At least as dangerous to the Umayyads and Abbasids were those sections of the population which accepted hereditary monarchy but believed that the only legitimate caliphs were the Prophet's direct descendants, in other words the bloodline of his daughter Fatimah and her husband, Ali. These people were the ancestors of today's Shi'i religious community, though even in the eighth century the precise boundaries and beliefs of Shi'i Islam were still far from sharply defined. Many descendants of Fatima and Ali – known as the Alids – lived contentedly under Umayyad and (even more so) Abbasid rule. The Abbasids, descended from Muhammad's uncle, were fellow members of the Hashem clan and intermarriage between Alids and Abbasids was frequent. In addition, even those Shi'i who kept as far as possible from the Abbasid regime did not always agree on who was the legitimate Alid caliph. A dispute as to who was the rightful successor to the greatly respected Shi'i leader ('imam/caliph') Jafar al-Sadiq, who died in 765, caused a permanent split between a minority 'Ismaili' group (whose hereditary leader is the Aga Khan) and the Shi'i mainstream.[7]

Nevertheless, in the ninth century a distinct school of Shi'i doctrine about the caliphate emerged. The true caliph must be from Ali's bloodline and should be nominated by his predecessor. His authority was absolute and his status semi-divine. Although he could not in principle change Muslim doctrine, only he could interpret it and he did so on the basis of a superhuman and esoteric wisdom and insight that came directly from God. The eschatological and millenarian hopes attached by Shi'i to their caliph could only endure because he lived in his followers' imagination and never actually bore the burdens of rule. When a Shi'i caliphate was established in tenth-century Egypt by the Fatimid dynasty, the monarchs faced immense difficulties in living up to the expectations generated by their creed. Since the Fatimids were from the minority Ismaili sect of Shi'ism, most Shi'i in any case regarded their rule as illegitimate from the start.

In 873, when the eleventh Shi'i caliph in the direct line from Ali died, mainstream Shi'i (subsequently defined as imami) believed that his successor had gone into hiding to escape murder by the Abbasid regime and would only return at the end of time as the 'Expected One' (*Mahdi*) to usher in the reign of justice on earth (in other words the victory of Islam), the time of Resurrection and the Day of Judgement. In many societies in history monarchs who died sudden or violent deaths (especially at aristocratic hands) lived on in popular mythology. They spawned 'Pretender myths' in which after miraculously surviving death they re-emerged to regain their thrones and protect their people from injustice. At one level, the Shi'i myth of the hidden imam was a Pretender myth on an apocalyptic scale. On occasion in the following centuries, claims that a *Mahdi* had reappeared threatened political stability in the Islamic world. The most important such occasion was the eruption on to the political scene at the end of the fifteenth century of the Safavid dynasty and empire which in the short term threw Middle Eastern international relations into chaos and in the longer run resulted in the emergence of Iran as a Shi'i state and nation.[8]

The first Islamic imperial monarchy was established in 661 by the founder of the Umayyad dynasty, Mu'āwiya, after victory in the civil war that followed the killing of his cousin Caliph Uthman in 656. Before becoming caliph, Mu'āwiya had been governor of Syria for almost twenty years and had established a strong hold over the province, including the military forces that faced the Byzantine enemy on Syria's northern borders. Compared to most imperial monarchies, the Umayyads were initially rather modest. Mu'āwiya was constantly on the move during his nineteen-year-long reign, cultivating the support of the Syrian tribal chiefs on which his regime partly rested. Court ceremony was minimal and the monarch was easily accessible. Only after a war of succession within the Umayyad dynasty and the accession in 685 of Mu'āwiya's distant cousin Caliph Abd al-Malk did the Umayyad dynasty put down strong institutional roots. The fact that the able Abd al-Malk ruled for twenty years mattered greatly. Arabic replaced Greek, Syriac and Persian as the lingua franca of imperial administration. An all-imperial and stable silver coinage was minted. Dependence on tribal leaders was much reduced by the creation of an army recruited from Syria and paid by the caliph largely out of Iraqi revenues. From start to finish the basis of Umayyad power was the support of Syrian military forces which the caliphs used to control Iraq's resources and revenues. The regime collapsed in the 740s when rivalries over succession between the Umayyad princes became intertwined with factional and tribal divisions within the Syrian army. In a manner not dissimilar to Tang China, the Umayyad princes' habit of marrying daughters of elite families quickly turned succession struggles into battles between aristocratic clans to control the throne.[9]

Civil war among the Umayyads opened the way to a successful rebellion rooted initially in the vast eastern province of Khurasan, which stretched all the way from central Iran to northern Afghanistan and the Chinese border with Central Asia. Khurasan's size and remoteness made it difficult to control for any regime centred in Iraq or Syria. In addition, to an even greater extent than in the empire's other provinces, the caliphate had often come to terms with native princes who retained their hold in their regions and could mobilize powerful military contingents should they decide to rebel. If the caliph or his governors squeezed too hard in their efforts to extract revenue then rebellion became likely. Although the Khurasani Iranian elite began to convert to Islam under the Umayyads, pre-Islamic Iranian traditions and identities persisted. The princely courts preserved an aristocratic culture. Songs and poems based on ancient Iranian stories were recited by wandering poets, a literary tradition that was to form the basis of the *Shahnameh*, the Persian national epic composed around the year 1000. The endurance of Iranian high culture and imperial traditions was to leave a powerful mark on the whole Middle East down to the modern era.[10]

Nevertheless, although there were some 'native', Iranian aspects to the Khurasani revolt, its core element was still the Arab military garrison of the province. Above all, these troops were mobilized against the Umayyad regime by appeals for a return to the purer, stricter and millenarian Islam of the Prophet. A key part of this call was the belief that a truly Islamic order could only be restored by a regime headed by one of the Prophet's own family, the Hashim. The fundamental ways in which Umayyad dynastic rule had departed from the Prophet's example and message could most easily be ascribed to the fact that the Umayyads had usurped the leadership of Islam from its rightful caliphs. Political deftness and opportunism placed the Abbasids, descendants of the Prophet's uncle, on the throne rather than the family of Muhammad's son-in-law, the Alids. The new dynasty owed much to its chief agent in Khurasan, the charismatic Abu Islam, who embodied and united both the Islamic–millenarian and the Khurasani nativist strands in the rebellion. One of the first moves of the founding father of the new dynasty, the Caliph al-Mansur, was to have Abu Islam killed since his great personal authority and following in Khurasan and Iran was a threat to caliphal power.[11]

Al-Mansur was not the first Abbasid caliph but his elder brother, Abu al-Abbas, died after only four years on the throne in 754 without an adult son to succeed him. Fortunately for the Abbasids, al-Mansur was 'a political operator of genius' who ruled for twenty-one years. Born in relative obscurity, he had learned the game of politics during the rebellion against the Umayyads. In these years he became a shrewd judge of men and forged alliances with a number of able generals and officials who had distinguished themselves in the course of the Abbasids' rise to power. This group of old comrades became his inner circle of advisers. As his treatment of Abu Islam showed, where necessary al-Mansur could be ruthless and unsentimental, but he was not by nature a cruel or arbitrary man. His anger was terrifying but purposeful, even theatrical. Notoriously tight-fisted, he was an exceptionally competent and conscientious administrator. In a manner beloved of Arabic story-tellers but familiar too from the histories of other dynasties, the shrewd, mean, hard-headed founder was succeeded by a charming, kindly, pious and open-handed heir, in this case the Caliph al-Mahdi, who unlike his father was also a generous patron of the arts. The reign of Mahdi's son, Harun al-Rashid (r. 786–809) is generally taken to be the high point of the Abbasid Empire.[12]

The Abbasid dynasty created an altogether more magnificent version of imperial monarchy than the Umayyads. One authority on the new regime notes 'the Abbasids' claims to be the imams of a universal monarchy, modelled in many respects on Sasanian imperial rule, but legitimated by their claims to be the inheritors of the authority of the Prophet'. The moon crescent with an inner star, to this day the emblem of Islam, was ever-present in late Sasanian throne buildings and was soon adopted by Arab conquerors. In time the new rulers introduced 'the Iranian political tradition of many of the Abbasids' military supporters, with its lavish court ceremonial, its use of gold, silk, perfume and wine as the luxurious symbolic markers of aristocratic status and the tradition of dynastic succession to power'. The huge palaces built by

the Abbasids in and around Baghdad drew their inspiration from surviving Sasanian buildings. For example, only a few miles from Baghdad
stood the enormous palace of the shahs at Ctesiphon. Its huge brick
arch was the largest pre-modern brick span anywhere in the world. For
the caliphs this was a source of inspiration but also competition. In
other words, a revolution designed in part to rid Islam of the excesses of
Umayyad monarchy had placed in power a dynasty whose monarchical
style far exceeded that of its predecessor. At a pinch one might compare
the evolution of Islamic politics from the Umayyads to the Abbasids to
a similar evolution in Roman politics from the Principate to the Dominate. Like Augustus the early Umayyads camouflaged the reality of
dynastic monarchy behind a facade of modesty and loyalty to tradition,
which in their case meant both Islamic and Arab tribal custom. The
Abbasids represented imperial monarchy in full Iranian glory. Combined with the fact that many subjects saw the Alids as the rightful heirs
to the caliphate, the splendour, refinement and increasing inaccessibility
in their vast palaces of the Abbasids was a potential threat to the dynasty's legitimacy in Muslim eyes. Muhammad had not brought Islamic
truth to humanity in order to restore the Sasanians.[13]

The core of Abbasid power in the dynasty's first sixty years was the
Khurasani army, which had overthrown the Umayyads in the late 740s
civil war. Now settled in Iraq and renamed the Abna (literally 'the sons',
meaning 'the sons of the revolutionary army'), it controlled Iraq's
resources on behalf of the Abbasids and itself. Iraq was by far the caliphate's richest and most valuable province. Still the proverbial garden
of Eden, it yielded four times more revenue than Egypt and five times
more than Syria. A regime which controlled Iraq's revenue could dominate all but the inaccessible mountain regions of Syria. A ruler who held
Iraq and Syria could usually secure Egypt, an especially valuable prize
since its population was concentrated in a small area adjacent to the
Nile and its southern and western borders were easily defended. Egypt
was both a wealthy province and also relatively cheap to defend and
govern, so an unusual proportion of its revenues could be remitted to
the imperial capital. An additional benefit of holding Egypt was that
Arabia – and therefore the Holy Places of Mecca and Medina – depended
for survival on Egyptian grain. Although of no military or fiscal significance, holding the Holy Places was very important in terms of legitimacy.
A regime with a secure hold on Iraq, Syria, Egypt and Arabia still needed

to show wisdom and restraint in governing Khurasan, but the real danger to the empire's survival came when its centre weakened or imploded as a result of factional battles at court, in the army or within the dynasty. As in almost all empires, battles over the succession were the likeliest cause of implosion. If the centre weakened, then all the centrifugal tendencies inherent in pre-modern empire would be unleashed. Warlords would surface in every region. Provincial governors would use their household troops and provincial networks to set themselves up as hereditary monarchs.[14]

These were the realities of Abbasid imperial governance inherited by the twenty-one-year-old Caliph Harun al-Rashid when he succeeded his brother in 786. Because of his role in *The Thousand and One Nights* at the high point of the Islamic empire's power and magnificence, Harun is the most famous of Abbasid rulers. But among the caliphs, he was neither the most gifted, learned nor politically astute. Following what was now a convention, the Caliph al-Mahdi had appointed his eldest son, Hadi, as his direct heir with Harun designated as Hadi's successor. As was usually the case, once on the throne the new ruler moved to overturn his father's will and appoint his own son as heir. The sudden death of Hadi after barely a year on the throne saved the succession for Harun. During his brother's reign Harun had good reason to fear for his life and there is credible evidence that he would have been happy to renounce his rights to the throne in return for a private life of security and luxury. Both his mother, the formidable Dowager Empress Khayzuran, and his chief adviser, Yahya the Barmakid, were made of sterner stuff: they had tied their fortunes to his cause and did all they could to oppose Hadi's plans.

As this suggests, Harun lacked self-confidence. As a young man, he was shy and retiring. One veteran courtier recalled that, even as a mature adult, Harun had 'one of the mildest countenances' of any caliph. He seems to have avoided face-to-face disputes whenever possible and sometimes to have been lost for words when they happened. Yahya was a highly intelligent and efficient senior official who had been appointed governor of Harun's household when the prince was still a boy. Yahya's father had served as 'prime minister' in the last years of Caliph Mansur's reign and had preserved this position under al-Mahdi until his death. Both Yahya and his wife had been close friends of al-Mahdi and his wife, Empress Khayzuran. The infant Harun is even said to have been breast-fed by the vizier's wife: if true, this made him the 'milk-brother' of Yahya's sons, al-Fadl and Jafar – a powerful link in this society. The young caliph Harun called Yahya 'my father' and deferred to him in all matters of government. One source reports the caliph's instructions to Yahya in the following terms: 'I have invested you with the rule of my flock . . . Appoint to office whom you will and remove whom you will. Conduct all affairs as you see fit.'[15]

From the early 770s until their destruction in 803 the Barmakid family played a great, and in Harun's reign dominant, role in government. The family came from the Khurasani native elite and for generations had been the guardians of a famous Buddhist shrine in the foothills of the Hindu Kush. After conversion to Islam they had intermarried with a number of Khurasani princely families. They were one of the leading non-Arab Muslim families from Khurasan to play a key role in the revolt which overthrew the Umayyads and placed the Abbasids on their throne. Subsequently the family provided the Abbasids with three generations of loyal, highly cultured and very competent advisers and ministers. The Barmakids' talent for propaganda and cultural patronage served the Abbasids well. First Yahya and then his son al-Fadl also played crucial roles as governors in the east. Their political sensitivity added to their local knowledge and contacts secured Khurasan's loyalty to the Abbasid regime. After their disgrace in 803 both the overall effectiveness of Abbasid government and its hold on Khurasan suffered badly. Harun died in 809 while on an expedition to crush rebellion in the province, caused above all by the heavy-handedness and corruption of Kurasan's Iraqi (Abna) governor.

The story of Harun's relationship with the Barmakids is fascinating and dramatic. For my purposes its interest goes beyond the specifically Abbasid context. For the first time we can look in some detail at the relationship between an emperor and his chief minister. Whether the chief minister is called 'prime minister', 'vizier', 'favourite' or some other title matters little: this relationship recurred frequently in the history of imperial monarchy and is a key theme running through this book. The relationship was both political and personal. Like any relationship between two people it was therefore to some extent in each case unique. Nevertheless, certain elements were constant. Of these, the most basic was the chief minister's insecurity. It was in the nature of imperial monarchy that the vizier's position could never be secure or institutionalized.

At its core was total dependence on the emperor's support and complete nakedness in the face of his anger.

For a monarch, having a chief minister could be an immense relief. Even the workaholic Abbasid founder Caliph al-Mansur once scolded his ministers for never living up to the example of the great Umayyad vizier, Hajjaj bin Yusuf (d. 714): 'Would that I could find someone to rely on, as they did him, and give myself a break from rulership.' Mansur's ministers were no doubt too tactful to suggest that any of them who had presumed to adopt Hajjaj's role would not have survived for long. The legitimacy of the Abbasids – and of most of the monarchies I study – was far too strong for a dynasty to fear overthrow by a powerful minister. In the Abbasids' case, at least at this time, even a coup to replace the caliph by another Abbasid was almost unthinkable. On the other hand, a monarch who left the business of government to his vizier might himself feel that he was not fulfilling his God-given responsibilities and would certainly be criticized – seldom of course to his face – by his courtiers to this effect.[16]

The control that a vizier would exert over patronage and policy would make him widely hated and envied. In Harun's case, his chamberlain al-Fadl bin al-Rabi loathed the Barmakids and had considerable control over access to the monarch. He allowed poisonous talk against the Barmakids to be poured softly but continually into Harun's ear. In the Abbasid regime, as almost always in pre-modern empires, political power brought great wealth. Disgracing a vizier might in some cases be driven in large part by a wish to regain this wealth for the treasury. A wise vizier did not flaunt his riches under the monarch's nose. Even if the vizier was personally capable of such restraint, however, there were limits to how far abstinence could go without undermining his position. Political grandees were expected to be rich and generous. They needed wealth to build up clienteles. Hospitality, gifts, pensions and rewards for those who proclaimed the vizier's virtues in whatever media fitted a specific culture were essential. Knowing where to stop required the sense of balance of a tightrope dancer.

Like Harun, many young monarchs ascended the throne lacking self-confidence and in awe of their mentor. As confidence grew, the desire to shake off the mentor's control was natural. In Harun's case he could not simply wait for Yahya to die, since the vizierate had become semi-hereditary in the Barmakid clan. Yahya's younger son, Jafar, was not

just a senior political figure but also Harun's closest friend from boy-
hood. As young men they had spent long evenings together, watching
singers and dancers, discussing poetry and consuming exquisite food
and wine. Intimate friendship with a monarch could be a tricky business. A relationship with a man who could end your life with a flick of
his fingers could never be entirely equal or easy. The emperor himself
could be torn between a human need for friendship, princely arrogance,
and the requirement to preserve authority and dignity by maintaining
distance and deference. An insecure man might be especially inclined to
demand both friendship and deference. Inevitably, preserving a balance
became far harder when politics intruded, and the ruler's intimate friend
was also his chief minister. Nevertheless, Harun's decision in 803 to
throw his 'father' Yahya into gaol, execute Jafar, and destroy the Barmakid family does not do him credit and damaged his dynasty's
interests.

The years between the destruction of the Barmakids in 803 and the
death of Harun in 809 were increasingly dominated by the question of
succession. Harun's senior wife – in all but official title empress – was
Zubayda, granddaughter of Caliph al-Mansur. Quite apart from her
high status, she was a powerful personality who exerted a great influence on her husband. Unsurprisingly, their only son Muhammad
al-Amin was designated heir. But in line with what was becoming a
caliphal convention, al-Amin's slightly older half-brother, Abdullah al-
Mamun, was proclaimed heir to the caliphate after al-Amin. Very
unusually, al-Mamun was not merely made governor of Khurasan (from
which his mother's family came) but also granted almost total control
over the province during his brother's reign. Harun was probably motivated in part by memory of his own persecution at the hands of his elder
brother. By building up al-Mamun's autonomous power, Harun may
well have sought to strengthen him against attempts to change the
succession.

Probably, less personal motives counted for more. It was difficult for
a ruler in Baghdad to retain control over Khurasan. The caliph had
nothing like the Chinese bureaucracy to unite and govern his vast
empire. His provincial governors were essentially viceroys – dependent
on their local networks, their households and the military garrisons to
secure and tax the extensive territories entrusted to them. Armed resistance was a constant threat. Having eliminated the Barmakids and

experienced the chaos wrought by an Iraqi (i.e. Abna) governor of Khurasan, Harun seems to have opted for a dynastic solution. He must have been aware of the great dangers of putting an imperial prince in total control of a vast and rich province. He may well have believed that by promising al-Mamun subsequent inheritance of the whole caliphate he was removing the danger of secession. Mutually binding oaths were an old Arab custom, dating back to the pre-Islamic days when no state existed to enforce obligations. Harun forced his sons to swear public and solemn oaths to uphold the succession settlement, publicized these oaths across his empire, and placed the documents in Islam's most holy place, the Ka'bah in Mecca.[17]

Harun died in 809 while leading his Abna army to help al-Mamun's government restore complete caliphal control across Khurasan and its borderlands. His last orders were that the army should continue its march after he died. Few rulers could command beyond the grave, however, and the Abna army promptly returned to Iraq on the orders of al-Amin's government in Baghdad. By early 811 full-scale civil war had begun between the half-brothers and their factions. On paper, victory ought to have gone to al-Amin, who controlled Iraq, the central Abna army and almost all the other provinces save Khurasan. Why victory went instead to al-Mamun remains uncertain, above all because we have very little information about military operations. Al-Mamun benefited enormously from having the services of the war's finest general, the young Khurasani aristocrat Prince Tahir ibn Huseyn. The speed, force and boldness of Tahir's strategy and tactics wrecked the confidence and morale of his opponents. Possibly Tahir's army had cavalry trained in steppe warfare in its ranks, and this gave it an edge over the Abna army consisting mostly of infantry, but we cannot be sure. Neither the young caliph al-Amin nor any of his commanders had the charisma to restore unity and confidence to his armies after Tahir's shattering initial victories. By the autumn of 813, after a siege lasting over a year, Baghdad was about to fall to al-Mamun's forces with the Caliph al-Amin trapped inside.[18]

The besieging forces were divided into two armies, one commanded by Tahir, the other by Harthamah bin Ayan, who had behind him decades of loyal service in the households of al-Mamun's father and grandfather. Al-Amin was desperate to surrender to Harthamah, in the correct belief that he would be treated with mercy and honour by his family's old retainer. By now, however, the caliph's court was a wasps' nest of people often concerned only to secure their future with the victors. Al-Amin's negotiations with Harthamah were betrayed to Tahir, whose soldiers ambushed and capsized the caliph's boat and took him prisoner.

One of Harthamah's lieutenants, Ahmad bin Sallam, also a captive of Tahir's forces, was alone in a guardroom when the caliph was brought in, 'unclothed, wearing drawers, a turban veiling his face, and a tattered piece of cloth on his shoulders'. Having fallen in the river, al-Amin was shivering with cold and wetness but, above all, fear. The caliph recognized Sallam as another old Abbasid retainer. '"Come close to me," he said, "and hold me. I feel very frightened." So I held him to myself. His heart was beating so hard that it was about to burst his chest and come out.' Many minutes passed. Then a group of Persians entered the room with drawn swords, though initially each hung back by the door seeking to push the others forward. The first blow was struck by the slave of one of Tahir's lieutenants. Al-Amin tried desperately to defend himself with a cushion, crying out 'I am the cousin of the Messenger of God . . . I am the son of Harun. I am the brother of Mamun', but by now the assassins' courage had returned and they fell on him and slit his throat. Tahir sent al-Amin's head to al-Mamun so no uncertainties could surround the ex-caliph's fate. Al-Mamun is reported to have been distressed by his brother's death but he understood political realities, telling his grieving vizier, 'what is past is past. Use your ingenuity to find an excuse for it.' Although for some time subsequently suspicious of Tahir and his sons, in time al-Mamun came to see that their support was important for his regime even after victory in the civil war. He was correct. For two generations the Tahir family supplied the Abbasids with loyal viziers in Baghdad and governors in Khurasan in a manner very similar to the previous achievement of the Barmakids. Their status, networks and local knowledge kept Khurasan under Abbasid rule for decades.[19]

Abdullah al-Mamun, the victor in the civil war, was one of the most interesting and remarkable Abbasid caliphs. Although no portraits exist of the caliphs, the adult al-Mamun was once described as being 'of middle stature, pale-complexioned, handsome and with a long beard', the latter being a mark of virility and beauty for Arab men, as was the black mole on al-Mamun's cheek. He was a monarch who could be both majestic and informal, according to the context. When in informal mode the caliph could be witty and shrewd, behaving and speaking in simple and accessible style. He liked wine though never drank to excess, and in personal terms he was strict in his observance of other Islamic norms and practices. Like most monarchs, al-Mamun was besieged by petitioners seeking favours: unsurprisingly, though in no sense reclusive, he once commented that solitude could be as congenial as sociability. This hints at a key element in al-Mamun's personality which was to have important political consequences. He was the most scholarly and intellectual of all the Abbasid caliphs.[20]

Al-Mamun was famous for his erudition and his intellectual curiosity. Although no doubt this was in part an innate element of his personality, it also owed much to his education and upbringing. Harun al-Rashid took a personal, humane and intelligent interest in his eldest sons' education. They were of course to be trained in the proper behaviour expected of princes: this included how to speak elegantly and confidently in public, together with the need to behave with self-control and dignity, always showing proper respect to older and senior men. But Harun also insisted on a rigorous education which implanted habits of hard work, self-discipline and precision, but also analytical skills. The core of this education was careful study not just of the Qur'an itself but also of Arabic grammar and style. Deep study of the intricacies of the Arabic language was seen as crucial for a sophisticated understanding of Holy Scripture.[21]

Al-Mamun's education had left him not just very interested in Qur'anic scholarship but also confident in his own expertise on the subject. Yet the young prince was also educated in secular – largely Persian – high culture and especially poetry. Al-Mamun's guardian was Jafar the Barmakid, in whose household he grew up. The Barmakids were sophisticated patrons both of Iranian high culture and of Islamic scholarship. Jafar held periodic debates among scholars, using Greek traditions of argument and dialectics to resolve thorny religious questions to which the Qur'an gave no clear answer. Al-Mamun's strong support as caliph for the so-called Mutazilites – who believed that philosophy was a vital aid to the understanding of ultimate truths – can certainly be traced to his years in Jafar's household. So too can his support for scientific experiments and, most important, for the translation into Arabic of the classics of Greek, Indian and Iranian science, medicine, mathematics and philosophy. From the ninth century onwards the Arab caliphate played a vital role in not just preserving ancient wisdom from a number of civilizations, but also in the cross-fertilization, evolution and transmission of this wisdom across a vast swathe of Eurasia and north Africa. Christian European science and philosophy in particular came to owe an extraordinary debt to the caliphate, and no caliph played a bigger role than al-Mamun in encouraging this process.[22]

His father's destruction of Jafar and the Barmakids must have come as a shock to the seventeen-year-old al-Mamun and was a first introduction to the vicious world of court politics. The young prince's new mentor was al-Fadl ibn Sahl, from a prominent Khurasani family recently converted to Islam but still very conscious of their Persian heritage. Since al-Fadl had been a protégé of the Barmakids and shared their values and political skills, the young al-Mamun will probably have found him congenial. When al-Mamun was appointed governor of Khurasan, al-Fadl went with him as de facto chief minister of the province and played the leading role in guiding al-Mamun through the crisis years before and during the civil war. To what extent (as most sources suggest) al-Mamun was dominated by al-Fadl, or whether (as is argued by a minority) the young caliph was already skilful at delegating responsibility to his chief minister while manoeuvring behind his back, we cannot be sure. After al-Mamun's armies captured Baghdad in 813 the decision was made to remain in the city of Merv, in eastern Khurasan, and run the empire from there. This is often put down to al-Fadl's fear that if al-Mamun returned to Baghdad his own dominance over the caliph would be undermined. Whoever made the decision, its result was disastrous. It is very difficult to run an empire from a capital city in a remote border region. Empires where this was done successfully possessed strong and long-established institutions and traditions rooted in a stable alliance between the central government and local elites. This was far from the case in the Abbasid caliphate, and least of all in 813, when civil war had encouraged provincial governors and warlords to set themselves up as independent rulers.[23]

It was only after al-Mamun executed al-Fadl and returned to Baghdad in 819 that the process of reconquering the provinces and restoring political stability began. Prince Tahir ibn Huseyn and his sons – previously pushed aside by al-Fadl – played a key role in this process. So did al-Mamun's half-brother, the formidable prince and later caliph al-Mutasim. Al-Mamun once wrote to al-Mutasim about the Abbasids:

'you have well realized that there are no outstanding qualities among them, even though the odd one of them retains a regard for personal honour.' The one exception in al-Mamun's view was al-Mutasim himself, whose powerful personality and record as a successful general were undeniable.[24]

Al-Mamun would in all circumstances stand out among the Abbasids for his intellectual interests but what made him truly extraordinary were three decisions he took as caliph after winning the civil war. The first was his appointment of a non-Abbasid as his heir: his choice, Ali ibn Musa, was not just a prominent Alid but also the man most Shi'i regarded as the true caliph and imam. Although Ali was a highly respected religious scholar who had never engaged in overt opposition to the Abbasids, many of his close relations had played key roles in rebellions against Abbasid rule. After Ali ibn Musa's death al-Mamun was partly reconciled with the Abbasids but throughout his life he did everything possible to forge a close alliance with the Alids and to boost the status of the Prophet's son-in-law above all other caliphs. On his deathbed al-Mamun did nominate an Abbasid as his successor but here again his choice ran against convention. Most caliphs put great effort into securing the succession for their son. In al-Mamun's case his son Abbas was an experienced and successful general with an army under his command. Nevertheless, al-Mamun chose as his heir his half-brother, al-Mutasim. But it was al-Mamun's decision strongly to assert the caliph's supremacy in determining Islamic doctrine, and his attempt to force all prominent religious scholars (ulama) publicly to recognize that supremacy, which was probably most shocking for his subjects.

We cannot be certain about al-Mamun's motives. It may even be that his choice of al-Mutasim as heir occurred through the mere chance that his brother rather than his son was present at his deathbed and used this to manipulate the succession. Most historians, however, believe that al-Mamum's three decisions were linked to his overriding concern that the authority of the emperor-caliph was in sharp decline and must be restored – if necessary by drastic means.

A leading historian of al-Mutasim's reign writes of al-Mamun's 'growing awareness ... of the real problem of the caliphate, already emptied of its original religio-political meaning, when the institution first emerged under the immediate successors of the Prophet, and then gradually losing popular support'. The chaos brought by the civil war among the Abbasids and the subsequent murder of Muhammad al-Amin could only have further weakened respect for the dynasty. Al-Mamun was steeped not only in the Persian tradition of monarchy but also in Greek, Hellenistic and Persian traditions of political thinking that stressed the ignorance of the masses and their acute need for strong authority if chaos and injustice were to be avoided. For him to preach a return to the more egalitarian and anarchic world of the Prophet and his Companions was inconceivable. Forging an alliance with the Alids and the exalted Shi'i vision of the caliphate was far more promising. As to his final choice of his brother rather than his son as heir, this was probably in al-Mamun's mind driven by the need to sacrifice personal feelings to the good of the caliphate as an institution. His brother was the more experienced general with probably the stronger personality and the more formidable army. He had the support of the Abbasid family and almost certainly therefore of Baghdad's elites. To reject his claims in favour of al-Mamun's son might well be to unleash a second civil war, which could easily destroy both dynasty and empire.[25]

A similar logic probably applied as regards al-Mamun's religious policy. Previous Abbasid monarchs had worked with the religious scholars and increasingly allowed the latter to develop consensual understandings of Islamic doctrine. At the beginning of the Abbasid era, Caliph al-Mansur had rejected a call from one prominent official, Ibn al-Muqaffa, for the monarch himself to take the lead in unifying and codifying Islamic law. In the eighty years that separated al-Mansur's refusal and al-Mamun's decision to reassert caliphal authority in religious matters Islamic society and religious scholarship had matured. One sign of this was that, whereas authoritative versions of Hadith, in other words the judgements of the Prophet and His Companions, sometimes cited rulings by Umayyad caliphs, no Abbasid caliph was ever invoked as an authority in legal Hadith.[26]

Three of the four great founders of the mainstream schools of Islamic law were already dead by the time al-Mamun ascended the throne. The fourth, Ibn Hanbal, was to be the most famous opponent of al-Mamun's policy. Ibn Hanbal was a 'literalist', or in present-day terms a 'Fundamentalist'. For him all truth lay in the Qur'an and Hadith and this truth was self-evident from their texts. There was no room in Ibn Hanbal's interpretation either for al-Mamun's support for philosophy and logic as an aid to finding religious truth or for the claim that the caliph must have the last word on matters of Islamic doctrine. Ibn Hanbal suffered imprisonment and a flogging for his stand, but Baghdad's masses were on his side and that of 'literalism'. They too had no time for 'Greek' philosophy. In the end, al-Mutasim's grandson Caliph al-Mutawwakil abandoned support both for 'philosophy' (i.e. the Mutazilites) and (implicitly) for the caliph's claim to be the final judge in all matters of Islamic doctrine. Correctly, al-Mutawwakil believed that by now these claims had been rejected by the great majority of his subjects and were merely further weakening the caliphate's legitimacy. His retreat reflected not just realities specific to the mid-ninth-century caliphate but also more general truths about an emperor's relationship with elites, institutions and mass religious beliefs. In the first Islamic century, before doctrines were codified or deep-rooted institutions established, the caliph not just could but sometimes had to play an active role as religious leader. Once a religion had taken root, however, an emperor challenged its doctrines and 'priesthood' at his peril.[27]

By the 850s al-Mutawwakil was living with more immediate and deadly legacies of the reigns of al-Mamun and al-Mutasim. One result of the civil war of 811–13 was that the Abna army, the foundation of early Abbasid power, had been destroyed. Al-Mamun and – even more so – al-Mutasim replaced it by employing Turkic slaves and mercenaries. Armed with composite bows and the skills of steppe cavalrymen these Turks were formidable soldiers. In principle they were also more dependable politically, since they were not linked to factions in society or government. The basic point about these Turkic soldiers was that they were loyal to their warrior leader, at least as long as he paid and rewarded them. Al-Mutasim was a formidable general and in his last years al-Mamun too was careful to lead campaigns against the Byzantines and reinvigorate the caliphate's claim to be warriors of Islam. By the reign of al-Mutawwakil, however, the Turks' loyalty to the caliph rather than their own generals was much more questionable. Al-Mutawwakil was not a warrior-caliph. Both he and his vizier were also increasingly aware of their dangerous dependence on their Turkic soldiers and generals. Fatally, their attempts to escape from this dependence became tied up with conflict between the caliph and his heir. The coup of 861 in which Turkic guardsmen murdered the caliph and placed the heir on the throne led to a decade of political chaos and the caliphate's loss of control of most of its provinces.

From 861 begins the long decline of the Abbasid dynasty. In broad outline this followed a pattern seen many times in the history of imperial monarchy. The over-concentration of power in the court and among the emperor's slaves made a regime acutely vulnerable to court politics. Succession struggles were the most frequent cause of conflict. Once the centre weakened or imploded it was in the nature of most empires that regional elites and warlords went their own way, sometimes recognizing the theoretical sovereignty of a distant emperor but usually refusing to share local revenues with him. It is true that Baghdad remained a great cultural and commercial centre for many more centuries. There were also moments when the decline of Abbasid power was temporarily reversed, though the dynasty's hold beyond Iraq was gone for ever after 861. In the longer run even in Iraq the Abbasids became almost Japanese-style priest-kings, providing legitimacy for the dynasties of military strongmen who exercised actual power. After the fall of Baghdad and the killing by the Mongols of Caliph al-Musta'sim in 1258, a pale shadow of the Abbasid caliphate continued to exist in Cairo under the aegis of the Mamluk regime. Themselves slave-soldiers of Turkic origin but with no pedigree, the Mamluks welcomed the extra legitimacy they gained in international relations by their claim to be protectors of the caliphate. When the Ottomans captured the Holy Places and then Cairo in 1517 they no longer had need of this cover and took for themselves the title of caliph. The last Abbasid caliph, Muhammad al-Mutawwakil III, surrendered to the Ottomans not just his title but also the sword and cloak of the Prophet, which reside in the great Topkapi palace-museum in Istanbul to this day. In return he was given a pension, lived in dignified retirement in Istanbul, and was even allowed to spend his last years in his native Cairo.[28]

10

Charles V and Philip II: The First Global Emperors

In most of Eurasia empires rose and fell during the thousand years before 1500 CE. Western Europe, the heartland of Latin Christendom, was an exception. Charlemagne's empire, created towards the end of the eighth century, did not last beyond the reign of his son. Apart from this brief though important Carolingian interlude, no true empires existed in Latin Europe from the collapse of the western Roman Empire in 476 CE until the reign of Charles V in the early sixteenth century. Geography was one important reason why western Europe avoided empire. Ever since Montesquieu, scholars have contrasted the vast plain of northern China to western Europe's long coastline and many peninsulas and islands, arguing that this landscape encouraged a multiplicity of independent realms rather than empire. Compared to the vast core of Asia, Europe appears a relatively small cul-de-sac. Linked to this idea but probably more important was the fact that western Europe is as far as it is possible to be in Eurasia from the nomadic warriors of the steppe who founded so many of Eurasia's greatest empires. China, the Middle East and even northern India were not just closer but also much richer and more enticing targets for nomadic conquerors. The politics of Latin Christendom also impeded empire. In China, for example, political and spiritual leadership were fused in a single person, the emperor. In Europe these roles were split between the pope and the Holy Roman Emperor. From the eleventh to the fourteenth century the struggle for supremacy between pope and emperor divided Europe. The fact that both the imperial and papal monarchies were elected also made it much harder for them to dominate European elites and impose some version of empire on western Europe.[1]

The vast empire consolidated under Charles V in the 1510s was therefore a source of wonder to most Europeans and a cause of worry to many. If the territories ruled by Charles are not defined as an empire, then no empire ever existed in history. Elected Holy Roman Emperor in 1519, even in purely formal terms Charles was Europe's only imperial monarch. He poured out one million florins and a flood of pensions and gifts to sweeten the seven imperial electors whose votes decided who should be emperor and to beat off a challenge by his greatest rival, King Francis I of France. He also made political concessions to the German princes. His latest biographer considers all of this to have been an excellent investment. The emperor had far less power in Germany than the French or English monarchs possessed in their own kingdoms, but he could still tap into some military and fiscal resources and enjoyed great status and political influence.

Charles's strength above all lay in the realms he had inherited from his ancestors. From his grandfather Emperor Maximilian came the Habsburg hereditary lands in Austria and south-west Germany. From Maximilian's wife, Mary of Burgundy, Charles inherited the very rich Low Countries. Above all, Charles's mother, Joanna 'the Mad', was the sole heiress to the crowns of Castile and Aragon. With the crown of Aragon came not just north-western Spain but also southern Italy. With Castile, Charles inherited not only most of the rest of the Iberian Peninsula (everything but Portugal) but also the huge new empire that the Spanish were carving out in the Americas, not to mention their outpost in the Philippines. Magellan discovered what became the Strait of Magellan and its route to the Pacific six days after Charles's coronation as Holy Roman Emperor by Pope Clement VII on 24 February 1530. Charles V was therefore not just the first European emperor in almost 700 years, he was also the first truly global emperor in history. A unique and astonishing aspect of this empire was that it had been acquired by the Habsburgs not through conquest but by dynastic marriage and inheritance. Only in Latin Europe could this have been possible. This is just one example of how dynasty and the dynastic principle mattered more in Europe's history than in the history of any other region of Eurasia.[2]

The origins of European uniqueness lay in the 'barbarian' kingdoms that emerged in western Europe during and after the Roman Empire's collapse. Spurred on by conflicts far to the east on the steppe, many tribes (some themselves nomadic, others not) had migrated into Rome's European provinces. There the leaders of tribal war-bands and confederations established their own kingdoms after Rome's demise. In the

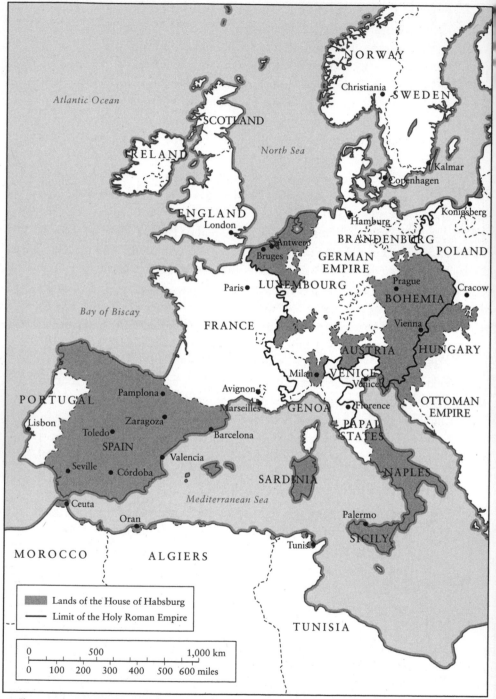

Charles V's Empire in Europe

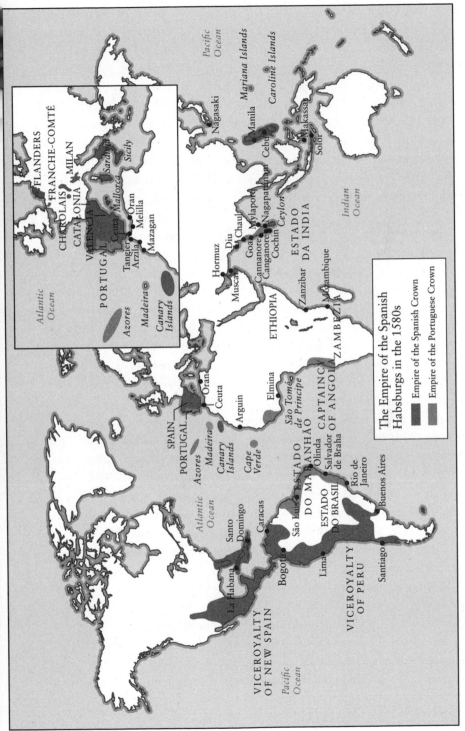

Philip II's Empire

long run, much the most significant was the kingdom of the Franks, ruled first by the Merovingian and then by the Carolingian dynasties. The Carolingians ruled over France and most of what later was called Germany. They left a deep imprint on both countries. The Viking warriors who conquered Normandy and became fully autonomous vassals of the French king in the tenth century were themselves initially a warband of seaborne semi-nomads. By the time their descendants conquered England in 1066 they had largely assimilated the religion, culture and political values of the west Frankish (i.e. French) warrior-landholding elite. After 1066 they created an Anglo-Norman political and social order largely on the French model, though with important local peculiarities.[3]

'Feudalism' as it evolved under the Carolingians was in many ways the adaptation of the Frankish war-band to the realities of exploiting and governing a sedentary society. The Eurasian war-band existed to provide its leader with formidable but also fully loyal military support. Its foundation was a personal and mutually binding bond between leader and follower. The leader repaid his military retinue's loyalty by providing his followers with booty and other rewards. If he conquered a territory, then he used the commanders of his war-band as trusted viceroys and governors. The Frankish kings deployed their leading war-band lieutenants in this way. Ruling a settled and largely agricultural people, they soon distributed lands rather than booty to their military retinue. Not only was booty scarce and land in plentiful supply, but creating a network of loyal Frankish landowners allowed the king to control his new kingdom. Since long-distance commerce and large towns had mostly disappeared with the demise of the Roman Empire, it was impossible even to imagine ruling through a salaried bureaucracy and army. Very important for Europe's subsequent development was the fact that the feudal contract was conditional. Only a lord who carried out his side of the contract could expect loyal service from his vassal.[4]

War is a dangerous, difficult and uncertain business. A dynasty whose sole claim to legitimacy was successful leadership in war could not expect to last long. The conversion of the Frankish King Clovis in 506 to the papal definition of Christian doctrine (i.e. not like the Visigoth king to Nestorianism or some other 'heretical' Christian sect) was a vital moment. As anointed king the monarch was unique among laymen. He became a semi-sacred figure, the heir of David, Solomon and the other

Old Testament monarchs. The Catholic Church even blessed the subsequent claim of the French and English monarchs to possess almost magical powers to cure a disease – scrofula – by the royal touch, a dramatic compromise with the traditions of pagan royalty. Saint Gregory of Tours (b. 539) compared Clovis's conversion to that of Constantine. At the king's baptism a dove was said to have descended from heaven with the holy oil for his anointment and the power to cure scrofula. A direct parallel was drawn with the descent of the Holy Ghost at Christ's baptism. In the centuries before a royal bureaucracy developed, the Church and its bishops were key allies of the king in governing his realm. Kings and bishops shared both an ideal and an interest in defending the peace and the laws of the kingdom against the violent feuding of the warrior aristocracy. When towns and trade began to grow from the twelfth century onwards merchants also supported this goal. Their taxes allowed the king to create the administrators and judges who could begin to turn the aspiration for peace and law into reality.[5]

The growth of the economy and the state administration was accompanied by increasing intellectual sophistication, not least as regards politics and government. In the early centuries of the Frankish kingdom, the realm was seen as little more than the dynasty's patrimony. Once royal officials and lawyers came into existence, so too did the first outlines of something one might describe as a state. The recovery first of knowledge of Roman law and then of ancient Greek philosophy by the end of the twelfth century contributed enormously to thinking about public authority and the state. Aristotle's *Politics* was especially influential. The emergence of universities in the thirteenth century greatly enriched intellectual debate. It was in this century that Saint Thomas Aquinas forged what was to remain for centuries the official Catholic synthesis of Christian doctrine and classical wisdom as regards the political and moral order. In medieval Europe lawyers, scholars and churchmen developed over the generations a concept of the king's two bodies – the first the physical body of the monarch and the second the immortal body politic of the kingdom. Few Roman or Chinese scholars would ever have seen their empires as a dynast's patrimony or needed to draw this distinction.[6]

Desiderius Erasmus was perhaps Europe's most famous 'public intellectual' of the early sixteenth century. Charles V, Francis I of France and Henry VIII of England competed for his praise and (sometimes) his services. Erasmus's book *The Education of a Christian Prince* was published in 1516 and was dedicated to the future emperor Charles V. The book was seen as the last word on how to form and educate a young prince so that he could become a virtuous and effective, legitimate monarch. Machiavelli might have provided a handbook showing parvenu Italian princely bandits how to hang on to their power, but true monarchs must base their authority in religious and ethical principles and must share a sense of moral community with their subjects. Erasmus drew heavily on classical sources, especially Cicero, Seneca, Aristotle and Plato. He reinforced their thrust with references to the Old Testament and to Christian charity. One feature of Erasmus's book was its almost Confucian disdain for the warrior and his ethos. For the Christian monarch, he wrote, war must be absolutely the last resort. 'Soldiering . . . is a very energetic kind of idleness, and much the most dangerous, since it causes the total destruction of everything worthwhile and opens up a cesspit of everything that is evil.' Chivalric tales of romance and martial valour were a particular abomination for Erasmus. 'Today,' he wrote, 'we see a great many people enjoying the stories of Arthur and Lancelot and other legends of that sort, which are not only tyrannical but also utterly illiterate, foolish, and on the level of old wives' tales.'[7]

Unfortunately for Erasmus, he was not living in China. The European social elite was a military and landowning class, of which the monarch was the leader. War was endemic in Europe's multi-state and anarchic world. Rulers spent most of their working lives either fighting and planning wars or agonizing over how to finance them. Military expenditure was by far the biggest item in any major state's budget. Along with the provision of justice to his subjects, command in war was almost a European monarch's *raison d'être*. In general, a king gained more prestige from valorous and victorious leadership on the battlefield than from his wisdom, his piety or the splendour of his court. This was especially true as regards his prestige in the eyes of the aristocracy. Since few monarchs could govern without aristocratic support this mattered greatly. Rulers knew too that domestic stability was often best preserved if aristocratic energies could be directed outwards.

Aristocrats were also simply the world in which monarchs lived, whose values and pastimes they shared, and for whose opinion they cared most in personal terms. To the extent that they could have companions and even friends, they drew them from this circle. Charles V and his contemporaries Francis I and Henry VIII dreamed of glory on the battlefield and competed between themselves to achieve it. After Francis I started his reign in glorious style by victory at Marignano in 1515 he insisted on being knighted on the battlefield by the Sieur de Bayard, a paragon of chivalry acknowledged throughout Europe. All three rulers loved the paraphernalia of chivalry, whether in the form of heraldry, chivalric tales and legends, or membership of knightly orders such as the knights of the Garter or the Golden Fleece. Among his fellow knights of the Golden Fleece, even Charles V relaxed and shed some of his imperial aloofness. The three monarchs also excelled in the paramilitary sports of hunting and jousting, taking pride in the skill and courage they exhibited and the risks they took. Francis I's successor, Henry II, was killed in a joust in 1559. His death contributed greatly to plunging France into thirty-five years of intermittent civil war.[8]

The Chinese emperor was in part a priest-king who in principle dwelled in a realm far above his elite officials. The Ottoman sultan in the empire's greatest era presided over a household and government manned by men who were his slaves. The anointed European monarch of the sixteenth century was not merely *primus inter pares* within the aristocratic elite but he was not nearly as far removed from it as was the case in many imperial monarchies. In sixteenth-century Castile, for example, the heads of the thirty-five aristocratic grandee families were addressed as 'cousin' by the king and permitted to wear their hats in his presence. In every kingdom a grey area existed between king and nobles which was populated by cadet and illegitimate branches of the royal family, as well as by aristocratic families who had intermarried with the reigning dynasty at some point in the past. This grey area was smallest in England and much larger in France, partly because of the existence of numerous families of foreign princes (e.g. the house of Lorraine) whose lands had been absorbed into France over the centuries. In Germany the situation was even more scrambled. In principle only the emperor was fully royal and sovereign. Next in the hierarchy came the handful of electoral princes, but, for all their power, none of them, for example, had the right to grant titles to their subjects since this remained an imperial prerogative. Despite already having provided two Holy Roman Emperors, when the electoral college was created in 1356 the Habsburgs were deemed insufficiently ancient and powerful to be given membership. They were relegated to the second tier of the imperial aristocracy.[9]

Monarchy and aristocracy operated according to the same principle. They were families in power, in other words, dynasties. As such they were obsessed by genealogy and by pride in the antiquity and glory of their lineage. The greatest Castilian aristocrat at the courts of Charles V and Philip II was the Duke of Alba, who won both renown and notoriety as the Habsburgs' leading general. Alba was famous for his rock-hard devotion to the Habsburg cause. Nevertheless, his biographer records that 'over and above his loyalty to the Crown Alba nurtured an even more profound loyalty to his family and lineage'. As one should expect of Holy Roman Emperors, the Habsburgs led the way as regards pride in their family's antiquity and the greatness of its history. In addition to being the grandson of Emperor Maximilian, Charles V was the descendant of both Charlemagne and Godfrey of Bouillon, who was crowned in 1099 as the first crusader-king of Jerusalem. Genealogists in the Habsburg service wove together family history and myth with the long-established legends about the origins of the many kingdoms over which they ruled.[10]

Charlemagne's empire and the Holy Roman Empire that succeeded it had always been seen as the direct heirs of ancient Rome. They therefore assimilated the ancient Romans' myths of origin, which linked the city's foundation to Aeneas and the Trojans. The chivalric order of the Golden Fleece, a key element in binding together the Burgundian dynasty and aristocracy, celebrated the dynasty's heroic Trojan origins and held up the Argonauts as early paragons of aristocratic chivalry and loyalty. After Constantine's conversion to Christianity centuries of scholarly effort went into weaving together Roman and Old Testament history. Charles V's grandfather Emperor Maximilian I bullied the theological faculty of the University of Vienna into recognizing his claim to descent from Noah. The Old Testament provided the creation myth of Latin Christendom. The history of European literature begins with Homer's saga about the destruction of Troy. Habsburg mythology and genealogy linked the dynasty to both. To the modern mind such genealogical obsessions appear laughable, but they mattered greatly in pre-modern Europe. What hold they had on the imagination of the masses it is impossible to say, but they clearly impressed monarchs and aristocrats. Human beings on their deathbeds are inclined to think about where they belong in a cosmos far greater than their own brief lives. Of course, as he lay dying Maximilian I was consoled by Christian priests' promise of eternal life to a ruler who had lived and reigned in communion with Christ. But the emperor also summoned his chief genealogist and had him recite aloud his family tree.[11]

The Burgundian dukes were a cadet branch of the French royal dynasty, the House of Capet, which ruled France from 979 until 1848 and – as I write this chapter – still reigns in Madrid. Charles V therefore had to compete with his arch-rival, King Francis I, for genealogical precedence. Lesser dynasties such as the Tudors had to comfort themselves with 'scraps' such as the Arthurian legend and descent from the saint-like but ineffective King Edward the Confessor. For both kings and aristocrats, dynasty was a source of pride but also obligation. Henry VIII of England might yearn to live up to the tradition of military glory established by Edward III and Henry V, but, even as the nobility first crystallized in twelfth-century France, Guy de Bazoches proudly traced his family line back to Clovis and bade his nephew 'ponder on what sort of man you should be when you have such great forefathers'.[12]

The monarch and aristocrat inherited both a landed property and a public office. In most countries an aristocrat was not just a landowner but also the hereditary source of local justice in his manorial court. The monarch governed the state, but his kingdom was also from another angle a dynastic possession whose fate was determined by the vagaries of family inheritance. In 1505 the Castilian Cortes (assembly) made the connection between royal and aristocratic inheritance explicitly: 'The crown is a national entailed estate (*majorat national*) and the noble entailed estate (*majorat*) is a domestic kingdom.' By 1500 male primogeniture was the system of inheritance both of the English and French monarchies and of their countries' leading aristocratic families. In Germany dividing the inheritance between legitimate sons remained the norm for princes and aristocrats. Charles V's younger brother Emperor Ferdinand I, who succeeded him in 1556, split his realms between his three sons (Maximilian, Charles and Ferdinand). Only biological chance reunited them in the person of Ferdinand II (elected Holy Roman Emperor in 1619), thereby creating what subsequently came to be called the Habsburg (i.e. Austrian) Empire.[13]

An expert on the origins of European statehood comments that 'in the same way as the right of property and inheritance was a fundamental principle of law in individual countries, the right of a dynasty to a certain principality or kingdom was fundamental to international politics.' Monarchs and aristocrats lived within the same legal, religious and cultural norms. These included Christian monogamy, a ban on divorce, and the exclusion of illegitimate children from inheriting property. In the latter case church and aristocratic concerns fully converged by the end of the twelfth century. Extremely high mortality rates, especially among children, were another constant. Royal and aristocratic families obsessed about retaining their status by only marrying their social equals. From the thirteenth century this meant that members of ruling families increasingly only married into other royal dynasties, who were by definition foreign. Apart from the desire to raise the status of royalty, there were also good political reasons not to encourage the ambitions of aristocratic families by giving them royal connections. Intermarriage between royal dynasties could also be a means to encourage and celebrate peace between warring states, as well as to strengthen the sense of a common European and Christian identity and code of conduct despite the rivalries and conflicts between the continent's rulers and states. But unless princesses were excluded from all rights of succession, intermarriage between royal dynasties could have dramatic consequences for international relations in Europe and for the formation of European states.[14]

As regards royal succession, France was exceptional in barring the throne not just to women but also to men descended from royal princesses. This was the so-called Salic Law. In theory dating back to Frankish times, in reality this law was concocted during a succession dispute which arose in 1316 between the child daughter of the deceased King Louis X and the king's younger brother. The brother won for political rather than legal reasons and became Philip V. As was common in pre-modern Europe, what began as a political expedient in time gained the sanctity accorded to custom and became a core principle of constitutional law. The French royal dynasty, the house of Capet, was also exceptional in its fertility and ruled for almost one thousand years without dying out in the male line, a very unusual achievement among royal and aristocratic families. In 1589 when the reigning Valois branch of the Capetians died out, the throne was inherited by a very distant cousin, Henry of Navarre, who then ruled as Henry IV. The last king of France from whom Henry IV descended in the male line was Louis IX (Saint Louis), who had died in 1270.

Only in Europe could dynastic law and legitimacy stretch this far.

Nevertheless, although Henry of Navarre's legal right to the crown was enormously important, it did not suffice to guarantee him secure possession of his throne. To do this Henry decided in 1593 that he must convert from Protestantism to Catholicism, which was the religion of the great majority of his subjects. In the French case, therefore, the community imposed its religion on the king, but this was not the norm in the sixteenth century. In 1555, for example, the Peace of Augsburg established the principle in the Holy Roman Empire that the prince's religion usually determined that of his subjects, though the latter had the right to emigrate and live under a ruler of their own religion. This principle was confirmed in the Peace of Westphalia, which ended the Thirty Years War in 1648. To an extent which seems astonishing to contemporary minds, not just the survival of states and very significant geopolitical outcomes but also the religion of whole peoples could be determined by dynastic chance and competition. This added an extra and vicious dimension to many wars between dynasties in the sixteenth and seventeenth centuries.

Although the Habsburgs planned their marriages with the greatest political care, only very improbable biological and medical chance led to the agglomeration of Charles V's great empire. When similar chance led in 1526 to the acquisition by his brother Ferdinand of the kingdoms of Bohemia and Hungary the dynasty seemed doubly blessed. Nevertheless, this huge accumulation of territories had its dangers for the Habsburgs. Inevitably the scale of Habsburg power scared not just foreign rulers but also many of their own subjects. Fear could breed suspicion, resistance and hostile coalitions. Even seemingly natural allies such as the papacy and the Catholic princes of the Holy Roman Empire often opposed Habsburg policy. In addition, the way in which their empire had been put together meant that the Habsburgs' strength was less than outward appearances suggested. The same laws that gave these territories to the Habsburgs also restricted their authority within them.

In the medieval era most European lands evolved laws, customs and institutions that strictly constrained a ruler's power. These constraints encompassed the monarch's 'feudal' contract with the nobility but also the autonomy of the clergy and the self-governing rights granted to urban corporations. Although the extent and institutional form of these constraints differed greatly from land to land, in most cases the ruler could not punish his subjects without due legal process nor tax them without their consent. Whether backed by law or just convention, strong opposition also faced any ruler who distributed offices and pensions to foreigners. A maze of representative and judicial institutions existed to uphold these rights and customs. On assuming power the ruler usually had to swear to preserve these institutions, laws and customs. In general, for reasons of both principle and prudence, the Habsburgs were fastidious in honouring this obligation. Even when subjects rebelled and thereby released the monarchs from their oaths, after defeating and punishing rebels both Charles and Philip usually preserved the existing constitutional order. Not just these two most famous Habsburgs but all the dynasty's monarchs in the years between 1519 and 1648 saw themselves as legitimate and therefore law-abiding sovereigns. Neither in their own minds nor in reality were they absolute monarchs, unconstrained by law, institutions and custom.[15]

These constraints added to the enormous difficulties faced by Charles V in governing his empire. Like every emperor, he was forced to rule huge territories and diverse peoples, as well as to defend long borders. His empire even in Europe was widely dispersed and had no capital. Charles scurried between Spain, the Netherlands, Italy and the Holy Roman Empire to meet one crisis after another. In this era and culture the monarch's personal presence was often crucial in a crisis if resources were to be mobilized, policies executed, proud aristocrats wooed and opposition overawed.

Charles's two greatest enemies were France and the Ottoman Empire, whose armies and fleets sometimes combined forces against him in the Mediterranean. France had double Spain's population and more than double its resources and revenues. In Charles's reign American gold and silver far from covered the shortfall. France was also strategically well-placed geographically between the emperor's two richest and most crucial possessions, Castile and the Netherlands. Meanwhile in Charles's reign the Ottoman Empire was at the apogee of its power and confidence. Its revenues are reckoned to have been four times those of Charles's Spanish and American possessions. The 85,000-strong Ottoman standing army vastly outnumbered the regular forces of all Europe's leading monarchs combined. Even in the 1550s the imperial ambassador compared European mercenary armies very unfavourably with the Ottoman troops in terms of discipline, endurance and in many cases skill. Perhaps worst of all for Charles was religious schism in the Christian world. One advantage of ruling an empire made up of so many autonomous units was that it was difficult for opposition to unite across the different corporate groups and territories. Protestantism now provided a force which could mobilize and unite opposition on a wide scale. With the salvation of men's souls at issue, political conflicts became more bitter and irreconcilable.[16]

In this era the costs of war boomed. Armies grew much larger. Training and coordinating pikemen, infantry equipped with firearms, cavalry and artillery required skill and experience. Almost incessant warfare meant that mercenaries offered their services in a seller's market. Above all, it was in this era that European military technology began to outpace that of the rest of the world. The two main areas where Europe stood out were the construction of near-impregnable 'Italian-style' fortresses and of purpose-built warships capable of delivering massive artillery broadsides. Both were hugely expensive, though their construction did often generate useful economic activity. As rulers were forced to extract more taxes from their subjects political tensions inevitably rose. The Habsburgs led Europe first in borrowing huge sums from bankers at ever more extortionate levels of interest and then in declaring bankruptcy.

A vicious circle quickly developed. To besiege formidable, modern fortresses required big armies and ponderous siege trains. This slowed down warfare. Decisive victory and the conquest of territory became harder to achieve. Climate had always shortened the campaigning season. Now financial constraints did the same. The fruits of seemingly decisive victories on the battlefield could easily slip away as unpaid mercenary armies dissolved. The sacking of Rome in 1527 by Charles's unpaid soldiers cost 8,000 civilian lives and damaged the emperor's prestige. When Philip II's unpaid troops in the Netherlands went on the rampage in 1576 they for a time united the entire population against Habsburg rule. Against the Ottomans in the Mediterranean and the Anglo-Dutch, Charles V and Philip II were forced to wage war at sea, with all the dangers and uncertainties this entailed in the early decades of war between sailing fleets. Storms wrecked Charles's assault on Algiers in 1540 and Atlantic winds, tides and storms impeded potentially very dangerous Spanish intervention in Ireland in the 1590s and 1601. By this later period Europe was also edging into the 'Little Ice

Age', which brought misery and political instability in its wake for much of the seventeenth century. The obstacles and frustrations facing any ruler attempting to impose his will across the European continent were vast.[17]

If one looks at Habsburg rule across the whole era from Charles V's assumption of power (king of Spain from 1516, Holy Roman Emperor from 1519) until the end of the Thirty Years War in 1648, then it is probably a fair generalization to say that the dynasty's success depended above all on its alliance with the top echelon of the aristocracy. In 1517 Charles arrived in Castile for the first time in his life, speaking no Spanish and surrounded by Burgundian courtiers. In 1520 he departed for Germany to assume his responsibilities as newly elected Holy Roman Emperor having alienated most sections of Castilian society. The dangerous rebellion which followed was crushed by the Castilian magnates, who preferred Habsburg rule to social and political radicalism. Thenceforth Charles was very careful not to antagonize the leading aristocratic families of both Spain and the Netherlands.[18]

In Germany his task was harder because Charles's power as monarch was far less and because it was here that the Protestant challenge first erupted in the 1520s. The two great Habsburg efforts to roll back German Protestantism came in the 1540s under Charles and in the 1620s and 1630s under Ferdinand II. Both emperors overreached and alienated potential allies but they also faced fundamental problems. Many princes had converted to Protestantism out of deep personal conviction as well as, sometimes, dynastic self-interest. In addition, the victory of Catholicism in Germany required greater imperial power, but Habsburg efforts in this direction cost them the support even of many Catholic princes. Similar difficulties confronted Philip II's rule in the Netherlands, where Protestantism was spreading quickly in the 1560s, as was always likely to happen in Europe's most urbanized region. An effective Catholic response required the fundamental reforms in the organization and resources of the Church which Cardinal de Granvelle was attempting to implement, but these reforms themselves alienated key interests and infringed many inherited rights and customs.[19]

By the late sixteenth century Catholicism was under siege also in the Habsburg lands in central Europe, in other words Austria, the Czech provinces and Hungary. The great majority of the landed nobility and the urban elites had converted to Protestantism, and Protestant sympathizers dominated most of the provincial assemblies (diets). The remarkable success of Catholicism in largely reconquering this vast area in the first half of the seventeenth century was owed to the rejuvenation and dynamism of the Counter-Reformation Church and the unremitting support it enjoyed from the Habsburgs after Ferdinand II's accession in 1618. The Jesuits in particular invested great and successful effort in educating young aristocrats, including the future Ferdinand II and many other Habsburgs. The emperors ensured that patronage and power flowed only to loyal Catholic aristocrats. The tight alliance between the Church, the Habsburg dynasty and the aristocratic magnates who came to dominate landowning and political power in the provinces was the bedrock of the Habsburg Empire for the next hundred years and remained very important right down to the empire's demise in 1918.[20]

A key thread running through this book is how emperors managed their families. Among imperial dynasties the Habsburgs (with inevitable individual exceptions) rank very high as regards solidarity, loyalty and effective support for the reigning monarch. This was especially true in the reign of Charles V, despite the fact that the emperor sometimes bullied his siblings, undermined their authority and exploited their devotion to him. First Charles's aunt Margaret and then his sister Mary (the widowed queen of Hungary) acted as his viceroys in the Netherlands. Both were highly intelligent, able and effective. Mary in particular combined total loyalty with an almost unique willingness to offer in strict confidence useful criticisms of her brother's policies. Castile was the core of Charles's power but he was able to spend most of his reign elsewhere, appointing his son Philip as viceroy with no qualms as to his loyalty. Of course, it helped greatly that (unlike most princes outside Europe) Philip could be certain that one day he would inherit his father's empire. Most remarkable was Charles's relationship with his only brother, the Archduke and later Emperor Ferdinand. For almost all Charles's reign Ferdinand acted as his deputy and designated successor in the Holy Roman Empire. In 1524 the emperor wrote to Ferdinand that 'there is no one in the world whom I love and trust as much as you', and subsequently Charles advised his son that Ferdinand was the man whom above all others in the world he could trust for wise advice and absolute loyalty. This loyalty was sorely tested when in the last years of his reign Charles attempted to go back on earlier promises and pass the imperial crown to Philip. Ferdinand's patience, calm, generosity and loyalty under extreme provocation was all the more remarkable because he knew that Charles's effort would not just break the Habsburg family apart but would also face insuperable opposition from the prince electors.[21]

To his credit, Philip himself dropped all pretensions to the imperial succession at the first possible moment. Through little fault of his own he was much less lucky than his father when it came to using his family to run his empire. His eldest (and for almost all Philip's reign only adult) son was the physically deformed and mentally defective Prince Charles (don Carlos), whom in 1568 the king was forced to lock away and exclude from the succession. Such embarrassments were the price one sometimes paid for adhering to the principle of primogeniture. Philip's much-loved and able younger sister Joanna insisted on becoming a nun. As Viceroy of the Netherlands, the king was forced to fall back on Charles's illegitimate daughter, Margaret of Parma. Margaret had neither the authority nor the ability of Mary of Hungary. As opposition mounted in the 1560s, Margaret and Philip's trusted lieutenant in the Netherlands, Cardinal de Granvelle, disagreed fundamentally as to whether it should be confronted or appeased. Similar divisions existed at Philip's court. Combined with the physical distance between Brussels and Madrid this contributed to paralysis in the face of growing crisis and played a big role in the coming of the Dutch revolt. Twenty years later, on the other hand, Margaret's son, Alexander Farnese, was to serve Philip well as a formidable soldier and viceroy.

As regards the Austrian branch of the dynasty, though Philip remained always on good terms with his uncle Ferdinand I subsequently relations cooled. Emperor Maximilian II (r. 1564–76) was a difficult man who never forgave perceived slights. The attempt by his uncle (and father-in-law) Charles V to exclude him from the imperial succession always rankled. His son and successor, Rudolph II (r. 1576–1612), was even less satisfactory: politically inept, deeply immersed in the occult world and astrology, and in increasingly precarious mental health. From Philip's perspective what mattered most was that both rulers disliked the Counter-Reformation and allowed the spread of Protestantism throughout Austria and Bohemia. Only in 1618, twenty years after Philip II's death, did the accession of Ferdinand II restore unity between the Spanish and Austrian branches of the Habsburgs in defence of intransigent

Counter-Reformation principles. Habsburg dynastic solidarity was the backbone of the Catholic cause during the subsequent Thirty Years War.[22]

In the end, however, the dynastic principle almost had the last laugh on the Habsburgs. The desire to bind together the Spanish and Austrian branches of the dynasty had resulted in a degree of intermarriage rare even in Europe. This policy, pursued over many generations, resulted in mental problems, infertility, physical disabilities and child mortality on a scale remarkable even in that era. Philip II's heir, don Carlos, had only four great-grandparents instead of the normal eight. Two of his grandparents were children of Charles V's mother, the insane Queen Joanna of Castile. The Spanish branch of the dynasty expired in 1700 at the death of the physically handicapped and impotent Charles II, the only son of Philip IV who survived to adulthood. The Spanish Empire was divided according to a somewhat modified version of legitimate family inheritance, with the biggest share going to a cadet branch of the French royal house, who were descended from Louis XIV's wife, the daughter of King Philip IV of Spain. Charles V and Philip II would have recoiled with horror at the thought of this outcome to all their endeavours. Forty years later, in 1740, the Austrian branch of the family also expired in the male line with the death of the Holy Roman Emperor Charles VI. The Austrian lands only survived almost intact in Habsburg hands thanks to the extraordinary courage and resolve of Charles VI's daughter, the Empress Maria Theresa. In both 1700 and 1740 the expiry of the two branches of the Habsburgs had great implications for European geopolitics and the balance of power between the continent's dynastic states. Hugely costly conflicts resulted that lasted for many years and might with some justice be described as world wars.

One interesting angle on Charles V's reign is to look at how the emperor's modus operandi changed over time. This says something about Charles himself, but the manner in which his attitude to governing evolved over the stages of his life was typical of many monarchs. The emperor was well educated by excellent tutors, one of whom subsequently became Pope Adrian VI. As an adolescent, Charles was more interested in martial sports and chivalric tales than in learning. Later in his life he sometimes regretted the gaps this left. His governor, the baron de Chevres, came from the very aristocratic Croy family and had a great influence on Charles until the baron's death in 1521. In some ways this influence was for the good: after he came of age, Chevres encouraged the young monarch to work hard and feel a great sense of responsibility. Unfortunately, like many aristocrats, Chevres had a limitless appetite for patronage which he dispensed among his relations and clients. In Castile he persuaded Charles to grant the plum archbishopric of Toledo to his nineteen-year-old nephew, wrecking the monarch's standing with the Castilian aristocracy. Subsequently Charles recognized the stupidity of this act and the dangers for a king of falling under the influence of a favourite and allowing him to control patronage.[23]

Charles's leading adviser in the 1520s was his chancellor, Mercurino di Gattinara, and the emperor accepted with admirable humility the old man's frank criticisms of his working methods. Nevertheless, Charles consulted widely and did not allow himself to be controlled by Gattinara. He read documents carefully, gathered opinions, reflected deeply and often with painful slowness, but he was very hard to budge once he had made a decision. With time came growing confidence in his own judgement and an increasing stubbornness, which in honest moments he himself admitted as a weakness. By the 1540s he was decreasingly likely to listen to advice that he didn't want to hear. This became especially true after his defeat of Francis I in 1544–5 and the German Protestants in 1548, and even more so after the death of the last of his senior advisers, Nicholas de Granvelle, in 1550. Although Granvelle was to some extent succeeded by his son, the future cardinal, the veteran emperor was far less likely to listen to the advice of a younger man and Granvelle junior was shyer to offer it. An emperor unwilling to listen to contrary opinions was unlikely to receive them. The serious military defeats suffered by Charles in 1549–52, and the foolish attempt to impose Philip as his successor in the Holy Roman Empire, followed. Nevertheless, it would be unfair to end an account of Charles's reign on a negative note. Despite exhaustion, illness and melancholy Charles summoned the resolution to beat back a French attempt to exploit their victory in the 1552 campaign. In the end he had the wisdom to remove himself from German affairs and allow Ferdinand to make the necessary compromises with the Protestants. Charles achieved the dream of many ageing emperors by abdicating and shedding the burdens of his position, handing his possessions peacefully to his heirs and retiring to the palace-monastery of Yuste in Extremadura to prepare for the afterlife. Given the enormous challenges Charles had faced, it was a considerable achievement to preserve his entire inheritance for his heirs.[24]

It is sometimes asked whether Charles V and Philip II operated according to what in contemporary jargon is called a grand strategy. This means a defined set of overall goals and priorities, policies geared to achieving these ends, and a plan of how to mobilize the political and economic resources necessary for success. In reality, no pre-modern monarch thought or planned in these precise terms. What Charles undoubtedly did possess was a vision. His dream was to fulfil his role as emperor by leading the community of Christian princes on a crusade that would end the Ottoman threat and liberate the Holy Land. Meanwhile in his domestic policy he would defend the unity of the Christian community and the doctrines bequeathed by the Gospel and the great ecumenical councils that had steered the Catholic Church since the fourth century. At the same time he would encourage fundamental reforms of church practice, whose necessity he freely recognized. In his own lands he would rule with the justice and mercy required of a Christian king. In essence this vision differed little from the ideal of Saint Louis (Louis IX), paragon of medieval monarchs. The parallel brings out how deeply conservative and traditional were Charles's core beliefs.[25]

Unlike Saint Louis, Charles V never actually went on crusade but his vision was nevertheless not just an escapist fantasy. The rivalry between France and the Bourbons was the key political cleavage in Christendom. Disputes over Milan and the Netherlands were its main flashpoints. After defeating Francis in the campaigns of 1543–4, Charles proposed to end their antagonism and foster a united Christendom by marrying his daughter to Francis's son and granting them possession of either Burgundy or Milan. The scheme fell through but it was visionary, principled and perhaps also politically wise. By 1548, when he wrote the last of his three testaments for his son, Philip (whom he left behind as regent when leaving Spain in 1538, 1543 and 1548), Charles's views on France had hardened.

In this testament he told Philip that no concessions would assuage French ambitions and the Habsburgs' lands must be defended to the last inch. But the emperor feared that it might be impossible for his heir to retain his grasp on the Netherlands while mostly based in Spain. Perhaps therefore it might be wiser to grant the Netherlands to another

Habsburg, who would rule the territory autonomously while swearing to adhere to the head of the family's foreign policy.

In Charles's opinion, holding Genoa and Milan was the key to dominating Italy. The pope must be obeyed on all issues of Catholic doctrine but his ambitions as a territorial sovereign were often malign and must be opposed. The final testament also revealed the hardening over time of Charles's attitude towards the German Protestants. He now wrote that only force could check their advance. Philip's leading biographer calls the 1548 testament highly perceptive and the grand strategy best suited to preserve Philip's inheritance intact, but perhaps this is to stretch the term 'grand strategy' too far. The emperor understood only too well the inherent uncertainty of politics and the extent to which the ruler of a vast empire was buffeted by unexpected circumstances and challenges. In an earlier testament he had warned Philip that it was impossible to give him detailed guidance on policy, 'for there are more exceptions than rules in politics'.[26]

Unlike Charles V, Philip II did not have the title of emperor. This went to his uncle Ferdinand and subsequently passed down the line of his descendants in the Austrian branch of the dynasty. No European in Philip II's era doubted, however, that the Spanish king was very much the head of the Habsburg dynasty. Philip's resources, power and ambitions were far greater than those of his Austrian cousins. In the early seventeenth century the Spanish king ruled an empire of 4.4 million square miles, much more than double the extent of the contemporary Ming Empire in China, one-third larger than the Ottoman Empire at its zenith, and vastly greater than the possessions of the Austrian Habsburgs. In Philip's reign the contribution of American silver to the Habsburgs' treasury grew exponentially and peaked. Even in Europe, Philip retained the two most important parts of his father's empire, Castile and the Netherlands, whose revenues were the key to Charles's power. He also ruled half of Italy and dominated most of the peninsula. Philip saw Castile as his homeland but even Charles had chosen this kingdom as his place to retire and be buried. In no sense did either man see himself as king of Spain. This is to read nationalist assumptions back into a much earlier history. No kingdom of Spain existed either in reality or in the minds of these Habsburg monarchs. In down-to-earth terms it was far easier for them to draw resources from the Americas than from Aragon. Philip's perspectives were barely if at all less universal than his father's. He inherited from Charles the same belief that his duty lay in sustaining the one true and universal Church. This meant the duty both to convert the Americans to the Catholic faith and to use American resources to reassert Catholicism's dominance in Europe. Spanish rule in the Americas had enormous, long-term geopolitical and cultural consequences. In the terms that this book defines the words 'empire' and 'emperor', Philip was unequivocally an emperor and ruled one of the largest and most important empires ever known.[27]

Philip faced somewhat lesser challenges than Charles. Since he was not the Holy Roman Emperor, he was not directly responsible for confronting the German Protestants. This task could be postponed until the Habsburgs had defeated their other enemies and could again unite their strength to resume the battle in Germany. This moment came in 1619 and brought decades of war to Europe. Nor was Philip responsible for defending the Hungarian border against the Ottomans. By the last quarter of the sixteenth century Ottoman relative power had somewhat declined and its main thrust was against Persia and the Austrian Habsburgs, rather than in the central and western Mediterranean. The truce agreed with Philip II in early 1577 lasted for the rest of his reign. Most important, between the death of Henry II in 1559 and the consolidation of Henry IV's position in the 1590s France was torn by religious conflict and was unable to sustain a meaningful foreign policy. France had been the most persistent and dangerous obstacle to Habsburg efforts to reassert the dominance of their dynasty and Counter-Reformation Catholicism in Europe. With France eliminated as a great power Philip II had a golden opportunity. To a great extent this was lost as a result of the Dutch revolt. The Dutch revolt and its consequences were therefore the most important challenge and failure in Philip's imperial project.

In the Netherlands, Philip faced a quintessentially imperial problem. No emperor found it easy to manage rich societies with deeply rooted local elites on the periphery of his empire. Distance imposed severe constraints on decision-making, especially in times of crisis. Revolts might well find effective support from great-power rivals. All these factors bore on the Dutch revolt, for whose outbreak Philip himself also bears part of the blame. At least in retrospect it seems obvious that a minimalist strategy based on preserving the alliance with the regional aristocracy would have been far preferable to Philip's efforts to impose policies by force. In the decades after Alba's army was first committed to the Netherlands in 1566 it sometimes appeared that the rebellion was on the point of extinction, but it always flared up again, not least because of the depredations of the Spanish army. Without the support of local elites, it was impossible to pay the vast costs of the occupying army from local taxes. The war contributed greatly to Castile's already crushing tax burden and Philip's bankruptcy. Worst of all, Spanish operations in the Netherlands drew Philip into war with England. In 1580 the king acquired through inheritance Portugal and its empire, a potentially enormous windfall. This made Philip a much greater world emperor even than Charles. The Portuguese kings' empire and power had never matched that of the Habsburgs. Even so it dwarfed the tiny overseas possessions of the French, Dutch and English. Now Europe's second-greatest overseas empire had fallen into the hands of the man who already ruled one of the largest empires on earth. However, in the 1580s English and Dutch naval raids on the Iberian coast and colonial trade inflicted huge losses, overstretched Habsburg resources and robbed the king of most of the potential benefits of his new acquisition.

Correctly, Philip's advisers warned him that it was impossible to defend a far-flung empire at all the places which a highly mobile, maritime enemy might choose to strike. For the first time a European monarch faced the classic dilemma of Chinese emperors. The ocean was an even wider and more open highway than the steppe. It allowed unparalleled mobility to British and Dutch seaborne raiders. Like the nomads of the steppe but to an even greater extent, the pirates of the sea could criss-cross enormous spaces in pursuit of profit and plunder. They could also concentrate their forces easily and had a range of stationary and juicy targets from which to choose. It was impossible for a sedentary empire to defend all these targets adequately. Divided by the oceans, the internal communications of the Spanish Empire were vulnerable to sea 'nomads' to a degree that was seldom true in land empires. Only an offensive strategy, in other words the invasion of England, had any chance of success. French and Ottoman distraction made it possible to mount such an operation. Although in strategic terms Philip's Armada – his grand-scale plan to invade England – made sense, at the lower, operational, level the difficulty of mounting such a complex amphibious campaign was immense, as Philip's leading military and naval advisers warned.[28]

If the king ignored this advice, this owed much to a combination of stubbornness and desperation, no doubt encouraged by increasing age. But there also lurked in Philip's mind – as indeed in that of his father and the Castilian elite as a whole – the belief that his cause was also that of God and would therefore in the end triumph against all obstacles. Behind this conviction there lay the belief that, if God had granted Spain and the Habsburgs so many victories and so enormous an empire, then He must have done so with some great purpose in mind. To some extent this was a Spanish and Habsburg variation on the theme of imperial power and hubris. It was also a Christian variation on the widespread assumption in pre-modern times that Heaven in some form intervened in events on earth, rewarding rulers who upheld its principles and punishing those who infringed them.[29]

Anglophone historians have usually much preferred Charles V to his son. The exuberant and chivalrous Burgundian youth is contrasted – usually implicitly – with the sinister black-clothed recluse weaving plots behind the blank stone walls of his palace-monastery, the Escorial, near Madrid. Aged twenty-five, Charles wrote that 'I would not like to go without performing some great action as a monument to my name . . . I have done nothing so far to cover myself with glory.' Philip II was probably too self-controlled to speak in this way. Even Charles's vices – his susceptibility to female charms and his love for iced beer and oysters – make him seem human when contrasted to the austere and tidy figure of Philip II. There were significant differences between the two men. Charles had the more charismatic personality and was often able to attract great loyalty and affection among his entourage. At times he could even be witty at his own expense. Philip's character owed at least as much to his mother as his father. During the first twelve years of his life in Spain Charles had been absent most of the time. Philip's mother, Isabella, on the contrary was a constant presence. Famous for her beauty, her delicacy and her reserve, the empress-queen was the embodiment of the aristocratic female ideal. 'Isabella was a formidable and imperious woman, known for her iron self-control, and from her Philip inherited his extraordinary self-discipline and his regal composure.' He will have needed all this self-discipline even at the age of twelve, when his mother died suddenly and his father departed for northern Europe again, leaving him behind as the nominal regent of Spain.[30]

As monarchs, the greatest difference between father and son was that Charles revelled in the role of warrior-king. He led his army on nine campaigns, most of them victorious. Contemporaries recorded that on campaign Charles unwound, shed some of his troubles and became lighter-hearted and more sociable. By contrast, though Philip was glad to have earned his spurs in the campaign of 1557 he never subsequently showed any wish to lead his army in battle. He was the quintessential royal chief bureaucrat, weighed down by the burdens of administration and operating most happily through written reports rather than face-to-face meetings. His best-known contemporary biographer describes his personality as obsessional: drowned in detail and unable to delegate; inflexible and with a tight control on his emotions; hard-working but often inefficient. The criticism is no doubt partly fair. But Philip's obsession with control and detail was partly born of deep suspicion about the hidden intrigues and machinations of rival individuals and factions in his court and government. These suspicions were often well-founded. In one notorious case a key adviser camouflaged his own disloyalty so craftily by blackening a rival that he persuaded Philip to order the latter's death. When the full story came out and the truth spread across Europe the enemies of Spain and Catholicism used it with glee to blacken the king's reputation.[31]

Even so, it would be a mistake to exaggerate the differences between the two monarchs. Neither man was exceptionally intelligent or imaginative: one should not expect this in hereditary monarchs selected on strict principles of primogeniture. Charles like Philip was often accused of stubbornness and immersion in details. It was Charles, not Philip, who was subject to fits of deep depression. By royal standards both men were remarkably chaste and faithful to their wives. There is no evidence of Charles's infidelity to the Empress-Queen Isabella, whom he loved deeply and whose death shattered him. His illegitimate children were born before or after his period of marriage. Both Charles and Philip were willing to lie and kill in defence of what they saw as a holy and legitimate cause. To the extent that Philip was more ruthless, this owed at least as much to different eras as to differences between the two rulers' personalities or morals. The Council of Trent put the last touches to the doctrines of intransigent Counter-Reformation and broke up in 1555. Thenceforth the ideological battle-lines in Europe were sharply drawn and the struggle between the rival religious camps became more ruthless and less susceptible to any conceivable compromise.

The monastery-palace of the Escorial was Philip's great creation and his pride and joy. One might almost say that it was his consolation and respite from the burdens of rule. He lavished personal attention on its construction and decoration, as well as on the collections it housed. Both Philip and Charles had fine artistic taste. Above all, they admired Flemish art and sought to introduce it into Spain, which in that era was something of a provincial backwater in Europe. The Escorial was austere by the standard of most palaces, including other Spanish royal residences where Philip actually spent most of his time. Since it was above all a monastery and royal mausoleum the Escorial's relative austerity is unsurprising. Philip chose the spot because of the superb mountains and forests by which his new monastery-palace was surrounded and which he loved. He was also a passionate gardener. In his day the Escorial was surrounded by superb gardens. Philip also loved fishing and hunting in the nearby ponds and forests. He was the greatest collector of paintings, books and exotic plants in Spain. Nor was he altogether without a sense of humour. He once secretly arranged for the monks in the Escorial to be visited in their cells by his pet elephant, much to their astonishment. Philip was certainly not exuberant and he felt the loneliness of power. Like many monarchs he kept his emotions under tight rein, revealing them fully only in his relations with his wives, sisters and daughters, to whom he was devoted. The picture of the king listening patiently and with an encouraging smile to modest petitioners, never interrupting them and always giving them the opportunity to speak first, is an attractive one. He was also punctilious in always kissing the hands even of the youngest and most junior of priests.[32]

Neither Charles nor Philip were theatrical monarchs, at least in their roles as Spanish kings. The great ceremonies associated with Charles, and above all his superb coronation in Bologna by the pope in 1530, were linked to his position as emperor. By French or English standards the Castilian kings did not go in for much ceremony. They had no splendid throne, sceptre or crown and they assumed power without any coronation. As kings of Castile, Charles and Philip were in no sense hidden away in the style of many non-Christian monarchs of Eurasia, but by European standards they lived a relatively quiet and secluded existence. Confident in their dynastic legitimacy, they felt no need to embark on Tudor-style publicity or personality cults. Neither man was blessed with a commanding physical presence. Charles was even ugly, with physical deformities that left his mouth hanging open, a prominent lower jaw and front teeth that had been knocked out in a hunting accident. To offset these disadvantages he cultivated not just a beard but also a calm, restrained but majestic manner that impressed those who met him and aged better than the more outgoing, ebullient and public style adopted by Henry VIII and (to a lesser extent) Francis I. Above all Charles and Philip were similar in their total dedication to their common dynastic, Christian and imperial ideal and identity, in which they sublimated their individual personalities. They served this cause with unstinting hard work and resolution, in a way that was by turns admirable, moving and terrifying.[33]

It is useful and interesting to study these Habsburg monarchs not just because of the importance of their empire and era, but also because the sources allow us to gain insights into their personalities and their inner thoughts about the business of government. Among many sources, probably the best are the testaments that Charles wrote for his son, in 1538, 1543 and 1548. The first testament, written in 1538 when Philip was only eleven, was repeated and developed in the other two. The testament of 1548, largely a survey of the international position, has already been discussed. I will conclude this chapter by looking briefly at the two memoranda that Charles drew up in 1543 as part of his second testament. Both documents were confidential but the second, in which the emperor discussed the strengths and weaknesses of his top ministers, was for Philip's eyes alone.

The memoranda combined comments about personalities and some more general thoughts about governing the empire. Philip was urged to keep a sharp eye on the treasury, 'which is today the most important department of state; the treasury has a clear knowledge of the means which are at your disposal'. He must be especially cautious about infringing the rights and privileges of the kingdom of Aragon, since the local elites were extremely touchy and excitable on this issue. As regards military leadership, he should put most trust in the advice of the Duke of Alba but should follow Charles's example in keeping Alba out of the top government council, since 'it is best not to involve grandees in the government of the kingdom', above all because of their tendency to regard government as a bottomless pit of patronage for their networks of relatives and clients. It was vital for Philip not to become the creature of either of the two 'parties' that dominated the court. He must employ members of both groups but stand outside and above them. To do so required the employment of competent ministers whose loyalty he could trust.

There followed an evaluation of the key ministers in terms of their knowledge, intelligence and reliability. Each one was an individual who must be controlled, motivated and used in the right role according to his expertise and trustworthiness. Charles was not a cruel master. None of his leading advisers was executed or even disgraced. Most of them held their positions for many years. The emperor accepted that high office would be used as a means to acquire wealth. Of course, Charles was not a modern chief executive officer. As monarch he stood far above his ministers. They could neither replace nor overrule him. Opinions and objections regarding policy would be offered only if they were invited and in usually very deferential terms. Nevertheless, much of Charles's memoranda would ring true to a contemporary political leader or even the leader of a large corporation. To achieve anything the emperor needed to work through men and institutions. From his earliest childhood Charles had been taught that he must take advice before making decisions and must choose honest advisers, not flatterers. So, we find God's anointed telling his son about the foibles of one minister and the manner in which past events had shaped the ambitions and resentments of his colleagues; about how vital two ministers were to the effective governance of Spain and how best to cajole them into working together in harmony; about how to encourage and reward honest criticism but, in one case, how much to trust a minister but beware his wife. The top echelon of government was a small village whose inhabitants Charles knew very well.

The person to whom Charles was writing in 1543 was not yet adult. He was the emperor's only son and the person on whom the future of dynasty and empire depended. Charles 'managed' all members of his family by using moral blackmail. He could do this effectively because from childhood they had internalized the lessons taught to them about family solidarity and the debt of loyalty owed to the dynasty's head. Inevitably, this blackmail was most extreme in the emperor's treatment of his heir. After a very brief bow to the fact that his sixteen-year-old son could not forsake all the recreations of youth, Charles reminded Philip that the fact he was now a married prince and his father's regent in Spain 'make you a man long before your time'. Philip's responsibility to God and to his own soul required that he must always put duty first. Some of the advice offered by Charles would no doubt have been endorsed by most monarchs when seeking to train their heirs and will by now be familiar to readers of this book. Philip was urged never to make decisions on the basis of 'passion, prejudice or anger', to be 'calm and reserved' in his bearing and to 'listen to good advice and take heed of flatterers as you would of fire'.

But Charles's urgings went beyond even those of the normal royal father. He reminded Philip that he was the only son he would ever have, which was no doubt a reference to the dead Empress-Queen Isabella, whose memory her husband and her son so revered. He must keep himself chaste, healthy and capable of producing heirs. 'Think what troubles might not ensue if your sisters and their husbands came to inherit what was yours.' Philip was warned against over-indulgence as a young man even in marriage (let alone with other women) and was reminded of the sad fate of his uncle, whom Charles described as dying early as a result. To avoid such temptations of the flesh and the emotions, Philip must steel himself to spend considerable time away even from his young wife. Since the requirements of ruling a vast empire had taken Charles away from his wife for many years, he no doubt thought that this warning was a useful preparation for his son.

Amidst the strains and temptations of kingship, it was vital to preserve one's moral compass. For this it was essential to choose as confessor a tough and fearless friar without personal ambition, who in the strict privacy of the confessional would tell home truths to the monarch and keep him true to his duty to serve God as both ruler and man. This gave the confessor a legitimate and at times important role in policy-making, something which remained a feature in Habsburg governance down to 1648 and even beyond. In the 1530s and 1540s, for example, one issue which greatly troubled Charles was the mistreatment of the American natives by the colonists. A number of prominent clerics close to the emperor (including his confessor) were intensely concerned with this question. It seems that Charles himself believed that the storms that wrecked his assault on Algiers in 1541 were God's warning about the sins committed by Spanish colonists in Latin America and his own failure to protect his native South American subjects. The emperor's efforts to rein in the colonists and impose imperial justice led to a revolt which almost lost Peru for the crown. Subsequently the demands of justice had to be reconciled with the king's need for revenue and the impossibility of tight royal supervision over communities and elites living at a huge distance from Madrid. These were problems familiar to most emperors. Nevertheless, in his later testament of 1548 Charles pressed Philip in the name of God and justice to protect the native Americans from the greed and cruelty of their Spanish colonial masters, which the tyranny of distance and the nature of colonial governance made it so hard to check.

The emperor's injunctions and moral qualms were not feigned. He knew that duplicity, violence and compromises with the realities of this world were necessary for a ruler who served God's cause. But his conviction that his dynasty had a divinely imposed mission and that God protected their endeavours sustained him and drove him on. 'God grant, my son,' he wrote, 'that you may so live and act with His help that He will be rightly served, and that He will receive you at last in Paradise after your days on earth. This is the constant prayer of your loving father.' Philip proved wholly loyal to his father's cause and bequest. To fulfil this mission he imposed great burdens and constraints on himself. Trying to evaluate the influence of genes, education and parental example on a man who died four hundred years ago is an impossible task. But if, as is sometimes suggested, Philip II was an 'obsessional personality', then the great pressures put on him in his youth must surely have had an effect.[34]

11

Emperors, Caliphs and Sultans: The Ottoman Dynasty

In the sixteenth century much of Eurasia was ruled by three Muslim dynasties. The Ottomans dominated the Near East, north Africa and south-eastern Europe. The Safavids reigned in Iran (including at times much of what we now call Iraq), and it was under their rule that the Iranian state and most of the population converted from Sunni to Shi'i Islam. Meanwhile, for the first time in more than a thousand years, almost all the Indian subcontinent formed a single empire, ruled over by the Mughals. The Mughals were the descendants of two of the greatest conqueror-emperors in history, Chinggis Khan and Timur. The Safavids claimed descent from the Prophet Muhammad and his son-in-law Ali. In comparison to these towering figures in Eurasian and Islamic history the Ottomans, whose ancestors were the leaders of a small Turkic war-band, were nobodies. Nevertheless, the Ottoman dynasty long outlived both the Safavids and the Mughals. Ruling for 650 years, the Ottomans have a good claim to be the greatest of all Islamic dynasties, matched only by the Abbasids.[1]

In the course of 650 years, the nature of the Ottoman monarchy changed and the power actually exercised by the monarchs waxed and waned. From their emergence in the thirteenth century until 1453, the Ottoman monarchs were the leaders of an exceptionally successful war-band, operating on the borders between the Christian and Muslim worlds in Anatolia and south-eastern Europe. The monarchs behaved according to the generally informal and relatively egalitarian code of war-band leaders. Conquest of Constantinople (Istanbul) in 1453 and of the Egyptian Mamluks in 1517 transformed them into the rulers of one of the world's greatest empires. Replacing the Mamluks as rulers and guardians of Mecca and Medina made the Ottomans the pre-eminent dynasty in Sunni Islam. The years between 1453 and the end of the sixteenth century are generally seen as the apogee of the Ottomans. The three most famous Ottoman sultans – Mehmed II (r. 1444–6, 1451–81), Selim I (r. 1512–20) and Suleyman I (r. 1520–66) – reigned in this era. They were formidable political and military leaders, as well as increasingly majestic and remote emperors.

The first half of the seventeenth century was a time of crisis for both empire and dynasty. One element of this crisis was the fact that for much of this period the monarchs were children or mentally defective. Stability was restored in the 1650s by the Grand Vizier Mehmed Koprulu, whose family dominated Ottoman government for decades, with the unequivocal support of Sultan Mehmed IV (r. 1648–87). The political order stabilized by the Koprulus lasted until the end of the eighteenth century and is sometimes called 'Ottoman constitutionalism'. The power of the monarchs was strongly constrained: political life was dominated by the *ulama* (senior judges and religious scholars), provincial notables (*ayans*), and the military garrison of Istanbul (Janissaries). The Janissaries were closely tied to Istanbul's merchants and artisans, as well as to conservative religious groups (Sufi lodges) in the capital.

Ottoman constitutionalism was ultimately undermined by its failure to sustain the empire's military power or defend its borders against the Russian Empire. Defeat in three wars between 1768 and 1812 resulted in a reassertion of centralized monarchical power as the only means to preserve the empire against external invasion and internal rebellion. This process began under Selim III (r. 1789–1807) and after his overthrow and murder was carried forward in 1807–8 more successfully by his cousin Mahmud II (r. 1808–39). This era in the history of the Ottoman monarchy lasted for a century. The last Ottoman autocrat, Abdul Hamid II (r. 1876–1909), was overthrown by the so-called Young Turks in 1908–9. These were mostly army officers and members of the civilian professional classes committed to socio-economic modernization, 'meritocracy' and Turkish nationalism. Initially they preserved the Ottoman dynasty as powerless symbols of imperial glory and unity. Defeat and the loss of empire in the First World War, followed by allied occupation of Istanbul, resulted in a Turkish nationalist backlash, led by Mustapha Kemal (Atatürk). He portrayed the dynasty as responsible for religious obscurantism, political backwardness and Turkish weakness and subservience towards Christian Europe. Between 1922 and 1924 he stripped

The Ottoman Empire c. 1550

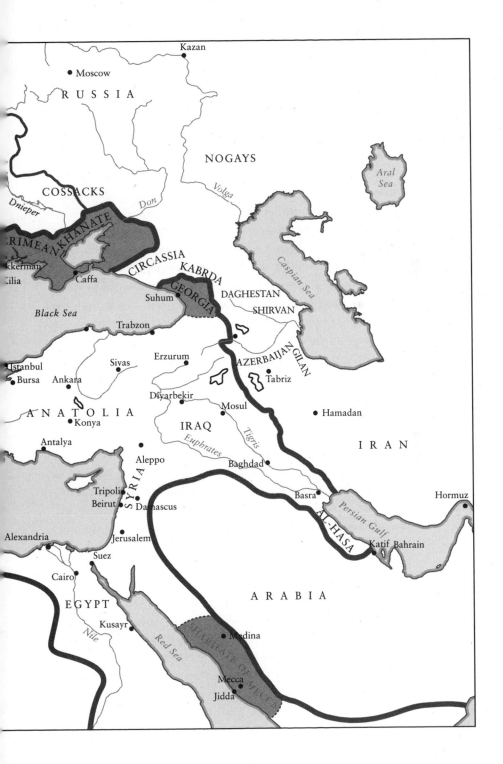

the Ottomans of their roles first as monarchs (sultans) and then as religious leaders (caliphs).[2]

Over the centuries the Ottomans drew on many sources of legitimacy. Initially, in a manner common to Turko-Mongol war-band leaders who had converted to Islam, they proclaimed themselves to be *'ghazi'*, in other words warriors fulfilling the Prophet's call to extend the Islamic faith across the world. The dynasty never abandoned their claim to be *ghazi* but in time added other elements of legitimacy better suited to the rulers of a sedentary realm. The Seljuk dynasty created the first great Turk Empire in Iran and Anatolia in the eleventh century. The Ottomans claimed to have been granted their core territories by the last Seljuk rulers. They borrowed from the Seljuks the Persian-Islamic conception of rulership rooted in the so-called 'circle of justice'. This boiled down to the argument that the wealth of a society and the power of its armies could only be sustained if monarchs ruled with justice and equity. The Ottomans also adopted the Seljuks' claim to descent from the mythical ancestor of all the Muslim Turks of western Asia, the world-conquering Khan Oguz. In the Turko-Islamic world God was believed to speak directly to human beings in their dreams. A core Ottoman legend described the dream of the dynasty's founder, Osman I, that God had planted the seed of a great tree in his bosom which grew to cover the whole earth with its shade. This legend illustrated God's promise that the Ottomans would one day rule all humanity. As widespread was the legend of the Red Apple (*Kizil-Elma*), which rested in Justinian's monument before the great cathedral of Hagia Sophia in Constantinople and symbolized worldwide dominion. These legends spread deeply into popular folklore, linking the dynasty to the mass of its Turkish subjects.[3]

The city of Constantinople had a huge place in the imagination of the Near Eastern world. It was *the* imperial city and the centre of the universe. The first Muslim siege of the city occurred in 650. For eight hundred years Constantinople's great walls defied one Muslim ruler after another. Its fall to the Ottomans in 1453 transformed the dynasty's status in its own eyes and those of the Islamic world. The city's conqueror, Mehmed II, had long since hoped to be a new Alexander. He undoubtedly believed the words addressed to him after the city's fall by the famous Greek scholar George of Trabzon: 'he who by right possesses the city (Constantinople) is the emperor of the Romans ... he who is and remains emperor of the Romans is also emperor of the entire earth.' A century later Mehmed's descendant Suleyman I would never address Charles V as emperor because he considered himself to be the sole heir to the Roman imperial tradition, ruler of the city that had been the empire's capital for over a millennium, and on a higher plane altogether to a near-powerless and provincial Holy Roman Emperor of the German Nation – which was Charles's official title.

At least as fundamental in its impact on Ottoman identity and legitimacy was the conquest of Medina and Mecca by Mehmed II's grandson Selim I. As sovereign and guardian of the Holy Places the Ottoman sultan became unequivocally first among Sunni Islamic rulers. To cite only some of the titles now appropriated by Selim, he was the 'Shadow of God', the 'Messiah of the Last Age' and the 'Alexandrine World Conqueror'. At a moment when the Sunni community was challenged by the new Shi'i empire of the Safavids, Selim was also 'the Renewer of Religion' and the great shield of Sunni doctrinal orthodoxy.[4]

Another title acquired by the Ottomans after their defeat of the Mamluks was 'Caliph'. After the annexation of Egypt the last Abbasid caliph was sent into honourable retirement in Istanbul. Selim I never used the title 'caliph' but his son Suleyman I did so on occasion. The key figure behind promoting the idea of the Ottoman caliphate was the former Grand Vizier Lutfi Pasha. Lutfi had lost his position and was fortunate to escape with his life after a violent clash with his wife, who as the daughter of Selim I had a sense of her own autonomy and status that a Muslim husband found hard to stomach. Possibly, it was in an effort to regain favour that he subsequently wrote a learned treatise arguing that the caliph did not need to be from the tribe of the Prophet – as the Abbasids had been – but could merit the title if he was a virtuous Muslim ruler who protected and supported Islam's holiest sites, Medina and Mecca. Although the Ottomans who succeeded Suleyman I retained the title, they did not make great play of their position as caliph until the reign of Abdul Hamid II in the dynasty's last decades. With his dynasty and empire threatened by both internal enemies and European imperialists the intelligent and able Abdul Hamid used his position as caliph to enhance the Ottoman monarchy's authority in the eyes of his own subjects, foreign powers and the worldwide Islamic community.[5]

It is difficult to get behind the official mask of Ottoman sultans and gain a sense of their personalities. This is certainly true of the dynasty's two greatest warrior leaders, Mehmed II and Selim I, the conquerors respectively of Constantinople and the Holy Places. Just occasionally a personal detail emerges. Members of the dynasty were given a practical training in some technical skill. Mehmed II was a trained gardener, with special enthusiasm for growing vegetables. What leaps out from every source is that both Mehmed and his grandson Selim were formidable, ruthless and effective autocrats: they were willing to sacrifice anything for the sake of their own power and that of their dynasty. Mehmed II in 1479 codified the already frequent practice whereby on ascending the throne a new sultan killed his brothers. The regulation stated that 'whichever of my sons inherits the sultan's throne, it behoves him to kill his brothers in the interests of world order. Most of the jurists have approved this procedure. Let action be taken accordingly.' Although the regulation was not binding on later sultans, in fact new sultans did follow this rule until the early seventeenth century. Selim I killed both his brothers and seven nephews on ascending the throne. He also, almost certainly, killed his father, Bayazid II, which in Turkic eyes was a more serious crime and was indeed 'the one clear and authenticated case of usurpation in the long history of the dynasty'.[6]

Many Ottoman sultans were given nicknames, most of which were flattering. Selim I was known to posterity as 'the Grim'. One senior official called Selim 'the ferocious lion . . . looking for a caracal . . . the man-eating king of the beasts'. The sultan's rages were notorious and terrified his family and entourage. Not only did he execute most of his Grand Viziers, he was also reported to have kicked around the head of one of them after the latter's execution to drive home the lesson. But although Selim's rages were real and frightening, his use of terror was usually considered a display of tactics rather than evidence of an uncontrollable temper. He often respected honesty and competence, especially from scholars, even when it led to questioning of his commands. In retrospect, Lutfi Pasha, who served as Grand Vizier under Selim's son, wrote that Selim used terror and strictness successfully to curb nepotism, corruption and incompetence within the civil and military administration. He contrasted Selim's tight-fisted control over public finance with the licence allowed by his son and grandson when it came to the corruption and extravagance of elite officials. Lutfi had an axe to grind with Suleyman I and Selim II but there is probably some truth to his comment. In all societies, histories of reigns and rulers were almost always written by members of the elite. The ruler's much-praised mildness and generosity usually meant generosity to them, often at the expense of ordinary subjects. In the lower reaches of society, a formidable autocrat who disciplined the elites and kept taxes down was generally welcomed.[7]

Selim came to the throne in 1512 after a bitter struggle with his eldest brother, Ahmed, and his father, Bayazid II. Bayazid was a gentler, more pious and less active ruler than either his father, Mehmed II, or his son Selim I. By 1511 he had been on the throne for thirty years, was well into his sixties, and was longing to settle the succession issue, escape to a quiet old age and abdicate in Ahmed's favour. Most high officials in Istanbul supported Ahmed. The sultan's middle son, Prince Korkud, had a high reputation as a scholar. In 1508 he had written a well-known work, 'The Erring Soul's Summons to Virtuous Works', which was both a personal search for religious truth and a plea to be allowed to pursue a life of contemplation and to remove himself from the world of politics. Unfortunately for Korkud, Ottoman tradition did not allow this freedom to princes, nor did Islam have the equivalent to the archbishoprics and cardinals' hats which might sometimes provide a Christian prince with a means of escape and immunity from political struggles.

Selim, the youngest son, was much tougher than his elder brothers. In the time-honoured tradition of Ottoman politics, he put together a coalition to support his cause in the succession struggle. This included elites from the region where he served as governor, frontier nobles in Europe who disliked the growth of centralized bureaucratic power under Bayazid, and Sunni religious leaders (*ulama*) who suspected Prince Ahmed and his sons of heterodox and even pro-Shi'i opinions. When the succession crisis reached its denouement in 1511–12 the decisive factor was the Janissaries' support for Selim. More than factional allegiance and corporate interest was involved. In these years the Ottomans faced an existential threat in the east from the growing power and aggression of the Safavid Shah Ismail. The Janissaries and their leaders were correct to believe that Selim was far better suited to face this threat than either his brothers or Bayazid. Their attempt to support Selim while preserving the life of Korkud failed, since it ran up against both the logic of Ottoman succession politics and the harsh and unforgiving personality of Selim I.[8]

The Safavid dynasty were leaders of a Sufi sect which originated in northern Iran and north-eastern Anatolia. To define that era's Sufism is difficult because its many sects had radically different beliefs, rituals and traditions. Many sects had dynasties of hereditary 'saints' as leaders. All of them sought a direct, emotional connection between the individual disciple of the sect's leader and God. They stressed inner belief over mere adherence to the outward forms of Islam laid down by the religious scholars (*ulama*) and the law (*sharia*). Some sects preached little more than a deeper and more intense piety than that shown by the average Muslim. Membership of these sects was wholly compatible with respect for the social order, the *ulama* and the *sharia*. By the fifteenth century some Sufi sects were wealthy and powerful. They included monarchs among their supporters and disciples. Even respectable sects often encouraged religious exercises such as collective chanting of religious formulas accompanied by breathing disciplines, dieting and ritual movements. At the extreme anti-establishment end of the Sufi movement some sects practised music, dancing, intoxicants and even orgies as a way to escape from reason, law and the vanities of this world, and to experience a direct, ecstatic communion with God. By the late fifteenth century the Safavids belonged fully to the radical wing of Sufism. Their rituals and their messianic message appealed to many Turkic nomadic tribesmen in the region, whose Islamic beliefs and practices often bore little resemblance to the doctrines established by orthodox *ulama*. Some Safavid practices – including ritualized cannibalism – may have owed more to elements in these tribesmen's Turko-Mongolian shamanistic heritage than to Sufism.[9]

If the Sunni political and religious establishment feared and despised Safavid savagery, it was appalled by the sect's adoption of Shi'ism in the fifteenth century. At a popular level, and especially in the Sufi world, the distinction between Sunni and Shi'i was often blurred. Apocalyptic and messianic currents existed on both sides of the divide and often overlapped. These currents gained strength in northern Iran after the region was devastated by the Mongols in the thirteenth century and the Black Death in the fourteenth. As the Islamic millennium approached, both religion and astronomy were drawn on to support predictions that the end of the world and the final judgement were just over the horizon. This was a favourable context for the emergence of a charismatic and prophetic leader.

The Safavid synthesis of Sufi and Shi'i beliefs proclaimed Shah Ismail to be the *Mahdi*, the representative of the hidden Shi'i twelfth imam and the precursor of the end of the world and God's final judgement of mankind. Especially in his religious poetry, Ismail came close to claiming that he was God himself, and many of the raw, nomadic tribesmen who followed his banner regarded him in this light. Religious messianism gave great unity, elan and power to the Safavid armies. As usual with charismatic leaders and millenarian political movements, the enormous initial impetus could not be sustained. Such leaders and movements promise miracles on earth, but in time reality intrudes. In the Safavid case what Max Weber called the routinization of charisma had vital longer-term consequences. For much of the sixteenth and seventeenth centuries the Ottomans were faced with a formidable enemy on their eastern flank. Without the Safavid threat they might well have taken Vienna and established a foothold in central Europe and southern Italy. Even more important from our contemporary perspective, the conversion of Iran to Shi'ism sharpened the age-old geopolitical rivalry between the great power that dominated the eastern Mediterranean and one that was based on the Iranian plateau.[10]

In the first years of the sixteenth century the Ottomans did not have the leisure to think long term. The Safavids were a huge, immediate danger. Between 1500 and 1512 Shah Ismail conquered not just most of Iran but also Baghdad and all of Mesopotamia. Worse still from the Ottomans' perspective, he had much potential support in Ottoman Anatolia. Many Anatolian nomadic tribes resented the efforts of the increasingly bureaucratic Ottoman regime to control and tax them. Many Ottoman Sufis shared beliefs and practices with Safavid Sufism. These included elements among the rank and file of the Janissaries, the core of the Ottoman army. In 1511 a serious pro-Safavid revolt broke out in Anatolia. Both Bayazid II and his chosen heir, Prince Ahmed, seemed too weak and too distracted by the succession issue to respond to this threat. Ahmed's son Prince Murad sympathized with the Safavid and Shi'i cause. In these circumstances it is not surprising that key members of the Ottoman elite, including the Janissary generals, looked to Prince Selim for salvation.[11]

Selim justified their confidence and thereby also justified the pitiless Ottoman approach to succession. Faced with an existential threat in 1510–14 the Ottomans produced a leader who rose to the occasion.

The 1511 rebellion was crushed and further revolt deterred by near genocidal levels of repression in some districts of Anatolia. Selim's policy preserved eastern Anatolia for his dynasty. He went on to crush the Safavids at the battle of Chaldiran in 1514, in large part because (unlike his enemy) he used firepower effectively on the battlefield. He also tricked the Safavids into fighting him at a time and on ground of his choosing. The Safavid threat was deflated for decades and never again put the actual survival of the Ottomans at risk. Selim then went on in 1516–19 to destroy and annex the Mamluk Empire, including the Holy Places. As all the great revealed religions loved to underline, God soon humbled even the greatest emperors. Selim died suddenly in 1520 at the peak of his vigour, leaving his throne to his only surviving son, Suleyman I, who ruled for almost forty-six years, the longest reign in Ottoman history. This reign is usually seen as the Ottoman apogee in terms not only of military power and victory, but also as regards internal legal and institutional consolidation, as well as the flowering of a distinct Ottoman high culture. Suleyman I is the most famous of all Ottoman sultans.

Suleyman was a warrior-king, who led his armies on twelve campaigns and won victories that led to the conquest of Serbia, Hungary and Mesopotamia. Ottoman troops defeated the Safavids and Habsburgs on battlefields 700 miles or more from Istanbul. From their bases in the port of Suez and Yemen they checked the Portuguese attempt to dominate the Indian Ocean. In the first twenty years of Suleyman's reign the sky seemed the limit, and the sultan dreamed of capturing Rome, Vienna and Tabriz, thereby creating a near-universal empire beyond the scale even of the early Arab caliphate. As was the case with all empires, in the end distance, topography and rival states imposed limits on expansion. The Ottoman forward bases in the west and east were Belgrade and Baghdad, 364 and 828 miles respectively from Istanbul. A combination of distance, logistics and poor communications undermined attempts to take Vienna and destroy the core of Habsburg power in Austria. On the Iranian plateau, the Ottomans found that they could neither feed their armies on long campaigns nor force the Safavids to give battle. A grudging recognition set in by the 1540s that the empire had reached its natural limits and that coexistence with the Habsburgs and Safavids was necessary.

The greatest achievements in the second half of Suleyman's reign were domestic. Though always known to European posterity as 'the Magnificent', in Turkey he is famous as 'the Law-Giver'. His law code, never fully matched by any other Muslim regime, was an all-encompassing and sensitive blending of the *sharia* and Ottoman decree-based statute. The beautiful mosques and other buildings constructed by his court architect, Sinan, with their extraordinary lightness, their exquisite yet austere refinement, their superb carpets and Iznik tiles, are the most lasting and famous monuments to Ottoman aesthetics and this civilization's sense of beauty. A literary and poetic high culture evolved in Suleyman's reign drawing heavily on Persian traditions but expressed in a newly refined Ottoman Turkish language. Intellectuals and cultural luminaries fleeing Safavid Iran contributed to this process. The sultan was himself a cultured man who played a significant personal role in archaeological and literary projects. Above all, he believed that they redounded to the Ottomans' international standing and – at the height of Ottoman power – he had ample resources to finance them. Nevertheless, Suleyman was not by most accounts as fine a poet as the founder of the Moghul dynasty, Emperor Babur. Nor was his personal contribution to making Turkish a medium for high literary culture as great. But whereas he is regarded as an ancestor by the contemporary Turkish nation and state, no powerful forces in contemporary India regard Babur or his native Chaghatay Turkish language as part of their heritage or identity. As always, present-day realities and the demands of the contemporary nation can easily distort our sense of historical judgement and perspective.[12]

Not surprisingly, Suleyman's personal impact is clearer as regards the evolution of Ottoman laws and institutions. The new law-code emerged from the collaboration between Suleyman and his chief religious and legal adviser, the famous scholar Ebusud, who served as head of the empire's religious establishment (chief mufti/*seyhulislam*) from 1545 until 1574. The sultan believed deeply and sincerely in the truth and wisdom of Islam. The great respect in which he held religious scholars in general, and Ebusud personally as the finest embodiment of this profession, created what one might almost call a semi-equality between them and was the foundation for a strong and genuine friendship. Together the two men expanded, restructured and refined the empire's judicial and educational system. A hierarchy of religious schools (*madrasas*) was created, stretching all the way upwards from provincial towns to the great imperial foundations in Istanbul. The impressive complex of mosques, schools and charitable institutions built for the sultan by Sinan and named the Suleimaniye formed the apex of this system. Although some of the system's graduates became teachers (*ulama*) in the schools, many others served as judges (*kadis*), climbing a career ladder that began in small towns and ended with the two chief judges of Europe and Asia (*kadiaskers*) who sat on the imperial council (*divan*), which was the highest administrative and judicial body in the empire, made up of anything from five to eight members and presided over by the Grand Vizier.[13]

Separate from the religious, educational and judicial establishments was the state's administrative apparatus, which was responsible for managing the system of taxation and military recruitment that was the core of Ottoman government and power (and of most other empires). Even at the end of Suleyman's reign the central bureaucracy was made up of barely two hundred officials, though of course these were supported by an array of copyists, messengers and janitors. These two hundred elite officials ran a system of correspondence, record-keeping and accounts which was exceptionally sophisticated and efficient for this era. A vital part of their work was the land surveys, tax assessments and military personnel records on which rested the state's ability to recruit and fund its army. In 1528 the most expensive part of this army was the 37,000 cavalrymen who held land-grants (*timars*) in return for military service. Unlike in Europe, these land-grants never became the cavalryman's private property to sell or to bequeath to his son. On the contrary, in Suleyman's era the military service system was tightly regulated by the state. Almost two-fifths of all state revenue went into supporting the *timariots*. In return the *timariots* not only formed the core of the Ottoman army but also played a key role in supporting tax collection, law and public order in the countryside.[14]

The core of the Ottoman system of government was the sultan's household. This is unsurprising: in pre-modern monarchies the royal household was generally the centre of government, but in both scale and quality the Ottoman imperial household was something special. Most of its members were slaves, recruited by the so-called *devsirme* system. Under this system, once every three to seven years Christian boys (aged from eight to twenty) were conscripted from the empire's European provinces, converted to Islam, and became slaves of the sultan. This contravened Islamic law's ban on forced conversion and the enslavement of Muslims, but no senior religious scholar seems to have had the temerity to protest. Once grown, most of the boys became Janissaries, of whom there were roughly 12,000 in the ranks in the 1560s. At that time the Janissary corps had good claim to be the most skilled, disciplined and motivated infantry in the world. The minority of more promising boys were sent to the pages' school within the inner court of the Topkapi Palace, where the sultan lived when in Istanbul. There they stayed for two to eight years, subject to tight supervision and discipline and almost cut off from the world beyond the palace walls. In time the less able boys became soldiers in the six Guards cavalry regiments. Although their subsequent careers were mostly military, some Guards cavalry officers were also seconded to administrative roles.[15]

The pages' school combined military, physical and intellectual education. The regime was strict and was designed to create obedient and loyal servants of the sultan. The intellectual training was excellent and rigorous. It included the Turkish, Arabic and Persian languages, as well as Turkish, Islamic and Persian history, literature and poetry. To graduate near the top of one's class required great intelligence, self-discipline and commitment. The best graduates were taken into the inner service of the sultan. As always in monarchies, closeness to the ruler was everything. The cream of the pages served in or around the sultan's private apartments. The longer a man remained in these positions, the likelier he was to gain the sultan's notice and favour. In time a page might move from a senior position in the household to a provincial governorship and thence to a vizierate and membership of the imperial council (*divan*).

A classic example of a successful product of the *devsirme* was Rustem Pasha, Suleyman's longest-serving Grand Vizier. Before his conscription, Rustem had been an illiterate swineherd in the Balkans. He ended his career not just in the empire's top office as Grand Vizier but also as the husband of Princess Mihrimah, Suleyman's only and greatly loved daughter. Marrying imperial princesses had its dangers. Uniquely among Ottoman women, they could divorce their husband, chase his concubines from the house, and ban him from marrying other women. Nor did marriage to a princess guarantee one against disgrace or execution at the sultan's hands. But the great political advantages a marriage could bring are illustrated by Rustem's career.

His wife had enormous influence with her father and unlimited access to her mother, the sultan's adored and extremely powerful wife Hurrem. The idea that an emperor might marry his daughter to a slave of peasant origin flouted the most fundamental principles of the European social and political order. It set the Ottoman version of emperorship apart even from the Mughal and Qing dynasties, both of which like the Ottomans employed harems. Some European observers admired Ottoman meritocracy. Defenders of European aristocratic principles argued that the Ottoman case illustrated the connection between equality, slavery, social climbing and despotism.[16]

In public Suleyman knew how to look and behave like an emperor. Even in the mid-1550s when he was almost sixty Suleyman still looked majestic and dignified. By then he had ceased to drink alcohol and his – by Ottoman standards – frugality and temperance slowed down the signs of old age. His gestures and countenance were described as 'majestic' by a European witness, who wrote that Suleyman was surrounded by 'great pomp and magnificence' and dressed in 'a robe of cloth of gold, embroidered most richly with the most precious stones'. By now Ottoman court ritual had moved far from the simple household manners of a war-band leader. The sultan did not speak in public and adopted 'an idol-like posture'. His Janissary guards were equally immobile, sometimes for hours on end, and their discipline and appearance made a great impression on foreigners, as was intended. Almost uniquely for an Ottoman sultan, we do have some insights into the man behind the royal facade in Suleyman's case. Above all that is because of his relationship with Ibrahim Pasha, his favourite and Grand Vizier in the first half of his reign. Still more revealing is his relationship with his wife and children.[17]

Ibrahim Pasha was the son of a Greek fisherman. Two years older than Suleyman, he was given to the young prince as a slave and became his closest friend. A good violinist and singer, he also attracted Suleyman because of their shared interest in ancient history. On ascending the throne in 1520 Suleyman waited until he had gained personal standing in the eyes of top officials by successful military leadership, which led to the fall of the island of Rhodes, long a Christian thorn in the Ottomans' side. He then appointed Ibrahim straight from a position in his household to be Grand Vizier. This was an unprecedented move which so infuriated the expected heir to the position that he staged a rebellion from his base as governor of Egypt. By appointing Ibrahim, Suleyman asserted his own control over government while delegating the boring details of administration which he detested. The two men communicated in person or by letter every day. Ibrahim had access even to the sultan's bedroom, which was a shocking infraction of Ottoman convention. The Grand Vizier was a highly intelligent and charismatic man, as well as a competent general and administrator. He was a man of culture and intellectual curiosity, and a great patron of scholarship and the arts. Ibrahim also had a flair for spectacle and propaganda which he used to promote the sultan's image as world-conqueror and universal emperor. Both Grand Vizier and sultan shared this vision and ambition in the heady, early years of Suleyman's reign.

In March 1536 Ibrahim was suddenly killed on Suleyman's orders despite having just led a victorious campaign against the Safavids and having spent the hours before his death sharing a seemingly friendly feast with the sultan. There is here a parallel with the Caliph Harun al-Rashid's sudden destruction of the Barmakids. No one can be sure why Suleyman acted in this way. Subsequently, when asked to allow similar intimate access to his Grand Vizier and son-in-law, Rustem Pasha, the sultan refused, adding 'once is enough for doing something crazy'. Perhaps Suleyman merely meant that his treatment of Ibrahim had encouraged him to be arrogant and presumptuous. In the way of almost all 'favourites', the Grand Vizier was jealous of any conceivable rival whom Suleyman seemed to like too much and tried to destroy them or at least post them as far as possible from the court. Ibrahim's private secretary wrote subsequently that power had changed his master, making him more arrogant and less cautious. The many enemies and rivals any favourite accumulated will have done their best to bring his failings to Suleyman's attention. But perhaps the sultan's words should be seen as a comment on the unique difficulties of sustaining a relationship between an emperor and a man who was simultaneously his childhood friend, his lifelong chief minister and his slave. As always, events have to be seen within the specific context of the Ottoman court and political culture, in which the arbitrary execution of Grand Viziers and other ministers was hardly abnormal. Political life is very often the graveyard of friendships. This does not always lead to one friend having the other strangled as he sleeps.[18]

By the time Suleyman ascended the throne, long-established

convention decreed that the sultan should not marry and should produce children by intercourse with slave concubines. A woman who had
a son by the sultan was usually kept from his bed in future and was
absolutely banned from giving birth to a second boy. Her role was
transformed from mistress to mother. As her son approached puberty he
was sent from court to prove his mettle as a provincial governor. His
mother went with him to act as mentor and run his household. Even in
this most personal emotional sphere, the monarch was expected to subordinate the love he might feel for the woman to interests of state. If the
young prince won the inevitable conflict to succeed his father, then his
mother would become empress mother (*valide sultan*), the most powerful and respected woman in the empire. If he lost, he would die and his
mother would be relegated to some sad and obscure corner of the Old
Palace, the harem's retirement quarters. Once again in Suleyman's case,
we see how the sultan's personality and his need for friendship and love
overrode convention. In 1521 he fell in love with a slave concubine
called Hurrem, who was one of the roughly 10,000 Russians, Ukrainians and Poles captured every year between 1500 and 1650 in Crimean
Tatar slave raids and sold into the Ottoman Empire. In time Suleyman
married Hurrem and produced no more children by other women.[19]

This had a dramatic impact on Ottoman court politics and above all
on the politics of succession. For Suleyman's eldest son, the able and
popular Prince Mustafa, whose mother was the concubine Mahidevran,
Suleyman's infatuation with Hurrem was a deadly threat. Succession
politics was a zero-sum game. Hurrem knew that if Suleyman died
while Mustafa still lived, there was every chance that the Janissaries
would put him on the throne. His seniority, experience, charisma and
ability all made this likely. In that case her sons would die. Suleyman
knew this too and for that reason killed Mustafa and both his sons
in 1553. There is a poignant account of a conversation between the sultan and his youngest son, Cihangir, of whom Suleyman seems to have
been very fond. Cihangir was born deformed and his parents' few surviving letters show their concern for his health. They spent as much time
as possible with him. Cihangir got on with his half-brother Mustafa
and is reported to have asked Suleyman once whether this, together
with his deformity, would save his life if Mustafa inherited the throne.
Suleyman responded that in this case Cihangir would certainly not be
spared. His fate was in fact unlikely to be different if the throne was

taken by either of his full brothers, Bayazid or Selim, though just conceivably if Hurrem was still alive at this point a mother's pleas to her son, the new monarch, might preserve the life of a brother whose deformity more or less ruled him out as a threat.[20]

It is difficult to put oneself in the mindset of a father who knew that his sons were almost bound to kill each other one day. No doubt, human beings adapt to tradition and convention. Most royal fathers in all eras were much inclined to see their children as pawns in the dynastic power-game. It is also true that the history of monarchy is very often the story of rulers who sacrificed personal emotions to the cause of dynasty and the logic of power. In many cases the office seems to have so much dominated its incumbent that signs of independent personality almost disappear, though this can be an optical illusion caused by lack of sources. Before Suleyman most Ottoman sultans barely knew their sons, who were sent away with their mothers when still children to serve as provincial governors. But Suleyman was different: in his case we can feel a human need for love and friendship, above all within the family circle. The early death of his first son by Hurrem, Prince Mehmed, caused him great sorrow. The grim realities of succession politics must surely at times have weighed heavily on him.

Within thirty years of Suleyman's death in 1566 the Ottoman Empire entered a period of crisis that only ended in the 1650s. An element in this crisis was perhaps climate change: the Little Ice Age is often seen as responsible for wrecking agriculture in the empire's Anatolian bread-basket, forcing part of the peasantry to turn to begging and banditry for survival. The influx of American silver caused massive inflation, which reached its peak in 1588–97 and 1615–25. Anyone living on fixed incomes was ruined: this included officials and *timariot* cavalrymen, which inevitably caused confusion in the state's administrative and fiscal machine. Long wars with the Habsburgs and Safavids were hugely expensive and ended without victory, booty or conquered territory. By the 1590s the Habsburgs had closed the gap with the Ottomans as regards military power. The rival military machines fought each other into stalemate on the battlefield and mutual bankruptcy. To meet Habsburg superiority in infantry – which increasingly displaced cavalry as the dominant military arm – the Ottomans recruited large numbers of foot-soldiers, whom they were barely able to pay even when on campaign. Discharged every winter and definitively at the end of the war in

1606, these soldiers swelled the forces of banditry. In Istanbul a furious competition developed between the Janissaries and the Guards cavalry to defend their share of a shrinking fiscal pie. Socio-economic chaos was intertwined with a political crisis in the palace and the top level of government. The political history of 1574–1656 is extremely complicated but it was mostly a tale of ineffective leadership and the growing power of court factions, interspersed with ferocious efforts by a handful of sultans to reassert autocratic power, in part by generous use of terror. A key factor in the political crisis was that – largely by biological chance – every sultan who ascended the throne in the first half of the seventeenth century was either a child or mentally handicapped.[21]

The political crisis can to some extent be traced back to the accession of Suleyman's grandson Murad III in 1574. His father, Selim II, had broken with tradition by only appointing his eldest son and chosen heir, Murad, to a provincial governorship. His five other sons were kept in Istanbul and were killed immediately on Murad's accession. With the Habsburgs and Safavids poised to exploit a traditional Ottoman war of succession, it was too dangerous to allow armed competition between rival princes. As Grand Vizier, Murad inherited Sokollu Mehmed Pasha, who had held this position since Suleyman's reign. Selim II had been happy to delegate most government business to Sokollu, who was his son-in-law. Inevitably, after long years in power, Sokollu and his clients dominated the government machine. Control over patronage was the first principle of power for almost any chief minister or 'favourite' in any pre-modern monarchy. Filling key positions with loyal clients was also often the only way to ensure that commands were obeyed and the government machine functioned. Unsurprisingly, the new monarch resented Sokollu's power. Even more resentful were the clients whom Murad had gathered during his years as provincial governor and heir apparent. Among Sokollu's greatest enemies were the sultan's mother, Nurbanu, and his favourite concubine, Safiye. Murad was very close to both these able and ambitious women, who themselves had built up networks of clients whom they needed to satisfy.

In complete contrast to most of his ancestors, Murad III never left Istanbul during his twenty-three-year reign, and for most of the time he lived deep in the palace in his harem. Only very seldom did he even show himself at Friday prayers, the one occasion on which the population of the capital could previously rely on seeing their monarch. Murad was neither lazy nor stupid, and he was a relatively diligent ruler. But his seclusion in the harem unavoidably increased the influence both of his womenfolk and of the eunuchs who were their main link to the outside world. They, together with other disgruntled courtiers, encouraged Murad to appoint a distinguished elder statesman, Semsi Pasha, as his 'private' councillor (*mutalib*). When Semsi died he was replaced by Doganci Mehmed Pasha, a senior household officer who had drawn close to Murad during imperial hunts because of his position as chief hawksman and subsequently head of the imperial stables. Murad very seldom met his Grand Vizier and insisted that all correspondence was in writing and that no appointments could be made without his sanction. First Semsi and then Doganci saw all correspondence and worked tirelessly against first Sokollu and then – after his murder by a frustrated petitioner in 1578 – all subsequent Grand Viziers.

As a result, the office of Grand Vizier lost its power. The average tenure of Grand Viziers in Murad's reign sank to less than two years, a pattern that continued until the 1650s. In a manner repeated in the history of many monarchies, although the ruler, his womenfolk, his eunuchs and his courtiers could destroy a chief minister, they could not themselves co-ordinate or direct government policy or the administrative machine unless the monarch was exceptionally able and hard-working. Sokollu's demise left a hole at the centre of the Ottoman polity. As a result, government dissolved into a war of factions for power and patronage. Inevitably the situation worsened in the first half of the seventeenth century, when monarchs were very often children or simpletons.[22]

Three sultans attempted to reassert royal power in the fifty years that followed Murad III's death. Mehmed III and Murad IV both had some success in reviving monarchical authority and Ottoman power but died young of natural causes. Osman I's case was more interesting. His story is important because it illustrated the risks that faced any monarch who flouted Ottoman conventions and challenged the interests of key social groups. Osman shocked conservative opinion by riding around Istanbul in everyday clothing and conversing with ordinary citizens. By now a monarch was expected to be rarely seen, let alone heard, and to surround himself with ceremonial dignity. Still worse, Osman insisted on marrying a daughter of one of the leading *ulama* families in Istanbul, a move even more radical than Suleyman's marriage to Hurrem. For a free Muslim woman of high status to enter and preside over the sultan's harem was an extraordinary break with precedent. Like many young emperors anxious to assert themselves and gain political leverage, Osman decided to lead his army to war in person, in his case against the Poles. The Janissaries' indiscipline and incompetence wrecked the campaign and persuaded Osman that radical military reform was essential. By going on a pilgrimage to Mecca he planned to escape his enemies in Istanbul, acquire prestige as a royal pilgrim, and recruit new military forces in the provinces. Aware of his intentions, the Janissaries overthrew and murdered their seventeen-year-old sultan in 1622, the first such regicide in Ottoman history. Most of the political and religious establishment welcomed and justified his overthrow, though not his murder.[23]

Amidst the chaos, the Ottoman dynasty very nearly died out in the first half of the seventeenth century. Partly as a result, on occasion sultans no longer killed all their brothers on coming to the throne but instead kept them under house arrest in a special quarter of the harem, known as 'the cages'. The first time this happened was on the accession of the child sultan Ahmed I in 1603 when his brother Mustafa's life was preserved. On Ahmed's death in 1617 Mustafa was put on the throne in preference to Prince Osman, Ahmed's son, although he was far from fully sound of mind. In time fratricide ended for good and succession between brothers became the Ottoman rule, but in the first half of the seventeenth century everything remained in flux. Many sultans still did kill their brothers. This was especially true of those monarchs who sought to restore the power of the sultanate. Murad IV (r. 1623–40) was a would-be autocrat who imposed his authority on the political elite through terror and led his armies in war. Before he left Istanbul and departed on campaign he killed all but one of his brothers and half-brothers. The one exception was Prince Ibrahim, whose mother (Kosem) begged for her son's life, arguing that since he was mentally deficient he could pose no threat. In 1640 Murad IV died suddenly, aged twenty-seven, without sons, and Ibrahim became sultan.

Events showed that the new sultan was indeed mentally deficient. His ministers reported to him as if to a child. In the first year of his reign the sultan's mental problems were not the chief worry, however. If the dynasty was to survive, its last remaining male had to have sons. Ibrahim's uncle, the crazy Sultan Mustafa I, had resolutely refused to have anything to do with women and Ibrahim appeared to be headed in the same direction. In desperation help was sought from, among others, Cinci Hoca, a quack and sorcerer who had been educated in a religious school (*madrasa*). Cinci succeeded only too well in curing Ibrahim's impotence by offering him a cocktail of aphrodisiacs, pornography and seductive females. Poor Ibrahim became obsessed with sex, staged vast and expensive orgies in his palace, and showered rewards on his favourites, promoting Cinci Hoca to one of the top judicial posts in the empire, to the fury of the religious and legal establishment. Ibrahim's neglect of business and his waywardness reduced both the army and the fiscal system to chaos in the course of a few years, which showed how dependent the Ottoman polity was on a powerful emperor or Grand Vizier. Since he had by now produced three sons and was therefore superfluous, Ibrahim was overthrown and killed in 1648. He was succeeded by his seven-year-old son, Mehmed IV.[24]

Mehmed's mother, Hadice Turhan, was twenty-one and had no political experience. Although she was the mother of Ibrahim's eldest son, the sultan had never shown her special favour. Amidst his orgies, she had been relegated to a hidden corner of the harem. The political and religious leaders who removed Ibrahim therefore asked Mehmed's grandmother, the formidable, intelligent and experienced empress mother Kosem to resume the role of regent that she had played in the first years of Murad IV's reign. Unfortunately for Kosem, Hadice Turhan was an intelligent young woman who quickly learned the political game. Key political figures who resented Kosem's close alliance with the Janissaries encouraged Hadice Turhan to resist the regent's monopoly of power and patronage. Aware of the danger, Kosem sought to destroy Hadice Turhan and replace Mehmed IV by a younger brother whose mother would be no threat. The plot was betrayed, Hadice Turhan struck first and Kosem was killed. Although Hadice Turhan's position as regent for her son was now secure, she inherited an empire in a state of deep crisis and potential collapse. The army was in disarray, the treasury empty, revolt was brewing on all sides, and by 1656 Istanbul itself was blockaded by the Venetian navy and its population (not to mention its Janissary garrison) was growing hungry and mutinous.

Hadice Turhan was well aware that she could not herself run the government or impose coordination and obedience on the military and administrative machine or the political elites. Apart from anything else, even an empress mother – the freest and most privileged woman in the harem – was banned from meeting any man face to face but her eunuchs. Occasional conversations with the Grand Vizier conducted discreetly from behind a screen or listening from behind a curtain to debates in the imperial council (*divan*) were not sufficient to manage Ottoman government and high politics. If Hadice Turhan had been older, with daughters married to senior statesmen, her position would have been much stronger. Lacking this, she badly needed a tough and loyal Grand Vizier, and in 1656 she at last found one in the person of Mehmed Koprulu. He restored order partly by the traditional method, in other words terror. But he combined this with intelligence, realism and resolution. After his death in 1661, Mehmed Koprulu was succeeded by his son Fazil Ahmed. When Fazil died in 1676 he was succeeded as Grand Vizier by Mehmed Koprulu's favourite son-in-law, Kara Mustafa. Kara was a childhood friend of Fazil Ahmed and had acted as his loyal and effective deputy for years before becoming Grand Vizier.

Not since the first half of the fifteenth century had son succeeded father as Grand Vizier. The three decades in which Koprulu Grand Viziers ruled the empire restored Ottoman political stability and military power. Crete was conquered and with it came total Ottoman domination of the Aegean. Poland was also defeated. The Koprulu regime's strength was based on the close alliance of the royal and Koprulu households. In the sixteenth century the sultan's household had been far bigger than that of any member of the political, religious or judicial elite. By 1650 this was no longer true. The households of leading viziers, governors and military commanders had expanded greatly in scale and power. One element of this – important both symbolically and in day-to-day reality – was that the Grand Vizier himself and his household had moved out of the imperial Topkapi Palace compound and established themselves elsewhere in Istanbul as an alternative focus of power. By throwing the monarchy's full weight behind the Koprulus, first Hadice Turhan and then Mehmed IV restored order, coordination and purpose to Ottoman government. This sounds easy and obvious. In reality it required from Hadice Turhan and her son self-discipline, acceptance of some Koprulu policies and appointments which they did not always like, and a fixed determination to ensure that rival personalities, ambitions and intrigues in the court, the harem and the political elite were kept under strict control.

Hadice Turhan comes across as a rare hero of Ottoman court

politics. She combined wisdom and toughness with humanity and insight into other people's strengths and weaknesses. She did not allow personal vanity or ambition to cloud her judgement. When Mehmed IV came of age he made clear that he did not want his mother to continue her involvement in politics. Mehmed himself lived in Edirne (Adrianople), where he could indulge his passion for hunting and escape the threat of the capital's periodically mutinous Janissaries. Between 1666 and 1676 Mehmed never once visited Istanbul. Hadice Turhan moved back to the capital in 1668 and her presence and patronage, not to mention the charitable foundations she created and supported, helped to fill the gap. She was the only person in the empire who could on occasion recall the sultan to his duty and away from his fondness for hunting.

Ottoman conventions about succession between brothers and the ending of fratricidal practices were not yet set in stone. After the birth of his sons, Mehmed IV (and even more so their mother) wished to kill his half-brothers in order to ensure the succession for their own children. Hadice Turhan led the successful opposition to Mehmed. In the Topkapi Palace she kept her stepsons, the princes Suleyman and Ahmed, under the close protection of herself and her own trusted guards.

Shortly after her death Mehmed IV and Kara Mustafa overreached themselves by attempting to capture Vienna in 1683. Although the siege almost succeeded, the stark danger of an Ottoman eruption into central Europe allowed the Habsburgs to create a mighty coalition of the German princes, Venice, the Pope, Poland and Russia. This coalition saved Vienna and then drove the Ottomans out of Hungary and Transylvania. As a result, Kara Mustafa was executed in 1683 and Mehmed IV was deposed in 1687. Having spent all forty-six years of his life hidden in the harem, Prince Suleyman emerged into the daylight as Sultan Suleyman II.[25]

Suleyman remarked later that, when he was escorted from the harem to ascend the throne, he believed he was being taken out for execution. He added that every day of his life since his earliest consciousness as a child, he had feared that this day might be his last. His fear was realistic. A lifetime immersed in a similar state of terror had contributed greatly to the mental problems of Mustafa I and Ibrahim I. By their standard, Suleyman II was remarkably sane, sensible and decent. But a lifetime spent in the 'cages' deep in the harem was a poor preparation for leadership. Once confined to the 'cages' Ottoman princes were not allowed to produce children. Only a ruling sultan had this right. So long as his father lived and ruled as sultan, a prince could enjoy a relatively free life and education in the palace. But the sultan was likely to die before his sons reached adolescence. By the second half of the seventeenth century fratricide had ceased and the rule was established that succession to the throne went to the eldest surviving brother of the deceased sultan.

None of Istanbul's leading teachers, scholars or elite officials could enter the harem and contribute to a prince's education. Therefore, whatever education a prince received came largely from the harem eunuchs. A few palace eunuchs were cultured men, but life in the 'cages' could not remotely provide a prince with adequate intellectual training to rule a great empire. A prince also had no first-hand knowledge of Ottoman society, no training in government, and little experience in human relations. He was absolutely barred from forming a network of friends, clients and allies with whom he could exchange ideas and with whose help he could rule effectively on coming to the throne. In hereditary monarchies, succession often brought renewed energy to government, together with new ideas and new men hitherto excluded from power. With a son's accession could arrive a new generation of statesmen and advisers. The Ottoman system combined the disadvantages of placing an often already ageing brother on the throne without the usual compensation of deep experience. Unsurprisingly, whereas Mehmed II, Selim I and Suleyman I remain well-known in contemporary Turkey, only historians recall the names of seventeenth- and eighteenth-century sultans.[26]

The Ottoman political system in these two centuries is sometimes described as 'the Second Ottoman Empire' or – in my view misleadingly – as 'Ottoman constitutionalism'. A fundamental difference from either the preceding or following eras was that the power of the sultan was strongly constrained. The historian who coined the term 'Second Ottoman Empire' called it an era of proto-democratization and described the constraints on royal absolutism as its most fundamental condition. The system of succession was one such constraint. In the seventeenth and, still more, eighteenth centuries sultans who challenged key social groups and vested interests in Istanbul were deposed. These interests included the households of leading statesmen, the religious and judicial elite, and the growing bureaucracy. In many ways the most important vested interest, and the one which gave muscle to opponents of royal autocracy, was the Janissaries.[27]

With the withering away of the Guards cavalry after the 1650s the Janissaries became the only sizeable military force in Istanbul. During the sixteenth century their number grew greatly, initially because new developments in warfare required the Ottomans to field far more infantry than in the past. To help support themselves and spare the state's revenues, the Janissaries were even encouraged to take up part-time trades in the capital. In the seventeenth century the *devsirme* ceased to operate and Janissaries were recruited from the Muslim population. Soon the monarchy lost control over the recruitment process. In the end, tens of thousands of artisans, merchants and shopkeepers bought entry to the Janissary rolls in search of the status, pensions and tax and legal privileges that went along with being a Janissary. Few of these men trained as soldiers or could be used in wartime. On the other hand, the Janissary corps forged close ties to the bazaar, the craft guilds and the Sufi sects which played key roles in the lives of Istanbul's population. The Janissary corps became in a sense the 'armed consultative assembly of the nation', if by 'nation' one means the population of the Ottoman capital.[28]

Like all regimes that are rooted in deference to established interests, the Ottoman polity was conservative. For most of the second half of the seventeenth century and until 1768 it was politically stable and offered a good deal of personal security to the population of Istanbul. Life was relatively predictable and was ruled by law, convention and tradition. For many Ottoman subjects this was a comfortable time to live, even a golden age. Among its beneficiaries were the Ottoman princes. If life in the 'cage' was frustrating, it was better than being strangled by one's brother when he ascended the throne. Although sultans were frequently deposed they were usually allowed to retire into a comfortable version of house arrest. Political conservatism matched 'the generally conservative make-up of Ottoman culture'. Cultural conservatism was rooted partly in deep allegiance to Sunni Islam. Although Christians and Jews were generally treated with admirable tolerance, the Ottoman dynasty and elite had seen themselves since the early sixteenth century as the world's leading champions of the true version of the Islamic faith. In both elite and popular circles openly borrowing ideas drawn from non-Muslim societies was condemned. Above all, Ottoman elites had a tremendous sense of pride in their dynastic empire, born of its longevity, grandeur and past conquests. They believed that the Ottoman Empire was wholly exceptional and that its glorious history showed that it enjoyed God's blessing. The usual response to setbacks was to see them as temporary and brought about by mistakes made by individuals and the sinfulness of mankind. The usual solution offered was a call to return to the principles of the Ottoman 'Golden Age', generally seen as the era of Suleyman I.[29]

While the Ottomans were looking inwards and backwards the military and fiscal power of the major European states was growing. It was in the eighteenth century that the military advantage swung decisively in Europe's favour and against the Ottomans. As regards weaponry, the key developments were the bayonet and lighter field artillery, which greatly enhanced the potential firepower and mobility of European armies. More important than the weaponry was the evolution of tactics and training to use these weapons to full effect. Victory on a European eighteenth-century battlefield came from superior firepower and shock tactics, which could only be delivered by close-order formations. Infantry, which became the key arm of a fighting force, had to be trained to move in close order across a battlefield, deploying smoothly between columns, lines and squares. Only well-trained and disciplined troops could achieve this in the heat of battle. Even harder was the coordination of infantry, artillery and cavalry on the battlefield. Also essential were the planning and logistics responsible for feeding tens of thousands of men and horses, enabling them to campaign over long distances but converge at the point of battle. Every level of warfare from basic tactical training and drill up to strategic planning and command required military professionals. Only states with effective fiscal machines could sustain the large and expensive professional armies required for European eighteenth-century war.[30]

The core of the Ottoman forces had traditionally been the Janissaries. By 1700 at a conservative estimate the size of the corps had quintupled since Suleyman I's death but most Janissaries were by now useless as soldiers. Towards the end of the century some 400,000 men were on the Janissary payroll (i.e. drawing monthly pay and daily rations), of whom 40,000 were useable in war, and even they were poorly trained and disciplined. The Janissary corps had largely turned into a strange combination of a welfare system, an investment fund and a tax evasion scam, designed to serve the interests of Istanbul's civilian population. Not only was a large proportion of the military budget being wasted but the Janissaries repeatedly used their military muscle on the streets of Istanbul to block attempts either to restore their own corps' military effectiveness or to create new military formations which would in time make clear the Janissaries' redundancy and challenge their monopoly of force in Ottoman internal politics.[31]

The second main element in the Ottoman army had traditionally been the *timariot* cavalry, who were 'paid' by land grants in return for their service. In the late sixteenth and early seventeenth centuries inflation often made the income from these grants insufficient for a cavalryman to feed his family and equip himself for war. More important in the long run were the changes in warfare that made these cavalrymen increasingly redundant when the Ottomans were fighting European enemies. This was not a uniquely Ottoman problem. In Europe knights and their retainers, the core of medieval armies, also lost their value. In eighteenth-century Europe the descendants of the feudal knights – in other words the land-owning aristocracy and gentry – very often served as professional officers in their monarchs' armies, thereby making a crucial contribution to the state's military effectiveness. They were also vital to provincial and local government through their manorial courts and their roles as magistrates and members of local elected assemblies. This alliance between landowning elite and monarchy was the backbone of the early modern European state. The *timariots* were the backbone of Ottoman provincial administration between roughly 1420 and 1580 but they never evolved into either professional army officers or local landowners and officials. This contributed hugely to the weakness of both the Ottoman army and Istanbul's control over local society.[32]

In the seventeenth and eighteenth centuries power increasingly slipped from the sultan and the Ottoman central government into the hands of local elites. This was in part the result of a deliberate policy of decentralization. Most of the fiscal system was privatized through the creation of tax farms (*malikane*), which from 1695 were leased out – initially very profitably – on a lifetime basis. These tax farms soon fell into the hands of local elites (notables/*ayan*). In addition to the power these elites already possessed through their landowning, their wealth and their networks of clients and allies, they now gained the enormous extra power of assigning and collecting taxes. Inevitably, more and more of the taxes raised stuck to local hands and never reached Istanbul. By the eighteenth century the central government also relied on local elites to recruit soldiers for wartime service and to maintain order in their districts. The notables/*ayan* therefore now commanded what were in effect private armies thinly disguised by being notionally in the sultan's service. These armies were poorly trained and disciplined, and therefore of little use in the field against the Russians and Austrians, but they greatly strengthened the notables' power in their home regions.

Given their scale and the nature of pre-modern communications all empires de facto were ruled on a very decentralized basis. All faced the basic conundrum that local elites naturally preferred to hang on to resources and revenues for themselves, rather than transfer them to a distant emperor and central government. Coercing, persuading and enticing local elites to transfer part of these revenues to the central authorities was usually the greatest and most difficult task of an emperor. Rulers who lost control over the empire's military and fiscal systems were unlikely to survive for long. This was especially true if, like the Ottomans, the empire was situated in a vulnerable geopolitical position and faced powerful neighbours. By the eighteenth century the Ottoman regime was failing in the most basic and crucial task of empire. Unfortunately for the Ottomans, they were doing so while their northern neighbouring empires were developing their fiscal and military machines and increasing central control over provincial elites and resources. Ottoman rulers and elites had failed to note or understand these developments.[33]

The result was revealed during the war with Russia between 1768 and 1774. The Ottoman elites were deeply shocked and surprised by their defeat. The decades before 1768 had been a period of economic prosperity and political stability. The empire had not been at war for thirty years. Moreover, that last war, at least on the Austrian front, had ended in Ottoman victory and the recovery in the 1739 peace settlement of key territories lost to the Habsburgs in 1718. The war against the Habsburgs' Russian allies had not gone so well but had ended without major disasters. Facing the Russian threat, the Ottomans relied less on their field armies than on a string of powerful fortresses along the north coast of the Black Sea and the lower Danube. Their garrisons often still preserved some military skill and value. To reach these fortresses the Russian army had to cross the vast and largely unpopulated territory of what we now call southern and south-western Ukraine. Feeding and supplying the army, let alone moving its cumbersome siege artillery, across this expanse was difficult. Underestimating this challenge had led Peter the Great to defeat and near disaster at Ottoman hands in 1711.

What the Ottomans failed to grasp was that Russian colonization of the Ukrainian steppe meant that by 1768 its bases were closer to Ottoman territory. The Russian generals had learned lessons from previous campaigns as regards supplying and moving their armies across the southern steppe. By 1750 the Russian army was a match for any other European military machine. In the war of 1756 to 1762 it had learned precious lessons from fighting Frederick the Great's Prussia. Between 1762 and 1768, under the overall direction of Catherine II, these lessons were absorbed into military regulations and training. The younger generation of generals who emerged from the Seven Years War were among the finest in Russian history. The most famous are Peter Rumiantsev and Alexander Suvorov. These men were not just great battlefield commanders. They had studied, discussed and written about war. One issue to which they had given serious thought was how to adapt a modern European army to fighting a non-European (i.e. Ottoman) enemy in a military theatre of operations that differed significantly from the battlefields of Germany and western Europe. By contrast, Ottoman military thinking had barely advanced since 1550. In 1768, in traditional fashion, the army was commanded by the Grand Vizier, in this case a civilian with no military experience.[34]

The result was a complete Ottoman defeat which was then repeated in the war against Russia between 1788 and 1792 and again between 1806 and 1812. The impact of these wars on Ottoman finances was catastrophic. The indemnity agreed as part of the 1774 peace alone amounted to half of all Ottoman annual revenue. The war of 1788–92 was even costlier. When Selim III launched his reforms in the 1790s the government's bankruptcy was a big additional obstacle to success. The wars increased the centre's dependence on regional elites, who to a great extent controlled the collection of taxes and the recruitment of soldiers. The geopolitical consequences of defeat were also severe. For three hundred years the Black Sea had been an Ottoman lake. The Ottomans controlled the sea's commerce at little expense in terms of providing security. Within ten years of the Russian annexation of Crimea in 1783 a great naval base had been constructed at Sevastopol and the Russian fleet now dominated the Black Sea. Naval power meant domination of trade routes, crucial help as regards transport and logistics for Russian armies operating in the Balkans, and a potential threat to the Ottoman capital. Seen in a broader context, the Russian victories were the prelude to a process which in the course of the next 130 years would see the ethnic cleansing and often the massacre of the majority of the Muslim population of Crimea, the north-west Caucasus and the Balkans, in other words of millions of former Ottoman subjects or members of communities that had lived under Ottoman protection. Military history is not simply the frivolous story of kings and battles: it has devastating consequences for ordinary men and women.[35]

In 1789 Sultan Abdul Hamid I (r. 1774–89) died and the throne passed to the next generation, in the person of his twenty-eight-year-old nephew Selim III. During the first thirteen years of Selim's life his father, Mustafa III (r. 1757–74), was on the throne and the young prince lived in relative freedom and even sometimes accompanied his father to meetings with viziers and on other official business. Even when his uncle succeeded to the throne and Selim retired to the 'cages' he was allowed sufficient freedom to retain contact with key figures in government and maintain his outdoor exercise regime. By now the regime in the 'cages' was more relaxed than in earlier times. Selim's freedoms were partly curtailed in 1785–6 when a plot was revealed to place him on the throne, but the young prince still had unlimited access to books and not all his lines of communication to the outside world were completely broken. When Selim ascended the throne, the Ottoman Empire was engaged in its second disastrous war with Russia. Selim's eighteen-year reign was dominated by his attempt to push through reforms that would restore Ottoman military power. The core of the reforms was the attempt to create a new army formed on European principles. Neither the sultan himself nor the key reformers were greatly influenced by the ideas or the culture of the European Enlightenment. Another generation or more would pass before the westernization of the Ottoman elite's values and culture truly began. In Selim's era the thrust was still narrowly technical and above all military.[36]

The sources do not allow us to gain a deep and all-round sense of Selim but some aspects of his personality do emerge: the emperor was a competent poet and a fine musician and patron of music. He was a

member of the Mehlevi Sufi order and in traditional Ottoman monarchical style would roam the streets of Istanbul in disguise in order to see
for himself how his people were faring and correct acts of injustice by
his officials on the spot. Selim was devoted to his sister and his mother,
who is sometimes described as trying to protect him from bad news and
from awareness of hostility to his reforms in society. This feeds into the
opinion, widespread among contemporary accounts, that Selim was a
decent, humane and sensitive man with correct ideas about reform but
that he lacked the toughness and the stamina to impose discipline on his
advisers or to crush his conservative enemies. There may well be some
truth in this view but one needs to be aware of the age-old myth that lay
behind it: the monarch was virtuous and in principle all-powerful but
his entourage were villains who sabotaged his good intentions. It does
appear that Selim started his reign full of energy, optimism and some
naïvety about the prospects of his reform programme. As sultan, he
learned during years of bitter experience how constrained were his real
powers and how great were the obstacles to his reforms. Inevitably,
frustration and exhaustion grew. The revolt which overthrew him in
1807 might perhaps have been crushed had Selim moved quickly and
decisively in its early stages. His response to the crisis suggests a tired
ruler who had lost faith in his reforms, his advisers and maybe in
himself.[37]

Selim had reason to despair. The vested interests he faced were formidable and aversion to reform based on 'infidel' principles ran deep in
Ottoman society. The groups of advisers and officials who supported
his reform programme were divided by personal ambitions and factional allegiances. Their commitment to reform was sometimes
half-hearted and easily subordinated to personal interests. The reform
programme was being introduced at a time when the state was bank-
rupt and the existing military budget was to a great extent wasted on
the Janissaries. To fund his new army Selim had to impose many new
taxes which were publicly earmarked for its support. In public eyes the
reforms above all meant higher taxes. During Selim's entire reign the
Ottoman Empire was pulled inexorably into the great power wars and
rivalries of the Revolutionary and Napoleonic eras. Domestic and external challenges fed off each other. Probably the most powerful notable in
the Balkans was Osman Pasvanoglu. Years of failed efforts to buy off,
co-opt or deter Pasvanoglu finally persuaded Selim that a major effort

was needed to destroy him and regain control of the large de facto king-dom he had carved out for himself in the northern Balkans. An army of 80,000 men, formed both of Ottoman troops and of the militias loyal to Osman's local rivals, besieged his fortress capital in Vidin for months. Then, in 1798, Napoleon's invasion of Egypt forced Selim to abandon the campaign, send his army to Egypt, and recognize Osman Pasvan-oglu as a vizier and as viceroy of the northern Balkans. Far from satisfying Pasvanoglu, this merely encouraged him to expand his private kingdom at Ottoman expense.[38]

Selim III was replaced by his first cousin Mustafa IV, the elder son of Abdul Hamid I. In the spate of coups and counter-coups that occurred in the following year both Mustafa IV and Selim III were killed. Before his own overthrow and execution Mustafa even ordered the killing of his younger brother Mahmud, the last surviving male Ottoman. Prince Mahmud and therefore the Ottoman dynasty survived by a hair's breadth, escaping his murderers by fleeing to safety over the roofs of the Topkapi Palace. Subsequently he ruled for thirty years as Mahmud II. After his terrifying escape Mahmud was understandably careful not to alienate the groups that dominated Ottoman politics at his accession, namely the Istanbul political elite, the regional notables and the Janis-saries. Slowly and cautiously he played these forces off against each other, began to build up his own group of supporters in Istanbul and among the provincial elites, and created a smaller version of Selim's military forces in a manner least likely to arouse the fears and jealousies of the Janissaries, namely as an artillery corps and a unit of the navy. He quietly supported a propaganda campaign in the 1820s to undermine support for the Janissaries in Istanbul society, exploiting their repeated failures on campaigns against foreign enemies and Greek rebels. In 1826 he destroyed the Janissary corps in a dramatic coup whose success depended on meticulous secret planning and the support of his marines and artillerymen.

Selim III had treated Mahmud well and allowed him a good educa-tion and considerable freedom. He encouraged his young cousin to love music and even sometimes taught him himself. Mahmud comes across as a tougher, more boisterous and more extrovert person than Selim. He enjoyed alcohol and practical jokes. Above all, he revelled in soldiers and soldiering. Yet, the two sultans' political commitments were the same. After disposing of the Janissaries, Mahmud drove forward Selim's programme of military reform and recentralization of political power. Carried further by Mahmud's descendants, these efforts had re-created by 1914 an effective state administration and army which were able to offer sterling resistance to the Russians, British and French in the First World War.[39]

12

The Mughals: India's Greatest Dynasty

The Mughal (Timurid) dynasty reigned in India from 1526 until 1857, though the second emperor (Humayun) spent much of his reign (1530–56) in exile and the Mughals from the early eighteenth century exercised little real power. At its peak in the seventeenth century the Mughal Empire contributed well over one-fifth of total global economic output. This huge wealth allowed the emperors to support a superb high culture – literary, artistic and architectural. This culture was above all 'Persianate', originating in what one might call 'Greater Central Asia', meaning in today's terms the five former Soviet Central Asian republics, north-eastern Iran (Khurasan) and Afghanistan. As the word 'Persianate' implies, the dominant element in this culture was Persian, but the 'Persianate' cultural region drew also on Islamic and steppe elements. Once established in India, the Mughals generously supported native Sanskrit-based culture too. Mughal high culture was therefore an exceptionally interesting synthesis, with its own unique and original aspects.[1]

The first six Mughal emperors were men of many talents. Dynastic genes apart, their quality often owed much to the ferocious competition between an emperor's sons to succeed their father. The princes who won this contest required political and military skills of a high order. Their powerful, vivid and fascinating personalities come down to us from contemporary sources, including in two cases their own autobiographies. But the wars of succession were always costly and potentially destabilizing. Moreover, the empire's dependence on the personality of its monarch carried unavoidable risks. Some historians blame Aurangzeb, the last of the six great emperors, for the collapse of Mughal power in the early eighteenth century. Among Aurangzeb's greatest mistakes was to reign for too long. When he died in 1707 he was eighty-nine years old and had reigned for almost fifty years.[2]

The founder of the Mughal Empire was Zahir al-Din Muhammad Babur, known to history as Babur (the Tiger). Born in 1483, Babur was the great-great grandson of Timur (Tamerlane) and a direct descendant also of Chinggis Khan. In the century since Timur's death his empire had both shrunk dramatically and fractured between his many descendants. The Timurid princes combined great pride in their ancestry with a total lack of dynastic solidarity. In the tradition of steppe politics they saw themselves as having equal rights to Timur's heritage and fought each other incessantly to secure it. Inheriting his small principality in the Fergana Valley (Uzbekistan) at the age of eleven in 1494 on his father's death, Babur himself immediately faced an invasion by an uncle to steal it. Civil war among the Timurids allowed their great rivals, the Uzbek tribal confederation, to conquer more and more of Central Asia. In Babur's youth the head of this confederation was Shibani Khan, another descendent of Chinggis. For two decades after 1494 Babur's efforts were concentrated on trying to defend and then regain his family's realm in Central Asia. The Uzbek khan was a bitter enemy also of the Iranian Shah Ismail. Acting as a client of the Safavids, Babur twice succeeded in regaining not just his own patrimony but also his uncle's city of Samarkand but on both occasions the Uzbeks regrouped and drove him out again.

At times Babur lived the life of a wandering and near penniless refugee, leading a tiny and bedraggled war-band. His fortunes were partly restored when he seized a chance opportunity to capture Kabul in December 1504. There he established what soon became the only surviving Timurid principality. Babur welcomed loyal Turkish and Mongol kinsmen, retainers and allies to Kabul but his principality's meagre resources greatly curtailed his ambitions to restore his dynasty's glory. Blocked by the Uzbeks from any hope of recapturing his ancestral homeland to the north, Babur's ambitions turned southwards to the immensely rich farmland of the Punjab and the north Indian plain. After a number of exploratory raids, in 1525 Babur invaded India and in the next three years smashed his enemies in two great battles and established a tenuous hold on most of the north Indian agricultural heartland. Babur thoroughly disliked the people, culture, food and climate of his newly conquered lands. As he once wrote, 'Hindustan is a place of little charm. There is no beauty in its people, no graceful social intercourse,

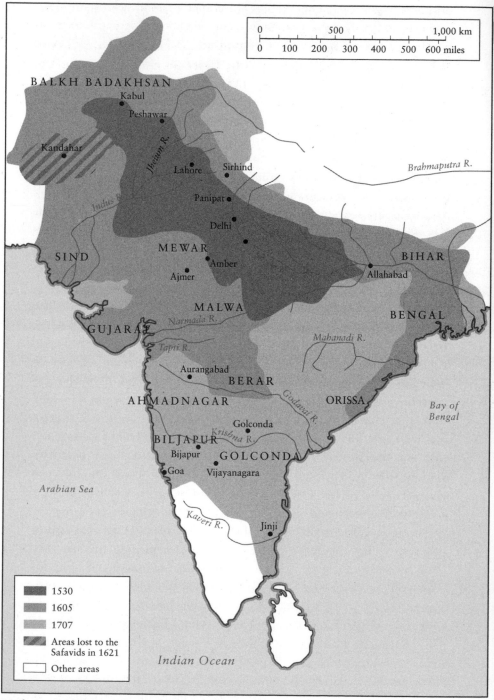

The Mughal Empire

no poetic talent or understanding, no etiquette, nobility or manliness. The arts and crafts have no harmony or symmetry. There are no good horses, meat, grapes, melons or other fruit ... The one nice aspect of Hindustan is that it is a large country with lots of gold and money.' The vast wealth of his new empire allowed Babur to restore his dynasty's grandeur, draw loyal Turkic and Mongol allies to his court, and establish himself as the Timurid dynasty's undoubted head.[3]

First and foremost Babur was a warrior and a princely dynast. Next only to his determination to restore his dynasty's grandeur, however, came Babur's ambition to become a respected poet in his native Chaghatay Turkic language. This is a reminder that, if the Timurid dynasty's broader political history in the fifteenth century was one of failure, it was far more successful in the role of cultural patronage. For many centuries Greater Central Asia had been one of the world's scientific, intellectual and cultural centres. Before the arrival of Islam, its cultural heritage combined native Achaemenid and Zoroastrian elements with Hellenistic influences introduced by Greek generals and settlers in the era of Alexander of Macedon. Muslim rulers of the region from the tenth century onwards encouraged the resurgence of Iranian tradition. Firdausi's *Shahnameh* was the single greatest monument to pre-Islamic Iran and its publication was vital to the preservation of much of ancient Iranian culture and memory. Typically, the Ghaznavids, a Muslim Turkic dynasty of steppe origin, supported the publication and lured Firdausi (940–1020) to their court as one of its leading ornaments. The region also benefited from being drawn into the Islamic cultural community that stretched from Spain to Central Asia. In the tenth and eleventh centuries some of the world's greatest philosophers, scientists, historians and mathematicians lived in Greater Central Asia.

Devastated by the Mongol invasion and the Black Death, the region staged a cultural renaissance under the fifteenth-century Timurids. Timur's grandson Mirza Taraghay (Ulughbeg) founded the famous observatory in Samarkand and was one of the century's greatest astronomers and mathematicians. Under his cousin Husayn Bayqara (r. 1469–1506), Herat became the greatest cultural centre in the Islamic world. Husayn's close friend and adviser, Nizam al-Din Harawi (1441–1501), usually known under his pen-name Navai, was not just a great patron of music, poetry and art but also himself a famous poet. It was Navai who through his poetry almost single-handedly turned his native

Chaghatay Turkish into a literary language. Navai was Babur's hero and role model. The emperor wrote both his poetry and his autobiography in Chaghatay Turkish, in the process speaking to us with a directness and humanity that disappears in the ornate Persian of court poets and writers of the era. For Babur, writing in his ancestral Chaghatay Turkish reflected pride in his Timurid heritage. In the disarming manner that makes his autobiography such fun to read, the emperor also ruefully confessed that he felt himself to be a very bad poet when writing in Persian and obeying the conventions of Persianate literary culture.[4]

Babur's career in many ways mirrored that of Mahmud, who had established the Ghaznavid dynasty as the first Central Asian Islamic rulers of northern India in the early eleventh century. Like the Timurids, the Ghaznavids were driven out of their Central Asian homeland, in this case by the Seljuk Turks. Mahmud put down roots in the Kabul region before using this as a base for the conquest of northern India. As was the case with Babur, it was only the weakness of the regimes ruling northern India at the time that made conquest possible. This reflected geopolitical realities. To invade India directly from Central Asia was very difficult since the invader would have to cross the high passes of the Hindu Kush before traversing Afghanistan and forcing his way through the Khyber Pass. Even an invader who held Kabul and used it as a base still faced a stiff challenge. Any stable regime which controlled the resources of northern India could garrison the mountain passes and keep an invader at bay. In the thirteenth century the Delhi sultanate even successfully blocked Mongol attempts to invade the subcontinent. Babur's invasion succeeded in part because he exploited divisions within the Afghan Lodi regime that ruled northern India in the 1520s and its deep unpopularity with many of its Hindu Rajput aristocratic subjects. His initial step was of necessity to conquer the Punjab and hold it as a base for future operations. In this he was greatly helped by the fact that the Lodi regime's governor of Punjab went over to the Mughals the moment their army arrived in the region.

Babur crushed the main Lodi army in the vicinity of Delhi at the battle of Panipat in 1526 and the Rajput princes at Khanua in the following year, though in both cases his army was heavily outnumbered. His victories were owed to the formidable Mughal military machine and the skill with which Babur coordinated its different elements on the battlefield. The core of his army were his Mongol mounted archers – the word

'Mughal' is in fact a local rendering of 'Mongol'. Babur combined their long-established tactical skill and mobility with infantry and artillery on the European and Ottoman model. Babur had Ottoman military experts in his household and he used battlefield tactics very similar to those employed by the Ottoman Sultan Selim I against the Safavids at the battle of Chaldiran in 1514. In the centre of his line he created field fortifications behind which he deployed his cannon and musketeers. The core of these fortifications was wagons tied together by chains. At Panipat and Khanua, Lodi and Rajput attacks broke down with heavy losses in the face of these fortifications and the firepower concentrated behind them. The demoralized enemy armies then disintegrated when faced with the counter-attack of the Mughal cavalry both from behind the wagon-camp and on the flanks. A military historian comments that 'North India saw the first coordinated deployment of mounted archers, field artillery, handgun-bearing infantry, and heavy cavalry . . . the effect was devastating for the local armies.'[5]

Babur's greatest biographer compares his mentality to that of the Italian elite in the era of Machiavelli and the Renaissance. Cold-eyed political realism and ambition were combined with great aesthetic sensibility and intellectual curiosity. His autobiography, the *Baburnama*, reveals him as 'an openly aggressive, unapologetic member of a warrior class whose profession was conquest and rule'. Babur describes his devastation of the Kabul region and his use of terror in order to deter resistance to his rule and to enable him to extract sufficient resources to sustain his war machine. He was much more a war-band leader than an emperor – relatively egalitarian, charismatic and delighting in the camaraderie of the military camp. Crucially for such a leader, he was a skilful, successful and lucky general, generous in his distribution of the booty that success brought. His powerful, vivid, uninhibited and egotistical personality leaps from the pages of the *Baburnama*. In fact, 'Babur himself and probably most Turco-Mongol warriors saw egotism as a manly virtue.' But he was much more than just a great warrior-king. His intellectual curiosity was encyclopaedic and his descriptions of Indian animals and vegetation were precise, detailed and scientific. Among memoirs written by monarchs, the *Baburnama* stands out for its honesty and the extent to which it reveals the inner man. Babur never saw or proclaimed himself to be a *ghazi* or warrior of Islam until the eve of the crucial battle of Khanua in 1527. Since almost all his previous foes had been Muslims this had not been an option. But when he saw the size of the Hindu Rajput army confronting him at Khanua, Babur realized that he and his troops needed all the help they could get. Now proclaiming himself a *ghazi*, he promised publicly that he would renounce alcohol for ever if only God would give him victory. Two years later, in one of the little asides that pepper the *Baburnama*, he wrote that his craving for wine was so strong it brought him close to tears.[6]

When Babur died in 1530 the Mughals' hold on northern India was insecure. The efforts of his eldest son, Humayun, to consolidate Mughal rule were sabotaged by his brothers' attempts to seize as much as possible of Babur's patrimony. As a result, Humayun was driven out of India by the Afghan leader, Sher Khan Sur, and took refuge in Iran as a client of the Safavids. Only the sudden and unexpected deaths of both Sher Sur and his son Islam Shah gave Humayun the chance to regain northern India. After Islam Shah's demise in 1554 a chaotic succession struggle raged in Delhi, with five rulers occupying the throne in just one year. Humayun retook Delhi in 1555 but died from an accidental fall in his library a year later, leaving the throne to his thirteen-year-old son, Akbar. Akbar was to rule for forty-nine years and it was in these decades that the Mughals put down roots in India and created the institutions and the legitimacy which gave their regime permanence. This followed a pattern long-since established by imperial dynasties. For a dynasty to survive, it was vital that the founding conqueror was succeeded by a highly competent heir who could consolidate the dynasty's hold on its newly won lands. Akbar followed in the footsteps of the Achaemenid King Darius I, Emperor Tang Taizong and the Abbasid Caliph al-Mansur. He was as great a ruler as any of this famous trio and was indeed one of the most impressive emperors in history.

Akbar's son and successor, Emperor Jahangir, described his father in the following terms: 'In stature he was of medium height. He had a wheaten complexion and black eyes and eyebrows. His countenance was radiant and he had the build of a lion, broad of chest with long hands and arms ... His august voice was very loud and he had a particularly nice way of speaking.' Akbar had extraordinary energy, stamina, courage and toughness. He was famous for riding and taming enraged and uncontrollable elephants whom his own most-experienced mahouts were too terrified to mount. Akbar was illiterate and dyslexic but made up for this deficiency by his astonishing memory and great intelligence, and his sensitive grasp of the personalities and motivations of his key advisers. The emperor was a naturally sociable and charming person, who enjoyed his public role and was always described as accessible, friendly and open. He stood halfway on the spectrum between his grandfather Babur, the war-band leader, and his grandson Shah Jahan, the majestic, distant and awe-inspiring emperor of the universe. To some extent this evolution in the nature of monarchy was a familiar story among conquest dynasties which came to rule sedentary societies and empires, but Akbar's style of rule also reflected his personality. A man of such great power but also personal charisma and ability could afford to be accessible, kindly and straightforward without for a moment risking any loss of his majesty.[7]

Akbar was a warrior-king. A fine strategist, he was an inspiring leader on the battlefield and a good comrade in camp. He was also an efficient and hard-working administrator, as well as a political leader famous for his love of justice, good judgement, and choice of loyal and effective lieutenants. Together with his great friend and minister Abul Fazl, he was also a master of propaganda. Given his personality, it is hardly surprising that Akbar was an extremely active and hands-on leader. As a young man he would roam the streets incognito in order to gauge public moods and see how his officials treated ordinary subjects. The emperor was skilled with his hands and fascinated by mechanical devices. Among other hobbies, he worked at carpentry. While inspecting his numerous building projects, he sometimes quarried the stone himself. More conventionally for a monarch, he was an avid huntsman and sportsman, revelling in boxing and fights between animals, and owning a menagerie of pets, spanning the whole spectrum from dogs to elephants and cheetahs.[8]

There was also a quieter, more introspective and thoughtful side to Akbar, who suffered from attacks of melancholy and mild epilepsy. He was devoted to his mother and to many other senior harem ladies and loved his children, with whom he spent an unusual amount of time for a monarch. The inner Akbar was partly revealed in his deep love and appreciation of painting. As a boy, Akbar had been trained as a painter. In his reign the imperial workshops grew greatly in scale and quality. They developed a unique style, partly because they merged Persian, Indian and European styles and techniques. Akbar inspected his workshops at least once a week, launched many projects and took a close interest in their execution. He once wrote, 'there are many that hate painting, but such men I dislike. It appears to me as if a painter had a quite peculiar means of recognizing God; for a painter in sketching anything that has life, and in devising its limbs, one after the other, must come to feel that he cannot bestow individuality upon his work, and is thus forced to think of God, the giver of life, and will then be increased in knowledge.'[9]

Akbar was deeply interested in religious questions. His personal search for God is a theme that runs through his life and was accompanied at times by spiritual difficulties and doubts. The Timurids were by tradition Sunni Muslims and supporters of the Naqshbandi Sufi sect. On the spectrum of Sufism the Naqshbandis stood at the most respectable 'establishment' end. They combined personal piety and good works with respect for the social order, its hierarchies and conventions. But the emperor's mother, to whom he was devoted, was a Shi'i Muslim. Akbar himself was always far more interested in the Sufi world of inner spirituality than in the Sunni *ulama* and religious doctrine. He became a close disciple of the head of the Chishti Sufi order, Shaykh Salim, who served as the emperor's spiritual adviser, playing the role of royal confessor in the Catholic world. His eldest son, the future Emperor Jahangir, was born in Shaykh Salim's home. Akbar's great palace at his new city of Fatehpur Sikri was built around Shaykh Salim's tomb. By 1577 Akbar was practising the arduous exercises and austerities of a Chishti devotee. These included not just strict dieting but on occasion walking barefoot for scores of miles 'across the scorching sands of Rajasthan' to visit Chishti shrines. The Chishti order was far more ascetic, otherworldly and inclined to mysticism than the Naqshbandis. Their beliefs and practices overlapped with those of some Hindu spiritual leaders. Shaykh Salim had almost as many Hindu as Muslim followers.[10]

In 1577 Akbar opened the House of Worship at his court in Fatehpur Sikri. Here he presided over debates between representatives of various elements of Islamic religious opinion, but also Brahmins, Christian Jesuit monks, Zoroastrians and Jains. There were few precedents or equivalents of debates of this quality at any other imperial court in history. Jahangir recalls that 'my father often used to hold discussions with the wise men of every religion and sect, particularly with the pundits and learned men of India ... he had sat so much with sages and learned men in discussions that no one could guess from his appearance that he was illiterate. He comprehended the subtleties of prose and poetry so well that it is impossible to imagine any better.' Father Monserrat, a Jesuit who attended these debates, found the emperor very erudite and well-informed on theological issues. In time, however, the Jesuits came to share the dismay of their Muslim counterparts as Akbar increasingly rejected monotheistic dogmatism in favour of an eclectic spirituality that sought to combine the insights of all the major religions.[11]

Akbar's personal search for God had a great impact on his regime's religious policy and ideology. Mughal policy also simply adapted to the reality of ruling a country whose overwhelming majority were Hindus. In Akbar's reign the Mughals ceased to be a conquest dynasty and became one rooted in Indian soil. Compromise with the majority and tolerance of their religion were essential. In the 1570s a number of special taxes and constraints on non-Muslims were abolished. In time Akbar's religious policy went far beyond mere tolerance. In 1579 the emperor issued a decree making himself the final arbiter in all matters of Islamic doctrine. This was to assert a position not seen within Sunni Islam since the days of the Abbasid caliph al-Mamun. Since al-Mamun's time Islam had become deeply influenced by the Sufi movement. Akbar and his chief adviser, Abul Fazl, were to some extent seeking to create an imperial Sufi sect with Akbar as its saint. Elaborate rituals inducted key figures at court into the sect as disciples. On a personal level, these disciples met Akbar's need for companions and friends. Some of the emperors we encounter in this book created similar groups for similar reasons but in their own dynastic and cultural idiom. More important, imperial Sufism was designed to raise the monarchy's sacred status and legitimacy in the eyes of its subjects of all confessions. Official policy chimed with some messianic and millenarian aspects of Sufi Islam. With the Muslim millennium approaching in 1591 these tendencies were especially strong. The emperor was described as a *mujtahid*, in other words a divinely inspired religious leader who would restore and inspire Islam in its second millennium.

Official ideology also tapped into traditions of Iranian and Hindu sacred monarchy, in which the ruler was identified with the sun, light and *farr*, in other words an almost superhuman charisma directly bestowed by God. Astrology played an important part in imperial ideology. In this era the belief that Heaven's plan for mankind might be revealed through studying the stars was very widespread. As we have seen, the Habsburg emperor Rudolph II, Akbar's contemporary, believed this passionately. Even the very orthodox Philip II did not deny this possibility. Astrology was even more systematically studied in the Muslim world than in the Christian one. Iranian astrological tradition especially stressed the vital significance for events on earth of the conjunction of the planets Saturn and Jupiter. It was in terms of these widely held astrological beliefs that Akbar was hailed as the 'Lord of the Conjunction' and the inaugurator of a new era in mankind's history. Similar titles were ascribed by their court astrologers to the Safavid shah Ismail and the Ottoman sultans Selim I and Suleyman I.[12]

Part of Akbar's ideology of sacred monarchy was watered down or abandoned in the reigns of his grandson Shah Jahan and – especially – his great-grandson Aurangzeb. This was in particular true when it too grossly violated Islamic norms. But the memory of Akbar loomed over the dynasty until its fall, penetrating deeply even into village folklore. Meanwhile more secular elements of Akbar's regime survived until the collapse of Mughal power in the early eighteenth century.

The most obvious example of this was the enormous territorial expansion that occurred under Akbar. In his reign Mughal rule was consolidated and deepened on the north Indian plain which formed the empire's heartland. The rich provinces of Bengal and Gujarat, together with strategically important Rajasthan were conquered. Of course, military power played a key role in the empire's advance. The Mughal military machine showed impressive adaptability in triumphing despite the alien terrain of Bengal's jungles, swamps and rivers. This required the creation of a fleet and the adoption of amphibious warfare tactics and logistics, all of which were totally new to the Mughal troops and their leaders. By the 1570s the Mughal army's reputation and size were so formidable that enemies often refused to meet it in the field, instead taking refuge in fortresses and engaging in guerrilla warfare.

These tactics slowed the Mughal advance but did not stop it. Indian fortresses were sometimes formidable obstacles, extending over great areas, girded by immensely thick walls, and perched in hilly and inaccessible spots. This was, for example, the case with the huge fortresses of Chittor and Ranthambor, which were held by the Sisoya family, Akbar's most formidable and persistent enemies among the Rajput princes. At Chittor in 1568, Akbar 'carved a huge gash in the mountain on which the city sat so that the great siege guns could be placed and fired from point-blank range'. After the defenders refused to surrender even after their walls were breached, the city had to be stormed at great cost to the attackers. In revenge and as a warning to others Akbar ordered the massacre of the garrison. Terror worked. When Ranthambor's walls were breached in the following year the garrison promptly surrendered to avoid a similar fate.[13]

Although on rare occasions Akbar used terror to achieve his aims, much more often he employed military power as a form of leverage. Rulers and elites who surrendered without last-ditch resistance were co-opted into the Mughal system of rule and allowed to retain much of their local power. This policy was applied with special success to the Rajput (i.e. Hindu) leaders of Rajasthan. Bringing them into the Mughal elite gave the Mughals control of the routes between the north Indian plain and the ports and commercial wealth of Gujarat. It brought into the Mughal service the best native cavalry in India. For many generations the Rajputs formed a large section of the imperial ruling elite. Their martial ethos and cult of unlimited loyalty to their overlord served the emperors well, not least because it reduced the monarchs' dependence on their sometimes fickle core elite of Turkic and Mongol warrior-nobles. One strand in the Mughal incorporation of Rajput elites into the imperial nobility was bringing their daughters into the imperial harem. The mother of Akbar's heir, the Emperor Jahangir, was a Rajput princess.[14]

As was generally the case with empires, the nature and roles of the imperial nobility were closely tied to how the 'agrarian surplus' was squeezed out of peasant farmers and redistributed. In the core of their empire the Mughals perfected an efficient and moderate system of taxation of agricultural production based on regular land surveys. Outside the north Indian plain taxes were often fixed since regular land surveys were beyond the administration's capabilities. In peripheral regions 'taxation' meant periodic tribute payments. However raised, vast sums poured into the imperial treasury. These were partly used to support elite, 'imperial' military units (imperial guards, artillery, key garrisons) and much of the administration. Most of the revenue was redistributed among the imperial nobility (*mansabdaris*), largely in return for recruiting, paying and organizing the overwhelming majority of the empire's military forces. In addition to commanding their military forces on campaign, nobles were required to serve in government posts and support their own households. How large the revenues *(jagirs)* assigned to a nobleman were depended on his rank. Meritorious service resulted in promotion in rank and an increase in *jagirs*.

To some extent it is right to see the Mughal nobility as an aristocracy. It had much of the mentality and many of the values generally associated with hereditary warrior-aristocratic elites. Nevertheless, this was a service elite, not a hereditary aristocracy on the European model. Promotion (and more rarely demotion) in rank depended on the emperor alone. *Jagirs* were not a nobleman's property and were assigned to him for a few years only. Except in the case of the Rajputs they were never hereditary. A fixed policy existed of rotating a noble's *jagirs* from region to region, thereby creating an all-imperial elite and stopping nobles from putting down deep local roots. When a nobleman died most of his wealth reverted to the emperor, who generously returned part of it to his family. His son usually entered the imperial service but initially received a more junior rank and smaller *jagir* than his father. Until the system began to break down at the very end of the seventeenth century, the noble would have to serve with merit if he was in time to attain the same wealth and rank as his father. With its shallow roots in Indian society and its rather limited pedigree the Mughal nobility was at most a hereditary aristocracy in the making. It was only later, as loyal clients of the British, that some families of the Mughal nobility became hereditary aristocrats in the full sense of the word. Like most empires, the British one in India was based in part on alliance with the native aristocracy. In the British case this alliance was also 'natural' and conformed to the situation in Britain itself, where in the eighteenth and nineteenth centuries the aristocracy became and remained the richest, most powerful and most admired hereditary ruling elite in Europe.[15]

The Mughal system gave the emperor greater control over a much wider territory than any previous rulers in Indian history. Nevertheless, one must be wary of terms such as 'autocracy' and 'centralization' when applied to the Mughal system of rule. The empire was vast and in much of it the monarch's authority was barely noticeable. Although his control over the core and densely populated north Indian plain was relatively tight, much of the empire was covered by forests, mountains, hills and jungles. A Dutch traveller commented that the emperor 'is to be regarded as the king of the plains and open roads only'. In addition, almost five million of Akbar's subjects possessed private weapons, and in many cases these were muskets. Most of these men were peasants who hired themselves out on a seasonal basis on the vast Indian military labour market. Armed resistance to intrusive government was an everyday reality. The emperor was also constrained by the fact that at the local level power belonged to the landowners (*zamindars*). Except in Rajasthan (i.e. Rajput country), these men were not in most cases deeply integrated into the administration, nor did they usually share the values or loyalties of the imperial nobility. Mughal power meant that the *zamindars* had no alternative but to hand over part of the rural surplus to the imperial government, yet many would only continue to do so as long as that power was real and visible. That was one reason why the emperor periodically went on great tours across his dominions, accompanied by his splendid court and thousands of soldiers.[16]

Comparisons with other empires illustrate the limits of Mughal power. Indian *zamindars*, except for the Rajputs, had little of the Roman elites' identification with the imperial state and empire-wide civilization. India had no equivalent to the iron frame provided by the Confucian administrative machine in China until the British created the Indian civil service in the nineteenth century. By the sixteenth century the Confucian ideology of imperial unity dated back 2,000 years, and for much of this period empire had prevailed as the actual system of rule. By the early modern era the Chinese civil-service examination system tied the entire provincial elite to the all-imperial values and loyalties of the Confucian bureaucracy. India was also unlike early modern Europe where the whole hereditary landowning class was usually closely aligned with the monarchy. This alignment was tightest in countries such as Russia and Prussia where much of the landowning class served for at least part of its life as officers in the monarchs' armies. Akbar's achievement in building the Mughal system of rule was spectacular. But no one ruler or reign could create deep-rooted institutions and values which were the product of centuries of political, cultural and social evolution in other regions of the world.

In the saga of the Mughal emperors, Akbar and Aurangzeb traditionally stand out, the former as hero, the latter as villain. Akbar is commonly seen as the empire's true founder, Aurangzeb as the individual who did more than anyone else to destroy it. In the eyes of modern, Congress-Party-oriented Indians who seek to sustain a secular, supra-communal political order, Akbar is a hero for treating all religions equally. Aurangzeb is a villain for moving the empire away from pluralism and back towards the privileging of Islam. He is even more of a villain in the eyes of India's present Hindu nationalist leaders. By contrast, the two men who reigned between Akbar and Aurangzeb – the emperors Jahangir and Shah Jahan – were once wittily described as the Rosencrantz and Guildenstern of the list of Mughal emperors. In reality, by the standards of most monarchs in history, both Jahangir and Shah Jahan were major figures, with clear-cut and powerful personalities.[17]

Jahangir, who ruled from 1605 to 1627, lacked his father's vast energy and activism. Although a wise manager of patronage and the ruling elites, he never commanded his armies on campaign and took a relaxed attitude to his day-to-day responsibilities as ruler. In large part he could afford to do so, since he inherited from his father an effective and smooth-running government machine. Even in 1622, when his health was fading, Jahangir could still react swiftly and decisively in an emergency, in this case to the major threat to his throne caused by the revolt of his son Prince Khurram (the future emperor Shah Jahan). Jahangir had an aesthete's eye for beauty, especially in jewellery and portraiture. He was a generous patron of Persianate and Sanskrit culture. He loved travelling around his empire and was a passionate huntsman.

The emperor's main problem was drink and drugs. All three of Akbar's sons were alcoholics and opium addicts. Princes Murad and Daniyal died early as a result. In his sometimes endearingly honest autobiography Jahangir recalls that he drank in excess until aged thirty, with the result that his hands shook so much that he had to be fed with a spoon by his attendants. 'These days,' he added, 'I drink only to promote digestion', and only in the evening. On the other hand, he still took his twice-daily dose of opium in order to remain composed. Although not an especially cruel ruler, Jahangir could be quick-tempered: under the influence of alcohol and opium he could sometimes no doubt be as comfortable a neighbour as 'Snowflake' and 'Innocence', the man-eating pet bears of the Roman emperor Valentinian I. Unsurprisingly, by the time he reached his late-fifties Jahangir's health was very poor. As a result, even more than before he devolved responsibility for government to his favourite wife, Nur Jahan, who 'had more affection for me than any other'.[18]

As in most hereditary monarchies, Mughal royal women sometimes played important political roles. Since they were neither threats nor competitors, an emperor could trust his female relations and allow himself warm, emotional relationships with them in a manner that was never possible with his sons or brothers. Especially under the first three emperors, senior imperial ladies enjoyed more freedom than was the case in the Chinese and Ottoman harems. Akbar's highly intelligent and independent aunt even led a pilgrimage to Mecca. The only human being before whom an emperor prostrated himself was his mother. Mothers, sisters and aunts were often trusted confidantes, as well as diplomats who helped to resolve disputes within the family. Nevertheless, Nur Jahan stood out among Mughal princesses for her personality and the power she wielded. Contemporary reports agree that she was a capable, independent and intelligent woman of rare beauty. Her marksmanship on hunting expeditions was famous. In one day in 1617 atop an elephant she killed four tigers with six shots and no misses. Jahangir poured wealth on his wife. She managed personally her great landed estates and her extensive network of political patronage. Already before Jahangir sickened in the 1620s Nur Jahan was the key power behind the throne. She promoted her father and her brother, Asaf Khan, into top posts in court and government. Very unusually, her position as almost co-regent was not kept private but was sometimes even recorded in official documents.[19]

If Nur Jahan and Jahangir had produced children of their own, then the whole pattern of court politics would have been transformed. In their absence, Nur Jahan initially forged an alliance with her husband's ablest son, Prince Khurram (Shah Jahan), whose mother was a Rajput princess. The relationship between two such ambitious, determined and powerful personalities as Nur Jahan and Khurram was always likely to unravel. By 1620, as Jahangir's health and energy declined, Nur Jahan became much the most powerful person in the empire. However, neither she nor her clients could have any illusions about how soon this power would evaporate when the emperor died and Khurram ascended the throne. Nur Jahan therefore began to switch her support to Jahangir's youngest son, Prince Shahriyar, to whom in time she married her only child by her first marriage.

Prince Khurram was thirty years old in 1622, impatient for power, arrogant, and well able to compare his own vigour with his father's obvious decrepitude. There followed revolt, defeat, and an only partial reconciliation between father and son. When Jahangir died in Kashmir in November 1627 Khurram was far away to the south, on campaign in the Deccan. He secured the throne above all because of the political skill and trickery of his father-in-law (and Nur Jahan's brother), Asaf Khan. As always in court and dynastic politics, questions of personal ambition, family relations and political considerations were intertwined. We cannot be certain why Asaf Khan opted for his son-in-law rather than his sister, to whom he owed so much. One factor which will certainly have weighed heavily was Asaf's knowledge that his daughter, Nur Mahal, was deeply loved by her husband, Prince Khurram. Probably he reckoned that his future status was better guaranteed by relying on his daughter than by allying himself with his sister and her son-in-law, with whom his relations were polite but distant. This calculation proved correct. Shah Jahan (Khurram) lavished rewards on Asaf and retained him as one of his closest advisers for the rest of his life. When his beloved wife, Nur Mahal, died in 1631 after giving birth to her fourteenth child, the emperor was devastated. His beard and moustache began to turn white and a gap was left in his life that was never to be filled. Shah Jahan, always deeply interested in architecture, personally planned and oversaw the construction of her mausoleum, the Taj Mahal, which remains to this day the greatest monument not just to the Mughal dynasty (and its exquisite aesthetic taste) but also to any monarch's love for a woman.[20]

Khurram had been born in 1592. Of his four grandparents, only one, Akbar, was a Muslim. The young prince was brought up at Akbar's court. Having seen all his sons take to alcohol and opium, the emperor no doubt wished to supervise the education of the next generation, who were his dynasty's future. Khurram stayed away from drugs and (mostly) drink for the rest of his life. The education of Mughal princes was rigorous and tough. Khurram was taught literature, mathematics, languages and history, especially the history of his own ancestors and their campaigns. He began lessons in archery aged five and by the time he was eight was being trained in musketry and the skills of horsemanship and cavalry warfare. A fiercely martial society demanded that its princes should have the qualities of a lion. Ruling the Mughal Empire was not for the faint-hearted. Mughal princes were trained from childhood to be independent, tough and ruthless. Khurram absorbed this lesson well. To do him justice, he absorbed other lessons too: as emperor he showed himself to be hard-working, self-disciplined, effective, and very conscious of the responsibilities of his office.[21]

Like most Mughal princes, as a young man Khurram was sent out to gain military and political experience by commanding armies and governing provinces. Khurram's greatest achievement in these years was his conquest of the Mewar kingdom, whose ruler was the head of the Sisoya dynasty, the greatest of the Rajput princes. Khurram treated his defeated enemy with tact, politeness and generosity. This was a matter of political calculation but it also reflected the respect of one military aristocrat for another. The heir to the Mewar throne, Prince Karna Singh, became Khurram's loyal friend, subject and ally for life, and a key member of his network.

As emperor, Khurram sought to live up to his title 'Shah Jahan', in other words 'Ruler of the World'. Although he mostly dropped the explicitly un-Islamic elements of Akbar's ideology of sacred kingship, he rejoiced in the title 'Lord of the Conjunction', with its millennial, cosmic and astrological connotations. Both the style and substance of his rule was imperial. Shah Jahan abandoned Jahangir's relative restraint and embarked on a policy of all-round territorial expansion. The peacock throne that he commissioned to celebrate his accession took seven years to construct and was inlaid with a mass of precious jewels at astronomical cost. A contemporary European jeweller viewed the peacock throne with awe, commenting probably correctly that 'it is the richest and most superb throne which has ever been seen in the world'. For Shah Jahan, as for most emperors, inspiring among foreigners the sense that his own dynasty stood above all others in wealth and splendour was the main reason for pouring resources into the creation of such splendid symbols. Like all emperors, the god-like, still and iconic figure on display to the public was also a human being. After thirty years as ruler, like so many monarchs, Shah Jahan was undermined by a combination of old age and the politics of succession. After the revolt of his sons and Aurangzeb's seizure of power, he was deposed and spent the last seven years of his life in humiliating and not always comfortable confinement.[22]

Aurangzeb's evil reputation is in most respects undeserved. Ruthlessness in succession struggles and the elimination of defeated brothers was by now the rule of the Mughal political game. Aurangzeb went no further in this direction than his father. Subsequently he reintegrated some of his brothers' children into the dynasty by marrying them to his own descendants. Not even remotely did Aurangzeb match the determination of some Ottoman sultans to eliminate not just brothers but also all their male offspring. Nor did the emperor seriously persecute his Hindu subjects. In an empire that contained thousands of temples he destroyed a few dozen. No forced conversions were attempted and non-Muslims retained their position in the imperial nobility. On the other hand, Aurangzeb did make clear that he saw himself as a Muslim monarch. The special tax on non-Muslims, abolished by Akbar, was reinstated after a gap of a century. Some ceremonies linking the monarchy to Hindu tradition were discontinued.

Aurangzeb was a skilful general, a hard-working administrator, and a ruler very conscious of his duty to provide justice to all his subjects. But he lacked the charisma, the conviviality or the human touch of Akbar, Babur or even Jahangir. His austerity and self-discipline slipped easily into rigidity. The one great recorded love of Aurangzeb's life was a Hindu slave-songstress. When she died, he was distraught but subsequently commented that her death was a good thing since his love for her had threatened the iron self-discipline and self-control which was essential to his success as general, political leader and monarch. His tactlessness and insensitivity in dealing with key Hindu leaders on occasion cost him dearly. On his deathbed, aged almost ninety, he demanded that he be buried in the simplest of graves as a sinner and a political failure.[23]

Although Aurangzeb's personality and mistakes undoubtedly made a significant contribution to the decline of the Mughals, deeper structural factors familiar to historians of empire mattered more. These included the perennial problems of succession, territorial overstretch, and the impact of ageing monarchs who occupied the throne for too long. Even more important was the fundamental challenge facing most empires, namely the monarchs' relationship with provincial landowning elites which was crucial to the empire's political stability and the viability of its patronage, fiscal and military machine. As already noted in this chapter, the Mughals' compromise with the provincial landowners, the so-called *zamindars*, was fragile. The crisis created by the linked problems of succession, over-extension and the ruler's old age undermined this relationship and thereby struck at the empire's foundations.

Akbar was fortunate that by the time he succeeded his father,

Humayun, all his paternal uncles were dead. His only sibling, his half-brother Mirza Hakim, was an infant. Mirza was assigned the Kabul region as his share of his father's inheritance and when he reached adulthood in the late 1570s he became a threat. By then, however, Akbar had ruled for twenty years and had consolidated his power across the whole of northern India. In 1582 he invaded Afghanistan and annexed it to his empire. Although Mirza Hakim's challenge was defeated with relative ease, it nevertheless represented a significant threat to Akbar. The most fundamental point about Akbar's reign was that he turned a Central Asian conquest regime into a political system rooted in the Indian subcontinent. As almost always occurred in the history of the steppe empires, important elements within the elite resented this process which challenged both their material interests and their cultural and ideological values. Mirza Hakim defined himself as the defender of Timurid tradition and Central Asian kingship. He appealed to Turko-Mongol aristocrats who hated the way in which Akbar was bringing Indian Muslims and Rajput Hindus into the imperial nobility. The Naqshbandis were also natural allies of Mirza. More broadly, he attracted support from orthodox Muslims suspicious of Akbar's religious policies. Similar issues re-emerged in the late 1650s during the bitter struggle between Shah Jahan's sons that ended with the triumph of Aurangzeb.[24]

During Akbar's reign conventions were established that changed the rules of succession politics. The empire was considered indivisible and no permanent appanages would be granted to princes. The right to succeed to the throne would henceforth be restricted to the ruler's sons, thereby avoiding the previous free-for-all between uncles, nephews and cousins which had undermined the Timurid dynasty's hold on Central Asia. These conventions were of course not set in stone like, for example, the French Salic Law. In the succession struggle to succeed Shah Jahan suggestions were sometimes made that the empire might be divided in traditional steppe style, with one son possessing paramount status as emperor but his brothers exercising de facto autonomy in their regional kingdoms. In the end, however, the principle of imperial unity under a single, theoretically all-powerful monarch prevailed.

As Shah Jahan aged, competition grew between his four adult sons over the succession. The emperor's eldest son was Prince Dara Shukoh. His name, which means 'Majestic as Darius', illustrates the Mughals' identification with an ancient tradition of Near Eastern imperial monarchy whose most spectacular embodiments were the great Achaemenid emperors. Shah Jahan made clear his support for Dara Shukoh as his successor, granting him much greater wealth and honours than his brothers. This was probably more than just a question of personal preference, though the strong support for Dara Shukoh of the emperor's eldest and favourite daughter, Jayanara, no doubt influenced Shah Jahan. The emperor was probably trying to nudge his dynasty towards a new convention by which the monarch chose which son would be his heir. Conceivably, he even pondered the advantages of male primogeniture. Shah Jahan kept his eldest son close beside him at court, where the institutions of central government and most of the empire's greatest nobles were located. His younger sons, Shuja, Aurangzeb and Murad, were sent out to govern, respectively, the crucial and wealthy regions of Bengal, the Deccan and Gujarat.

Unsurprisingly, the younger brothers resented the emperor's attempt to change the rules of succession and secretly allied against Dara Shukoh. Marriages were arranged between the children of Shuja and Aurangzeb. Aurangzeb agreed with his younger brother Murad that the latter would rule autonomously in western India (including Murad's power base in Gujarat) under the largely nominal paramountcy of Aurangzeb himself as all-Indian emperor. When the news spread in October 1657 that Shah Jahan had fallen critically ill and seemed on the point of death, Shuja in Bengal proclaimed himself emperor. Dara Shukoh sent the cream of the imperial army to Bengal where they crushed Shuja but he failed to recall them in time to confront the combined armies of Aurangzeb and Murad as they converged on Delhi. Although Dara Shukoh's huge wealth enabled him to field a second great army against his brothers, his troops were less battle-hardened and less loyal than theirs, and Dara himself had neither experience nor natural ability as a general. By contrast, Aurangzeb had commanded armies ever since his adolescence. He had also forged a powerful sense of unity and loyalty among his leading lieutenants, a wide network of allies within the Mughal elite and his soldiers. Dara Shukoh was defeated in the battle of Dharmatpur near Delhi on 15 April 1658 and, though fighting continued for a year, this victory proved decisive. Aurangzeb imprisoned his father. He captured, humiliated and killed Dara Shukoh. Once victory was assured over Dara, he tricked, double-crossed and killed Murad.

1. Ashurbanipal killing a lion.

2. The earliest known pillar erected by Ashoka.

3. Marcus Aurelius shows his clemency towards the vanquished.

4. Taizong receiving the ambassador of Tibet.

ذكر حوادث سنة خمسين

5. Muʿāwiya I ibn Abī Sufyān meeting his councillors.

6. Otto, between military men on one side and two clergy on the other. On the facing leaf, four figures resembling the Magi approach him, symbolizing the four provinces of his empire (Germany, France, northern Italy, the Slavic east).

7. Entrants undertake Imperial Chinese civil-service exams.

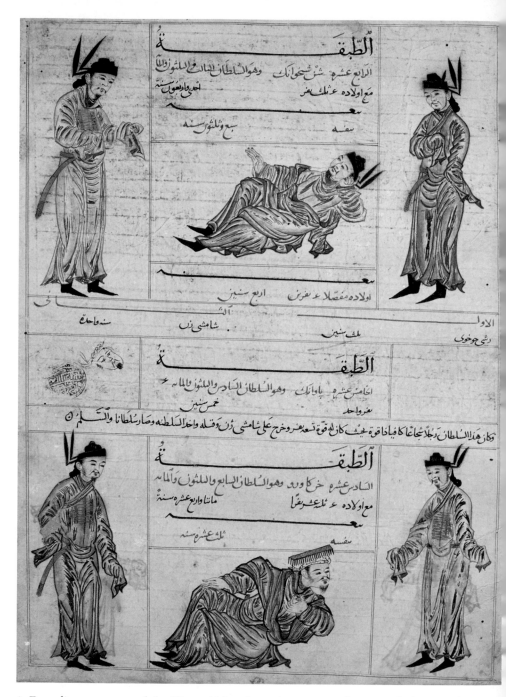

8. Founding emperors of the Qin and Han dynasties, portrayed in an early fourteenth-century history book owned by the son of Timur, Shahrukh.

9. Babur celebrates the birth of his son and successor, Humayun, in the royal gardens at Kabul.

10. Maximilian I with his wife Mary of Burgundy and their family. Below them are Philip's sons, the future emperors Charles V and Ferdinand I.

11. Suleyman the Magnificent with his faithful Janissaries during the Conquest of Belgrade.

12. In El Greco's painting *The Adoration of the Holy Name of Jesus*, Philip II is shown kneeling, at bottom centre.

13. Prince Khurram (later Shah Jahan) weighed in gold and silver before Jahangir.

14. Louis XIV portrayed in triumph as the Roman god Apollo.

15. The Kangxi Emperor, fourth ruler of the Qing dynasty, seated at his writing desk.

16. The Yongzheng Emperor portrayed as an ascetic.

17. Peter the Great.

18. Maria Theresa.

19. Standing before the tomb of Peter the Great, Catherine gestures towards the banners and other trophies of Russian victory over the Ottoman fleet in 1770.

20. Kaiser William II. Behind him is the imperial family, with Empress Auguste Victoria and Crown Prince Friedrich Wilhelm; before the steps of the throne is Chancellor Otto von Bismarck.

1. The Meiji Emperor presented with a portentous eagle.

2. The Empress Dowager of China, Cixi.

23. Nicholas II.

24. Alexander the Great statue in Thessaloniki, Greece.

25. Japanese Emperor Naruhito visits the Geku, Outer Shrine of the Ise Grand Shrine.

The war to succeed Shah Jahan tells one much about both the Mughal Empire and the politics of succession in imperial monarchies. Aurangzeb and Dara Shukoh felt for each other a deep and personal hatred which combined political rivalry with sibling jealousies and resentments. In more structural terms the war showed that the emperor's support and control over the central army and government were not enough to guarantee victory and could even be a disadvantage. In their role as regional viceroys, princes possessed enormous resources and gained priceless political and military experience. If they had the natural ability to exploit these opportunities then they became formidable challengers for the succession. Dara Shukoh seems not to have fully understood the sources of power in Mughal politics and to have been too confident in his own superior resources and abilities.

Dara Shukoh and Aurangzeb were very different personalities but they also represented rival visions of the empire's future. Dara followed Akbar's path in seeking both personal fulfilment and ultimate religious truth in a synthesis of Islamic and Hindu religious and mystical traditions. Unlike Akbar, he was a scholar, pouring much of his energy into writing works on theology. He combined the arrogance natural to imperial princes with the particularly unbearable haughtiness of a clever and devout man who believes that he is not just more intelligent but also more holy than other people. His behaviour frequently infuriated members of the Mughal elite. Dara lacked the maturity or self-discipline to curb his tongue and was much inclined to witticisms about aristocrats and courtiers. Proud warrior-nobles, deeply conscious of their public honour, never forgave these slurs. He even on one occasion committed the ultimate insult of hitting an aristocrat with his shoe. Aurangzeb was skilful in exploiting his rival's behaviour, as well as his heterodox religious views. He portrayed himself as an experienced and effective general and administrator who was at the same time both personally modest and respectful of the Mughal regime's core values.[25]

Of course, many elements in the struggle to succeed Shah Jahan were unique to the personalities of the rival princes and the context of Mughal politics, but there were also parallels with other eras and regimes, even in the seemingly totally remote world of the battle to succeed Lenin in the Soviet Union of the 1920s. As Trotsky and Dara Shukoh discovered, to be the front-runner in a succession struggle is often to unite all other candidates against you. Trotsky was more intelligent and certainly more of an intellectual than Joseph Stalin. This is by no means always an asset in the political world. His intellectual arrogance and his witticisms at the expense of the Russian former workers, peasants and lower middle-class men who increasingly dominated the party-state apparatus did not help his cause. Stalin, by contrast, like Aurangzeb, portrayed himself as a modest man, respectful of the ruling elite and their values. Interest in ideas and in the great questions of international socialism also to some extent blinded Trotsky (like Dara Shukoh) to the real sources of power in Soviet politics. Stalin on the contrary focused exclusively on the struggle for power and dedicated himself to the crucial but unglamorous control of promotions and appointments within the Bolshevik apparatus, constructing a formidable network of allies and clients in the process.

At one level the comparison between Stalin and Aurangzeb is absurd. Stalin was operating in a post-revolutionary situation in which all existing political institutions and conventions had been destroyed. He headed a new regime dedicated to a millenarian plan to transform mankind. Aurangzeb was a hereditary monarch operating within the conventions of an established political, religious and social order. But even when comparing seemingly incomparable eras and regimes some constants about human beings and political power are revealed. That is indeed one of the underlying themes of this book.

In recent years historians have tended to defend the Mughal system of succession. It is true that Mughal conventions shielded the empire from some of the potential dangers of succession wars. The number of competitors was limited to sons. Young princes were brought up as lion cubs and were expected to have the qualities of a lion. By most dynastic standards Mughal emperors were extraordinarily forgiving when their sons rebelled in order to improve their chances of inheriting the throne. Partitioning the empire among candidates was ruled out. The elimination of all losers meant that conflicts over succession ceased for a generation. Although defeat was fatal to a prince this was not true as regards his supporters. New emperors never carried out purges of their brothers' clients. They were regarded not as traitors but as men who had served their masters in the manner that duty required. Loyalty to patrons and heads of extended households was a core political and ethical principle of the Mughal elite. The new monarch reintegrated able and influential men back into the imperial system of rule. Often that applied too to the male, let alone female, descendants of his brothers. Meanwhile the competition for power between princes with regional power bases enhanced and ensured the political and military abilities of a future emperor. Success required the ability to build and sustain political networks. It also required stamina, courage and a hard-nosed immersion in politics. The succession process integrated into the imperial central ruling group fresh blood, much of it drawn from groups and regions outside the existing elite in Delhi.

One might at a pinch argue that democratic politics too is a version of (admittedly unarmed) civil war and that the Mughal competition for power was superior as a training in the actual ability to govern. On the other hand, even a brief comparison with the Ottoman Empire shows that the Mughal system of succession was only affordable because of the empire's unusual degree of geopolitical security. No outside great power had the means to exploit Mughal succession struggles in a way that threatened the empire's existence. The closest the Mughals came to war with a great-power rival was their attempt to retake Kandahar from the Safavids in 1652 and 1653. The failure of this attempt was a humiliation but Kandahar in Safavid hands was no threat. The Mughals controlled far greater resources than any ruler of Iran could possibly match. Moreover, Safavid attention was largely focused on conflict with the Ottomans. Given the appalling communications between Kandahar and Punjab the city could in any case never serve as the base for an invasion of India.[26]

Nevertheless, succession struggles consumed resources and temporarily weakened the state. Most emperors reigned for decades so these costs proved acceptable once every other generation. But in the years following Aurangzeb's death in 1707 emperors came and went at great speed. In 1719 four men sat on the throne, two of whom died almost immediately and one of whom was murdered. At this point the costs of succession conflicts became exorbitant, especially since they coincided with what one might describe as a crisis brought on by the empire's territorial over-extension.

By the end of Akbar's reign all of northern and much of central India was in Mughal hands. Further expansion faced severe geographical obstacles. As regards the empire's northern frontiers this became obvious in the reign of Shah Jahan. The emperor pursued his dynasty's old dream – dear even to Akbar and Jahangir – of recapturing its ancestral homeland in Central Asia. All the Mughal emperors, for example, subsidized the upkeep of Timur's tomb in Samarkand. Shah Jahan's attempt to reconquer the region was dynastic identity politics writ large and expensive. Since the Mughals held Afghanistan, extending their power beyond the Hindu Kush was not as wholly unrealistic as would have been the case had they tried to mount the operation from Punjab. Even so the logistical obstacles were enormous. The army could not live off the land north of the Hindu Kush and needed to sustain and protect supply lines stretching back over the high mountain passes to Kabul. Part of the problem was that the army, like the regime it served, was now rooted in India. The Mongol mounted archers who had been a key element in Babur's army had largely disappeared, which made dealing with the raids of mobile nomad enemy cavalry difficult. For the Mughal soldiers and generals (not to mention princes Murad and Aurangzeb whom Shah Jahan appointed to command operations) the campaigns seemed not just gruelling and frustrating but also pointless. The regions beyond the Hindu Kush were far poorer and harder to exploit than their Indian homeland. Military operations in the region could never hope to repay their costs.[27]

The two-year campaign north of the Hindu Kush in 1646–7 cost half the empire's annual revenue but did the Mughals no lasting harm. Vastly more expensive were the campaigns to conquer south-central India (the Deccan region), which had begun even before Shah Jahan became emperor and which continued until the death of Aurangzeb. Moreover, if the financial costs were exorbitant, in the end the political ones were worse. Admittedly, the push to conquer the Deccan was much more reasonable than attempting to campaign beyond the Hindu Kush. The region was richer and more accessible. Almost all regimes which controlled northern India for any time attempted at some point to move southwards. Not only were parts of the Deccan wealthy but if the whole region was securely held, the road was open to the narrow but rich coastal plains and ports of south-east and south-west India. Nevertheless, the Mughal push to conquer the Deccan faced many obstacles.

In large part these were the products of geography, topography and distance. Much of the region consisted of mountains and forests. The western Deccan in particular was an area of mountains and hills on which perched the forts of a horde of local warrior-gentry. Like most empires, the Mughals found it easiest to conquer a state and co-opt its elites into their own imperial system. It was not easy to employ this method in the western Deccan, where conditions were more anarchic and power was widely dispersed. Military operations in the Deccan soon descended into a war of sieges and ambushes. Dragging siege guns around the region was a slow and frustrating business. Geared by now to warfare in the plains, the Mughal army was hard pressed to respond to the raids and ambushes of the Maratha light cavalry, who were its main enemies. With no geopolitical rivals of any note and having not faced a major challenge on the battlefield for a century, the Mughal military machine had in any case lost much of its edge. As campaigns dragged on endlessly with often little reward, many of Aurangzeb's generals lost their commitment and energy.[28]

For Aurangzeb, conquest of the Deccan became the object of his life and an obsession. In 1682 he transferred himself, his court and key elements of his central government far southwards into the Deccan, where they operated from the vast, mobile and tented headquarters that substituted for a capital city for the rest of Aurangzeb's reign. Neither he nor they returned to the empire's heartland before he died twenty-five years later. At a time when the empire's core fiscal and military institutions were coming under increasing strain in the Mughals' north Indian heartland this was very unfortunate. Raising taxes from the land, assigning them to nobles holding *jagirs*, and periodically rotating these nobles around the empire was a complex business in both administrative and political ways. The imperial officials who ran this system required supervision if corrupt collusion with nobles and local landowners (*zamindars*) was to be held in check. Aurangzeb was too far away and too obsessed by the campaign in the Deccan to do this job properly.[29]

The whole system of rule depended on the ability of imperial officials to persuade and coerce the *zamindars* to hand over part of the rural surplus. The growing wealth of many provinces in the second half of the seventeenth century made *zamindars* richer and less obedient. One relatively small but not insignificant element in the weakening of the centre's hold was the fact that the emperor, far away in the Deccan, could no longer make periodic tours around the empire's core provinces. These had been theatres of imperial benevolence and patronage but also power. By the 1690s nobles were increasingly claiming that the only way in which they could wring the promised revenues from their *jagirs* was if they resided in them for years on end. This inevitably made them

disinclined to accept rotation. An additional problem was that Aurangzeb attempted to conquer the Deccan by the traditional Mughal
combination of carrot and stick. The carrot entailed trying to suborn
and co-opt the Deccan's elites with generous grants of *jagirs*. Since much
of the Deccan was being ravaged by Maratha raids and its crops and
animals consumed by the Mughal armies, these *jagirs* had to be found
in the north. This put great extra strain on the already shrinking reserves
of land and revenue.

As Aurangzeb aged, problems worsened. The emperor had always
been imperious, inflexible and even obsessive. Such character traits seldom improve with age. By the 1690s many members of the Mughal elite
realized that the effort to conquer the south was becoming dangerously
counter-productive. With Aurangzeb now in his eighties, even the emperor's own age group, let alone elder statesmen or relations whose advice
might have carried weight, were dead. Younger members of his entourage
were mostly 'flattering upstarts much too intimidated by the stubborn
octogenarian to dare suggest a change of policy'. Among Aurangzeb's
sons, the intelligent Prince Muazzam had long since become convinced
that the attempt to conquer the south by military force was hopeless and
dangerous. After failing for years to persuade Aurangzeb, his efforts to
undermine his father's policy resulted in his imprisonment.[30]

By the time the emperor died, even some of his great-grandchildren
were adults. Inevitably, some of these younger men became deeply frustrated. Equally inevitably, the emperor feared for his throne and security.
His key policy to protect himself against his sons and grandsons was
radically to reduce their incomes, and therefore the size of their households and personal military followings. The increasing shortage of land
and revenue for *jagirs* provided an excellent excuse for this policy. In
previous reigns the emperor's sons had been vastly richer than any
nobleman, but when Aurangzeb died in 1707 this was no longer true. In
a manner that would previously have been inconceivable, key noblemen
remained neutral in the conflict to succeed Aurangzeb, and then bar-
gained with the new emperor, Bahadur Shah, as near equals. Bahadur
was an able man. Had he reigned for the previous Mughal average of
twenty-five years the monarchy might well have regained power. Since
he came to the throne at the age of sixty-four this was hardly likely.
After his death in 1712 rival elite factions fought to put their client
Mughal prince on the throne. Of course, the last thing these factions

wanted was a Mughal with the personality and desire to take back power for the dynasty. Henceforth Mughal princes spent their adolescence and early manhood in the harem. Inevitably their potential as leaders was severely diminished.[31]

The weakening of the monarchy, implosion of central authority and transfer of power to regional warlords is a familiar tale in imperial history. Of course, many Mughal provincial governors seized the opportunity to set up hereditary dynasties in their own region. Sometimes they almost were forced to do this. In the past they had relied on the emperor's assistance in order to control local *zamindars* and govern their provinces. Now they had to manage on their own. They needed the resources to maintain patronage networks, deter or coerce recalcitrant *zamindars*, but also carry out the functions (e.g. adjudicating local disputes) which made their rule legitimate in local eyes.

While retaining the resources to manage their provinces, some governors remained loyal to the Mughal dynasty. Nizam al-Mulk was the governor of Gujarat, the Deccan and Malwa. He was an out-and-out Mughal loyalist. Although by 1722 his power meant that no one could have stopped him from going his own way and setting up his own dynasty, he chose instead to accept the position of chief minister to the emperor Muhammad Shah. He took the post with a reform programme which included removing the *jagirs* of nobles who were no longer performing useful service, stamping out corruption in the administration, and regaining control over the tax system and the crown's former lands from the local power-holders who had appropriated them. This programme had much in common with Mehmed Koprulu's successful drive to reverse Ottoman decline in the 1640s. Pressure from court factions and favourites turned Muhammad Shah against Nizam al-Mulk and his reforms. As a result, Nizam returned to the Deccan and set up the autonomous state of Hyderabad, which survived as the greatest of Indian princely states until the demise of British rule in 1948.[32]

In time-honoured fashion the implosion of the state that dominated the great northern plain of India opened the way to invasion by a semi-nomadic cavalry army over the north-western frontier. In 1739 Nader Shah sacked Delhi, carrying off the peacock throne (and much more) to buttress his newly established dynasty's legitimacy as shahs of Iran. Nader was the son of a herdsman from the semi-nomadic Afshar tribe in northern Khurasan, where the Persian and steppe worlds met. Like many a war-band leader before him, he had built his power on his skill as a military and political leader, on personal charisma, luck and terror. He exploited the chaos that resulted from the decline and fall of the Safavid dynasty, whose last shah was deposed in 1722. After conquering Iran he led his army through Afghanistan into northern India. Timur (Tamerlane) was his hero and his model. Eight years after taking Delhi, Nader Shah died. Like so many war-band empires, his did not survive its founder's demise.[33]

Only ten years after Nader's death, in 1757, Robert Clive won the battle of Plassey. By 1765 the rule of the East India Company was established in Bengal. Subsequently the British used Bengal as the base from which in time their rule spread across all India. In geopolitical terms this represented a revolutionary departure from Indian tradition. The Indian subcontinent had always been conquered by war-band leaders bursting across its north-western frontier. Now, for the first time in history, it had been conquered by sea power. The British conquest of India was a huge step towards European domination of the globe. We saw the first stage of this process in chapter 10 with the Spanish conquest of central and southern America in the reigns of Charles V and Philip II. Two hundred and fifty years after the Spanish conquest began, European might had grown enormously. The British stood at the forefront of European power and progress. Their naval, military, commercial and financial strength by 1815 dominated the Atlantic region, which itself was becoming the hub of the global economy. American silver had been the initial foundation of Europe's trade with China and India. Now Indian opium, backed by the power of the Royal Navy, became a key weapon in British attempts to invade and dominate the economy of China. The Opium War of the 1840s was a key stage in this process. By now British power had been hugely enhanced by the Industrial Revolution. Britain and with it the rest of the globe had entered the modern age, which was also the great era of European imperialism.

The nineteenth century represented a fundamental break with the past. Nevertheless, far from everything in European and British imperialism was new. On the contrary, both generally and specifically in India, European empire in many respects followed age-old imperial patterns. Britain's power was the most important reason for its conquest of India, but the establishment of British rule was greatly helped by the implosion of the Mughal Empire that had occurred in the previous generation and had little to do with external forces. A similar process of cyclical imperial decline eased European victory over the Ottomans and the Qing. Traditional imperial geopolitics still mattered greatly. British rule in India benefited from the natural rampart of its mountainous northern frontiers. At the beginning of the nineteenth century a senior Russian general, Levin von Bennigsen, wrote that the British position in the subcontinent was invulnerable. The modern, European-style army that the British had created in India could not be defeated by a cavalry army invading over the north-west frontier in traditional style. Logistics, terrain and distance ensured that no modern infantry and artillery-based army could invade through Afghanistan. It could only come by sea, which British maritime dominance made impossible. British–Russian imperial rivalry in Asia was a thread running through international relations between 1815 and 1914. Its reality was best expressed by the fate of the three greatest Asiatic dynastic empires. The British monopolized the Mughal inheritance. For decades after the 1840s they were the dominant European influence in China. Meanwhile they blocked Russia from swallowing the Ottoman Empire.[34]

British rule in India was rooted in a strong sense of cultural superiority and civilizing mission. Most British officials saw themselves in this respect as heirs of Rome. Nevertheless, as in all successful empires, the conquerors knew that they had to adapt their methods of rule to local realities and traditions. They also understood that they needed the cooperation of native elites. Any doubts on this score were reinforced by the lessons of the rebellion of 1857. British rule in India was rooted in hierarchies of both class and race but these could sometimes be ambiguous. Like most complex imperial systems, the British system of rule also had its ironies and subtleties.

My godfather, Christoph von Furer-Haimendorf, became a renowned anthropologist and spent much of his life studying the tribal peoples of India. In origin his family came from the lesser nobility of the Holy Roman Empire. Among his closest friends were intelligent and highly cultured members of the Muslim Hyderabadi aristocracy who threw in their lot with the Congress Party in the hope of creating an independent India which would stand above communal divisions. They had similarities to Hubert Butler, the Protestant gentleman, Gaelic scholar and Irish patriot whom I mentioned in the Preface and in whose house I spent so many childhood summers. In 1939 the Second World War caught up with Haimendorf as he did his research in India, making him technically an enemy alien. In the eyes of British officialdom – in whose ranks he also had many friends – my godfather was a trusted albeit slightly exotic variation on the Etonian or Wykhamist theme. He was interned 'within the confines of the Government of India', a large place and not one which he had any wish to depart in the middle of a world war. When the Japanese army reached the north-east frontier of India in 1942 it turned out that Haimendorf was not just the greatest expert on some of the tribes that straddled the front line but also the European most trusted by the tribal leaders. So the British appointed him their official agent in the area. Subsequently, he used to delight in recounting how one of his responsibilities was periodically to sign forms recording that enemy aliens in his area – of which he was the only example – were under secure observation. Franz Kafka and Nikolai Gogol, respective witnesses to Austrian and Russian imperial bureaucracy, would have understood the joke.

13

China's Last Dynasties: The Ming and the Qing

China's last two dynasties, the Ming and the Qing, fit into a recurring pattern of Chinese imperial history. Like the Han and the Song, the Ming dynasty was ethnic Chinese. The Qing (Manchus) by contrast was a conquest dynasty, whose origins lay beyond China's northern frontier in the world of the warrior horseman. In military terms the conquest dynasties were usually more formidable than the 'native' Chinese ones. This enabled them to create much larger empires which stretched far beyond China's ethnic borders. Native Chinese dynasties ruled a country that was already vast by European standards, but empire reached its greatest extent under the Qing. In 1800 it stretched over 4.4 million square miles with a population which was already well over 300 million. By contrast, all western Europe covered 888,000 square miles and its largest kingdom, France, was only 211,000 square miles in size. Even by the standards of the other great Eurasian empires of its day the scale of the Qing empire was unique. The Ottoman Empire was much less (2.1 million square miles) than half its size and its population was ten times smaller. At their apogee the Mughals ruled over 1.5 million square miles and less than 200 million people. Only the Russian Empire in 1800 (8.8 million square miles) exceeded the Qing in territory, though the tsar had roughly one-eighth as many subjects as the Chinese emperor. China's imperial tradition represented the victory of human institutions and ideas over nature. Inevitably, that victory came at a cost.[1]

The reader will by now be familiar with the key institutions of Chinese empire – in other words the emperor and the bureaucracy – and with the Confucian doctrine and ancient traditions that defined their relationship. The fall of the Song and China's subsequent rule by alien Jurchen and Mongol regimes was proof for the neo-Confucians that

The Ming and Qing Empires

Heaven had punished the Chinese for their abandonment of the true Confucian path and the Song monarchs' flirtation with Legalism. The neo-Confucians' great hero among ancient Chinese philosophers was Mencius/Mengzi (372–289 BCE), the least Legalist and Realist of all the major ancient thinkers in the Confucian tradition. Mencius put his emphasis on cultivating the ethical and humane instincts of the inner man. As regards politics, he argued that serving the people's welfare was the origin and sole source of legitimacy of all governments. The founder of the Ming dynasty, Zhu Yuanzhang (the Hongwu Emperor, r. 1368–98), based his regime's legitimacy on the claim that he had expelled the Mongols and restored true Chinese Confucian principles. For the most part he adhered strictly to the canon established by the Song-era founders of neo-Confucianism, Cheng Yi and Zhu Xi. But the emperor disliked Mencius's 'democratic' ideas and refused to allow him to be quoted in the official texts. Minister of Justice Qian Tang courted suicide by protesting that 'this humble subject would die for Mencius, and in dying would be greatly honoured'. Many of his official colleagues did die in this cause during Hongwu's ruthless purges.[2]

Hongwu's son, the Yongle Emperor (Zhu Di), ruled from 1402 until 1424. He was the dynasty's 'second founder', successfully consolidating and legitimizing the Ming regime's hold on Chinese society. Yongle was one of royal history's 'wicked uncles' who usurped the throne of a young and innocent nephew. As a result, he was always anxious to legitimize his rule in disapproving Confucian eyes. One concession he made to the literati was to allow Mencius a place of honour in the official canon, which was second only to Confucius himself. Thenceforth both the Ming and Qing regimes supported neo-Confucianism wholly and unequivocally as the state's official ideology. They placed its key texts at the centre of the civil-service examination system which played a crucial role in forming the values and beliefs of Chinese elites down to the twentieth century. All male elite education was geared to the civil-service examinations. Although the examination system had its earliest origins under the Tang and had blossomed under the Song, its scale and impact increased enormously under the Ming and the Qing. The Ming extended the exam system right down to county level and made passing the exam the only way to enter the higher ranks of the civil service. The overwhelming majority of candidates failed even to become 'licentiates', in other words to gain the licence to sit for the exams at provincial level.

Far fewer still passed the provincial and metropolitan-level exams, thereby acquiring the right to compete at the highest level of all, the palace examinations.[3]

By 1500 a million candidates were sitting exams at various levels at any time. Numbers grew still greater under the Qing, in whose time it was reckoned that candidates enrolling for county-level tests had a 0.01 per cent chance of graduating with a palace degree. A successful candidate at palace level needed to have mastered more than 600,000 Chinese characters from both the ancient and contemporary scripts. Most candidates at county level barely dreamed of reaching this pinnacle. For them it sufficed to become a licentiate, which provided a stipend, tax exemptions and legal privileges, together with great prestige and status in local society. But a licence was not acquired for life. To preserve one's status it was necessary to submit oneself to periodic requalifying tests. The large numbers of licentiates and the much larger group of failed candidates absorbed not just neo-Confucian ideas and values but also the norms prescribed by the examination system for how to think and write in the correct fashion.[4]

In the palace examinations the chief examiner was the emperor himself. He set a few questions, read a handful of the best scripts, and presided over graduation ceremonies. For a minority of emperors who were determined to be their own prime ministers, participation in the examination system was a way to get to know the brightest, most ambitious and most hard-working younger generation of elite officials. The Yongle emperor, very much an autocrat, employed a handful of the most impressive palace-degree graduates in his private secretariat (known as the Grand Secretariat) within the palace's Inner Court. These men acted as trusted advisers on the whole range of policy issues but also helped to supervise the bureaucratic machine and ensure that it implemented the emperor's commands effectively. For most emperors, serving as examiner above all had a symbolic purpose: they acted the Confucian emperor's role as supreme teacher and moral guide to his people. Another bow to Confucian legitimacy was daily attendance at a lecture on aspects of Confucian thinking delivered by a senior official or a member of the Hanlin Academy, the seat of the empire's most respected Confucian scholars and teachers. This was a parallel to the sermons preached to Christian contemporary monarchs.

Unlike a Christian monarch, the emperor was his realm's chief 'priest', presiding in person over a range of daily rituals and sacrifices both privately inside the palace and – on the major festivals – amidst great parade and splendour beyond the palace gates. These rituals might combine in various mixes Confucian, Buddhist and Daoist elements. Ming emperors made daily visits to the Hall of Venerating the Ancestors to pay homage to their forebears. The Qing monarchs on occasion also participated in Manchu shamanic rituals. Ritual and carefully scripted behaviour extended well beyond the narrow sphere of religious prac-tice. Of course, the court's great ceremonies, audiences and parades were choreographed down to the last detail and were enacted with close attention to the emperor's every movement and gesture. Confucian doc-trine placed enormous emphasis on proper and proportionate behaviour in all aspects of life, and especially in human interaction. Harmony on earth was embodied in correct, ritualized behaviour. Although some of these norms had been reimagined by the neo-Confucians, they were presented as being handed down from ancient days and therefore bear-ing the near-sacred quality that Chinese thinkers ascribed to precedent and antiquity. Since the emperor's proper behaviour not merely pro-vided a guide to his subjects but also guaranteed harmony between Earth and Heaven, his every act was liable to criticism by his civil ser-vants. Officials were fully aware of the potential for controlling the emperor's behaviour by warning him that his misdeeds would cause the heavens to fall.[5]

Unsurprisingly, supposedly autocratic monarchs sometimes took great exception to this criticism. The founders of dynasties and their immediate successors were generally men of action, with experience of life beyond the court. In new dynasties precedent and convention might not yet have taken deep root across the full range of government. The rulers of conquest dynasties might on occasion evade Confucian stric-tures by retreating into their own ancestral customs. But in the later generations especially of a native dynasty the constraints imposed by Confucian officials might sometimes appear unbearable to the man on the throne. The longest-ruling Ming emperor was Wanli, who reigned from 1572 until 1620. Driven to distraction by the criticisms and cabals of his officials, 'as an emperor who actually carried on a strike against his own bureaucrats over a long period of time, Wan-li has come down in history without any close parallels'.[6]

Wanli ascended the throne in 1572 at the age of nine. Any child emperor grew up amidst exceptional and dangerous pressures. For a timid child who lacked self-confidence, having to perform in public was a great strain. Even Louis XIV, usually described as temperamentally suited to his royal role, burst into tears when he forgot his lines during a public ceremony. A Chinese emperor faced special difficulties, which reached their extreme in the Ming era. The founder of the Ming dynasty, Zhu Yuanzhang (the Hongwu Emperor), had bequeathed to his descendants an extreme version of autocratic rule. No fewer than 185 types of official business had to be reported to the emperor in person. Of course, a child could not in reality decide these issues, but propriety required that the forms were preserved. A sufficiently disciplined and docile child could perform the ritual and symbolic acts that took up so much of the time of a Chinese emperor. By all accounts Wanli was an exceptionally disciplined, obedient and well-behaved child: he fulfilled his ritual role admirably. Apparently, he devoted seven of every ten days to his education in the Confucian classics, and the other three days were given over to performing rites and presiding over audiences with ministers.

Louis XIV was fortunate in having a mother who showed him great love and warmth. Both Wanli's mother and his father's senior wife, the dowager empress, stressed discipline and austerity as core principles of his education. Apparently, his mother sometimes used to punish him 'by making him kneel if he was inattentive in his studies. She used to get him up for his predawn court audiences.' The two dowager empresses entrusted supervision of Wanli's education to the court's senior eunuch, Feng Bao, who headed the key directorate of ceremonies in the inner court. Like many Ming-era eunuchs, Feng was well educated and highly cultured. He employed the finest Confucian teachers to instruct Wanli. The boy emperor was brought up on his own and without siblings. His only playmates were young eunuchs, but Feng put strong curbs on their games with the boy monarch for fear that they would not show him due respect and might lead him astray.

The child emperor's leading mentor was the intelligent and experienced Grand Secretary, Zhang Juzheng. He leavened Wanli's strictly Confucian ethical education with advice on the practice of governing men and empires. By all accounts Wanli was an exceptionally – indeed precociously – intelligent student, very quick to learn. He was among other things an outstanding calligrapher, a skill he greatly enjoyed. Although Zhang treated Wanli well, he discouraged him from spending too much time on even such a 'distraction' as calligraphy. So long as

Zhang lived, Wanli deferred to him and praised him. Perhaps it is un-surprising that after Zhang died in 1572, the nineteen-year-old emperor cut loose. Many of us in our own lives will have encountered examples of spectacular delayed rebellion by young adults subjected to exces-sively disciplined, pressured and protected upbringings.[7]

After Zhang died he was discovered to have amassed a large fortune while in office. There was nothing unusual in this but the discovery may well have come as a shock to the young and still naïve monarch, who had been strictly educated in Confucian principle but thus far had no personal experience of men and politics. Like so many emperors he will have noted the disparity between the high-flown ethical claims of Con-fucian officialdom and the behaviour of many Confucian officials. The much-proclaimed Confucian principle of frugality was very often absent in the exquisitely cultured and expensive lifestyle of elite officials. Inevitably, denunciations of Zhang poured in from rivals who envied his ten-year hold on power. Wanli's disillusion and cynicism grew. Exposure to the everyday reality of an emperor's duties will not have helped matters. Ming government drowned in paper and procedure. The emperor was faced by a tidal wave of memoranda and reports. Especially when submitted to the monarch, their style was arcane, even liturgical. 'These papers were as a rule lengthy, with technical discourse mingled with doctrinal polemics. Even with careful reading, it was dif-ficult to grasp the main issues and peripheral subtleties, not to mention the number of administrative terms and long lists of proper names.' After Zhang's death Wanli attempted for some years to work conscien-tiously on government business, but in time a sense of frustration, powerlessness, alienation and despair seems to have overcome him. In the last thirty-one years of his reign he never once left Beijing.

To manage the bureaucratic machine the Ming monarchs increas-ingly used eunuchs from their inner court as a private secretariat. This exposed them to hard criticism from officialdom. Producing sons to continue one's lineage was at the heart of the Confucian value system. Eunuchs were therefore even more despised by Chinese elites than was the case in most cultures. In the Ming era the brightest eunuchs were well educated in their special palace school by top-class teachers from the Hanlin Academy. But although his eunuchs were competent to act as the emperor's assistants, they were just as inclined as ordinary offi-cials to form factions. During their education and service eunuchs might forge many links with the bureaucratic elite, so factions could cut across the divide between the inner court and the government machine. Once again, the rhetoric of Confucian officials conflicted with their behaviour. By Wanli's time a Ming emperor who wished to control policy and appointments faced a daunting challenge.

The final straw for Wanli seems to have come when the bureaucracy blocked his plan to make his son by his beloved consort Zheng the heir, in the process setting aside the claims of his eldest son by another consort. For officialdom primogeniture embodied the principles of hierarchy and seniority that were central to the Confucian value system. It also promised stability. Typically, Wanli reacted in the worst possible way. He lacked the determination or confidence to impose his candidate on the bureaucracy and very grudgingly accepted his eldest son as heir, meanwhile both neglecting the crown prince and (contrary to all precedent in the Ming era) keeping Zheng's son close by him at court as a constant source of potential threat and instability. He also essentially withdrew from government business, refusing to meet ministers, sign documents or make appointments.[8]

The traditional story about Wanli stops at this point. It is a tale of irresponsibility and selfishness, intertwined with moments of avarice and cruelty. Recent research suggests, however, that although Wanli gave up in despair as regards internal affairs, he remained an interested and effective leader in diplomatic and military matters. The evidence suggests that in this sphere he was much more effective than the Emperor Huizong of the Song dynasty, whose failings had contributed to disaster in the 1120s. Predictably, his civil officials blocked Wanli's wish to lead his armies in the field. In this case they were able to point to the awful precedent of his ancestor the young emperor Yingzong (Zhu Qizen), whose thirst for military glory had ended in his capture in 1449 during a campaign against the Mongols. Although barred from commanding in the field, Wanli remained very interested in his army, securing it adequate resources and promoting able generals. A military historian has commented that between 1570 and 1610 the Ming army was probably more effective than at any time since the dynasty's first two reigns. Like many leaders, Wanli came to despair of the factionalism, pettiness and stalemate of domestic politics but he enjoyed playing a role on the international stage. He was strongly committed to preserving the pre-eminent position of his dynasty and the Chinese Empire in East Asia. He also believed that in military and diplomatic affairs he retained the freedom and the power to act effectively.[9]

In 1592 the government faced its greatest crisis in Wanli's reign when a large-scale rebellion in the Shaanxi region coincided with a massive Japanese invasion of Korea. Within weeks the Korean king, a Ming client, was driven from his capital. Wanli reacted swiftly and effectively. He determined strategic priorities, appointed able generals, allowed them considerable autonomy, and allocated them the resources necessary for their tasks. He also strengthened the Korean king's back and restored Korean morale by his immediate and effective assistance. As a result, the rebellion was crushed and Korea recaptured. Ming officialdom looked down on generals and feared their political ambitions. During the war civilian ministers were much inclined to claim credit for success, while seeking to constrain the generals' authority and smother them in criticism for any perceived slowness or failure. At one moment of crisis, as denunciations of his commanders poured in from civil officials and censors, Wanli resolved matters by noting that 'anyone else who wishes to add another gratuitous remark to this confusion' would find themselves without a career and in very uncomfortable exile. The emperor's role in imposing his will as regards policy, backing trusted generals and silencing factional conflicts was the basis of Chinese victory in the war against Japan.[10]

Like every dynasty, the Ming had its own style of governing. The dynasty's founder, Zhu Yuanzhang (the Hongwu Emperor), had ruled for thirty years, from 1368 until 1398. Like the founder of the Han dynasty, Liu Pang, he was of peasant origin and rose to power as the leader of a rebel band. After establishing himself on the throne the Han founder showed moderation and ruled in concert with a long-serving group of trusted lieutenants. By contrast, Zhu Yuanzhang was an out-and-out autocrat who killed thousands of his officials in repeated purges designed to consolidate and maximize his power and assuage his paranoia and insecurity. Although his successors never resorted to his level of violence, Ming political culture – and above all the monarchs' treatment of their officials – was much more despotic and brutal than had been the case under the Song dynasty, which the Ming claimed as their model. Hongwu's son, the Yongle emperor, was very able and some later emperors were competent and responsible, but on the whole the Ming provided fewer distinguished monarchs than most Chinese dynasties and ran their government much less effectively than their successors, the Qing. One problem was that by demanding that his descendants follow his lead in acting as their own prime ministers, Hongwu created expectations and conventions that most later Ming monarchs could not sustain. In line with Chinese custom, the Ming system of succession gave priority to the sons of the empress and operated by strict rules of primogeniture. This guaranteed that the throne would at times be occupied by men of limited ability who could not hope to rule in Zhu Yuanzhang's manner.

In 1644 Beijing fell and the last Ming emperor committed suicide. The dynasty's demise owed much to massive peasant revolts brought on by the devastating economic impact of the 'Little Ice Age'. Crucial too was the paralysis of the government machine which was owed to furious infighting between bureaucratic factions. As with the Song, the civil bureaucracy's attempts to control the army reduced military effectiveness and alienated many generals. Once again in Chinese history pressure built up on the northern front in the dynasty's last decades. By the 1600s the main threat came from the growing power and confidence of the Manchu tribal confederation, headed by the charismatic and skilful war-band leader Nurhaci. Faced by peasant revolt and bureaucratic obstruction some senior Chinese generals ended by going over to the Manchus, seeing them as a less bad alternative than anarchy and governmental paralysis.

Nurhaci himself and the core of the tribal conglomerate that came to be called Manchu were Jurchens, in other words the descendants of the warrior cavalrymen who had defeated and captured the Song emperor Huizong in 1127 and had then ruled northern China until they were subjugated by the Mongols. Their ancestral homeland was in northern Manchuria. The Jurchens traditionally herded cattle, fished, farmed and hunted. They were formidable mounted warriors – excellent horsemen and mounted archers, tough, disciplined and ferocious. Like most successful warrior confederations, in time Nurhaci's Jurchens incorporated into their ranks many other tribes. For example, in the era of Mongol rule the Khitan people disappear from history. Many of their descendants served Nurhaci. In 1635 Nurhaci's son Hong Taiji proclaimed himself first emperor of the Qing dynasty. At the same time he created the name 'Manchu' as a term to include all the tribal cavalrymen who accepted his leadership.

Subsequently, as part of their campaign to legitimize themselves in Chinese eyes, the Qing always denied that they had overthrown the Ming. They argued that internal rebellion caused by the dynasty's loss of Heaven's mandate was responsible. Of course, the Qing claim was self-serving, but it was even so partly true. It was a peasant rebel army that had taken Beijing in 1644, forced the Ming emperor's suicide, and subsequently sacked the city. Key members of the Chinese elite had supported the restoration of public order and imperial unity by the Qing. Without their support the Manchu conquest of China would have been impossible. The new dynasty rooted its legitimacy among its Chinese subjects in the claim that it had ended anarchy and restored Confucian order and rectitude in China.

Nevertheless, the Qing were a conquest dynasty and fitted into the long-established pattern whereby warrior cavalrymen from northern Eurasia conquered and ruled the sedentary peoples living to their south. Although never themselves nomads in the strict sense of the word, the Manchus' military qualities were those of the steppe nomads. Their speed and mobility caused many problems for the more static Ming armies. Typically, on the path from war-band leader to semi-sacred monarch the Qing monarch became more distant, more majestic and more autocratic. Also typically, in their efforts to root themselves in the sedentary lands they had conquered the Qing risked alienating the Manchu warriors on whom their power traditionally rested. The dynasty – like many nomad dynasties before it – strove to preserve the warrior culture, solidarity and distinctiveness of their own Manchu people both because the Qing always saw themselves as sharing this identity and because the separate identity of the Manchu community played a key role in the dynasty's system of rule.

Briefly stated, the key to Qing success was that they used Chinese political institutions and ideas to tame the aristocratic and tribal element in Manchu politics, and then employed the tamed Manchu elite to help them direct and control the Chinese bureaucracy. This sounds wonderfully simple. In fact, it was a complex process that required great political sensitivity and skill, as well as many compromises and accommodations. The latter ran the whole gamut from balancing appointments to key posts between Chinese and Manchus to evolving a new style of imperial clothing which combined traditional Chinese colours and symbols with Manchu-style tailoring. The new rulers forced all their male

Chinese subjects to shave their foreheads and tie their hair behind in a long queue as a mark of submission and loyalty. In time the Qing were able to present themselves as near-universal emperors who were simultaneously Confucian sage-kings, Mongol khans, Buddhist wheel-turning rulers (*chakravartin*) and hereditary chiefs of the Manchus. The dynasty's success owed much to the fact that for almost 140 years it was headed by three exceptionally intelligent, skilful and hard-working monarchs: the Kangxi Emperor (r. 1661–1722); his son, the Yongzheng Emperor (r. 1722–35); and Yongzheng's son, the Qianlong Emperor (r. 1735–96).[11]

At the heart of the Qing system of rule were the so-called Eight Banners, each of which had Manchu, Mongol and Chinese divisions. From one angle the Banners were an enormously expanded and regulated war-band. From another they were the descendants of the supra-ethnic decimal units into which many nomadic empires (including the Mongols) had divided their subjects for purposes of war and administration. The Banners ran the lives not just of warriors but also of their families. They sought to guarantee the families' livelihood so warriors could be mobilized whenever needed for the state's military service. The first Manchu Banners were established in 1615 and by 1642 the whole Banner system was in place. The Chinese Banner units always had least prestige in Qing eyes but were crucial in attracting, organizing and rewarding Han Chinese who either lived in districts conquered by the Qing before the 1640s or had defected from the Ming armies and administration. By the mid-eighteenth century the Qing were deeply rooted in Chinese society and the Chinese Banner units were both redundant and expensive. They were therefore wound down and finally abolished in 1756.

The Mongol Banner survived until the dynasty's fall and was a key component of the successful Qing strategy of recruiting and holding the allegiance of Mongol elites. Coming from semi-nomadic warrior horsemen, Mongol culture was far closer to that of the Manchus than to the Chinese. During the reigns of Nurhaci and his son many Mongol tribesmen had joined the Qing armies. After the Qing had conquered all of Mongolia, they divided the region into four relatively weak hereditary khanates and ruled it indirectly. Mongol aristocrats were given positions of honour at court and frequently intermarried with the Qing imperial family, a privilege never allowed to Chinese. The excellent cavalry which the Mongol princes supplied to their Qing overlords played a crucial role in the conquest of Xinjiang in the eighteenth century. In many respects the Mongols' position in the Qing Empire was similar to that of the Rajputs in Mughal India. They were privileged and trusted allies, incorporated into the regime and well rewarded for their loyalty.[12]

There was never any doubt that the Manchus were the senior Banner units and the core of Qing power. Nurhaci and his son Hong Taiji gave the Manchus not just a name but also their first written language and an organization – the Banners – which cemented their identity and enabled them to govern, unite and dominate China while retaining a degree of separateness. The Qing emperors always stressed their equal favour and fairness to their Chinese, Manchu and Mongol subjects. They assimilated, patronized and gloried in Chinese high culture. Nevertheless, they never forgot that they were a conquest dynasty and people, who made up much less than 2 per cent of the empire's population. Insecurity bred a degree of solidarity and watchfulness among the Qing family and the Manchu community.[13]

Beginning with Hong Taiji in 1635 and continuing throughout the eighteenth century the emperors constantly stressed the need for the Manchus to retain the martial skills, cultural traits and loyalties which made up their heritage. More than any other individual, Kangxi was responsible for bringing the Chinese into the Manchu regime and legitimizing Qing rule in Chinese eyes. Nevertheless, even after thirty-five years on the throne, in 1707 he privately warned a trusted Manchu lieutenant never to forget that 'learned Chinese do not want us Manchus to endure a long time – do not let yourselves be deceived by the Chinese'. The monarchs expected a special loyalty and felt a special sense of community with their Manchu Bannermen. In their private correspondence with trusted Manchu officers the emperors often expressed 'a kind of solicitude and easy familiarity rarely seen in communications with Chinese officials'. In the Manchu language even the very imperious Qianlong sometimes spoke of himself and his lieutenants as 'us Manchu officials'. No Qing monarch would have dreamed of identifying himself with Han Chinese bureaucrats in these egalitarian terms.[14]

Manchu culture respected lineage and hereditary status. Command of Banner companies was transmitted from father to son. A hierarchy of hereditary aristocratic titles was held by members of the Manchu elite. These titles were usually only retained for a specified number of generations. In many cases a family was demoted one grade on the aristocratic ladder with each generation unless the title-holder himself earned merit through service. Regardless of titles and formal status, members of elite families had far easier access to the emperor and his patronage than ordinary Manchus. This was partly balanced by the possibility, open to all Manchu Bannermen, of service in the 1,500-strong Imperial Bodyguard with its splendid uniforms, prestige and esprit de corps. Service in the Bodyguard brought one directly under the emperor's eye. Intelligent Guardsmen might be employed on special missions and in some cases went on to make spectacular careers at court and in government. Although titles and lineage conveyed social status and hinted at respectable wealth, the Qing elite nevertheless was a service nobility, whose power derived entirely from the monarch. In the top echelons of the Qing regime Manchu elites were also balanced by senior Chinese officials who had risen through the bureaucracy by a system rooted in success in examinations and meritorious service.[15]

At the heart of the Manchu elite were members of the Qing dynasty. In polygynous dynasties the imperial 'family' could grow into a clan of immense size whose upkeep was a heavy burden on the state. By 1615 the Ming royal clan had consisted of well over 200,000 members and ate up 143 per cent of the state's total income from the land tax. In China, as elsewhere, managing the emperor's close male relations was a challenge. In the Ming era, the heir's younger brothers were sent to the provinces as boys and lived there for their entire lives. Carefully watched and forbidden any political role or influence, many of these regional princely courts played a useful role as cultural centres and patrons. As was generally the case, the Qing managed their clan more efficiently than the Ming. Even after over 250 years of Qing rule, the Aisin Gioro clan was fewer than 100,000 strong and ate up much less state revenue. Qing princes had a rigorous education in Chinese high culture and some of them became famous connoisseurs and patrons. But the emperor's brothers were not exiled from Beijing and played a prominent role in court ceremonies. Although most princes lived largely private lives devoted to cultural pursuits, they were not completely banned from government office. In a few cases an emperor's trusted brother or uncle played a vital political role, especially in times of uncertainty and crisis. After 1723 there were no major succession crises and (unlike the Ming) in the Qing era there were no cases of princes staging revolts or usurping the crown, though in the last years of Kangxi's reign great tensions among his sons over the succession suggested that this might happen.[16]

The Kangxi emperor came to the throne aged seven in 1661 and ruled for sixty-one years. Thanks in large part to Kangxi's intelligence, political skill and hard work the Qing were transformed in these decades from a conquest regime into one that had put down deep roots in China and had won the respect and allegiance of much of the Chinese elite. There was nothing inevitable about this achievement. In 1661 though the last remnants of Ming resistance had been mostly squashed, the central government exercised only nominal control over all of China south of the River Yangzi, which was ruled by three Chinese military viceroys (the so-called Three Feudatories) who had defected to the Qing during the years of conquest. The Jurchen, ancestors of the Manchus, had conquered north China in the 1120s but had never succeeded in extending their rule south of the Yangzi. The same could very easily have happened to the Qing. The greatest conquest regime in Chinese history, the Mongols (Yuan) had ruled China for less than a century partly because they had failed to draw the Chinese elite into government or to legitimize their rule in its eyes. Kangxi was an avid and intelligent student of history and dedicated himself to avoiding the mistakes of the Mongols and Jurchen. His success was of great long-term importance. In his reign Tibet and Taiwan were brought under Chinese rule. Under his son and grandson the powerful empire created by Kangxi used its resources to advance deep into Inner Asia, conquering the huge region now known as Xinjiang. The Qing Empire was almost five times larger than its Ming predecessor. Today's enormous and powerful People's Republic of China is the heir of the Qing, rather than Ming, Empire.

Thanks above all to the writings of the Anglo-American historian Jonathan Spence, even historians who know no Chinese have access to Kangxi's thoughts about himself, the world around him and rulership in his own words. The emperor was a man of high intelligence, great intellectual curiosity and exceptional energy and stamina. In this he was comparable to Akbar, the 'Second Founder' of the Mughal Empire. Unlike Akbar, Kangxi was neither illiterate nor dyslexic. Given the enormous place of the written word in the Chinese bureaucratic empire, an illiterate ruler would have found it very hard to oversee the governmental machine or earn the respect of his officials. In addition, although Kangxi was very capable of honest introspection, he does not seem to have shared Akbar's sometimes tortured pursuit of personal religious truth and meaning. He never questioned neo-Confucian values in the way that Akbar forged a personal and heterodox attitude to Islamic dogma. Kangxi had absorbed traditional Chinese thinking about wise and benevolent rulership and strongly identified with his vocation as emperor. The great sense of responsibility he felt for his subjects' welfare and his dynasty's reputation and survival fuelled a lifetime of extremely hard work, which faltered only in old age. In his final valedictory statement he claimed with considerable justice to 'have worked with unceasing diligence and intense watchfulness, never resting, never idle . . . day after day'.[17]

Kangxi always attempted to know enough about an issue to avoid complete dependence on expert advice. One of the first questions he had to decide as emperor was whether to base the calendar – a key imperial responsibility with sacred, cosmological aspects – on the calculations of his official Chinese astronomers or those of the Jesuits who lived in Beijing. Kangxi opted for the Jesuits because the empirical evidence they advanced proved their case in his eyes. Facts, evidence and realities always counted most for Kangxi. Typically, he then devoted many hours in an already packed schedule to learning the principles of European mathematics and astronomy from a Jesuit whom he appointed as his tutor. Kangxi believed in seeing problems himself and personally interviewing the officials charged with surmounting them. This was the main rationale behind the numerous tours he undertook across China's provinces. The emperor was also a good judge of men and a good boss. Most of his key appointments turned out well. Faced by obstruction, let alone resistance, Kangxi could be tough and even ruthless, but he encouraged and rewarded honest and efficient officials, and protected them from unjust and malicious criticism. On occasion he treated long-serving and trusted officials not only with justice but even with kindness and something approximating to friendship. Kangxi's relative indulgence towards his subordinates in part reflected his personality but it also had political grounds. Consolidating the Qing regime and winning the loyalty of key individuals and elites could often require indulgence towards a degree of nepotism and corruption.[18]

Kangxi revelled in his role as warrior-king but in comparison to 'second founders' such as Tang Taizong and Ming Yongle he actually spent very little time on campaign. The most crucial war in his reign was the eight-year struggle to destroy southern China's Three Feudatories and reunite the empire. This war erupted in 1673 when the nineteen-year-old emperor ignored the advice of most of his ministers and attempted to clip the powers of the three southern autonomous warlords. Near disaster followed and for a time the survival of the Qing regime was in doubt. Had the Qing fallen, Kangxi would have gone down in history as one of those brash young monarchs who had ruined their inheritance by pursuing military glory and disdaining the counsel of experienced ministers. Instead, his gamble paid off and the Qing gained effective control of all of southern China.

With his customary and endearing frankness Kangxi subsequently admitted that he had miscalculated the risks and was personally responsible for the war's initial disasters. When victory finally came, he made public his refusal to accept congratulations or new honorific titles since 'eight years of bitter war', whose 'scars were not yet healed', had 'resulted from my miscalculations'. All attempts by officials to cover up this truth 'by finding other scapegoats for the errors' were wrong. 'The responsibility . . . all of it – was mine.' Such public confession of error is rare among mere politicians, let alone emperors. It reflected not just Kangxi's attractive personality but also the Confucian principle of self-criticism and inner spiritual development at its best. Although Kangxi wanted to take command in person, he listened to the pleas of his ministers and directed the war effort from Beijing. Among his main roles were to provide sufficient men and resources to his generals and to retain an appearance of complete calm and confidence in moments of defeat and despair. One key to victory was the emperor's acknowledgement that the Manchu princes and generals who initially led his armies were out of their depth when faced with the military and political realities of waging civil war across the terrain of southern China. In time he had the sense and flexibility to replace them with equally loyal but much more competent Chinese commanders.[19]

In 1696–7 Kangxi finally got his wish to lead his armies on campaign, on this occasion against the Oirat (west Mongolian) khan Galdan, who had long been a thorn in the Qing's side. The emperor wrote that the key to defeating elusive nomad armies on the northern steppe was 'to attend closely to details of transport and supply. You can't just make guesses about them, as they did in the Ming dynasty.'

Although he defined the campaign's overall goals and strategy, he consulted his experienced generals closely on how to achieve success. Long-distance campaigns against the nomads were a gruelling experience and Kangxi was proud that he had shared the sufferings of his soldiers. He ascribed Galdan's destruction to meticulous planning and the 'inflexible will' that had overcome all obstacles and doubts. Kangxi's joy at his victory was huge. He wrote to a trusted eunuch in his Inner Court that 'my great task is done. In two years I made three journeys, across deserts combed by wind and bathed with rain, eating every other day . . . Heaven, earth and ancestors have protected me and brought me this achievement. As for my own life, one can say it is happy. One can say it's fulfilled . . . I've got what I wanted.' Galdan's destruction was indeed a major strategic and political gain for the Qing, but Kangxi's joy was probably owed in large part to the fact that he had lived up to his ideal and self-image of warrior-king. Many years later, reflecting on the need to reform the military examination system, Kangxi told his officials that 'I have dealt with a very large number of military matters. I have personally led military campaigns and I deeply understand the way of generalship.' He took great pride in being able to say this.[20]

Kangxi's father was an admirer of Chinese high culture. During his brief reign he sought to integrate a number of Chinese traditions and institutions into the Qing system of government. When Emperor Shunzhi died suddenly aged only twenty-three the Manchu grandees who dominated the child Kangxi's regency council reversed his changes, seeking to restore Manchu dominion within a conquest regime. A small example of the new era was that the child emperor had to be taught the rudiments of neo-Confucian doctrines and Chinese literary culture secretly by two old palace eunuchs who were hangovers of the Ming era. One of the first things Kangxi did on taking power and liberating himself from the regents was to throw himself into the intensive study of Chinese literary language and culture, as well as of neo-Confucian writing. In time he came to be a considerable connoisseur and patron of Chinese painting, calligraphy, poetry and landscape gardening. He himself became a respectable poet and calligrapher. Yet in no way did Kangxi's love of Chinese culture imply any distancing or disparagement of his Manchu identity. On the contrary, he was a passionate horseman and archer, loved the simple life of the hunt, and was very committed to preserving the Manchu traditions of his people. The emperor was a man who lived comfortably and productively in two cultures, both of which he treasured.

For Kangxi, acquiring learning and refinement in these aspects of Chinese high culture gave acute personal joy and satisfaction but it also had vital political benefits. Chinese literati could respect an emperor who identified so strongly and impressively with their own aesthetic and ethical values. In 1677, as part of his deep interest in Chinese culture, Kangxi established the Southern Study inside his palace, and this became a haven for outstanding scholars from the Hanlin Academy. Some of these men became the emperor's intimates, accompanied him wherever he went, and advised him on policy as well as literary culture. In a further olive branch to elite literati, in 1679 Kangxi staged a special top-level examination open only to the most distinguished and erudite scholars. The successful graduates were loaded with honours, brought into the Hanlin Academy, and given the task of producing the official history of the Ming. Of course, such a history was far from a purely academic enterprise, but Kangxi encouraged the compilers to do pains-taking research and pay due respect to the achievements especially of the earlier Ming monarchs. When doing so he repeated the Qing mantra that his dynasty had not overthrown the Ming. On the contrary, they had saved China and Confucian civilization from anarchy after the Ming lost the Mandate of Heaven and were driven from their capital by a rampaging peasant mob.[21]

In 1711 a scandal erupted in Jiangsu province over corruption in the provincial examinations which had led to the success of rich and well-connected candidates whose scholarship was clearly inferior. This swiftly turned into a war of mutual denunciations and indictments between the scholarly Chinese Governor of the province, Zhang Box-ing, and his superior, Gali, the abrasive and down-to-earth Manchu Governor-General of the region. The Lower Yangzi delta where Jiangsu province was located was China's richest region. Among its wealthy and largely autonomous local elite Qing rule was tolerated rather than liked. Both Boxing and Gali were highly respected in their respective Chinese and Manchu elite worlds. The confrontation between the two men was therefore dangerous and struck at the accommodation on which Qing rule rested. The two-man top-level committee which Kangxi despatched to adjudicate the dispute was interested in politics not justice. Its mem-bers were intent on not annoying Gali and his powerful backers. The

Governor-General was in fact guilty of large-scale corruption, but the committee largely exonerated him and called for Boxing's dismissal and punishment. In the normal course of Chinese bureaucratic politics an emperor would probably have had little choice but to endorse this judgement.

However, Kangxi had a trick up his sleeve. In the previous decade he had been developing what later was called the Palace Memorial System. Initially in the provinces but later even in Beijing a small number of men whom the emperor trusted were encouraged to report secretly and directly to him on important issues. They did so outside all bureaucratic channels with correspondence being carried by the emperor's most trusted palace eunuchs. Kangxi thereby acquired additional, speedy and secret information from sources he trusted. In the Jiangsu area one of the emperor's informants was Tsao Yin (Cao Yin), the director of the state's textile factories and overseer (censor) of the salt trade in the region. These were difficult and responsible positions, only occupied by men in whose honesty and efficiency the emperor had confidence.

Tsao Yin was Kangxi's 'bondservant', a category that roughly translates into hereditary household servant or even slave. Like most bondservants, Tsao's ancestors were ethnic Chinese who had been captured and semi-enslaved when the Qing overran southern Manchuria in the 1610s. As in the Ottoman Empire, the Qing monarch's bondservants were often both his household minions and his trusted lieutenants whom he placed in important posts. Tsao Yin's father had been the successful and much respected Textile Commissioner in Nanjing for twenty-one years. Even more to the point, Tsao's mother had been Kangxi's wet-nurse. In Chinese and Manchu culture this was often an important bond and the emperor always took an affectionate interest in her well-being. Tsao and the young prince had frequently played together as boys. For all the huge gap in the two men's status, Kangxi's letters to Tsao show warmth, trust and concern. The fact that both men shared and even embodied the culture, refinement and pastimes of the Chinese literati elite added a touch of mutual and equal respect to their relationship. Tsao's secret reports to Kangxi revealed to him the realities behind the scandal in a way that no ordinary bureaucrat would have dared to do. The Governor-General was cashiered, whereas Governor Boxing was simply moved sideways to a position of equivalent status. The story had two key implications. First, the emperor would treat senior Chinese and Manchu officials justly and equally. Second, he had acquired a powerful new weapon with which to supervise his bureaucrats.[22]

By the time the Jiangsu scandal erupted in 1711 Kangxi was already worn down by the perennial nightmare of ageing monarchs, the succession. In 1674 Kangxi's beloved first wife and empress Xiaozhang had died giving birth to a boy, Prince Yinreng. Perhaps this circumstance explains in part the emperor's extraordinary devotion over the years to his son. Kangxi records that 'I, the Emperor, was his warm old nurse. I taught him to read myself.' Probably the emperor spoiled his son. In 1678 the eighteen-month-old prince was already proclaimed heir-apparent. No doubt this partly reflected Kangxi's devotion to the child and to the memory of his wife. Undoubtedly too it was a bow to Chinese custom at a time when the war against the 'Three Feudatories' was going badly and Kangxi needed the Chinese elite's support. But a boy who was designated heir was the target for endless flattery and temptation. Kangxi made the situation worse by telling Yinreng as early as the mid-1690s of his wish to retire when the time was right and pass the burden of rule to his heir. This further increased the appetite and the impatience of the faction that formed round the crown prince. Much of the Manchu elite – not to mention Yinreng's half-brothers – disapproved of Kangxi's bow to Chinese traditions of primogeniture and the designation of young children as heirs before they had proved their mettle. Yinreng therefore became the target of much spite and gossip. After years of closing his ears to tales of Yinreng's misdeeds and depravity, Kangxi finally stripped him of his position as heir and imprisoned him in 1708 in an emotional semi-public spectacle that ended with the emperor collapsing to the floor and weeping.[23]

Kangxi's troubles were far from over. By removing Jinreng he opened the field to ferocious intrigues between other sons and their supporters to secure the succession. Briefly, Kangxi favoured his eighth son, Prince Yingssu, and appointed him heir, only then to recoil in horror and lock him up too when it was discovered that Yingssu's faction – without the prince's knowledge – was plotting to murder the former crown prince. In his remorse Kangxi persuaded himself that his beloved Yinreng had been unfairly blackened by his enemies, or even perhaps subjected to a spell. In April 1709 Yinreng was restored as heir but quickly reverted to his former ways. When the heir was again demoted and imprisoned in

1712 the struggle over the succession reached new heights. Having failed with two appointed heirs, Kangxi resolved not to appoint a new one until he neared death.

By 1722 the leading candidates appeared to be Prince Yinti, who had inherited most of Yingssu's faction, and Kangxi's fourth son, Prince Yinzhen, the future Yongzheng emperor. The rival princes had the same mother, so on this occasion a succession struggle was not linked to murderous intrigues in the harem. When Kangxi suddenly fell ill in December 1722 and died within ten days Yinzhen was in Beijing and Yinti was far away in the west, commanding armies in Tibet. Probably Kangxi nominated Yinzhen on his deathbed and Yinzhen was immediately proclaimed emperor in Beijing without opposition, but uncertainty about his accession's legitimacy destabilized politics in the first half of his reign. In Tibet Prince Yinti commanded large armies and enjoyed vice-regal powers. In his situation an Ottoman or Mughal prince would have marched on the capital. But Qing convention was different: succession was decided within the family, not on the battlefield. One historian notes 'the impressive solidarity observed among the Manchu elite'. This partly reflected awareness of the Manchus' vulnerability: civil war between princes in an empire where Manchus faced a far more numerous and highly sophisticated Chinese population would have threatened the survival of the regime. Manchu elites had the biggest interest in avoiding this but even simple Bannermen in the early eighteenth century lived much better than Chinese peasants. Middle-ranking Manchu families had slaves.[24]

One reason for believing that the emperor chose Yinzhen as his successor is that Kangxi was in general an excellent judge of people and, as the Yongzheng emperor, Yinzhen proved a successful choice. Yongzheng fully supported the key principles of his father's reign: these included the Manchu–Chinese balance, maintaining the identity of the Manchu Banners, and wholehearted support for neo-Confucianism. His great priority was to make the Qing machinery of government more effective. When he ascended the throne in 1722 a new broom was needed. Inevitably, after decades on the throne, the ageing Kangxi's grip had weakened. The old emperor himself bemoaned the fact that his excellent memory, vital for the way he had always done his job, was now fading. Kangxi had usually been an indulgent boss, for both personal and political reasons. As he aged and his energy declined, official corruption grew. Rivalries over the succession had undermined discipline and encouraged the factional strife that was always one of the Chinese bureaucracy's weaknesses.

The new emperor immediately tackled these cancers with energy, thoroughness and determination. With the regime already over eighty years old and rooted in Chinese society, Yongzheng could afford to take a harder line on corruption. He was also a man in his forties, with considerable experience of men and politics. He warned one senior official who, in the emperor's opinion, was trying to pull the wool over his eyes that 'you must know that I am not a ruler who was born and grew up deep in a palace. I had forty years of worldly affairs' before ascending the throne. Like Emperor Ming Wanli, Yongzheng noted the frequent contrast between the high-flown ethical claims of Confucian officials and their behaviour, but he reacted in a much more mature and competent fashion. The emperor was a paragon among imperial rulers as regards his close and effective control over the bureaucratic machine. He was his empire's chief administrator and chief personnel officer. His priorities were personnel policy, managing the flow of information, and ensuring that policies were not just proclaimed but also implemented effectively. He drove his officials hard and could be harsh with them. The strict Yongzheng imposed his will on the bureaucracy, but he never resorted to the executions and humiliating public beatings of officials which scarred Ming government. In the cause of efficient governance he drove himself harder than anyone else, working long hours deep into the night. Like his father, Yongzheng had internalized Confucian teachings about rulership. He had a deep sense of his responsibility to guide and protect his ordinary subjects and to promote their welfare.[25]

Yongzheng's reign began with a major turnover of key personnel such as provincial governors and commanders of Manchu garrisons and Banners. Much dead wood had accumulated in Kangxi's last years and the factions that had supported rival claims to the throne stood ready to sabotage the new monarch's policies. Yongzheng placed enormous importance on selecting the right men for responsible posts. He once wrote, 'if we obtain the right people to govern, then there is no task that cannot be satisfactorily accomplished. Without such people, although we play with documents and manipulate words, nothing can be accomplished.' In a vast empire where so much authority had to be delegated to officials operating far beyond the emperor's eye, these words had special force. Yongzheng had strong doubts about the way in which elite bureaucrats were currently recruited and promoted. It was politically impossible to challenge the examination system, but the emperor believed that its graduates too often preferred literary excellence to professional skill and hard-nosed determination to look at facts on the ground and achieve results. Within the bureaucracy he viewed the promotion system as haphazard and corrupted by patron–client networks. He opened up new channels for promotion, in many cases personally interviewing men recommended by his lieutenants as well as all candidates for important jobs. Hundreds of records of these interviews conducted by the emperor have been published in recent years: each record contains a brief résumé of the candidate followed by Yongzheng's grading of his suitability for the post and comments, which were shrewd, to the point and far from merely formulaic.[26]

The greatly expanded Palace Memorial system was at the heart of Yongzheng's management of his administration. In Kangxi's time the system had been relatively small-scale and haphazard. Yongzheng extended it to a wider range of officials in Beijing and across the empire: the number of memorials he received in a year was ten times greater than in Kangxi's reign. On many days he received, read and commented on fifty to sixty such memorials. Yongzheng used the memorial system to speed up decisions on key issues, extend his supervision over his administration, and evaluate, encourage and criticize his officials. The criticisms could be blunt. In one not untypical moment of exasperation the emperor returned a memorial to a senior official with the comment, 'you are as dumb as wood and stone! I don't think you are a human being at all.' Officials soon learned not to waste Yongzheng's time on insignificant issues or flowery literary language. He sometimes warned miscreants that he had received information about their misdeeds and was keeping a careful watch. But the memorials also often contained warm words of praise and encouragement. They convey the sense that the emperor was attempting to cultivate personal loyalty and a shared commitment to the public good between himself and trusted officials. Above all, the Palace Memorial system allowed Yongzheng to maintain an intense, detailed and secret conversation on policy with his senior officials. Key policies such as the reform of provincial finance emerged from this give and take. In an empire of China's size and variety it was vital that central policy should be adapted to local realities and needs.[27]

When Yongzheng ascended the throne the treasury was empty despite there having been peace for many years. The financing of provincial government was a source of immense inefficiency and corruption. The most basic problem was that government was under-funded, but the political pact between the Qing and Chinese elites included low taxation so Yongzheng could not tackle this problem at its root. He could and did remedy the additional problem that far too little revenue was retained at provincial and local levels to pay officials and sustain administration. This led to a range of semi-legal and covert demands on the local population. Since it was impossible to audit these levies they varied greatly from place to place and were an easy cover for official corruption and extortion. As a prince, Yongzheng's first recorded official mission was to inspect the grain reserve stores which local government was supposed to maintain in order to combat famines. In the district he inspected he found that almost 40 per cent of the stores were wholly or partly empty because of the bankruptcy and corruption of the local administration. When drought and famine recurred the consequences for the local peasantry would inevitably be catastrophic. Yongzheng's insistence on reforming local government finance was driven by acute awareness of such failings and dangers. Typically of Yongzheng, the work was gruelling and brought no glory but it was important. His reform both increased and regularized the revenues sustaining local administration, in the process improving efficiency, reducing corruption, and sustaining the viability of provincial government for decades. His sharp eye and insistence on discipline in the administration soon returned the central treasury to surplus.[28]

Yongzheng's intensely active role in government inevitably resulted in the growth of his personal secretariat in the Inner Court. Simply to handle the flow of memorials, archive them and follow up on the decisions that the emperor made required a growth in the number of staff and a more systematic approach. When renewed war broke out with the Dzunghars (western Mongols) the flow of documents into the Inner Court grew sharply. In 1731 Yongzheng reproached himself bitterly for the fact that the lack of system and consultation in the Inner Court had contributed to a serious military defeat. As always, there was a pay-off: a small staff and informal procedures in the Inner Court's 'secretariat' might maximize the emperor's freedom of action and encourage personal loyalty to him among his closest officials, but it did so at the risk of mismanaging the information, consultation and decision-making process which was vital to effective leadership of so great a government machine and so vast an empire.

Crucial too was the death in 1730 of the emperor's key adviser and de facto deputy, his brother Prince I (Yinxiang). The emperor was devastated. Yongzheng wrote 'there was nothing, no matter how great or small, that the prince did not take charge of and manage, nothing that he did not attend to in all detail and deal with in such a satisfactory fashion that my heart was completely at peace.' He added that 'it is utterly impossible for me to describe my sorrow in pen and ink. Now I have lost my mental bearing.' Yongzheng once wrote, 'one man's strength is not sufficient to run the Empire.' He worked immensely hard and felt all the solitude that is the inevitable lot of any leader, let alone of an imperial leader whose sacred office imposed maintaining a distance from his subjects. A loyal and intelligent brother who was also deeply involved across the whole range of policy was a companion and friend whom no minister could fully replace. But Prince I's death did have some advantages. Subsequently Yongzheng developed within his Inner Court an apparatus – given the title of Grand Council – which not just managed business efficiently but also stood ready for the day when the emperor was no more. The basic point was that no normal monarch could be expected to work as hard as Yongzheng and no human being could continue to do so over the course of a long reign.[29]

Yongzheng was very far from being just a tough-minded administrator interested only in the practicalities of government. Unlike most of his brothers he never boasted of skill in archery or horsemanship. He was not a military man. Like all the Qing princes he received a thorough education in Chinese philosophy and culture. Among his many brothers he stood out for his deep immersion in philosophical questions and his knowledge of Chinese classics, language and history. Yongzheng was a rather emotional, moody and melancholy child and adolescent. Kangxi once chided him for these weaknesses and Yongzheng as emperor had his father's remarks framed and placed on his desk. Probably Yongzheng's later intense commitment to Chan (Zen) Buddhism with its strict discipline of calm meditation was one way in which he sought to keep these emotions in check. But his interest in Buddhism went far beyond mere exercises to achieve calm and self-control. Yongzheng had a good knowledge and appreciation of Confucian, Legalist and Taoist writings but his greatest religious commitment was to Buddhism. After his death, his former princely palace became a centre for Tibetan Buddhism in Beijing.

As emperor Yongzheng took a close interest in the work of his court artists and craftsmen. The main themes of court artwork in his reign 'were largely drawn from Daoism, mythology, legends, and auspicious symbolism, a world in which the emperor was deeply immersed'. His comments on the work produced were very numerous and – as was his usual style – mostly short and to the point. Nevertheless, they were intelligent, informed and showed detailed knowledge and interest across a range of issues. Here was no dilettante. Nor was Yongzheng's interest in painting, ceramics and a wide range of other arts and crafts mere posturing to win applause. His taste was exquisite. One historian of Chinese imperial patronage of the arts calls Yongzheng 'the most intriguing and multi-faceted of the Qing emperors'.[30]

Predictably, Yongzheng managed the succession to the throne efficiently. He carefully educated and mentored his chosen heir, the future Emperor Qianlong. Yongzheng established the rule that an emperor would choose his heir but keep the name secret in a sealed box, only to be opened upon his death. This system would never have worked in the Ottoman or Mughal courts, but under the Qing it functioned effectively, at least so long as the reigning emperor was an adult capable of independently choosing a successor. Although not as intelligent as his father or grandfather, Qianlong proved a competent and diligent monarch with a strong sense of the responsibilities inherent in his office. After sixty-one years on the throne he abdicated in 1796 so as not to infringe filial piety by reigning for longer than his grandfather. Unlike in Charles V's case, this abdication was a sham. Qianlong continued to dominate the political world until his death in 1799.

In a sense the charade sums up one side of Qianlong and his reign. He set out to be the perfect Confucian and Manchu monarch, where possible even exceeding the historically mandated measures of success and virtue. For example, the emperor sought to be a paragon among literati. Since Chinese Confucian gentlemen wrote poetry so did Qianlong – in his case producing a one-inch-thick book of usually rather mediocre poems every year. But it would be unfair to dismiss all Qianlong's efforts in this manner: he was a fascinating ruler who had many cultural and political achievements to his credit. He deserves a much more careful study than considerations of space and balance allow me in this book. One familiar problem of Qianlong's reign resulted from the fact that the emperor lived to the age of eighty-eight. In his last years Qianlong's energy inevitably faded and corruption grew apace. A more fundamental problem was that by the 1780s China was facing challenges that could not be surmounted by traditional methods. Internally, this meant above all the huge growth in population and the failure of the state machine to expand and evolve to serve the growing population's needs. In external affairs it meant the growing might of the European powers, and especially Britain.[31]

To some extent in the period 1780–1840 China followed the same path as the Ottoman Empire. Power was decentralized and the central government's authority and resources were weakened. Traditional military forces – in this case the Banner troops – were allowed to lose their military value while remaining a heavy burden on the treasury. All this happened at a time when growing European power stood ready to exploit any weakness in Asian empires. Nevertheless, the Qing had a better excuse than the Ottomans for allowing these developments. The Banner system was vital to the legitimacy and governance of Qing China in a way that was not true of the Janissaries' role in the Ottoman state. The Ottomans had been in direct military and political competition with Christian Europe for centuries before 1768. They ought to have been more aware of military developments among their historical enemies. By contrast, for China the European threat was well over the horizon before the nineteenth century. The only European power with which the Chinese had significant political relations was Russia. For over a century these relations had been peaceful and in the distant East Asian theatre Russian power had little menace. Above all, in the late eighteenth century the Ottomans' nemesis – Russia – was a pre-modern Eurasian empire like their own. The catastrophic defeat that struck the Qing Empire in the 1840s during the Opium War owed much to the fact that its British enemy was able to make use of the unprecedented power generated by the Industrial Revolution. China, along with the rest of the world, was entering a new era.

Qianlong himself was very interested in military affairs. Although he never commanded armies personally in the field, the emperor sought to win military glory for his empire and dynasty. As the heir to the Manchu military heritage he saw this as both his duty and his due. He also believed that the Qing's legitimacy in Chinese eyes was linked to their warrior reputation and their expansion of China's empire. His greatest and most lasting triumph was the destruction of the Dzhungar Mongols and the annexation of Xinjiang (Chinese Turkestan) in the 1750s. Although China's hold on this vast region was subsequently strengthened by large-scale Han immigration, it remains to this day a semi-colonial region, scarred by conflicts between the indigenous people, Han immigrants and the Chinese state. In Qianlong's time, it was the geopolitical consequences of Xinjiang's conquest that mattered most. For two thousand years China's overwhelming geopolitical challenge had been to defend its northern borders against nomadic warriors. Now this threat was gone. Euphoria, self-satisfaction and complacency were in the circumstances understandable. The neo-Confucian Chinese monarchy was conservative to its core. The greatest stimulus to reform was always likely to be external threats. Now all such threats had seemingly disappeared.

History tends to play nasty tricks on those who think it is over. Within a century the Qing were confronted by the immense challenge of Western power on their previously secure southern coastline. When disaster occurred in the 1840s Opium War the Chinese faced a European enemy whose pre-modern military system had been brought to perfection during the Napoleonic Wars and had then gained additional strength thanks to the Industrial Revolution. Chinese junks faced British steamships armed with massive firepower. The Qing cannot fairly be blamed for having failed to prepare adequately for war against so revolutionary and unprecedented a threat. The demise of military nomadism, the emergence of industrial-era warfare, and the domination of the globe by the European powers represented a fundamental break in Eurasian geopolitics and global history.[32]

14

The Romanovs: Dynastic, Russian, European and Eurasian Emperors

The founders of the Russian Empire were the rulers of Moscow, an initially small principality formed in the last decades of the thirteenth century. Moscow's rulers were descendants of Rurik, the semi-mythical Viking chieftain who had ruled the area around Kiev towards the end of the ninth century. At a pinch one might describe these Vikings as river-borne nomadic war-bands. In the following four centuries Rurik's dynasty came to rule over much of today's European Russia, Belarus and Ukraine. Since the Rurikids divided their realms between their sons, by 1200 a maze of mostly tiny principalities covered this vast territory. The most powerful Rurikid by then was the Grand Prince of Vladimir, who dominated the north-eastern territories ('Great Russia') which became the core of the Muscovite and then Russian state. Moscow's princes were a junior branch of the grand princes of Vladimir. For almost 250 years after the Mongol invasions of the 1240s most of the Rurikid lands were part of the empire of Chinggis Khan and his successors. The Chinggisids ruled their Slav subjects indirectly, using the Rurikid princes to extract tribute and transmit it to the ruling khan.

During the fourteenth century Moscow's rulers emerged as the most powerful princes in 'Great Russia'. Their position as 'Grand Princes' was recognized both by the Tatar/Mongol khan and by the Orthodox Church, whose patriarch (originally located in Kiev) moved to Moscow for good in the first half of the fourteenth century. A crucial factor in Moscow's rise was the fact that whereas rival principalities were divided among many heirs, over four long generations biological chance kept the whole Muscovite inheritance united. This good fortune ended in 1425 when Vasily I died, leaving his adult younger brother and his ten-year-old son (Vasily II) as rival candidates for the throne. The vicious twenty-year civil war that followed brought anarchy and the intervention of outside rulers, but Vasily II's final victory established the inheritance of the undivided realm by male primogeniture as the unchallenged 'law' of the realm.

In the century that followed Vasily II's victory Moscow made the first steps towards empire. The fall of Constantinople to the Ottomans in 1453 left Moscow's rulers the only independent Orthodox monarchs and allowed them to claim the Byzantine imperial heritage. This included the title of tsar (a corruption of 'caesar') and Byzantine imperial rituals, symbols and ideology. All the other Rurikid principalities of Great Russia were absorbed by 1520, as was the vast and wealthy trading state of Novgorod. Ivan IV – 'the Terrible' (r. 1547–84) – conquered the main successor states to the Mongol Empire in Europe, the Muslim khanates of Kazan and Astrakhan, in the 1550s. His subsequent attempt to conquer Livonia (today's Latvia and Estonia) and plant Russian power on the shores of the Baltic Sea overstretched his realm's resources and resulted in economic and political crisis. Ivan's reaction to this crisis was massive purges of the ruling elite, including the killing of the junior branch of the Muscovite dynasty and – perhaps – of his eldest son and heir. One plausible explanation for his extreme and counter-productive cruelty is that his brain was increasingly affected by the mercury he took to counter a painful and debilitating disease of the spine. Largely thanks to Ivan, in 1598 the Moscow dynasty died out, unleashing two decades of anarchy, civil war and foreign intervention known as the Time of Troubles, which culminated in an attempt to set up the Polish king's son as ruler in Moscow. The Orthodox and proto-nationalist revolt that ensued drove out the Poles and elected as tsar Michael Romanov, a member of an aristocratic family prominent since Moscow's creation and one which had intermarried with the reigning dynasty. Memory of the Time of Troubles greatly strengthened the belief that only a powerful and legitimate monarchy could save the Russians from domestic anarchy and foreign domination. This memory was one of the foundation myths of the Romanov dynasty and empire.[1]

Inevitably the political system and traditions of the Muscovite principality were deeply influenced by its geographical setting. No other great sedentary empire in history had a heartland in so northern a latitude, so far from the centres of international trade and culture. Moscow was some 1,300 miles north-east of Constantinople, which was at the centre of trading routes that linked the Mediterranean region to Asia

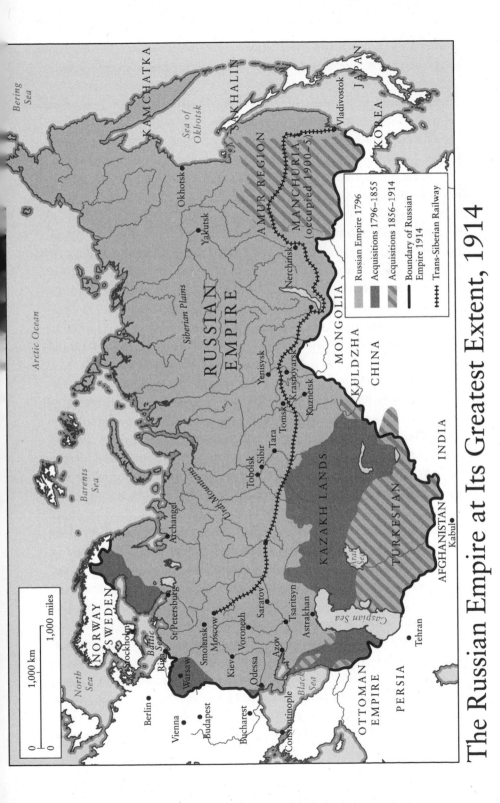

The Russian Empire at Its Greatest Extent, 1914

Legend:
- Russian Empire 1796
- Acquisitions 1796–1855
- Acquisitions 1856–1914
- Boundary of Russian Empire 1914
- Trans-Siberian Railway

Bering Sea
Arctic Ocean
Barents Sea
Sea of Okhotsk
North Sea
Baltic Sea
Black Sea
Caspian Sea
Aral Sea

NORWAY
SWEDEN
KAMCHATKA
SAKHALIN
JAPAN
KOREA
Vladivostok
AMUR REGION
MANCHURIA (occupied 1900–5)
MONGOLIA
KULDZHA
CHINA
INDIA
TURKESTAN
AFGHANISTAN
Kabul
PERSIA
Tehran
OTTOMAN EMPIRE
Constantinople
KAZAKH LANDS

RUSSIAN EMPIRE
Siberian Plains
Ural Mountains

Okhotsk
Yakutsk
Nerchinsk
Yenisysk
Krasnoyarsk
Kuznetsk
Tomsk
Tara
Sibir
Tobolsk
Archangel
St Petersburg
Stockholm
Riga
Smolensk
Moscow
Warsaw
Berlin
Vienna
Budapest
Bucharest
Kiev
Voronezh
Odessa
Azov
Saratov
Tsaritsyn
Astrakhan

1,000 km
1,000 miles

from ancient times. It was even further from the Atlantic, which became the centre of the global economy from the eighteenth century. In civilizational terms Moscow was perched on the furthest periphery of the Orthodox and Byzantine community, which itself by 1450 was much the junior partner in the European and Christian world. Distance from the great trade routes and cultural centres meant relative poverty, few towns and small numbers of merchants, professional men and skilled craftsmen. States able to tap into international trade could place smaller tax burdens on their people. The overwhelming majority of the tsar's subjects even in 1700 were peasants, whose 'surplus' had to sustain the monarchy and its armies. In most of the world's great 'agrarian' empires peasant farmers lived in densely populated and fertile river valleys. In Russia by contrast the peasantry was thinly sprinkled across a vast but infertile zone. Even in 1750 the empire's population was smaller than that of France. Distance and climate placed a high tax on all the operations of the Russian state, economy and people. Fixing the population to the soil – in other words serfdom – was the only way to sustain the state, its armed forces and the warrior-landholding elite.

There was nothing at all inevitable in the rise of a powerful state in the Muscovite heartland. If such a state did emerge, however, geography more or less determined how it would seek to expand its power and territory. One reason for the foundation of the city of Moscow was its good water communications with Russia's greatest river, the Volga, and thereby its links to the Baltic and Caspian seas. Any state rooted in Moscow would seek to control these waterways and their outlets to the sea, in order to stop its trade being constrained, taxed and interdicted by rival powers. Even more elemental was the drive to expand out of the poor soils of the Muscovite heartland towards the much more fertile land of the steppe. Still, the geographical location of the Russian heartland did offer some advantages. Its dense network of rivers flowed slowly across a flat landscape and were in most cases easily managed and navigated by the standards even of the Nile, let alone the Yellow River. The remote and densely forested terrain offered some security against nomadic armies. It was even better security against early modern European infantry and artillery-based armies which found it hard to feed themselves on Russian soil and even harder to move across Russia's vast distances, especially in spring and autumn when all roads dissolved into mud.

Above all, Russia benefited after 1500 from its peripheral location in the European state system, which facilitated its expansion across the whole of northern Asia. Russia would gain enormous wealth from Siberia's fur, silver and gold, and other minerals. The Russian military and metallurgical industry was created in the Urals in the reign of Peter I 'the Great' (r. 1682–1725) and was based on the region's vast resources of iron and timber. In comparative imperial terms the native forest peoples of Siberia offered weak opposition to Russian expansion. Already by the end of the seventeenth century the Russians had reached the Pacific Ocean and had achieved a stable compromise with the Qing Empire, which contributed among other things to the rapid demise of Mongol military nomadism. Not until the emergence of Japan at the end of the nineteenth century did Russia face a serious military threat to its Asian territories. Essentially the Russians had moved into the geopolitical void created by the collapse of the Mongol Empire. Comparisons with the Ottoman experience are illuminating. When the Chinggisid Ilkhanate disintegrated in Iran it was in time replaced by the Safavid dynasty, which quickly became a formidable enemy on the Ottomans' eastern frontier.

The basic geopolitical imperatives of the Muscovite and then Russian state – in other words control of river-borne trade routes and expansion on to the rich soils of the steppe – were far harder to achieve and faced major opposition. Expansion southwards ran head-on into nomadic warrior communities, above all the Crimean Tatars. Scores of thousands of Russians and Ukrainians were netted by the Crimean slave raids that occurred regularly between 1500 and 1650. Europe's first slave-based sugar plantations were in Cyprus with captured Russians and Ukrainians providing the labour. Most of Moscow was burned down in a Crimean Tatar raid as late as 1571. Building and manning the fortified lines that protected Russian colonization as it advanced across the steppe from the sixteenth to the eighteenth centuries could only be achieved by a state capable of mobilizing resources and manpower on a considerable scale. Behind the Crimean Tartars stood their overlord, the Ottoman sultan. In military terms the Ottoman Empire was more powerful than Russia until the eighteenth century. In 1711 the Ottomans came close to destroying Peter the Great and his army and forced the tsar to make a humiliating peace. Even later in the eighteenth century it took enormous military and logistical efforts to secure Russia's hold on the northern shore of the Black Sea and thereby make possible the economic development of southern Russia and Ukraine.

For a state rooted in the Moscow region, access to the Baltic was always likely to be an earlier and more credible priority than advancing across the steppe to challenge Ottoman dominance of the distant Black Sea coastline. From early days Russia's rulers fought on two fronts – northern and southern. Managing diplomatic relations in order to exploit opportunities as they arose in one of these theatres and avoid simultaneous two-front wars required diplomatic skill and experience. In the early eighteenth century Russia fulfilled its long-held goal of establishing its control over the south-eastern shore of the Baltic Sea. Opening up the trade routes to the booming economies of western and central Europe led to enormous economic gains but it also embroiled Russia in direct competition with the European great powers. Right down to 1917 the single greatest priority for Russian tsars was to maintain the empire's security and status in competition with the economically and culturally more advanced great powers to its west. This continued to be true for the tsars' communist successors. Any state whose roots lay in the bare Muscovite heartland and which evolved through surmounting these geopolitical challenges was unlikely to be a model of liberty and benevolence.

Once again, comparisons with the Ottomans are to the point. The Russian and Ottoman empires were located on the immediate periphery of Latin Europe in an era (1500–1918) when European power grew enormously and came to dominate the world. The Russian people paid a high price for the creation of an often ruthlessly exploitative state and its military machine. On the other hand, as we have seen, Ottoman failure to sustain the state's military power led in time to the killing or ethnic cleansing of millions of Muslims in the empire's northern borderlands and European domination and even colonization of the Islamic heartlands. By the traditional measure of empire – in other words military power and glory – Russia did much better than the Ottomans in the eighteenth century. Leadership was a major factor in Russian success and Ottoman failure in this geopolitical competition. Two longer-term structural factors were also vital to Russian success: first, the creation of an effective but ruthless system to control and mobilize Russian manpower through serfdom and conscription into the armed forces: and, second, the rapid westernization of Russian elites. In long-term historical perspective it is easy to see the awful hatreds and brutality of the Russian Revolution as in part a belated revenge against exploitative but also culturally alien rulers. There were no easy or cheap answers to the geopolitical challenges faced by the Russians or Ottomans in the early modern and modern eras.[2]

The core of the Russian political system was an exceptionally close alliance between a powerful monarchy and the hereditary military and landholding elite. The thirteenth-century prince of Moscow was the perfect example of a war-band leader. By the end of the sixteenth century he had evolved into a distant and divinely appointed emperor surrounded by the rituals of absolute and hereditary monarchy. His territorial conquests had allowed the tsar to create a royal army consisting of cavalrymen granted land in return for military service and a smaller number of full-time, salaried infantry known as musketeers (*strel'tsy*). The parallels with the Ottoman case are clear.

The ideology, symbols and rituals of Russian imperial monarchy were drawn from the Byzantine Orthodox tradition. In the Byzantine Empire the Orthodox Church's celebration of absolute and semi-sacred monarchical power was balanced by the political culture inherited from imperial Rome. The dynastic principle was weak, the overthrow of emperors and dynasties by military coup and mass disturbances on the streets of the capital a recurring story. Imported to Russia where the dynastic principle was strong, Byzantine ideology contributed to the formation of a mighty monarchy whose rulers were sometimes depicted in messianic and almost Christ-like terms. Unlike his peers in Latin Europe, the tsar did not face a web of laws, institutions and conventions protecting the lives and property of the elite, and often granting aristocrats a say in legislation and taxation. Peter the Great's reign showed the awesome power of a very competent and determined tsar. In 1722 he was able simply to decree the replacement of the old rule of male primogeniture by a new law giving the reigning monarch the right to choose his own successor from among the members of the dynasty. No eighteenth-century French king would even have dreamed of abolishing the Salic Law governing succession to the throne. No law or institution had restricted Ivan IV's reign of terror directed against the Russian aristocracy.[3]

Ironically, Ivan IV's reign illustrated graphically both the extent and the limitations of autocratic power. The only result of his actions was the destruction of his dynasty and the near-destruction of the Muscovite state. A key lesson learned from his reign and the Time of Troubles was that the political system could only function if tsar and elite collaborated. The new Romanov regime did everything in its power to restore their traditional alliance. A remarkable number of the families supposedly destroyed by Ivan resurfaced within the political and social elite. The fourth Romanov tsar, Peter the Great, was in many ways an astonishingly original and even revolutionary figure, with immense personal charisma. He transformed Russia's international status, central government institutions, and the mentality and culture of the Russian aristocracy. But Peter had no intention of destroying the traditional elite and would have ruined any chance of achieving his goals had he attempted to do so. His success depended on reforming and strengthening the alliance between the monarchy and Russia's traditional elites so that it could meet the changing military, political but also cultural requirements of the early modern world.

At Peter's accession the uselessness of the traditional cavalry regiments risked making the landholding-military elite redundant. Peter's institutional and cultural reforms transformed this elite into the officer corps of his Europeanized army and state. Henceforth service as an officer in the emperor's army or fleet became a badge of honour and an expected cultural norm for Russian noblemen. The tsar's unconventional 'career' and mindset allowed him to discover and recruit into his entourage some able individuals from outside the traditional elite. These included both foreigners and Russians from non-elite backgrounds. Nevertheless, the top military and civilian office-holders in 1730 still mostly came from traditional landholding families. Even in the reign of the last Russian emperor, Nicholas II (r. 1894–1917), over one-third of Russia's ministers, top officials, diplomats, judges, senior generals and admirals came from families belonging to the pre-Petrine Russian elite. The last 'prime minister' (i.e. Chairman of the Council of Ministers) of imperial Russia, Prince N. D. Golitsyn, came from a family that had played a key role in the Russian court and politics in the early fifteenth century.[4]

The Russian hereditary, military and landholding elite – obsessed with genealogy and very conscious of a collective elite identity – had far more in common with the European aristocracy than with Confucian bureaucrats or the slave-soldiers who formed the core of the Ottoman ruling elite at the empire's sixteenth-century highpoint. It had some similarities with the Manchu and Mughal nobilities but was much older, more deeply rooted in its society, and more secure in its possession of landed property. In the fourteenth century the Muscovite aristocracy – meaning the small group of *boyar* families – owned their land outright and without any service obligations. By the seventeenth century all landholders were obliged to serve in the tsar's armies if the need arose, but estates which had originally been held as temporary tenures in reward for military service had by now become hereditary family property. Only in the second half of the eighteenth century did landed estates become outright property along European lines and without any legal obligation to serve. This was part of the broader Europeanization of the Russian elites, started quietly under Tsar Alexei (r. 1645–76) and driven forward with enormous gusto by his son Peter the Great. Even in 1789, however, the Russian elite was more geared to serving the state and had fewer legal and political rights than the French, let alone British, aristocracy and gentry.[5]

Such comparisons help to situate Russia and its elites in global history, but they have their dangers. It makes little sense to judge the Russian aristocracy as failing to meet Latin European aristocratic norms that had evolved in a different context. Before the eighteenth century the Russian elites did not measure themselves by European models. They operated according to their own traditions, needs and priorities. The basic point was that an aristocracy that sat on its estates in the bare Muscovite heartland would have doomed itself to poverty and insignificance. On the contrary, the alliance of monarchy and service-oriented aristocracy fuelled Russia's growth from an impoverished, small principality to an empire that covered one-sixth of the world's land surface. As a result, the Russian elites acquired not just wealth but also an honoured place in world history. Their literary, musical and artistic culture – combining Russian, European and imperial elements – became one of the ornaments of modern, global civilization. These were no small achievements. On the other hand, the fusion of Western and Russian traditions was the source of tensions which were both creative and at times devastating in their impact.

The Russian Empire reached its apogee in the 'long eighteenth century', in other words between 1689 and 1815. Two of its rulers in this era, Peter I and Catherine II 'the Great' (r. 1762–96), dominate public perceptions of eighteenth-century Russia and loom almost larger than life. Before looking at these two extraordinary monarchs it is worth pausing to explain the society and political system which they ruled. This makes clear the opportunities, constraints and dangers they faced. It tells us what they could and could not do.[6]

At the centre of the political system stood the autocratic sovereign, unconstrained by laws or institutions, and the source of all legitimate authority. To challenge the Romanov dynasty's right to rule was unthinkable to members of the eighteenth-century elite. On the other hand, Peter I's abolition of the old convention of succession by male primogeniture weakened the legitimacy of individual rulers. Although monarchs almost always nominated an heir, succession crises occurred in 1727, 1730 and 1825. In 1741 and 1762 coups overthrew monarchs within a year of their accession. In 1801 Paul I was assassinated after just four years of rule. The muscle for these coups was provided by the regiments of the Guards, whose noble officers were often linked to key figures at court and in the government. Wise rulers knew how to use their 'autocratic' power but also to understand its limitations. They were careful not to tread too hard on the interests and sensitivities of the aristocracy, and in particular of key courtiers and Guards officers. A foreign policy perceived by powerful members of the elite to be contrary to Russian interests also played a big role in the overthrow of Peter III in 1762 and of his son, Paul I, in 1801.[7]

The Russian elite was always divided between a group of rich and powerful families which dominated the court and a much larger and poorer group of landholding families whose lives revolved around life on their estates in the provinces and service in the tsar's armies. It is reasonable to call the former group 'aristocrats' and the latter 'gentry'. The main allies of the monarchy and the chief beneficiaries of its growing wealth and territory were the aristocrats, but competent monarchs made sure never to become the servants of any aristocratic faction. To some extent they balanced not just individuals and factions but also aristocrats and gentry against each other. In 1730 key aristocratic courtiers chose Duchess Anna of Courland, the daughter of Peter the Great's half-brother Ivan V, to occupy a throne made vacant by the sudden death of the young Peter II. They attempted to impose constitutional constraints on the monarchy, which in practice would greatly have enhanced the power of leading aristocratic families like their own. Anna defeated this attempt in part by appealing beyond the narrow aristocratic elite to a broader gentry group that had gathered in Moscow to greet the new reign. Few members of the gentry welcomed the prospect of court patronage and promotion in the state's military and civil service falling into the hands of a few aristocratic magnates and their clients. More than just self-interest was involved. Supporters of autocracy pointed out the damage that rule by aristocratic oligarchy was doing to the international power and status of neighbouring Poland and Sweden.

For two hundred years before Peter I's reign, Russian tsars had usually married women from respectable gentry families. The difficulty of persuading foreign royal brides to convert to Orthodoxy was one constraint on choosing European princesses. To marry Russian aristocrats was both to invite great jealousy within the court elite and to elevate the status of an aristocratic family to possibly dangerous levels. A carefully vetted bride from the gentry was a much safer option. After her marriage, the bride's close relations would be brought into the court elite. Often, they proved key allies of the tsar, linked by special bonds of blood and dependence. This tradition ended with Peter I. Thenceforth the Romanovs intermarried almost exclusively with European royal dynasties. However, it took some time for this new custom to take root. In 1727 the eleven-year-old Peter II, grandson of Peter the Great, ascended the throne. Prince Alexander Menshikov, one of Peter I's leading lieutenants and now the dominant figure in government, immediately tried to marry off his own daughter to the young tsar. This grab for power infuriated other key political figures and quickly led to Menshikov's overthrow. Instead, Peter II was betrothed to Princess Catherine Dolgoruky, whose family were bitter enemies of Menshikov and dominated the government after his fall. Completely unlike Menshikov, who had been promoted by Peter I's favour despite very humble origins, the Dolgorukys were an ancient princely family descended from Rurik. Had Peter II lived and produced heirs the Dolgoruky family would probably have dominated the court for at least one generation. Conceivably, had the Romanov family died out – which very nearly happened in the eighteenth century – the Dolgorukys might even have succeeded them on the throne. Peter II's unexpected death from smallpox aged only fourteen wrecked their ambitions.[8]

For all but two of the following sixty-six years Russia was ruled by female monarchs. Empress Anna (r. 1730–40) was a widow. Elizabeth (r. 1741–62), the daughter of Peter the Great, and Catherine II 'the Great' were officially unmarried though both may actually have contracted secret marriages to their main favourites, respectively Kirill Razumovsky and Grigorii Potemkin. For an empress officially to marry any man was to grant him enormous power and status, thereby greatly diminishing her own position and infuriating rival courtiers. Favourites and their families often played a role similar to that of the relatives of royal brides in the pre-Petrine era. The favourites were almost always drawn from respectable gentry families but not from the court aristocracy. The families of Elizabeth's two greatest favourites, Razumovsky and Ivan Shuvalov, played vital roles in politics and government. The same was true as regards Catherine II's longest-lasting favourites, Grigorii Orlov and Potemkin. The Orlovs were at the centre of the conspiracy that brought Catherine to power in 1762 by overthrowing her husband, Peter III. For the next decade, when her throne remained insecure, their network ensured the loyalty of the Guards regiments. Grigorii's brother Alexei, the most formidable of his many able siblings, disposed of the imprisoned Peter III on Catherine's behalf and occupied a variety of positions in her regime, most notably as commander of the Russian fleet which amazed Europe in 1769 by sailing from the Baltic to the eastern Mediterranean and destroying the Ottoman navy. The greatest of all Catherine's favourites, Potemkin, served as her formidable and totally loyal viceroy of southern Russia – including all the territories newly conquered from the Ottomans – in the second half of her reign.[9]

Placing a mistress in the monarch's bed had always been a route to power and wealth not just for her but also often for her family. In eighteenth-century Russia this rule still applied but, instead of beautiful young women, handsome young Guards officers now competed to catch the empress's eye. The job of favourite was not always comfortable. By the 1780s favourites were trying to satisfy the sexual and emotional needs of a woman old enough to be their grandmother, with 'uncle' Potemkin from time to time peering over their shoulder in a remarkable menage à trois. On the other hand, even a short spell as favourite brought lavish rewards. Most gentry families could only rise into the aristocracy by distinguished service, especially in the army. The eighteenth-century army fought enough wars and was enough of a meritocracy for some sons of the gentry to win fame, high rank and sometimes wealth. The most famous general in Russian history, Field

Marshal Alexander Suvorov, followed this path. Most gentry officers never rose beyond the rank of major and retired after years of service to manage an estate or serve as a middle-ranking official in the provinces. For the usually poor sons of the gentry a military career brought in essential extra income as well as status.

Meanwhile the gentry officer and landowner made a crucial contribution to the state's effectiveness. In 1763 the Russian government employed 16,500 officials, one thousand more than in Prussia, a country that was just one per cent the size even of Russia-in-Europe. Without the noble landowner – whom one emperor described as the state's involuntary tax collector and conscription agent in the village – the tsarist regime could not have functioned. Dominated by landed noblemen, the army was also a reliable and irreplaceable force for repressing serf rebellion and maintaining the highly exploitative system of rule on which both the state and the gentry depended. The army and its officers were at the centre of the regime's legitimacy and system of rule. The officer's uniform was a badge of noble status and honour. The army's many victories in the eighteenth century bathed the state's alliance with the gentry in the prestige and the spoils of success. Like its early modern European rivals, Russia solved the conundrum that had brought down so many other dynasties and empires. Its army was formidable in the face of foreign enemies but its noble officers were fully loyal to their warrior-king and dynasty. Coups in eighteenth-century Russia were kept strictly within the court and the Guards. No Russian general dreamed of marching on St Petersburg in support of a candidate from the Romanov family, let alone of seizing the throne for himself.

When the Romanovs conquered vast new territories in the seventeenth and eighteenth centuries their landowning elites fitted snugly into the imperial order. They ran local government and many of their sons joined the imperial army and bureaucracy, in the process becoming loyal servants of monarchy and empire. Sometimes – especially in the case of well-educated Protestant nobles from Russia's Baltic provinces and abroad – they brought with them skills which were in short supply in Russia. A monarch might also welcome the fact that some of these 'foreigners' lived outside the Russian aristocracy and its networks of clients and allies. In a manner dear to all emperors, they were 'his men'.[10]

Less important to the state than the landowners but still very significant was the Orthodox Church. Above all, the Russian national Church legitimized the monarchy through its prayers, sermons and rituals. Although a pure product of Enlightenment agnosticism, Catherine II spent great time and effort participating in church services and displaying her loyalty and generosity to Orthodoxy in public. She learned a lesson from her husband, Peter III (r. 1762), who had contributed to his downfall by on occasion openly ridiculing the Church. The Orthodox Church in Byzantium and elsewhere had never enjoyed as much autonomy from royal authority as was the case with Catholicism in much of Latin Europe. Peter I increased the Church's dependence by abolishing the patriarchate and running the Church through a Protestant-style committee of archbishops headed by a royal procurator. The fate of the Church's vast landed property tells one something about where power lay in imperial Russia. In Protestant Europe during the Reformation most church land was expropriated, usually in time becoming aristocratic property. In Catholic Europe the Church usually retained its lands. Only in Russia did the monarchy (in Catherine II's reign) expropriate church lands and then just keep them and the peasants who dwelt on them for itself. One result was that by the early nineteenth century roughly half of the Russian peasantry were not private serfs, instead owing all their dues and services to the state or the Romanov family. Over the course of the eighteenth century the taxes and dues paid by these so-called 'state peasants' became the single largest source of revenue for the treasury.[11]

Peter the Great created the eighteenth-century Russian system of government though he built on strong and deeply rooted foundations inherited from Muscovite history. Peter's father, Tsar Alexei (r. 1645–76), died leaving two sons and many daughters by his first wife, Maria Miloslavskaya. Peter was the only surviving son of Alexei's second wife, Natalia Naryshkina. In the last three decades of the seventeenth century Russian politics to a great extent boiled down to a struggle between the Miloslavsky and Naryshkin factions to control power and patronage. The key to victory was to place 'your' prince on the throne. The Naryshkins won in large part due to medical and biological chance. Alexei's eldest son, Tsar Fedor III, died childless in 1682 at the age of twenty. His younger son Ivan V was severely handicapped both physically and mentally.

Mostly for that reason not just the Naryshkin faction but also the

Patriarch of the Orthodox Church and key 'independent' aristocrats chose Peter as tsar in 1682, even though he was a ten-year-old child. The Miloslavsky faction struck back by using a revolt by the Moscow musketeer (*strel'tsy*) regiments to force an alternative arrangement. Peter and Ivan in theory now ruled jointly. Real power belonged to Ivan's older sister Sophia, the most formidable of Alexei's daughters by Maria Miloslavskaya. The musketeers occupied a position in Moscow akin to that of the Janissaries in Istanbul. They were by now more or less useless as soldiers but were a powerful force in domestic politics, linked to conservative and xenophobic religious sects and fiercely protective of their own corporate interests. During their revolt in 1682 they terrorized Peter and his mother and they killed some prominent members of the Naryshkin family and faction. Peter did not forget this. After the musketeers staged another revolt in 1698 Peter punished the rebels with great brutality and abolished the musketeer corps.

The 1682 settlement was a compromise, albeit one which favoured the Miloslavskys. Russian court politics was not a zero-sum game. Remembering the horrors of Ivan IV ('the Terrible') and the Time of Troubles, the ruling elite sought consensus and the avoidance of bloodshed. The anarchy and murder unleashed by the musketeers in 1682 was potentially a threat to all aristocrats. During Sophia's regency (1682–9) Peter and his mother lived freely on their estate at Preobrazhenskoe just outside Moscow, surrounded by allies and clients. Sophia does not seem to have even thought of killing Peter, and the Moscow elite would have been appalled had she attempted to do so.

The clock was ticking against Sophia. Once Peter came of age and married, Muscovite convention would make it hard for a female regent to deny him the right to rule. The Miloslavskys' prospects depended on the decrepit Tsar Ivan producing sons. If he did so, then it might perhaps be possible to destroy the Naryshkin faction and confine Peter to secure but honourable exile in a monastery. Sophia's chances would be increased given military victory in Russia's ongoing war with the Ottomans. Praskovia Saltykova, whose family was closely allied to the Miloslavskys, was dragooned into marrying Ivan V in 1684. It is unlikely that poor Praskovia, said to be the most beautiful woman in Russia, much enjoyed this fate. Subsequently, rumour suggested that Ivan was impotent and that Praskovia's five children were fathered by an Italian doctor whose services the Miloslavskys had procured. In the event the rumour was far less important than the fact that all five of her children were girls. Meanwhile the two campaigns launched against the Ottomans' Crimean clients in 1687 and 1689 ended in disaster. When Peter reached the age of seventeen and married in 1689 the game was up. When the final confrontation came between the regent and Peter, the Moscow elite backed the tsar. Sophia, not Peter, ended her days in a monastery. With Sophia safely out of the way, Peter and the Naryshkin faction were happy to preserve the facade of dual rulership with Ivan V. From Peter's personal perspective, Ivan performed a useful role by participating in the lengthy Orthodox and neo-Byzantine ceremonies that enveloped the Russian monarchy and which Peter himself so disliked.[12]

Peter's unusual childhood and adolescence had an important influence on his reign. Tsar Alexei died when Peter was only four, so the young prince was never subject to a father's direction or control. From the age of ten, though co-tsar, Peter lived away from the Kremlin at the suburban estate of Preobrazhenskoe. He seems to have enjoyed a remarkably free and untutored adolescence. Always passionately interested in military matters, he poured much of his energy into forming two 'play' regiments, named after the neighbouring villages of Preobrazhenskoe and Semenovskoe. Their ranks were filled by a strange combination of the sons of aristocrats from the Naryshkin faction and the estate's stable-boys and other young servants. Initially playmates, many of these boys (including Alexander Menshikov) subsequently became members of Peter's inner circle and loyal agents in his drive to transform Russia. Joined in time by foreign mercenary officers, the two units survived until 1917 as the senior regiments of the Imperial Guards and formed the core and model for the new army created by Peter during his twenty-six-year reign.

It was during his adolescent years that Peter forged close links with the many foreigners living in Moscow. Already in Alexei's reign most of the army was made up of 'new model' regiments whose soldiers were Russian conscripts but whose officers were European mercenaries, employed to train their soldiers in European tactics, drill and weapons. Many European merchants also lived in the foreigners' quarter of the capital, which was located not far from Preobrazhenskoe. Peter's realization that western Europe was much more advanced than Russia in terms of technology, organization and ideas developed as a result of his immersion in Moscow's foreign community. His contacts with these foreigners not only had a vital influence on Peter's thinking, they also had immediate political consequences. Among the many foreign mercenary officers whom Peter got to know in Moscow the most senior was the Scot General Patrick Gordon, who became the tsar's close and trusted friend. When Moscow's musketeers revolted in 1698, Peter was in western Europe on his extraordinary eighteen-month expedition to learn first-hand about international relations, modern technology and European culture. The revolt was crushed by the new model regiments, commanded by Patrick Gordon. No Russian 'Janissaries' would block Peter's programme of rapid and radical borrowing from western Europe.

For Peter, military matters were 'the foremost of worldly activities'. Given his definition of a monarch's role it was inevitable that the primary focus of his reforming programme was on the armed forces but he soon realized that military reform without parallel changes in government institutions and elite mentalities was impossible. For much of his reign the urgent demands of war imposed short-term responses to emergencies and ruled out a coordinated reform programme. The Great Northern War against Sweden began in 1700 and lasted until 1721. The decision to take Russia to war was Peter's alone. The context seemed favourable. Denmark and Poland were Russia's allies. Sweden was isolated and its new king, Charles XII, was only fifteen. In fact, Charles and Sweden proved formidable enemies. The Swedish army was one of the best in Europe and it was sustained by an effective administrative and fiscal system. The war began badly for Peter when his army was routed in 1700 at the battle of Narva. In a series of brilliant campaigns, by 1706 Charles had knocked Denmark and Poland out of the war and was preparing to invade Russia.

Under the enormous strains of the war the Russian administration buckled. Peter and his lieutenants raced from crisis to crisis, overcoming emergencies, sorting out bottlenecks and enforcing obedience by immense personal effort and frequent recourse to coercion. Only as the war began to wind down in the last years of his reign was lasting institutional reform possible. Between 1718 and Peter's death in 1725 a swathe of reforms transformed central government institutions, the management of the Orthodox Church, the fiscal and military recruitment systems, and the rules governing succession to the throne – to name only the most significant legislation. In 1722 a law for the first time defined what it meant to be a noble in Russia and how men might acquire nobility through service to the state. A new capital city of St Petersburg emerged from the marshes of the Baltic coastline as a symbol and model of the European values and manners that Peter sought to imbed in the Russian elite. His reforms provided the foundations of Russian government and elite culture throughout the eighteenth century and in many respects down to 1917.[13] The superb Russo-European city of St Petersburg is probably the most important monument still in existence to an emperor's vision and its impact on his country and the world.

One of Peter's biographers describes him as 'something of a freak of nature'. At six foot seven inches he towered over most of his contemporaries. Official portraits show him as handsome and regal. The tsar's eyes were 'full of fire and animation'. But his small hands and feet and his narrow shoulders were out of proportion with his enormous body. Worse still, his face was subject to frequent strong tics and twitches. They became most alarming when Peter fell victim to one of his terrifying outbursts of anger. Of all the monarchs we have so far encountered in this book, only the Chinese emperor Tang Taizong made the same overwhelming physical impact on those whom he met. For Russians, this impact was all the greater because Peter was without a beard and dressed in European style, breaking radically in this case too with royal precedent. Peter was a man of titanic and volcanic energy, stamina and willpower. Almost all of this he concentrated on his task of defeating the Swedes and transforming Russia's government, armed forces and elite culture. Unlike most monarchs, he did not even find relief in hunting.[14]

Peter could not sit still. Rather like the Mughal emperor Akbar, if he saw a carpenter or stonemason at work he yearned to join in. Unlike Akbar, there was no contemplative side to Peter and no search for a personal religious truth or aesthetic ideal. In part this was simply a matter of personal character but it also reflected broader realities. Wholly unlike the Persianate or Chinese high cultures inherited by Akbar and Kangxi, pre-Petrine Russia had no secular high culture of note. Its sense of beauty and its search for meaning lay in the icons, the music and the world of contemplation of Russian Orthodoxy. Although Peter remained always a firm but unphilosophical believer in Christ and his teaching, he rejected many Orthodox rituals and conventions as mummery and superstition, not to mention as obstacles to progress. Only well after his death would the revolution he launched lead to the creation of a splendid secular high culture in Russia, though one still often shot through with religious values and motifs.

Peter's most notorious assault on Orthodox propriety was the 'All-Mad, All-Jesting, All-Drunken Assembly' which he set up in 1690 and which met periodically for the rest of his reign. In part this was a private drinking club where Peter let down his hair and indulged his love of alcohol in the presence of trusted friends and associates. A ruler who worked as hard as Peter and who sought to impose radical reform on a conservative society needed relaxation and companionship and felt even more alone than most monarchs. But the Assembly also served as a bonding mechanism which brought together and secured the personal loyalty to Peter of its members, many of whom became his key lieutenants. Heavy drinking and strange rituals play similar roles in officers' messes and student fraternities. To some extent Peter's All-Drunken Assembly fulfilled the same role as Charles V's Knights of the Golden Fleece and Akbar's imperial Sufi order. Given the enormous demands Peter placed on his lieutenants and the obstacles they faced, the tsar had extra need to secure the loyalty, unity and commitment of his inner group of helpers. The carnivalesque rituals they performed, mocking the Church's rituals and the stuffy ways of the old *boyar* elite, were a collective affirmation of loyalty to the tsar and the cause of Westernization.[15]

The behaviour of the All-Drunken Assembly was far from private. It was also only one of the many ways in which Peter shocked the sensibilities of traditional Muscovites. Given the extent to which he angered many members of the Muscovite elite and the great sacrifices he demanded from Russian society it is worth asking why he was not overthrown and how he succeeded in achieving most of his goals. Coercion is a necessary but far from sufficient answer. So too is the great potential power of an unequivocally legitimate tsar. But Peter was not Ivan IV, who would terrorize his subjects in an increasingly random and counterproductive manner. As far as possible, he worked with members of the traditional elite. His overriding goal – defeat of Sweden and establishing Russian power in the Baltic region – was an age-old and often frustrated Russian ambition.

Peter pursued that goal with great intelligence and skill. He proved an excellent diplomat and strategist. He chose effective generals and as he faced the greatest crisis of his reign in 1706 – namely Charles XII's invasion – he joined with his leading military advisers to devise a defensive strategy which first stymied and then destroyed the Swedish army. Success legitimizes almost any ruler or strategy. A true warrior-king, at the decisive battle of Poltava in 1709 Peter commanded in person with the skill, courage and sang-froid of a heroic warlord. His soldiers loved a monarch who shared their dangers and possessed an ability to bond with 'ordinary' men to a degree that was rare among hereditary monarchs. The leading contemporary Western expert on Peter comments that the victory at Poltava and the subsequent surrender of almost the entire Swedish army 'decided not only the outcome of a war but also the outcome of Peter's reign, for it enormously strengthened his hand. As for most other monarchs of the early modern era, nothing did so much for his power and prestige as stunning military victory.' As always, chance played its role too. If the bullet that passed through Peter's hat at Poltava had been two inches lower his place in history and Russian memory would have been very different.[16]

Perhaps the greatest tribute to Peter was that his legacy survived his death, despite the fact that for the next almost four decades Russia was governed by a succession of mostly mediocre rulers. At least in retrospect, most of the Russian elite gloried in his achievement and absorbed the European culture he had promoted. Most eighteenth-century Russian monarchs made great play of identifying themselves with the emperor and his legacy. During this century Russia grew enormously in population, wealth and power, in large part because of the international trade routes and fertile agricultural regions opened up by the state's military power. 'In the Russian empire per capita income of the entire population rose to levels unimagined in Peter I's time, increasing by 70 per cent between about 1720 and 1762 and by 70 per cent again by 1802.' As always, prosperity made life far easier for rulers. Allies could be bought and the hostility of potential enemies assuaged. Catherine II rewarded the key conspirators who brought her to power by the coup of June 1762 to the tune of 1.5 million rubles, in other words almost ten per cent of the state's annual revenue.[17]

Catherine's life reads like a fairy story. A girl of fifteen from a minor and by no means wealthy German semi-royal family was taken to Russia to marry the heir to the throne. In time she learned to enjoy the luxuries and survive the intrigues of a brilliant but treacherous court. Her husband – boorish and only interested in soldiers – proved a disappointment but she consoled herself by taking three interesting lovers over the course of her first twenty years in Russia: her friends smuggled her into their love-nests dressed as a man. One of these lovers was a handsome, intelligent and refined young Polish aristocrat – Stanislas Poniatowski – whom Catherine subsequently placed on the Polish throne. In 1762, aged thirty-three, Catherine gave birth to a son by (probably) Grigorii Orlov in April, overthrew her husband in a coup in June, and was crowned in a sumptuous coronation in Moscow in September. Subsequently, in her thirty-six-year reign she became famous in the classic role of emperors as law-giver and creator of institutions. Passionately – even obsessively – committed to writing, she produced plays, librettos for opera and satirical essays. The greatest minds of the European Enlightenment such as Voltaire and Diderot corresponded with her and celebrated her genius. Her armies went from victory to victory, conquering immensely valuable territories for her empire.

The apogee of Catherine's glory came in 1787 when she inspected her newly conquered territories in the south. The first half of the journey took her down the river Dnieper from Kiev in a flotilla of splendid barges. Grandest of all was the empress's boat, incorporating a superb bedroom suite hung with Chinese silks, a library, a dining room to seat seventy guests and an orchestra. The Prince de Ligne, one of Europe's most prominent and sophisticated aristocrats, wrote that nothing to equal this had been seen since the time of Cleopatra. Catherine was escorted around her southern territories by their viceroy, Grigorii Potemkin, the greatest of her lovers. Catherine's taste in men tended to bounce between virile military heroes and sensitive, cultured (but equally handsome) aesthetes. Potemkin was a glorious combination of both, with his own unique and original genius. Ligne encountered many of Europe's most famous and outstanding people in the course of a long life: he called Potemkin 'the most extraordinary man I ever met'. Catherine called him 'my pupil, my friend, almost my idol', a description which says much about her nature and how it was reflected in her love life. In Crimea, Potemkin led Catherine around ancient Greek ruins and the sub-tropical gardens and exotic palaces of the khans. Here was a combination of Ovid and *The One Thousand and One Nights* from the Baghdad of the Abbasids. This was in fact a good metaphor for Catherine's entire life and reign.[18]

If Catherine's life reads like a fairy story, that in large part reflected its reality. But it also owed something to the fact that Catherine told the story of her life that way in her memoirs and her correspondence. The empress was a child of the Enlightenment. She knew how to craft an autobiography with herself as heroine and she did so with a sharp eye to the audience. She cared greatly for her historical reputation and glory. She was a consummate actress, and one sometimes has the feeling that she was acting herself in the great play of her life and greatly enjoying the role. For a monarch these were priceless qualities. Theatre was intrinsic to great monarchies. A monarch needed to be able to act a role: to charm, woo, persuade, frighten and inspire. It helped enormously if he or she enjoyed the job. Enjoyment contributed to stamina, and stamina was vital for a human being fated to do a job for life. But an effective monarch needed both to be an actor and be able to stand back from the role. Falling victim to the illusions of the royal theatre could be fatal.

Catherine was supremely able to avoid such pitfalls. She was a highly intelligent, tough, self-disciplined and self-aware realist. From her German, Protestant education she imbibed a strong work ethic. As empress she worked hard, rising early every morning and devoting hours to government papers. For a monarch, managing people was even more important than understanding the complexities of policy and administration. As a young woman of no outstanding beauty Catherine had learned how to appeal, listen and please. Life as crown princess had taught her to judge character but conceal her opinions. Experience and sensitivity, combined with a voracious reading of history, helped her to understand people and politics. The empress was justly famous for her choice and skilful use of able lieutenants. It helped that she had not been born on the steps of a throne. She knew that she had usurped the crown not only from her husband but even in a sense from her son, Paul. This bred caution and alertness, valuable traits in any ruler.[19]

Catherine's programme was summed up in her address to the representatives of the estates and peoples of her empire, a unique gathering which she summoned to Moscow in 1767: 'Russia is a European power.' As regards imperial power politics, Catherine faced one insurmountable taboo. In this and all other empires known to me a woman could not command her armies in battle. Actually, she was fortunate to be excused from this temptation since command in the field was a difficult and risky enterprise which lured some male monarchs to their destruction. In the crucial war of her reign, the 1768–74 conflict with the Ottomans, Catherine acted as an effective supreme commander. She set up and chaired a supreme war council. Its members offered the best advice and expertise available in Russia, but in the end it was Catherine who decided. Russian strategy was not blurred by conflicting opinions and ambitions, as had occurred in the Seven Years War. The empress was fortunate in having at her disposal some of the greatest generals in Russian history, but she had to recognize their talents amidst the babble of conflicting factions and she gave them the resources but also the freedom to achieve their victories.

Especially in the second half of the war Catherine came under enormous strain. Alarmed by Russia's victories, Prussia and Austria threatened to intervene. A devastating plague epidemic struck Moscow. A huge revolt exploded under the leadership of Emelian Pugachev among the Cossacks, serfs and native peoples of the Urals and Volga borderlands. The pressure on Catherine to concede a compromise peace to the Ottomans in order to concentrate on other threats was immense, but she stood firm. Her calculation of the dangers, strengths and weaknesses of her position proved exact. Her favourite, Grigorii Orlov, showed courage and competence in taking command in Moscow and managing the plague epidemic. Even with most of its army at war, the Russian state and social order proved much too strong to fall to peasant and Cossack rebellion. Clever and ruthless diplomacy diverted the Austrians and Prussians towards joining with Russia in the partition of Poland. Catherine's faith in her generals was justified: their victories in 1774 finally forced the Ottomans to accept her peace terms, which brought Russia crucial prizes.[20]

In domestic policy Catherine pursued but deepened Peter's agenda of Europeanization. She loved St Petersburg and lavished attention on it, seeing it as a well-ordered, rational and European model for Russia's future. Like Catherine, many monarchs sought to immortalize themselves in stone. But Catherine's building projects in her capital were also a statement about Russia's identity. Her 'Instruction' (*Nakaz*) for the 1767 assembly set out her vision for Russia as a prosperous, tolerant, educated and law-abiding part of the European cultural and political universe. The 'Instruction' was always more of a vision than a programme and the more deeply Catherine understood Russian realities, the more this became the case. The empress disliked serfdom but she knew that even the most cultured and European aristocrats at her court would turn against her if she challenged it. Nor did she have any means to replace the serf owners by government police, fiscal or military recruitment officers. The lesson of the Pugachev rebellion was that provincial Russia was drastically under-governed. Kazan province, overrun by Pugachev, had eighty permanent state officials and a population of 2.5 million. Catherine's top priority came to be the expansion, rationalization and proper funding of local government but she understood that little could be achieved unless local elites were encouraged to play a major role in administration, policing and justice. This was the purpose of the corporate institutions she created for provincial nobles, the role she designed for these bodies in local government, and her efforts to raise the cultural and educational level of the Russian gentry.[21]

The empress was a great traveller. She was brought up in Germany and spent her first seventeen years in Russia confined to the imperial court, so it was vital for her to see first-hand the realities of her empire. She also travelled to show herself to her subjects and inspect how her reforms were progressing. Catherine enjoyed her travels but she worked hard and briefed herself thoroughly in advance about the places and people she would be encountering. Sometimes provincial Russian realities were a great shock. Even more stunning were the non-Russian regions. After visiting Kazan for the first time in 1767 she wrote to Voltaire about the complexities of legislating for an empire: 'what a difference in climate, peoples, customs and even ideas! Here I am in Asia; I wanted to see it with my own eyes. There are twenty peoples of various kinds in this town, who in no way resemble one another. And yet we have to make a coat that will fit them all.' The improving and systematizing spirit of the Enlightenment found empire an alluring but also potentially dangerous challenge. Empire in general meant diversity. Its scale usually precluded close surveillance by central government. Trying to impose the Enlightened mix of state-led 'improvement' and homogenization on an empire could stir up great opposition. Catherine was too cautious and realistic to push the Enlightenment project to extremes. Nor did she have a government machinery capable of attempting this except in narrow fiscal-military terms. Her friend and ally, the Habsburg Emperor Joseph II, was less constrained and less cautious.[22]

Catherine's name resonates in the contemporary West above all as a woman with an exciting sex life. Being a female ruler caused few ripples in Russia by the 1760s since for almost all the years between Peter the Great's death and Catherine's accession the empire had been ruled by women. The young Princess Sophia of Anhalt-Zerbst was given the name 'Catherine' on converting to Orthodoxy in honour of Empress Elizabeth's mother, Catherine I, the second wife of Peter the Great. In 1725, the court faction that placed Catherine I on the throne faced the unprecedented challenge of legitimizing the rule not just of a woman but also of a woman who was the daughter of an Estonian peasant but had become Peter's mistress, his closest companion and subsequently his wife. The leaders of state and Church had devised a number of strategies to do this: one of them was to boost the existing cult of St Catherine of Alexandria, the fourth-century martyr. In the Russian society of that era, appealing to precedent and specifically to the Bible made the greatest impact on minds. St Catherine was praised for the manly courage evident in her martyrdom, which made her worthy to rule. Both she and, by association, Empress Catherine I were acclaimed by the church hierarchy for 'bearing in thy feminine body the manly wisdom of the mind'. As always where Orthodoxy and her legitimacy were concerned, Catherine II was assiduous in cultivating the saint's cult. In a more mundane manner, the previous empresses' love lives also created welcome precedents. Empress Elizabeth had been famous for her lovers. She had plucked her greatest love, Kirill Razumovsky, from the ranks of the imperial choir. Catherine wrote that he was probably the most handsome man that she had ever met.[23]

Easy access to all the most beautiful objects of one's sexual desire was one of the perks of power in almost all political traditions. Catherine had no man above her to stop this rule from applying in her case too. No doubt many divorced grandmothers would enjoy having the pick of handsome young officers as an antidote to loneliness and ageing. Catherine's upbringing had left her with few sexual inhibitions. At the risk of gross generalization, the sexual mores of Germany's Protestant upper class depended greatly on whether a family was influenced by Pietism. Emerging in the mid-seventeenth century, the Pietists called for a return to the pristine faith of Luther, to an inner world of spirituality and a life of hard work, charity and sincerity in society. They despised the 'French' model of loose morals and luxury. Brought up by a distinctly un-Pietist mother in a court culture that took Louis XIV's Versailles as its model, the young princess encountered many examples of illicit sexual relationships in her childhood and adolescence. Empress Elizabeth's court was even more free-wheeling in this respect. A deeply unattractive and indifferent husband necessitated a search for sexual fulfilment – even possibly for an heir to the throne – from other sources. As empress, Catherine never ran anything remotely like a harem. Serial monogamy was more or less her rule. She seems to have had no more than a dozen lovers. Most of her relationships ended when her young lovers sought other women. This must have been increasingly painful as age fed her insecurities, but she always treated her ex-partners generously. The manner in which she overflowed with love and enthusiasm for new partners and the traumas she suffered when these relationships broke down are rather touching.[24]

On the whole even Catherine's least inspiring favourites did little harm. Amidst the strains of rulership they provided her not just with sexual escape but also with the companionship she craved. Only in her last years were her relationships with men barely older than her grandchildren a source of embarrassment. Her last lover, the empty and pretentious Platon Zubov, interfered in government affairs in unprecedented and annoying fashion. But by then, after more than thirty years on the throne, Catherine's grip was beginning to weaken. Moreover, 'Uncle' Potemkin was no longer alive to provide emotional support and keep bumptious young favourites in their place. Even Zubov was a storm in a very small teacup in comparison to the impact on Ottoman politics of Suleyman's love for Hurrem. The obsession of the ageing Emperor Tang Xuanzong for the beautiful young consort Yang Yuhuan took one of history's greatest empires far down the path to destruction.[25]

Probably the fairest and most revealing comparison is with Catherine's contemporary, King Louis XV of France (r. 1715–74). The fact that Louis had a string of mistresses was hardly unusual in the history of Christian monarchies. The villa he maintained near his palace at Versailles where he entertained many young women, some of them semi-prostitutes, went well beyond Catherine's behaviour and was a source of scandal. Unable either to obtain absolution from his confessor or to control his sexual desires, Louis no longer 'touched' sufferers from scrofula, in the process contributing to the desacralization of the French monarchy. In one respect Louis was unluckier than Catherine. In France there already existed a scurrilous underground press and a civil society avid to read its scandalous tales. Nothing like this yet existed in Russia. The king's most famous and important mistress was Madame de Pompadour. Intelligent, well-educated and charming, she was in many ways a worthy female equivalent to Potemkin but, as a woman, could not play anything like his public role in war and government. Her male protégés were deeply implicated in creating the unpopular alliance with Austria in 1755–6 and then in leading French armies in some of the most humiliating defeats on the battlefield in the Seven Years War. As bad, Madame de Pompadour was closely linked to a financial group, the Paris brothers, who made fortunes by supplying the French armies amidst these disasters. Her name was associated in French minds with corruption, defeat, libertinism and humiliation. In contrast, Grigorii Potemkin and the Orlov brothers played leading roles in Catherine's greatest military triumphs.[26]

In November 1796 Catherine died and was succeeded by her son Paul I. He ruled until March 1801 when he was overthrown and killed in a coup which had widespread support among the St Petersburg aristocracy and Guards officers. So far in this chapter we have looked at the Romanov dynasty in the persons of its greatest monarchs. To some extent this bias towards successful emperors exists in other chapters too. It is useful to look at Paul as a case study in failure. In addition, conspiracy and assassination frequently occurred in the history of imperial monarchy. Of course, there were elements in the coup that overthrew Paul that were unique, but the history of his downfall also had aspects that were generic to court politics.[27]

Paul's personality played a key role in his overthrow. The emperor was not stupid and had been well-educated but his temperament fitted him badly for his job. He could be charming, well-informed and kind but he was subject to strong mood swings. At times these led to terrifying and violent bursts of anger, as well as to a suspiciousness that came close to paranoia. Some emperors we have encountered were also moody. Qing Yongzheng partly cured this through the discipline of Zen Buddhist meditation. Jahangir took opium and other emperors sometimes indulged in debauchery in order to keep their demons at bay. Paul's refuge was the spartan military mindset and austere self-discipline of his hero, Frederick II of Prussia. As age and the burdens of his office took their toll, it became increasingly obvious that this was not enough to sustain Paul's inner balance and calm. His violent mood swings affected his policy-making and his management of his ministers, generals and courtiers. Men demoted and disgraced almost on a whim might be restored to favour when Paul's mood changed. His strong and changeable emotions made the tsar a bad judge of character and loyalty. For example, one senior general whom he had disgraced was Baron Levin von Bennigsen. In a better mood, Paul was persuaded to reinstate Bennigsen and allow his return to St Petersburg. The man who persuaded him to do this was Count Peter von der Pahlen, the Governor-General of the capital and someone the emperor greatly trusted. Bennigsen became one of the key figures in the conspiracy that overthrew and murdered Paul. Pahlen was the conspiracy's leader.

Emperor Paul lacked not just emotional intelligence but also political nous and wisdom. A wholehearted autocrat and militarist, he took the army and military discipline as his model. The most dangerous illusion for any emperor was to believe the official rhetoric that he was all-powerful. In some respects Paul had the mentality of a corporal: he tried to regulate even what aristocratic ladies wore at private balls in St Petersburg. Paul disliked and distrusted the Russian aristocracy. He once said that there were no *grands seigneurs* in Russia except for men who were talking to the emperor and even they lost this status when the conversation ceased. He was partly correct: the Russian aristocracy was more dependent on the monarchy than was the case in France, let alone England. But he was also partly wrong and he paid for his mistake with his life. His arbitrary demotion and disgrace of key members of the elite hit their careers and ambitions but his behaviour also infringed their personal and corporate sense of honour and dignity. For example, he ended nobles' exemption from corporal punishment and reduced the role of elected nobles in local government. Paul's efforts were in direct conflict with the policy of earlier rulers to inculcate European culture and values into the Russian elite. They also conflicted with even older assumptions among the Russian aristocracy that they had the right to be their emperor's closest counsellors.

Paul's third key failure was in the realm of diplomacy and war, which in Russia as in most imperial monarchies was an emperor's core policy-making responsibility. Alarmed by growing French power, in 1798 Paul had gone to war against the French Republic in alliance with Britain and Austria. When the war went badly, the emperor blamed his allies and withdrew from the coalition. By late 1800 he had gone to the other extreme and was on the verge of allying Russia to France. He banned all trade with Britain, a devastating potential blow to the Russian economy and the state's finances since the British were by far Russia's most important export market. In a bizarre echo of an earlier nomadic era of warfare, he ordered a Cossack expeditionary corps to march through Afghanistan and threaten British rule in India. Most of Paul's advisers believed with good reason that his policy of alliance with France was contrary to Russia's interests and was bound to fail. General Bennigsen subsequently set out the reasons why this was the case in an intelligent, well-informed and convincing paper. Years later in his memoirs he wrote that he was moved by the sight of Paul's young daughters weeping over the body of their dead father and kissing his hand. But for the military and political elite of this (and any other) empire, *raisons d'état* might often compete for first place against personal and group interests but very seldom with sentiment.[28]

The best insider account of the events leading to Paul's overthrow is that of Countess Dorothea von Lieven. She lived at the heart of the imperial court and knew its secrets. Her mother had come to Russia from their native Wurttemberg with Paul's fiancée, the future Empress Marie, as lady-in-waiting and intimate. Dorothea's mother-in-law was Countess Charlotta von Lieven, the empress's closest friend and the governess of the imperial children. Catherine II had appointed this Pietist Baltic German noblewoman to this plum position because she believed that Charlotta would protect her grandchildren from the vices and temptations of the court. Dorothea's husband, Christopher, was the head of Paul's military secretariat. Since Paul ran the army personally and with obsessive attention to detail, Christopher was in most respects his chief military adviser and spent more hours with him every day than almost any other person. Christopher Lieven had good reason for gratitude to Paul. Among other things, the emperor had appointed him to his extremely powerful position at the age of twenty-two. Family tradition also pushed in the direction of loyalty. Along with much of the rest of the old feudal warrior-landowning class, in the seventeenth century many Lievens had become officers in a royal army, in their case the army of the Swedish kings. They prided themselves on having the loyalty unto death of a war-band leader's bodyguard. Among a whole menagerie of generals in the family, their paragon was an ancestor who, in the era before they became Russian subjects in 1721, had thrown himself in the path of a cannonball to save the life of his chief, the Swedish king.[29]

Christopher Lieven was tugged in opposite directions by his loyalty to Paul on the one hand and his fundamental disagreement with his policies on the other. Christopher was a professional soldier with a Lutheran conscience. He disliked the alliance with Napoleon. The orders despatching the Cossacks to India went out under his name and he hated the knowledge that he was sending most of them to their deaths on a futile adventure. Moreover, the Lievens were loyal to the Romanov dynasty as much as to Paul. Since the Romanovs were at war with themselves this posed problems. By 1800 Paul's paranoia had grown to include suspicion of his wife and his eldest son, the Grand Duke Alexander. One of Paul's first acts as emperor had been to promulgate a law of succession establishing the principle of male primogeniture and naming Alexander his heir. However, by the winter of 1800 he was muttering dark hints about the fate of Peter the Great's son, Alexei, whom the tsar had imprisoned and tortured to death. Paul now appeared to be cultivating his thirteen-year-old nephew, Prince Eugene of Wurttemberg, as a possible alternative heir. Charlotta Lieven was deeply loyal to the empress and was a positive tigress in defence of her charges, the imperial children. Christopher Lieven was close to the Grand Duke Alexander and was an officer in his regiment, the Semenovsky Guards. In the end he resolved the conflict of loyalties by taking to his bed with a surprisingly incurable illness in the hope that matters would resolve themselves before he needed to re-emerge. This happened on 11 March 1801 in the shape of Paul's overthrow and murder.

In the event, staying in bed proved the wisest tactic. No conspiracy to overthrow a tsar had any hope of success unless it could secure the support of a plausible successor. In 1801 the only possible successor was Alexander. After some hesitation he had lent his backing to the coup. Alexander was much less ambitious for power than his grandmother had been before the coup of 1762. For him the crown was a fate, not a choice. He had even dreamed of escaping his fate and living privately near the Rhine with his wife. But he was horrified by Paul's despotism and the disasters towards which his foreign policy was leading Russia. Alexander had insisted that his father's life must be spared and that he must be allowed a comfortable retirement. Pahlen had agreed, knowing full well that this promise could never be honoured. A living Paul would remain a mortal threat, not least because of his popularity among the ordinary soldiers of the Guards, whom he had often treated generously. No doubt some of them rather liked seeing their officers subjected to the arbitrary despotism which was often their own lot.

Alexander felt deep remorse at his father's death and never forgave the conspirators. A man like Christopher Lieven whose role in the affair was almost as equivocal as Alexander's own was much more acceptable to him, and even more so to the Dowager Empress Marie, whose opinions counted for much with the new tsar. Lieven remained a key military and diplomatic adviser to Alexander throughout his reign. The emperor died in 1825, to be succeeded by his younger brother, Nicholas I. When Charlotta Lieven died in the following year Nicholas was one of her four pall-bearers. Famous for his austere self-discipline, this was one of the very rare moments when he shed tears in public. All Dorothea's former charges were devoted to her. The Grand Duchess Anna, later queen of the Netherlands, recalled that it was Charlotta's 'unique privilege to scold the family ... this is granted neither by decree nor by hereditary title'. Even as an adult Nicholas I called her *Mutterkins*. Like most empresses in history, Marie had been a cool and remote mother to her young children. Charlotta had filled the emotional void. At its innermost core imperial monarchy was a family affair. Intimate relationships with members of the family counted immensely.[30]

For the true courtier, an emperor's tears were more recognition than the highest of orders or decorations. They took on some of the odour of the holy oil with which the monarch was anointed at his coronation. For some courtiers monarchical recognition and closeness became an end in itself and almost a devotional cult. But most courtiers in history were a hard-headed crew. They believed that tears would be followed by more tangible rewards. This certainly happened in the Lievens' case. From Catherine II to Nicholas I, four Romanov monarchs in succession lavished estates, titles, 'pensions' and positions on them. By the end of this wave of extravagance they were probably the richest landowners in the Baltic provinces, first-rank princes, and owned in addition big estates in Russia itself and the core of what became the Ukrainian coal-mining industry. The Lievens were an old family, who had been chieflings worshipping pagan gods in the forests of Livonia before the German knights arrived. By the time their homeland was annexed by Russia in 1721 they had become respectable barons and occasionally counts, but the imperial monarchy of the Romanovs was their El Dorado. The keys to El Dorado lay in the love of a mother and her children for their 'nanny'. To which one might add – in parenthesis – that the emotional balance of an emperor and solidarity among his siblings were key factors in the stability of hereditary monarchies. A governess who helped to achieve this played a more than purely private role. By dynastic standards, Nicholas I's relationship with his brother and predecessor, Alexander I, and his son and successor, Alexander II, were exceptionally warm and trusting.[31]

Alexander I ruled for twenty-four years. He was one of the most intelligent, complex and fascinating rulers in Russian history. His childhood and education were dominated by his grandmother Catherine II. She poured on to him her long-repressed maternal instincts and oversaw his education on the most advanced Enlightenment principles. It was Catherine who chose as his chief tutor the Swiss republican Frederick La Harpe. La Harpe gave Alexander a splendid education based above all on classical history and philosophy with some room too for French literature. His philosophy of education owed much to Rousseau. La Harpe's aim, as he explained to Catherine, was to teach Alexander as much of the humanities and sciences as was necessary to understand their basic principles and their importance but above all to make him aware that he must be 'an honest man and an enlightened citizen'. The heir must be educated to understand that power was given to him only in order for him to provide justice, liberty and security to his subjects and to do everything possible to increase their prosperity. La Harpe's greatest hero and role model was Marcus Aurelius. Here was the most just and public-spirited of emperors, who would have restored the republic had the Rome in which he lived made this possible. The parallels to an Enlightened Russian emperor living amidst autocracy and serfdom were clear. Alexander remained close to La Harpe for his whole life, commenting that 'I owed him everything' and once even saying 'had there been no La Harpe there would have been no Alexander'. La Harpe's principles dominated Alexander's plans for reforming Russian government and society.[32]

By 1810 Alexander's mind was beginning to turn towards religious answers to life's puzzles and problems. The immense strains which this sensitive and highly strung man bore with courage and steadfastness in the face of Napoleon's invasion of 1812 took him deeper in his search for religious truth and meaning. His was a search for a personal faith: it owed little to Orthodoxy or the official Church. Instead, it was based on intense reading of the Bible and of the writings of Christian mystics, most of whom were Catholics. Many people in Alexander's generation trod a similar path from Enlightenment to renewed Christian commitment. In part this was a reaction to the furies unleashed by the French Revolution and the following twenty-five years of international and civil war. Alexander's promotion of the Holy Alliance had much in common with Woodrow Wilson's crusade in 1918–19 for the League of Nations. After years of carnage both men sought ethical and institutional guarantees of international peace and security. Alexander's quest for a personal faith also paralleled Emperor Akbar's Sufi mysticism and the attraction of many Chinese emperors to Buddhist meditation. In Alexander's day it was still almost impossible for a European to move beyond the tradition of Christian thought and practice but within that tradition the emperor's views were ecumenical. He once wrote: 'Let us practice the Gospel – that is the main point. I do believe that all communions will one day be united.' In the last months of his life he was in secret communication with the Vatican as regards the coming together of the Catholic and Orthodox faiths.[33]

Alexander was a complicated man who lived in an era of immense conflict and change. Of course, his life and reign had many twists and turns. But two patterns running through the study of emperors provide some insights. Like many young monarchs, Alexander came to the throne aged twenty-three with interesting ideas and the best of intentions. He was steeped in the late-Enlightenment culture of simplicity, sensibility and friendship. His mother warned him that his simple and friendly behaviour had its dangers. A young monarch facing experienced and wily ministers needed to cultivate distance and to protect himself by the 'magic of grandeur' that surrounded his office. La Harpe reminded him that 'the emperor has to have an air' and that 'it was impossible for him to have true friends'. In 1801–5 Alexander gathered a tiny group of like-minded friends – the so-called Unofficial Committee – to advise him on a programme of radical reform, but the young men had no experience of turning ideas into policies and little understanding of how the government machine worked. Since the ideas they were discussing – the abolition of serfdom and the introduction of a constitution – were revolutionary in the Russian context their discussions had to remain a total secret, which was a further obstacle.

Also like many young monarchs, Alexander yearned for military glory.

From his earliest days, he had been reminded that he had been named partly after Alexander of Macedon. In 1805 he accompanied his army on campaign. At the battle of Austerlitz against Napoleon he listened to the advice of bumptious young aristocrats in his entourage and overrode the cautious, defensive strategy of his commander-in-chief, Mikhail Kutuzov. The result was disaster.[34]

The middle period of Alexander's reign was his time of greatest achievement, as was often the case with monarchs. Rulers by that point had gained experience of men, institutions and politics. Naïve enthusiasm had dissipated but exhaustion and disillusion had not yet replaced it. In Alexander's case these years saw the implementation of major and lasting reforms in central government and education, as well as the emperor's skilful and courageous leadership in the struggle to defeat Napoleon and create a stable international order in Europe.

After 1815 Alexander became increasingly exhausted and frustrated by the business of government. It was rather a comedown from liberating and reordering Europe to coping with the nitty-gritty of domestic administration and the difficulties of achieving results in the teeth of bureaucratic incompetence and powerful vested interests in society. Alexander's major domestic initiative in the last decade of his reign was an attempt to transform military conscription. The system he inherited wrecked the lives of countless peasants and their families by forcing young men into lifelong military service. Hundreds of thousands of potentially productive young men were removed from the economy in peacetime. Meanwhile when war came Russia had no trained reservists to mobilize. By settling much of the army into so-called military colonies and turning them into part-time farmers Alexander attempted to solve these problems. He had grandiose plans to introduce schools and welfare services in the colonies. The initiative collapsed in the face of resistance by both peasants and soldiers, and the frequent incompetence and brutality of the officials tasked with its implementation. There were similarities with the failure of the Song bureaucracy to implement the equally sweeping goals of the 'New Policies' in China seven hundred years before. The abject collapse of what Alexander saw as a rational and benevolent policy fed into his growing pessimism about human beings and the possibility of improving their lot by government policies. In this book we have encountered earlier emperors experiencing similar exhaustion and frustration, and a similar turn to religion and the inner world in response: Emperor Tang Xuanzong in the early eighth century comes immediately to mind.

After only two months on the throne Alexander had written to La Harpe that 'what gives me most difficulty and work is to reconcile individual interests and hatreds, and to make everybody cooperate for the single goal of generally being useful'. Very many leaders of large corporations and almost all heads of government no doubt felt and feel the same. But Alexander was less thick-skinned and power-hungry than most leaders who fight their way to power. Doomed to do the job for life, he felt the strain of leadership with increasing despair. After 1815 the emperor came increasingly to prefer female company to male, not in search of sex but simply because he found most men he encountered to be obsessed by ambition, rank and favour whereas women in his experience were more inclined to sincerity, emotion and the inner life. In 1819 he told his brother Nicholas, 'more than ever Europe needs young sovereigns with all their energetic strength; for me, I am no longer what I was, and I believe it my duty to retire before it is too late'. In Alexander's case, this was not posturing. The longing to escape was genuine but Russian precedents and political realities made abdication very difficult.[35]

As always, the key problem was the succession. Alexander and his beautiful wife, Princess Louise of Baden, had been married aged sixteen and fourteen and a half respectively. In time adolescent love cooled and Alexander looked to other women. True to his principles of sincerity and friendship (but also to the practices of his grandmother's court) he was indulgent when his wife – known in Russia as Empress Elizabeth – took lovers. When she bore a girl by her great love, a young Guards officer, Alexander recognized the child as his own, heaving a sigh of relief that it had not been a son, with all the consequences that might have had for the succession. The inner circle of family and courtiers knew the truth. The heir to the throne was Alexander's brother, the Grand Duke Constantine. He seems to have arranged the murder of his sister-in-law's lover to avoid possible further complications. Matters grew more confused when Constantine himself married a Polish noblewoman and resigned his rights to the throne in favour of Paul's third son, the future Emperor Nicholas I. Nothing in the empire's laws permitted such an abdication and the matter was kept a close secret. When Alexander died suddenly and far from his capital in 1825 chaos ensued.

A group of radical Guards officers attempted to stage a coup. Some wanted to impose a constitutional regime on the Romanovs, others to establish a republic. The coup was crushed but its memory hung over the whole thirty-year reign of Nicholas I. Had it succeeded, a tradition of military putschism might have entered Russian politics – as was happening in these years in Spain. In that case, Russian history might have taken a very different path.[36]

Like many emperors, Alexander found it easier to achieve success in external affairs. The levers of foreign policy – his army and diplomats – were relatively simple and under his exclusive control. He used them with great skill to achieve the defining triumph of his reign, the destruction of Napoleon's empire and the creation of a European order which made Russia far more secure than at any time since 1793. The emperor was personally responsible for formulating the grand strategy and conducting the diplomacy that made this victory possible. He believed that the only way to destroy Napoleon's huge army was to lure it deep into the Russian interior, wearing it down in a war of attrition that played to Russian strengths and Napoleon's vulnerabilities. This was the first stage of Alexander's two-stage strategy. He knew that simply expelling the French from Russia would not bring lasting security. If Napoleon was given respite to recover from the disaster of 1812 and retain his hold on Germany and central Europe, then in even the medium run Russia would lack the resources to protect herself against his mighty empire. Therefore, Alexander immediately advanced into central Europe in 1813 and drew Austria and Prussia into a victorious coalition that drove the French back across the Rhine and then toppled Napoleon. Both stages of Alexander's strategy were unpopular among Russian elites. It took all of his intelligence, resolution and subtlety to execute his plans but it also required the power of an autocrat.[37]

Alexander's strategy for domestic reform was much less successful. By now the 'progressive agenda' he imbibed from La Harpe had gone well beyond the Enlightened Despotism of Catherine's day and looked to the end of serfdom and the creation of a constitution. Alexander believed in both principles but the challenge was obvious since autocracy and serfdom were the foundations of his regime. Most of his ministers and senior officials owned serfs. In the provinces the government still depended on the help of the landowning class to police, tax and administer the population. Even the supposedly autocratic monarch in practice often had great difficulties in getting his policies executed in the enormous expanses of Russia. His administration was riddled with factions. Would not the creation of an independent elected legislature further weaken the monarch and enhance faction and division? The landowning aristocracy and gentry were by far the richest, most cultured and most powerful groups in Russian society. They would dominate any legislatures that constitutional reforms created. They were precisely the groups most committed to the defence of serfdom. The failure of Alexander's reform agenda was owed to objective circumstances. It increased his growing sense of exhaustion and disenchantment after 1815.

In key respects Alexander's defeat of Napoleon ended a cycle of Russian history that had begun with Peter the Great or even before. Peter's overriding goal had been to modernize Russia so that it could compete with the European great powers. In 1815 Russia had achieved this goal. Most observers recognized it as the most powerful state on the European continent. At a high level of generalization one could even make some comparisons between the regime of Nicholas I of Russia (r. 1825–55) and that of Emperor Qing Qianlong of China after the elimination of the nomad threat from the north. In both cases governments that felt confident in their geopolitical security had no reason to engage in potentially destabilizing radical reforms.

Unfortunately for both regimes, the onset of the Industrial Revolution in the first half of the nineteenth century revolutionized warfare and transformed the European and global balance of power. The Qing dynasty learned this first in the Opium War and the Romanovs in the Crimean War of 1854–6. Russia's enemies, the French and British, moved, fought and communicated with the technology of the industrial era. They travelled to the Crimea by railway and steamship. Russian reinforcements arrived there by the old pre-industrial method – in other words they walked or rode. Across the whole gamut of sources of power – from weapons to financial resources and communications technology – Russia was revealed as backward. The rulers of Russia's empire had no wish to follow the Mughals, the Ottomans and the Qing into decline and likely partition at the hands of the European powers. After 1856 they launched a programme of modernization that began with the abolition of serfdom. This programme was essential to their survival but it propelled them into a modern world that posed great new challenges both to empire and to hereditary monarchy. As empires go, the Romanovs' empire had been a great success. The problem now was to transform a successful pre-modern empire into a viable modern polity.

15

Europe on the Eve of Modernity: The Habsburgs, the French Revolution and Napoleon

With the long-awaited death of the incapable and childless Charles II in 1700 the Spanish branch of the Habsburgs ceased to exist. At this moment the Holy Roman Emperor was Leopold I, Charles's cousin. Leopold came to the throne in 1657 and died in 1705. The great historical enemy of the Habsburgs was France's Bourbon dynasty. Its most famous ruler was Louis XIV, who reigned from 1643 until 1715. Although Leopold was called an emperor and Louis merely a king, this did not mean that the French monarch, or any other European king, recognized the Holy Roman Emperor as having a superior rank or status. In European international law and diplomacy after the Treaty of Westphalia that ended the Thirty Years war in 1648, all sovereign monarchs had equal rights. Once Russia established itself as a European great power in the eighteenth century, the Habsburgs were finally forced to recognize not just the equal status of the tsar but also the fact that there were now two emperors in Europe.

Within the Holy Roman Empire the emperor did have a status superior to all other rulers, including the seven prince-electors. Leopold I also drew some rather small material advantages from his position as emperor. His real power rested on his position as hereditary king of Bohemia and Hungary, and hereditary prince of the Austrian, Alpine and Adriatic territories held by the Habsburgs. Nevertheless, in 1700 all these hereditary possessions combined had half the population of France and provided one-sixth as much revenue and one-tenth as many soldiers. Louis XIV also stood first in Europe in terms of soft power. Its embodiment was the palace and court society of Versailles, unrivalled in their scale and magnificence, and copied across Europe. In Louis's reign French high culture and the French language acquired the pre-eminent position in Europe that they were to retain until deep into the nine-teenth century. At his coronation the Bishop of Soissons had hailed Louis as 'the first of all kings on earth' and the theme was repeated end-lessly throughout his reign in sermons, rituals, poetry and painting. He was the Augustus of his age, the heir to imperial Rome and the Sun King. Louis saw himself as the greatest monarch in the leading region of the world, and one whose power was uniquely blessed by the only true God.[1]

Beyond question Louis XIV saw himself as king of kings and was enormously powerful. Does this make him an emperor? In my Introduc-tion, I defined empire in terms of power, territorial extent and diversity of peoples. If France's power was imperial in scale, its territories were not. At little more than 190,000 square miles in extent, it was dwarfed by its contemporaries, the Mughal and Qing empires. Louis did not face the age-old imperial conundrum of how to control elites and viceroys operating at huge distance from his capital. France's overseas colonies were still so insignificant that Louis XIV forgets to mention them in his Memoirs. Diversity is a more complex issue. The French kingdom was clearly less diverse in population than most of the great empires thus far encountered in this book. Nevertheless, the languages spoken by much of the population of western and southern France were incom-prehensible to a Parisian. Regions had different laws, institutions, taxes and loyalties. A leading historian of Old Regime France writes that 'rather than thinking of France as a coherent nation-state, we might do better to consider it a polyglot empire, with a wide range of local inst-itutions adapted to many local cultures'. As this suggests, the modern Western mind juxtaposes empire and nation. Louis XIV's France was neither a fully fledged empire nor a true nation in our usual contempor-ary understanding of these concepts. From the perspective of a Qing monarch, both Louis XIV and Leopold I were at best rather paltry emperors. Rather than fighting fruitlessly about what constitutes a true definition of empire, perhaps the most interesting point is that the case of Louis XIV's France suggested that, in terms of power, the future might lie not with vast and sprawling empires but with medium-scale polities which were easier to control, exploit and develop.[2]

Both as human beings and rulers, the contrast between Leopold and Louis was stark. Louis was the model and inspiration for many Euro-pean monarchs from the mid-seventeenth to the mid-eighteenth

The Habsburg Lands in 1748

centuries. His panache and charisma were famous. His every word and movement radiated majesty. He made the parade of military glory, mistresses and great palaces the fashion for a modern monarch. Leopold was small, ugly and short-sighted. He had minimal presence, was resolutely chaste and completely un-martial. One ambassador wrote that his swollen lips contributed to giving him the look of a camel, though most camels do not wear spectacles. The difference between the two men was to some extent embodied in their main palaces. Louis's Versailles was superb, ostentatious and in parts almost pagan in its celebration of the king's superhuman qualities and triumphs. His path of military glory and conquest loomed large in its decoration. By contrast, the Hofburg, Leopold's main palace, was cramped, pokey and modest – almost a metaphor in stone for the Emperor Leopold's personality. The Hofburg was squeezed into Vienna, a far smaller city than Paris and one which in Leopold's time was still almost a frontier town, encircled by walls. In the famous siege of 1683 Vienna came within a whisker of falling to the Ottomans.[3]

Leopold's grandfather, Ferdinand II (r. 1619–37), had reasserted the Habsburgs' deep commitment to Catholicism and the Counter-Reformation. Ruling in the first half of the Thirty Years War, he saw himself as a warrior for the faith, a true heir of Charles V and Philip II. Educated by the Jesuits, he was a devout Catholic who usually spent one hour in prayer and spiritual reading after he woke, and then attended two masses, one of them dedicated to the repose of the soul of his first wife. Most of his Sundays and Feast Days were given over to religious reflection, ceremony and devotions. Ferdinand was convinced that his dynasty's flourishing was rooted in God's support for a family that had committed itself so totally to His cause. One of the most famous images and memories of Ferdinand came from a moment of defeat and acute crisis in the Thirty Years War. The emperor for an hour lay 'stretched out on the floor in front of the cross', praying that he might devote himself only to God's glory, in whose cause he would bear all the tests and sufferings imposed on him with not just humble submission but also with the true joy of a penitent. Subsequently, Ferdinand recalled that 'his prayers had rendered him hopeful and completely calm within'. It was widely believed among his subjects that Christ Himself had spoken to the emperor from the Cross, reassuring him that 'I will not desert you'. In Ferdinand's reign the Eucharist, the Cross and the Immaculate Conception of the Virgin Mary became core elements of Habsburg ideology and identity.[4]

Ferdinand II's definition of dynastic identity ruled his descendants until the mid-eighteenth century. Leopold I was the perfect embodiment of this identity. Devout, rather introspective and with no charisma or talent for theatre, the emperor's personality was influenced by the fact that, as a second son, he had been trained for a career in the Church and for dutiful submission to his elder brother, the presumed future emperor and head of the dynasty. When both his brother and his father, Ferdinand III, died in quick succession Leopold suddenly found himself doing a job for which he was ill-suited by training or character. His biographer calls him 'a quiet young gentleman content to let things run as they had done in the past'. Forced to learn the business of rulership on the job, it is hardly surprising that Leopold initially lacked confidence in his own ability or judgement. In time, experience bred in him a degree of well-informed and cautious realism. He became a good judge of men. One element in his style of rulership never changed: Leopold had absolutely no hankering for military glory. When the Turks besieged Vienna in 1683 the emperor retreated safely to the rear, entrusting his armies to Prince Charles of Lorraine. In this case too, Leopold was an extreme example of a Habsburg trait: few emperors tried to command their armies in war. On the other hand, in a dynasty famous for its appreciation of music, Leopold was the most talented of all Habsburg musicians, a composer of sacred works. The emperor's personal modesty was combined with enormous pride in his dynasty. In Leopold's eyes the most crucial aspect of his duty was to maintain God's blessing on the Habsburgs by defending the Catholic faith, setting a personal example of chastity and charity, and fulfilling 'the quasi-sacramental character of his high earthly office'. The latter above all meant leading the many rituals, processions, pilgrimages and ceremonies that linked Catholicism to the dynasty and its lands.[5]

At a pinch one might describe Leopold as the closest a European emperor could come to the ideal of Confucian monarchy. The comparison is not as far-fetched as it might seem at first glance. At the same moment that some Jesuits were educating Leopold I, others were in Beijing attempting to convert Emperor Kangxi and the Chinese elite to Christianity. By then Jesuit missionaries had been in China for a century. Most of them admired Confucianism as a system that promoted ethics, high culture and social order. They believed that Catholicism could live happily alongside Confucian practices and complement them. To an extent there are parallels here to the admiration of the poet Matthew Arnold – whose father Thomas was the father of the modern English public school – for the Stoic ethics and culture of Marcus Aurelius. Arnold believed that adding Christian doctrines of salvation and love to the Stoicism of Marcus provided the ideal basis for the formation of the contemporary British and imperial ruling class. Of course, some Confucian traditions such as ancestor-worship had their problems for a Jesuit, but the missionaries were convinced that these could be nuanced. In a sense the alliance of the Catholic Church, and especially the Jesuits, with the Habsburg dynasty provided a precedent. The Habsburgs did not literally worship their ancestors in Confucian style but their sense of identity and mission were driven by a deeply held belief in their dynasty's destiny, illustrated by its history and earned by its age-old service to supernatural truths.[6]

Leopold's oldest son and successor, Joseph I (r. 1705–11), was very different and was the least typical Habsburg of this era. He even lacked the usual physical attributes of the dynasty, the protruding jaw and lower lip. Uniquely among Habsburgs, Joseph was not educated by Jesuits. He never visited the great Marian shrine at Mariazell, the key symbol of the devotion of his dynasty and empire to the Virgin. His many love affairs and his appetite for military glory left Leopold aghast. So too did some of his ideas about modernizing the Habsburg system of rule. When Joseph died suddenly in 1711 leaving only two daughters the dynasty reverted to type in the shape of his brother, Charles VI (r. 1711–40). Charles had been the Habsburg candidate for the Spanish throne and between 1705 and 1711 had fought in Spain to secure his rights there. On leaving for the front, he left instructions for his wife that reminded her of the Habsburgs' devotion to God and the Virgin Mary and stated that 'on account of this devotion, he had witnessed the rise and preservation of his dynasty'. Charles remained sure until he died that he was the legitimate king of Spain and many Spanish émigrés remained members of his entourage. Dearest to Charles's heart was his massive project to turn the abbey at Klosterneuberg into his own Escorial. The greatest living British expert on the eighteenth-century Habsburgs calls Charles 'lugubriously pious and bigoted'.[7]

The Habsburg alliance of dynasty, aristocratic magnates and Church had its costs. The Council of Trent had defined Catholicism in terms diametrically opposite to Protestantism. Against the culture of the written word, Scripture and reason it had elevated the senses, symbols and mysticism. In theology the Habsburg trinity of the true presence of Christ in the Eucharist, the mystery of the Cross and veneration of the Virgin Mary were core elements in the attack on Protestantism. Religion overlapped into culture. 'Visual, tactile, theatrical and emotional, this is the culture of images: anything associated with the Word is conspicuously absent.' Repression and mass emigration took their toll: in Bohemia and Moravia alone, in the 1620s roughly 150,000 people emigrated, including one-quarter of the nobility. 'As the casualties had included Protestantism, the bourgeoisie, the towns and urban culture', the Habsburg Empire became 'essentially static, conservative and defensive'. Between the reigns of Ferdinand II and the second half of the eighteenth century the Habsburg lands produced not a single philosopher or scientist of note. They became in European terms an economic and intellectual backwater.[8]

The impact of backwardness on Habsburg power was enhanced by the fact that the dynasty's aristocratic and ecclesiastical allies took a vast share of the empire's wealth. In Moravia, one of the empire's richer provinces, a fifth of the rural population lived on the estates of the princes Liechtenstein, and more than half the remaining population on lands owned by the great monasteries. In mid-seventeenth century Hungary thirteen aristocrats owned 37 per cent of all the land. Monasteries owned half of all the province of Carniola. Aristocrats and abbots dominated the provincial estates which administered the various provinces. A truly Habsburg administration existed only in Vienna. In some geopolitical contexts this might not have mattered. In the multi-polar world of European geopolitics the limited resources flowing to the central government made the empire vulnerable to predators.[9]

On the surface Charles VI's empire looked strong. His share of the Spanish Empire included the rich southern Netherlands (i.e. today's Belgium) and all southern Italy, giving the Habsburgs domination of the peninsula. Meanwhile, under the inspiring leadership of Prince Eugene of Savoy the Habsburg armies had conquered the whole of Hungary and Transylvania, as well as the region around Belgrade. As usual, increased territories meant greater military commitments: the Habsburgs' borders (even excluding the Netherlands and southern Italy) stretched for 2,500 miles. But most of these borders had good natural defences, meaning mountain ranges. The core of the empire within the mountains was integrated in strategic, economic and cultural terms by the River Danube and its tributaries. On the other hand, even the Danube had its limits: unlike the Rhine, the river did not flow through Europe's economic heartland. Nor did the Habsburgs control its outlets into the Black Sea.

Above all, the empire was surrounded by potential enemies whose combined resources greatly exceeded its own. External invaders might find allies among the disaffected elites of some Habsburg provinces. If Hungarian rebellion was a near-perennial threat, at the empire's moment of supreme crisis in 1741-2 the estates even of Bohemia and Upper Austria swore allegiance to the newly crowned Holy Roman Emperor, the Bavarian elector Charles Albert, in an effort to retain their lands and curry favour with what appeared to be an invincible invader. France was already much richer and more populous than the Habsburg Empire in 1700. With the cadet branch of the Bourbons established in Madrid, the Austrians after 1714 faced a strong risk of simultaneous French invasions of the empire's core down the upper Danube and Franco-Spanish invasions through northern Italy down the River Po. Although the Ottomans in the eighteenth century were much less of a threat than in the past, they were still capable of defeating the Austrians in 1737–9 and could force a major diversion of Habsburg troops if acting together in wartime with their traditional allies, the French. Much more serious was the threat in the north. Swedish intervention in the Thirty Years War had stopped Ferdinand II's hitherto victorious armies from imposing Habsburg domination throughout Germany. After defeat by Peter I's Russia the Swedish threat faded, only to be replaced within a generation by the even greater threat of Prussia.[10]

Prussia ought not to have been a serious threat. In 1740 the Habsburg emperor ruled 20 million subjects and the king of Prussia only 2.25 million. Located on a sandy and infertile plain, Prussia had few natural resources and no natural defences against outside attack. During the Thirty Years War the Hohenzollerns had been forced to look on helplessly as their territories were devastated by rival foreign armies. The Great Elector, Frederick William of Brandenburg-Prussia (r. 1640–88), learned a harsh lesson in power politics. During his long reign he laid the foundations of the formidable eighteenth-century Prussian state. He created a central administration to oversee the many separate provincial institutions. He squeezed much greater revenues from the provincial estates, using this income to create a strong army. Faced by a looming threat of war with France and needing the Hohenzollerns' support, in 1701 the Emperor Leopold I allowed them to assume royal status as kings in Prussia. Even so, in 1700 there was nothing inevitable about Prussia's emergence as the great power of northern Germany. The electorate of Saxony, for example, was richer than Prussia and had an army of equal size. Its ruler was also king of Poland.

The reign of Frederick William I (r. 1713–40) transformed the situation. Frederick William eliminated his father's expensive court, lived frugally, avoided all cultural projects, and invested every penny in 'hard power', creating a formidable army of 80,000 men and a large surplus in his treasury. At its peak in his reign, the army is reckoned to have enlisted over 7 per cent of the Prussian population in its ranks at a time when roughly 1.5 per cent of Charles VI's subjects served in his army. The Saxon elector-kings turned Dresden into one of the jewels of

European culture but by 1740 their army was one-third the size of Prussia's. Frederick II (r. 1740–86) used this army, whose infantry was the best-trained in Europe, to conquer Silesia in the 1740s. This was the richest province in the Habsburg Empire, containing one-third of the empire's industry and contributing a third of all Habsburg revenues. Its acquisition almost doubled the Prussian population and made Prussia a great power. Very soon, the efficient Prussian administration had doubled the revenues raised from Silesia by the Habsburgs without needing to increase taxes. Contemporaries sometimes called Prussia a barracks state and Europe's Sparta. One should not push such comparisons too far. The king's control over society was far from total. Among the obstacles in his path were private property, the Protestant conscience, the almost autonomous world of the noble estate, and the civil society that was growing up in urban Prussia in Frederick's reign. Nevertheless, much more even than Louis XIV's France, Prussia was a striking example of how a medium-sized kingdom could manage, develop and tax its resources more effectively than a huge empire.[11]

Royal leadership was crucial to Prussia's rise. The Great Elector and kings Frederick William I and Frederick II were among the ablest (and least pleasant) hereditary monarchs in history. Frederick II was not just a first-class political leader and chief administrator but also the most famous general of his age. In addition, he was a political thinker, historian, writer, composer and flautist of merit. Just as Louis XIV had defined the marks of kingship in the Baroque era, so Frederick II was the model Enlightened monarch. The Habsburg Empress Maria Theresa (r. 1740–80) regarded him as a monster because of his open atheism, his ruthless pursuit of Realpolitik, and his theft of her richest province. To her horror, her son Joseph II (r. 1765–90) saw him almost as a role model in his total dedication to his state, his utilitarian conception of kingship, his caustic wit and his military glory. Frederick shunned all ritual and ceremony, barely participated in court society, and concentrated on his role as chief executive officer of the Prussian state and commander of its armies. Joseph sought to emulate him in this.[12]

Frederick's wars had a devastating impact on society. The Prussian exploitation of occupied Saxony in the Seven Years War was sufficiently ruthless to fund roughly one-third of the war effort. The conflict cost the lives of one-tenth of Prussia's own population. War in Europe was very far from being just 'the sport of kings'. It was nevertheless far short of warfare in the Chinese era of Warring States, in which, for example, Qin commanders could order the killing of all 400,000 men of the surrendered army of a great-power rival. This was far beyond the imagination or moral compass even of a free-thinking Machiavellian such as Frederick II. In geopolitical terms there was another crucial difference between Prussia and the Qin. The 'iron' state created by the Hohenzollerns united Germany in 1871 and in the twentieth century made two devastating attempts to conquer Europe. Unlike the Qin, Prussia was not placed on the edge of its international system of states and thereby able to draw on the resources of an extensive hinterland. To its east lay the great Eurasian empire of Russia, whose intervention was of decisive importance in stopping the German drive to create a European empire.

In the late 1730s the Habsburg Empire seemed ripe for plucking. Deprived of Prince Eugene's inspiring leadership, its armies had deteriorated. Naples was lost to the Bourbons and Belgrade to the Ottomans. The state's bankruptcy forced the abandonment mid-stream even of Charles VI's pet project to build a new Escorial palace in the monastery of Klosterneuburg. Worst of all, Charles had produced only daughters, the elder of whom was the future empress Maria Theresa. No woman could be Holy Roman Emperor, so the Habsburgs lost the status and the access to some of the empire's resources that went along with this title. Although Charles made little attempt to secure this title for Maria Theresa's husband, Prince Francis Stephen of Lorraine, he did put great effort into securing the succession to all the Habsburgs' own lands for his daughter. The so-called Pragmatic Sanction guaranteeing Maria Theresa's rights was agreed by the estates of all the Habsburg lands, as well as by most of the European powers, including France and Prussia. Whether rival powers would abide by this promise once Charles was dead was always moot. The electors of Bavaria and Saxony, who had married daughters of Charles's elder brother, Joseph I, had some reason to argue that their wives' claims were better than Maria Theresa's.

As heiress to the Habsburg lands, Maria Theresa was the most eligible bride in Europe. Had she rather than her cousin Maria Amalia married the Bavarian heir European history might have taken a different turn. Uniting the lands of Germany's two leading Catholic dynasties would have created a powerful bloc against Prussian expansionism. Although Protestants were at the forefront of economic and cultural development in eighteenth- and nineteenth-century Germany, much of the heartland of the Industrial Revolution in western Germany and Silesia was in Catholic-majority areas. By 1900 their numbers, their geographical position and their economic, intellectual and cultural dynamism had made the Germans the leading people on the European continent. The key question was whether German power could be utilized for Europe's benefit rather than for its destruction. Just possibly a super-state incorporating most German Catholics but also the other peoples of central Europe within the Habsburg imperial tradition of respect for diversity, multi-ethnicity and law might have gone some way to resolving this conundrum. It could hardly have done worse than the twentieth-century heirs to the Prussian tradition.

Dynastic chance ruled out a Bavarian marriage for Maria Theresa. In both personal and genetic terms she was better off with Francis Stephen of Lorraine as her husband. The prince was the grandson of Vienna's saviour in 1683. He had been brought up at the Austrian court and the young couple fell in love and lived in a happy marriage that lasted until Francis Stephen's death in 1765. Charles VI and his wife, Princess Elizabeth-Christine of Brunswick-Wolfenbuttel, were not closely related and nor were Maria Theresa and Francis Stephen. She gave birth to sixteen children, of whom ten outlived her. Many of these children turned out to be highly intelligent and competent. By contrast, the marriage of Maria Theresa's likeliest Bavarian bridegroom, the future elector Maximilian Joseph III, was childless. Had he married his cousin, Maria Theresa, the genetic consequences might have been unhappy.

Maria Theresa received an education not much inferior to the average German Catholic prince of her generation. The main difference was that she was taught nothing about law. As the more enlightened Austrian aristocrats were beginning to realize, the typical Catholic – which generally meant Jesuit – education rooted in knowledge of classical history, Aristotle and Aquinas was inferior to that now offered to Protestant elites in the north German universities. Like her Catholic male peers Maria Theresa knew nothing about Thomas Hobbes, René Descartes, Samuel von Pufendorf or Christian Wolff – key sources of modern German ideas about politics, administration, philosophy and law. Life at court as a young woman taught her something about managing personal relations and patronage within the elite: in Vienna as in almost all monarchical regimes this was the stuff of politics. But although Charles

VI gave Francis Stephen a place in his political and military councils, he allowed his daughter no role in either.

Maria Theresa deeply loved Francis Stephen and called him 'the best of husbands' but once she succeeded her father in October 1740 she immediately made it clear who was boss. The fact that from 1749 Francis was Holy Roman Emperor and Maria Theresa merely empress consort was irrelevant. More than ever, Habsburg power was rooted in their hereditary lands, not in the Holy Roman Empire from which they derived their imperial title. Throughout her reign Maria Theresa acted as chief political officer and chief administrator of her empire. This fitted her intense sense of her duty and right as head of the dynasty and heiress to the Habsburg tradition. It suited her strong-willed and powerful personality. She worked hard both as head of the bureaucratic machine and final decision-maker, and as the manager of personnel and patronage. She carried out the ceremonial duties of her office conscientiously. Meanwhile she gave birth to sixteen children and was a much more emotionally involved and 'hands-on' mother than the average eighteenth-century queen. As this suggests, the empress had great stamina and toughness. She possessed both intellectual and emotional intelligence. She had an instinctive grasp of the human psyche and combined this with common sense, beauty and warmth. With rare exceptions she chose able lieutenants and inspired great and sustained personal loyalty among her top advisers.[13]

Within a year of her accession Maria Theresa faced an acute crisis. French, Prussian, Bavarian and Spanish armies occupied parts of her empire. In the winter of 1741–2 it seemed probable that the Habsburg Empire would be dismembered, leaving Maria Theresa as little more than queen of Hungary. The Habsburgs were saved in part by skilful diplomacy which divided their enemies and secured assistance from the British and Dutch. The empire's 'strategic depth' allowed it to mobilize great resources from its southern (Border/Grenze) and eastern (Hungarian) provinces, untouched by invasion. This was possible only because the Ottomans remained neutral and unthreatening. Maria Theresa showed great courage, energy and political skill in responding to the crisis. The most famous episode in this response was her coronation in Hungary which she combined with an unprecedented, direct and emotional appeal to Hungarian elites for support. One historian calls her handling of the Hungarian parliament 'a public relations coup'. It certainly showed at their best her theatrical qualities and her ability to play on public emotions. The years 1740–5 were Maria Theresa's glory years. Subsequently her friend and mentor, Count Emmanuel Silva-Tarouca, recalled that in this period the young empress had needed to 'learn the ABC of rulership'. She had worked hard enough for four people and produced a child every year, yet somehow she had found the energy to ride too fast, dance, go out in society, and lift the spirits of all who met her by her charm, energy and conversation. 'She found the time to do everything and to do it well.'[14]

Peace finally came in 1748 at the price of ceding Silesia, and for the next fifteen years Maria Theresa concentrated her energies on regaining the province and punishing Frederick II for his perfidy. Preparation for revenge against Prussia occurred in three main areas: domestic administration and finance; military; diplomatic. The empress carried out radical administrative reforms in the Austrian and Bohemian provinces that doubled state revenue. She exploited the guilt of some provincial estates for their disloyalty during the war and the fear that all of them felt at the prospect of conquest by Frederick's Protestant and exploitative regime. The new revenues were used to create an army equal in size and not much inferior in quality to the Prussian. Most remarkably, Count (later Prince) Wenzel Anton Kaunitz, one of eighteenth-century Europe's shrewdest statesmen and diplomats, created an Austrian–French–Russian–Swedish coalition against Prussia. Wooing Louis XV away from centuries of French hostility to the Habsburgs was his crowning achievement.[15]

The allied coalition was far superior in power to Prussia and ought to have triumphed in the Seven Years War of 1756–63. It failed to do so because of the incompetence of French generals, the difficulties of co-ordinating Austrian and Russian military operations, and bad luck. The caution and factional divisions within the Habsburg high command were also important. As a woman all the empress could do, sitting in Vienna, was to urge aggression on her generals and implore them to sacrifice their personal ambitions to a higher (i.e. her) cause. By contrast, as sovereign and battlefield commander Frederick II could squash factional infighting and impose his own aggressive mindset on his generals. The enormous costs of the Seven Years War and the failure of the seemingly invincible coalition turned Maria Theresa against war and foreign policy adventures for the rest of her reign. But it in no sense reduced her faith in Kaunitz, who in the 1760s and 1770s became her most influential adviser not just on foreign policy but also on key domestic issues as well.[16]

In 1765 Francis Stephen died, throwing the empress into despair. He was succeeded as Holy Roman Emperor by their eldest son, Joseph II. Devoted to reason, utility and Realpolitik, the new emperor had little interest in this position. Far more important to him was his appointment as co-regent of the Habsburg lands. Although Maria Theresa retained the final say on policy, in the last fifteen years of her reign Joseph's influence became increasingly strong. Mother and son were seldom in agreement. In part this was just the clash of two strong-willed personalities, both of whom were brought up to exercise sovereign power. The generation gap between them resulted in disagreement on key policies, especially where questions of religion were concerned: Maria Theresa was the devout product of Counter-Reformation Habsburg piety and Baroque culture, whereas Joseph became a disciple of Enlightenment utilitarianism and reason. As regards foreign policy, Joseph's bellicose pursuit of Realpolitik often appalled and alarmed his mother. Their manner of ruling was also different. Maria Theresa operated through personal relationships and the cultivation of loyalty and trust. Joseph was notoriously inept at human relations and tended to regard governing as a matter of pulling the levers of the bureaucratic machine. Extra volatility and emotion were added to their relations by the fact that in their own way mother and son loved each other, were obsessed by each other, and interpreted disagreement as rejection and even betrayal.[17]

Prince Kaunitz represented the third pillar in this extraordinary triumvirate. Joseph shared his mother's admiration for Kaunitz's intellect: this remained true even after Maria Theresa's death when Joseph was sole ruler and Kaunitz was almost the only adviser to whom he paid any degree of deference. During the co-regency the chancellor became the intermediary and balancer between the two Habsburgs. This tried his nerves but increased his influence and indispensability. Kaunitz himself was an eccentric and vain person, hyper-sensitive to perceived slights. He was also a neurotic hypochondriac, terrified of fresh air and rain, and much inclined to take to his bed in moments of crisis. The relations between the three figures at the head of Habsburg government were peppered with emotional tantrums and threats to resign, withdraw and abdicate. They had the makings of a good opera. The characters and the libretto of this opera are wonderful but their fascination should not distract one entirely from underlying features of the regime they headed. It never crossed Maria Theresa's mind to try to exclude Joseph from the succession. Nor could Joseph even imagine the possibility of displacing his mother by extra-legal means. Bringing the army into dynastic politics was equally unimaginable. European dynastic right was by now deeply rooted in universally accepted ideas of law and legitimacy. Their long reign as rulers of the Holy Roman Empire – of all empires in history the one most immersed in constitutional law – added a specifically Habsburg emphasis to this European tradition.[18]

For all the tantrums and the disagreements of its top leaders, much was achieved by the Habsburg regime in the last years of Maria Theresa's reign. Central government revenues grew from 35 million florins in 1763 to 50 million by 1780. The army grew to 300,000 men and a line of fortresses was built in Bohemia which stymied Frederick II's attempted invasion in 1778–9. The coordination and efficiency of central government institutions increased markedly and for the first time its growing apparatus at provincial and district level allowed it to intervene effectively in the lives of its peasant subjects. A key underlying motif of Maria Theresa's reign was that the state needed to take a larger share of the peasant surplus if it was to survive in the competitive world of European geopolitics. As the bureaucracy spread downwards, Maria Theresa became more aware that simply squeezing the peasantry harder would be both immoral and ineffective. The horrendous famine of 1770–1 rammed home this point. So too did Joseph's detailed accounts of his inspection tours in the provinces. In the last years of her reign Maria Theresa was moving in the direction of radical reforms designed to improve the peasantry's legal rights and prosperity.

Her greatest success probably lay in the transformation of primary education, a cause to which she was deeply committed. By the end of her reign the monarchy had over 200,000 students in 6,000 schools, together with a rapidly growing cadre of well-trained teachers. Maria Theresa's main guide as regards educational reform was Johann Felbiger, an Augustinian abbot but a Prussian subject. Here as in so many cases the empress drew on expertise from outside the core Habsburg lands and their traditions. By the 1770s, however, her efforts had created a well-educated home-grown bureaucratic elite committed to the reformist but moderate agenda of the German Enlightenment. Its watchword was state-led reform to raise the economic, legal and cultural position of the masses, thereby increasing overall economic prosperity and government revenues.

Franz von Greiner belonged to this new elite and was a key figure at the centre of Habsburg government who steered radical reform of primary education past its many critics in the administration and the aristocracy. Greiner is a fine example of a man who combined the public-service values and professional competence of a modern state official with a deep personal loyalty and almost religious veneration for his sovereign. His wife was Charlotte Hieronymus, Maria Theresa's dresser, hair stylist and reader, who had become the most devoted and trusted of all the empress's domestic servants. Maria Theresa 'rescued' a number of Protestant orphans, converted them to Catholicism, and took responsibility for their education and careers. Charlotte Hieronymus was the most intelligent and successful of these children. The story of Franz von Greiner and Charlotte Hieronymus encapsulates Maria Theresa's dual role as chief executive officer of the Habsburg state and Catholic mother of her people.[19]

Maria Theresa's views on her role as empress and on how to be an effective ruler are best understood in her own words through the two testaments she wrote in the 1750s and through the instructions she gave to her eighteen-year-old son, Leopold, when he departed to take up his position as Grand Duke of Tuscany. Her view on sovereignty was the traditional one of a Habsburg dynast. The dynasty ruled through God's support and blessing, given because the Habsburgs had served His cause over the generations. Her key conviction was 'to trust in God alone, whose Almighty power has chosen me for this position without any desire or action of my own, and who therefore will have made me worthy to fulfil this calling which has been imposed upon me'.

The near-catastrophe of the early 1740s had taught her that if the Habsburgs and their mission were to survive, deep reforms of the state bequeathed to her by her father were essential. At the core of these reforms had to be a bigger share for the crown of the empire's revenues which had to come at the expense of the elites. The empress was in no sense a social leveller. The aristocracy were her natural allies whose rights and status must be respected. Monarchy and hierarchy were essential to the survival of a just, orderly and prosperous society. But within that social order the monarch was the mother of her people, their only protector against injustice and oppression. To place that responsibility above all private interests and feelings was, she told Leopold, essential for legitimate monarchy and for the flourishing of their dynasty and its mission.[20]

Maria Theresa wrote that she would not attempt to give her son detailed advice on how to rule Tuscany because a ruler could only act upon close knowledge of his country and people. Leopold must dedicate himself to acquiring this knowledge and he must take no major decisions before he had done so. There were no short cuts for the good ruler: hard work was essential. To stand above and arbitrate between the conflicting views and interests of his advisers the monarch had to go into matters in detail, build up his knowledge and experience, and form his own opinions. 'The truth gets through to those of us who sit on thrones only with great difficulty, or it is so camouflaged that one cannot recognize it.' Leopold must never retain among his councillors anyone who had lied to him or deliberately covered up the whole truth. He must make their demotion public, as a deterrent to others. He must not give his trust quickly or easily to anyone but once he had tested a minister carefully he must back him entirely and unconditionally. Keeping tabs on his officials was necessary but publicly undermining them or going behind their backs to their subordinates destroyed efficient governance and was always a mistake. He must never promise anything to petitioners or advisers on the spot and without consideration. He must learn to say no politely and without harming people's self-esteem. He must also be tough with miscreants and punish where necessary, without hardening his own personality or forgetting the benevolence inherent in his position as monarch. He must be a model of upright behaviour, morals and religious observance for his subjects to follow. In her normal fashion when writing even to her grown-up children the empress also reminded him to say his prayers at night, send her and her private doctor daily reports if he suffered even minor illness, and to banish nude statues and paintings from all his homes and palaces.[21]

Maria Theresa's death in 1780 was followed by ten years of Joseph II's sole rule. Radical reforms, previously checked by his mother's caution and conservatism, now followed one another at great speed. Religious toleration and full civil rights for Protestants and Jews came first. There followed a great reduction in the obligations owed by peasants to their lords, which threatened bankruptcy for many of the lesser nobles. Unlike his mother, Joseph extended his religious and agrarian reforms beyond the core territories of his empire. He tore up the constitutions of Hungary and the Belgian provinces, imposing new, streamlined and authoritarian institutions allowing minimal possibilities for local input. In his foreign policy he botched his second attempt to swap Bavaria for the Austrian Netherlands, in the process allowing Frederick II to form and lead a league of almost all the major princes of the Holy Roman Empire directed against Habsburg aggression. The Russian alliance signed by Joseph in 1781 dragged Austria into war with the Ottomans in 1787 at a moment when domestic opposition was coming to a head. By late 1789 the Netherlands were in full revolt with the Habsburg army and administration driven out. Rebellion was boiling in Hungary with its leaders looking to remove the Habsburgs and find an alternative foreign king. Prussian invasion in support of the Hungarians appeared imminent. Meanwhile indignation seethed among the elites of the Austrian lands and Bohemia. Faced by the danger of his empire's disintegration, Joseph withdrew many of his main reforms. When he died in February 1790 he had placed on his tombstone an inscription stating that he was a monarch who had failed in everything he attempted.

Much can be said in Joseph's favour. He was a very hard-working servant of the state and the common good, sacrificing all his leisure and shortening his life by his tireless labour in this cause. Some of his most important progressive reforms survived: these included religious toleration and the radical humanization of the criminal code. Other reforms designed to improve the peasants' lot provided beacons for the future. The Josephist ethos of public service and enlightened progress retained its hold on the bureaucratic elite down to the empire's fall in 1918. Joseph's repeated and exhausting tours of inspection across the whole extent of his empire in order to discover realities on the ground struck a chord in the public imagination and memory. So even more so did his accessibility and kindness to the hundreds of thousands of ordinary subjects whose petitions he received and whom he interviewed in the course of his travels. These memories of 'the people's emperor' contributed to the dynasty's legitimacy throughout the nineteenth century. Joseph saw his openness to petitioners as a means to check the public pulse and control misconduct by his officials. Admitting that officialdom could nevertheless sometimes pull the wool over his eyes on his occasional visits, he added that 'if you return several times, you see the changes, you listen to the complaints, you get to know (whom) to employ in the future, you judge the actions of the others ... and finally you judge – more or less – the capacity and zeal of the ministers'. He might have added that his on-the-spot inspections had alerted the central government, not to mention his mother, to the realities of ordinary subjects' lives far from the capital and to the sufferings and injustices which they endured.[22]

Not all Joseph's mistakes were his alone. In her last years Maria Theresa was planning radical agrarian reforms to improve the lives of the peasantry. Kaunitz was co-author of Habsburg foreign policy in the 1780s and no less aggressive than the emperor. The Russian alliance was the cornerstone of this policy and there were good reasons to support it. The Russo-Prussian alliance of the 1760s and 1770s had obvious dangers for Austria. The 1781 Austro-Russian alliance gained Russian support for Austria in the event of further Prussian aggression. Neither Kaunitz nor Joseph had illusions about Russian ambitions in the Balkans but they believed that it was safer to join Russia, seek to restrain her, but if necessary share the spoils with her when the Ottoman Empire was dismembered. The alternative – remain paralysed by a Prussian threat in the rear while Russia swallowed the Ottoman Empire – was unappealing. Joseph and Kaunitz did not expect the Ottomans themselves recklessly to attack Russia in 1787, thereby triggering the obligation to come to her aid. Nor did they anticipate that – when crisis loomed with Prussia in 1790 – the Russians would be tied down in war with both the Ottomans and the Swedes.

Nevertheless, it is impossible to deny that Joseph's radical and aggressive moves simultaneously on many fronts always risked disaster. Maria Theresa was far too cautious and realistic to expose her empire to such risks. She was careful never to confront the Hungarian elites and to satisfy herself with the generous revenues received from the Belgian provinces without challenging their archaic constitutions or the conservative mindset of their elites. She warned Joseph on these points. In her instructions for Leopold in 1765 she stressed one of the key principles of her rule: despotism did not work in the Habsburg Empire (or Tuscany). Success required winning hearts and minds. Joseph refused to listen to this message. He ignored the pleas of veteran, loyal and enlightened advisers that his policies were leading to disaster.

In part this reflected his stubborn, self-righteous and arrogant personality. As his sole reign began, Princess Eleonore Liechtenstein, who knew him better than almost anyone else, predicted trouble because 'his hobby-horse is to be always right'. The emperor was an intelligent man and he was convinced of his intellectual superiority to those around him. This is a dangerous failing in monarchs, since no one is in a position to challenge or contradict them. In diplomatic and military matters Joseph listened and even occasionally deferred to Kaunitz and Field Marshal Franz Moritz von Lacy, but in domestic policy he acted the autocrat. In addition, the emperor was incapable of putting himself in other people's shoes and could be almost autistic as he trampled on their feelings. One of the few people he considered both his intellectual equal and his friend was his brother Leopold. Unfortunately, Joseph treated his siblings even more despotically and abrasively as head of the dynasty than he behaved towards ordinary subjects. He totally alienated Leopold by the ruthless insensitivity with which he insisted on reincorporating Tuscany into the Habsburg Empire and claiming control of the education and careers of his sons.[23]

Ineptitude as regards personal relations was combined with the dangers inherent in Enlightenment ideas for any ruler of an empire. Joseph believed in system, uniformity and rationalization as key principles of statehood. But his empire was made up of diverse, historical communities whose rule he had assumed as a result of laws rooted in history, convention and family inheritance. The Habsburg Empire was not a state and its diverse lands were a patchwork of inherited private property, rights and privileges similar in principle to the laws that gave hereditary sovereignty to the Habsburgs. The empire could not be governed or preserved by appealing only to abstract principles of natural law, utility and reason. In this sense Joseph's policies were a dead end, not a path to the future.[24]

Joseph married twice. His second marriage was loveless, childless and brief. Although equally brief, his first marriage, to Princess Isabella of Parma, was the emotional high point of his life. Isabella's mother was Princess Louise Elizabeth of France, the favourite daughter of King Louis XV. Like almost all the marriages of Maria Theresa's children, this one was designed to prop up the core of Austrian foreign policy, namely the alliance with France. One year younger than Joseph, Isabella was superior to him intellectually and in a different universe as regards emotional intelligence and maturity. In Vienna she formed a deep friend-ship with his most intelligent, intellectual and artistic sister, the Archduchess Maria Christina. Maria Christina's husband, Prince Albert of Saxony, called Isabella 'this truly astonishing woman, who was still less than twenty years old' when she arrived in Vienna but who 'was not only endowed with all the admirable qualities of the heart, but . . . possessed also all the information and talents which could be hoped for in the most accomplished of young men . . . The careful education which she had received . . . had given her understanding not only in fields nec-essary to a lady of her rank but also in the abstract parts of mathematics and even in tactics. She combined this with some special talents, such as for music – she played the violin perfectly – and for drawing and paint-ing, and for certain crafts, in which she would direct the workmen whom she employed; and she wrote with facility and uncommon wit.'[25]

Among Isabella's writings which have survived are works on trade, education, contemporary French philosophy, religious meditations and autobiographical snippets. Among the latter are her reflections on the life of a royal princess: 'Her fate is unquestionably most unhappy,' she wrote. 'The rank she holds, far from procuring her the least advantage, deprives her of the greatest pleasure of life, which is given to everyone (else), of company . . . Obliged to live in the middle of the great world, she has, so to speak, neither acquaintances nor friends. This is not all. In the end the effort is made to establish her. There she is, condemned to abandon everything, her family, her country – and for whom? For an unknown person, whose character and manner of thinking she does not know . . . sacrifice to a supposed public good, but in fact to the wretched policy of a minister who can find no other way for the two dynasties to form an alliance which he pronounces indissoluble – and which, immediately it seems advantageous, is broken off.' Joseph's love for Isabella, initially awkward and callow, became deep. Contrary to all court and dynastic precedent, as she lay dying of smallpox, he insisted on staying with her throughout her illness. Devastated by her death, he was further trauma-tized by the death in 1770, aged eight, of their adored only daughter. All monarchs are lonely and Joseph's character, political commitments and work ethic made him exceptionally so. Had his wife and daughter lived, he would probably have become a more emotionally balanced man, better capable of understanding other people's feelings and opinions. This in itself could have had important political consequences. In addition, Isabella might well have become a trusted source of political advice and realism.[26]

When Joseph died in February 1790 with the Habsburg Empire facing an existential crisis, it was extremely fortunate that the throne was inherited by the forty-three-year-old Archduke Leopold, who had twenty-five years' experience of governing Tuscany. Leopold was the most intelligent of Maria Theresa's sons. Paul Schroeder, the justifiably renowned historian of international relations, calls Leopold 'one of the most shrewd and sensible monarchs ever to wear a crown'. Destined to inherit his father's grand duchy of Tuscany, he received the education of a future ruler, not of a younger son. Leopold was six years younger than Joseph. By the time he reached adolescence the Viennese Enlightenment had advanced. He was educated by better teachers than his brother, let alone his mother. Leopold remained a great reader throughout his life. His intelligence and erudition impressed some of the greatest minds of his day. He was passionately interested in science, technology and economics, but he also had great respect for philosophy and, especially, for history. His commitment to the education of his children and to the radical improvement of public education in Tuscany was famous. Also famous was his increasingly energetic womanizing, which became almost his main emotional release from the strains of ageing and ruling.[27]

Leopold was fortunate to inherit the rule of Tuscany in 1765. The Habsburg-Bourbon alliance brought an almost unique generation of peace to a peninsula over which the two dynasties had fought for centuries. The grand duchy was a maze of archaic jurisdictions and privileges. In 1764 it had suffered a severe famine, the last great famine in Italian history. Leopold's educational, legal, economic and cultural policies turned it into a laboratory for Enlightened reform and gained him the respect of progressive opinion across Europe and North America. Benjamin Franklin was one of his many correspondents. Leopold shared most of Joseph's views on religion. Some of his policies aimed at reducing papal control over the clergy went further than even reformist Tuscan clerics were prepared to follow. Unlike his brother, when Leopold realized this he compromised in good time and without needing to have his hand forced. This reflected a basic difference of personality between the brothers which had a major impact on how they ruled. Leopold was far more balanced, cautious and sensitive to criticism and opposition. He was much more prepared to swallow his pride and, where necessary, retreat. He possessed some emotional intelligence and was capable of empathy.

For the first thirty years of his life Leopold was mostly on good terms with Joseph. Then their relationship soured, though Leopold's discretion and Joseph's insensitivity meant that the emperor never understood the depth of his younger brother's anger. A key issue was Joseph's determination to bring Tuscany back into the Habsburg Empire once Leopold inherited the throne. Leopold saw this as a threat to his life's work but he could do nothing to oppose the head of the dynasty and the man in whose hands lay the future careers and marriages of his enormous brood of children. More basically, the political principles of the two men diverged sharply. Leopold shared none of Joseph's enthusiasm for war and armies. He believed that the annexation of more territory by the Habsburgs would probably be counter-productive and could only come as a result of risky and expensive wars. Leopold was also a committed constitutionalist. As he wrote to Maria Christina, good ideas could not be imposed. Society must be consulted and convinced. Representative institutions were essential to good government. Leopold was a methodical, efficient and cautious administrator and reformer. Even in his small grand duchy he tried out reforms patiently in one district before applying them everywhere. He saw Joseph's strategy of launching multiple radical reforms simultaneously across the entire Habsburg Empire as inherently inefficient and dangerous. As events proved him right in the late 1780s, his fears grew that Joseph would destroy the Habsburg Empire and his family's heritage.

Leopold's desire to stay away from Vienna until Joseph died made good sense. Rightly, he feared to be compromised by any association with his brother's policies. If the spiral down to catastrophe was to be avoided, it was essential that his subjects felt that a complete break had occurred with Joseph's death. When this happened in February 1790, Leopold immediately made clear in his proclamations and meetings with provincial elites that he was strongly committed to government by consent and that he rejected Joseph's more radical and contentious policies. In reality, the new emperor by no means opposed all his brother's measures. Some he succeeded in retaining and others he hoped to reintroduce more gently when the time was ripe. But Leopold was acutely conscious of the vital need to place himself at the head of the opposition movement, thereby seeming to direct events rather than being perceived as simply conceding to popular demands, suggesting weakness and thereby inviting further pressure. His promises quickly satisfied elite opinion in the Austrian and Bohemian lands. His key priorities became the danger of Hungarian rebellion and Prussian invasion, together with the need to reconquer Belgium and end the war with the Ottomans.

Leopold quickly realized that the first step had to be détente with Prussia, even if that required rejecting territorial gains at Ottoman expense (which anyway he saw as having little value). Moderation and clever diplomacy achieved this aim through the Austro-Prussian convention of Reichenbach in July 1790. With the threat of Prussian help gone the Hungarian rebels toned down their demands. A compromise was achieved which amounted basically to a restoration of the status quo on Maria Theresa's death. Although even Leopold's enthusiasm for constitutions was dented by the Hungarian gentry's intransigence, he was careful to camouflage his victory and allow the Hungarian noble opposition to retreat with its pride intact. With the Prussian and Hungarian issues resolved, the reconquest of the Belgian provinces proved easy. Leopold's three coronations as Holy Roman Emperor, king of Hungary and king of Bohemia symbolized the end of the domestic crisis. This came just in time before the international implications of the French Revolution burst on Austria and Europe. Leopold died suddenly on 1 March 1792. Not even his great intelligence and political skill could have averted the deluge which was to sweep over Europe in the following twenty-three years of war and turmoil.[28]

A study of the Habsburg dynasty in this era would be incomplete without some attention to Maria Theresa's daughters. She, Joseph and Leopold regarded most of them as pawns in the dynasty's foreign policy. To support the alliance with France, three of them were married to Bourbon princes. The exception was the Archduchess Maria Christina, her mother's favourite, who was allowed to make a love match to the sixth son of the Elector of Saxony, was deluged in gifts, and was allowed exceptional access and influence by the empress. Maria Christina was highly intelligent and a gifted musician and painter. Born on her mother's birthday, she seems to have been regarded by Maria Theresa as almost a reincarnation of herself. Inevitably her siblings were jealous of the influence and patronage allowed her by their mother. In Joseph's reign Maria Christina and her husband, Duke Albert, served as joint governors of the Netherlands, following an old Habsburg tradition but the emperor allowed them no power and ignored their sensible advice and warnings. Despair at Joseph's policies led to reconciliation between her and Leopold, who was her junior by five years. Their alliance was based on common political views and a common desperation to save the Habsburg inheritance, but it was speeded by the decision of the childless Maria Christina to make Leopold's son, Charles, the heir to her large fortune. Charles suffered from epilepsy and was disparaged by Joseph. Leopold and Maria Christina better appreciated his qualities. Subsequently, he became Austria's best senior general of the Revolutionary and Napoleonic era.[29]

Maria Amalia, four years younger than Maria Christina, was married to Duke Ferdinand of Parma, a Bourbon on both his father and mother's side, who was six years younger than his bride. He was the brother of Joseph's beloved first wife. Maria Theresa always had doubts about Amalia, whom she considered her most headstrong and disobedient daughter. As duchess, she and her husband horrified the empress by openly defying not just her but also Ferdinand's grandfathers, the kings of France and Spain. When the marriage was arranged everyone had the highest hopes of the young Duke Ferdinand. Like his sister Isabella, he had been splendidly educated and had shown in his childhood and adolescence great intelligence and willingness to learn. His education had been entrusted to outstanding teachers who were disciples of the French Enlightenment. What followed had much in common with the story of the Ming emperor Wanli. A boy celebrated as a prodigy who seemed to have absorbed willingly an intensive and disciplined education of the highest standard subsequently 'dropped out' and proved a vast disappointment. In Ferdinand's case revolt took the form of rejection of everything connected to Enlightenment and a life spent in prayer amidst humble religious pilgrims. As was sometimes the case with popular religion, prayer and abstinence were interspersed with bouts of carousal and self-flagellation. The only thing to be said in Ferdinand's favour was that a duke of Parma could cause far less trouble than an emperor of China.[30]

The archduchess Maria Carolina, second youngest of Maria Theresa's daughters, was married to King Ferdinand of Naples, the son of King Charles III of Spain. Unlike in the case of his first cousin

Ferdinand of Parma, no one in Vienna was under any illusions that the Neapolitan king would be an especially pleasing partner for the young archduchess. He had an ugly face, a body that was out of proportion and a shrill voice. Much worse, he was totally uneducated. His parents had left him behind in Naples (aged ten) as king when his father inherited the Spanish throne. On occasion in this book we have come across princes who benefited from escaping a conventional palace education. Ferdinand was an example of how such an escape could go horribly wrong. The king could barely string together an intelligent sentence. Subsequently, Joseph reported in disgust after a visit to Naples that what the king liked 'was horseplay and practical joking, endless contrived hunting, badinage and games with his attendants, slapping ladies' bottoms'. Leopold said the same after a similar visit, though he added that the king did have some amiable qualities even if he was a child of nature. Poor Maria Carolina showed heroic fortitude in managing Ferdinand, bearing him many children and essentially running his government. At times the going became almost unbearable.

One aspect of the life of this 'child of nature' was regular excursions to the brothels of Naples, with predictable consequences. In 1786 Leopold reported to Joseph that 'for nine years the king has been ill with various venereal diseases, which are not completely cured, and has passed them on to the queen. She has been seriously ill with them several times, especially during her pregnancies and confinements. Her son Gennaro and two of her daughters have been seriously affected. She has finally had to undergo proper treatment, having had fainting fits and very painful bouts of urine retention and a gangrenous sore in the vagina.' Recently, while she was again both ill and pregnant, Ferdinand had forced himself on her once more. Unsurprisingly, relations between the royal couple had suffered. Maria Carolina's brothers were suitably sympathetic but in their eyes Austria's influence in southern Italy had to take priority over a sister's feelings.[31]

The empress's youngest daughter, Maria Antonia (Marie Antoinette), was the prize in her mother's strategy to cement through marriage the Habsburg-Bourbon alliance. When in 1770 she married the heir to the French throne, the future Louis XVI, Marie Antoinette was fourteen and a half, Louis was fifteen. Since Louis's mother and grandmother were dead, she was immediately the senior royal lady at court. Four years later she was queen. The young princess was badly educated for her future role and the French court was a snake-pit. It was much more opulent than the Habsburg court and the young queen was easily tempted into extravagance. As financial crisis hit France in the 1780s she became known as Madame Deficit. The French high aristocracy was more arrogant and independent than its Austrian equivalent. Many of the top positions at court had been held by the same princely and noble families for generations. Marie Antoinette caused great offence by redistributing some of these posts in her household to her friends. Above all, she was seen as the representative of an Austrian alliance which was unpopular both in and beyond court society. In fact, she had no influence on French foreign policy and not much on domestic politics, until Louis's nervous breakdown in 1787 forced a more active role on her but perception mattered more than reality. As usual, a queen who was politically unpopular was accused of sexual depravity. The underground pornographic press and its avid readership had been fed on accounts of Louis XV's mistresses. Now it turned all its attention on Marie Antoinette.[32]

The political ineptitude of the queen's husband was a far more important cause of her downfall than any mistakes she made. Louis XVI was not stupid and he was well-educated, kind and well-meaning. He was deeply interested in history and a good linguist, and had a sharp understanding of international relations. He had subscriptions, for example, to both the *Spectator* and *Hansard*, and read every word of key debates in the British parliament. Unfortunately, by temperament Louis was unsuited to being a king, let alone an autocrat. As with the Ming emperors, he was saddled with a dynastic 'founder' and model who insisted that a true monarch must be his own prime minister. In his case this was Louis XIV, whose personality and ruling style loomed over his successors. Louis XVI's attempt to play a role for which he was unsuited contributed greatly to a lack of coordination, uncertainty and finally paralysis in the French government. In his memoirs, which became a bible for his successors, Louis XIV had cautioned that decision-making could be agonizing but must not be avoided or postponed: 'uncertainty sometimes leads to despair; once one has studied a matter for a reasonable amount of time it is necessary to decide.' Of all his ancestor's precepts, this was the one Louis XVI found it hardest to follow. Wavering, uncertainty and delay – dangerous at all times – became a fatal weakness in a time of crisis and revolution.[33]

In Louis XVI's reign the challenge facing a French king was severe. The growing power of Britain in the west and Russia in the east undermined French pre-eminence in Europe. French elites blamed the king for relative decline but rejected the policies necessary to avoid it. The decision to end the competition with the Habsburgs and concentrate resources on fighting Britain's growing naval and colonial power was wise but unpopular. The compromise between crown and elites on which the old regime rested needed to be renegotiated to allow an increase in revenue and a rationalization of government and law. Attempts in this direction were denounced as despotism. Nevertheless, the king's position was not hopeless. Comparisons with Alexander I of Russia's position as he contemplated constitutional reform and the emancipation of the serfs are to the point. Alexander had no groups in society to which he could look for support and he risked not just his own overthrow but also the destruction of the state if he embarked on these reforms. Conservative opponents of reform could argue plausibly that it would destroy Russia's military power, along with its international status and security.[34]

A French king had more room for manoeuvre. A large, literate and cultured middle class existed. Within the noble elite there were many who sympathized with Enlightened reform. Nor were privileged members of French society always united in defence of the same privileges. In the French context, Enlightened reform was essential if the country's military power and international status were to be preserved. A skilful king fully committed to Enlightenment principles might perhaps have built a coalition to sustain a reform programme. It is no doubt unrealistic to expect a monarch as extraordinary as Peter the Great to have emerged from the cultural world of the Bourbon dynasty and the court of Versailles. Probably a figure of this uniqueness and originality was not needed. My hunch – and such judgements can never be more than informed hunches – is that if Louis XVI's brother-in-law, Leopold of Tuscany, had inherited the French throne in 1774, there might well have been no French Revolution.[35]

Certainly, it is hard to imagine Leopold (and many other monarchs) blundering as badly as Louis XVI did in 1789. In times of crisis resolute, self-confident and consistent leadership is vital. Decisions must be made quickly, amidst great strain, and on the basis of uncertain information. Perhaps it is relevant that Louis XVI was the least military of all the Bourbons. During 1789 he floundered, unable to make decisions himself but an obstacle to anyone who sought to act decisively in his name. When the Estates General met in May 1789 it was vital that the king take the lead of the reform agenda. Instead, he was inactive, surrendering the initiative to the deputies and allowing tensions between nobles and the Third Estate to become uncontrollable. After wavering between reformist and 'aristocratic' advisers he moved towards the conservative side in June. Troops began to be concentrated in the Paris region. The dismissal of the powerful finance minister, Jacques Necker, was the spark that caused the storming of the Bastille and the government's loss of control in Paris. Necker's enormous popularity made such an explosion predictable. Typically, he was dismissed before most of the regiments summoned to Paris had arrived. Perhaps this was done to force the king's hand: Louis was not trusted to hold firm to the conservative course he had adopted. One of the most interesting contemporary historians of Imperial China writes that 'at times of crisis, when swift and resolute decision-making was required, many emperors proved completely inadequate, fluctuating between competing court factions, acting erratically and hastening their dynasty's demise'. This is a good description of Louis XVI's role in the coming of the French Revolution.[36]

The Revolution transferred sovereignty from a monarch blessed by God and history to the people. It defined the nation as the people in collective, political form. In revolutionary ideology the nation took on a secular sacredness, though one whose rhetoric had religious undertones. For millennia hereditary, sacred monarchy had been the most durable and successful form of polity on earth. In eighteenth-century Europe its dominance seemed so well-established that it could often be taken for granted. After 1789 this could never be true again. Ideological struggle became a key issue in politics. Conservatives sought to combat revolutionary principles not just by formulating counter-revolutionary political ideas but also by reasserting the role of ritual, spectacle and mystery as means to legitimize and popularize monarchy. Nineteenth-century monarchy rejected the Enlightenment model of rulership embodied by Frederick II and Joseph II.

If the principle of national sovereignty was dangerous for all hereditary monarchies, it was especially so for emperors, who usually ruled over many peoples. If each of these peoples exercised its rights as a sovereign nation then not just the monarchy but the empire itself was doomed. Since the people was now the sovereign, defining who exactly these people were and excluding 'outsiders' became of vital importance. In a world largely made up of empires and multi-ethnic states the potential for chaos was great. By the last decades of the nineteenth century this threat was becoming clear to Europe's rulers. In the 1890s Theodore Martens, the chief legal adviser to the Russian Foreign Ministry, wrote that the principle of nationalism – in other words that every people must have its own state – was a recipe for chaos in eastern Europe, a region dominated by empires. He was correct. It has taken two world wars, genocide and ethnic cleansing to turn the region into something approximating the west European model of the nation state.[37]

The potential danger of nationalism to regional and global order was not immediately self-evident in the rhetoric of the French Revolution, which made common citizenship the key to membership of the nation. In reality, the revolutionary leaders and their followers were Frenchmen who gloried in a specifically French nationalism and took for granted the existence of a French identity rooted in history, language and culture. The origins of this identity stretched back deep into the Middle Ages. Joan of Arc became a national saint for her expulsion of English plunderers from France's sacred soil. In the eighteenth century what one historian calls 'a cult of the nation' – *La Patrie* – spread in France. Louis XVI's veteran foreign minister, the comte de Vergennes, wrote that 'the Frenchman, proud of the name he glories in, sees the entire nation as his family, and sees his zealous sacrifices as a religious duty towards his brothers. He sees the *patrie* as the object of his worship.' Intellectual and cultural developments in the eighteenth century combined with age-old xenophobia to create this nationalism not just in France but in much of western Europe. On both sides of the Channel it was fed by the repeated wars between France and England in the century before the Revolution. If democracy was one heir of the Revolution, nationalist strife was another. Amidst the enormous excitement generated by the Revolution individuals might be willing to sacrifice themselves for an idea. Rather soon, the reality reasserted itself that most men were not prepared to die for the purely civic nation, unconnected to the pull of ethnic and historical identity. One immediate result of the Revolution was the attempt by a charismatic general to conquer Europe in the name of the French nation.[38]

Chaotic times breed charismatic leaders. Amidst uncertainty and stunningly rapid change populations often seek security in a charismatic leader, protector and guide. The French Revolution destroyed the age-old institutions and beliefs on which political power had rested. The comforting security of habit, custom and inertia disappeared. The Revolution resulted in civil war, terror and wars with all the other European powers. Amidst the chaos, men of ambition had chances inconceivable in more settled times. Unlike most of the would-be charismatic leaders who emerge in such eras, Napoleon actually was a genius. He was not just one of the greatest generals in history – winning an astonishing sixty-one of his seventy battles – he was also a shrewd politician and an exceptionally efficient chief administrator. In addition, he created and directed a first-rate propaganda machine. This machine cultivated among the French a sense of personal and emotional identification with the emperor, in a manner that was unlike the traditional awe for the king. The ordinary citizens with whom Napoleon came into most everyday contact were his soldiers. For a man whose regime was based on military support and who saw martial glory as a vital ingredient of its legitimacy the relationship with his troops was vital. Even some hereditary monarchs cultivated a degree of camaraderie on campaign that was never seen at court in peacetime. The image of 'the Little Corporal' that Napoleon promoted went well beyond this.

Napoleon was beyond question a charismatic leader in the spirit of Alexander of Macedon. He was a man so superior in his personality and achievements as to seem touched by destiny, fortune or the gods. Also according to the model of ancient Greek charismatic heroes, he was a warrior-leader. Whether he fits Max Weber's conception of charisma linked to the tradition of the Old Testament prophets is a more interesting and debatable question. Napoleon was a child of the French Revolution. In the areas of Europe he conquered or dominated some revolutionary principles were introduced. These included the career open to talents, the secularization of church property and equality before the law. On the other hand, Napoleon was a pragmatist and a man of order, not a Jacobin or an ideologue. His rule in France sought to end ideological conflict, depoliticize the population and achieve a stable compromise between Old Regime and Revolutionary principles. Charismatic prophets are more inclined to preach permanent revolution. To find their equivalents in modern European history one needs to wait for Lenin, Mussolini and Hitler.[39]

Leadership is one of this book's major themes. Throughout it I pick up on Max Weber's famous distinction between traditional, charismatic and 'rational', rules-bound leadership. Another of my book's key themes is hereditary monarchy. Napoleon is a fine example of a charismatic leader who attempted to found a royal dynasty. His second marriage, to a Habsburg, Marie Louise, subsequently Duchess of Parma, demonstrated that he sought acceptance from Europe's old dynasties, while at the same time portraying himself as a super-monarch, not just a king but an emperor on the scale and model of ancient Rome. His regime's propaganda was saturated with Roman themes and symbols. Of course, Napoleon's own enormous ambition and ego was a key factor in his drive to found a dynasty. So too were his often deeply conservative and family-oriented values. Nevertheless, political calculation also played a crucial role. Hereditary monarchy remained the best way to give stability and longevity to his regime, after a decade in which institutions had been uprooted and leaders had come and gone with dizzying speed. Few members of the French elite could be expected to commit themselves to Napoleon's cause or serve him loyally so long as the long-term survival of his regime seemed insecure. Hereditary monarchy was their guarantee.

Part of Napoleon's enduring fascination is also owed to another great theme of this book – namely the relationship between structure and agency, between the heroic individual and the context in which he or she is forced to act. The turning point in Napoleon's attempt to dominate Europe came in the Russian campaign of 1812. Until then he seemed fortune's child. Astonishing and repeated success bred hubris and in familiar ways this was followed by nemesis. Napoleon made a number of key mistakes in the Russian campaign that resulted in his army's annihilation and opened the way to a coalition of all the European great powers that led to his fall. Failure in 1812 was also due to problems familiar to empires that over-extend themselves. Like Chinese emperors in Korea twelve hundred years before, Napoleon was operating at a huge distance from his empire's core in terrain that he did not know and which was unsuited to his style of warfare. Like the Koreans, the Russian political and military leaders planned and waged a campaign that played to their strengths and the emperor's weakness.

Napoleon's most powerful adversaries, the British and Russians, were also examples of predatory empires, intent on expanding their power and wealth. The basic point in their favour was that it was by now far easier to create an empire on or beyond Europe's periphery than at its core. Centuries of warfare had made the European military-fiscal machines the most formidable in the world. Outside Europe these armies could be used against less powerful states. Any attempt to create an empire within Europe would entail fighting a coalition of great powers possessing state-of-the-art armies. A crucial reason for Napoleon's defeat was that British sea power locked French imperialism into Europe. Hard-power factors were not the only obstacle faced by a would-be emperor of Europe. No empire had united western Europe since the days of Charlemagne, one thousand years before. Three hundred years after the printing of vernacular Bibles it was far too late to think of imposing an all-imperial language on Europe. Many of the dynasties and regimes facing Napoleon had deep roots in their communities' history and identity. In India, by contrast, the British moved into the void left by the Mughals. None of the regimes they faced were deeply rooted. Even more important, for reasons explained earlier, Indian geopolitics favoured the British once they had created a formidable modern army supported by the Indian taxpayer but backed up by British control of the seas.

European geopolitics was a far greater challenge to a would-be emperor. By abandoning the Austrian alliance and committing themselves to a two-front war on land and sea the French made their own final defeat probable. It was difficult but possible to conquer Germany, Italy and the Low Countries, in other words the territory of Charlemagne's empire and of the founder states of the European Union. A would-be emperor was then confronted by two great-power centres on Europe's eastern and western flanks, namely the Russians and the British. These two great powers would almost certainly ally against him since his power threatened their security and ambitions. It was very hard to mobilize sufficient power from Europe's Carolingian core to defeat these two peripheral enemies simultaneously. The challenge was all the greater because the would-be emperor needed different types of power. Against the English he required a navy sufficient to control the Channel. To beat the Russians he needed a military and logistical machine able to conquer and control the Russian heartlands south and east of Moscow. Napoleon failed to overcome this challenge, as did the Germans in the twentieth century.

Napoleon's greatest enemy was Britain. The Anglo-French wars that began in 1689 only ended in 1815. Victory over Napoleon was the decisive step towards Britain's global pre-eminence in the nineteenth century. The spoils of victory were great. During the Revolutionary and Napoleonic wars the British conquered much, though far from all, of the former Mughal Empire. In 1815 the revenues of British India were greater than those of either the Russian or Austrian empires. In this period Spain's American empire revolted against colonial rule. Britain was able to dominate Latin American markets without even having to pay the costs of direct rule. During the war Napoleon had attempted to force Britain to make peace by denying access to European markets. His attempt failed in part because by now so much of British trade was trans-oceanic. Unlike Napoleon the British did not wish or need to conquer Europe. On the contrary, they supported a balance of power on the European continent which provided the United Kingdom with security on the cheap and thereby enabled a relatively small (by imperial standards) island people to concentrate their resources on creating a worldwide empire. To Britain's already overwhelming naval, financial and commercial power were added from the 1820s the formidable extra resources that derived from her being the first industrial nation. The next chapter is devoted to the European empires that dominated the globe in the nineteenth century, with Britain in the lead.

16

Emperors and Modernity:
1815–1945

This chapter studies emperors and imperial monarchy between 1815 and 1945, in the era when Europe dominated most of the world and when society and politics were transformed by the Industrial and French revolutions. To make this immensely complex period comprehensible I have divided the chapter into five sections. The first looks in broad outline at the context in which European emperors operated and the challenges they faced. During this era Europe's most powerful empires were the British, German and Russian. In sections two, three and four I look at these three imperial monarchies in turn. Choosing the British, German and Russian imperial monarchies has the additional advantage that they adopted different strategies for survival. The British became constitutional monarchs who performed a symbolic role as representatives of nation and empire. The Russians clung hardest to the traditional role of sacred and autocratic rulership. The Germans adopted a hybrid, halfway position between autocracy and constitutionalism. In section five I look at non-European imperial monarchies in this era. I start with the Ottomans and the Qing but devote most attention to the Japanese imperial monarchy, which combined native, Confucian and Buddhist elements with imported European influences. Of all non-Western polities, Japan was most successful in adapting to a world dominated by European ideas, technology and power. By 1900 it was the only non-Western great power. Japan is a fitting place to finish this book. In August 1945 Emperor Hirohito's decision to end the Second World War was the last time any monarch whom one can legitimately call an emperor made a major impact on world history.

The Industrial Revolution transformed the societies ruled by emperors and the international context in which they operated. All the empires so far studied in this book were rooted in agrarian or pastoralist societies, though they did also usually encourage and tax long-distance trade. The world of industry, urbanization and mass literacy that grew up in the nineteenth century presented all hereditary monarchs – let alone hereditary rulers of empires – with vast and unprecedented challenges. The machinery of government became far larger and more complex. Eighteenth-century Europeans at last caught up with twelfth-century China as regards the scale and complexity of government. In the nineteenth century they surpassed it. Only the most extraordinary human being could serve as head of state and head of government in this era for the whole of an adult lifetime. Even emperors who remained in principle autocrats devolved much of the business of government to ministers, reserving for themselves only the final say as regards appointments and decisions they considered crucial. Like the Song emperors of twelfth-century China, their personal role was greatest as regards diplomacy and war, and in moments of crisis.

Industrial-era society was even harder to manage than the machinery of government. Civil society – in other words a range of autonomous groups and institutions beyond the state's control – already flourished in eighteenth-century western Europe but the industrial era hugely expanded and strengthened it. Newspapers were at the core of civil society and shaped public opinion. In the nineteenth century they grew enormously in their impact and their autonomy from political control, above all thanks to dramatic technological changes in printing and photography and to the emergence of a mass readership. No monarchy could afford in the long run to ignore or confront public opinion. This was a crucial element in a broader picture. Traditionally the key allies – though also sometimes rivals – of hereditary monarchy had been aristocrats and priests. The Industrial Revolution created many powerful new groups and interests which monarchs had to recognize and accommodate.

Whatever survival strategy it adopted, a monarchy was certain wherever possible to make identifying the dynasty with nationalist feeling among its core population a top priority. This strategy was not wholly new. Viscount Bolingbroke had written *The Patriot King* in early eighteenth-century England and George III had worked successfully to place the initially alien Hanoverian dynasty at the centre of English and British patriotic sentiment and national identity. The eighteenth-century Bourbons had attempted with less success to identify themselves with

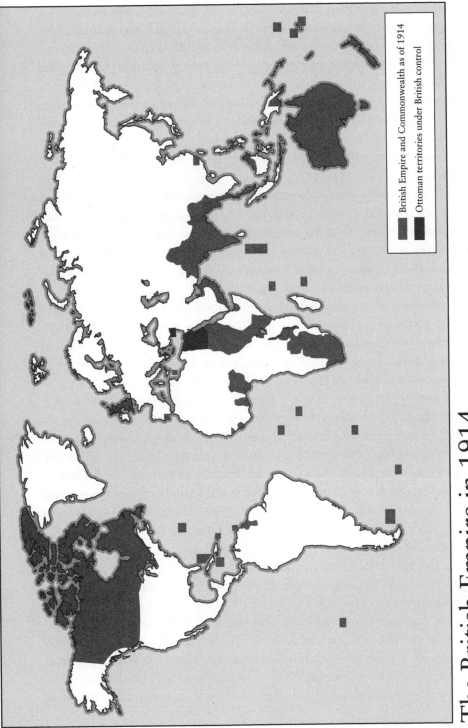

The British Empire in 1914

British Empire and Commonwealth as of 1914

Ottoman territories under British control

French patriotic pride and glory – not least because of their humiliating defeat by both Britain and Prussia during the Seven Years War. The idea of the nation took on a radical meaning in the context of the French Revolution because it was part of an ideological package that included popular sovereignty, republicanism, legal equality and democracy. Although republican nationalism remained a force in parts of nineteenth-century Europe, over the decades nationalism increasingly moved to the right of the political spectrum. A key turning point was the success of the Hohenzollerns and the House of Savoy in uniting Germany and Italy behind their leadership.[1]

By 1900 it seemed clear that nationalism was the most potent and popular ideology both to combat socialism and to reunite societies transformed and riven by capitalism and urbanization. It was also the most effective way to legitimize governments, elites and monarchs in the new world of mass politics. Governments used many means of propaganda, including above all the new systems of mass public education, to inculcate nationalist sentiment among their subjects, but nationalism also came from below. The nation offered a sense of community to people living isolated lives in the mega-cities created by the Industrial Revolution. To some extent it could act as a substitute for religion in providing individuals with a sense of purpose, dignity and belonging, as well as a place in a collective afterlife. To brief and humdrum lives it could sometimes even offer a touch of heroism and a place in history. The impersonal and ever more intrusive bureaucratic state could be dressed up and legitimized by the fairy tale of nation as family writ large. Monarchs had always been portrayed as their people's father or mother. Now they could be depicted as mothers and fathers of the national family. Rulers who lived exemplary family lives best suited this trend. Female monarchs often shone in this role, with Queen Victoria in the lead.[2]

The only European imperial dynasty which did not attempt to ally itself with nationalism was the Habsburgs. Traditionally, the dominant ethnic group in the empire had been the Germans but they made up less than one-quarter of the total population. Still worse from the Habsburgs' perspective, German nationalists among their subjects increasingly sought to break up the empire and unite in a Great German nation state ruled from Berlin. As a result of these unique circumstances there grew up in the Austrian half of the empire an impressive system for managing multi-ethnicity through compromise and legally guaranteed rights not just for individuals but also for ethno-linguistic communities. After the so-called compromise of 1867 the empire was essentially divided in two, which is why it is sometimes called the Dual Monarchy. Emperor Francis Joseph acted in parallel as emperor of Austria and king of Hungary, while retaining full control over foreign and military policy. In their half of the empire Hungarian nationalism was allowed free rein. This infuriated the non-Hungarians and weakened their loyalty to the Habsburgs. On the other hand, Hungarian nationalism's loyalty to the dynasty and the empire was also equivocal. The inability of the Habsburgs to appeal to nationalist sentiment weakened the empire in reality, and even more so in the perception both of its rulers and of outside observers. The pessimism this bred in ruling circles in Vienna contributed greatly to the reckless desperation evident in the decision for war in 1914.[3]

So too did shifts in the European balance of power rooted in the spread of the Industrial Revolution across Europe from its cradle in the continent's north-western periphery. The initial impact of the Industrial Revolution had been further to strengthen Britain, and thereby to reinforce the balance of power on the continent that served British interests. Once the Industrial Revolution spread eastwards its impact on international relations in Europe became far more destabilizing. By 1914 many intelligent Europeans believed that if Germany was Europe's potential hegemon today, then Russia would have assumed this role within a short generation. Germany's rulers themselves often believed this and launched a war in 1914 to stop this process in its tracks. The First World War destroyed the German, Russian, Austrian and Ottoman empires and was almost the last act in the long history of imperial monarchy.

International relations in the fifty years before 1914 must also be seen in the context of what today we call globalization. The European nation state that blossomed in the first half of the nineteenth century was the most powerful polity yet seen in history. Its ability to organize, mobilize and enthuse its subjects across a large territory was unprecedented. Nevertheless, by the 1870s the realization began to dawn among European statesmen and 'public intellectuals' that being a leading European nation state would not be enough to secure one's position as a great power in the twentieth century.

By now European prosperity was tightly linked to overseas markets and raw materials. A European power's global economic interests therefore had to be protected. The triumph of the United States in the Civil War (1861–5), followed by its rapid economic and demographic growth in the following decades, convinced intelligent European observers that only states with continental-scale resources would be able to hold their own against this competitor in the twentieth century. Simultaneously, technological development – above all, the railway – was making it possible to colonize and develop continental heartlands. This was the geopolitical basis for the 'Age of High Imperialism' between the 1870s and 1914. Intellectual currents also favoured the scramble for empire. Social Darwinism encouraged the belief that securing colonies was a mark of the manliness and vigour required if a people were to survive in the struggle for existence. Modern 'scientific' perspectives became easily intertwined with the age-old conviction that success on earth reflected the will of Providence. More fundamentally, possessing an empire was widely seen as determining whether a people would rank among the 'world-historical' nations best suited to determine mankind's future. Paradoxically, the era that spawned nationalism and doomed traditional sacred imperial monarchy also encouraged the creation of global empires. Nationalism appeared to be the key to domestic legitimacy and effectiveness, but international security, status and power required empire. How to square this circle was one of the greatest challenges facing emperors and statesmen in the decades before 1914.[4]

Sacred hereditary monarchy and empires had dominated world history for millennia. In the course of the 130 years covered in this chapter such empires disappeared. The realms of Haile Selassie in Ethiopia and the newly minted Pahlavi dynasty in Tehran – the only possible post-1945 candidates for emperorship – were small in size and importance when compared to the great imperial monarchies studied in this book. Nevertheless, the story of emperors and imperial monarchy between 1815 and 1945 is far from unimportant. On the contrary, some emperors had a major impact on world history in ways that sometimes resonate to this day. The whole of this chapter is a comment on the remaining importance of emperors, but it is at this point worth pausing on the Brazilian case – which is probably unfamiliar to most readers – to illustrate both the fact that emperors mattered and that just how much they mattered remains in many cases an open and debated question.[5]

In 1807 Napoleon's army invaded Portugal and the royal family fled to Brazil. When King Joao VI was forced to return to Portugal in 1816 he left his son, Dom Pedro I, behind as regent. Dom Pedro quickly understood that the only way to preserve the Braganza dynasty's rule in Brazil was to head the independence movement. He therefore proclaimed himself emperor. The imperial title was supposed to reflect Brazil's vast size and its aspiration to future greatness. It also reflected Dom Pedro's desire to associate himself with Napoleon, as a modern monarch devoted to stability and order but respectful of the French Revolution's appeal to citizenship and meritocracy. The imperious, hyperactive and charismatic Dom Pedro was forced to abdicate in 1831 after clashing with the Brazilian elites and parliament. His eldest daughter, Maria da Gloria II, succeeded him in Portugal after her liberal supporters triumphed over the deeply conservative and clerical factions headed by her uncle Dom Miguel. In Brazil, Pedro I was succeeded by his five-year-old son, Dom Pedro II. The latter ruled for fifty-eight years, in many ways one of the longest and most successful reigns in the history of imperial monarchy.

Dom Pedro II ought to have been mad or at the very least ineffective. On his father's side his genes were Braganza and Bourbon. His mother was the daughter of the Habsburg emperor. He had no more great-great-grandparents than Charles V. His mother died when he was an infant. His father abdicated and departed to Europe overnight without time to say goodbye. The five-year-old emperor became the centre of violent struggles between political factions. One casualty was his adored governess, whom the child had called 'mama'. At the same time, terrified that Brazil might go the way of Spanish America and disintegrate, the political elite treated the child as a semi-sacred totem pole, surrounded by ceremony and deference. Unsurprisingly, as a teenager, the young emperor seemed rather odd to visiting foreign princes. Remarkably, the most lasting impact of his early years was an unusual degree of introspection and a passionate interest in books and scholarship. As emperor, Dom Pedro had all the hallmarks of a Victorian-era liberal. He was as intelligent, high-minded, progressive and committed to educational and cultural improvement as Queen Victoria's husband, Prince Albert. Dom Pedro dreamed that one day Rio might be a copy of the Parisian intellectual and cultural world he so admired. Perhaps he was even too intellectual and Enlightened in some respects – refusing to adopt the public pomp and ceremony which became an increasing attribute of successful monarchy in the second half of the nineteenth century. On the other hand, within the limited resources of the Brazilian government he did everything possible to create educational and cultural institutions. He pushed the Brazilian elites as far and as fast as they would tolerate in the direction of abolishing first the slave trade and then slavery.

On the surface the Brazilian political system looked British. It had political parties called 'Liberal' and 'Conservative', a prime minister and cabinet drawn from those parties, and a parliament to which the cabinet was partly responsible. In practice it was far more like eighteenth-century Britain. Parties were factions, dominated by patrons and avid above all for patronage. Elections were 'managed' by the government and Dom Pedro was Brazil's real ruler – as had been the case with Britain's first three Hanoverian kings. As ruler he achieved a great deal. For example, it was he, not the ministers, who steered his country to victory in the gruelling war between Paraguay and the Triple Alliance of Brazil, Argentina and Uruguay. Inevitably, a fifty-eight-year-long reign strained the ruler's stamina and the patience of ambitious politicians. The nineteenth century witnessed changes in ideas and culture at what was, by historical standards, unprecedented and dizzying speed. Dom Pedro's Parisian erudition and culture made him seem a very modern man in the Brazil of the 1850s but thoroughly old-fashioned by the 1880s. By then mass politics and a popular press had emerged, at least in Rio and a few other towns. Since the monarch was the country's political leader he was deluged with criticism and libel. Dom Pedro was finally removed in a military coup in 1889. The army that he had created to win the war against Paraguay saw its status and funding decline sharply after peace returned. This was in any case not a European traditional army officered by nobles linked to the crown by ancient loyalties. Some officers saw themselves and the republic as harbingers of progress, science and meritocracy. Most were inspired by much narrower and more selfish motives.

Neither Dom Pedro nor his heiress, Princess Isabel, made serious efforts to oppose the coup or work for the monarchy's subsequent restoration. Dom Pedro was probably the most intelligent and certainly the most intellectual hereditary emperor anywhere in the world in the years between 1815 and 1945. He always said that he would have preferred to be president of a republic. That cuts to the heart of the dilemma facing a far-sighted and ambitious nineteenth-century emperor. Such a man was likely to sense that the institution he represented was living on borrowed time and that his role in history was to smooth the path to his own disappearance. Dom Pedro often stated that what constrained him from departing the political scene was his belief that Brazil was not yet ready for democratic republicanism. Similar excuses have been made by many other rulers in modern times. In Dom Pedro's case it might fairly be added that his pessimism was largely borne out by Brazil's subsequent history. On the other hand, the fact that Brazil's generals and politicians dared to remove Dom Pedro was in a real sense the measure of his success. In 1831 there was a strong probability that without the monarchy Brazil would disintegrate into a maelstrom of rival provincial republics headed by strongmen. By 1889 this was unthinkable and the country's unity was secure. If Brazil does ever overcome its enormous internal problems – many of them inherited from the colonial legacy and slavery – and realize its potential, then recognition of Dom Pedro II and his place in world history will grow greatly.[6]

In the eighteenth century Britain's 'free' constitution was widely admired by Enlightened Europeans. Nevertheless, though her laws and representative institutions made Britain unique among the European great powers, British kings still ruled as well as reigned. To be sure, government was only possible with the consent of the House of Commons but that could usually be arranged. Political parties in the modern sense with clear ideologies and extra-parliamentary organizations did not exist. The Commons was split into a number of factions centred on political leaders and aristocratic patrons. The electorate was small and many seats were in reality the property of powerful aristocrats. Parliamentary factions and their patrons were usually more interested in patronage than policy and the government had great resources at its disposal when it came to patronage, bribery and corruption. One firm rule of eighteenth-century British politics was that governments almost never lost general elections.

All this changed between the end of the American War of Independence in 1783 and Queen Victoria's accession in 1837. Many administrative reforms were carried out in the name of efficiency, honesty and economy that greatly reduced the role of patronage and corruption in politics. Political parties formed. In 1832 electoral reform abolished many of the 'pocket' and 'rotten' boroughs and greatly increased the electorate. In

1834 King William IV lost confidence in his Whig (liberal) government, replaced it with the opposition Conservatives and called an election. The Whigs won and he was forced to accept them back into office. The lesson was learned and Victoria never repeated her uncle's move nor tried to reassert the diminishing power of the crown. With much wider extensions of the franchise in 1867 and 1884–5 and the consolidation of mass-based political parties the queen's power was further reduced. Even now, the monarchy was not completely powerless even in hard political terms. In the early twentieth century Edward VII (r. 1901–10) exercised an important influence on foreign policy by nudging into top diplomatic positions men who shared his belief that Britain needed to draw closer to France and Russia in order to check German ambitions. Nevertheless, by then easily the most important role of the monarchy was symbolic.[7]

Since hereditary monarchy is in its nature a deeply flawed system of rule, British political development was a hopeful sign for humanity. Choosing the ruler by the lottery of hereditary succession is a self-evidently risky procedure in all eras and contexts. Given the challenges facing modern government it became near-suicidal. Hereditary monarchical sovereignty had survived for so long as much as anything because other political systems had in practice usually proved unworkable. The shift to parliamentary government was only possible because the British elites had the resources and the wisdom to evolve political institutions and conventions that could fill the gap previously occupied by the monarch. In the nineteenth century they adapted these institutions and conventions to bring ever wider sections of the population into the political system. In the new era of mass literacy, urbanization and the spread of democratic ideas this was vital for political stability and legitimacy.

The best-known text on the new monarchy was Walter Bagehot's *The English Constitution*, written in 1865. He divided government into 'efficient' and 'dignified' sections and placed the monarchy in the latter. As regards the crown's political role, he stated that 'the sovereign has, under a constitutional monarchy such as ours, three rights – the right to be consulted, the right to encourage, the right to warn. And a king of great sense and sagacity would want no others.' Inculcated into generations of princes, this became the core doctrine of British monarchs. Far from being a starry-eyed royalist, Bagehot was almost a republican. His book exposes the weaknesses of liberalism even at the apogee of its power and confidence. Bagehot believed in government by the rational, intelligent and well-informed upper 'ten thousand'. 'The masses are infinitely too ignorant to make much of governing themselves, and they do not know mind when they see it.' For that reason, magic wands and symbols needed to be waved under their noses if they were to obey the government of the 'ten thousand' and perceive it as legitimate. Of these, at least in Britain, where custom and inertia were powerful, the monarchy was the most potent. In time, Bagehot believed, education and culture would make the masses more rational and the need for traditional and magical symbols of authority less necessary.[8]

In fact, Bagehot overestimated the rationality of the twentieth-century electorate and underestimated the monarchy's durability and inventiveness. In part, the British monarchy's survival depended on its retreat from overt politics. Even those on the left who disliked it believed that there were more important enemies to slay. In addition, much of British society right down to 1945 remained deeply conservative, hierarchical and deferential in most of its core values. Monarchy and religion had always been tightly connected in Britain as elsewhere. Until the 1960s the United Kingdom mostly remained a Christian nation and 'there is poll evidence that in 1964 around 30% (of the population) believed that the Queen had been chosen by God and some 35% in the mid-1950s'. In that context it is hardly surprising that Bagehot wrote in the 1860s that 'the immense majority of the Queen's subjects' believed that she 'ruled Britain "by God's grace"'. Of course, educated Britons did not see their monarch as 'sacred' in the traditional sense but most of them supported monarchy as a force for unity, stability and the preservation of a national identity rooted in history. In Britain as elsewhere, many people had deep doubts about the ugliness, materialism and atomization of the new industrial world. The Industrial Revolution had introduced fundamental and astonishingly rapid changes in the economy and society. The monarchy symbolized a stability and a respect for traditional values for which many Britons yearned.[9]

The monarchy did not just survive as a pillar of conservatism. It also adapted itself in important ways to the new era. It tailored its behaviour to suit bourgeois tastes and exploited modern technology to spread its message. Especially from the 1870s, as democracy and the mass-circulation press took root, the monarchy renovated or even invented a range of ceremonies, rituals and other public activities designed to make it the symbol of national unity, decency, family values and grandeur. The area around Buckingham Palace was redesigned to enhance royal parades and spectacles. The Anglican Church's shift in the direction of semi-Catholic ritualism and the British musical renaissance were mobilized in monarchy's cause. This is the era of Edward Elgar's 'Pomp and Circumstance'. King Edward VII proved a committed and effective showman. For example, he revived the defunct ritual of personally opening each new parliamentary session in full royal regalia. The monarchy became a wonderful and gorgeous pageant that glamourized the nation's story. Modern technology allowed ordinary people like the courtiers of old to imagine themselves to be both spectators and participants.[10]

Empire played an important role in increasing the monarchy's prestige in British eyes. Exotic imperial contingents at royal ceremonies enhanced the theatre and reminded watchers that monarchy was linked to British worldwide grandeur and status. Native princes arriving to pay homage to the British monarch reinforced the principle of hierarchy. The Diamond Jubilee of 1897 was the greatest and most imperial of all London's royal festivals. Unlike in the 1887 Golden Jubilee, pride of place was given to representatives of Britain's empire rather than to Queen Victoria's royal relations in Europe. As always, empire was associated with military power. The monarch's role as commander-in-chief of the armed forces gained extra lustre. So too did the military principles of hierarchy, discipline and obedience. The usually upper middle-class products of British public schools could play the role of pre-modern rulers as district officers in India and across the empire. Empire thereby served the cause of fusing aristocratic and bourgeois values and consolidating the ruling class. For the many people who disliked aspects of industrial-era mass society, the romance of empire was soothing balm.[11]

The monarchy also helped to legitimize British rule in the colonies. The cult of monarchy seeped into all of empire's pores. The non-White colonies were themselves usually hierarchical societies with traditions of sacred monarchy. They found allegiance to a monarch more natural than to an abstraction such as a republic. If native elites gained most from this, even the rank and file of Indian regiments, though sometimes unimpressed by their British officers, appear to have felt genuine loyalty to their monarch and great enthusiasm when they were rewarded or spoken to by the king-emperor in person. In the non-white colonies British officials exercised direct control. The symbolism of monarchy was an adjunct to hard power. On the contrary, by 1900 London exercised minimal direct power in the self-governing White dominions and relied on symbols and emotional links to build loyalty. Common allegiance to the monarchy was almost the only constitutional bond and it was often sustained by powerful sentiment. In 1904 the Governor-General of Australia commented with some astonishment on the contrast between Australians' sometimes equivocal feelings about England and empire and their extraordinary affection for a monarch whom almost none of them had ever met.[12]

This helps to explain why Edward VIII's abdication in 1936 was so serious a matter. Faced with the looming threat of world war, Britain needed the support of the dominions and feared anything that would weaken their allegiance. Canada, the greatest of the White dominions, had no need of military protection from Britain. On the other hand, the British connection and specifically the monarchy were elements in the Canadian defence of its separate identity against American economic and cultural power. In the brief period between George VI's coronation and the outbreak of the Second World War his main foreign visit was to Canada. Amidst great pomp, circumstance and public enthusiasm the king traversed the entire continent from east to west. His effort was generously repaid. During the war the Canadian navy came to assume most of the responsibility for the western sector of the North Atlantic. Of the two British armies which invaded France in 1944 and fought their way across northern Europe, one was Canadian.[13]

With monarchy reduced to a symbolic role, the intellectual and political calibre of the monarch became far less important. Sir Alan ('Tommy') Lascelles was Assistant Private Secretary to three monarchs and Principal Private Secretary to two and an aristocrat by birth. His cousin, the Earl of Harewood, had married the only daughter of George V. Lascelles was totally committed to Britain's political stability at home and greatness in the world. For him, the monarchy's value lay in its service to these two causes. He had the courtier's close-up view of royalty and was unsentimental about the personalities of the kings whom he served. He once described George V as a 'poor little man', adding that the king 'was far and away and without any question the most physically repulsive man he had ever seen'. In only slightly more charitable terms, he recalled decades after George V's death that 'he was dull, beyond dispute' but that 'he was not a *bad* man in any sense of the word – he wasn't, like so many of his predecessors, a glutton, a lecher, a seducer of other men's wives, or a spendthrift; he was scrupulously fair to his ministers, of all parties; even his stamp-collecting resulted in his leaving an heirloom worth God knows how many thousands. In fact, he did his dreary job as well as he could, and as long as he could.'[14]

Probably, Lascelles would have agreed that George V's rather average ability combined with his strong sense of duty best suited the 'dreary job' that he had inherited. The British monarchy certainly did not want a man of the extravagant and eccentric genius of Richard Wagner's patron, King Ludwig II of Bavaria (r. 1864–86). King Leopold II of Belgium (r. 1865–1909), Queen Victoria's first cousin, was far saner than Ludwig but just as undesirable. Leopold was one of the most intelligent, ambitious and unpleasant monarchs in the nineteenth century. His role as constitutional king of what he himself described as a 'small country, small people' did not satisfy his talents or ambitions. Many constitutional monarchs searched for popularity and liked to be told that if their country became a republic, they would be elected its president. When an unwary flatterer spoke to Leopold in these terms, the king turned to his chief medical adviser with the words, 'What would you say, doctor, if someone greeted you as a great veterinarian?'[15]

In typical nineteenth-century fashion, Leopold tried to realize his ambitions through empire and was constantly on the search for colonies he might acquire. He finally struck lucky in the 1880s during the 'Scramble for Africa'. Leopold exploited his contacts across Europe and Belgium's position as a small, unthreatening and neutral country. He carefully cultivated international – and especially British – public opinion by claiming to be motivated by a mission to convert and civilize the natives. He came away from the 1884–5 Berlin Congress that divided up Africa among the European powers with the Congo as his personal possession, a territory bigger than England, France, Germany, Italy and Spain combined. This amounted to a private, royal empire. Leopold was a modern man and monarch. In the Congo he sought not just status and an outlet for his energies but also the maximum possible profit. He used terror and forced labour on a grand scale in order to wring profits from Congolese ivory and rubber equivalent to well over one billion dollars in today's money. By one estimate his private royal and commercial empire cost Congo roughly ten million deaths in his lifetime. Part of this profit went into turning the gardens and buildings of the royal palace at Laeken into Leopold's version of Versailles. Before the nineteenth century the Saxe-Coburgs had been a minor dynasty with little wealth. After Leopold II's efforts they could begin to emulate their wealthy Dutch royal neighbours, the house of Orange.

The international scandals that erupted over Leopold's rule in the Congo made the king increasingly unpopular in Belgium in the last decade of his reign. Given European values in that era, it is perhaps unsurprising that Leopold's well-publicized sexual exploits were a greater source of unpopularity. Aged sixty-five, the king became obsessed by a sixteen-year-old courtesan, Caroline Lacroix, who accompanied him not very privately on his travels for the rest of his life. British public opinion was more censorious than Belgian and a British monarch might not have got away with such flagrant misbehaviour. As Prince of Wales, the future Edward VII had sometimes sailed dangerously close to the wind in his full-time pursuit of beautiful women. When he ascended the throne in 1901 a shrewd observer commented that Edward had 'certain qualities of amiability and of philistine tolerance of other people's sins and vulgarities which endear him to rich and poor, to the stock exchange Jews, to the turf bookmakers and to the man in the street. He will make an excellent king for a twentieth-century England.' This turned out to be correct but as heir to the throne, amidst his many romantic scrapes, Edward had owed much to the self-discipline and loyalty to the crown of his wife, Alexandra. With her silence and support Edward was able to sustain a popular image as a devoted father and family man. Had the very popular Alexandra allowed herself in public to utter criticisms of her husband or suggest estrangement then Edward's reputation might have been damaged irreparably.[16]

Alexandra's grandson Edward VIII (r. 1936) was unwilling to subordinate personal feelings and private life to royal duty. The result was abdication. His younger brother George VI (r. 1936–52) was sustained by his love for his wife and children and the closeness of their family circle. He embodied admirably and sincerely the monarchy's claim to represent family values, which since Victoria's day had become a core element in its mass appeal. On the other hand, George VI was less rugged than his father, George V. His brother's abdication also catapulted him on to the throne without political or psychological preparation for his new role and in the midst of the growing international crisis that led to war in 1939. He did his duty bravely but his stammer and chain-smoking betrayed how heavily the burden of being even a constitutional monarch could bear down on an individual. In his case it contributed to death at the age of just fifty-six.[17]

The British were not the only Europeans to manage peacefully the transition to constitutional monarchy and democracy. The same process occurred independently in the Low Countries and Scandinavia. Nevertheless, Britain's position as the world's greatest empire and first industrial nation gave its move towards democracy a unique resonance and importance. Although many European monarchs before 1914 hoped to follow the British model, this was often difficult to achieve. Britain's system of government drew great legitimacy from the fact that the United Kingdom was the richest, most powerful and most envied country on earth. A Scotsman could take great pride and derive many benefits from belonging to such a country. The Union, founded in 1707, was blessed by time and success. British institutions – monarchy, parliament, law courts and local magistrates – were deep-rooted and enjoyed great legitimacy in public eyes. The British ruling class was united on fundamental principles, wealthy, and had long experience of government. No other European polity shared all these strengths.

It is to some extent possible to see Europe in 1900 as divided between a wealthy 'First World' core in the continent's north-west and a more numerous 'Second World' periphery to their south and east. For all this Second World's diversity, it shared fundamental features whose similarity was thrown into sharp focus when all countries across Europe's periphery faced the challenge of modernity and mass politics. By First World standards, middle classes were small and peasantries enormous, poor and often hungry for land. Regions were less integrated into the national community and states were weaker and more brittle. Intelligentsias looked to France, Britain and Germany for inspiration and compared their own usually corrupt and factionalized politics unfavourably with an idealized picture of politics and government in Europe's First World core. As mass socialist movements developed in the few cities and threatened to extend into the countryside all the elites but especially rural landowners feared for their property.

In most respects Italy stood at the top of the list of Second World countries. Nevertheless, the Italian state was weak by First World standards. To take but one key example: even by 1914 the education system had not yet succeeded in inculcating a strong sense of Italian identity or loyalty to the royal state into most of the peasantry or even into the urban population of southern Italy. The kingdom of Italy dated back only to the 1860s. Many Catholics and most southerners saw the Piedmontese takeover of the peninsula more as conquest than voluntary unification. The most powerful conservative force in Italy was the Catholic Church. Since the annexation of Rome and the Papal state in 1871 it had been the enemy of the new Italian kingdom. In Austria and Germany by 1900 mass Catholic political parties had emerged on the right of the political spectrum. Their size, organization and mass appeal made them worthy competitors of the socialist parties that were emerging on the left. In northern Italy socialism gained mass support from the 1890s. The Italian regime's inability to mobilize mass Catholicism against the socialists was a major weakness.

The new Italian monarchy's legitimacy was rooted in its claim to have united Italy, thereby serving the national cause. Unfortunately, the royal army's role in the so-called Risorgimento had been less than glorious. By far the most heroic episode in the Risorgimento had been the conquest of Sicily by the charismatic republican Giuseppe Garibaldi. The Austrians had won all the battles against the king's army in 1849 and 1866. The unification of Italy had been owed above all to outside powers – to France in 1859 and to Prussia in 1866 and 1871. After unification Italy became the sixth and least of the European great powers. Nationalist opinion yearned to live up to this position. In a manner typical of this era, Italy's rulers saw the pursuit of empire as a means to acquire status, glory and legitimacy. The attempt to conquer Ethiopia resulted in humiliating defeat in 1896. Occurring at the same time as growing labour unrest in the north, the disaster in Ethiopia rocked the Italian regime. A fearful King Umberto I (r. 1878–1900) responded by installing a tough general as his prime minister to restore the state's authority.[18]

In 1900 Umberto was assassinated by an anarchist. His son, Vittorio Emanuele III (r. 1900–46), quickly abandoned his father's line. In the fourteen years between his accession and the outbreak of the First World War he went out of his way to stress that he was a constitutional monarch who left politics to the politicians. The king accepted the extension of the franchise to most male Italians. He even allowed his civilian ministers to determine appointments in his military entourage, a move inconceivable not just in Germany but even in many fully constitutional monarchies. In these years he sometimes annoyed Russian diplomats by warning them of the dangers to Tsar Nicholas II in playing so strong and overt a role as political leader. By contrast, the king boasted of the way in which many trade unionists, moderate socialists and former radical republicans had come to accept the Italian constitutional monarchy. In complete contrast to Nicholas, during the First World War Vittorio Emanuele exercised significant quiet influence behind the scenes, but in general, and always in public, he stuck firmly to his symbolic role as constitutional king.

In the crisis-ridden years that followed the war the king found it impossible to sustain this strategy. The Russian Revolution and the fate of the Romanovs were a terrifying warning to all monarchs. In 1919–21 there seemed a great danger, especially among the more fearful members of the elite, that Italy might go Russia's way. When Mussolini's fascists marched on Rome in 1922 the decision as to whether to use the army to stop them rested in the king's hands alone. Vittorio Emanuele failed to defend the constitution, appointed Mussolini to the premiership, and then sustained him during his sometimes murderous and flagrantly illegal consolidation of the Fascist regime. The political context was of course crucial to the king's decision. But one also cannot ignore the impact of the diminutive and totally un-charismatic king's personality, and above all his lack of self-confidence. It may simply have been easier for the king to allow Mussolini to take power than to repress his movement and take upon himself the responsibility of political leadership in a situation where he could not rely on consistent support from the socialists, the right-wing nationalists or the Catholic mainstream. Perhaps he was influenced by the threat that his cousin the Duke of Aosta, a heroic military leader in the First World War, might act as a surrogate king in the Fascist cause. Both literally and in terms of charisma the tall and imposing duke towered over the tiny king. Undoubtedly, Vittorio Emanuele also feared to unleash a civil war between the royal army and right-wing paramilitaries, many of whom were former front-line soldiers. The fact that the Fascist leaders had abandoned their early republicanism and now proclaimed their allegiance to the monarchy was no doubt a vital factor too.

Very possibly Vittorio Emanuele was also swayed by a world-weary contempt for the petty ambitions and vendettas of the liberal political elite. Many years later his great-nephew recalled being alone with the king on a journey from Rome to the family's summer country retreat, a journey that took them past the estates and villas of many leading politicians. Vittorio Emanuele pointed out the nepotism practised by one villa-owner, the corruption of a second and the mistresses of a third. Like most monarchs of this era, the king had been brought up as a soldier and without much respect for party politicians. He had no taste for spectacle, magnificence or the glittering world of a court and Roman high society. His critics whispered that, had he not been born to inherit a throne, he would have settled happily into the life of a republican-leaning accountant or small-town bank manager. Vittorio Emanuele was devoted to his wife and lived a simple, almost cosy and distinctly bourgeois private life. By temperament and training he was not a natural politician, let alone an inspiring leader. Vittorio Emanuele's alliance with Fascism kept the socialists at bay and in some respects gave the monarchy renewed legitimacy. Of the world's six monarchs who ruled great powers in 1914, only Italy's king did not have the title of emperor. This came with Mussolini's conquest of Ethiopia in 1936, to the gratification of Italian nationalists and their king.[19]

Until the Fascists came to power Italy operated under a mixed constitution, in which power was in principle divided between the monarch and an elected parliament. This was the norm in most of Europe in the second half of the nineteenth century. The exact balance of power between monarch and parliament varied between polities both in constitutional principle and, even more, in political practice. Granting civil rights and political representation was a recognition of the growing strength of civil society. At a minimum, parliaments had a considerable say as regards budgets and legislation. Executive power – especially as regards foreign and military affairs – remained in the hands of the monarch. Many upper- and middle-class Europeans expected power to gravitate in time towards democracy as populations became more educated, prosperous and politically 'mature', thereby needing less the guardianship provided by the monarch and his officials. But powerful interests and ideological currents opposed these liberal assumptions and hoped to retain the monarchy as a cover for a more radical and populist variant of authoritarian nationalism. Before 1914 Italy was moving towards liberal democracy. With the Fascist ascent to power it took a radical turn in the opposite direction.

The most important 'mixed monarchy' in Europe was Prussia and the German Empire created and largely dominated by Prussia after 1871. Before the 1848 revolution Prussia and Piedmont were absolute monarchies. Both states adopted mixed constitutions in the aftermath of the revolution and this was an important step towards the alliance the two monarchies forged with the middle classes and with German and Italian nationalism. In 1846 between 50 per cent and 60 per cent of the Prussian population were reckoned by the government to be living at or below the subsistence level. The combination of a spiralling population and the impact of the new industrial-era technology was depressing living standards and threatening public order. The 'Hungry 40s' were also a time of poor harvests, potato blight and economic recession. In these circumstances it is not surprising that much of the middle class was terrified by the growing power of mass radicalism on Berlin's streets in the summer of 1848 and by the calls of the radical, 'Jacobin' wing of the German revolutionary movement for universal male suffrage. The Hohenzollerns and their state offered a safe haven, especially if – as was the case – the monarchy was willing to accommodate some liberal demands. In subsequent decades the urban working class became more prosperous and better educated. They also became better organized and joined the ranks of the growing socialist movement in large numbers. In many bourgeois eyes the monarchical state remained a comforting presence in the era of mass politics and of a powerful Social Democratic Party still in principle committed to republicanism and Marxist revolution.[20]

'Mixed monarchy' had inherent weaknesses. A bit like in the contemporary United States, the division between the executive and legislature could sometimes paralyse government. In the case of the nineteenth-century monarchies, however, the situation was worsened by the fact that the executive and legislature based their authority on conflicting principles of legitimacy. Monarchs ruled by God's grace and historical, dynastic right. Parliaments derived their authority from the votes of the people. As serious, the constitutions of mixed monarchies left enormous power in the hands of monarchs who were often unable even sometimes unwilling to exercise it. A hole resulted at the centre of government. In addition, dynasties which still played a major political role could not adopt the British monarchy's strategy to survive the challenges of modernity, whose key principle was to move outside and above the political sphere and play a largely symbolic role. In the era of mass politics, party conflict and freedom of the press, not doing this had obvious dangers. Max Weber correctly wrote that hereditary monarchs were inherently unsuited to the new world of modern party politics and the mass media. He added that monarchs who attempted to play an overt political role put not just their dynasties but the state itself at risk.[21]

Between 1849 and 1866 the Prussian mixed monarchy faced many of these problems. By 1862 monarch and parliament were at loggerheads over control of the army and William I (r. 1861–88) was contemplating abdication. In desperation he appointed Otto von Bismarck, seen as a reactionary by most educated Prussians, as prime minister. Over the next nine years Bismarck won the battle with parliament and opened the way to military reforms which made Prussia's army the best in Europe. His brilliant diplomacy together with the army's prowess won decisive victories over Austria and France and united Germany under the Prussian crown. Prussia-Germany became continental Europe's leading great power. The manner and the terms of unification won liberal support for the Prussian monarchy, while preserving the power and the interests both of the Hohenzollerns and of the Prussian elites. The consequences for German and European history were immense.

When William I succeeded his childless brother as king in 1861 he was already sixty-four years old. No one expected him to live for another twenty-six years. His longevity was of vital importance since Bismarck's survival in office depended entirely on the king. The relationship between William I and Bismarck was as important and as interesting as the one between Louis XIII and Richelieu. The two men did not always agree on policy and William usually gave way, even when convinced that his views were correct, as they often were. Bismarck got his way by taking to his bed, claiming that he was at death's door, threatening to resign and indulging in an astonishing display of tantrums, tears and emotional blackmail. William once famously remarked that 'it is very difficult to be emperor under Bismarck'. Most monarchs would not have tolerated this situation for twenty-six years. To do so required William's unusual degree of patience, self-discipline, selflessness and modesty. In 1879 he commented that 'Bismarck is more necessary than I am'. Perhaps age was a factor: the old king feared political turbulence and clung to his experienced minister. Undoubtedly too, William was in awe of Bismarck's genius and fearful about the consequences if he retired.

There were good reasons for both awe and fear. Bismarck was a political genius who showed immense skill and achieved astonishing results in both foreign and domestic policy between 1862 and 1871. On the other hand, the political system he created for the newly united Germany was a monster. Managing the mixed Prussian constitution was hard. Bismarck now created an all-German parliament (the Reichstag) based on universal male suffrage, since he believed that the mass rural electorate could be relied on to support the conservative cause against urban liberals and radicals. This calculation was mostly correct. Between 1871 and 1914 a mass agrarian and conservative party emerged and played a key role in German politics. On the other hand, rapid industrial development meant that by the early twentieth century more than two-thirds of the population lived in towns and cities. By 1914 the socialists were the largest party in the Reichstag. A Prusso-German monarch had somehow to coordinate the activities of the German Reichstag, a far more conservative Prussian parliament elected on a narrower franchise, an executive branch which in principle was not responsible to any parliament, and armed forces which were independent of any civilian control and subordinate only to their commander-in-chief, the king-emperor. Bismarck more or less succeeded in controlling and coordinating this monster, but no subsequent chancellor ever did so.[22]

William I's longevity mattered so greatly because the heir to the throne, Crown Prince Frederick, was more liberal than his father and was known to distrust Bismarck. Controversy still rages as to how liberal Frederick actually was and whether he would have dismissed the chancellor had he come to the throne between 1871 and 1888. Frederick had a strong sense of the monarchy's grandeur and rights, and he was as passionately committed to the army as his father. Liberalism in nineteenth-century central Europe differed from English liberalism, let alone from the word's connotations in contemporary America. As a good Prussian liberal, Frederick had his doubts about universal suffrage, was as suspicious of socialism as was Bismarck, and was even more hostile to Roman Catholicism in the era of Pius IX and papal claims to infallibility. As emperor, Frederick would also have been constrained by political realities. By the 1880s liberalism was becoming a minority cause in Germany, with less popular support than the mass agrarian, Catholic and socialist movements. Nevertheless, one point is certain. As Prussia's king, Frederick would never have appointed Bismarck in 1862 and would have replaced him had he come to the throne at any time in the following four years. It was in these years that Bismarck achieved his fundamental goals of displacing Austria as the dominant power in Germany and winning a compromise peace with Prussian liberals on the crown's terms.

Had Frederick come to the throne after 1866 and kept Bismarck in office he would have lived a miserable life between the chancellor's hysterics on the one hand and the strong pressure from his wife, Victoria, the Princess Royal, to remove Bismarck. The crown princess and later empress was the daughter of Britain's Queen Victoria and her husband Albert, the prince consort. Outspoken and often tactless, she made no secret of her belief in the superiority of all things English. Frederick adored her, calling her 'my life's only true joy'. He admired his wife's intelligence and strong personality. As befitted an Englishwoman, Victoria's liberalism was more radical than her husband's, but Frederick usually deferred to her. In the inner circles of the Prussian elite this fact was well-known and damaged his reputation. Had he ever dismissed Bismarck, anti-English sentiment and denunciations of 'the Englishwoman' in elite circles would have surged. In the event, the issue was never put to the test. When William I died in 1888 Frederick himself was already dying of cancer and reigned, as Frederick III, for only three months.[23]

Victoria loved Frederick but her husband's death was not just a personal tragedy, it was also the end of what she perceived as her life's mission, the encouragement of English and liberal principles in Germany. The fact that her son William II had rejected both his mother and her principles was a huge additional source of grief. Victoria adored her father, Prince Albert, and was his favourite child. Her sense of mission in Germany was in part a vow to his memory since the mission was to a great extent the one that he had laid out for her. After twenty years in Britain, Prince Albert had come to admire the British constitution but he always remained a German prince and deeply interested in German affairs. His vision was of a Germany united and led by a reformed and liberal Prussia. Such a Prussia would rule by moral example as well as by power. Albert would never have forced a Prussian marriage on his daughter and was delighted by her love for Frederick, whom in time he came greatly to like and to mentor. But he always saw his daughter as playing a major political role in Germany through the great influence she had over her husband. Albert's mission for Victoria was in many ways more far-reaching and potentially dangerous than the role Maria Theresa assigned to her daughter Marie Antoinette at Versailles. Victoria's role was not just to keep Prussia as England's friend but also to push Prussia and Germany towards a liberal and English-style future.[24]

William II ascended the throne in 1888 aged twenty-nine. The last German emperor is one of the most studied and debated monarchs in history. It is impossible in this book to provide anything more than a sketch of his personality and his significance. One useful way to gain insights into William's character is to compare him to former Prussian monarchs. He himself identified with his grandfather William I. He launched a major public campaign to establish the first emperor in German memory as 'William the Great', calling Bismarck and the architect of Prussian military victory over France and Austria, Field Marshal von Moltke, mere 'pygmies' and 'lackeys' in comparison. For neither the first nor last time most educated Germans cringed at the ludicrous and bombastic claims of their monarch and the emperor's campaign failed. Some large and pompous statues were erected in William I's honour, but it was Bismarck, not the old emperor, who enjoyed cult status in nationalist and conservative circles. The modest and realistic William I would also have cringed. William II had none of the austere self-discipline either of his grandfather or of the traditional Prussian upper class. He loved acting the part of Prussian warrior-king and playing this role became part of his identity, but William II completely lacked the inner steel, the resolution or the focus of the seventeenth- and eighteenth-century founding fathers of his dynasty's greatness.

William was in many ways much closer to his great-uncle Frederick William IV (r. 1840–61). Frederick William's weaknesses included 'excitability', 'nervous unsteadiness and unpredictability', 'rashness' and 'flights of fancy'. These were also very evident in his great-nephew. Frederick William finally went mad. There were many members of the elite who believed that William II was never entirely sane. Frederick William enjoyed making speeches, shone in this role, and had a knack for grasping the mood of his audience. In this too he was followed by William II, who had a gift with words, though a less sure hold either on his tongue or on the impact his words would have. In the new mass-media age these words were now carried to far wider audiences, whose sympathies were often very different to those whom William was addressing. Frederick William knew that post-1815 Prussia was much broader than the Hohenzollerns' old eastern heartland and tried to speak to his new subjects in the Rhineland and Westphalia and secure their loyalty. William sought to redefine what empire meant and to be a modern emperor for all Germans. In his reign the meaning of empire and emperorship shifted. In 1871 the imperial title signified that Prussia's monarch ruled over the kings of Bavaria, Saxony and Wurttemberg. It implied some element of continuity with the old 'Holy Roman Empire of the German Nation'. These meanings did not disappear under William II but they were overshadowed by a conception of world empire that fitted the era of globalization and high imperialism. William's passionate interest in maritime affairs and modern technology meant nothing to traditional rural Prussian nobles. His liking for ostentation and luxury repelled them.

Beyond question, William II's character was more flawed and unpleasant than Frederick William's. His leading biographer writes of the emperor's 'superiority complex – a brittle, narcissistic amour-propre combined with an icy coldness and an aggressive contempt for those he considered weaker than himself'. The arrogance of power was combined with deep personal insecurities linked above all to his twisted relationship with his mother Victoria, a proud woman ashamed to have given birth to a partly crippled first child and heir. To do William justice, he mastered with great courage his physical handicaps and the painful cures to which he was subjected since childhood. He was intelligent and could sometimes be interesting and charming in company. Perhaps one might add in his defence that his era – the age of mass politics, industrial capitalism and imperialist geopolitics laced with 'scientific', racist ideas – was far removed from the more innocent world of simple piety and Romantic fairy tales in which Frederick William IV dwelled.[25]

How powerful was William II? Historians have debated this ever since his reign. The one certain answer is that he was less powerful than the letter of the Prussian and German constitutions, let alone his own boastful rhetoric, suggested. His ministers echoed this rhetoric because they knew their master's acutely sensitive pride demanded it but also because acting in this way allowed them in practice to manage William and reduce his actual role in government. William was served by civil and military secretariats which might in principle have been used effectively to support his personal control over government and policy. In practice their leaders were above all devoted to protecting both the political system and William himself from the potentially disastrous impact of his own sometimes extravagant statements and behaviour. The German and Prussian government machines were large, growing and complex. To have any chance of running these machines their chief executive officer required a mastery of detail, an ability to focus, and a willingness to work consistently and hard. William lacked all these characteristics.[26]

Nevertheless, all senior appointments were made by the emperor. No chancellor, minister or top general who seriously annoyed him would long survive in office. William sometimes chose poor candidates whom he liked for key positions. The younger Helmuth von Moltke, Chief of the General Staff in 1914, for example, was a military courtier and an avid fan of spiritualism who lacked the talent or the temperament for this vital role. William's power over key appointments made it likely that ambitious men would tailor their actions to his prejudices. Even so, it is difficult to think of significant domestic policies that were initiated by William and negotiated past his ministers and the German and Prussian parliaments. Although his role was greater in foreign policy, even here the initiative usually came from his chancellors. William II's biggest impact even as regards foreign affairs lay less in what he did than in what he failed to do. In the German Empire only the emperor could coordinate diplomatic, military, naval and domestic policy. Vague pronouncements about Germany's pursuit of a 'world policy' and parity with Britain were far from sufficient. William's failure to define a clear grand strategy, match means to ends in realistic fashion, and then hold his diplomats, generals, admirals and ministers to this strategy cost Germany dear.[27]

The emperor's most important personal initiative was the creation of a massive navy. In domestic political terms his initiative proved a great success. The navy was a perfect symbol for the new German Empire. As part of the armed forces it represented a core traditional element in imperial monarchy. On the other hand, naval power had nothing to do with Prussian tradition and had long since been a cause dear to liberal and middle-class Germany. The officers of William's navy shared most of the values of the army's still mostly noble officers but came in the great majority of cases from middle-class families. This strengthened and symbolized the alliance of nobility and bourgeoisie in the new imperial state. The Navy League which was established in 1898 to support the fleet was a large and sophisticated modern organization that mobilized huge public support not just for the navy but also for the monarchy and its values. Within a year of its creation the League had over one million members. Warships incorporated the most advanced modern technology. Naval power was associated with globalization, commerce and empire. Warships carried the flag around the globe in a manner impossible for armies. Great battleships also had an austere beauty and fascination that made them cultural as well as political icons. The naval race against Britain to build battleships took on some of the characteristics of an international steeplechase, watched avidly by the British and German publics.[28]

William depended on Admiral Alfred Tirpitz to devise and manage the naval construction programme and to manoeuvre it through an initially suspicious parliament. It was Tirpitz who masterminded the creation of the Navy League. The emperor's relationship with Tirpitz was often difficult. Both men needed each other but often differed as regards what kind of ships they wanted and how best to employ them in war. After this led to his dismissal in 1916, Tirpitz went on to form the Fatherland Party, which in 1917–18 had more public support than any other political movement in Germany. Tirpitz allied himself to generals von Hindenburg and Ludendorff, whose victories had gained them great public confidence. Together by 1917 this triumvirate enjoyed such widespread support that William had no option but to bow to their wishes. The emperor had lost his position as Germany's leader. The monarchy could not control a mass movement and organization that it had itself sponsored. The hard-line militarist and ultra-nationalist leadership that displaced the emperor by 1916 led Germany to a defeat that a more intelligent and flexible civilian leadership might well have avoided. They then succeeded in pinning the blame for defeat on their socialist and liberal enemies.[29]

The basic problem with the fleet was that its construction compromised German foreign policy and dangerously increased Germany's isolation among the great powers. The strategic thinking behind the fleet's creation was in part plausible and legitimate. Globalization and industrial development had linked vital German interests to overseas trade and markets. In any conflict with Britain these interests were indefensible against British naval power. No European great power liked to accept this degree of vulnerability. One problem was that Germany lacked the resources – and above all a federal tax system – which would enable it to compete simultaneously with France and Russia on land and Britain on the seas. In addition, the idea that a powerful German navy would act as a source of leverage in relations with Britain backfired in spectacular fashion. Instead, it persuaded the British to patch up old colonial rivalries with France and Russia and join them in a partnership designed to check Germany. This in turn contributed to German paranoia about encirclement and isolation. When the arms race on land accelerated in 1912 sensible members of the German elite understood that Britain had won the naval competition, but it was difficult to admit this publicly. Nor were either William II or Tirpitz willing to abandon their dreams of naval power. The best biographer of William's father, Frederick III, on the whole plays down the consequences of Frederick's early death. Nevertheless, he writes that 'it appears almost inconceivable that Emperor Frederick and Empress Victoria would have adopted a policy of colonial and naval expansion understood to antagonize Britain'. Given the crucial importance of these policies, this is a significant comment about the role of William's personality in German history.[30]

German elites and public opinion became increasingly critical of William II's leadership. The attempt to drive William out of politics began in 1906 after Germany's defeat in the First Moroccan Crisis. On the right and much of the centre of the political spectrum this setback was often ascribed to the emperor's weakness and lack of resolution at a time when Russia's defeat in the war against Japan and subsequent revolution gave Germany a decisive military advantage. The attack was led by Maximilian Harden, one of Germany's leading public intellectuals, who edited the journal *Die Zukunft* ('The Future'). Harden exploited yet one more incautious outburst in the press by William, in this case a foolish interview which was published in Britain's *Daily Telegraph* in 1908. Above all, he used sexual scandal, in this case homosexuality, in the emperor's entourage, to undermine William's standing. Prince

Philipp zu Eulenberg, the emperor's dearest friend, was his main target.

There were many parallels here with the nearly simultaneous campaign by the national-liberal Russian politician and newspaper owner Alexander Guchkov to use the Rasputin affair to blacken Nicholas II and drive the Romanovs into a purely English-style symbolic role. In both cases the traditional world of a royal court confronted a free and scandal-mongering press, ambitious politicians and a parliament guaranteed free and public debate. Both Harden and Guchkov believed that a hidden group of courtiers and personal friends were deciding key appointments and policies. This was actually far truer in the case of Eulenberg than Rasputin, whose influence on policy was minimal. Nevertheless, Harden exaggerated even Eulenberg's influence on policy. In both cases the biggest result of the campaigns was to do great damage to the prestige of monarchy and monarch. In Russia this proved fatal. Harden's campaign had less devastating results but was also not without costs. He saw Eulenberg and other homosexuals in William's entourage as weaklings and believed that their elimination would allow German foreign policy to develop its full power and virility. This illustrates a more general point. Harden's attack on William was a battle between traditional monarchical and modern mass politics, but 'modern' did not always mean wise or peaceful. Eulenberg had been one of William's most pacific advisers. His removal played a role in Germany's descent into the First World War.[31]

William's part in the outbreak of the First World War is the most notorious and contested episode in his life. The events of July and August 1914 have special significance for this book both because the First World War destroyed the world's most powerful imperial monarchies and because this was almost the last time that emperors made crucial foreign-policy decisions. The immediate cause of the war was the assassination of Archduke Francis Ferdinand and his wife Sophie on 28 June 1914. Nine months before, the Habsburg ministerial council had decided that the first opportunity must be taken to destroy Serbia as an independent state. This entailed great risks of war with Russia which could only be faced if German support was forthcoming. The ministers agreed that this would only be the case if Austria had been flagrantly challenged by some Serbian action. The assassination offered precisely that golden opportunity. It also killed the member of the tiny decision-making group in Vienna which was the most powerful advocate of peace. In a broader sense Austria's clash with Serbia was part of the story of the conflict between empire and nationalism. At the same moment that this conflict in south-eastern Europe was leading to a war that would destroy the continent, it was also – in the form of the Ulster Question – paralysing British domestic politics. Austrian behaviour in the July 1914 crisis had some parallels with British and French policy during the Suez Crisis of 1956. Imperial elites facing geopolitical decline and growing nationalist challenges reacted with a combination of desperation, arrogance and miscalculation. The key difference was that in 1956 Big Brother in Washington said no. In 1914 Big Brother in Berlin said yes.[32]

German decision-making in 1914 was influenced by the pervasive sense of cultural pessimism and recklessness that reigned in conservative circles and which has worrying echoes in contemporary America. Nevertheless, in the July Crisis only three men really mattered in Berlin. They were the Chief of the General Staff, General Helmuth von Moltke; the chancellor, Theobald von Bethmann Hollweg; and William II. Moltke mattered least. He gave the same advice in 1914 as he had given during the Balkan crises of 1912–13, in other words to strike now when the military advantage remained on Germany's side and before it moved irrevocably towards Russia. During the Balkan Wars the civilian leadership overruled Moltke. In 1914 they supported him. The key figure here was Bethmann Hollweg. During the July Crisis the emperor always sought his advice and acted in accordance with it.

The chancellor was an honourable man and by no means an adventurer or a militarist but he shared the geopolitical assumptions and the nationalist values of his time and class. In other words, he was committed to making Germany a country of equal worldwide status and long-term historical significance as Britain and, if possible, the United States. Maybe he was influenced by the advice of his chief foreign policy adviser, Kurt Riezler, that the other great powers so feared a European war that Germany could risk a high level of brinkmanship in a crisis. Perhaps the chancellor's deep pessimism about future international relations in Europe also owed something to the recent death of his beloved wife. Amidst the awful strains of managing William II and the chaotic German political system Bethmann Hollweg had relied on her as a consolation and a backbone. By temperament he was inclined to melancholy and had the personality of a bureaucrat with academic inclinations, rather than that of a thick-skinned brawler and politician. The chancellor had been showered with attacks from the right, accusing him of unmanly weakness and cowardice. It is absurd and terrifying that the death of a wife could help to plunge the world into a war that cost millions of lives and nearly destroyed European civilization. That does not necessarily mean it is not true.[33]

William II shares some of the blame for the disaster. Faced by a hugely important crisis, the German government's response was lamentable. The supposedly more backward Austrians and Russians managed a full discussion of options in their respective councils of ministers, which included all their empires' key civilian and military leaders. In Germany it somehow seemed more essential that William's summer cruise not be postponed even for a day. No collective meeting of all the key leaders happened. Contemporary technology made it possible to recall the ambassadors from St Petersburg, London and Paris to attend such a meeting. Count Pourtalès could have repeated points made in his earlier despatches: no Russian government could stand aside if Austria invaded Serbia, but no Russian minister was likely to want war now or in any predictable future, if only because the risk of revolution was too great. Prince Lichnovsky could have contributed his view from London: Anglo-German relations had improved and there was every reason to expect further improvement given growing tension between Britain and Russia. On the other hand, no one should expect British neutrality if Germany attacked France. Meanwhile Ambassador von Schoen could have added two additional points: due to demographic and economic factors France's relative power was in decline; in addition, politics was moving leftwards and Raymond Poincaré's strongly nationalist and pro-Russian leadership was unlikely to endure much longer. These realistic arguments for optimism ought to have been thrown into the balance against Bethmann Hollweg's deeply pessimistic analysis of international relations in a council where all the opposing views were represented.

Even had William II chaired such a council, this might have achieved nothing. From the earliest history of hereditary monarchy there could be inherent problems when monarchs chaired ministerial councils. Walter Bagehot summed up the problem pithily: 'no man can argue on his knees'. Ministers would be slow to contradict the monarch's known opinions, especially in front of other ministers. An insecure monarch or one who stood on his dignity might well resent even argument, let alone contradiction. Louis XIV's advice to his son and heir is to the point. The wise king must listen much more than he speaks. He must encourage contrary views. A monarch must not resent a minister's criticisms or fear that his advisers might be cleverer than himself since the power and majesty of his office raise him well above them and allow him to make the final decisions. In short, the monarch needed modesty, self-discipline and a degree of inner self-confidence and balance.

Of all emperors in history, William II was least likely to follow this advice. The emperor was notorious for talking, not listening, and he was acutely sensitive to any perceived slight or criticism. Phillip zu Eulenberg, who probably understood William best, warned an incoming foreign minister in 1897 that William took all disagreement personally, hated to be seen to follow advice, deeply needed praise, and in general must be treated 'like a good, clever child'. Ministers learned not to argue with him, to put up with his bluster and posturing, and to expect in times of crisis that theatrical bombast would in time give way to timidity and retreat. Many senior generals expected precisely this in July 1914. They were right. As the risk of European war rose, William sought to retreat. By then he had unleashed a chain of events that it was difficult to stop. If Bethmann Hollweg and Moltke sabotaged his efforts to back down in the last two days of July 1914, they did so partly in the knowledge that a retreat at this point would have a disastrous impact on the Austro-German alliance and on the monarchy's prestige among German elites and public opinion.[34]

Among the European great powers, Russia clung longest to the traditional model of sacred and absolute monarchical sovereignty. In part this reflected the backwardness of Russian society in comparison to Britain and Germany. Even in 1900 more than 80 per cent of the population were barely if at all literate peasants whose mental world remained pre-modern and religious. The survival of sacred and autocratic monarchy also owed much to the ideals and political strategies of Russia's rulers. These strategies were driven partly by commitment to Russian traditions but also, most crucially, by the belief that Western-style liberal and democratic principles would lead inexorably to conflicts between social classes and ethno-national groups that would destroy

Russian society and the multi-national Russian Empire. In terms of per capita income Russia even in 1914 stood towards the bottom of what I have described as Europe's Second World periphery. It was also one of the handful of great empires that dominated most of the globe. In the twentieth century almost no state in the Second World enjoyed a peaceful transition to democracy. Between the two world wars almost all of them were governed by authoritarian regimes of the right or the left. None of the empires that existed in 1914 have survived. Russia's rulers faced enormous challenges as they sought to turn what had been a successful pre-modern empire into a viable twentieth-century polity.

Alexander II (r. 1855-81) was in many ways the most liberal of the Romanov monarchs. In the wake of Russia's defeat in the Crimean War of 1853-6 he believed that modernization along Western lines was essential if Russia was to survive as a great power. He liberated the serfs, introduced a Western-style legal system, relaxed the censorship, and introduced representative institutions of local government in the provinces elected on a wide if unequal suffrage. Nevertheless, Alexander believed strongly in his people's faith in sacred monarchy and tailored his political strategy accordingly. In 1861 he told Otto von Bismarck, then the Prussian envoy in St Petersburg, that 'throughout the interior of the empire the people still see the monarch as the paternal and absolute Lord set by God over the land; this belief, which has almost the force of a religious sentiment, is completely independent of any personal loyalty of which I could be the object. I like to think that it will not be lacking too in the future. To abdicate the absolute power with which my crown is invested would be to undermine the authority which has dominion over the nation. The deep respect, based on an innate sentiment, with which right up to now the Russian people surrounds the throne of its Emperor cannot be parcelled out. I would diminish without any compensation the authority of the government if I wanted to allow representatives of the nobility or the nation to participate in it.'[35]

The emperor believed that only an imposing and legitimate monarchy that stood above society could arbitrate the deep differences in values and interests between his subjects. In 1861, the year of emancipation, it was the potential war between nobles and peasants that most worried Alexander. Two years later, as revolution erupted in Poland, it would have been the monarchy's role in preserving the empire that most occupied Alexander's mind. His grandson Nicholas II (r. 1894–1917) faced even worse rural and national conflict, as well as a growing struggle between workers and capitalists in the cities. Like his grandfather, he believed that an imposing authoritarian state was essential if class and national conflicts were not to tear Russia's society and empire to pieces. He continued to hope that peasant monarchism would sustain and legitimize the state. Unfortunately for him, by the early twentieth century peasant mentalities were beginning to change. The programme of modernization pushed by the state was undermining the regime's social and ideological foundations. Creating new foundations for Russian statehood and empire was a great challenge and a source of bitter conflict between rival political groups and ideologies.

Nicholas II shared many of his grandfather's political beliefs and calculations. Nevertheless, there were important differences between the two emperors. Alexander II saw himself as a great European monarch, a *grand seigneur* writ large, and the first gentleman in Russian society. He moved easily in the Petersburg aristocratic world. At times he had a touch of his uncle Alexander I's sense of frustration and even shame that backward Russia seemed so unready for 'civilized', European reforms. Already in the reign of his son and successor, Alexander III (r. 1881–94), the monarchy moved in a more nationalist and populist direction. Nicholas II followed his father not his grandfather in this respect, though he remained very much a European gentleman in his values and behaviour. To some extent the nationalist and populist trend was a response to changing political realities in the new world created by the Industrial Revolution, but Nicholas's Russian patriotism and populism were wholly sincere. Alexander II's religion was conventional and superficial. His personal life in the last half of his reign was dominated by his infatuation for his mistress, Princess Catherine Dolgorukova. By contrast, Nicholas loved his wife Alexandra and remained faithful to her. He was also a deeply committed Orthodox Christian. At the core of the emperor's political beliefs was his sense of communion between the Orthodox tsar and people. As father and guardian of the Orthodox community it was his duty to retain the last word on decisions that would determine his people's fate. His inner spiritual world had a purity which ill-suited him for a life in politics. So too did his military training and his respect for the officer's code of obedience, loyalty and self-sacrifice. Unlike Alexander II, Nicholas II had no one among his ministers or even in Petersburg high society whom one could truly describe as a friend. His wife's shyness and unpopularity in high society increased Nicholas's isolation from Russian elites as well as Alexandra's increasingly hysterical belief that the monarchy's only true support lay in the Orthodox peasantry.[36]

Nicholas's political stance was rooted in nineteenth-century Russian conservative political thinking. Slavophilism was the most influential, vibrant and potentially popular conservative ideology in nineteenth-century Russia. Its central tenet was Russia's uniqueness as a civilization set apart from Latin Europe. Russia's prosperity and indeed survival depended on recognizing this truth and ruling in accordance with its own identity and traditions. Slavophiles argued that these had been better preserved among the peasantry than the educated elites, let alone in the pro-Western radical intelligentsia. At the heart of Russian identity was the Orthodox Church. The tsar was the guardian and protector of the Church and the Orthodox community against Russia's external and internal ('un-Russian') enemies. Unlike the Latin Church, ruled over by papal absolutism, in Slavophile texts the Orthodox Church was portrayed as operating on the basis of community decision-making and consensus, which was embodied in the great ancient councils of the Christian Church.

According to the Slavophiles, collectivism, community-feeling and consensus had spread from the spiritual world into Russian culture and society. A key example of this was the Russian peasant commune. When serfdom was abolished in 1861 the commune was preserved as a traditional national institution which would provide ordinary Russians with a social security net and protect them from the ravages of liberal capitalism. Most peasant land was owned collectively by the commune, was periodically redistributed according to the size and needs of families, and was inalienable. The commune was responsible too for policing and justice in the village. When a working class developed rapidly in the 1890s the state security police set up government-run trade unions to help workers defend their rights and their well-being against their employers. The headquarters of police trade unionism was in Moscow under the protection of the city's Governor-General, the Grand Duke Serge Alexandrovich, who was Nicholas II's uncle and brother-in-law. Moscow symbolized the old, pre-Petrine Russia and was always the heart of the Slavophile movement. Anti-semitism was a more 'modern' element in Serge's thinking and his political agenda. There are some similarities between Russian conservative thought and the ideas behind Mussolini's corporate state. Had the White military counter-revolution triumphed in 1918–20 or had the monarchy survived into the 1920s then it is likely that elements of Italian Fascism would have taken root in Russia.[37]

The most interesting defender of this neo-Slavophile vision of Russia's future was Lev Tikhomirov, a former revolutionary and terrorist leader who had recanted and moved to the right of the political spectrum in the late 1880s. His book *Monarkhicheskaia gosudarstvennost* (*Monarchical Statehood*), published in 1905, was one of the last defences of traditional sacred monarchy to see the light of day in Europe. Religion – and in the Russian case Orthodoxy – was at the centre of Tikhomirov's thinking. Like almost all conservatives, he believed that without the hope and the ethical principles drawn from religion human beings would fall into nihilism, despair and extreme egoism. Society would disintegrate. He wrote that, for all its theoretical commitment to science and reason, the revolutionary movement was actually a fanatical counter-religion but one without a firm ethical basis. Therein lay part of its danger because for historical and religious reasons Russians sought and needed faith, certainty and a strong commitment to absolute truths. They could easily be led astray by the revolutionaries. For the foreseeable future, he wrote, 'a Russian, by the nature of his soul, can only be a monarchist or an anarchist'. Tikhomirov was by no means a total reactionary. He recognized Peter the Great's achievement and the need for many of Alexander II's reforms. He denounced the existing regime's attempt to control and stifle autonomous social groups, but added that the revolutionaries bore great responsibility for this because they exploited every move to allow greater freedom as an opportunity to destroy the entire existing political, religious and social order. In an empire with seventy different nationalities, democratic party politics was certain to encourage polarization and disintegration. In Russia even more than in western Europe or north America, democracy would lead to disaster since in any system based on counting votes party politicians would exploit social and national divisions. Moreover, among the mass electorate 'the majority will always be found among the stupidest, less conscientious, less creative and, finally, less influential parts of the population'.[38]

Society must, in Tikhomirov's view, be organized into corporations. All subjects must belong to a corporation. The traditional organization of Russian society into social estates provided a foundation and model but needed to be adapted to fit the very different modern world that was emerging in Russia. A key part of this strategy was to extend the principle of corporatism to the new working class that was growing rapidly in Russia's cities. Torn from the traditional and religious world of the village, these former peasants were being thrown into the alien, soulless and exploitative world of modern capitalism. Most of them lived in conditions which made even family life impossible. They needed protection, guidance and organization if their lives were to have structure or meaning. The most important of all Russian corporations was the Orthodox Church, which must be freed from state regulation and given the autonomy and the resources to fulfil its mission as the bedrock of Russia's unity and its ideals. The emperor was the supreme guardian of this unity and ideal. He must not attempt to be the chief executive of the apparatus of government. This role demeaned him and was in any case impossible to fulfil in the modern context. The emperor was Russia's conscience and its guarantee that government would not abandon Russian core principles and ideals. This would allow Russia to preserve its unique identity and to fulfil its mission in world history. For all his strong support for the corporate state, Tikhomirov was not a Fascist, let alone a German National Socialist, in embryo. He was a conservative whose core beliefs were rooted in religion, not race. The closest contemporary parallel to his vision of Russian monarchy is Iran's supreme leader and guardian.[39]

Nicholas II was in many ways a conservative Slavophile. His sincere if sometimes naïve populist instincts clashed with other elements in his make-up. The Romanovs' traditional allies were the Russian aristocracy and gentry. This was the world in which Nicholas himself was brought up and to which he belonged. The great majority of the people with whom he came into regular contact were from this world. Although increasingly ill at ease in the more fashionable and 'fast' end of Petersburg high society, he felt most at home in the officers' messes of his Guards regiments, where aristocratic and military values merged.

Like all members of the Russian elite, Nicholas was also a European. Even Slavophilism had many of its intellectual roots in German conservative thought of the Romantic era. The emperor was among other things a European gentleman of the Victorian era, with all that entailed in terms of values, behaviour and constraints. His wife, Alexandra, was Queen Victoria's granddaughter.

The various strands in Nicholas II sometimes came into conflict when confronted by Russian realities. This was true during the revolution of 1905–7 when the monarchy came close to destruction. A dangerous strand in the revolution was the peasantry's drive to expropriate the estates of the aristocracy and gentry. Although the traditional elite's landholdings had decreased sharply since 1861, in some Russian provinces they still owned much (though never even remotely most) of the agricultural land. Agreeing to the expropriation of the big estates was the vital first step to consolidating the 'union of tsar and people' and bringing it into line with modern populist politics. Instead, Nicholas decided that private property must remain inviolable. There were good pragmatic grounds for his decision: expropriation would have set back the modernization of Russian agriculture and risked bankrupting the treasury. It would also have struck at not just the interests of Russian elites but also at the general belief among Europe's upper and middle classes that the sanctity of private property was at the heart of European civilization and had been a key cause of Europe's rise to dominion over the world. During the 1905 revolution a number of popular and potentially large parties sprang up on the right of Russian politics. Nicholas flirted with these groups but never dreamed of placing himself at their head or treating them as anything other than very junior allies.[40]

Nicholas II's stance during the 1905 revolution says much about the limits of populist monarchism. Hereditary monarchs whose dynasties have ruled for centuries have different political instincts to populist demagogues and leaders. Their power is rooted in different social groups, different values and different tactics. At a minimum they are less hungry, less innovative and less ruthless. Max Weber was partly making this distinction when he juxtaposed traditional and charismatic leadership. Early twentieth-century European (and Russian) monarchs also operated in part according to Weber's third type of leadership, which is usually called 'legal-rational'. Unlike many earlier royal dynasties which we have encountered in this book, they faced tightly regulated systems of succession, large and rules-bound bureaucracies, and a body of written constitutional law. The Italian Fascist case shows that monarchy could for a time share power with a radical populist movement and its leader, but this was in the post-war era when pre-1914 dynastic confidence had been severely shaken. Although the House of Savoy was an ancient dynasty, the post-1861 Italian liberal monarchy was in any case a new and rather modest institution when compared to the Romanovs and even the Hohenzollerns. It lived under the shadow of its much more ancient and awe-inspiring neighbour monarchy in the Vatican. Moreover, relations between the monarchy and Fascism were always fraught, unstable and full of suspicion. In 1943 Vittorio Emanuele removed Mussolini and brought down the Fascist regime.[41]

Nicholas II's title was not just 'Emperor' but also 'Autocrat of all the Russias'. The tsar was not the king of Italy, let alone the emperor of Japan. Russian tradition and political culture expected him to rule as well as reign. There had never been an equivalent of the Ottoman Grand Vizier or the German chancellor in Russia. Especially in times of crisis, the monarchy's strongest adherents looked to the tsar for leadership. Amidst the deep political crisis caused by the strains of the First World War, for example, Empress Alexandra called on her husband to prove himself 'the Autocrat without wh. [i.e. which] Russia cannot exist'. Nicholas's personality was ill-suited to the role of autocrat. Fate imposed a life at the epicentre of politics on a man who disliked politics and politicians. Although determined and sometimes stubborn, Nicholas was at heart a kind and sensitive person who was repelled by the ambitious and aggressive men who abound in the political world. He feared to fall under their control and fought to defend his independence.[42]

Personalities aside, for reasons explained earlier in this chapter, a twentieth-century monarch had little chance of acting effectively as head of government. The burdens of rulership and the complexity of government were simply too great. Russia was an extreme example of a general trend. Even if one excludes junior clerks, messengers and janitors, the number of civil servants in St Petersburg alone had increased from 23,000 in 1880 to 52,000 by 1914. The Russian state was attempting to play a far more interventionist role in society and economy than was the case in the First World. It had little alternative if Russia was to modernize at sufficient speed to employ its booming population and defend itself against First World rivals. At a time when the still small British treasury was wedded to laissez-faire, the Russian Ministry of Finance was devising and overseeing the rapid modernization of industry and communications. After 1906 the Ministry of Agriculture ran a vast parallel programme designed to transform the economy, education, culture and landholding system in the villages where more than 80 per cent of Russians still lived. Russia had Europe's largest and most sophisticated security police, a branch of government always very hard to control because of the secrecy with which it operates. Nicholas's efforts to rule as an autocrat over this sprawling and complex apparatus were unavailing but they stopped any 'prime minister' from doing the job effectively. The hole at the centre of government proved especially disastrous in both real and symbolic terms amidst the enormous difficulties of the First World War.[43]

When he ascended the throne in 1894 Nicholas II had little experience of government or politics. He revered his father Alexander III and shared his political goals and principles. Domestic affairs remained on the path set by Alexander until the first years of the twentieth century, at which point began the crisis that nearly toppled the monarchy in the 1905 revolution. Meanwhile Nicholas licensed his uncle Grand Duke Serge Alexandrovich to experiment with so-called 'police socialism' in the Moscow region and, in time-honoured royal fashion, concentrated most of his own energy on foreign affairs. Above all, this meant the Asia-Pacific region where – correctly – the emperor saw Russia's future to lie. By developing Siberia and colonizing it with Russians the government could combine the advantages of nation and empire, thereby solving the key challenge that faced all rulers of European great powers. During its centuries of expansion, Imperial Russia had benefited from never facing a hostile great power on its eastern border. The rise of Japan and its attempt to establish itself on the Asian continent in Korea and Manchuria was a new and very unwelcome danger. Unfortunately, the emperor underestimated the power and resolve of the Japanese. Rejecting the advice of more cautious and experienced ministers, he led Russia into the disastrous defeat at Japan's hands in 1904–5. This was Nicholas's most important independent initiative as 'autocrat' and it fatally damaged his prestige. However, even had policy been more wisely directed, the basic strategic dilemma would have remained. In 1909 his war minister warned Nicholas that if Russia faced simultaneous threats from Japan and Germany it would be paralysed. Had the Japanese struck north not south in late 1941 when Hitler was approaching Moscow, we all might be living in a different world.

On top of already mounting domestic opposition, the humiliating defeat by Japan led to revolution within Russia. This in turn led to the creation of a parliament and the so-called era of constitutional politics. The basic dilemma that had faced Nicholas since he had ascended the throne was sharpened but not fundamentally changed. In 1914 urban and educated Russia made up less than one-fifth of the population of 170 million, but in absolute terms and relative to other European countries this was a large number. Urban and elite Russia was often sophisticated. This was a world of high technology, of newspapers with circulations sometimes well above 100,000, and of an avant-garde high culture involving such figures as Chagall, Stravinsky and Scriabin. It was a society that sometimes seems post-modern without ever having been securely bourgeois and modern. It looked on a system of government rooted in eighteenth-century principles of bureaucratic absolutism and more ancient concepts of divine-right monarchy as hopelessly out of date. In his left ear Nicholas heard the advice from his more liberal ministers that any attempt to deny this society the civil and political rights taken for granted in Europe was certain to lead to revolution. This advice was correct. His ministers were too tactful to add that the emperor's senior and middle-ranking officials were now mostly the graduates of higher educational institutions. Liberal reform was essential even to retain their loyalty. The rapid turnover of ministers in 1915–17 owed much to the fact that most senior officials had lost confidence in Nicholas II and his political line. The monarchy fell in March 1917 when Nicholas was abandoned even by his senior generals.

Thus far this interpretation of events is the one familiar to the English-speaking world but, unfortunately for Nicholas, matters were not so simple. In the emperor's right ear he heard the warning from his more conservative and authoritarian ministers that Russia faced simultaneously the threat of peasant, worker and national revolution. They also warned him that the underground revolutionary movement could never be reconciled and was committed to the destruction of the Russian Empire, private property and the entire existing social order. It had assassinated his grandfather, the most liberal of Russian tsars, and it could easily kill him too. Liberalization, let alone democratization, would undermine the police state which was essential for the preservation of society and empire, at least until modernization had created a strong middle class and prosperous peasant farmers. Unfortunately for

Nicholas, they too were probably correct. To find a way down the narrow pathway between these rival truths was extremely hard.

Even so, the Old Regime might perhaps have survived into the 1920s had it not been for the First World War. This brings one back to a key theme running throughout this book, namely the importance of diplomacy, geopolitics and war. Before 1914, as in the late 1930s, German power and ambitions were the greatest threat to Russia. Any Russian government had two options in the face of this threat. It could seek agreement with Germany and try to deflect it westwards against the French and British, hoping for a lengthy stalemate in the west during which Russia could modernize its economy and stabilize its internal political situation. This was the strategy urged on Nicholas II by Peter Durnovo and Serge Witte, the two ablest statesmen of his reign, both of whom believed that war with Germany would lead to socialist revolution in Russia. It was the strategy adopted by Stalin in 1939, which ended in disaster. Having eliminated France and driven the British back over the Channel in a lightning campaign, Hitler was able to unite the resources of the European continent against the Soviet Union in 1941.

The alternative strategy, an alliance with the French and British to deter German aggression, was the one adopted by Nicholas II before 1914. Most of his senior advisers, as well as most of Russian public opinion, supported this strategy of deterrence. It was designed precisely to avoid the situation faced by Alexander I in 1812 and Stalin in 1941, in other words the domination of the European continent by an empire whose power and aggression was bound to be a fearsome threat to Russian security. This strategy also ended in disaster for Russia, though the war that erupted in August 1914 would probably have been avoided if Britain's commitment to deterrence before 1914 had been unequivocal and credible. 'Unequivocal' would have required a defensive military alliance with France and a unilateral guarantee of Belgian independence. 'Credible' would have meant conscription and an army sufficiently large to give a military alliance teeth. Unfortunately, the traditions and illusions of the British people made this impossible. Among the many victims of the war that followed were Nicholas II, his wife and five children, who were massacred at Ekaterinburg in the night of 16/17 July 1918.[44]

The European takeover of the world began with the conquest of the Americas in the sixteenth century. In most of the anglophone colonies of settlement (North America and Australasia) native societies were destroyed or marginalized. Indigenous societies and cultures survived somewhat better in Latin-speaking South America and in New Zealand. Almost all of Africa was conquered by Europeans in the nineteenth and twentieth centuries, though the subjection of the ancient imperial monarchy of Ethiopia to Italian rule was very brief. In Africa indigenous peoples survived European imperialism and in time regained control over their entire continent. In Asia the picture was more mixed. South Asia, in other words the Mughal inheritance, fell to the British. The three other great Asian imperial monarchies – Persian, Ottoman and Chinese – came under great pressure from European imperialism, suffered many humiliations and significant loss of territory, but nevertheless survived into the twentieth century. Although the Ottoman and Qing dynasties were overthrown in the first quarter of the twentieth century, the modern armies and other state institutions they had created subsequently played a vital role in preserving the independence of their core territories in the teeth of foreign imperialist attacks.[45]

Many useful comparisons can be made between the Asian imperial monarchies as regards both the challenge of Western imperialism and their response. European ideas and ideologies threatened the legitimacy of traditional monarchy. This became a serious danger as these ideas spread among Asian elites and growing middle classes. Simultaneously, integration into the global, Western-dominated economy imposed enormous strains on Asian societies. In China, for example, it greatly widened the existing gap between the commercial world of coastal and southern China, the political elite in Beijing, and China's vast agrarian hinterland. Repeated defeats and humiliations at the hands of the Western imperial powers wrecked the legitimacy of the dynasties and their regimes. Unequal treaties deprived these regimes of control over trade policy and opened their markets to a flood of Western imports. Foreigners resident in their empires acquired extra-territorial rights which gave them not just protection but also advantages in their competition with domestic merchants and manufacturers.[46]

In 1922–4 the former Ottoman general Mustapha Kemal (Atatürk) dethroned the last Ottoman sultan and caliph, who could easily be depicted as a puppet of British imperialists who had destroyed the Ottoman Empire and were threatening to dismember the Turks' Anatolian homeland. The Qajars were finally removed in 1925, in part because they had proved wholly incapable of standing up to British imperialism. The Qing suffered a similar delegitimization. In their case the fact that the dynasty was non-Chinese and had ruled by balancing Han-Chinese and Manchu elites made it doubly vulnerable to the charge that it had failed to defend China's pride, status and territory against Western imperialism.

Atatürk became the first president of the Turkish Republic, but General Reza Khan founded a new imperial dynasty – the Pahlavis – that ruled Iran for the next half-century. Like Atatürk and Reza, General Yuan Shikai commanded his country's main army in 1912 when the Qing dynasty was overthrown. Like Reza, he quickly pronounced himself emperor and sought to found a dynasty. Unlike Reza, who was 'an ignorant but astute peasant', Yuan was a well-educated and sophisticated man with a long and successful career as a general, diplomat and provincial governor. Yuan was defeated by a combination of modern and very traditional challenges. Coastal southern China was far more modern and sophisticated than Iran – there was, for example, no electricity even in Tehran when Reza came to power. China's new middle classes – like their equivalents across most of Asia – rejected hereditary emperorship as an anachronism. Meanwhile, in time-honoured fashion, Yuan Shikai's sons quickly fell out as regards who was to succeed their father, which was a pressing issue since Yuan was already fifty-six years old when he seized the throne. Many provincial military commanders rejected Yuan's authority and his claim on their regions' tax resources. When the new emperor was shown up as powerless to defend China against renewed Japanese aggression his regime quickly folded.[47]

Among Asian imperial monarchies, the Ottomans mounted the most long-lasting and interesting response to the challenge of Western-style modernity. Under Mahmud II (r. 1808–39) and his successors the regime pursued a policy of modernization designed to preserve the empire against the European imperial powers. To sustain this programme the Ottoman government trained and employed thousands of officers, officials, engineers, doctors and other professionals. By the late nineteenth century these groups had acquired a great sense both of corporate solidarity and of their own key role in their country's future. Their secular, scientific and often Turkish nationalist values had little in common with the dynastic, religious and historical loyalties that had traditionally sustained the Ottoman monarchy. The intelligent and wily Abdul Hamid II

(r. 1876–1909) well understood that the growing power of these new professional groups threatened to relegate the Ottoman dynasty to a purely symbolic role or even dispense with it altogether as an obstacle to personal ambitions and society's progress. To avoid this fate, he attempted to raise the monarch's status far above all mundane political forces by placing great emphasis on – even to an extent resurrecting – the sultan's role as caliph of the global Islamic community. Abdul Hamid correctly believed that in a still overwhelmingly rural and peasant society most of his Turkish subjects identified with religion and dynasty, not with new-fangled European ideas about national identity rooted in ethnicity and language.[48]

By 1900 many of the empire's Christian peoples had already acquired their independence, while others seemed likely to do so sooner rather than later. In this context it was crucial to consolidate loyalty to empire and monarchy among the sultan's Muslim subjects, who included millions of Arabs and Kurds. Stressing the sultan-caliph's role as head of the worldwide Islamic commonwealth served this purpose. It was also a useful strategy to employ against the European great powers which intervened constantly in Ottoman internal affairs in order – so they claimed – to protect the sultan's Christian subjects. The British, Russian and French empires contained scores of millions of Muslims, for some of whom the caliph's name had great meaning. In 1908–9 Abdul Hamid's regime was overthrown by the so-called Young Turks, who ruled the empire from then until its demise. They relegated the monarchy to a purely symbolic and ceremonial role but retained it as a key force for holding together the multi-national empire and enhancing its status in the international sphere.[49]

Had the Ottoman Empire survived, in the longer term tensions would have grown between the Young Turks' ethno-linguistic and even racial version of Turkish nationalism and the policies needed to preserve a multi-national empire. Nevertheless, it was geopolitics and specifically the First World War which in fact destroyed both the dynasty and the empire. Although Mahmud II and his successors rebuilt the Ottoman state, they could not regain the empire's old position as a great power. All Ottoman statesmen and ministers in the monarchy's last century understood that survival required playing the European great powers off against each other and finding loyal patrons among them. For excellent reasons the Ottomans mostly aligned themselves with Germany in the empire's last four decades. Had the Germans won the First World War – which very nearly happened – the Ottoman Empire would almost certainly have survived for a few more decades at least. Allied victory and subsequent plans to undermine Turkish control even of Anatolia destroyed the dynasty. Between 1919 and 1923 the British and French occupied Istanbul and used the sultan as their puppet. This was a factor, for example, in the mass 'khilafat' (i.e. caliphate) resistance movement that swept British India in these years. The killing of protesters at Amritsar in April 1919 on the orders of General Dyer is the best-remembered event in this struggle. When Atatürk abolished the Ottoman caliphate in 1924, British and French imperialists could breathe a sigh of relief. But for many Muslims worldwide who faced the pressures of European imperialism and the more complex challenges of Western modernity the disappearance of the caliphate left a void.[50]

Unlike the Ottomans, the Qing could not claim leadership over a great international religion. On the other hand, Han Chinese made up a far larger percentage of the Qing population than was true of Turks in the Ottoman Empire. In addition, geography meant that European pressure on the Ottomans began generations before a similar process started in East Asia. For all these reasons, though the Qing lost part of their empire's peripheral territory during the nineteenth century, the scale of their losses was much smaller than in the Ottoman case. Like the Ottomans, the Qing learned that survival required both the rebuilding of the state's military–fiscal machine on Western principles and playing the imperialist powers off against each other. By 1914 the greatest threat to China was increasingly from Japan, above all because the Japanese were the only great power whose strength and ambitions were focused on East Asia. By greatly decreasing European power in East Asia the First World War made China more vulnerable to Japan.

By the 1860s it had become evident to the better-informed members of the Japanese elite that if Japan was to avoid the fate of most of Asia and retain its independence then fundamental reforms that introduced Western technology, institutions and ideas were essential. The rapid growth of Japan's economy and military power in the decades following the so-called Meiji Restoration of 1868 astonished the world and undermined assumptions that successful modernity was a European monopoly. The reasons why – uniquely among non-European peoples – Japan had leaped into the ranks of the great powers by 1914 are many and complex. One vital point was that Japan – an ethnically homogeneous, relatively small territory surrounded by seas – fitted the European model of the ethno-national state better even than any European polity. It was easier for a government to transform such a country than was the case with a vast, polyglot and loosely administered empire. Again following European logic, having secured its independence, in the 1890s Japan began to acquire a sizeable overseas empire. Considerations of security and status required this, as did national pride.[51]

The Japanese monarchy before the Meiji Restoration fused traditional native shamanic rituals (Shinto) with Confucian and Buddhist concepts imported from China between the sixth and eighth centuries CE. Its foundation texts were the *Kojiki* (*Record of Ancient Matters*) and the *Nihon Shoki* (*Chronicles of Japan*) compiled in the early eighth century. At their core was the myth of origin of the imperial dynasty and the Japanese race. The emperor (*Tenno*) was the descendant of the sun-goddess Amaterasu, who sent her grandson Ninigi down to rule on earth and gave him the sacred mirror, sword and beads that remain the regalia of the line of emperors who according to the dynastic legend descend from him and rule Japan to this day. Similar myths of origin recur across much of east and north-east Asia. The antiquity and sacred genealogy of the dynasty were always central to its legitimacy and were entwined in folk religion. The dynasty's antiquity impressed even the Chinese. The Ming dynasty's founder called the Japanese 'just insular barbarians; yet their dynasty is everlasting and the court offices are handed down in unbroken succession. This is indeed the way of antiquity.'[52]

From the first half of the ninth century Japan's emperors no longer held political power. Their role became to legitimize the rule of the country's power-holding, military dynasties, the last of which, the Tokugawa shoguns, ruled from 1600 until 1868. The Tokugawa's first shogun confirmed ancient tradition by decreeing that apart from religious rituals, 'the emperor is to be engaged in arts, the first of which is scholarship'. To a Western observer, the commitment of Emperor Hirohito (r. 1926–89) to studying marine biology and writing poetry seems exotic, but scholarship and poetry were part of the tradition of Confucian monarchy which the Japanese had imported from Tang-dynasty China. In the millennium between the ninth century and the Meiji Restoration the life of an emperor was usually very depressing. Reigning emperors very seldom left the 220-acre compound of the imperial palace in Kyoto. Since imperial children were too sacred to be touched or viewed by a doctor their life expectancy was dramatically low even by pre-modern standards.[53]

From the tenth century until the Meiji Restoration the emperors did not even use the title '*tenno*'. In reality, even in the brief period when they exercised power they had never been emperors in the sense used in this book – Japan was too small, its people were too homogeneous, and its ruler was never remotely as powerful as his contemporaries the Tang-dynasty emperors of China. The Japanese imperial dynasty lasted so long in part precisely because it was powerless. It was therefore no threat but a useful source of legitimacy for the men who actually ruled Japan. The fact that they preserved the imperial dynasty and never sought to usurp the throne reflects their respect, and that of Japanese elites, for the emperors' religious and historical legitimacy. The monarchy also survived because Japan was an island, protected by the sea from the reach of the steppe nomads, though only just. The *Kamikaze* (divine wind-spirit, i.e. typhoons) that destroyed the Mongol invasion fleets in 1274 and 1281 were seen by the Japanese as confirmation that heaven protected their sacred land.

The monarchy was enormously useful to the Meiji-era reformers. Radical and unpopular reforms imported from abroad could be legitimized under the slogan of returning power to Japan's oldest and highest native institution, the emperor. The Japanese Meiji-era constitution of 1889 located sovereignty in the emperor. Ito Hirobumi, the constitution's chief architect, wrote that 'the Sacred Throne was established at the time when the heavens and the earth became separated (*Kojiki*). The emperor is Heaven-descended, divine and sacred.' The dynasty was described as not just eternal but also as the head and ultimate ancestor of the Japanese race. The idea that the monarch was metaphorically speaking the father of his people was common in many cultures. Japan took this conception to its furthest possible limit. The emperor was in principle both the political and religious head of his people. Unlike in Europe or Islam, the Meiji-era leaders did not have to manage autonomous religious leaders.[54]

Best of all, the emperor was much too sacred to be mired in the dirt of politics, nor did dynastic tradition encourage him to fill the role of head of government. His sovereignty was therefore an excellent cover for the ruling oligarchs. The principle of monarchical sovereignty allowed them to reject popular sovereignty and democracy without embroiling them in the thankless task of trying to control a would-be royal autocrat. Until the First World War the emperor's sovereign authority was to a great extent wielded by an informal council of elder statesmen, the *Genro*. Senior German and Russian officials looked to Japan with envy. In 1912 the chairman of the Russian State Council said to a confidant that 'among Petersburg statesmen there had more than once arisen the question of how to protect the throne from chance backstairs influences and to form around it a special Supreme Council (on the Japanese model)'. This reflected the lack of confidence of much of the governing elite in Nicholas II's ability. To be fair, it also reflected the age-old tendency of bureaucratic elites to seek to monopolize power and reduce the monarch to a symbolic role as merely a source of legitimacy.[55]

The emperor who gave his name to the Meiji era ascended the throne in 1867 aged fourteen and reigned until 1912. It is impossible to gain much sense of the human being who presided over this momentous era in Japanese history. For example, Meiji seems to have got on well with his wife, Empress Shoken, but the couple were childless. His children were born of concubines, the last eight of them having the same mother, Sono Sachiko. We know nothing about her or her relationship with Meiji. The emperor embodied traditional Confucian values of austerity, duty and moral virtue. He stayed in his palace in Tokyo through the sweltering heat and humidity of the Japanese summer rather than retire to the hills because he believed he should share the discomfort of his subjects and provide a good example of duty, self-discipline and self-sacrifice. He combined a Confucian ethic with spartan military values and customs drawn both from samurai traditions and from the ethos of the European officer corps of his day. These military traditions played no part in the history of his dynasty but were at the heart of the Meiji-era synthesis of native and foreign elements. As in contemporary Europe, from the 1880s the Japanese monarchy was increasingly involved in spectacle, ceremony and rituals – some of which were ancient but many either new or reinvented. An area in central Tokyo, Nijubashi, was re-developed to stage these ceremonies and great military parades were held in the fields and parade ground in the Aoyama district, close to the emperor's palace. Meiji was tough and healthy. His longevity and the enormous advances made in his reign added to his prestige. So too did Japan's victories over first China and then Russia under his nominal command.[56]

Japan was a mixed monarchy, with its constitution partly borrowed from Germany. Sovereignty and executive power belonged to the emperor, but parliament had a significant role in legislation and the budget. Unsurprisingly, it also shared the faults of these hybrid political systems. The armed forces were free of any civilian control, being nominally subordinated to the emperor, which made them in practice autonomous. Japan did not even have a figure equivalent to the German chancellor. Rather like Bismarck, the *Genro* filled the gap at the centre of government, but after they had died it loomed ever wider. Lack of coordination between army, navy, diplomacy and domestic government were crucial factors in Germany's blundering towards the First World War. They played an even bigger role in causing Japan's descent into the Second World War. The army pulled Japan into war in China in the 1930s against the wishes of the civilian government. In time this embroiled Japan in a war with the United States that the more realistic diplomatic and naval leaders knew it could never win. But by 1941 the price of peace with the USA would have been a humiliating withdrawal from China that the army as well as much of the naval and civilian leadership (not to mention Japanese public opinion), could not stomach. In the Japanese political context of 1941 it was far easier to make the tactically brilliant but strategically reckless decision to attack Pearl Harbor than to retreat under the pressure of the American oil embargo.

Subsequently, Emperor Hirohito was often blamed for Japan's slide towards war and defeat in 1945. This was hardly fair. None of the creators of the Meiji political system had ever envisaged that an emperor would play the leading and coordinating role of a German kaiser or a Russian tsar. He was not even expected to play the active guardianship role envisaged by Tikhomirov. Occasionally, Emperor Meiji operated behind the scenes in support of a minister or policy but in general and always in public he remained silent, benevolent and neutral. Even under Meiji, despite his experience and enormous prestige, 'for all the re-iterated declarations of absolute loyalty to the throne, the emperor's ministers disregarded his wishes when they found them inconvenient'. Matters had worsened dramatically by the 1930s for reasons similar to parallel developments in Europe. The era of mass politics had arrived and was putting unprecedented pressure on the political system. The frustrations and gridlock inherent in hybrid constitutional systems eroded respect for parliaments, party politicians and the existing constitution among the population. Above all, the Crash and the Depression resulted in sharp polarization between socialists on the left and ultra-nationalists on the right.[57]

Unlike Vittorio Emanuele III, Emperor Hirohito did not deliberately hand power to ultra-nationalists but increasingly they took over the officer corps of the armed forces from below. Imbued with a strong belief in Japan's spiritual uniqueness and superiority, radical nationalist officers disobeyed orders, assassinated civilian and even military leaders, and in 1936 staged a coup that killed some of the emperor's key advisers and came close to succeeding. Still worse, these officers had widespread support among the masses, in elite circles and even within the imperial family. The call to take the leadership in Asia, drive out the Europeans, and thereby assume a grand role in histor, had strong support across the Japanese political spectrum in 1941. Not just Japanese tradition but also the fate of the Romanovs was a disincentive against an emperor taking a strong independent line in politics. When in 1937 Hirohito contemplated intervening personally to tilt the balance against the military extremists he was warned by the last of the *Genro*, Prince Saionji, that the monarchy must not endanger itself by active political engagement. Only in the apocalyptic circumstances of August 1945 did Emperor Hirohito decisively enter the political arena to end the Second World War, and even then this only happened because his civilian and military ministers were split down the middle on the issue of peace or continued war and requested his intervention.[58]

17

Afterword

This book is about the past. Hereditary imperial monarchy belonged to a world in which authority was believed to come from Heaven, antiquity and legitimacy went together, and hierarchy was taken for granted. The pre-industrial economy could not generate the wealth or sustain the levels of education and urbanization which stable democracy usually requires. The main exceptions were some city states but in the long run these were never able to defend themselves against larger external enemies. Imperial monarchies were also rooted in the assumption that the mass of the population was too uneducated, too busy scraping a livelihood, too foolish or too sinful to be allowed a say in government. There is no point in reading this book in a mood of sustained indignation that the past world did not operate according to contemporary political principles. Indignation needs to be suspended and the past to be understood on its own terms.

That does not mean that the history of imperial monarchy is totally irrelevant to today's world. In the Middle East some powerful hereditary monarchies still exist. The impatient and arrogant young crown prince of Saudi Arabia, imbued with a sense of mission, is a type I have encountered in my research for this book. In the First World monarchs now play an almost purely symbolic role as representatives of the sovereign nation, though monarchies still need to strike a balance between the mystery that depends on remoteness and the pressures to turn them into a permanent public theatre. Potentially, monarchs who stand above partisan politics and link the present-day nation to its roots and its long-term future retain their value. Traditional values of community, self-sacrifice and self-discipline may well be needed badly when faced by the great pressures that climate change will place even on rich, First-World societies. Monarchy could symbolize these traditions and values.

On the other hand, young royals face all the traps of modern celebrity culture. Young people nowadays take for granted their right to choose their own path in life. Only young princes and princesses have imposed on them a tightly choreographed lifetime role, played out in a fishbowl under intense public scrutiny. Some of them are bound to reject their role in the national fantasy or play it badly.

Geopolitics, empire, sovereignty and leadership are key themes in this book. Inevitably, they remain crucial despite the disappearance of imperial monarchy. Before 1914 the key to a great power's success seemed to lie in somehow combining the strengths of the nation (solidarity, commitment and legitimacy) and of empire (continental-scale resources, power and security). This has not changed. Better than any other empire, China has evolved most of the way towards becoming a nation while retaining most of the territory ruled by the Qing emperors. This is the geopolitical foundation of its power. Current policies in Xinjiang in some respects follow in the tradition of nineteenth-century empires' efforts to impose a homogeneous 'national' identity on as many of its subjects as possible. At the other end of Eurasia, Europeans face the risk of having no say in vital issues such as climate change and international trade unless they create institutions that can speak with continental-scale resources behind them. How to create legitimate and effective pan-European institutions in the continent that invented modern nationalism remains the EU's major problem. Success or failure may well be judged by how effectively the EU responds to the potentially enormous challenge on its southern front that the combination of Africa's growing population, climate change and migration is likely to create.

It has taken two world wars, genocide and ethnic cleansing on a grand scale to transform the map of eastern and central Europe from empire to nation. The Middle East is engulfed in what is to some extent still a post-Ottoman crisis. The European model of ethno-linguistic nationhood does not easily fit a region traditionally dominated by Islam and empire, with different religious, ethnic and linguistic communities living cheek by jowl. Most large countries in Asia remain more like empires than the European model of the ethno-national polity. If Asia catches the disease of European ethno-nationalism the planet might well not survive the resulting chaos.

India is the best example of the danger. Modern India is the product of the Mughal and British empires. For two generations after independence the Congress Party and the anglophone elites associated with it ruled India thanks to the legitimacy and the institutions they had created in the successful fight against British rule. Memories of this fight have now faded and democratic politics has put down ever deeper roots in the population. The result has been the growing appeal to ethnonationalism, which in India often means Hindu communalism and targeting the Muslim minority as the enemy within. The end of empire in South Asia resulted in partition and the creation of two bitterly hostile neighbours, India and Pakistan. After fighting many wars, both countries are now armed with nuclear weapons. Climate change is going to put great pressure on peoples and governments everywhere. South Asia will be one of the regions worst affected, especially if water becomes an increasingly scarce resource with access to it becoming a growing cause of cross-border, international conflict. China too faces acute possible shortage of water. So does Pakistan, which is already politically unstable. A number of paramilitary, 'terrorist' groups shelter under the wing of its military leaders. In the next few years biological weapons of mass destruction will become much more readily available to non-state organizations. The risk that an act of terrorism could escalate into a devastating war, as happened in 1914, is merely the worst of a number of possible nightmare scenarios for South Asia.[1]

The spread of the Industrial Revolution across the globe from its beginnings in Britain has transformed and destabilized international relations in the last two centuries. The rise of China is the latest act in the drama. Apt and frightening parallels are often drawn with the rise of Germany and Europe's descent into war in 1914. It proved impossible peacefully to integrate the growing power of European, capitalist and semi-liberal Germany into the global order that before 1914 was largely steered from London. China is a far greater challenge. Beijing's role in determining the world's future has revolutionary implications as regards not just who holds power but also which values predominate. In previous eras it is hard to imagine that American–Chinese rivalry would not have ended in war. The existence of nuclear weapons makes the risks of war immense and the chances of anything that could meaningfully be called victory extremely doubtful. That is the key reason why all-out war between Washington and Beijing remains improbable. Improbable does not mean impossible. Plentiful room remains for miscalculation, accident and failed brinkmanship. Like a virus, war has the horrible habit of reinventing itself in order to survive. New technologies raise the possibility of limited and therefore winnable war. In a crisis where decisions need to be made in minutes cyber warfare has the potential to undermine military command and control systems.

The competition between China and the United States has become an ideological struggle. The United States (and some other Western countries) are denouncing Chinese efforts to infiltrate their economies, steal their secrets and influence public opinion. I suspect that American-style democracy is a greater and more intrusive threat to China's internal stability than anything attempted by Chinese policies towards the First World. China's rulers must surely see it that way. In my first chapter I described the United States as the heir of Aristotle and Chinese Confucian bureaucracy as the heir of Plato. There is just enough truth to this idea to make it more than a glitzy catchphrase. It does at least point to the fact that communism has little to do with the current American–Chinese competition, though it is a useful slogan in domestic American politics. Leaving aside ideology, the history of the United States and China makes sharp differences between the two superpowers' instincts and perspectives inevitable. China's history is the story of acute vulnerability in the face of the steppe nomads and ecological disaster, together with catastrophic loss of life when dynastic power disintegrated. On the contrary, no great power was ever born under a luckier star than the United States. The USA has long coastlines on the world's two greatest oceans. It has never had a serious geopolitical rival in its entire hemisphere. Colonists arriving from eighteenth-century Europe's most advanced and enterprising country had the resources of a continent at their disposal. The Americans exploited this opportunity with wonderful energy, intelligence and enterprise. In politics their greatest achievement was to combine the continental scale required by empire with the preservation of local, republican self-government. This was the beauty of American federalism.

Nevertheless, for all their differences, the United States and China share one obvious similarity – they are superpowers. In the era of climate change the contrasting strengths and weaknesses of empire and nation become even starker. Communities will probably need a strong degree of solidarity, discipline and self-sacrifice to weather this crisis. Governments will need legitimacy. It is easier to achieve this in a small-scale, ethno-linguistic and historical nation state. On the other hand, it is the great powers that will be the key to whether or not the world overcomes the unprecedented challenges of climate change. They are the greatest polluters. They alone have the power to make a difference on a global scale, and this will become even truer if geo-engineering comes on to the agenda. Their competition and conflicts could make any coordinated response to climate change impossible.

Empires were always hard to govern because of their size and diversity. In the pre-modern world emperors were helped by the fact that the responsibilities of government were narrow and empire's survival usually depended on holding the allegiance of the small social elite whose systems of local patronage and coercion were in general the everyday reality of power for most of the population. In the modern era of big government and mass politics this is no longer true. In his memoirs Barack Obama writes that his time as president taught him how extremely limited was the power of a modern democratic leader when it came to domestic policies, 'especially in big, multi-ethnic, multi-religious societies like India and the United States'. The problem is that climate change seems certain to demand radical and painful policies from governments and peoples. With all its astonishing achievements, technology on its own will not meet the challenge of climate change. Effective and intelligent government will also be essential. That may be hard to find even as regards internal policy. Persuading one's own electorate and foreign states to subscribe to a coordinated global response to climate change will be much harder.[2]

This book was written amidst the coronavirus pandemic and it was hard not to view this crisis as a small, early foretaste of much greater crises to come. Responses to the Covid pandemic raised the nasty suspicion that Chinese authoritarian state capitalism may prove better suited to our times than American democracy. In that context it is worth recalling that the fate of the empires studied in this book in the end above all turned on how effectively they responded to external challenges. Nevertheless, it is far too early to draw final conclusions from the pandemic and they are in any case unlikely to be black and white. The failure of the Chinese central government in the pandemic's initial phase was the product of the centre's inability to control local officials or gain an accurate sense of what was happening in Wuhan. Every Chinese emperor faced this problem. The absence of an autonomous press and judiciary is even more harmful in empires than in smaller countries. In their absence, only a powerful autocrat working through intrusive and often crude police measures can hope to control his officials and ensure the execution of policies and the protection of ordinary subjects. Powerful autocrats can devastate societies, wreck economies and terrify neighbours. They seldom improve with old age, as this book has frequently illustrated. Behind the facade of neo-Confucian righteousness China's last truly great emperor, Yongzheng, combined a strong sense of the responsibilities of his office with flashes of humanity and a surprisingly wry self-awareness. It would be comforting to know that President Xi Jinping shares these qualities. On the other hand, it does not seem to me self-evident that every senior official who fears the impact of American-style democracy on China must necessarily be either a villain or a communist. Awareness of the immense challenges climate change will impose on China must strengthen such fears.

The American people are as convinced as any Confucian emperor of the superiority of their political system (democracy) and the virtue of their sovereign (themselves). Beyond question, democracy is a more suitable political system in the modern world than monarchical neo-Confucianism. The essential virtue of the sovereign is a necessary myth in any political system. Even so, the history of imperial monarchy suggests that government functions best when the sovereign takes his own virtue with a pinch of salt. In all political systems succession struggles are a time of weakness. The American electoral cycle means that such struggles are never-ending. Long-term planning and policy become even harder than in most other democracies. Parts of the American political class have shown that they need no lessons from the courtiers of old when it comes to ruthless self-interest, tunnel vision, and a fixed determination to flatter the sovereign and tell him only what he wants to hear. To do them justice, controlling the sovereign was never easy. In the last resort it is simpler to assassinate an emperor than to retire or tranquilize a people.

Unfortunately, the American sovereign currently has many reasons to be angry. *Inter alia*, First-World liberal democracy cohabited comfortably with global capitalism in part because the First World took most of the benefits for itself and dumped most of the costs on the Third World. The shift in the global balance of power is sharing the burdens more fairly. China's growing power is one aspect of this. Another is the rise of a billion or more Asians into the middle class at the same time as workers in the First World are suffering. Within the First World those elements which were 'losers' in the West's rise to global dominance – above all the descendants of African slaves – are raising their voices. The livelihoods, status and identity of White electorates are threatened. Given the rapid growth of hereditary inequality and privilege in the United States, 'ordinary' Americans have good reason to suspect polite lullabies about meritocracy. For elites and the political class to encourage increasingly pre-modern levels of inequality while preaching democracy and populism is bound to create great tensions. Pre-modern societies and governments were legitimized by explicitly inegalitarian ideologies which enjoyed widespread acceptance.

Watching Donald Trump at work when I was writing this book made me think more kindly of emperors. Trump appeared to share the last German emperor's characteristics – narcissism, bullying, bombast and the inability to keep his mouth shut being the most obvious – without William II's periodic flashes of intelligence and the residual ethical constraints left over from a Victorian education. Along with much of the old elite, in the bitterness of exile William subsequently blamed defeat and revolution in 1918 partly on the Jews. Anti-semitism was the most 'successful' and catastrophic conspiracy theory in modern Western history. Thus far, the falsehoods and fantasies encouraged by Donald Trump seem mild by comparison. But when the young William first began to play with anti-semitism in the 1880s the genocide of the 1940s would have been unimaginable.

Unlike Donald Trump, most of the rulers studied in this book had an exalted sense of their office and the behaviour it required – sometimes of course much too exalted. They usually had some sense of commitment to something beyond their own egos – even if sometimes only to their dynasties. Almost always they were educated to feel responsible for – if never to – the societies they ruled. Most of them had some ethical and religious principles, even if these often weakened in the face of the necessities and temptations of politics and power. Of course, I am not arguing for sacred, hereditary monarchy as the answer to today's challenges. That would require someone much more eccentric even than myself. Most contemporary First-World leaders are far superior to Donald Trump. The problem is that they need to be much superior not just to him but also to all the emperors in history. Climate change poses challenges to government of a magnitude never previously encountered. If today's leaders fail in rising to that challenge, then all other human aspirations will also fail. Moreover, no emperor ever faced the prospect of ending human existence in the course of a weekend-long international crisis that drew him away from the soothing influences of his harem or his golf course.[3]

Notes

1. BEING AN EMPEROR

1. As regards empires, the fullest, up-to-date history is Peter Bang, Christopher Bayly and Walter Scheidel (eds), *The Oxford World History of Empire*, Oxford, 2021. The most comprehensive and easily understood one-volume survey is Jane Burbank and Frederick Cooper, *Empires in World History*, Princeton, NJ, 2010. The closest thing to a comparative study of structure and agency in imperial monarchy is Alois Winterling (ed.), *Zwischen Strukturgeschichte und Biographie. Probleme und Perspektiven romischen Kaisergeschichte*, Munich, 2011.

2. I consulted Per Saugstad, *A History of Modern Psychology*, Cambridge, 2018, on the application of modern theories of psychology to the heroes of this book. But only very seldom do we know enough about these people to apply such theories to their cases with any confidence. Pierre Monnet and Jean-Claude Schmitt (eds), *Autobiographies Souveraines*, Paris, 2012, is a good introduction to autobiographical writings by monarchs in the premodern world.

3. On the origins and early history of the Japanese monarchy see Ben-Ami Shillony, *Enigma of the Emperors*, Folkestone, 2005, chs 1–5, pp. 1–38. On monarchy and the Shinto religion see Helen Hardacre, *Shinto: A History*, Oxford, 2017. For anthropological studies of pre-historical monarchy see especially David Graeber and Marshall Sahlins, *On Kings*, Chicago, IL, 2017, 'Introduction', pp. 1–22, and Sahlins, ch. 1, 'The Original Political Society', pp. 23–69, and Kent Flannery and Joyce Marcus, *The Creation of Inequality*, Cambridge, MA, 2012.

4. On magic, astrology, Julian and Joseph see later discussion in this book: ch. 2, pp. 4–5, ch. 5, pp. 72–5, ch. 12, pp. 254–5, ch. 15, pp. 356–7, 359–64. On the decline of magical thinking in the face of science and reason see e.g. Stuart Clark, *Thinking with Demons*, Oxford, 1997; Toby E. Huff, *The Rise of Early Modern Science: Islam, China and the West*, Cambridge, 2017; Keith Thomas, *Religion and the Decline of Magic*, London, 1971; and Michael Hunter, *The Decline of Magic*, New Haven, CT, 2020.

5. Friendship, its possibility or otherwise for a monarch, and its political consequences, is a thread that runs through this book. It is discussed in the Roman context, e.g. by Daniel J. Kapust, *Flattery and the History of Political Thought*, Cambridge, 2018, esp. ch. 1, pp. 30–63. It resurfaced strongly in the 'era of the favourite' in early modern Europe: see e.g. J.H. Elliott and L.W.B. Brockliss (eds.), *The World of the Favourite*, New Haven, CT, 1999. To the point are Louis XIV's comments in *Mémoire de Louis XIV*, Paris, 1806, (ed) J.L.M. de Gain-Montagnec, pp. 60–2.

6. Manfred Kets de Vries, *The CEO Whisperer*, Cham, 2021, p. 4.

7. The key text on Louis XIII is A. Lloyd Moote, *Louis XIII: The Just*, Berkeley, CA, 1989. J.H. Shennan, *The Bourbons: The History of a Dynasty*, London, 2007, is the best introduction to the dynasty: ch. 4, pp. 61–94, covers Louis XIII.

8. Kets de Vries, *CEO Whisperer*, p. 157; J.H. Elliott, *Richelieu and Olivares*, Cambridge, 1984, p. 38.

9. Barack Obama, *A Promised Land*, London, 2020, e.g. pp. 228, 319, 534; David Runciman, *Where Power Stops*, London, 2019, pp. 92–3.

10. Runciman, *Where Power Stops*, p. 9; Kets de Vries, *CEO Whisperer*, pp. 11, 117. Of the many texts I read on leadership, the three I found most valuable were Kets de Vries, *CEO Whisperer*, Nannerl O. Keohane, *Thinking about Leadership*, Princeton, NJ, 2010 (the quote is from p. 69), and Keith Grint, *Leadership: A Very Short Introduction*, Oxford, 2010.

11. Louis XIV, *Mémoires*, Part I, pp. 8–9, 114, 121, 140–1, 150–2, 164–6, 176–7, 185 (examine self strictly); Part 2, pp. 16–20, 90–2 (appointments).

12. N. Machiavelli, *The Prince*, ed. Q. Skinner and R. Price, Cambridge, 1998, pp. 6, 67, 82–3.

13. For Weber's own views on authority and charisma, see above all Max Weber, 'The Profession and Vocation of Politics', pp. 309–69, in P. Lassman (ed.), *Weber: Political Writings*, Cambridge, 1994. There is a vast literature on Weber and charisma: a good place to start is Thomas E. Dow, 'The Theory of Charisma', *The Sociological Quarterly*, 10:3, 1969, pp. 306–18.

14. The quotation is on p. 8 of Eva Horn, 'Narrating Charisma', *New German Critique*, 38:3, 2011, pp. 1–16.

15. The essential introduction to the comparative history of dynasty and dynasties is Jeroen Duindam, *Dynasties: A Global History of Power, 1300–1800*, Cambridge, 2015.

16. On Africa and female rule, apart from Duindam, *Dynasties*, see also Jeroen Duindam, *Dynasty*, Oxford, 2019, pp. 52–8. On women, monarchy and power see e.g. Scott Wells and Ping Yao, 'The Gendering of Power in the Family and the State', pp. 55–75, in Craig Benjamin (ed.), *The Cambridge World History*, Cambridge, 2015: vol. IV, *A World with States, Empires and Networks, 1200 BCE–900 CE*. The overall editor of *The Cambridge World History* is Merry Wiesner-Hanks.

17. Wells and Ping Yao, 'The Gendering of Power', is excellent on these points. A good introduction to the roles played by women at royal courts is Anne Walthall (ed.), *Servants of the Dynasty: Palace Women in World History*, Berkeley, CA, 2008. There are countless biographies of female rulers but a far smaller number of comparative studies of female rulers and rulership in specific eras, regions and cultures. These we will encounter in later chapters. On Chinese attitudes to female rule see e.g. Keith McMahon, *Women Shall Not Rule: Imperial Wives and Concubines in China from Han to Liao*, Lanham, MD, 2013.

18. On the Ottoman harem, see Lesley Pierce, *The Imperial Harem*, Oxford, 1993. On the Qing dynasty, Evelyn S. Rawski, *The Last Emperors*, Berkeley, CA, 1998, esp. ch. 4, pp. 127–59.

19. Carolyn Harris, *Queenship and Revolution in Early Modern Europe*, Houndmills, 2016, is an interesting comparison of the roles and fates of Henrietta Maria and Marie-Antoinette.

20. Jacques LeGoff, *Saint Louis*, Notre Dame, IL, 2009, pp. 62–3: the foreign-born regent, Queen Blanche, was accused of diverting French revenues to help her foreign relatives, of clinging to power and of immorality – i.e. sexual relations with the papal legate. For more on Blanche and her role, see Lindy Grant, *Blanche of Castile: Queen of France*, New Haven, CT, 2016.

21. All these points are discussed at greater length in later chapters. The most vital sources are Pierce, *Imperial Harem*, Rawski, *Last Emperors*, and Russell E. Martin, *A Bride for the Tsar*, DeKalb, IL, 2012.

22. The best introduction to the issue of succession remains the Introduction by Jack Goody (pp. 1–56) in Jack Goody (ed.), *Succession to High Office*, Cambridge, 1966. For the specific examples given here see the relevant later chapters of this book. There are some parallels with succession in the animal world: see e.g. Stephen Moss, *Dynasties*, London, 2018, esp. ch. 2, pp. 73–123.

23. All biographies of rulers discuss their education and upbringing. Comparative studies of royal education are far rarer: two good ones are Pascale Mormiche, *Devenir prince. L'école de pouvoir en France XVIIe–XVIIIe siècles*, Paris, 2009, and Aysha Pollnitz, *Princely Education in Early Modern Britain*, Cambridge, 2015.

24. Antony Black, *A World History of Ancient Political Thought*, Oxford, 2016, pp. 13–20, best sums up the reasons for the dominance of ancient political thinking by sacred, hereditary monarchy. Much of his book is an extended commentary on this theme.

25. The key sources are cited in note 3. In addition, see Louis XIV, *Mémoires*, Part 1, pp. 237–9; Part 2, pp. 55–6.

26. Sarah Allen, *The Heir and the Sage*, Albany, NY, 2016, p. 10. On ancient dynasties and popular legends, see above all Richard van Leeuwen, *Narratives of Kingship in Eurasian Empires, 1300–1800*, Leiden, 2017.

27. Aristotle, *The Politics and the Constitution of Athens*, (ed.) Steven Everson, Cambridge, 1996, pp. 86–7, 108, 174. Plato, *The Republic*, (ed.) G.R.F. Ferrari, Cambridge, 2000, pp. 122, 175, 190. For discussion of Chinese political ideals, bureaucracy and emperorship see ch. 6.

28. Baron Charles de Montesquieu, 'Réflexions sur la Monarchie Universelle en Europe', passim, but esp. p. 19, in *Deux Opuscules de Montesquieu*, Paris, 1891. On the history of public debt see David Graeber, *Debt: The First 5,000 Years*, New York, 2011, and James MacDonald, *A Free Nation Deep in Debt: The Financial Roots of Democracy*, New York, 2003.

29. By far the best comparative study of universal empire is Peter Bang and Darius Kolodziejczyk (eds), *Universal Empire: A Comparative Approach to Imperial Culture and Representation in World History*, Cambridge, 2012; see also Peter Fibiger Bang, 'The King of Kings: Universal Hegemony, Imperial Power, and a New Comparative History of Rome', ch. 14, pp. 322–49, in J.P. Arnason and K.A. Raaflaub (eds), *The Roman Empire in Context: Historical and Comparative Perspectives*, London, 2011.

30. Clifford Geertz, *Negara: The Theatre State in Nineteenth-Century Bali*, Princeton, NJ, 1980, pp. 4, 13.

31. A vast and contentious topic. The single best guide in my opinion is C.A. Bayly, *The Birth of the Modern World, 1780–1914*, Oxford, 2004.

32. On the caliphate see ch. 9. On Eurasian geopolitics see Victor Lieberman, *Strange Parallels: South-East Asia in Global Context, c. 800–1830*, 2 vols, Cambridge, 2003, and Jos Gommans, 'The Warband in the Making of Eurasian Empires', ch. 4, pp. 297–383, in Maiake van Berkell and Jeroen Duindam (eds), *Prince, Pen and Sword: Eurasian Perspectives*, Leiden, 2018.

33. Anthony Kaldellis, *The Byzantine Republic: People and Power in New Rome*, Cambridge, MA, 2015, pp. xiv–xvi.

34. On Song ethno-nationalism see Nicholas Tackett, *The Origins of the Chinese Nation*, Cambridge, 2018. An earlier study of Chinese ethno-nationalism is E. Dikotter, *The Discourse of Race in Modern China*, London, 1992. Graham Allison, *Destined for War: Can America and China Escape Thucydides's Trap?*, New York, 2017, became a best-seller. Even my *Russia against Napoleon: The Struggle for Europe, 1807–1815*, London, 2011, is constructed around the question as to why modern Russians obsess about 1812 but forget 1813 and 1814. The statistics on the Ming and Qing empires are from vol. 1 of Peter Fibiger Bang, Christopher Bayly and Walter Scheidel (eds.), *Oxford World History of Empire*, Oxford, 2021: ch. 2, Walter Scheidel, 'The Scale of Empire: Territory, Population, Distribution', pp. 91–110: here p. 92.

35. Peter Fibiger Bang, 'Empire – A World History', *Oxford World History of Empire*, ch. 1, pp. 1–87, here p. 78; Peter Vries, *State, Economy and the Great Divergence: Great Britain and China, 1680s to 1850s*, London, 2015, links the intensive governance possible in a medium-sized country to Britain's growing lead over China in this era in economic terms.

36. Machiavelli, *Prince*, pp. 6, 67, 82–3.
37. The potential bibliography is especially vast: see e.g. on fiscal systems Andrew Monson and Walter Scheidel (eds), *Fiscal Regimes and the Political Economy of Pre-Modern States*, Cambridge, 2015. An interesting way to approach the idea of royal justice is, so to speak, upside down: Nikos Panou and Hester Schadee (eds), *Evil Lords: Theories and Representations of Tyranny from Antiquity to the Renaissance*, Oxford, 2018.
38. In recent years the literature on royal courts has increased enormously in both quality and quantity. The place to start is Jeroen Duindam, Tulay Artan and I. Metin Kunt (eds.), *Royal Courts in Dynastic States and Empires*, Leiden, 2011. On hunts see Thomas T. Allsen, *The Royal Hunt in Eurasian History*, Philadelphia, PA, 2006.
39. The quotation is from p. 209 of Alan Strathern, *Unearthly Powers: Religious and Political Change in World History*, Cambridge, 2019.
40. My comments on the training of beauty queens and models are owed to conversations with my daughter-in-law, Raine Baljak, who was the beauty queen of a sizeable chunk of her native Philippines and works as a model (as well as doing a university degree and running a business!). See e.g. her lecture on what it takes to be a beauty queen and model, available on YouTube at https://youtube.com/mef9MKEJnno or www.rainebaljak.com.
41. For Finer's comment see S.E. Finer, *The History of Government*: vol. 1, *Ancient Monarchies and Empires*, Oxford, 1997, pp. 472–3.

2. CRADLE OF EMPIRE

1. Antony Black, *A World History of Ancient Political Thought*, Oxford, 2016, p 34; Amanda Podany, *The Ancient Near East: A Very Short Introduction*, Oxford, 2014, p. 27.
2. W.G. Lambert, 'Kingship in Ancient Mesopotamia', pp. 54–70, in John Day (ed.), *King and Messiah in Israel and the Ancient Near East*, London, 2013.
3. Podany, *Ancient Near East*, pp. 40–6.
4. Gojko Barjamovic, 'Mesopotamian Empires', pp. 120–60 (quotation from p. 138), in Peter Fibiger Bang and Walter Scheidel (eds), *The Oxford Handbook of the State in the Ancient Near East and Mediterranean*, Oxford, 2013; Podany, *Ancient Near East*, p. 103.
5. Bleda S. During, *The Imperialization of Assyria*, Cambridge, 2020, p. 142.
6. Jon Taylor, 'Knowledge: The Key to Assyrian Power', pp. 88–97 (here pp. 93–4), in Gareth Brereton (ed.), *I am Ashurbanipal, King of the World, King of Assyria*, London, 2018.
7. Ibid, p. 88.

8. Judith Bunbury states that 'Egypt ... is a product of the Nile, the world's longest river': Judith Bunbury, *The Nile and Ancient Egypt*, Cambridge, 2019, p. 2.

9. Black, *Ancient Political Thought*, pp 20–1. The comparison between Egypt and Mesopotamian monarchy is drawn largely from the editors' Introduction (pp. 3–32) but also from other contributions in Jane A. Hill, Philip Jones and Antonio J. Morales (eds), *Experiencing Power, Generating Authority*, Philadelphia, PA, 2013.

10. Arielle P. Kozloff, *Amenhotep III: Egypt's Radiant Pharaoh*, Cambridge, 2012, pp. 2–4, 242–52; Ronald T. Ridley, *Akhenaten: A Historian's View*, Cairo, 2019, p. 216.

11. The story told in this and the previous paragraph owes everything to Kozloff, *Amenhotep*.

12. My two key texts were Ridley, *Akhenaten*, and Nicholas Reeves, *Akhenaten: Egypt's False Prophet*, London, 2019. Note that Kozloff believes that Akhenaten felt that Amun and the old gods had let him down: *Amenhotep III*, p. 2.

13. Cecily J. Hilsdale, 'Imperial Monumentalism, Ceremony, and Forms of Pageantry: The Inter-Imperial Obelisk in Istanbul', ch. 6, pp. 223–65, in Peter Bang, Christopher Bayly and Walter Scheidel (eds), *The Oxford World History of Empire*, Oxford, 2021, vol. 1: the quotation is on p. 233.

14. The bible for those interested in Russian ritual and ceremony is the two volumes of Richard S. Wortman, *Scenarios of Power: Myth and Ceremony in Russian Monarchy*, Princeton, NJ, 1995 and 2000.

3. THE PERSIAN EMPERORS AND ALEXANDER OF MACEDON

1. A. Shapour Shakbazi, 'The Achaemenid Persian Empire', pp. 120–41 (here p. 121), in Touraj Daryee (ed.), *The Oxford Handbook of Iranian History*, for the term 'historical romance'. Xenophon's book has even been rendered as a first-person autobiography and presented as a manual on leadership aimed at business schools by Larry Hedrick in his *Xenophon's Cyrus the Great: The Arts of Leadership and War*, New York, 2006.

2. For a fuller definition of this term see Antony Black, *A World History of Ancient Political Thought*, Oxford, 2016, pp. 13–20.

3. This paragraph is largely lifted from Prods Oktor Skjaervo, 'Avestan Society', pp. 57–119, in Daryee, *Iranian History*, but it also owes something to Abolala Sondaver, *The Aura of Kings: Legitimacy and Divine Sanction in Iranian Kingship*, Costa Mesa, CA, 2003.

4. Pierre Briant sums up the relationship between king and Persian aristocracy as a 'gift-service exchange' and discusses it at length and convincingly. Most

of this paragraph is drawn from Pierre Briant, *From Cyrus to Alexander: A History of the Persian Empire*, Winona Lake, IN, 2002, esp. ch. 8, pp. 302–54.

5. Ibid, p. 308.

6. Amelie Kuhrt, *The Persian Empire: A Corpus of Sources from the Achaemenid Period*, pt. III, ch. 11, docs. C 16 and 17, pp. 501–5.

7. The quotation from Plato is on p. 3 of Richard Stoneman, *Xerxes: A Persian Life*, New Haven, CT, 2015.

8. Robin Lane Fox, *Alexander the Great*, London, 2004, pp. 48, 64–5; Elizabeth D. Carney, 'Dynastic Loyalty and Dynastic Collapse in Macedonia', ch. 11, pp. 147–62, in Pat Wheatley and Elizabeth Baynham (eds), *East and West in the World Empire of Alexander*, Oxford, 2015: the quotation about religion is on p. 149. On Philip see Ian Worthington, *By the Spear: Philip II, Alexander the Great and the Rise and Fall of the Macedonian Empire*, Oxford, 2014.

9. Lane Fox, *Alexander*, p. 48. Lane Fox's biography conveys wonderfully the spirit of the man.

10. John Boardman, *Alexander the Great: From his Death to the Present Day*, Princeton, NJ, 2019, pp. 100–1. As usual when faced with an unfamiliar subject, I turned first to an Oxford *Very Short Introduction*, in this case Hugh Bowden, *Alexander the Great: A Very Short Introduction*, Oxford, 2010. From there I passed to Ian Worthington (ed.), *Alexander the Great: A Reader*, Oxford, 2012: a natural and rewarding move; Lane Fox, *Alexander*, p. 487.

11. Sarah Brown Ferrario, *Historical Agency and the 'Great Man' in Classical Greece*, Cambridge, 2014, pp. 341–2.

12. The quotations come from pp. 4–6 of Lucy Hughes-Hallett, *Heroes: Saviours, Traitors and Supermen*, London, 2004, but the whole of the Prologue and ch. 1 (on Achilles) are relevant to this paragraph.

4. THE ROMAN IMPERIAL MONARCHY

1. Henri Pirenne, *Mohammed and Charlemagne*. The first edition was published posthumously in French in 1935.

2. The ideas in the previous two paragraphs were almost entirely lifted from Edward N. Luttwak, *The Grand Strategy of the Roman Empire: From the First Century CE to the Third*, Baltimore, MD, 1990.

3. Stephen Mitchell, *A History of the Later Roman Empire A.D. 284–641*, Oxford, 2015, p. 56.

4. Although I have read a good deal about Augustus, I should record here my great debt to Jochen Bleichen, *Augustus: The Biography*, London, 2015. On the institution of emperorship, I am indebted to Fergus Millar, *The Emperor in the Roman World*, Ithaca, NY, 1992.

5. Peter Garnsey, 'Introduction: The Hellenistic and Roman Periods', ch. 20, pp. 401–14, in Christopher Rowe and Malcolm Schofield (eds.), *The Cambridge History of Greek and Roman Political Thought*, Cambridge, 2005, p. 411; Carlos F. Norena, *Imperial Ideals in the Roman West*, Cambridge, 2011, p. 316.

6. Peter Fibiger Bang, 'The Roman Empire', ch. 9, pp. 240–89, in Peter Bang, Christopher Bayly and Walter Scheidel (eds), *The Oxford World History of Empire*, Oxford, 2021, vol. 2. The quotation is from p. 273. Traditionally, a big contrast was made between the centralized and bureaucratic Han Empire and the much more decentralized Roman one. The contrast remains though the differences were less than are traditionally depicted. The best up-to-date comparisons are in Walter Scheidel (ed.), *State Power in Ancient China and Rome*, Oxford, 2015.

7. Christopher Kelly, *Ruling the Later Roman Empire*, Cambridge, MA, 2004, p. 192; Peter Eich, 'Late Roman Imperial Bureaucracy from a Comparative Perspective', ch. 4, pp. 90–149, in Scheidel, *State Power*, also made a significant contribution to this paragraph.

8. Kelly, *Ruling the Later Roman Empire*, pp. 192, 197–8.

9. Antony Black, *A World History of Ancient Political Thought*, Oxford, 2016, p. 185. Most of this paragraph is owed to Irtai Gradel, *Emperor Worship and Roman Religion*, Oxford, 2002.

10. This paragraph is drawn above all from ch. 4, pp. 161ff, of Olivier Hekster, *Emperors and Ancestors: Roman Rulers and the Constraints of Tradition*, Oxford, 2015.

11. Bleichen, *Augustus*, p. 31. The discussion and statistics are drawn from P. Garnsey and R. Saller, *The Roman Empire: Economy, Society and Culture*, Berkeley, CA, 1987, ch. 7, pp. 126ff, and Richard Saller, 'Family and Household', ch. 29, pp. 855ff, in Alan Bowman, Peter Garnsey and Dominic Rathbone (eds), *The Cambridge Ancient History*: vol. XI, *The High Empire. A.D. 70–192*, Cambridge, 2000.

12. *Marcus Aurelius: Meditations*, London, 2006: this edition translated by Martin Hammond with an Introduction by Diskin Clay, pp. 63, 89, 103–4.

13. This paragraph is largely lifted from Frank McLynn, *Marcus Aurelius: A Life*, Cambridge, MA, 2009. In discussing Marcus Aurelius I also owe a debt to Anthony Birley's biography: *Marcus Aurelius: A Biography*, London, 1966, and to the authors of chs 20 (Peter Garnsey), 22 (Malcolm Schofield), 26 (Miriam Griffiths) and 29 (Christopher Gill) in Christopher Rowe and Malcolm Schofield (eds.), *The Cambridge History of Greek and Roman Political Thought*, Cambridge, 2006.

14. *Marcus Aurelius: Meditations*, pp. 5, 6–8, 51–2.

15. Ibid, pp. 23, 71–2.

16. Ibid, pp. vii, 94.

17. The quotations are from Peter Sarris, *Empires of Faith: The Fall of Rome to the Rise of Islam, 500–700*, Oxford, 2011, p. 23. These are very complicated

issues and I owe a big debt both to Peter Sarris's work and to Gilbert Dagron, *Emperor and Priest: The Imperial Office in Byzantium*, Cambridge, 2003: the whole book is vital to my work but pt. 1 and pt. 2, ch. 4, pp. 125ff, are especially relevant to the role of Constantine.

18. H.C. Teitler, *The Last Pagan Emperor: Julian the Apostate and the War against Christianity*, Oxford, 2017, pp. 24–5.

5. ASHOKA, INDIA AND THE ORIGINS OF BUDDHISM

1. Antony Black, *A World History of Ancient Political Thought*, Oxford, 2016, p. 68. A brief and up-to-date guide to early Indian civilization is provided by the first two chapters (pp. 1–27) of Marc Jason Gilbert, *South Asia in World History*, Oxford, 2017.

2. A good introduction to the Axial Age is Bjorn Wittrock, 'The Axial Age in World History', ch. 5, pp. 101–19, in Craig Benjamin (ed.), *The Cambridge World History: vol. IV, A World with States, Empires and Networks, 1200 BCE–900 CE*, Cambridge, 2015. By far the best work on the *Arthashastra* is Mark McClish, *The History of the Arthashastra*, Cambridge, 2019. I follow his interpretation of the book's origins, history and authorship. Nayanjot Lahiri, *Ashoka in Ancient India*, Cambridge, MA, 2015, p. 63, writes that Ashoka will certainly have known the book. The evidence for this is lacking.

3. Upinder Singh, *Political Violence in Ancient India*, Cambridge, MA, 2017, p. 123.

4. The version of Kautilya, *The Arthashastra*, that I used was a 2016 edition, published by Eternal Sun Books, and printed in Great Britain by Amazon. The quotations are from pp. 30, 189 and 299.

5. Lahiri, *Ashoka*, pp. 63–4; Kautilya, *Arthashastra*, pp. 26–7, 188–90.

6. Black, *Ancient Political Thought*, pp. 76–7; Singh, *Political Violence*, pp. 120–1; Kautilya, *Arthashrastra*, pp. 16–21, 26.

7. Lahiri, *Ashoka*, p. 187.

8. The quotations are from the Thirteenth Major Rock Edict and are drawn from *A Translation of the Edicts of Ashoka*, which can be found at katinka-hesselink.net/Tibet/asoka 1b.

9. Lahiri, *Ashoka*, pp. 135–6.

10. Starting from great ignorance as regards Buddhism, my first recourse was to Damien Keown, *Buddhism: A Very Short Introduction*, Oxford, 2013. From there I graduated to Peter Harvey, *An Introduction to Buddhism*, Cambridge, 2013. Alan Strathern, *Unearthly Powers: Religious and Political Change in World History*, Cambridge, 2019, is much the best comparative study. Although his main concern is conversion to Christianity, he compares

the Buddhist case at length: e.g. pp. 3–5, 131ff, 151ff. Romila Thapar, *Asoka and the Decline of the Mauryas*, Delhi, 2012, esp. her Preword and ch. 1, pp. xv–xliii and 1–7.

11. Singh, *Political Violence*, pp. 44–5; Shonaleeka Kaul, 'South Asia', ch. 18, pp. 480–513, in Benjamin, *Cambridge World History*, vol. IV.

12. The quotations are from *Translation*, Tenth Major Rock Edict, Minor Rock Inscriptions-Schism Edict and Twelfth Major Rock Edict.

13. *Translation*, Tenth Major Rock Edict; John S. Strong, *The Legend of King Asoka: A Study and Translation of the Asokavadana*, Princeton, NJ, 1983, p. 143.

14. Strong, *Legend*, ch. 2, pp. 38–70.

15. On long-term influence and Nehru, see Singh, *Political Violence*, pp. 1–3, 25–30.

16. On the spread of Buddhism see Tansen Sen, 'The Spread of Buddhism', ch. 17, pp. 447–82, in Benjamin K. Kedar and Merry E. Wiesner-Hanks (eds), *The Cambridge World History*: vol. V, *Expanding Webs of Exchange and Conflict, 500 CE to 1500 CE*, Cambridge, 2015, and Harvey, *Introduction*, esp. pp. 100–2. On Buddhism, the contemporary West and psychiatry see Keown, *Buddhism*, pp. 138–41, and Manfred Kets de Vries, *The CEO Whisperer*, Cham, 2021, pp. 27–33.

6. THE ORIGINS OF CHINESE EMPERORSHIP

1. Yuri Pines, *The Everlasting Empire: The Political Culture of Ancient China and its Imperial Legacy*, Princeton, NJ, 2012, pp. 56–7.

2. This is to adopt the view of Michael Loewe, *Divination, Mythology and Monarchy in Han China*, Cambridge, 1994, esp. ch. 4, pp. 85ff, and Pines, *Everlasting Empire*, ch. 2, pp. 44ff. Mark Edward Lewis, *The Early Chinese Empires: Qin and Han*, Cambridge, MA, 2007, pp. 62–6, partly dissents. See too T. Corey Brennan, 'Toward a Comparative Understanding of the Executive Decision-Making Process in China and Rome', ch. 2, pp. 39–55, in Walter Scheidel (ed.), *State Power in Ancient China and Rome*, Oxford, 2015.

3. Pines, *Everlasting Empire*, p. 1.

4. Li Feng, *Early China: A Social and Cultural History*, Cambridge, 2013, pp. 117, 142–4. I also drew heavily in this paragraph on Sarah Allan, *The Heir and the Sage: Dynastic Legend in Early China*, Albany, NY, 2016.

5. Yuri Pines makes the point that no scholar ever advocated multi-polarity: *Everlasting Empire*, p. 19.

6. These are complex questions not easily summed up in a paragraph: see B. Schwarz, *The World of Thought in Ancient China*, Cambridge, MA, 1985, and Youngmin Kim, *A History of Chinese Political Thought*, Cambridge, 2018.

7. There is further complexity, including disagreement as to what constitutes a religion and whether Confucianism was a religion: Damien Keown, *Buddhism: A Very Short Introduction*, Oxford, 2013, pp. 5–16, has an admirably clear and succinct discussion of the first question. Yinzhong Yao, *An Introduction to Confucianism*, Cambridge, 2000, is a detailed account of the core principles and historical development of Confucianism.

8. Feng, *Early China*, pp. 241–2. On the Great Wall and the First Emperor see note 15.

9. Derek Bodde, 'The State and Empire of Ch'in', pp. 20–102 (here p. 56), in D. Twitchett and M. Loewe (eds), *The History of China*: vol. 1, *The Ch'in and Han Empires: 221 BC–AD 220*, Cambridge, 1986; Gideon Shelach, 'Collapse or Transformation? Anthropological and Archaeological Perspectives on the Fall of Qin', pp. 113–38 (here p. 129), in Yuri Pines, Lothar von Falkenhausen, Gideon Shelach and Robin Yates (eds), *Birth of an Empire: The State of Qin Revisited*, Berkeley, CA, 2014.

10. Dingxin Zhao, *The Confucian-Legalist State: A New Theory of Chinese History*, Oxford, 2015, pp. 266–8.

11. Lewis, *Early Chinese Empires*, p. 61.

12. The comparison to Augustus is made by Peter Fibinger Bang and Karen Turner, ch. 1, pp. 11–38, in Scheidel, *State Power*.

13. Dingxin Zhao, 'The Han Bureaucracy: Its Origin, Nature and Development', pp. 56–89, in Scheidel, *State Power*, here p. 80. My comment on thinking on emperorship in the pre-imperial era is taken from Yuri Pines, *Envisioning Eternal Empire: Chinese Political Thought of the Warring States Era*, Honolulu, 2009, esp. ch. 4, pp. 82ff.

14. I owe much in this paragraph and in the following paragraphs on Wudi to discussions with Peter Bang.

15. Lewis, *Early Chinese Empires*, ch. 6, pp. 128–39, summarizes Chinese relations with the Xiongnu. Nicholas di Cosmo, *Ancient China and Its Enemies: The Rise of Nomadic Power in East Asian History*, Cambridge, 2002, is the key text. For the debate on state activism in Wu's reign see pp. 89–93 of Kim, *Chinese Political Thought*.

16. Michael Loewe, 'The Former Han Dynasty', pp. 103–202, in Twitchett and Loewe, *History of China*, here pp. 153–5. In the same volume, Robert P. Kramers, 'The Development of the Confucian Schools', ch. 7, pp. 747–66, here pp. 753–7.

17. Hans Bielenstein, 'Wang Mang, the Restoration of the Han Dynasty and Later Han', pp. 223–90, in Twitchett and Loewe, *History of China*, here p. 226. Much of this paragraph is drawn from Robert Cutter and William Crowell, *Empresses and Consorts*, Honolulu, 1999.

18. Bielenstein, 'Wang Mang', p. 227.

19. Ibid, pp. 251–90; Patricia Ebrey, 'The Economic and Social History of Later Han', ch. 11, pp. 608–48, in Loewe and Twitchett, *History of China*.

7. NOMADS

1. Quoted in Christoph Baumer, *The History of Central Asia*, 4 vols: here vol. 1, *The Age of the Steppe Warriors*, London, 2012, p. 224.

2. See above all Ursula B. Brosseder, 'Xiongnu and Huns: Archaeological Perspectives on a Centuries-Old Debate about Identity and Migration', pp. 176–88, in Nicola di Cosmo and Michael Maas (eds), *Empire and Exchanges in Eurasian Late Antiquity*, Cambridge, 2018. Brosseder is cautious about the links, as is e.g. Barry Cunliffe, *By Steppe, Desert and Ocean: The Birth of Eurasia*, Oxford, 2015, p. 334.

3. The quote is from p. 27 of Peter Jackson, 'The Mongol Age in Eastern Inner Asia', pp. 26–45, in Nicola di Cosmo, Allen J. Frank and Peter B. Golden (eds), *The Cambridge History of Inner Asia: The Chingissid Age*, vol. 2, Cambridge, 2009. Most of the information in this paragraph is from 'Tatars', pp. 528–30, in Christopher P. Atwood, *Encyclopaedia of Mongolia and the Mongol Empire*, New York, 2004.

4. The quote is from Anatoly M. Khazanov, 'Pastoral Nomadic Migrations and Conquests', pp. 359–82, in Benjamin Z. Kedar and Merry E. Wiesner-Hanks (eds), *The Cambridge World History: Expanding Webs of Exchange and Conflict, 500 CE–1500 CE*, vol. 5, Cambridge, 2015, here p. 360; Cunliffe, *By Steppe*, p. 192, makes the point about predatory nomadism starting in the east.

5. The leading advocate of aristocracy as the guiding principle of the steppe polity is David Sneath, *The Headless State: Aristocratic Orders, Kinship Society and Misrepresentations of Nomadic Inner Asia*, New York, 2007. Peter Golden is among the doubters, commenting that although aristocracy existed it played a much smaller role than in sedentary states: see Peter B. Golden, 'Migrations, Ethnogenesis', ch. 6, pp. 109–19, in di Cosmo et al., *Cambridge History of Inner Asia*, vol. 2.

6. Christopher Beckwith, *Empires of the Silk Road*, Princeton, NJ, 2009, makes a strong argument for the importance and un-aristocratic nature of warbands. So does Jos Gommens, 'The Warband in the Making of Eurasian Empires', ch. 4, pp. 297–383, in Maaike van Berkell and Jeroen Duindam (eds), *Prince, Pen and Sword: Eurasian Perspectives*, Leiden, 2018.

7. The statistics and much of the discussion are drawn from Pita Kelekna, *The Horse in Human History*, Cambridge, 2009, ch. 5, pp. 135–64. On the nomads' bows see Mike Loades, *The Composite Bow*, Oxford, 2016.

8. The losses are stated in Christoph Baumer, *The History of Central Asia:* vol. 2, *The Age of the Silk Roads*, London, 2014, pp. 16–17.

9. Carter Vaughan Findley, *The Turks in World History*, Oxford, 2005, pp. 69–71, makes these comments about Nizam al-Mulk and adds that the empire was destroyed by succession struggles rooted in the universal nomadic belief that sovereignty belonged to the whole royal clan. On Ibn Khaldun see

Robert Irwin, *Ibn Khaldun: An Intellectual Biography*, Princeton, NJ, 2018, esp. ch. 3, pp. 39–64; Khazanov, 'Pastoral Nomadic Migrations and Conquests', p. 360; Beckwith, *Empires*, p. 339; Cunliffe, *By Steppe*, pp. 8–16, on the ecological vulnerability especially of the Mongolian nomads.

10. For a summary of Xiongnu history see e.g. Ying-Shih Yin, 'The Hsiung-nu', pp. 120–49, in Denis Sinor (ed.), *The Cambridge History of Inner Asia*, Cambridge, 1990, vol. 1.

11. This is a very inadequate summary of the history of a fascinating but little-known empire: see e.g. Baumer, *Silk Roads*, pp. 47–60; Craig Benjamin, *Empires of Ancient Eurasia: The First Silk Roads Era, 100 BCE–250 CE*, Cambridge, 2018, ch. 7, pp. 176–203.

12. The quote is from Findley, *Turks*, p. 68. Findley is an immensely useful guide to the history of the Turkish peoples, but his book is well supported by David J. Roxburgh (ed.), *Turks: A Journey of a Thousand Years, 600–1600*, London, 2005, which accompanied an outstanding exhibition at the Royal Academy of Arts.

13. My main sources for the last two paragraphs are Baumer, *Silk Roads*, ch. 5, pp. 173–206, and ch. 8, pp. 255–70, and Findley, *Turks*, pp. 43–8.

14. The quote is from Baumer, *Silk Roads*, p. 261.

15. The quote is from p. 119 of Paul Kahn, 'Introduction to the "Secret History of the Mongols"', ch. 14, in William Fitzhugh, Morris Rossabi and William Honeychurch (eds.), *Genghis Khan and the Mongol Empire*, Washington DC, 2013. Ch. 13, by Morris Rossabi, 'Genghis Khan', pp. 99–109, is also a very useful introduction to Chinggis's personality, rise and reign.

16. The two most useful introductions to Mongol warfare that I encountered are Timothy May, 'The Mongols at War', ch. 26, pp. 191–202, in Fitzhugh et al., *Genghis Khan*: 'Military of the Mongol Empire', and pp. 348–54 in Atwood, *Encyclopaedia*. The comparison with the Assyrians is in Cunliffe, *Steppe*, p. 422.

17. On the law code and 'testament' see Christopher Baumer, *The History of Central Asia: The Age of Islam and the Mongols*, vol. 3, London, 2016, pp. 274–8. On ideology and Tengri, see Anne F. Broadbridge, *Kingship and Ideology in the Islamic and Mongol Worlds*, Cambridge, 2008, ch. 1, pp. 6–25.

18. The quote is from Timothy May, *The Mongol Empire*, Edinburgh, 2018, p. 84. The pieces on 'Mongke Khan' and 'Mongol Empire', pp. 362–9, in Atwood, *Encyclopaedia*, are a fine introduction to the Mongol system of government and Mongke's efforts to consolidate it.

19. Barbara Forbes Manz, *The Rise and Rule of Tamerlane*, Cambridge, 1989, p. 1.

20. Barbara Forbes Manz, 'Temur and the Early Timurids to c. 1450', ch. 10, pp. 182–98, in di Cosmo et al., *Chingissid Age*, here p. 198; Irwin, *Ibn Khaldun*, p. 99.

8. IMPERIAL CIVILIZATION
AND CHINESE TRADITION

1. N. Machiavelli, *The Prince*, ed. Q. Skinner and R. Price, Cambridge, 1998, p. 82.
2. This interpretation is largely drawn from Andrew Eisenberg, *Kingship in Early Medieval China*, Leiden, 2008, ch. 6, pp. 167–94.
3. On locusts see Howard J. Wechsler, 'T'ai-tsung (r. 626–49) the Consolidator', in Denis Twitchett (ed.), *The Cambridge History of China*, vol. 3, pt. 1, Cambridge, 1979, p. 189. On Taizong as soldier, see David A. Graff, *Medieval Chinese Warfare 300–900*, London, 2002, pp. 161, 169.
4. The comments on Taizong as a military commander are largely drawn from Graff, *Medieval Chinese Warfare*, ch. 8, pp. 160ff, but also from Chinghua Tang, *The Ruler's Guide: China's Greatest Emperor and His Timeless Secrets of Success*, Stroud, 2017, ch. 7, pp. 67ff. See also a key article by Jonathan Karam Skaff, 'Tang China's Horse Power: The Borderland Breeding Ranch System', ch. 2, pp. 34–59, in Hyun Jin Kim, Frederik Vervaet and Selim Adah (eds), *Eurasian Empires in Antiquity and the Early Middle Ages*, Cambridge, 2017.
5. The information in these paragraphs is drawn partly from Wechsler, 'T'ai-tsung (r. 626–49) the Consolidator', pp. 193–9, and partly from Tang, *Ruler's Guide*, passim.
6. This paragraph is a summary of key points in Jack W. Chen, *The Poetics of Sovereignty: On Emperor Taizong of the Tang Dynasty*, Cambridge, MA, 2010.
7. The English translations of both documents are reproduced with a long and thoughtful introduction by Denis Twitchett, 'How to be an Emperor: T'ang T'ai-tsung's Vision of His Role', pp. 1–102, in *Asia Major*, 3rd Series, IX, 1996. For the recorded conversations see Tang, *Ruler's Guide*.
8. Twitchett, 'How to be an Emperor', pp. 16–24.
9. Ibid, pp. 22, 26–7, 29–32.
10. Ibid, pp. 56, 69.
11. Ibid, pp. 51–3, 55–8.
12. Denis Twitchett and Howard J. Wechsler, 'The Kao-tsung Reign and the Empress Wu: The Inheritor and the Usurper', pp. 242–89, in Twitchett, *Cambridge History of China*, vol. 3: the quotation is from pp. 244–5. The biography by N. Harry Rothschild is the best source on Wu and ch. 2, pp. 11–16, looks at the influence of the steppe tradition as regards her rise to power: N. Harry Rothschild, *Wu Zhao: China's Only Woman Emperor*, New York, 2008. Keith McMahon, *Women Shall Not Rule: Imperial Wives and Concubines in China from Han to Liao*, Lanham, MD , 2013, ch. 5, pp. 181–208, adds extra information on both Wu and the influence of the steppe tradition.

13. The statistics come from p. 329 of Richard Guisso, 'The Reigns of the Empress Wu, Chung-tsung and Jui-tsung (684–712)', ch. 6, pp. 290–332, in Twitchett, *Cambridge History of China*, vol. 3.

14. Rothschild, *Wu Zhao*, ch. 10, pp. 137–56, discusses Wu's relationship with Buddhism in detail. Peter Harvey, *An Introduction to Buddhism: Teachings, History and Practices*, Cambridge, 2013, pp. 284–6, makes interesting comparisons between the Buddhist, Christian, Muslim and Confucian treatment of women. Mark Edward Lewis, *China's Cosmopolitan Empire: The Tang Dynasty*, Cambridge, MA, 2009, ch. 8, pp. 207ff, discusses Buddhism in Tang China.

15. The basis for this account of Xuanzong's reign is Denis Twitchett, 'Hsuan-tsung (r. 712–56)', ch. 7, pp. 333–463, in Twitchett, *Cambridge History of China*, vol. 3. On An Lushan, nomadic culture and the Tang armies the account is supplemented by Skaff, *Sui-Tang China*, pp. 86–7, but esp. ch. 7, pp. 272ff, and Graff, *Medieval Chinese Warfare*, ch. 10, pp. 205ff. On consorts and lychees see McMahon, *Women Shall Not Rule*, ch. 6, pp. 211ff. On the creation of the East Asian world see Lewis, *China's Cosmopolitan Empire*, pp. 153ff.

16. Walter Scheidel, 'The Scale of Empire', *The Oxford World History of Empire*, 2 vols, Oxford, vol. 1, p. 103.

17. The case for an emerging Chinese elite ethno-national consciousness is taken almost entirely from a fascinating though controversial book by Nicholas Tackett, *The Origins of the Chinese Nation*, Cambridge, 2017.

18. On this see Nicholas Tackett, *The Destruction of the Medieval Chinese Aristocracy*, Cambridge, MA, 2014.

19. The statistics come from Tackett, *Origins*, p. 15. There are succinct introductions to neo-Confucianism as a socio-political system in Dingxin Zhao, *The Confucian-Legalist State: A New Theory of Chinese History*, Oxford, 2001, ch. 12, pp. 331ff, and as an intellectual system in Xinzhong Yao, *An Introduction to Confucianism*, Cambridge, 2000, pp. 96ff, but the key text is Peter K. Bol, *Neo-Confucianism in History*, Cambridge, MA, 2008. Ling Zhang, *The River, the Plain and the State: An Environmental Drama in Northern Song China, 1048–1128*, Cambridge, 2016, is an informative and well-told story of these efforts at water management. Although the author is rather critical of Song efforts, what strikes me is that no other government of that era could have attempted even one-tenth as much.

20. The statistics are from Charles Hartman, 'Sung Government and Politics', ch. 1, pp. 19–136 (here pp. 52–3), in John W. Chaffee and Denis Twitchett (eds.), *The Cambridge History of China: Sung China 960–1279*, vol. 5, pt. 2, Cambridge, 2015. The chapter is my main source on how the Song system of government worked, but for general background see Dieter Kuhn, *The Age of Confucian Rule: The Song Transformation of China*, Cambridge, MA, 2009.

21. This is a very brief summary of a complex issue: my key sources here were Ari Daniel Levine, *Divided by a Common Language: Factional Conflict in Late Northern Song China*, Honolulu, 2008, and Jacyoon Song, *Traces of Grand Peace: Classics and State Activism in Imperial China*, Cambridge, MA, 2015.

22. The key source is Patricia Buckley Ebrey, *Emperor Huizong*, Cambridge, MA, 2014, but see Jay Xu and He Li (eds), *Emperors' Treasures: Chinese Art from the National Palace Museum, Taipei*, San Francisco, CA, 2016, pp. 1–35, on Huizong as an artist, calligrapher and collector, and John W. Chaffee, *Branches of Heaven: A History of the Imperial Clan of Sung China*, Cambridge, MA, 1999, chs 2 and 3, pp. 21–63, on the lives of younger sons.

23. The key sources for this paragraph are Wang Tseng-Yu, 'A History of the Sung Military', ch. 3, pp. 214–49, in Chaffee and Twitchett, *Sung China*, and 'The Defence of the Northern Frontier', ch. 2, pp. 74–104, in Tackett, *Origins*.

9. THE ISLAMIC CALIPHATE

1. The best introduction to the Roman-Iranian rivalry is James Howard-Johnston, 'The Two Great Powers in Late Antiquity: A Comparison', ch. 4, pp. 157–226, in Averil Cameron (ed.), *The Byzantine and Early Islamic Near East*, Princeton, NJ, 1985.

2. The literature on the Arab conquests and early Islam is vast. The easiest English-language introduction to the conquest remains Hugh Kennedy, *The Great Arab Conquests: How the Spread of Islam Changed the World We Live In*, London, 2007, followed by Chase F. Robinson (ed.), *The New Cambridge History of Islam: vol. 1, The Formation of the Islamic World*, Cambridge, 2010. On Islamic political ideas, Gerhard Bowering (ed.), *Islamic Political Thought*, Princeton, NJ, 2015, followed by the narrative history by Antony Black, *The History of Islamic Political Thought*, Edinburgh, 2001, are probably the easiest places to start. Robinson, *New Cambridge History*, pp. 190–2, is one of many authors who stress the crucial importance of *jihad* in the Qur'an.

3. The succession struggle is an enormously contentious issue. Analysis is made even more difficult by the scarcity of contemporary evidence. I relied mostly on Andrew Marsham, *Rituals of Islamic Monarchy: Accession and Succession in the First Islamic Empire*, Edinburgh, 2009, pt. I, pp. 1–77; Jonathan Berkey, *The Formation of Islam: Religion and Society in the Near East 600–1800*, Cambridge, 2003, chs 1–8; Wilfred Madelung, *The Succession to Muhammad: A Study of the Early Caliphate*, Cambridge, 1997.

4. Andrew Marsham comments that hereditary monarchy was the 'perhaps inevitable' price for Islam's survival: Marsham, *Rituals*, p. 9. My comments

on the Qur'an are drawn mostly from Bowering, *Islamic Political Thought*, esp. the pieces by Roy Jackson, 'Authority', pp. 25–36, and Gerhard Bowering, 'Muhammad', pp. 152–68.

5. See ch. 1, note 13, for my key sources on Muhammad and the caliphate. As regards the place of Old Testament prophets in Weber's thinking about charisma the best introduction is Christopher Adair-Toteff, 'Max Weber's Charismatic Prophets', *History of the Human Sciences*, 27:1, 2014, pp. 3–20.

6. Hugh Kennedy, *The Court of the Caliphs: The Rise and Fall of Islam's Greatest Dynasty*, London, 2004, pp. 130–59, on Abbasid architecture and buildings.

7. Attempting to sum up in a paragraph the complex evolution of Islamic thought and religion is a big challenge: on the Shi'i I owe a great debt to Najam Haider, *Shi'i Islam: An Introduction*, Cambridge, 2014. On the history of the Alids, see Teresa Bernheimer, *The Alids: The First Family of Islam, 750–1200*, Edinburgh, 2013.

8. Apart from Haider, *Shi'i Islam*, this dangerously compressed paragraph owes much to Carol Kersten (ed), *The Caliphate and Islamic Statehood: Formation, Fragmentation and Modern Interpretations*, Berlin, 2015, 3 vols: here vol. 1, esp. ch. 2, Josef van Ess, 'Political Ideas in Early Islamic Political Thought', pp. 20–33, and ch. 4, Ira M. Lapidus, 'The Separation of State and Religion in the Development of Early Islamic Society', pp. 55–75.

9. The standard texts here are chs 5 and 6 (by Chase Robinson and Paul M. Cobb) in Robinson, *New Cambridge History*, vol. 1, pp. 173–268. My paragraph also draws greatly on a fascinating talk given in Cambridge on the Umayyad regime by Professor Andrew Marsham, who is writing a history of the Umayyad Empire.

10. Kennedy, *Court of the Caliphs*, p. 6.

11. Tayeb el-Hibri, 'The Empire in Iraq, 763–861', in Robinson, *New Cambridge History*, pp. 269–304 (here pp. 269–72, and Berkey, *Formation*, pp. 102–9, 174.

12. Kennedy, *Court of the Caliphs*, ch. 2, pp. 11–50.

13. Marsham, *Rituals*, pp. 184–6. On the crescent: Aziz al-Azmeh, *Muslim Kingship: Power and the Sacred in Muslim, Christian and Pagan Polities*, London, 1997, p. 68; Kennedy, *Court of the Caliphs*, p. 137.

14. Kennedy, *Court of the Caliphs*, p. 132, for the statistics on tax yields.

15. Ibid, pp. 58–79, is the best narrative on Harun's early reign and his relationship with the Barmakids: the quotation is from p. 63. But both the quotation and most of Kennedy's account is drawn from the superb *History* of al-Tabari: the most recent English-language version of al-Tabari is translated by C.E. Bosworth and is published in a multi-volume edition by SUNY Press, Albany, NY. The volume on Harun's reign is number 30 (1989) and it is the main source, together with Kennedy, for the following paragraphs.

16. The quote is from Tayeb El-Hibri, 'Redemption', p. 188

17. The texts of the oaths are in vol. 30 of Tabari/Bosworth, *The Abbasid Caliphate in Equilibrium*, pp. 185–95.

18. The suggestion that Tahir's army may have largely consisted of cavalry comes from Hugh Kennedy, as does the admission that certainty is impossible since evidence on warfare in the Arabic literature is very slight: Hugh Kennedy, *The Armies of the Caliphs: Military and Society in the Early Islamic State*, London, 2001, pp. 108–11.

19. The description of al-Amin's death and all the quotations are drawn from Al-Tabari, *The History of al-Tabari: The War between Brothers*, vol. 31, Albany, NY, 1992, translated and edited by C.E. Bosworth, pp. 182–96.

20. His entry in *The Encylopaedia of Islam*, Leiden, 1991, 2nd edn, vol. 6, pp. 331–9, calls him the greatest intellectual among the caliphs. The rest of this paragraph is drawn largely from Al-Tabari, *The History of al-Tabari: The Reunification of the Abbasid Caliphate*, vol. 37, Albany, 1987, translated and edited by C.E. Bosworth, pp. 244–6.

21. Michael Cooperson, *Al-Mamun*, Oxford, 2006, p. 4. Although I drew on a number of sources for this paragraph and the next, Cooperson was the key one.

22. Ibid, ch. 2, 'Education', pp. 17–37.

23. Kennedy, *Court of the Caliphs*, p. 88; Cooperson, *Al-Mamun*, e.g. ch. 4, pp. 57–79.

24. John A. Nawas, 'All in the Family? Al-Mu'tasim's Succession to the Caliphate as to the Lifelong Feud between al-Ma'mun and his Abbasid Family', ch. 16, pp. 281–90, in Kersten, *Caliphate*.

25. This paragraph owes most to Osman al-Bili, *Prelude to the Generals: A Study of Some Aspects of the Reign of Al-Mutasim*; the quotation is from p. 33.

26. P. Crone and M. Hinds, *God's Caliph: Religious Authority in the First Centuries of Islam*, Cambridge, 1986, p. 91. Muhammad Qasim Zaman, *Religion and Politics under the Early Abbasids: The Emergence of the Proto-Sunni Elite*, Leiden, 1997, is the fullest source on this issue. I have neither the space nor the expertise to go into the details of his dispute with Crone over the caliphs' relations with the *ulema*.

27. My guides on this subject were, above all, John A. Nawas, 'A Re-Examination of Three Current Explanations of al-Mamun's Introduction of the *Mihna*', ch. 15, pp. 265–80, and Muhammad Qasim Zaman, 'Defining the Role and the Function of the Caliph in the Early Abbasid Caliphate', ch. 14, pp. 235–64: both in Kersten, *Caliphate*, vol. 1.

28. These issues belong to later chapters, but see e.g. Mona Hassan, *Longing for the Lost Caliphate*, Princeton, NJ, 2016.

10. CHARLES V AND PHILLIP II

1. A recent and thought-provoking work comparing European multi-polarity to Chinese empire is Walter Scheidel, *Escape from Rome*, Princeton, NJ, 2019: his discussion of geography's impact is in ch. 8, pp. 219–366.

2. Geoffrey Parker, *Emperor: A New Life of Charles V*, New Haven, CT, 2019, p. 96.

3. Peter Sarris, *Empires of Faith: The Fall of Rome to the Rise of Islam, 500–700*, Oxford, 2011, pp. 84–8, 120–4; Jos Gommens, 'The Warband and the Making of Eurasian Empires', pp. 297–383, in Maiake van Berkell and Jeroen Duindam (eds), *Prince, Pen and Sword: Eurasian Perspectives*, Leiden, pp. 373–5.

4. I do of course realize that in dismissing the highly contentious question of feudalism in a single paragraph that also covers the Carolingians and the deep origins of European constitutionalism I am taking many liberties. My comments on feudalism owe much to the discussion in pt. 4, pp. 259ff, in David Crouch, *The Birth of Nobility: Constructing Aristocracy in England and France 900–1300*, Abingdon, 2005. On the Carolingians and warrior aristocracy I was partly guided by Johannes Fried, *The Middle Ages*, Cambridge, MA, 2015, esp. ch. 3, pp. 44–81, and Rosamund McKitterick, *Charlemagne: The Formation of a European Identity*, Cambridge, 2008, esp. pp. 224ff, but also by the chapter by Janet Nelson, 'Kingship and Empire', ch. 10, pp. 211–51, in J.H. Burns, *The Cambridge History of Medieval Political Thought c. 350–c. 1450*, Cambridge, 1988. Nelson comments inter alia on the contractual relationship between king and warrior aristocrats and this is a theme in much of the literature, not least in chs 9 and 15, pp. 174–210 and 423–53, by Ruan Caenegen and K. Pennington in Burns's volume.

5. On Saint Gregory and Clovis see e.g. Marie Tanner, *The Last Descendant of Aeneas: The Hapsburgs and the Mythic Image of the Emperor*, New Haven, CT, 1993, pp. 36–8.

6. On the king's two bodies the foundational text is Ernst Kantorowicz, *The King's Two Bodies*, Princeton, NJ, 1957.

7. Lisa Jardine (ed.), *Erasmus: The Education of a Christian Prince*, Cambridge, 1997, pp. 61, 65, 83.

8. One could choose very many sources: excellent especially on monarchs' values is Glenn Richardson, *Renaissance Monarchy: The Reigns of Henry VIII, Francis I and Charles V*, London, 2002, esp. pp. 3–4, 5–6, 27–8, 36–54. From a more structural perspective see Philip T. Hoffman, *Why Did Europe Conquer the World?*, Princeton, NJ, 2015: he comments that 'the business of rulers was war' and cites Machiavelli in claiming that military glory was a monarch's greatest source of prestige (p. 19). Lucian Bely agrees that military glory was much the greatest source of a prince's prestige within

the ruling elite: p. 87 in Lucian Bely, *La Société des Princes XVIe–XVIIIe siècles*, Paris, 1999.

9. Richardson, *Renaissance Monarchy*, p. 163, on hats and cousins. Bely, *Société*, is full of information on the various monarchies' ordering of the dynastic and aristocratic elites.

10. Henry Kamen, 'Alba: Statesman and Diplomat', pp. 31–49 (here p. 41), in Maurits Ebben, Margriet Lacy-Bruijn and Rolof van Hovell tot Westerflier (eds), *Alba: General and Servant to the Crown*, Rotterdam, 2013.

11. Tanner, *Last Descendant*, is the source for most of these paragraphs. The reference to Maximilian on his deathbed comes on p. 107.

12. For Bazoches's statement see Crouch, *Birth*, p. 126.

13. Bely, *Société*, p. 309. On inheritance in the European aristocracy and the spread of primogeniture see, above all, Hamish Scott, 'Dynastic Monarchy and the Consolidation of Aristocracy during Europe's Long Seventeenth Century', pp. 44–86. in Robert von Friedeburg and John Morrill (eds), *Monarchy Transformed: Princes and Their Elites in Early Modern Western Europe*, Cambridge, 2017.

14. Svette Hakon Bagge, *State Formation in Europe, 843–1789: A Divided World*, Abingdon, 2019, p. 35.

15. This is a common theme in most of the recent literature. Henry Kamen sums up this consensus: 'sixteenth-century Spain lacked any doctrine of absolute monarchy': Henry Kamen, *The Escorial: Art and Power in the Renaissance*, New Haven, CT, 2010, p. 147. This is also a key theme running through Robert Bireley, *Ferdinand II, Counter-Reformation Emperor, 1578–1637*, Cambridge, 2014.

16. The statistics on Habsburg, French and Ottoman revenues come from Martyn Rady, *The Habsburgs: The Rise and Fall of a World Power*, London, 2020, p. 66. The role of Protestantism in uniting opposition to the rulers of composite states/empires is the key theme of Daniel H. Nixon, *The Struggle for Power in Early Modern Europe*, Princeton, NJ, 2009. The comments come in the famous letters of Ogier de Busbeq, *The Turkish Letters 1555–1562*, Baton Rouge, LA, 2005. On Ottoman and European standing armies see James D. Tracy, *Emperor Charles V: Impresario of War*, Cambridge, 2002, p. 17.

17. It would be easy to produce a twenty-page bibliography for the issues covered in these two paragraphs. On the Military Revolution my preferred introduction is Clifford J. Rogers, *The Military Revolution Debate*, Boulder, CO, 1995. On European warfare in global context see Hoffman, *Europe*, and Tonio Andrade, *The Gunpowder Age*, Princeton, NJ, 2016. On the Little Ice Age and political stability see Geoffrey Parker, *Global Crisis: War, Climate Change and Catastrophe in the Seventeenth Century*, New Haven, CT, 2013.

18. My main sources on Charles V apart from Parker, *Emperor*, and Tracy, *Emperor Charles V*, are Karl Brandi, *The Emperor Charles V*, trans. C.V.

Wedgwood, London, 1939 and 1980, and the useful short introduction by William Maltby, *The Reign of Charles V*, Houndmills, 2002.

19. Apart from the biographies of Charles V and Ferdinand II already cited, my main source on the empire was Joachim Whaley, *Germany and the Holy Roman Empire*: vol. 1, *Maximilian I to the Peace of Westphalia 1493–1648*, Oxford, 2013.

20. The essential source for this paragraph was R.J.W. Evans, *The Making of the Habsburg Monarchy 1550–1700*, Oxford, 1979, but the short introduction to Habsburg history by Charles Ingrao is a useful supplement: *The Habsburg Monarchy 1618–1815*, Cambridge, 1994.

21. Parker, *Emperor*, p. 217. M.J. Rodriguez-Salgado provides brief portraits of the reigning family, though her depiction of Charles V applies only to his last years of physical decline and deep melancholy: *The Changing Face of Empire*, Cambridge, 1998, Introduction, pp. 1–12.

22. On these emperors see Rady, *Habsburgs*, chs 11–13; Paula Sutter Fichtner, *Emperor Maximilian II*, New Haven, CT, 2001; R.J.W. Evans, *Rudolph II and His World*, London, 1997.

23. Above all see Parker, *Emperor*, ch. 5, pp. 101–30, and Brandi, *Emperor Charles*, pp. 50–5, 131.

24. Brandi, *Emperor Charles*, pp. 204–14, 391–5, 610–18; Parker, *Emperor*, pp. 376–92.

25. On Saint Louis see Jacques Le Goff, *Saint Louis*, Notre Dame, 2009.

26. On Charles's plans in 1544 and the treaty of Crepy see e.g. Parker, *Emperor*, esp. pp. 308–12. For grand strategy see Geoffrey Parker, *The Grand Strategy of Philip II*, New Haven, CT, 1998, pp. 78ff; Brandi, *Emperor Charles*, p. 488.

27. The statistics are drawn from Scheidel, 'The Scale of Empire', in Scheidel, *Oxford World History*, vol. 1, pp. 92–3.

28. Parker, *Emperor*, ch. 17, pp. 305ff, covers the 'Enterprise of England'. On p. 306 he describes the memorandum by Juan de Zuniga which set out the arguments for an invasion as 'Spanish strategic planning at its best'.

29. A number of historians make this point but none better than Sir John Elliott: 'Power and Propaganda in the Spain of Philip IV', pp. 145–73, in Sean Wilentz (ed.), *Rites of Power: Symbolism, Ritual and Politics since the Middle Ages*, Philadelphia, PA, 1985. Although the main focus is on the first half of the seventeenth century, Elliott makes clear that his argument applies to the previous century too. See also on this point Parker, *Grand Strategy*, pp. 92–108.

30. Patrick Williams, *Philip II*, Houndmills, 2001, p. 11; Brandi, *Emperor Charles*, pp. 220, 238.

31. Parker, *Emperor*, ch. 14, pp. 247ff, Epilogue, esp. pp. 368–70. Juan de Escobedo was murdered in 1578 thanks to the intrigue of his rival, Antonio Perez.

32. This is drawn above all from Kamen, *Escorial*, esp. ch. 5, pp. 117–41.

33. On the Castilian monarchy's relative austerity see Elliott, 'Power and Propaganda', pp. 150–2; Kamen, *Escorial*, pp. 146–50. The comparison with Henry and Francis is from Richardson, *Renaissance Monarchy*, pp. 145–51.

34. The text of the 1543 memoranda is in Brandi, *Emperor Charles*, pp. 489–93. On America see also Parker, *Emperor*, ch. 13, pp. 342ff.

11. EMPERORS, CALIPHS AND SULTANS

1. For a comparative work on the three Islamic dynasties see Stephen F. Dale, *The Muslim Empires of the Ottomans, Safavids and Moghuls*, Cambridge, 2010.

2. The most recent one-volume history of the Ottoman Empire in English is Douglas A. Howard, *A History of the Ottoman Empire*, Cambridge, 2017.

3. O. Turan, 'The Ideal of World Domination among the Medieval Turks', *Studia Islamica*, IV, 1955, pp. 77–90; Colin Imber, 'The Ottoman Dynastic Myth', *Revue d'Études Turques*, 9, 1987, pp. 7–27; Rhoads Murphey, *Exploring Ottoman Sovereignty: Tradition, Image and Practice in the Ottoman Imperial Household 1400–1800*, London, 2008, esp. ch. 2, pp. 41–75.

4. For George of Trabzon's address see Abdurrahman Atcil, *Scholars and Sultans in the Early Modern Ottoman Empire*, Cambridge, 2017, p. 56. For Selim's titles see H. Erdem Cipa, *The Making of Selim: Succession, Legitimacy and Memory in the Early Modern Ottoman World*, Bloomington, IN, 2017, pp. 214–15.

5. Carol Kersten (ed.), *The Caliphate and Islamic Statehood: Formation, Fragmentation and Modern Interpretations*, 3 vols, Berlin, 2015: vol. 2, ch. 11, pp. 171–8, Hamilton A.R. Gibb, 'Lutfi Pasha on the Ottoman Caliphate'.

6. On the 1479 law of succession see Murphey, *Exploring Ottoman Sovereignty*, pp. 102–4. The quotations are from Franz Babinger, *Mehmed the Conqueror and His Time*, Princeton, NJ, 1978, p. 66, and A.D. Alderson, *The Structure of the Ottoman Dynasty*, Westport, CT, 1982, p. 62.

7. Cipa, *Making of Selim*, pp. 187–208. See also Kaya Sahin, *Empire and Power in the Reign of Suleyman: Narrating the Sixteenth-Century Ottoman World*, Cambridge, 2013, pp. 29–32.

8. See above all Cipa, *Making of Selim*, esp. ch. 2, pp. 62–108.

9. On Sufism see Lloyd Ridgeon (ed.), *The Cambridge Companion to Sufism*, Cambridge, 2015, esp. ch. 2 by Erik S. Ohlander, 'Early Sufi Rituals, Beliefs and Hermeneutics', pp. 53–73, and ch. 4, Ahuret T. Karamustafa, 'Antinomian Sufis', pp. 101–24. Antony Black, *The History of Islamic Political Thought*, Edinburgh, 2001, is also a useful guide for a newcomer to the field both to understanding Sufism and the Safavids, and to placing them within the broader Islamic context: see esp. ch. 12, pp. 128–34, 'The Politics of Sufism', and ch. 22, 'The Safavids', pp. 221–38. Colin P. Mitchell, *The*

Practice of Politics in Safavid Iran, London, 2012, ch. 1, pp. 19–46, is an excellent introduction to the formation and expansion of the Safavid movement and realm.

10. There is a good description of Selim's conflict with the Safavids in Alan Mikhail, *God's Shadow: The Ottoman Sultan Who Shaped the Modern World*, London, 2020, ch. 12, pp. 185ff.

11. Apart from Mitchell, *Practice of Politics*, ch. 1, see Cipa, *Making of Selim*, pp. 32–54.

12. A very inadequate summary, especially of Sinan's magnificent constructions: see e.g. Michael Rogers, 'The Arts under Suleyman the Magnificent', pp. 257–94 (the reference to Babur is on p. 267, but see my comments on Babur in ch. 12 in this book), in Halil Inalcik and Cemal Kafadar (eds.), *Suleyman the Second* [sic] *and His Time*, Istanbul, 1993, and pt. III, 'Culture and the Arts', pp. 407–592, in Suraiya N. Faroqui and Kate Fleet (eds), *The Cambridge History of Turkey*: vol. 2, *The Ottoman Empire as a World Power, 1453–1603*, Cambridge, 2013.

13. See above all Abdurrahman Atcil, *Scholars and Sultans in the Early Modern Ottoman Empire*, Cambridge, 2017, esp. ch. 10, pp. 188ff, but see also Madeleine C. Zilfi, 'Sultan Suleyman and the Ottoman Religious Establishment', pp. 109–20, in Inalcik and Kafadar, *Suleyman*.

14. Colin Imber, 'Government, Administration and Law', ch. 7, pp. 205–40, in Faroqui and Fleet, *Cambridge History*, vol. 2, is a good introduction. Kaya Sahin, *Empire and Power*, esp. pp. 220ff, adds telling details. The statistics for *timariots* and revenue come from H. Inalcik and D. Quataert, *An Economic and Social History of the Ottoman Empire 1300–1914*, Cambridge, 1995. There are now a number of excellent studies of senior officials: see especially Kaya Sahin's study of Celalzade Mustafa, *Empire and Power*, and Cornell H. Fleischer, *Bureaucrat and Intellectual in the Ottoman Empire: The Historian Mustafa Ali (1541–1600)*.

15. Muhammet Zahit Atcil, *State and Government in the Mid-Sixteenth-Century Ottoman Empire: The Grand Vizierates of Rustem Pasha*, PhD (University of Chicago), 2015, pp. 21–5; Linda T. Darling, 'The Sultan's Advisors and Their Opinions on the Identity of the Ottoman Elite, 1580–1683', pp. 171–81, in Christine Isom-Verhaaren and Kent E. Schull (eds), *Living in the Ottoman Realm: Empire and Identity, 13th to 20th Centuries*, Bloomington, IN, 2016.

16. The key source on the previous two paragraphs is Muhammet Atcil, *State and Government*. On the debate in Europe see e.g. Michael Curtis, *Orientalism and Islam: European Thinkers on Oriental Despotism in the Middle East and India*, Cambridge, 2009.

17. The descriptions are from Alan Fisher, 'The Life and Family of Suleyman I', pp. 1–19 (here pp. 1–3), in Inalcik and Kafadar, *Suleyman*, and from Leslie Peirce, *The Imperial Harem*, Oxford, 1993, p. 176.

18. On the relationship see Leslie Peirce, *Empress of the East: How a European Slave Girl Became Queen of the Ottoman Empire*, New York, 2017, pp. 150–8, 167; Sahin, *Empire*, esp. chs 2 and 3, pp. 49–100. The reference to Ibrahim's secretary is from Muhammet Atcil, *State and Government*, p. 52.

19. On the Ottoman harem and the politics of reproduction see Peirce, *Imperial Harem*. For the statistic on Slavic slaves see p. 284 of Inalcik and Quataert, *Economic and Social History*.

20. Peirce, *Empress*, pp. 118–22, 143, 235, 243–4, 257–84.

21. On inflation and its impact see I. Metin Kunt, *The Sultan's Servants: The Transformation of Ottoman Provincial Government, 1550–1650*, New York, 1983, esp. ch. 5, pp. 77ff. On the Little Ice Age's impact on Anatolia and military units in Istanbul see e.g. Jane Hathaway, *The Chief Eunuch of the Ottoman Harem: From African Slave to Power-Broker*, Cambridge, 2018, ch. 5, pp. 77ff (esp. pp. 77–8), but note that Wolf-Dieter Hutteroth does not believe that the Little Ice Age made a fundamental impact on the empire's stability: see pp. 20–3 in Hutteroth, 'Ecology of the Ottoman Lands', pp. 18–43, in Soraya Faroqui (ed.), *The Cambridge History of Turkey: The Later Ottoman–Empire, 1603–1839*, vol. 3, Cambridge, 2006. On comparative Austrian and Ottoman-military power and performance see e.g. Gabor Agoston, ch. 6, 'Empires and Warfare in East-Central Europe, 1550–1750: The Ottoman–Habsburg Rivalry and Military Transformation', pp. 110–35, in Frank Tallett and D.J.B. Trim (eds), *European Warfare 1350–1750*, Cambridge, 2010. A narrower study of the western Ottoman–Habsburg borderlands comes to the same conclusion, that the Austrians had achieved rough parity by the early seventeenth century: James D. Tracy, *Balkan Wars: Habsburg Croatia, Ottoman Bosnia, and Venetian Dalmatia, 1499–1617*, Lanham, MD, 2016.

22. My main source for the two previous paragraphs is a still unpublished PhD by Cumhur Bekar, *The Rise of the Koprulu Family: The Reconfiguration of the Vizierate in the Seventeenth Century*, London, 2018, esp. ch. 1, pp. 13ff, but see also Hathaway, *Chief Eunuch*, pp. 55–9, Peirce, *Imperial Harem*, pp. 92–7, and Murphey, *Exploring Ottoman Sovereignty*, pp. 130–1, 150.

23. See above all Baki Tezcan, 'The 1622 Military Rebellion in Istanbul: A Historiographical Journey', pp. 25–43, in Jane Hathaway (ed.), *Mutiny and Rebellion in the Ottoman Empire*, Madison, WI, 2002; Gabriel Piterberg, *An Ottoman Tragedy: History and Historiography at Play*, Berkeley, CA, 2003: ch. I, pp. 9–29, covers the events, whereas the rest of the book is a study of how they were interpreted by later generations.

24. The quotation and the basic narrative is drawn from Peirce, *Imperial Harem*, pp. 245–7, supplemented by Bekar, *Rise*, pp. 26–9, and George Junne, *The Black Eunuchs of the Ottoman Empire*, London, 2016, pp. 168–9.

25. The two key sources for the previous four paragraphs are Bekar, *Rise*, pp. 57–82, 94–6, 116–24 on Hadice Turhan, and ch. 4, pp. 146 on the Koprulu

household and the foundations of the Koprulu regime, and Peirce, *Imperial Harem*, pp. 25–63, 112, 143, 236–9.

26. For Suleyman's comments see p. 101 of Peirce, *Imperial Harem*. Her books are the best source on the harem. On the eunuchs and Ottoman culture see esp. ch. 9, pp. 193ff in Hathaway, *Chief Eunuch*, and Junne, *Black Eunuchs*, pp. 140–2, though his evidence comes largely from the nineteenth century.

27. Baki Tezcan, *The Second Ottoman Empire: Political and Social Transformation in the Early Modern World*, Cambridge, 2010, p. 77.

28. Ibid, p. 6. There is an immense literature on the Janissaries: a good, short but comprehensive introduction is Gilles Veinstein, 'On the Ottoman Janissaries (fourteenth–nineteenth centuries)', pp. 115–134, in Erik-Jan Zurcher (ed.), *Fighting for a Living: A Comparative History of Military Labour*, Amsterdam, 2013.

29. The quotation is from p. 52 of Christopher K. Neumann, 'Political and Diplomatic Developments', ch. 3, pp. 44–64, in Faroqui, *Cambridge History of Turkey*, vol. 3. Although one could cite many sources for the argument in this paragraph, it owes most to Ethan Menchinger, *The First of the Modern Ottomans: The Intellectual History of Ahmed Vasif*, Cambridge, 2017, esp. pp. 28–30.

30. The literature on eighteenth-century warfare is immense. I covered this issue from a Russian perspective in Dominic Lieven, *Russia against Napoleon: The Battle for Europe, 1807 to 1814*, London, 2009, and refer in my notes to part of the literature. See esp. pp. 93–5.

31. There is now a respectable literature on Ottoman military history. Virginia Aksan, *Ottoman Wars 1700–1870: An Empire Besieged*, Harlow, 2007, and Rhoads Murphey, *Ottoman Warfare: 1500–1700*, New Brunswick, NJ, 1999, are the places to start. Both have contributed many useful articles on this theme too. A valuable comparison between Ottoman and Russian military power is Gabor Agoston, 'Military Transformation in the Ottoman Empire and Russia, 1500–1800', *Kritika*, 12:2, 2011, pp. 281–320. The figure of 400,000 represents the number of pay coupons in circulation: Virginia Aksan, 'Whatever Happened to the Janissaries? Mobilization for the 1768–1774 Russo-Ottoman War', *War in History*, 5:1, 1998, pp. 23–36 (here p. 27); Tezcan, *Second Ottoman Empire*, pp. 198ff.

32. The quote is from Murphey, *Exploring Ottoman Sovereignty*, p. 266. The possible bibliography on this issue as regards the European nobility is immense: see Christopher Storrs and H.M. Scott, 'The Military Revolution and the European Nobility, c.1600–1800', *War in History*, 3:1, 1996, pp. 1–41.

33. I am of course aware that this paragraph will annoy many Ottomanists who have spent their lifetimes fighting (admirably) against the idea of Ottoman decline since Suleyman's time, who dislike military history and who have struggled against an authoritarian tradition in modern Turkey which seeks to legitimize itself partly by reference to the demands of military power and national security. Nevertheless, I believe the argument in this paragraph to be

true. By far the best coverage of these issues are chs 6 (pp. 118–34), 7 (pp. 135–56) and 8 (pp. 157–85) in Faroqui, *Cambridge History of Turkey*, vol. 3, on the relations between centre and periphery and on public finance.

34. The best English-language history of the war is Brian L. Davis, *The Russo-Turkish War, 1768–1774: Catherine II and the Ottoman Empire*, London, 2016, to which his *Empire and Military Revolution in Eastern Europe*, London, 2011, is a useful prelude and introduction. On the Ottoman side the key works are by Virginia Aksan, above all *Ottoman Wars*, esp. ch. 4, pp. 129ff, but also 'The One-Eyed Fighting the Blind: Mobilization, Supply and Command in the Russo-Turkish War of 1768–1774', *International History Review*, 15:2, 1993, pp. 221–38, and *An Ottoman Statesman in War and Peace: Ahmed Resmi Efendi 1700–1783*, London, 1995, ch. 3, pp. 100–69: the comment that Ottoman military thinking remained stuck in 1550 is on p. 130.

35. For the statistics on Muslim populations killed or expelled see J. McCarthy, *The Ottoman Turks*, London, ch. 10, pp. 329ff. On the indemnity see Menchinger, *First of the Modern Ottomans*, p. 143.

36. The key source on Selim before his accession is Aysel Yildiz, 'The "Louis XVI of the Turks": The Character of an Ottoman Sultan', *Middle Eastern Studies*, 50:2, 2014, pp. 272–90.

37. Aysel Yildiz, *Vaka-Yi Selimiye or the Selimiye Incident: A Study of the May 1807 Rebellion*, Sabanci University, PhD, 2008. Ch. 6.5 of the thesis, 'The Myth of Selim III', pp. 741ff, is currently the best discussion in the English language of Selim III's personality and its impact on his reign. It is not replicated in the author's much shorter book, *Crisis and Rebellion in the Ottoman Empire*, London, 2017, or even entirely in Yildiz, '"Louis XVI of the Turks"'. Coskun Yilmaz (ed.), *III. Selim*, Istanbul, 2010, contains an English translation of its chapters. They add something to our knowledge of Selim and the book is lavishly illustrated.

38. On Pasvanoglu see Fikaret Adanir, pp. 180–3, in Adanir, 'Semi-Autonomous Forces in the Balkans and Anatolia', pp. 157–85, in Faroqui, *Cambridge History of Turkey*, vol. 3, and Robeert Zens, 'Pasvanoglu Osman Pasha and the Pasalik of Belgrade, 1791–1807', pp. 89–104, in Hathaway, *Mutiny*.

39. There remains no good biography of Mahmud II, but Coskun Yilmaz (ed.), *II. Mahmud*, Istanbul, 2010, reveals more about Mahmud's personality than is possible in the sister volume on Selim cited in note 37.

12. THE MUGHALS

1. The meeting of Persianate and Sanskrit cultures in India, especially under the Moghuls, is the main theme of Richard M. Eaton, *India in the Persianate Age*, London, 2019. The theme is tackled in more detail in Audrey Truschke, *Culture of Encounters: Sanskrit at the Mughal Court*, New York, 2016.

2. The statistic on the Mughal Empire's share of the global economy comes from p. 1 of Andrew de la Garza, *The Mughal Empire at War*, New York, 2016.

3. *The Baburnama: Memoirs of Babur, Prince and Emperor*, ed. Wheeler M. Thackston, New York, 2002, pp. 352–3.

4. The best English-language introduction to the region's intellectual and cultural history is S. Frederick Starr, *Lost Enlightenment: Central Asia's Golden Age from the Arab Conquest to Tamerlane*, Princeton, NJ, 2013. On the Ghaznavids, Babur and Central Asian culture see Stephen F. Dole, *The Muslim Empires of the Ottomans, Safavids, and Moghuls*, Cambridge, pp. 17–20, and Stephen F. Dole, *The Garden of the Eight Paradises: Babur and the Culture of Empire in Central Asia, Afghanistan and India (1483–1530)*, Leiden, 2004, ch. 3, pp. 135ff, ch. 5, pp. 247–89, esp. pp. 247–54.

5. The quotation is from p. 34 of Pratyay Nath, *Climate of Conquest: War, Environment and Empire in Mughal North India*, New Delhi, 2019. These two paragraphs are largely based on Garza, *Mughal Empire*, esp. pp. 33–43, 102–4, 191–2.

6. *Baburnama*: the comments on his pledge of abstinence and later regrets are on pp. 380–3 and 436. Dole, *Muslim Empires*, p.72; Dole, *Garden*, pp. 13–14, 33–4, 106, 172, 349–51, 430.

7. The quotation comes from Wheeler M. Thackston (ed.), *The Jahangirnama: Memoirs of Jahangir, Emperor of India*, Oxford, 1999, pp. 35–7. Andre Wink, *Akbar*, St Ives, 2009, ch. 8, pp. 109–16, gives a good summary of Akbar's personality, as does Abraham Eraly, *The Mughal Throne: The Saga of India's Great Emperors*, London, 2000, pp. 163–79. Lisa Balabanlilar, *The Emperor Jahangir*, London, 2020, is much the best study of this emperor.

8. Abul Fazl was the author of the *Akbarnama*, the 'official history' of the emperor and his reign. Akbar himself supervised the work closely. It formed a key element in the image he promoted of himself and his regime. I ploughed my way through the first five volumes edited and translated by Wheeler M. Thackston: *The History of Akbar*, Cambridge, MA, 2015–19. The formal Persianate style in which the history is written makes it harder to follow than the almost deceptively simple accounts given by Babur and Jahangir in their autobiographies.

9. J.M. Rodgers, *Mughal Miniatures*, Northampton, MA, 2007, p. 61; see also Lisa Balabanlilar, *Imperial Identity in the Mughal Empire*, London, pp. 62–6.

10. Eaton, *India*, pp. 233–5; Balabanlilar, *Imperial Identity*, pp. 83–4.

11. *Jahangirnama*, p. 35.

12. These two paragraphs are to a great extent a precis of A. Azfar Moin, *The Millennial Sovereign: Sacred Kingship and Sainthood in Islam*, New York, 2012. Also very important is the piece by J.F. Richards, 'The Formulation of Imperial Authority under Akbar and Jahangir', ch. 3, pp. 126–67, in Muzaffar Alam and Sanjay Subramanyam (eds), *The Mughal State*, Delhi, 1998.

13. Garza, *Mughal Empire*, pp. 56–7, 116–24; Jos Gommans, *Mughal Warfare*, London, 2002, pp. 170–9.

14. On the incorporation of the Rajputs, see esp. Norman P. Ziegler, 'Some Notes on Rajput Loyalties during the Mughal Period', ch. 4, pp. 168–210, in Alam and Subramanyam, *Mughal State*.

15. All the standard works discuss the system of land revenue and the service nobility. See for example John F. Richards, *The Mughal Empire*, Cambridge, 1993, ch. 3, pp. 58–78, 'Autocratic Centralisation'. See also Gommans, *Mughal Warfare*, ch. 2, 'Warband and Court', pp. 39–64. On the British and European aristocracy see Dominic Lieven, *Aristocracy in Europe, 1815–1914*, London, 1992.

16. The quote is from p. 188 of Nath, *Climate*. The best introduction to the *zamindars'* role is S. Nurul Hasan, 'Zamindars under the Mughals', ch. 9, pp. 284–300, in Alam and Subramanyam, *Mughal State*.

17. Muzaffar Alam and Sanjay Subrahmanyam, 'Introduction', pp. 1–71 (here p. 19), in Alam and Subramanyam, *Mughal State*, for Rosencrantz and Guildenstern.

18. *Jahangirnama*, pp. 26–7, 49–50, 161; Eaton, *India*, pp. 244–72, provides a good account of Jahangir's record, qualities and defects as a ruler. Balabanlilar, *Imperial Identity*, p. 94, describes his 'interpretation of imperial duties' as 'minimalist'.

19. Eaton, *India*, pp. 247–8. On Nur Jahan, see Ruby Lal, *Empress: The Astonishing Reign of Nur Jahan*, New York, 2018.

20. There is a detailed account of the succession crisis in Fergus Nicoll, *Shah Jahan: The Rise and Fall of the Mughal Emperor*, London, 2009, ch. 9, pp. 145ff. On his reaction to his wife's death and his role in creating the Taj Mahal see ch. 11, pp. 181ff.

21. Nicoll, *Shah Jahan*, pp. 27–31; Munis D. Faroqui, *The Princes of the Mughal Empire, 1504–1719*, Cambridge, 2012, p. 7. There is a full, flattering but plausible account of Shah Jahan at work as monarch by one of his senior Hindu officials: see pp. 102–27 in Rajeev Kinra, *Writing Self, Writing Empire: Chandar Bhan Brahman and the Cultural World of the Indo-Persian State Secretary*, Oakland, CA, 2015.

22. Nicoll, *Shah Jahan*, pp. 89–90, 153–4; Moin, *Millennial Sovereign*, pp. 212–14. The quotation is from Eraly, *The Mughal Throne*, p. 311.

23. On Aurangzeb see especially Audrey Truschke, *Aurangzeb: The Life and Legacy of India's Most Controversial King*, Stanford, CA, 2017. Ch. 7, pp. 288–339, in Eaton, *India*, and ch. 10, pp. 205ff, in John F. Richards, *The Mughal Empire*, Cambridge, 1993, also helped me greatly in writing this paragraph.

24. Faroqui, *Princes*, pp. 137–42.

25. Faroqui gives the most complete account of the succession struggle, but see also e.g. Truschke, *Aurangzeb*, pp. 19–35, and Eaton, *India*, pp. 288–308. Supriya

Gandhi, *The Emperor Who Never Was: Dara Shukoh in Mughal India*, Cambridge, MA, 2020, is a fascinating study of the mind and thought of Dara.

26. Nath, *Climate*, pp. 91–9.

27. On the campaign north of the Hindu Kush see ibid, pp. 99–112; Gommans, *Mughal*, pp. 179–87.

28. Although Garza, *Mughal Empire*, only covers the period up to 1605, his last chapter (ch. 7, pp. 182–99) is good on the decline of the Mughal military system, above all due to the lack of worthwhile enemies. Nath, *Climate*, is above all concerned with north India, but his comments on the ecological constraints on military operations are very relevant to the Deccan too. See also Gommans, *Mughal*, pp. 187–99.

29. Kinra, *Writing Self*, is a valuable portrait of a (in this case rather admirable) senior imperial official.

30. The quote is from Eaton, *India*, p. 323; on Muazzam see Faroqui, *Princes*, pp. 303–8.

31. Faroqui, *Princes*, ch. 7, pp. 274ff.

32. On Nizam see Eaton, *India*, pp. 346–7.

33. The best guide to Nader Shah is Michael Axworthy, *Sword of Persia*, London, 2006.

34. A key text placing European expansion in the context of the cyclical decline of the great Eurasian empires is Christopher Bayly, *Imperial Meridian: The British Empire and the World, 1780–1830*, London, 1989. On the Russian angle see Dominic Lieven, *Russia against Napoleon*, London, 2009, pp. 64–5, and Dominic Lieven, *Towards the Flame: Empire, War and the End of Tsarist Russia*, London, 2015, pp. 197–8.

13. CHINA'S LAST DYNASTIES

1. The statistics are drawn from Peer Vries, *State, Economy and the Great Divergence: Great Britain and China, 1680s–1850s*, London, 2015, pp. 49–52. See David M. Robinson, *In the Shadow of the Mongol Empire*, Cambridge, 2020, for discussion of the Ming founders' complex relationship to the Mongol past.

2. For a brief introduction to Neo-Confucianism's place in the Confucian tradition see Xinzong Yao, *An Introduction to Confucianism*, Cambridge, 2000, pp. 70ff. For greater depth see Peter K. Bol, *Neo-Confucianism in History*, Cambridge, MA, 2008. See also Li Jia, 'Conflicts between Monarchs and Ministers', *Chinese Studies in History*, 44:3, 2011, pp. 72–89.

3. On Yongle see above all Shih-shan Henry Tsai, *Perpetual Happiness: The Ming Emperor Yongle*, Seattle, 2001.

4. The two previous paragraphs are a brief summary of a complex process: see Benjamin A. Elman, *Civil Examinations and Meritocracy in Late*

Imperial China, Cambridge, MA, 2013, esp. pp. 1–10, 50–1, 92–114, 146–8, 227.

5. See David M. Robinson, 'The Ming Court', ch. 1, pp. 21–60, in David M. Robinson (ed), *Culture, Courtiers and Competition: The Ming Court (1368–1644)*, Cambridge, MA, 2008, and James Laidlaw, 'On Theatre and Theory: Reflections on Ritual in Imperial Chinese Politics', ch. 12, pp. 399–416, in Joseph P. McDermott (ed), *State and Court Ritual in China*, Cambridge, 1999.

6. Ray Huang, *1587. A Year of No Significance: The Ming Dynasty in Decline*, New Haven, CT, 1981, p. 75.

7. The two previous paragraphs are based partly on Huang, *1587*, esp. pp. 7, 27–32, and partly on 727–8 of F.W. Mote, *Imperial China: 900–1800*, Cambridge, MA, 1999. Above all, they are based on discussions with my research assistant, Hantian Zhang. On Wanli's mother see p. 129 of Keith McMahon, *Celestial Women: Imperial Wives and Concubines in China from Song to Qing*, Lanham, MD, 2016.

8. On the eunuchs see e.g. Scarlett Jang, 'The Eunuch Agency Directorate of Ceremonial and the Ming Imperial Publishing Enterprise', pp. 116–79, in Robinson (ed), *Culture*, and Shih-shan Henry Tsai, *The Eunuchs in the Ming Dynasty*, Albany, NY, 1996.

9. Kenneth M. Swope, 'Bestowing the Double-Edged Sword: Wanli as Supreme Military Commander', pp. 61–115, in Robinson (ed.), *Culture*. His judgement on Ming military quality is on p. 76.

10. Ibid, p. 95; see also Kenneth M. Swope, *A Dragon's Head and a Serpent's Tail: Ming China and the First Great East Asian War 1592–1598*, Norman, OK, 2009.

11. A fine source on the Qing 'compromise' is Macabe Keliher, *The Board of Rites and the Making of Qing China*, Oakland, CA, 2019: the issue of ceremonial clothes is discussed on pp. 98–102 and 146–66.

12. On the Banners and Manchu identity see Mark C. Elliott, *The Manchu Way: The Eight Banners and Ethnic Identity in Late Imperial China*, Stanford, CA, 2001. On the Mongols' role see e.g. Pamela Kyle Crossley, *A Translucent Mirror: History and Identity in Qing Imperial Ideology*, Berkeley, CA, 1999, pp. 311ff, and Evelyn Rawski, *The Last Emperors: A Social History of Qing Imperial Institutions*, Berkeley, CA, 1998, pp. 66–70.

13. For background on the Manchus see Pamela Kyle Crossley, *The Manchus*, Oxford, 1997.

14. Elliott, *Manchu Way*, pp. 164–9.

15. The quote is from Rawski, *Last Emperors*, p. 81.

16. Ibid, pp. 88–126. On the Ming princes see Craig Clunas, *Screen of Kings: Royal Art and Power in Ming China*, Honolulu, 2013.

17. The key text is Jonathan Spence, *Emperor of China: Self-Portrait of Kang-hsi*, London, 1974: the quotation is from p. 170.

18. On mathematics, astronomy and the Jesuits, see Catherine Jami, *The Emperor's New Mathematics*, Oxford, 2012, esp. pp. 74–81.

19. Spence, *Emperor*, pp. 37–8.

20. Ibid, pp. 18–23; S.R. Gilbert, 'Mengzi's Art of War: The Kangxi Emperor Reforms the Qing Military Examinations', pp. 243–56 (here p. 250), in Nicola di Cosmo (ed.), *Military Culture in Imperial China*, Cambridge, MA.

21. The most informative source on these issues remains Lawrence Kessler, *K'ang-hsi and the Consolidation of Ch'ing Rule 1661–1684*, Chicago, IL, 1976, esp. ch. 6, pp. 137ff. See also Richard E. Strassberg, 'Redesigning Sovereignty: The Kangxi Emperor, the Mountain Estate for Escaping the Heat, and the Imperial Poems', ch. 1, pp. 1–39, in Richard E. Strassberg and Stephen H. Whiteman (eds), *Thirty-Six Views: The Kangxi Emperor's Mountain Estate in Poetry and Prints*, Washington, DC, 2016.

22. My sources on the scandal and Tsao are Jonathan D. Spence, *Ts'ao Yin and the K'angshi Emperor: Bondservant and Manchu*, New Haven, CT, 1966, esp. ch. 6, pp. 213ff, and R. Kent Guy, *Qing Governors and their Provinces*, Seattle, WA, 2010, pp. 248–58.

23. Spence, *Emperor*, p. 125. A full and balanced account of the struggles over the succession is Silas H. Wu, *Passage to Power: K'ang-hsi and His Heir Apparent 1661–1722*, Cambridge, MA, 1979.

24. Elliott, *Manchu Way*, p. 356.

25. As regards Yongzheng there is no equivalent of Jonathan Spence's book on Kangxi. On his personality and priorities, probably the best introductions are Pei Huang, *Autocracy at Work: A Study of the Yung-cheng Period, 1723–1735*, Bloomington, IN, 1971 (the quotation is from p. 116), and Jonathan Spence, *Treason by the Book*, London, 2001.

26. Guy, *Qing Governors*, pp. 121–2.

27. The quotation comes from p. 74 of Silas H.L. Wu, *Communication and Imperial Control in China: Evolution of the Palace Memorial System*, Cambridge, MA, 1970: ch. 7, 'Changes in the Palace Memorial System in the Yung-cheng Reign', pp. 66–78, is the main source for this paragraph. See also Beatrice Bartlett, *Monarchs and Ministers: The Grand Council in Mid Ch'ing China, 1728–1820*, Berkeley, CA, 1991, esp. pp. 45ff.

28. The key work here is Madeleine Zelin, *The Magistrate's Tael: Rationalizing Fiscal Reform in Eighteenth-Century Ch'ing China*, Berkeley, CA, 1984. Her chapter (ch. 4, 'The Yung-Cheng Reign', pp. 183–229) in W.J. Peterson (ed.), *The Cambridge History of China: The Ch'ing Dynasty to 1800*, vol. 9, Cambridge, 2002, is a useful introduction.

29. Bartlett, *Monarchs*, pp. 78, 134, for the quotations: her work is the key source on the evolution of the emperor's secretariat (i.e. the Grand Council). Wu, *Communication*, p. 90, on Prince I's death.

30. On Yongzheng and culture see Claudia Brown, *Great Qing: Painting in China 1644–1911*, Seattle, 2014, esp. pp. 45–8, and He Li, 'Qing Dynasty',

pp. 135–41, in Jay Xu and He Li (eds), *Emperor's Treasures: Chinese Art from the National Palace Museum, Taipei*, San Francisco, CA, 2016. On his education, temperament and culture see Huang, *Autocracy*, ch. 2, pp. 27–50, esp. pp. 28 and 33. On meditation and Zen Buddhism see Peter Harvey, *An Introduction to Buddhism*, Cambridge, 2013, pp. 217–23.

31. This is a deeply inadequate and unfair summary of Qianlong and his reign, but considerations of space allow no more. On Qianlong see e.g. Mark C. Elliott, *Emperor Qianlong: Son of Heaven, Man of the World*, New York, 2009, and Harold Kahn, *Monarchy in the Emperor's Eyes*, Cambridge, MA, 1971.

32. On Qing military culture see e.g. Joanna Waley-Cohen, 'Militarization of Culture in Eighteenth-Century China', pp. 278–95, in di Cosmo (ed.), *Military Culture*. On Chinese expansion see Peter C. Perdue, *China Marches West: The Qing Conquest of Central Eurasia*, Cambridge, MA, 2005. Amidst the vast literature on the Opium War, I was largely guided by Mao Haijian, *The Qing Empire and the Opium War*, Cambridge, 2016, and James M. Polachek, *The Inner Opium War*, Cambridge, MA, 1992.

14. THE ROMANOVS

1. Nancy Shields Kollmann, *The Russian Empire 1450–1801*, Oxford, 2017, is an excellent introduction to this era: her discussion of Ivan IV and mercury poisoning is on pp. 153–4. Also excellent is the more general introduction to Russian history by Paul Bushkovitch: *A Concise History of Russia*, Cambridge, 2012: chs 2 and 3, pp 19–58, cover the issues discussed in these two paragraphs. For more detail see Maureen Perrie (ed.), *The Cambridge History of Russia*: vol. I, *From Early Rus' to 1689*, Cambridge, 2006. The most recent English-language biography of Ivan IV by Charles J. Halperin makes clear just how little we really know about Ivan and the extent to which our assumptions are rooted in myth: *Ivan the Terrible: Free to Reward and Free to Punish*, Pittsburgh, PA, 2019.

2. I first made this argument in Dominic Lieven, *Empire: The Russian Empire and its Rivals*, London, 2000, esp. chs 4, 6,7 and 8. P.D. Curtin, *The Rise and Fall of the Plantation Complex*, Cambridge, 1990, ch. 1, is a useful insight into Russian slaves on Cyprus.

3. On the impact of Byzantine Orthodox traditions see Boris Uspenskij and Victor Zhivov, *Tsar and God and Other Essays in Russian Cultural Semiotics*, Boston, MA, 2012, ch. 1, 'Tsar and God: Semiotic Aspects of the Sacralization of the Monarch in Russia', pp. 1–112. Interestingly, they claim that European Baroque discourse on absolute monarchy was imported to Russia and understood literally, outside its cultural and political context. On Byzantine 'republicanism' see Anthony Kaldellis, *The Byzantine Republic: People and Power in New Rome*, Cambridge, MA, 2015.

4. Carol B. Stevens, *Russia's Wars of Emergence 1460–1730*, Harlow, 2017, on p. 235 stresses Peter's impact on noble attitudes to military service. On continuity and Peter I see B. Meehan-Waters, *Autocracy and Aristocracy: The Russian Service Elite of 1730*, New Brunswick, NJ, 1982. On the origins and family histories of Nicholas II's elite see Dominic Lieven, *Russia's Rulers under the Old Regime*, New Haven, CT, 1989, pp. 1–51, especially ch. 1, 'From the Tartars to the Twentieth Century'. On Golitsyn as a metaphor for continuity within the imperial governing elite see E. Amburger, *Geschichte der Behordenorganisation Russlands von Peter dem Grossen bis 1917*, Leiden, 1966, p. 519.

5. These comparisons are the stuff of this book. I made similar comparisons in Lieven, *Empire*, pp. 241–53. Kollmann, *Russian Empire*, pp. 219–21, makes similar comparisons with admirable succinctness.

6. Apart from the general histories already cited, a good introduction to early eighteenth-century Russian society and government is Lindsey Hughes, *Russia in the Age of Peter the Great*, New Haven, CT, 1998. On the second half of the century see above all John Le Donne, *Ruling Russia: Politics and Administration in the Age of Absolutism, 1762–1796*, Princeton, NJ, 1984, and Isabel de Madariaga, *Russia in the Age of Catherine the Great*, New Haven, CT, 1981. John Le Donne, *Absolutism and Ruling Class, 1700–1825*, Oxford, 1991, is a useful work of reference. Some contributions in Dominic Lieven (ed.), *The Cambridge History of Russia*: vol. II, *Imperial Russia, 1689–1917*, Cambridge, 2006, provide brief but excellent insights into aspects of Russian government and society.

7. For an original defence of Peter III (or more accurately, of his reign) see Carol Scott Leonard, *Reform and Regicide: The Reign of Peter III of Russia*, Bloomington, IN, 1993. Roderick E. McGrew, *Paul I of Russia, 1754–1801*, Oxford, 1992, is more orthodox but both fair and comprehensive.

8. The Bible on royal marriages in the pre-Petrine era (with some pages devoted to Peter's legacy) is Russell E. Martin, *A Bride for the Tsar*, De Kalb, IL, 2012.

9. Simon Sebag-Montefiore, *Prince of Princes: The Life of Potemkin*, London, 2000, is a fine study of Catherine's greatest favourite and his relationship with the empress.

10. On local government and the nobility see R.E. Jones, *The Emancipation of the Russian Nobility, 1762–1785*, Princeton, NJ, 1973.

11. Gregory Freeze, 'Russian Orthodoxy: Church, People and Power', pp. 284–305, in Lieven (ed.), *Imperial Russia*, is a good introduction to his many excellent publications on the Church and Orthodoxy in the imperial era.

12. Paul Bushkovitch, *Peter the Great: The Struggle for Power*, Cambridge, 2001, chs 2–4, pp. 49–169, is an excellent guide to the politics of this period. See too Lindsey Hughes, *Sophia, Regent of Russia 1657–1704*, New Haven, CT, 1990. On Praskovia and her marriage see Martin, *Bride*, pp. 220–2. The Miloslavsky

and Naryshkin factions left a strong mark on eighteenth-century court politics: see John Le Donne, 'Ruling Families in the Russian Political Order, 1689–1825', *Cahiers du monde russe et soviétique*, 28, 1987, pp. 233–322.

13. Hughes, *Sophia*, p. 383.

14. Ibid, p. 357.

15. The newest full work on the All-Drunken Assembly is Ernest A. Zitser, *The Transfigured Kingdom: Sacred Parody and Charismatic Authority at the Court of Peter the Great*, Ithaca, NY, 2004. Although full of interest, some of the complex symbolic meanings it attaches to the Assembly's activities might perhaps have flown rather high over the heads of Peter and his comrades, especially when they were in festive mood. Hughes, *Sophia*, pp. 249–57, is a useful down-to-earth addition to Zitser's account.

16. Bushkovitch, *Peter the Great*, p. 291.

17. The quotations are from Gary Marker, *Imperial Saint: The Cult of Saint Catherine and the Dawn of Female Rule in Russia*, De Kalb, IL, 2011, p. 8, and Kollmann, *Russian Empire*, p. 368. On her generosity to the conspirators see Simon Dixon, *Catherine the Great*, London, 2011, pp. 18ff.

18. The expedition to the south and indeed Catherine's entire relationship with Potemkin are wonderfully depicted by Simon Sebag Montefiore, *Prince of Princes*, esp. chs 23–5, pp. 351–77. On the Prince de Ligne see the biography by Philip Mansel, *Prince of Europe: The Life of Charles-Joseph de Ligne*, London, 2003.

19. The basis for any study of Catherine is her own voluminous correspondence and memoirs: many of these sources are available in English and French and are listed in Sebag Montefiore, *Prince of Princes*, pp. 598–9.

20. The best history of the war is Brian L. Davis, *The Russo-Turkish War, 1768–1774*, London, 2016. Madariaga, *Russia*, part iv, pp. 187–238, is excellent on the diplomacy of the war years but also on Russian foreign policy in general.

21. Madariaga, *Russia*, chs 18 and 19, pp. 277–307, discusses the reforms of local government and the nobility. The statistics on Kazan are from Dixon, *Catherine*, p. 228. Note Catherine's comment (Dixon, *Catherine*, p. 182) about her horror when she encountered representatives of the provincial gentry in 1767: 'the number of ignorant noblemen ... was immeasurably larger than I could ever have supposed.'

22. Dixon, *Catherine*, p. 169.

23. On Saint Catherine see Marker, *Imperial Saint*: the quotation is from p. 22. For Catherine's comment on Razumovsky see Dixon, *Catherine*, p. 48. On Catherine's love life as well as all other aspects of her personality and reign his book is full of insight and sense.

24. Tim Blanning gives an excellent, brief account of Pietism's evolution and impact in T.C.W. Blanning, *The Culture of Power and the Power of Culture: Old Regime Europe 1660–1789*, Oxford, 2002, pp. 55–8, 203–8.

25. In addition to sources already cited, Klaus Sharf, *Ekaterina, Germaniia i nemtsy*, Moscow, 2015, is full of insight and information regarding the impact of her youth and adolescence in Germany.

26. By far the fullest study of Louis XV is Michel Antoine, *Louis XV*, Paris, 1989. See esp. ch. 9, pp. 405ff, for the king's private life.

27. On Paul see McGrew, *Paul*, and Hugh Ragsdale (ed.), *Paul I: A Reassessment of His Life and Reign*, Pittsburgh, PA, 1979. On his mindset see also an especially shrewd chapter in Richard S. Wortman, *Scenarios of Power: Myth and Ceremony in Russian Monarchy*, vol. 1, Princeton, NJ, 1995, ch. 6, pp. 171–92.

28. I discuss Bennigsen's views on pp. 64–5 of Dominic Lieven, *Russia against Napoleon: The Struggle for Europe, 1807 to 1814*, London, 2009: my comments are largely based on the three volumes of his memoirs: *Mémoires du General Bennigsen*, Paris, n.d.

29. Dorothea's account was first published in *Istoricheskii Vestnik*, 5, 1906. It is republished in D.K. Burlaka, *Pavel I: Pro et Contra*, St Petersburg, 2014, pp. 333–49. For a recent study of Dorothea see John Charmley, *The Princess and the Politicians*, London, 2005. Voltaire remarks on this Lieven in his *Histoire de Charles XII, Livre Second*, pp. 113–14. See also R.M. Hatton, *Charles XII of Sweden*, London, 1968, p. 195.

30. S.W. Jackman (ed.), *Romanov Relations*, London, 1969, Grand Duchess Anna to Grand Duke Constantine, 2 April 1828, p. 149. Apart from Dorothea's account, part of this paragraph is family lore passed on by my great-aunt Alexandra Lieven, who died in London aged 96 when I was already in my twenties. Charlotta Lieven was her great-grandmother, Peter Pahlen her great-great-grandfather. The occasional (German-speaking) eccentric who wants more details can find them in Alexander von Lieven, *Urkunden und Nachrichten zu einer Familiengeschichte der Barone, Freiherren, Grafen und Fursten Lieven*, 2 vols, Mitau, 1910.

31. Marie-Pierre Rey, *Alexander I: The Tsar Who Defeated Napoleon*, de Kalb, IL, 2012, pp. 3–12, 67–83, gives a good account of Paul's reign, Alexander's role in the conspiracy and his subsequent remorse. 'First-rank princes' means *svetleishie knyaz'ya* as distinct from the far more numerous ordinary *knyaz'ya*.

32. The quotations are from S.V. Mironenko, the outstanding contemporary Russian expert on Alexander: they are in an article he wrote for the catalogue of an excellent exhibition on Alexander in the Hermitage in 2005: *Aleksandr I. 'Sfinks, ne razgadannyi do groba'*, SPB, 2005, pp. 10–59. Unfortunately, neither this article nor his other excellent works are available in translation.

33. The quotation is from Rey, *Alexander I*, p. 304. This is an excellent study, now available in a good English translation as well as the original French.

Alexander's religious search is well covered. His conversation with the Vatican comes on pp. 366–76.

34. The quotations are from ibid, pp. 93–4, and Mironenko, *Aleksandr I*, p. 67.
35. The quotation is from Rey, *Alexander I*, p. 309. The growing preference for female company is taken from V.M. Faybisovich, 'Aleksandr I – chelovek na trone', pp. 66–97, in Mironenko, *Aleksandr I*.
36. The most detailed account of the Empress Elizabeth's love and its sad conclusion is by D.I. Ismail-Zade, 'Aleksandr I i Imperatritsa Elizaveta Alekseevna', in Mironenko, *Aleksandr I*, pp. 98–115.
37. This is a key theme running through my *Russia against Napoleon: The Struggle for Europe. 1807 to 1814*, London, 2009.

15. EUROPE ON THE EVE OF MODERNITY

1. Jeroen Duindam, *Vienna and Versailles: The Courts of Europe's Dynastic Rivals, 1550–1780*, Cambridge, 2003, p. 85; A. Wess Mitchell, *The Grand Strategy of the Habsburg Empire*, Princeton, NJ, 2018, pp. 27–34. Peter Burke, *The Fabrication of Louis XIV*, New Haven, CT, 1992, pp. 179–81; Francois Bluche, *Louis XIV*, Oxford, 1990, p. 1.
2. James B. Collins, *The State in Early Modern France*, Cambridge, 2009, p. 8.
3. The description of Leopold is drawn from Jean Berenger, *Leopold Ier*, Paris, 2004, ch. 3, pp. 75–6.
4. On Ferdinand II see above all: Robert Birely, *Ferdinand II, Counter-Reformation Emperor, 1578–1637*, Cambridge, 2014. See pp. 179–80 for his daily religious routine. On Habsburg Counter-Reformation ideology – and specifically the Eucharist, Cross and Mary – the foundation work is Anna Coreth, *Pietas Austriaca*, West Lafayette, IN, 2004 (a translation of the original German work published in 1959). The quotations are from pp. 39–40.
5. This paragraph is based on Berenger, *Leopold*, above all pp. 75–106, and on the only modern biography of Leopold in English: J.P. Spielman, *Leopold I of Austria*, London, 1977: the quote is from p. 34. I also learned much about Leopold from discussions with Jeroen Duindam, whose more positive evaluation of Leopold runs against traditional views.
6. On the Jesuits in China there is a large literature: see e.g. Florence Hsia, *Sojourners in a Strange Land: Jesuits and Their Scientific Missions in Late Imperial China*, Chicago, IL, 2009. Specifically on Kangxi and the Jesuits see e.g. Catherine Jami, *The Emperor's New Mathematics: Western Learning and Imperial Authority in the Kangxi Reign*, Oxford, 2012. On Matthew Arnold and Marcus Aurelius see Marcus Aurelius, *Meditations*, Preface, p. xviii.
7. On Joseph I see above all C.W. Ingrao, *In Quest and Crisis: Emperor Joseph I and the Habsburg Monarchy*, West Lafayette, IN, 1979. The description of

Charles VI is by Derek Beales, p. 89, in Beales, 'Clergy at the Austrian Court in the Eighteenth Century', pp. 79–104, in Michael Schaich (ed.), *Monarchy and Religion: The Transformation of Royal Culture in Eighteenth-Century Europe*, Oxford, 2007.

8. The first two quotations come from T.C.W. Blanning, *Joseph II*, London, 1994, pp. 16–17. The absence of scientists and philosophers is from C. Ingrao, *The Habsburg Monarchy 1618–1815*, Cambridge, 1994, pp. 101–3.

9. See Ingrao, *Habsburg Monarchy*, p. 43, for Hungarian landowning and émigré numbers, and p. 135 for figures on monastic landowning in Moravia and Carniola. The statistic on the Liechtenstein estates comes from James van Horn Melton, 'The Nobility in the Bohemian and Austrian Lands, 1620–1780', pp. 110–43 (here p. 131), in H.M. Scott (ed.), *The European Nobilities*, 2 vols, London, 1995: vol. 2, *Northern, Central and Eastern Europe*.

10. Most of these statistics and many other points are drawn from Mitchell, *The Grand Strategy*: see esp. pp. 6, 27–34, 127–8, 155. On revenues compared to France see Duindam, *Vienna and Versailles*, p. 85.

11. These points are relevant to comparisons between inter-state relations in eighteenth-century Europe and China in the Warring States era: in her thought-provoking comparative study Victoria Hui rather overlooks the deep structural reasons why a European monarch had no chance of mobilizing his realm's resources in the manner of a king of Qin: *War and State Formation in Ancient China and Early Modern Europe*, Cambridge, 2005.

12. The statistics on Prussia and Austria are from Mitchell, *Grand Strategy*, pp. 160–1. On Saxony and Prussia, see T.C.W. Blanning, *The Culture of Power and the Power of Culture: Old Regime Europe 1660–1789*, Oxford, 2002, pp. 58–72. On Frederick II see T.C.W. Blanning, *Frederick the Great*, London, 2015. For Prussian history in this era see Christopher Clark, *Iron Kingdom: The Rise and Downfall of Prussia 1600–1947*, London, 2007.

13. All these points are drawn from the outstanding biography by Barbara Stolberg-Rilinger, *Maria Theresia. Die Kaiserin in Ihrer Zeit*, Munich, 2017: for her education and preparation for her future role, see esp. pp. 20–6 and 52–64. Jean-Paul Bled, *Marie-Thérèse d'Autriche*, Paris, 2001, is the next best study of the empress.

14. Stolberg-Rilinger, *Maria-Theresia*, pp. 118–20; Mitchell, *Grand Strategy*, pp. 167–8.

15. The key sources on military affairs are Christopher Duffy, *The Army of Maria Theresa: The Armed Forces of Imperial Austria, 1740–1780*, Doncaster, 1990; G.E. Rothenberg, *The Military Border in Croatia 1740–1881*, Chicago, 1986; Mitchell, *Grand Strategy*, pp. 169–73. On domestic reforms see Stolberg-Rilinger, *Maria Theresia*, pp. 193ff. A good recent study of the central government's relations with the provincial estates is William D. Godsey, *The Sinews of Habsburg Power: Lower Austria in a Fiscal-Military State 1650–1820*, Oxford, 2018.

16. Both Duffy, *Army*, and Mitchell, *Grand Strategy*, stress the mismatch between defensive mindset and offensive goals in the Seven Years War. Michael Hochedlinger, *Austria's Wars of Emergence 1683–1797*, Harlow, 2003, esp. ch. 11, pp. 246–64, provides a good narrative and analysis of military operations.

17. On the relationship between mother and son see Derek Beales, *Joseph II: In the Shadow of Maria Theresa*, vol. 1, Cambridge, 1987, esp. pp. 41–2, 148–9; Stolberg-Rilinger, *Maria Theresia*, esp. pp. 540–58, 745–8.

18. On Kaunitz see F.A.J. Szabo, *Kaunitz and Enlightened Absolutism: 1753–1780*, Cambridge, 1994. On the Holy Roman Empire the bible is the two-volume history by Joachim Whaley, *Germany and the Holy Roman Empire*, Oxford, 2012.

19. For the statistics see Ingrao, *Habsburg Monarchy*, pp. 189–91. On Hieronymus, Greiner and educational reform see Stolberg-Rilinger, *Maria Theresia*, pp. 365–70, 708–14.

20. Stolberg-Rilinger, *Maria Theresia*, pp. 217–21.

21. Adam Wandruszka, *Leopold II. Erzherzog von Osterreich, Grossherzog von Toscana, Konig von Ungarn und Bohmen, romischer Kaiser*, 2 vols, Vienna, 1963–5: here vol. 1, pp. 109–18; Stolberg-Rilinger, *Maria Theresia*, p. 221.

22. The outstanding authority on Joseph is Derek Beales: the quote is from vol. 2, p. 147, of his *Joseph II: Against the World*, Cambridge, 2009.

23. The quotation comes ibid, vol. 2, p. 23. Eleonore was one of Joseph's close circle of female intimates. For many years he was infatuated with her and dreamed of making her his mistress: on Eleonore herself, her circle and Joseph's personality see Rebecca Gates-Coon, *The Charmed Circle: Joseph II and the 'Five Princesses' 1765–1790*, West Lafayette, IN, 2015.

24. I owe this paragraph above all to Derek Beales, who first taught me about Joseph, Leopold and the Habsburg Empire of this era, but also to Timothy Blanning, *Joseph*.

25. Beales, *Joseph*, vol. 1, p. 72.

26. Ibid, pp. 69–82, provides a convincing and sensitive view of Isabella and her relationship with Joseph. The quotation is from p. 72.

27. The great source on Leopold remains Wandruszka's two-volume biography: my comments on the brothers' education are largely based on Wandruszka, *Leopold*, vol. 1, pp. 40–52, 89–95, and Beales, *Joseph*, vol. 1, pp. 43–62; Paul W. Schroeder, *The Transformation of European Politics 1763–1848*, Oxford, 1994, p. 64.

28. Schroeder, *Transformation*, pp. 64ff.

29. Stolberg-Rilinger, *Maria Theresia*, pp. 760–6; Wandruszka, *Leopold*, vol. 1, pp. 341–2, vol. 2, pp. 186–7, 202–18.

30. Stolberg-Rilinger, *Maria Theresia*, pp. 778–80.

31. Ibid, pp. 78–87; Beales, *Joseph*, vol. 1, p. 261, vol. 2, p. 501.

32. John Hardman, *Marie Antoinette*, New Haven, CT, 2019, is the best source on the queen. Carolyn Harris, *Queenship and Revolution in Early Modern Europe*, Houndmills, 2016, puts her fate in comparative perspective.

33. On Louis XVI see above all John Hardman, *The Life of Louis XVI*, New Haven, CT, 2016, and Munro Price, *The Fall of the French Monarchy*, London, 2002; Louis XIV, *Mémoire*, Fragments, pp. 169–70.

34. The most intelligent opponent of Alexander's reforms, Nikolai Karamzin, argued precisely in these terms: Dominic Lieven, *Russia against Napoleon: The Struggle for Europe. 1807 to 1814*, London, 2009, pp. 86–9.

35. The potential literature is immense. As a safe background to the political history of the era I started with Colin Jones, *The Great Nation: France from Louis XV to Napoleon, 1715–1799*, London, 2002, and went next to Julian Swann, *Exile, Imprisonment or Death; The Politics of Disgrace in Bourbon France*, Oxford, 2017. For a narrower focus on the crisis of the 1780s from the monarchy's perspective I found invaluable Julian Swann and Joel Felix (eds), *The Crisis of the Absolute Monarchy: France from the Old Regime to the Revolution*, Oxford, 2013.

36. Alexandre Maral, *Les derniers jours de Versailles*, Paris, 2018, is a wonderfully evocative and intelligent account of the crisis and Louis's role. Yuri Pines, *Everlasting Empire; The Political Culture of Ancient China and Its Imperial Legacy*, Princeton, NJ, 2012, p. 74.

37. On Martens see Dominic Lieven, *Towards the Flame: Empire, War, and the End of Tsarist Russia*, London, 2015, pp. 124–7.

38. David A. Bell, *The Cult of the Nation in France: Inventing Nationalism, 1680–1800*, Cambridge, MA, 2001, esp. pp. 103–5. Also excellent is T.C.W. Blanning, *The Culture of Power and the Power of Culture: Old Regime Europe, 1660–1789*, Oxford, 2002.

39. These two paragraphs owe much to David A. Bell, *Men on Horseback: The Power of Charisma in the Age of Revolution*, New York, 2020, as well as to Christopher Adair-Toteff, 'Max Weber's Charismatic Prophets', *History of the Human Sciences*, 27:1, 2014, pp. 3–20. My courage fails when faced by the vast literature on Napoleon: interested readers should consult the notes of my *Russia against Napoleon*. A good place to start a foray into Napoleon's relationship with the Revolution is David P. Jordan, *Napoleon and the Revolution*, Houndmills, 2012.

16. EMPERORS AND MODERNITY

1. On the eighteenth century and patriotism see discussion in the previous chapter and note 38.

2. The literature on nationalism is vast: a good introduction is John Breuilly (ed.), *The Oxford Handbook of the History of Nationalism*, Oxford, 2013.

3. I discuss these issues in far more detail in Dominic Lieven, *Empire: The Russian Empire and Its Rivals*, London, 2000, esp. ch. 5, pp. 158–200 and 461–4, and in Dominic Lieven, *Towards the Flame: Empire, War, and the End of Tsarist Russia*, London, 2015, esp. pp. 33–43. The most significant addition to the literature since I wrote these books is the thought-provoking work by Pieter M. Judson, *The Habsburg Empire: A New History*, Cambridge, MA, 2016.

4. This is really the key theme of ch. 1, pp. 17–45, of Lieven, *Towards the Flame*. My endnotes in that book contain references to sources and further reading. An excellent addition to the literature on this subject is Erik Grimmer-Solem, *Learning Empire: Globalization and the German Quest for World Status, 1875–1919*, Cambridge, 2019. A key work, unfortunately never translated, is S.Neitzel, *Weltmacht oder Untergang: Die Weltreichslehre in Zeitalter des Imperialismus*, Paderborn, 2000.

5. Arno Meyer, *The Persistence of the Old Regime: Europe to the Great War*, New York, 1981, is the classic statement on the survival of royal and aristocratic power. In my *The Aristocracy in Europe 1815–1914*, Houndmills, 1992, passim but esp. 'Conclusion', pp. 243–53, I argue that he pushes his argument much too far.

6. The key work here is the biography of Dom Pedro II by Roderick J. Barman, *Citizen Emperor: Pedro II and the Making of Brazil, 1825–91*, Stanford, CA, 1999. Also useful is Malyn Newitt, *The Braganzas: The Rise and Fall of the Ruling Dynasties of Portugal and Brazil, 1840–1910*, London, 2019. As background on Brazilian history see Boris Fausto and Sergio Fausto, *A Concise History of Brazil*, Cambridge, 2014.

7. On the eighteenth-century monarchy see e.g. Hannah Smith, *Georgian Monarchy: Politics and Culture, 1714–1760*, Cambridge, 2006. On Edward VII's role in foreign policy see Roderick R. McLean, *Royalty and Diplomacy in Europe, 1890–1914*, Cambridge, 2001, ch. 3, pp. 141–85.

8. Paul Smith (ed.), *Bagehot: The English Constitution*, Cambridge, 2001: the quotations are from pp. 60 and 186. David M. Craig, 'Bagehot's Republicanism', ch. 5, pp. 139–62, in Andrzej Olechnowicz (ed.), *The Monarchy and the British Nation 1780 to the Present*, Cambridge, 2007.

9. The quotation is from Andrzej Olechnowicz, 'Historians and the Modern British Monarchy', ch. 1, pp. 6–46 (here p. 246), in Olechnowicz, *Monarchy*; Smith, *Bagehot*, p. 37.

10. David Cannadine, ch. 4, 'The Context, Performance and Meaning of Ritual: The British Monarchy and "the Invention of Tradition"', pp. 101–64, in Eric Hobsbawm and Terence Ranger (eds), *The Invention of Tradition*, Cambridge, 1983.

11. The key source for both this and the following paragraph is David Cannadine, *Ornamentalism*, Oxford, 2001.

12. D. Omissi, *The Sepoy and the Raj 1860–1940*, London, 1994, pp. 107ff. The Governor- General is quoted by Max Beloff, *Imperial Sunset*: vol. 1, *Britain's Liberal Empire, 1897–1921*, New York, 1970, p. 98. Luke Trainor, *British Imperialism and Australian Nationalism*, Cambridge, 1994, argues that veneration of the monarchy was stronger in the 1900s than twenty years before.

13. Ashley Jackson, 'The British Empire, 1939–1945', ch. 22, pp. 558–81 (here p. 563), in Richard J.B. Bosworth and Joseph A. Maiolo (eds), *The Cambridge History of the Second World War*: vol. 2, *Politics and Ideology*, Cambridge, 2015.

14. Hugh Vickers (ed.), *James Pope-Hennessy, The Quest for Queen Mary*, London, 2018, p. 18. Duff Hart-Davis (ed), *King's Counsellor. Abdication and War: The Diaries of Sir Alan Lascelles*, London, 2006, pp. 433–4.

15. Both this and the following paragraph are based on Adam Hochschild, *King Leopold's Ghost*, London, 1998: the quotations are from pp. 36 and 39.

16. Jane Ridley, 'Bertie, Prince of Wales: Prince Hal and the Widow of Windsor', ch. 7, pp. 123–38, in Frank Lorenz Muller and Heidi Mehrkens (eds), *Royal Heirs and the Uses of Soft Power in Nineteenth-Century Europe*, London, 2016. The quotation is on p. 136.

17. On George VI see Sarah Bradford, *George VI*, London, 1989.

18. Basic reading on Italy in this period includes M. Clark, *Modern Italy, 1871–1945*, Harlow, 1996; C. Duggan, *Francesco Crispi*, Oxford, 2002; G. Finaldi, 'Italy, Liberalism and the Age of Empire', ch. 2, pp. 47–66, in M.P. Fitzpatrick (ed.), *Liberal Imperialism in Europe*, New York, 2012.

19. The two key and contrasting texts on Vittorio Emanuele are Frederic Le Moal, *Victor-Emmanuel III*, Paris, 2015, and Denis Mack Smith, *Italy and Its Monarchy*, New Haven, CT, 1989. They cover the crucial question of the king's surrender to Fascism on pp. 280–91 and 244–54 respectively. The essential text on the monarchy is Catherine Brice, *Monarchie et identité nationale en Italie (1861–1900)*, Paris, 2010. On Vittorio Emanuele and the First World War see Valentina Villa, 'The Victorious King: The Role of Victor Emmanuel III in the Great War', pp. 225–50, in Matthew Glencross and Judith Rowbotham (eds), *Monarchies and the Great War*, Cham, 2018. The description of the king's comments on the political elite comes from a discussion I had over dinner many years ago with Prince Nicholas Romanov. The prince's grandmother, a Montenegrin princess, was the sister of Vittorio Emanuele's wife, Queen Elena.

20. My two key texts on this era in Prussian history were David Barclay, *Frederick William IV and the Prussian Monarchy, 1840–1861*, Oxford, 1995, and Christopher Clark, *Iron Kingdom: The Rise and Downfall of Prussia, 1600–1947*, London, 2006.

21. I make these points in somewhat greater detail in Lieven, *Towards the Flame*, pp. 91–3. Weber, 'The Profession and Vocation of Politics', p. 163.

22. On Bismarck, see above all Jonathan Steinberg, *Bismarck: A Life*, Oxford, 2011, esp. pp. 196, 350, 358, 386, 403, 430: 2.

23. This discussion is based mostly on Franz Lorenz Muller, *Our Fritz: Emperor Frederick III and the Political Culture of Imperial Germany*, Cambridge, MA, 2011: the quotation is from p. 30. Muller believes that Frederick would have kept Bismarck in office in most of the years between 1866 and 1886. Jonathan Steinberg, *Bismarck*, e.g. pp. 381, 472, believes the opposite and also thinks that his accession would have resulted in significant political change.

24. Apart from Muller, *Our Fritz*, the best source on Albert's mission is Edgar Feuchtwanger, *Albert and Victoria: The Rise and Fall of the House of Saxe-Coburg-Gotha*, London, 2006, esp. pp. 34–7, 77–83, and ch. 7, pp. 121ff, 'The Prussian Marriage'. As general background see Stanley Weintraub, *Albert: Uncrowned King*, London, 1977.

25. John C.G. Rohl, *Kaiser Wilhelm*, Cambridge, 2014, pp. 9–10, 18. Behind this brief sketch lies the lifetime of research on William that fed into three large volumes of biography: *Young Wilhelm: The Kaiser's Early Life, 1859–1888*, Cambridge, 1993; *Wilhelm II: The Kaiser's Personal Monarchy, 1888–1900*, Cambridge, 2001; *Wilhelm II: Into the Abyss of War and Exile, 1900–1941*, Cambridge, 2007.

26. Oliver Haardt, *Bismarcks ewiger Bund*, Darmstadt, 2020, is partly a study of the exponential growth of the empire's central administrative machinery.

27. The leading English-language protagonists in the debate about William's role are Christopher Clark, *Kaiser Wilhelm II: Life and Power*, London, 2000, and John Rohl. Unlike some disputes between historians this one has been conducted with a civility that helps to illuminate the key issues. Two edited collections on William introduce one to a spectrum of interpretations by other historians: John C.G. Rohl and Nicholas Sombart (eds), *Kaiser Wilhelm II: New Interpretations*, Cambridge, 1982, and Annika Mombauer and Wilhelm Deist (eds), *The Kaiser: New Research on Wilhelm II's Role in Imperial Germany*, Cambridge, 2013.

28. An excellent introduction to many of these issues is Jan Ruger, *The Great Naval Game: Britain and Germany in the Age of Empire*, Cambridge, 2007.

29. Chs 8, 9 and 10, pp. 195–258, by Holger Afflerbach, Matthew Stibbe and Isabel V. Hull, in Mombauer and Deist (eds.), *The Kaiser*, provide a clear picture of William's shrinking power as the war progressed.

30. Muller, *Our Fritz*, p. 274. On the broader issue of German strategic thinking, Jonathan Steinberg, *Yesterday's Deterrent: Tirpitz and the Birth of the German Battlefleet*, London, 1965, remains a good place to start.

31. On the Eulenberg case and Harden, see Norman Dormeier, *The Eulenberg Affair*, Rochester, NY, 2015: pp. 41–53 are a good description of Harden

and his goals. See also Isabel V. Hull, 'Kaiser Wilhelm II and the "Liebenberg Circle"', ch. 7, pp. 193–220, in Rohl and Sombart (eds), *Kaiser Wilhelm II*. I have discussed the Rasputin affair in Dominic Lieven, *Nicholas II*, London, 1993, pp. 164–70 and 227–8, and *Towards the Flame*, pp. 104, 347. The most significant candidates for office whom Rasputin supported were Alexei Khvostov, Minister of Internal Affairs in 1915–16, and Alexander Protopopov, who occupied the same post in 1916–17. Khvostov was a former provincial governor and a right-wing member of parliament. Given Nicholas's political course the appointment of such a man was logical. As minister, Khvostov attempted to have Rasputin murdered. This is hardly a sign of belonging to his clique but it further blackened the regime's reputation. Protopopov was the deputy speaker of the parliament and had previously been recommended to the emperor for a ministerial post by its speaker, Michael Rodzianko. For a more detailed (and different) view see Douglas Smith, *Rasputin*, New York, 2016. Opposed to the normal English-speaking account are a number of recent works in Russian: see e.g. A.N. Bokhanov, *Pravda o Grigorii Rasputine*, Moscow, 2011.

32. Lieven, *Towards the Flame*, pp. 275–6, 315–20.
33. I discuss the July Crisis in far more detail in Lieven, *Towards the Flame*, ch. 7, pp. 313–42. For an excellent account see T.G. Otte, *July Crisis: The World's Descent into War, Summer 1914*, Cambridge, 2014. The only English-language biography of Bethmann is by Konrad H. Jarausch, *The Enigmatic Chancellor*, New Haven, CT, 1973, which is now rather out of date. My interpretation of Bethmann is based partly on conversations with my friend Professor Stieg Forster and even more on conversations with Bethmann's granddaughter Isabella von Bethmann Hollweg, who was a close friend of my aunt.
34. Bagchot, *English Constitution*, p. 62; Rohl, *Kaiser Wilhelm*, pp. xx, 19–20, 43, 67.
35. The quote from Bismarck is on p. 142 of Lieven, *Nicholas II*, but the whole of chs 5 and 6, pp. 102–60, is relevant to the discussion. The original source for Bismarck's words is l. Raschau (ed.), *Die politische Berichten des Fursten Bismarck aus Petersburg und Paris*, Berlin, 1920, vol. 2, pp. 129–30.
36. No adequate biography of Alexander II exists in any language. My own biography of Nicholas II contains suggestions as regards additional reading. Since I wrote *Nicholas II* much good work has been published in Russian, including a valuable article by S. Podbolotov, 'Nikolai II kak Russkii Natsionalist', *Ab Imperio*, 3, 2003, pp. 199–223.
37. The best brief introduction to Russian political thought and Slavophilism is Gary M. Hamburg, 'Russian Political Thought, 1700–1917', in Dominic Lieven (ed.), *The Cambridge History of Russia*: vol. 2, *Imperial Russia, 1689–1917*, Cambridge, 2006, ch. 6, pp. 116–44. On the Russian peasantry and the commune see David Moon, *The Russian Peasantry 1600–1930*, London, 1999. On popular monarchism see Maureen Perrie, 'Popular Monarchism:

The Myth of the Ruler from Ivan the Terrible to Stalin', pp. 159–69, in G. Hosking and R. Service (eds), *Reinterpreting Russia*, London, 1999. On police trade unionism see Jeremiah Schneiderman, *Serge Zubatov and Revolutionary Marxism: The Struggle for the Working Class in Tsarist Russia*, Ithaca, NY, 1976. For Italian comparisons see notes 16, 17 and 19 of this chapter.

38. L.A. Tikhomirov, *Monarkhicheskaia gosudarstvennost'*, St Petersburg, 1905 (reprinted 1992): the quotations are from pp. 406 and 579.

39. Inevitably, this is a dangerously brief précis of a complex set of ideas. A recent good biography of Tikhomirov is Aleksandr Repnikov and Oleg Milevsky, *Dve zhizni L'va Tikhomirova*, Moscow, 2011.

40. On Nicholas II see Lieven, *Nicholas II*, and pp. 93–105 in Lieven, *Towards the Flame*. On property in Imperial Russia a fine introduction is Ekaterina Pravilova, *A Public Empire: Property and the Quest for the Common Good in Imperial Russia*, Princeton, NJ, 2014.

41. On Mussolini see e.g. R.J.B. Bosworth, *Mussolini*, Oxford, 2010. For a good introduction to the relationship of the monarchy and Fascism both in Italy and in comparative perspective see Martin Blinkhorn (ed.), *Fascists and Conservatives*, London, 1990.

42. Alexandra to Nicholas, 22 August 1915, p. 171, in Joseph T. Fuhrman (ed.), *The Complete Wartime Correspondence of Tsar Nicholas II and the Empress Alexandra*, Westport, CT, 1999.

43. I discuss these issues at much greater length in Lieven, *Nicholas II*, pp. 102–31.

44. Nicholas and his reign are the subject of my *Nicholas II*, as well as my *Towards the Flame* and *Russia's Rulers under the Old Regime*.

45. Stephen R. Halsey, *Quest for Power: European Imperialism and the Making of Chinese Statecraft*, Cambridge, MA, 2015, pp. 1–51, is a useful introduction both to European imperialism and non-European states' response. Nevertheless, in his effort to defend the Qing he rather exaggerates their uniqueness and plays down Ottoman and Iranian successes.

46. The best short introduction to modernity's impact on (especially non-European) monarchy is pp. 579–93 in Jürgen Osterhammel, *The Transformation of the World: A Global History of the Nineteenth Century*, Princeton, NJ, 2014.

47. On Yuan see Odd Arne Westad, *Restless Empire: China and the World since 1750*, London, 2012, pp. 138–43, and Jonathan D. Spence, *The Search for Modern China*, New York, 1999, pp. 269–70. The quotation is from p. 22 of Abbas Milani, *The Shah*, Houndmills, 2011.

48. The key work on Abdul Hamid II and his use of Islam is Kemal H. Karpat, *The Politicisation of Islam: Reconstructing Identity, State, Faith and Community in the Late Ottoman State*, Oxford, 2001. See also Selim Deringil, *The Well-Protected Domains: Ideology and the Legitimation of Power in the Ottoman Empire 1876–1909*, London, 1998. There is an excellent modern

biography of Abdul Hamid: François Georgeon, *Abdulhamid II. Le Sultan Caliphe*, Paris, 2003.

49. On Pan-Islamism in the international context see David Motadel (ed.), *Islam and the European Empires*, Oxford, 2014, esp. ch. 6, Umar Ryad, 'Anti-imperialism and the Pan-Islamic Movement', pp. 131–49.

50. Mona Hassan, *Longing for the Lost Caliphate*, Princeton,NJ, 2016, passim but especially pp. 150ff for discussion of the khilafat movement. On the late empire's international position and its decision to enter the First World War see Mustafa Aksakal, *The Ottoman Road to War in 1914*, Cambridge, 2008, and M. Kent (ed.), *The Great Powers and the End of the Ottoman Empire*, London, 1996.

51. A good recent history of the Meiji Restoration is Mark Ravina, *To Stand with the Nations of the World: Japan's Meiji Restoration in World History*, Oxford, 2017.

52. Ben Ami Shillony, *Enigma of the Emperors*, Folkestone, 2005, pp. 6–7.

53. Ibid, pp. 90, 94.

54. Walter A. Skya, *Japan's Holy War*, Durham, NC, 2009, p. 45. M.B. Jansen, 'Monarchy and Modernisation in Japan', *Journal of Asian Studies*, August 1977, pp. 611–22, remains a short but useful guide to this issue.

55. A.N. Naumov, *Iz utselevshikh vospminanii*, 2 vols, New York, 1955: here vol. 2, pp. 216–17.

56. Much the fullest biography of Meiji is by Donald Keene, *Emperor of Japan: Meiji and His World, 1852–1912*, New York, 2002. On the monarchy's new public face see T. Fujitani, *Splendid Monarchy: Power and Pageantry in Modern Japan*, Berkeley, CA, 1996.

57. The quotation is from p. 536 of Keene, *Emperor*. Skya, *Japan's Holy War*, ch. 1, pp. 33–52, is excellent on the Meiji constitution.

58. The most recent work on these issues is Noriko Kawamura, *Emperor Hirohito and the Pacific War*, Seattle, WA, 2015: I agree with her judgements, though from a position of much less knowledge. The incoherence in Japanese grand strategy is well explained by Alessio Patalono, 'Feigning Grand Strategy: Japan, 1937–1945', ch. 6, pp. 159–88, in John Ferris and Evan Mawdsley (eds), *The Second World War*: vol. 1, *Fighting the War*, Cambridge, 2015. On support for Japan's wars in 1931–45 see Eri Hotta, *Pan-Asianism and Japan's War 1931–1945*, New York, 2007. On Saionji, see Lesley Connors, *The Emperor's Adviser: Saionji Kinmochi and Pre-War Japanese Politics*, Beckenham, 1987, pp. 168–79.

17. AFTERWORD

1. Footnoting these points is so impossible that I will resort to nepotism: see e.g. my brother Anatol Lieven, *Pakistan: A Hard Case*, London, 2012, and

Climate Change and the Nation State, London, 2020. On biological warfare see e.g. my colleague at Trinity, Martin Rees, *On the Future: Prospects for Humanity*, Princeton, NJ, 2018, ch. 2, pp. 61–82.

2. Barack Obama, *A Promised Land*, London, 2020, pp. 602–3.

3. Graham Allison, *Destined for War: Can America and China Escape Thucydides's Trap?*, Boston, 2017, is the best-known work on this issue for the general public. Christopher Coker, *The Improbable War: China, the United States and the Logic of Great Power Conflict*, London, 2015, seems to me a balanced assessment. On Trump see above all John Bolton, *The Room Where It Happened*, New York, 2020, and Jessica Matthews in *The New York Review of Books*, LXVII:13, August 2020, pp. 19–21.

Index